KAUFMAN & CO.

KAUFMAN & CO.

BROADWAY COMEDIES

GEORGE S. KAUFMAN
with
EDNA FERBER
MOSS HART
RING LARDNER
MORRIE RYSKIND

THE LIBRARY OF AMERICA

The paper used in this publication meets the
minimum requirements of the American National Standard for
Information Sciences—Permanence of Paper for Printed
Library Materials, ANSI Z39.48—1984.

Distributed to the trade in the United States
by Penguin Putnam Inc.
and in Canada by Penguin Books Canada Ltd.

Library of Congress Catalog Number: 2004044200
For cataloging information, see end of Notes.
ISBN 1–931082–67–7

———

First Printing
The Library of America—152

Manufactured in the United States of America

LAURENCE MASLON
SELECTED THE CONTENTS AND
WROTE THE NOTES FOR THIS VOLUME

Contents

THE ROYAL FAMILY

A Comedy in Three Acts

by

George S. Kaufman

and

Edna Ferber

THE SCENES

The action passes in the duplex apartment
of the Cavendishes, in the East Fifties,
New York.

ACT I
A Friday in November. Early Afternoon.

ACT II
Saturday. Between Matinee and Night.

ACT III
A Year Later.

ACT I

SCENE: *The scene is the duplex apartment of the Cavendish family, in the East Fifties, New York. The room is spacious and high-ceilinged—it is really two floors that one sees. At the rear is a balcony from which various doors open into hallways and bedrooms. A curved staircase leads to this balcony. The main room, downstairs, has three doors. One is the outer door, set at a right angle in a kind of recess at the back. Almost hidden under the curve of the stairway is a door that leads to the rear of the apartment—used only by the servants. On the left, the side opposite the outside entrance, is a double door into the library. It is a doorway of majestic height, and when these doors stand open one catches a glimpse of high and endless bookshelves.*

The room has about it nothing of the commonplace. At a glance one sees that it is lived in by an unusual family. It is rich, careless, crowded, comfortable. Almost cluttering it are deep cushioned chairs, little corner clusters of couch, table, lamp; photographs in silver frames are all about; magazines, cushions. A profusion of flowers. Tapestries and rich shawls hang over the balcony railing. A grand piano is partly under the balcony, slightly to the left. A colourful brocade is thrown over this, and a lamp stands on it, together with photographs, etc. All sorts of periods and styles have gone into the making of the room. Prominently placed is a portrait in oils of the late Aubrey Cavendish in his most celebrated role, all bristling mustachios, high stick, romantic cape, glittering orders, gold braid, silk and boots and swagger. The time is about one o'clock of a November afternoon. The Cavendishes, a family of actors, are only now stirring for the day.

At the rise of the curtain the stage is briefly empty. Immediately Della, the maid, comes from one of the bedrooms off the balcony, a breakfast tray in her hands. She looks a capable person, in the thirties, and intelligent enough to cope with the often surprising situations that arise in the Cavendish household.

She has some difficulty in manipulating both the tray and the door. Finally manages to close the door with her foot. Then she rests the tray on the balcony rail for a moment of readjustment

*before starting the length of the balcony to descend the stairs. As
she starts along the balcony Jo, the houseman, enters from the servants' entrance downstairs, also carrying a laden tray. He is
wearing a white housecoat. He is a man of about forty-eight or
fifty.*

*Jo goes straight toward the stairway and up, passing Della, who is
coming down. They pass about a third of the way up. As they are
a step or two past each other the telephone on the stage rings.
There is a brief glance between them, an unspoken "There's the
'phone." Della, downward bound, naturally is the one to answer
it. She looks about for a convenient place upon which to put her
tray. Goes to the telephone.*

DELLA: Hello!
  (*The house 'phone, somewhere in the servants' entrance,
  rings. Jo is at the top of the stairs. Della looks up at him; motions towards the doorway. Jo looks about in indecision, then
  puts the tray on the top step and comes hurriedly down. In
  the meantime Della is speaking on the outside 'phone.*)
Yes. . . . No, she's not up yet. . . . I say she's not up yet.
Well, I don't know. About an hour, maybe.
  (*Jo is now at the house 'phone, unseen. His conversation can
  be heard running through the rest of Della's talk.*)

JO: Hello. . . . You can sign
for them. . . . All right,
send him up and I'll sign
for them. (*He hangs up.*)

DELLA: Who is it, please? . . .
Mr. Who? . . . Will you spell
that, please? . . . W? . . .
Oh, Mr. Wolfe! . . . Yes,
Mr. Wolfe? . . . (*A more
personal tone.*) You know
how it is here when the
'phone starts. . . . Yes, certainly, Mr. Wolfe. I will. All
right.

  (*Jo, having finished his telephone conversation, has crossed
  rapidly and is well up the stairs.*)
DELLA: Who was on the house 'phone?
JO: Nothing. Only some flowers.
DELLA: (*A glance around the flower-laden room.*) Just what we
need. (*Reaches for the tray. Again the telephone.*) Hello! (*The*

sound of the back door buzzer.) The back door, Jo! (*Jo disappears into Julie's room.*) Hello! . . . Yes. . . . Who is it, please? . . . Oh. . . . Yes, she's up, but she can't come to the 'phone. She's taking her boxing. . . . Yes, I'll take . . . Dinner at Mrs. Sherwin's— (*Jo appears from Julie's room.*) Will you wait a minute, please? . . . Jo, that was the back door. Katie'll never answer.

JO: All right. (*He comes downstairs. Goes out at the rear.*)

DELLA: (*Again at the 'phone.*) Now what was that again? . . . Dinner at Mrs. Sherwin's, four thirty-six Park Avenue, November 26th, at seven. . . . Seven! I'll tell her, but Miss Cavendish has got to be in the theatre before eight— she always eats dinner six-thirty. . . . Yes, I will. (*Hangs up.*)

(*Jo enters again. In his arms, stacked high and tied together, are pasteboard boxes, very large ones at the bottom, smaller ones at the top. They reach almost to Jo's chin.*)

JO: Where do you want these?

DELLA: Who they for? Miss Julie? Take 'em up to her room.

(*Jo goes toward stairs. A hall-boy enters behind him, bundle laden. He pauses just a moment, peers around his stack of boxes to get his bearings.*)

Right on up.

HALL-BOY: There's more out there. (*Follows Jo up.*)

(*Della goes.*)

(*McDermott, the trainer, comes onto the balcony from Julie's room, whistling. A dapper, slim, quick ferret, with a left cauliflower ear and an amazing co-ordination of muscle. He reeks of the ring. He is wearing a white flannel sleeveless undershirt, trousers, a belt. Has on one boxing mitt, carries the other. He surveys Jo and the hall-boy, laden with boxes.*)

McDERMOTT: Somebody moving in?

JO: One side! Heads up!

McDERMOTT: G'wan!

(*Della comes on again, carrying additional boxes.*)

Je's!

(*Jo goes into Julie's room. The hall-boy still ascending the stairs. The doorbell rings. Della has an instant of indecision. Puts down her boxes. Starts for door. Telephone rings. Della*

*goes toward it. Changes her mind, continues to door. Tele-
phone continues. McDermott comes down, is met about one-
third of the way up by the hall-boy; solves the traffic problem
by leaping lightly over the railing. Jo reappears on balcony.
Comes down.*)

DELLA: Jo, answer the telephone.

JO: Let it ring!

McDERMOTT: (*To Della.*) Seen Miss Julie's mitts?

DELLA: In the liberry.

McDERMOTT: Where?

MESSENGER: (*Voice off. Very loud.*) Telegram for Cavendish!

JO: (*Picking up Della's pile of boxes.*) Only ring again if I do answer it. (*Starts for the stairs.*)

McDERMOTT: Where'd you say?

(*Della back from the door, with telegram and receipt pad in
hand.*)

DELLA: In the liberry. Jo, you got a pencil?

(*McDermott goes into the library.*)

JO: (*Over the top of his boxes.*) Have I got a pencil!

(*Hall-boy out of Julie's room. Down stairs.*)

DELLA: Well, I can't . . . Oh, for heaven's sake! (*In 'phone.*)
Will you hold the line a minute? (*To hall-boy.*) Boy, can you
sign for this and give it to that messenger?

(*Hall-boy takes pad, goes to outer door.*)

Hello! . . . Miss Julie Cavendish? . . . Well, she can't just
now.

McDERMOTT: (*Enters from library, whistling.*) I found 'em!

DELLA: Oh, I should think in about an hour.

McDERMOTT: I bet Jo was using them.

(*Jo enters from Julie's room. Starts down. He carries a pair
of women's shoes.*)

DELLA: All right. I'll tell her. (*Hangs up. The back door buzzer
sounds.*) What's that?

JO: I guess it's those flowers.

DELLA: I'll go. Here, you take this up to her. (*Hands him
telegram.*) Give me those. (*Takes shoes.*)

(*McDermott has taken off his gloves, put on the other pair.
Tucks original gloves under his arm.*)

(*Back door buzzer sounds again.*)

DELLA: Oh, all right, all right! (*She goes.*)

JO: (*Looks forward to a little talk with McDermott.*) How's the battler, huh? Pretty good?

MCDERMOTT: Say, I feel like I could take on the Woolworth Building! (*A few swift passes at Jo with his gloved hands.*) A little boxing wouldn't hurt you none. You got flat feet carrying trays. And look at that! (*Taps Jo's stomach.*) What do you eat for breakfast! Ostrich eggs!

JO: Say! Any fellow goes around boxing women for a living I guess I could take 'em on.

MCDERMOTT: Yeah! I've taken on some of the best in the world in my time.

JO: I know your record. You was known as Canvasback McDermott. (*Sweeps the floor with a gesture of his palm.*) You're right in your class now, all right. Running a gymnasium racket, hiring out as a punching bag for women to keep their figures.

MCDERMOTT: All right, and let me tell you something. I got women clients could make a jelly out of you, and what do you know about that!

JO: Yeah!

MCDERMOTT: Yeah. (*Points vaguely up the stairs.*) She give me a poke yesterday would have held you for the count.

JO: I'd like to see her try it.

MCDERMOTT: I trained a lot of stage people, but I never seen anybody pick it up quicker than Miss Cavendish.

JO: Say, acting ain't all they can do. Look at Tony.

MCDERMOTT: I seen him in pictures.

JO: Act, play the piano, fiddle, fence, box. I bet the old lady herself could take you on. Say, I been here upwards of ten years, and— (*The outer doorbell rings. Jo starts toward it, still talking.*) —and nothing they could do— (*Remembers telegram. Gives it to McDermott.*) Here! Take that, will you? You're going up to Miss Julie's room. . . .

(*McDermott is on his way up the stairs.*)

Say, do you think you could get me into the Garden Friday night? I've never seen this Delaney.

MCDERMOTT: Sure. Just mention my name. (*Takes the last few steps in a great leap. Disappears.*)

(*Jo opens the outer door. The well rounded tones of Herbert Dean are heard in greeting.*)

DEAN: Ah, good morning, Jo, my boy! Good morning!

JO: Good morning, Mr. Dean.

(*Dean strides into the room. Jo shuts outer door and follows.*)
(*Dean is about 57, very dressy, an excellent actor, beginning to show his age. The flower of the Lamb's Club. Necktie, shirt and handkerchief always blend. Massage has been his most active form of exercise. His appearance inevitably brings to mind the adjective "well-preserved." Clothes a shade too well tailored. His topcoat is one of those which define the waistline. His walking stick is London. Under his arm is a play manuscript. His entrance is a characteristic one, done in state. That springy walk. He makes straight for the centre of the room and stands viewing himself in the mirror.*)

DEAN: Well, well, well! Where's the family! Where's every-body! (*Drops 'script on table.*)

JO: They're not down, Mr. Dean. It's hardly half past one yet.

DEAN: (*Removes coat.*) I was up a full hour ago. Setting up ex-ercises! Cold bath!

JO: Yessir! You always took care yourself. That's how you kept your figger.

DEAN: Not bad, is it— For a chap of—uh—forty-five?

JO: Forty-five, sir! Oh, my no!

DEAN: Well, look here. They're all awake, aren't they? Miss Julie's awake?

JO: Oh, yes. Her and the trainer been exercising half an hour and more. She ought to be down any minute now.

DEAN: I see. I see. I want very much to talk to her before we're interrupted. How about my sister? She up?

(*A glance to balcony bedroom door. Jo is in alcove, hanging coat, etc., in closet.*)

JO: She's been stirring quite a while. Doesn't sleep so well lately, Mrs. Cavendish doesn't. Wide awake at eleven every morning.

DEAN: (*Dean has noticed the breakfast tray and drifts toward it, talking as he walks, but intent on the tray.*) Well, of course she's getting along in years. (*Feels the coffee pot to learn if it's hot. Dreamily picks up a breakfast roll. Butters it.*) Trouble is she won't give in. Pretends she's well.

(*Two long and determined peals of the doorbell. An appre-*

hensive look in Dean's face. Jo opens outer door to admit Kitty LeMoyne Dean.)

JO: Good morning, Mrs. Dean!

(Kitty, enters, ignoring Jo's greeting. About forty-eight, but doesn't believe it. An actress for many years, never more than mediocre. She is obviously in a temper. Comes directly over to Dean. Him she stands regarding with a baleful eye. They glare at each other. Dean turns away with a snort.)

(Jo, coming down, is in a genial mood and essays a pleasantry.)

That's funny. You getting here just a minute after Mr. Dean. He just got here a minute ago himself. *(He looks expectantly from one to the other, for appreciation of this coincidence. Something in their faces tells him that things are not so jolly.)* Well, I'll tell Miss Julie you're both down here.

(He retreats, somewhat gingerly. Della enters breezily. She is carrying an open box of flowers, so that the mass of blooms is plainly to be seen.)

DELLA: Good morning, Mrs. Dean! Mr. Dean! You two are out bright and early!

JO: Psst!

(A bit of warning pantomime from Jo to Della. Della gives Jo an uncomprehending look.)

DELLA: H'm? *(Della over to Kitty with box of flowers.)*

Did you ever see these kind of roses? I've forgotten what you call them.

(Kitty barely glances at the box. A movement of the lips that is a frigid imitation of a smiling assent.)

Well, I guess I'll take them up and show them to her. *(She goes upstairs.)*

(Jo picks up the tray that Della brought down earlier. Starts off with it.)

DEAN: Heh! Here, here! *(Dashes to tray. Snatches another roll.)*

JO: Why, you're hungry, sir! Won't you let me bring you a bite of breakfast!

DEAN: No, no, no, no! . . . I'll tell you what. You might bring me a cup of coffee.

JO: Yessir! I'll have it made fresh for you.

DEAN: Thanks, Jo. I wasn't permitted to finish my breakfast

this morning, what with one thing and another. (*With a meaning glare at Kitty.*)

JO: Yes, sir! (*A backward look around the edge of the upraised tray that inquires as to Kitty's possible need of refreshment.*) Perhaps—uh— (*Kitty's stony look defeats him. Jo goes.*)

    (*Kitty and Dean are alone. Dean takes a vicious and defensive bite of roll.*)

KITTY: And furthermore, Herbert Dean, if you think you can shut me up by sneaking off to this family of yours—

DEAN: Sneaking, my good woman! I believe I am privileged to walk out of my own home and call on my niece and my sister without asking your formal permission.

KITTY: If you think I'm going to stand by and see another woman play that part—

    (*Simultaneous.*)

KITTY: —you're mighty mistaken, that's all I can say! If you think you're going to do that play without me being in it you've got a lot to learn! That part was made for me! I'd be marvellous in it! And if you imagine for one minute, Herbert Dean—

DEAN: For Heaven's sake, Kitty, now let me alone on that, will you! It's not your kind of part, I tell you! You'd be all wrong in it! I've been waiting ten years to get a play like this— (*The 'script has been lying on the table. He picks it up for emphasis as he speaks.*) but I tell you it isn't for you! It's—

    (*Both stop at the sound of a door opening on the balcony. They glance up. Della appears. Dean throws the manuscript back on the table with a slam and turns away. Della comes down. She has just gone out at right and Kitty has taken breath for a renewal of the attack when the 'phone rings. Della returns.*)

DELLA: Hello! . . . Yes . . . Mr. Anthony Cavendish? Oh, no, Mr. Anthony Cavendish is not here. . . . Yes, he lives here when he's home, but he's in Hollywood. . . . I don't believe he's expected. (*Aside to Dean.*) Is Mr. Tony expected?

    (*A shrug only from Dean.*)

DELLA: No, he isn't expected. . . . Who is it, please? . . . The Graphic? Oh, yes.

DEAN: (*A warning whisper.*) You don't know anything!

DELLA: (*In 'phone.*) I don't know anything. (*Hangs up.*)

DEAN: What did they want?

DELLA: Said Mr. Tony. I told them he was in Hollywood.

DEAN: The Graphic? What's that young devil up to now?

KITTY: A Cavendish can do no wrong.

DELLA: I told Miss Julie you wanted to see her in a hurry. (*Della goes.*)

KITTY: In a hurry, h'm? Before I could get here!

DEAN: Now, Kitty, let's not go all over this again. Look at me! I'm all unstrung. I've had no sleep.

KITTY: You had as much sleep as I had.

DEAN: Whose fault was it! Let me tell you, madam, one more night like that and I move to the Lamb's Club.

KITTY: Move! Where do you think you live now!

DEAN: (*Picks up 'script.*) I won't have any more talk about it.

KITTY: No, I'm not allowed to say a word. But you send a 'script over for Julie to read last night—Julie and that sister of yours.

DEAN: And why shouldn't they read it! I have never done a play without consulting Fanny and Julie.

KITTY: Maybe that's why you never have a hit.

DEAN: I'll have one this time! I can see myself in every line of it, every gesture! Take the Nero scene! (*A pose.*) The Abraham Lincoln scene! As Frederick the Great! But you, my dear Kitty—the woman who plays this part must be— You see, your technique is more—uh—mellow—

KITTY: Are you by any chance telling me that I'm too old!

DEAN: Oh, my dear Kitty!

KITTY: Then I suppose I'm not a good enough actress! I was good enough to support Mansfield, though, wasn't I!

DEAN: Plenty!

KITTY: I'm as good an actress as your precious Julie, even if she is a Cavendish. And I'm better than that sister of yours ever was.

DEAN: My dear Kitty, please do not embarrass me by comparing yourself with Julie Cavendish, or with her mother, the greatest Lady Macbeth of her day.

KITTY: Oh, for— Listen! There are a few actresses whose name isn't Cavendish. Cavendish! Cavendish! I've had the royal

family Cavendished up to me for twelve years. God, but I'm
sick of them!

DEAN: You are sick of the Cavendishes! You are—the most distinguished . . . And who are you, I'd like to know, to be
sick of the Cavendishes! What were you when I married
you!

KITTY: I was understudying Mannering in "The Garden of
Allah."

DEAN: You were an off-stage noise!

(*Jo enters, with Dean's tray. Slight pause on threshold to
make certain battle is not too thick.*)

JO: Here you are, Mr. Dean. Nice hot pot of coffee, pick you
up right away. (*Puts tray on table. Draws up chair for Dean.*)

DEAN: Thanks, Jo, thanks. Coffee! That's fine!

JO: Hot buttered toast. (*Lifts a napkin.*)

KITTY: Oh, Jo!

(*Jo pauses.*)

I feel a little faint. (*An eye on the tray.*) Perhaps if I forced
myself to swallow a mouthful of coffee—

JO: Right away, Mrs. Dean. And a little toast?

KITTY: The tiniest sliver. . . . Or perhaps I ought to try to eat
an egg.

JO: I'd try, yes Ma'am. Soft boiled?

KITTY: I think—shirred. With just a thin curl of bacon.

JO: Thin curl of bacon. Yes'm. (*Turns to go.*)

DEAN: I—uh—h'm—I might have an egg, Jo, while you're
about it.

JO: Yes, sir. Same as Mrs. Dean's?

(*The sound of the outer door closing.*)

DEAN: Why—ah—

(*Gwen enters from outer door. She is in riding clothes; a slim
lovely young thing of nineteen. She is, perhaps, less a
Cavendish than any of the others of the family. Perry Stewart enters behind her and lingers a moment uncertainly in
the doorway.*)

(*Perry Stewart is a personable young fellow of about
twenty-eight. Piping Rocking, Long Island, bonds. He is
wearing an overcoat. His driving gloves are rather indicative of the Minerva at the curb.*)

GWEN: M-m-m! Jo, I've got to have some lunch. (*To the Deans.*) Hello! . . . Want some lunch, Perry?

DEAN: Lunch!

PERRY: Not a chance! If I'm going to dress and get back here I've got to blow.

GWEN: This is Perry Stewart. Oh, I guess you've met. My Uncle —and Aunt Kitty.

(*They exchange greetings.*)

KITTY: Been riding?

GWEN: Mm. It was marvelous. The ground was white with frost.

DEAN: I never cared much for Nature.

GWEN: Jo, what've you got to eat? . . . What's the matter, Kitty? Don't you like frosty mornings, either?

KITTY: I've just had one.

PERRY: Look here, don't you waste a lot of time on lunch. (*Looks at wrist watch.*) I'll be back here at half past two, and you're going to be ready.

GWEN: Very well, m'lord.

PERRY: No fooling, Gwen. It's an hour's drive, and a guest of honor has got to be on time.

GWEN: That sounds scarey.

PERRY: Well—you know—one thing she's fussy about is people being on time.

GWEN: I'll be sitting on the curb.

PERRY: She thinks actresses are temperamental, or something. So let's show her. (*To Dean and Kitty.*) Good-bye.

(*They say good-bye.*)

GWEN: Good-bye, Perry!

(*Perry goes. Gwen follows him a step or two into the alcove.*)

JO: (*To Dean.*) You said the same as Mrs. Dean's, sir? The eggs?

DEAN: Oh. Yes. A little bacon—chicken livers—anything.

GWEN: What've you got for me, Jo? Cold meat, or a chop—I don't care so long as it's food.

JO: Yes, Miss Gwen. (*Jo goes.*)

GWEN: Gosh, I'm hungry! I was up at half past seven.

DEAN: Half past what!

KITTY: I think he's awfully good looking, Gwen.

GWEN: I'll tell him.

KITTY: What's the function this afternoon? It sounds formal.

GWEN: Oh, no. Perry's mother's giving a tea for me out at Scarsdale, that's all. (*Is going up the stairs.*)

DEAN: Uh—Gwen. You might remind your mother that I am waiting. And also your grandmother.

GWEN: Sure.

KITTY: Incidentally, so am I.

DEAN: No more morning rides after this week, eh, Gwen, my child? Rehearsals. Rehearsals.

GWEN: I'm afraid so.

DEAN: You ought to be very proud, my dear. At your age, to be appearing with your mother. Quite an event! Quite an event in the theatre! (*Toast and napkin in hand, he gives the effect of a speech as his mood gains in warmth and splendor.*) Yes, sir! About to enter into your great inheritance! To come before the public as the descendant of a distinguished family! It is not a trust to be taken lightly, my dear. Remember that not only will all of us be watching you, but your gifted ancestors as well. (*A heavy "Ahem!" here.*)

(*Gwen has lingered politely near the top of the stairs. Fanny Cavendish's door opens and she enters quickly from the balcony. She speaks simultaneously with the opening of the door.*)

FANNY: I think that speech needs cutting, Bertie.

(*Fanny Cavendish is 72. Managerial, pungent, rather magnificent. Given to domineering and to reminiscence. Her clothes are rich but careless, and somewhat out-dated.*)

GWEN: (*Runs up the remaining stairs. Kisses Fanny's cheek lightly.*) How are you, baby? Feeling all right?

FANNY: Splendid. . . . Have a nice ride?

GWEN: Glorious! The sun over the—

FANNY: Spare me.

(*Gwen goes. Fanny starts down stairs. She walks with a cane.*) Yes, Bertie, they'd be up the aisles and out before you'd really got your teeth into it. (*Is descending stairs.*) Isn't that hat a little ingenue, Kitty?

DEAN: How are you this morning, Fanny? What did the new doctor say? Anything?

FANNY: What do they know? Parcel of fools! (*Descends the last step*.) Well, what brings you two love birds around at the break of day?

KITTY: Bert is calling one of his family conclaves.

DEAN: I'm here to see Julie, that's all.

FANNY: (*Easing herself into her chair.*) Family conclave, eh? Sounds very repulsive.

(*Dean attempts to assist her.*)

It's all right. Don't fuss, Bertie. I'm not helpless. (*Sits.*) Julie not down yet, eh?

DEAN: She is not. I've been waiting half an hour.

FANNY: That prize fighter's here, I guess. Boxing! Time I was Julie's age I didn't have to box to keep my figger. You could span my waist with your two hands.

KITTY: I like a nice womanly figure myself.

FANNY: You ought to be very happy.

DEAN: (*A pat on the shoulder.*) Well, Fanny, you certainly don't seem an invalid. You're looking splendid.

FANNY: Invalid? Well as I ever was. I'm going into rehearsal as soon as Wolfe can pick a cast.

DEAN: Now, now, Fanny. You've had a long siege of it. After a year's illness—

KITTY: Nearer two, isn't it?

FANNY: And what if it is! Two years out of a lifetime! I played fifty-three years without missing a performance, except when Tony was born.

KITTY: And surely when Julie was born!

FANNY: Not Julie! She knows her business better than that. Julie was born during Holy Week.

DEAN: But look here now, Fanny. What are you going to do? You haven't a new play, have you?

FANNY: Who said anything about a new play! I'm reviving "Mrs. Castlemaine."

DEAN: But that's rather old-fashioned, Fanny. New York won't come to see that, even with you in it.

FANNY: New York! You talk like a Follies girl! I'm going to take it on the road.

DEAN: The road? You're mad.

FANNY: I know your views, Bertie. You think Albany is somewhere in the Antipodes.

DEAN: I don't belittle the road. It's quite all right in its way. But my public is in New York.

KITTY: Or was, when last heard from.

FANNY: Well, I'm not like you, Bertie. I've been a trouper all my life, and I'm going to keep on trouping. I'd rather pack 'em into a tent in Texas than play highbrow matinees every Tuesday and Friday at the Teacup Theatre in New York.

DEAN: But you've been ill, Fanny. You can't stand what you used to. Those dreadful small town hotels! Sleeping in Pullmans!

FANNY: I did it when there weren't any Pullmans! When many a time I had to sit up all night—yes, with Julie asleep on one side, and Tony generally yelling his head off on the other.

DEAN: But that belongs to the past, Fanny. You're too important a figure to-day.

FANNY: (*In spite of her infirmity rises to her feet.*) I was Fanny Cavendish then, just as I am now. When the bills said Aubrey and Fanny Cavendish people knew what they were going to see. You had to know how to act— (*A slow turn toward Kitty.*) —when you went on the stage in those days.

KITTY: You had your method. We of the younger school have ours.

FANNY: Ah, youth, youth!

DEAN: (*In the manner of a formal announcement.*) If you do go back this season, Fanny, that's going to mean the whole family on the boards.

FANNY: The whole family?

DEAN: Except Tony, of course. You can't call pictures acting. But with you in "Castlemaine," Julie and Gwen in their play, and— (*A triumphant reach for the manuscript on the table. The doorbell rings.*) your humble servant as the star of—

FANNY: (*In a surprising shout.*) Della! Della! (*Turns to Dean again.*) What's that about your being the bright particular star?

DEAN: I sent the manuscript of my next play over to Julie last night.

FANNY: I know it.

    (*Della enters. Goes to outer door.*)

DEAN: Have you read it?

FANNY: Only the first ten scenes.
> (*Jo enters with Kitty's tray.*)

DEAN: Well?

FANNY: I was afraid to read the second act for fear you played two parts at once.

DELLA: (*At door.*) Good morning, Mr. Wolfe.

WOLFE: (*Off.*) 'Morning, my girl. Good morning.

JO: (*Speaks through others.*) Here you are, Mrs. Dean. All nice and hot.

KITTY: (*Tragically.*) Oh—food!
> (*The thought palpably repels her, though she begins to eat. Jo places tray left centre. One dish Jo transfers to Dean's tray.*)
> (*Oscar Wolfe enters, followed by Della, who waits. Wolfe is a figure of authority; dark, stocky, slightly gray, dressed with a picturesque richness. A rakish black velour hat. Altogether the entrepreneur.*)

WOLFE: Well, well! Good morning, show folks! Hello, Bert!

DEAN: Ah, Oscar! Just the man I want to see.

WOLFE: (*Shakes a chiding finger.*) Calories, Kitty! Calories!

KITTY: (*Her mouth full.*) I didn't have a bite of breakfast.

WOLFE: Fanny, my girl, how are you! (*Takes her hand, pats it warmly.*)

FANNY: What brings you around this hour?

WOLFE: What draws me here always but the one great passion of my life! You, my dear Fanny!

FANNY: (*With insistence.*) What are you here for?
> (*Wolfe removes coat. Jo takes it, also hat and stick.*)

WOLFE: The heartlessness of this coquette! The best years of my life I've given her.

DEAN: Ah—Oscar—just—

WOLFE: (*Not heeding Dean. To Fanny.*) Where's your gifted daughter?

FANNY: I thought so . . . Della, tell Julie.
> (*Gwen appears on the balcony. Della goes upstairs.*)

GWEN: My lunch ready? I'm dying. (*Wears silk riding shirt, breeches, mules and gay bathrobe.*)

JO: I'll bring it right in. (*Goes.*)

WOLFE: Hello there, young lady! How's the child actress!

GWEN: Well, if it isn't Oscar himself! Here at the first pale crack of dawn!

WOLFE: Crack of dawn, huh? Say, you good-for-nothing actors can sleep till noon. You know your poor old manager's done a day's work for you already. That's quite a costume! What are you supposed to represent?

GWEN: (*Jo enters with Gwen's tray.*) I'm the Spirit of Quick Lunch. . . . Bring it over here, Jo. Don't you want something, Mr. Wolfe? H'm? Haunch of venison or a couple of bear steaks?

FANNY: Jo! Time for my egg-nogg, isn't it?

JO: Yes, Mrs. Cavendish. They're beating it up.

WOLFE: (*A slow inclusive look around that takes in the three trays.*) Don't you ever get mixed up, Jo, about who wants breakfast and who wants lunch?

JO: Yes, sir, certainly do, Mr. Wolfe. Still, you get used to it.

WOLFE: Say, do you people realize that there actually are families in this town that sit down in a dining room all at the same time and eat a meal! Together!

FANNY: Quaint!

GWEN: I think it would be nice.

JO: Sure you wouldn't care for anything, Mr. Wolfe? Glad to get it for you.

WOLFE: No, not me, thanks, Jo. Lunch is a meal I never eat.
    (*Jo goes again.*)

FANNY: No. Just a little thick soup, and a mixed grill and coffee and French pastry at the Astor.

WOLFE: You're your old self this morning, Fanny.

FANNY: My old self, Wolfe, and ready to go back to work.
    (*A quick movement from Dean. He wants to speak of himself.*)

WOLFE: Now, now, Fanny! Not so fast!

FANNY: Don't you now—now—Fanny me! I know whether I'm well or not. You haven't time for anything nowadays but Julie and Gwen.

DEAN: (*Manuscript in hand, taps Wolfe on the shoulder.*) Oscar, I tried to reach you all day yesterday—

WOLFE: Yesterday? A crazy day. This is the last theatre I'll ever build. Contractors, plasterers, license commissioners!— Where the devil is Julie? She can't stay in bed *all* day. (*Up at balcony.*) Julie!

FANNY: Julie! (*A shout that tops Wolfe's.*)

JULIE: (*A voice from behind the bedroom door, balcony.*) I'm busy.

FANNY: Wolfe is here!

JULIE: Give him my love!

WOLFE: I'm in a hurry! (*Nothing from the upper regions. A moment's expectant pause. Wolfe turns away with an impatient shrug.*)

DEAN: Well, Oscar—I have finally found the play!

(*Jo enters with egg-nog; crosses to Fanny.*)

WOLFE: All right, all right. Later on. (*A hand on Dean's shoulder.*) You're a fine actor, Bert, but remember that last opus you handed me. . . . Well, well! What you got there, Fanny? Something good?

FANNY: Egg-nogg. I'm being built up.

WOLFE: Got a little schnapps in it, huh?

FANNY: Milk and eggs.

WOLFE: Say, to do you good it's got to have something in it. Let me send you a few bottles of sherry to-morrow. (*Scribbles hastily in a little note book taken from his pocket. As he writes.*) I got some fine Amontillado over at the office.

FANNY: That'll help.

DEAN: Now, Wolfe. (*Slips the manuscript under Wolfe's arm.*) There's the 'script.

(*Della comes onto the balcony from Julie's room, a great pile of garments in her arms, so stacked that she scarcely can see over them. Down the stairs and goes out.*)

WOLFE: All right. (*Up toward the piano. Tosses manuscript on piano.*) I'll keep it in mind. (*Strikes a note or two, idly.*)

DEAN: What a play! Richness, characterization, verisimilitude!

WOLFE: M-m-m-m! . . . I read it anyhow. (*A bar or two of music.*) That other piano as bad as this?

DEAN: I'll drop in on you first thing in the morning. Hear what you think. (*He goes back to his tray.*)

(*Kitty, too, returns to her tray.*)

(*Wolfe, becoming more interested in the music, runs another bar or two. Then he sits and concentrates a bit more on a few notes, preparatory to playing the thing he has in mind.*)

FANNY: What's the name of it again, Bertie? This masterpiece.

DEAN: "The Conqueror."

(*Another brief run on the piano from Wolfe.*)

FANNY: Are you going to do it soon?

DEAN: Oh, around the holidays, if that suits Oscar.

(*A glance toward Wolfe. Wolfe now is playing, lightly, a melodious, slightly sentimental air that continues for a few bars without interruption.*)

GWEN: (*During a moment's lull in the music.*) What's that?

WOLFE: I don't know. They were playing it in Vienna.

(*For a moment they give an ear to the music. Jo comes to Fanny with a plate of rolls. Fanny refuses. While the music is still playing, Jo crosses to Kitty, offers her the rolls. They have all resumed eating. Their attention is fixed on the food before them. A brief lull. The music softly continues. The tinkle of silverware and the clatter of china is distinctly heard.*)

(*The door of Julie's bedroom opens slowly. Julie appears, balcony. Julie Cavendish is 39, beautiful, slim, mature. She is wearing a smart, rather tailored afternoon gown. Is evidently dressed for the day. She comes out slowly, curious to know who is playing. She crosses the width of the balcony, stands at the railing, looking down. Her first glance is toward the piano. She sees Wolfe there. Her gaze encompasses the rest of the room. Four of its occupants are busily eating. One at a time, she takes them in.*)

JULIE: Have you a table for one, Jo, not too near the music?

(*Wolfe stops playing. Turns quickly to look up at Julie. Dean also looks up at her; and Kitty.*)

WOLFE: How do you ever make it on matinee days, Julie?

JULIE: (*Starts toward stairway.*) By being the star, Oscar. They wait for me.

KITTY: I was on the point of departure.

JULIE: Oh, please! Try some of the broccoli hollandaise. It's very nice this morning. (*She is leaning over the stairway rail, one hand posed just a little too carefully on the bannister.*) Or filet of sole Marguery.

FANNY: A very good entrance, Julie.

JULIE: Dear little mother! Wouldn't you like to go up and come down again?

(*Comes on down. Jo picks up Gwen's tray. Goes out with it. Gwen rises from her table, a bit of food in her hand, munching as she goes. She meets Julie at the foot of the stairway.*)

Have a nice ride, Gwen? (*A glance at her.*) Don't you look terrible!

(*Della enters, carrying a gay orange and purple figured box.*)

GWEN: I know it, Mother. I'm going right up and change.

JULIE: No. Wait a minute. (*Flicks open the telegram in her hand, holds it out.*) For lo, I bring good tidings! Guess what!

FANNY: Tidings?

GWEN: Well?

DEAN: What?

DELLA: (*Indicates hat box.*) A C.O.D. package, Miss Julie. Thirty-nine dollars.

JULIE: What?

DELLA: Thirty-nine dollars. A package.

JULIE: Thirty-nine dol—what did I buy for thir—such a strange sum. Who has thirty-nine dollars? (*Surveys the group rapidly.*) Oscar! Let her have it, will you? That makes—how much do I owe you now?

WOLFE: Enough.

(*McDermott appears from centre door, balcony. He wears coat, small black derby; little black bag in his hand. Starts down.*)

GWEN: Mother, I can't wait. You haven't any news, anyhow.

JULIE: Oh, but I have, Gwen, so come right back here. (*Glimpses McDermott coming swiftly down the stairs.*) I'll want you to-morrow, you know, Mac.

McDERMOTT: (*Shifts his hat slightly by way of deference.*) Yes, Miss Cavendish, we'll have a real workout to-morrow. Same time?

JULIE: No, come at eleven— No—Bendel! Ten? . . . Oh, my God, no! . . . Twelve . . . one . . . one, Mac.

FANNY: Matinee to-morrow.

JULIE: Oh, good Lord, I can't make it to-morrow at all, Mac . . . Monday.

WOLFE: Watch out there! You got rehearsals starting Monday!

JULIE: Wait a minute, Mac. So I have. Let me think . . . could you give me Sunday?

McDERMOTT: I don't generally work Sundays as a rule. But seeing it's you. One o'clock?

JULIE: One's fine. You're a dear.

McDERMOTT: So long! (*McDermott start to go.*)

JULIE: Good Lord! Mac! I can't Sunday! Make it to-morrow at twelve! I'll get it in some way!

McDERMOTT: Yes, ma'am. (*Leaves.*)

JULIE: Special fitting on Sunday, and it may take hours. Oscar, her second-act dress is going to be lovely. Cloth of gold, encrusted with turquoise. And of course the sable wrap will make it perfect.

WOLFE: Sable wrap?

JULIE: Why, of course. For the opera scene. She has to have a sable wrap.

FANNY: Wouldn't surprise me if the whole cast wore 'em. My day it was Fanny Cavendish's costumes by Fanny Cavendish. With one little dress and a guipure lace flounce I could be anything from Camille to The Two Orphans.

JULIE: I've seen that one little dress in the storehouse. The investment for whalebone and buckram alone would have kept me in sables a lifetime.

FANNY: A dress was a dress those days, and not a chemise.

GWEN: Mother, are you going to read that telegram or aren't you? Perry'll be here in ten minutes.

WOLFE: First let me tell you what I came about. Then I get right out.

(*A sigh of impatience from Gwen.*)

JULIE: No, no! You've got to hear this. We need you.

GWEN: Well, then, come on with it!

FANNY: Yes, Julie, I think you've built up a good suspense.

JULIE: (*Surveys her position.*) Am I centre? . . . It's dear little brother Tony again.

FANNY: Tony!

DEAN: I knew it.

WOLFE: What's he done now, that bum?

KITTY: Plenty, is my guess.

JULIE: Well, his telegram is rather sketchy, but as nearly as I can make out, I gather that he's killed somebody.

FANNY: Anyone we know?

JULIE: (*Reads.*) "Pay no attention to possible accounts of Deming incident injuries not fatal takes more than that to kill a lousy movie director I arrive New York Saturday

California police have no authority outside state on no condition talk to reporters Zeta Zaydak on this train but no
trouble so far as am locked in drawing room love to all of
you he was dirty hound anyhow. Tony." Good old Tony.

(*There is a moment's complete silence following the reading
of this.*)

KITTY: What did I tell you!

JULIE: It lacks a certain clarity, doesn't it?

FANNY: California police!

DEAN: What's this, what's this!

(*There now ensues a babel of sound—exclamations, conjec-
tures, questions. What's it mean? You know Tony. What's it
all about? Who's Zeta Zaydak? Read that again.*)

WOLFE: (*Comes over to Julie.*) Let me have that, Julie. Now,
just a minute, people. Let's get at this. This may not be so
funny.

FANNY: Do you think it's serious?

JULIE: Of course not, Mother. It never is.

WOLFE: (*Re-reading fragments of the telegram to himself, but
aloud.*) Possible accounts of Deming incident—

GWEN: Deming is his director.

WOLFE: Arrive New York Saturday.

DEAN: That's to-morrow.

WOLFE: . . . Zeta Zaydak on this train . . .

KITTY: She's that Polish hussy.

WOLFE: A fine business.

FANNY: What's she on the train for?

WOLFE: On no condition talk to reporters. . . .

JULIE: Have there been any reporters?

DEAN: Before you were down. The Graphic!

JULIE: The Graphic! Whatever we've done, we've always kept
out of the tabloids.

WOLFE: Who's kept you out, I'd like to know! Wolfe! If it
wasn't for me they'd have been running long ago a contest
Which Is The Craziest Cavendish.

JULIE: Here's another chance for you. What are we going to do?

WOLFE: Now, wait a minute. Let's look this over. Maybe it's
not as bad as it seems.

FANNY: No.

GWEN: Of course not, Grandma. Such a fuss because Tony's

punched some director. I'm sure to be late. (*On her way up the stairs. Escapes.*)

WOLFE: (*Still concentrating on the telegram.*) Now the way I figure it, it was like this. The fella says something Tony doesn't like. Tony knocks him down, of course. And to keep from having to answer a lot of questions about it, he gets on this train.

JULIE: With the picture half finished, naturally.

WOLFE: Omaha he sent this from. Omaha last night. That means he got to Chicago this morning. Naturally he got on the Century. To-morrow morning you'll be just one happy family.

JULIE: We've got to keep the newspapers off him. You know Tony and the papers. They've been laying for him ever since that Mauretania thing.

KITTY: I must say I don't blame them.

DEAN: Yes, he never should have thrown that reporter overboard.

WOLFE: A big mistake.

JULIE: We mustn't let them get at him this time. They're sure to know he's on the Century. They'll swarm on him at the station. He'll start to smash cameras. (*A gesture that says "Whoop!"*)

FANNY: That poor boy.

WOLFE: (*Snaps his fingers.*) I tell you how I fix it. He don't come into Grand Central. He gets off at 125th Street.

JULIE: It doesn't stop there.

WOLFE: To-morrow it will—for one second. (*Points wisely to himself.*) I get him off the train, I bring him here before the newspapers know it, he stays quiet a couple of weeks. If they find it out, he's having a nervous collapse—and nobody can see him.

JULIE: Oh, Oscar! That'll be wonderful! There you are, Mrs. C. Everything's grand.

FANNY: Everything grand! Who's this Zany woman! What's she doing on the train!

JULIE: Well—uh—Oscar, tell mother the facts of life.

WOLFE: (*Pats Fanny's shoulder.*) Satisfied, Fanny? Huh? Your boy ain't in danger?

FANNY: You're the manager.

WOLFE: Good! Now! If nobody else has got anything to do,

that you would like to have me wait until you do it—Julie, you don't want to take a massage first, or something? . . . No? . . . Well, then, do you mind if I waste just a minute of your time on my business!

DEAN: That's what I say! After all, we—

WOLFE: No, no, no, no, no! This is Julie. Julie, my girl, it is now— (*His watch.*) . . . My God! Five minutes after two! I want you downtown in my office—you and Gwen—three o'clock sharp.

JULIE: Downtown! What for?

WOLFE: Now, don't start to holler before I tell you. I'm not so stuck on it, either, but we've all got to do it.

JULIE: Do what?

WOLFE: Who do you think came in on the Mauretania last night?

JULIE: Wait a minute. (*Grips the arm of her chair; prepares for the worst.*) Well?

WOLFE: Out of a blue sky—St. John Throckmorton.

JULIE: Oh! Is that all?

KITTY: Who's he?

WOLFE: Who's he? Only the fellow that wrote Julie's new play, that's all.

DEAN: Oh, the author!

JULIE: *How* you scared me! . . . Send him back.

KITTY: I'd love to meet him.

WOLFE: Now, now, hold on a minute. We got to be nice to this fellow. He's given you a beautiful play here, and the point is he's going to write more of them.

FANNY: The less you have to do with authors the better.

WOLFE: Now, you do that for me, huh, Julie? Be there with Gwen at three?

FANNY: They tell you how to read your lines.

WOLFE: (*To Fanny.*) That's right! Make it harder! (*To Julie.*) We call it settled, huh? You'll be there? Remember this fella's come all the way over from England.

JULIE: But an English author! If he landed last night won't he be lecturing this afternoon?

WOLFE: If you comedians will keep still a minute I'll tell you what it is. This Throckmorton is a new playwright, and English to boot, and nothing will satisfy him he wants to read his play to the entire company.

(*A shout of derision from them all.*)
Now hold on a minute. This is a serious fellow—monocle,
spats, gardenia—everything. With him this is part of being
a playwright, reading the play aloud. The chances are he
saw one of those photographs in the Green Room of His
Majesty's Theatre, the whole company grouped around,
—Beerbohm Tree in the middle—and What's-his-name
reading "The Gay Lord Quex" to 'em— *You* should try to
talk him out of it. I spent the morning.

JULIE: I never heard anything so idiotic in my life! It's fantastic! But if you're really serious, and you want me to do this,
I'll sit through it—only it can't be this afternoon.

WOLFE: It's got to be this afternoon.

JULIE: Oh, no! Then the whole thing's off. It would take
hours. I have an appointment.

WOLFE: Julie, how often do I ask a favour? Now this fella has
got another play that I'm crazy to get hold of. If we're all
just a little bit nice to him—jolly him along—tell him how
good he is. What do you say? H'm?

FANNY: To hell with him!

JULIE: But Oscar, why in the name of heaven does it have to
be just this afternoon! Can't it be some other time!

WOLFE: Say, what's going on this afternoon! You going to be
married!

JULIE: (*A startled look.*) I can't, that's all, Oscar. I—can't! It's
got to be some other time.

WOLFE: To-morrow you got a matinee. Monday you begin rehearsals.

JULIE: Well—Sunday.

WOLFE: Sunday he's out at Otto Kahn's. I tell you there *is* no
other time. If you knew what you mean to him! He's all impressed about having you and Gwen in his first play. He
knows all about you. Everything you've been in—all of
you.

DEAN: Really!

KITTY: You don't say!

WOLFE: So you wouldn't even do this for your old manager,
huh? You got some little appointment—tea, or buy a hat—
and compared to that Oscar don't matter.

JULIE: Oh, now, Oscar—

WOLFE: Well—never mind. The next time you ask me to do something for you—I do it anyhow.

FANNY: I don't believe in humouring playwrights, but if it's such a favour to Oscar, that's different. . . . (*Turns to Julie.*) What're you up to that's so important this afternoon?

KITTY: I'd do it, busy as I am.

FANNY: Oscar's done a lot of things for you.

JULIE: (*A second's hesitation.*) You win, Oscar. At three o'clock — Enter Julie Cavendish, laughing.

WOLFE: That's my girl! (*Starts briskly toward the outer door, buttoning his coat with the air of one who has accomplished something. He talks as he goes.*) Now don't forget. Three o'clock at my office. (*He is putting on hat and coat. He takes out his watch again, his coat half on.*) It's now two-twenty. You and Gwen leave here quarter to three, sharp. All right? I can depend on it?

JULIE: I'll be there.

WOLFE: That's the way to talk. Good-bye, everybody! (*Starts out.*)

DEAN: (*Has picked up his manuscript, eager for a few last words to Wolfe about it.*) Heh! Oscar!

WOLFE: (*A little bewildered, glancing at the manuscript.*) What's this?

DEAN: (*Highly offended.*) Well, on my word! That is the play that—

WOLFE: Oh, yes, yes, yes, yes—

(*Into the alcove. Dean follows him rapidly. Kitty has been easing over toward Wolfe at the first sign of his departure. She now comes swiftly to the alcove, bent on pressing her own claim. They all talk at once.*)

DEAN: Now as I told you, there's a scene or two where I could use a better entrance. But that's a simple matter. The main thing is to get an absolutely— Kitty, for God's sake!

KITTY: You are going to remember about me, aren't you? I've played nearly all those parts and there isn't one—

WOLFE: Sure, sure! I read it to-night, give you a ring in the morning. Excuse me if I run! (*To elevator.*) Down!

(*The slam of the door.*)

(*Both Dean and Kitty break off. Dean strides on and across the room, hands in pockets, very disgruntled. Kitty follows him, bristling.*)

KITTY: I'm on to you, all right. You're afraid I'll give too good
a performance. You won't surround yourself with anything
but second-rate people—you don't want anybody that's
really good. Let me tell you I don't propose to be held
down artistically just because I'm married to Herbert Dean.
I'm important too, don't forget. Ask any producer in New
York—

DEAN: (*At the same time.*) Good God, Kitty, I've been a star
for years! It's simply that you're not suited to this play, that's
all. It's entirely the wrong kind of part for you. I should
think you'd want to help instead of hindering. I've got to
have peace of mind for this thing. You know very well you
drive me crazy by your infernal—

JULIE: (*Cutting in on the double conversation.*) Oh, stop it, you
two, will you! Stop it or get out of here! Go on in there and
argue! I've been a star, you've been a star—I can't stand it, I
tell you! Get out! Get out! Get out!

(*Takes an arm of each, and, while they are still arguing,
propels them rapidly into the library. Slams the door on
them. Turns swiftly, her back to the door, slumps a little
against it, exhausted. A deep breath. The telephone rings on
stage.*)

(*Julie's sigh breaks off in the middle.*)

Ah!

(*A mock nod of deference in the direction of the 'phone.*)

FANNY: Let it ring.

JULIE: Oh, you never can tell. (*Picks up the receiver.*) Yes! . . .
This is Julie Cavendish. . . . Yes, this is Miss Cavendish
speaking. . . . Yes? . . . Yes— (*To Fanny.*) You were right.
. . . Well, I'll tell you, it's very difficult for me to take part
in any benefit performances just at present. . . . December
third. . . . Well, you see, I'll be playing and rehearsing at
the same time. I'm afraid . . . Yes, I'm sure it's a very good
cause. . . . The Newark Newsboys. . . . Oh, yes. . . .
Well, I will if I possibly can. (*One of those mirthless laughs in
response to a bit of fulsome praise.*) That's very kind of you.
I'm so glad you enjoyed it. . . . No, I won't forget. . . .
Century Theatre, December third. (*Hangs up. To Fanny.*)
Mother, will you remind me? Bronchitis on December third.

FANNY: I shall do no such thing! If you said you'd play that benefit you'll play it, bronchitis or double-pneumonia.

JULIE: The honour of the family!

FANNY: Now, Julie Cavendish, what's all this mooning about? What was that big renunciation scene? "I can't this afternoon. I can't. . . . All right—I will! I—will." (*A gesture.*)

JULIE: Gilbert's back.

FANNY: Gilbert?

JULIE: Gil Marshall. He's in New York. I had a note from him; and some flowers.

FANNY: (*Slowly.*) So that's it.

JULIE: You see, it would have been nice to have had the afternoon clear.

FANNY: Was he going to come here?

JULIE: He's calling up at four to find out. Della will have to explain to him, that's all. A play reading! I'd better not tell him that.

FANNY: So! He's come back to New York to spend his millions, h'm? Wonder it hasn't been all over the papers again. What's that they call him?—South American Diamond King?

JULIE: Emerald, Mother. Much nicer.

FANNY: Emeralds or diamonds. When I think that if it hadn't been for me you'd have gone off to South America—given up your career—everything.

JULIE: I wonder what he's like now. He may have grown very charming. South America, and millions, and perhaps a little grey here. (*Touches her temple.*) Sounds rather romantic.

FANNY: No more romantic now than he was nineteen years ago! Ah! What a siege that was!

JULIE: And what a demon you were!

FANNY: I had to be. You thought because he looked serious and didn't say much that he was doing a lot of deep thinking. I knew it was because he couldn't think of anything to say.

JULIE: You certainly acted like a mother in a melodrama.

FANNY: I told him. I showed him that he couldn't hope to make you happy. A home and a husband for a girl like you! I said: "Here's a girl that's going to have fame and fortune—

the world spread before her. Do you think that you can make up to her for all the things you'd rob her of! You and your South America! You and your engineering! . . ."

JULIE: Yes, yes, I know, Mother. He went away, and we both lived happy ever after.

FANNY: How I ever got you where you are to-day is more than I know. You were always at the point of running off with some young squirt.

JULIE: But I never did. So it couldn't have been so serious.

FANNY: Serious enough for them! That young Earl of Pembroke who went off to Africa, and that Philadelphia fellow that shot himself—

JULIE: He was cleaning his gun.

FANNY: They were always cleaning their guns. And when you finally married Rex Talbot! . . . I'll never forget the goings-on then.

JULIE: Mother, out of the whole crowd of them, why did I marry Rex?

FANNY: He was the weakest, I guess.

JULIE: I always said I wouldn't marry an actor. And Rex wasn't even a good actor. What was there about him, Mother?

FANNY: Rex Talbot was a brilliant young loafer! And he had the most beautiful manners. He was the kind of man who could kiss your hand without looking silly.

JULIE: I guess that was what he was always doing when I needed him. That's one thing you will admit about Gil, Mother. He would have been dependable.

FANNY: When you're eighteen you don't marry a man because he's dependable.

JULIE: But when you're a little older, you begin to think that maybe—

FANNY: (*Quickly.*) What's that?

JULIE: Don't be alarmed. But I am curious to see him again. That's natural, isn't it? Only it can't be this afternoon—that's sure. I had it all staged so beautifully, too. I was going to wear my rose beige, and a hat with a brim, and be dignified and wistful, yet girlish withal.

FANNY: You can put on that act for him just as well after the show to-night. It's been nineteen years. What's a couple of hours more!

JULIE: No. Midnight isn't as kind to me as it used to be. I'm just vain enough to want to look my best.

FANNY: You are, eh?

JULIE: I want to look fresh and young and radiant.

FANNY: Is that all?

(*Gwen comes onto the balcony. She is smartly dressed in an afternoon frock, and on her arm she carries her coat. Her hat is in her hand. She is singing blithely and carelessly the newest jazz song hit. She comes quickly down the stairs.*)

GWEN: (*At the foot of the stairs.*) Has anybody seen my tan bag? (*Throws coat and hat on nearby chair.*)

JULIE: (*Remembering the engagement with Wolfe.*) Gwen, you're not going out?

GWEN: (*Goes swiftly to the library door.*) I left it down here somewhere last night when—
(*Opens the library door. Dean's voice and Kitty's are heard in conflict, Dean's rising clearly above Kitty's.*)

DEAN: —over my dead body—

KITTY: —a woman like Fanny Ward—
(*Gwen bangs the door shut with a bewildered and startled expression.*)

FANNY: (*Half to herself.*) Shouts and murmurs.

GWEN: But I think it's *in* there.

JULIE: Gwen, was it this afternoon that you were going out to Westchester? With Perry?

GWEN: Of course. He'll be along any minute.

JULIE: Gwen, you've just got to leave word for him, that's all. You can't go.

GWEN: Why not? What's the matter?

JULIE: We've got to go right down to Oscar's office. I promised.

GWEN: But, Mother—

JULIE: I know. I just forgot you were going with Perry. It's a reading of the play by Throckmorton. He got in last night. He's set on it. Wolfe made an awful fuss about it—a favour to him—we—

GWEN: Mother, that's absurd. You know I've had this date with Perry for a week. And it isn't—just an ordinary date. I've never met his mother. She's giving this tea just for me. It's the first time she's asked me. She's having all these people in. How can I—

JULIE: You can do it as well as I can, Gwen. I'm only doing it for Oscar.

GWEN: But it can be some other time.

JULIE: No—it can't. I've been all over it, and there isn't any other time. It's got to be this afternoon.

GWEN: (*Stamping childishly away from them.*) Oh, for the Lord's sake!

FANNY: He picked a good day for it, this Thingumbob.

GWEN: Why do I have to be there! I've read his old play!

JULIE: So have I, for that matter.

GWEN: (*On the verge of tears.*) Why didn't you tell me sooner? You knew I had this date—

JULIE: I'm sorry, Gwen, but I didn't know it myself until ten minutes ago. That's what Wolfe came to tell me, and I gave up something just as important—and more so. If you think it's going to be any fun for me to sit there and hear a play read—

GWEN: (*Who has not stopped for Julie's speech, so that both are speaking.*) —I wouldn't *care* if it wasn't Perry's mother, but she'll probably never ask me again. And I couldn't go if she did ask me. I'll be rehearsing all the time, and then I'll be acting, and it'll just go on like that forever. First thing you know I'll be an old woman—

> (*Two long rings at the doorbell, followed by a terrific hammering at the outer door. The clamour is enough to stop them, mid-speech.*)

JULIE: (*Startled.*) What's that! . . . Jo! . . . Della! (*Goes to alcove.*)

GWEN: What is it! (*Runs to alcove.*)

> (*Fanny pounds on the floor with her stick. Jo appears swiftly, followed by Della. Both go to alcove, Jo on a half run, Della walking very quickly. At the same moment the double doors of the library are thrown open as Dean and Kitty emerge, brought out by the unusual noise.*)

DEAN: What's the matter? What's going on?

KITTY: My, what a racket!

> (*With the others they go up toward outer door. They are huddled in a group as Jo opens the door. From off stage you hear their voices in surprise and alarm. Fanny alone is on stage.*)

JULIE: Tony!

GWEN: Tony!

FANNY: (*In a tone of unbelief.*) Tony?

DEAN: (*Over his shoulder, to Fanny.*) It's Anthony!

(At this point the group at the door breaks into a confused chorus of surprise, unbelief, amazement, interrogation. "But how did you get here!" "You were in Chicago this morning!" "We just got your telegram!" "What does this mean!" "I don't understand how you—" "Well, this is a surprise, Mr. Tony!" [Jo] "Well, of all people!" [Della] Tony's "sh-sh-sh-sh-sh!," attempting to silence them, sounds through this babel.)

(Tony enters, dramatically, elaborately stealthy, his look and gesture cautioning silence. He is wearing an all-enveloping fur coat, the collar of which is turned up so that his face is concealed. The brim of his soft felt hat is pulled down over his eyes. He comes down swiftly, almost in the manner of one who is backing away from something he fears. His face is turned away so that he is looking over his shoulder. His left coat sleeve, scarcely seen by the audience, hangs empty.)

TONY: Sh-sh-sh! Sh-sh, I tell you!

FANNY: Tony! It's really you!!

(Julie, Gwen, Dean, Kitty have followed a few feet behind him, bewilderment in their faces. They are still exclaiming. Jo and Della, laden with luggage, come down from the alcove entrance so that in the hallway one glimpses a hall-boy and a chauffeur, also carrying Tony's belongings. Distributed among these servants are a violin case, half a dozen bags and suitcases, very smart and glittering; an overcoat, a rug, golf sticks, hat-box, tennis racquet, fencing foils in a case, a pillow envelope. The barrage of questioning opens up again with Julie, Dean and Kitty in the lead. Gwen, after the first flurry of the entrance, remembers her own problem. And, while she is interested in Tony's explanation, etc., she is plainly disturbed about Perry Stewart.)

JULIE: But Tony, how did you get here? It isn't possible!

DEAN: My dear boy, this is rather bewildering!

KITTY: Well, you're a great one! Of all the surprises!

FANNY: If this is one of your jokes, Tony Cavendish—

TONY: Sh-sh! Be quiet will you, everybody! Shut up!

(*Complete quiet then, for a brief moment.*)

Somebody go out there— (*Points to the entrance.*) and lock the doors! Gwen! (*Indicating library.*) Take a look out of that window! See if there's a man out there in a long overcoat!

(*Gwen vanishes a second through library doorway. Appears again immediately.*)

Take everything up to my room, Jo!

(*Jo starts slowly up the stairs, laden with luggage, a glance over his shoulder to indicate that the hall-boy and the chauffeur are to follow him with their share of the burden. They follow.*)

Julie, have you got some change? I want a lot of change. (*Turns toward his mother. Tilts up her chin, gaily. Kisses her.*) How's America's sweetheart? Aren't you glad to see your baby boy?

JULIE: Tony, will you quiet down long enough to explain this trick entrance? How did you get here?

TONY: I'll tell you in a minute. First I want some money. (*Glances up toward chauffeur, hall-boy, Jo, on stairway. To Chauffeur.*) Let me see. You get twenty dollars. (*Aside to others.*) He brought me in from Mineola. . . . You get ten . . . (*To the hall-boy.*) And ten apiece for those fellows downstairs. How many are there?

HALL-BOY: Three, sir. Two, and the doorman.

TONY: All right. You take forty, and you get twenty. . . . And now remember, you fellows, if any of those reporters ask you, you didn't see me, I never came in here. You don't know anything about me. Do you get that?

HALL-BOY: Yes, sir.

CHAUFFEUR: I get you.

TONY: Julie, let them have the money, will you?

JULIE: Jo, you attend to it. My bag's on my dresser.

JO: I'll see to it.

(*At the end of his own last line Tony has started to throw off his fur coat, shrugging his left shoulder free and revealing his left arm in a silk sling. A little shriek from Fanny.*)

FANNY: Tony! Your arm!

JULIE: You're hurt!

DEAN: Is it a serious injury?

KITTY: (*At sight of the arm.*) Oh!

GWEN: (*Half aloud.*) Oh, Tony!

TONY: It doesn't amount to anything. I hit him too hard, that's all.

(*Fanny makes a pitying sound between tongue and teeth.*)

JULIE: How did it start in the first place?

DEAN: Let's hear about it.

TONY: Della, I'm starved. I haven't had a bite for twelve hours. Bring me everything you've got.

(*Della goes.*)

First I've got to have a hot bath. Come on up stairs, everybody, while I take a bath.

(*With Kitty and Dean in the lead, Kitty having one foot on the stairway, they all go up toward the stairs. Fanny is last.*)

JULIE: Tony, will you listen to me! How did you get here today? You were in Omaha yesterday.

TONY: I flew, of course. Came by aeroplane from Chicago.

DEAN: Aeroplane!

KITTY: Flew!

JULIE: Tony Cavendish!

TONY: I couldn't come on a train. They're watching the trains. I've got to lay low in this apartment till I sail.

FANNY: Sail!

JULIE: Sail where?

TONY: Europe, of course. To-morrow on the Aquitania. . . . God, I hate pictures. . . . I've got to have a bath. If you want to hear the rest of it come on up!

(*Tony starts again for the stairway, and Kitty and Dean mount quickly ahead of him. Julie follows just behind, with Fanny bringing up the rear. Gwen remains on stage. As they ascend the stairs, Tony, Julie, Dean and Kitty are talking constantly and simultaneously.*)

DEAN: What happened out there, Tony? How did you get into this fight?

TONY: He had it coming to him ever since we started to shoot. He put his girl into the picture and when she got stuck on me he got sore. The blow off came when we were out on location. Doing a desert scene and Deming picked out the worst camel in the pack, and said to me, "You ride that one." I took one look at it and said, "The hell I will!" He said, "Who's directing this picture, you or me?" I said, "You're directing the picture, but you're not directing me. I'm through with it, and you can take this to remember me by."

JULIE: Unless you've killed him, Tony, I don't see why they're making all this fuss. And as for your going to Europe, I think it's the most ridiculous thing I've ever heard of. And you walked out in the middle of a picture, of course. They'll probably sue you for a million dollars, and you'll never get another picture job. (*Over balcony railing to Gwen, just exiting.*) Get your things on, Gwen—I'll be right down.

KITTY: I've always heard things about those directors, though I must say I met David Wark Griffith and you couldn't ask for a more perfect gentleman. He said to me, Miss Le Moyne, he said, if you ever want to go into pictures, come right to me.

DEAN: Perfectly right to put the fellow in his place. Catch me letting any whipper-snapper tell me what to do. I'd show him!

(*At the top of the stairs Tony leaps ahead of the rest and is the first to exit through the curtained doorway. Dean and Kitty follow, then Julie. Fanny is sufficiently far behind the rest to cause her question to come out clearly as the uproar of the others dies away with their disappearance.*)

FANNY: Who's this train woman? Zickery Zackery. (*Disappears.*)

(*Gwen's mood throughout this scene has been one of thoughtful depression. After the general exit she drifts down toward the table where her hat and coat have been thrown. Without glancing at it she picks up her hat, listlessly. As she stands, thoughtful, the hall-boy and the chauffeur appear on the balcony and descend the stairs quickly. The hall-boy leads. He is counting a little sheaf of crisp bills. The chauffeur is just putting his bills into his pocket. They depart. Gwen merely glances at them, resumes her position. With a little spasmodic gesture that is almost despairing she crumples her hat in her hand. She slumps into a chair, beating one hand softly with the crushed felt hat. A deep sigh. She sits staring ahead of her. A brief moment of quiet and silence. Jo comes onto the balcony; descends the stairs. The doorbell rings. The sound electrifies Gwen into sudden action.*)

GWEN: I'll go, Jo.

> (*Jo leaves. Gwen tosses the hat aside. Hurries up into the alcove.*)

PERRY STEWART: (*Off. With exaggerated elegance.*) Why! Fancy meeting *you* here!

GWEN: Oh, shut up, Perry!

> (*The sound of the door closing. Gwen comes back immediately, followed by Perry. He is speaking the next line as he comes.*)

PERRY: Come on, get your bonnet on. I'd like to stop at the club and look at that horse, wouldn't you? It'll only take a minute.

GWEN: Oh, Perry!

PERRY: What's the matter?

GWEN: I can't go.

PERRY: What do you mean—you can't go!

GWEN: They're going to read the play down at Wolfe's office.

PERRY: What?

GWEN: The author's going to read the play. And of course they had to pick to-day.

PERRY: What are you talking about?

GWEN: I can't go with you, Perry. I've got to go to Wolfe's office to hear the play read. There's no way out of it. I've got to do it. Isn't that damn!

PERRY: You're joking.

GWEN: But, Perry, I'm not! I know it sounds silly—

PERRY: Silly! It's cuckoo! I never heard anything so ridiculous in my life. You can't mean you're breaking this date just to go and hear somebody read a play. . . . What play?

GWEN: The play! The play that goes into rehearsal on Monday. That mother and I are doing.

PERRY: Why, good God, you've read it a thousand times. You read it to me!

GWEN: But this is different. The author's going to read it.

PERRY: Well, let him—the silly ass! What do you care!

GWEN: (*A long breath.*) Now, Perry, please try to understand this. It's part of my job, and it's important.

PERRY: Important to hear some idiot read a play that you've read again and again!

GWEN: But it's more than that—it's a ceremony!

PERRY: Gwen, you know as well as I do that we planned this thing a week ago. Mother's no Victorian, but listen, you can't do a thing like this. She wouldn't understand.

GWEN: Perry, I want terribly to go! I made an awful fuss. But what could I do?

PERRY: You know, Gwen, this isn't the first time you've done this to me.

GWEN: Perry, please don't be unreasonable.

PERRY: I don't think I was unreasonable about New Haven, when we were all set to go to the game—

GWEN: But I explained. I told you. You said you understood. Wolfe suddenly 'phoned—I had to go down to see the chap he'd got as juvenile. If it was somebody I couldn't stand— And Wednesday I had to be photographed with Mother.

PERRY: Yes, I know. I know.

GWEN: Don't look so stern. You know this is all just because of the new play.

PERRY: Yeh. But there'll always be a new play. (*Looks directly at her.*) Won't there?

GWEN: I realize it's inconvenient sometimes. It is for me, too.

PERRY: But what are we going to do about it, Gwen?

GWEN: If I can't go—I can't.

PERRY: I'm not talking about that. I mean us! . . . Look here, Gwen. You're no blue-eyed babe. I haven't dropped down on one knee and said will-you-be-mine, but you know I'm absolutely crazy about you. Don't you?

GWEN: Uh-hm.

PERRY: But what are we heading for? That's what I'd like to know. How's it all going to work out?

GWEN: Why—I don't know. What is there to work out?

PERRY: After all, you marry the person that you'd rather be with than anyone else in the world. But where'll you be half the time? Rehearsing, or something.

GWEN: Now don't be fantastic! Rehearsals last three weeks.

PERRY: All right. And then what! You're at the theatre every night. Your work will just begin when mine is all over. You'll have dinner at six. I'll probably not even be home. By midnight you're all keyed up and ready to start out, but I've got to be at work in the morning. We'll be living in two different worlds!

GWEN: But those things adjust themselves. Lots of other people have got around it.

PERRY: I'd do anything in the world for you, Gwen. I'd die for you! But I can't be one of those husbands. Hanging around dressing rooms! Side-stepping scenery. Calling up the costumer. What am I going to do every night. See the show!

GWEN: But you wouldn't want me to be one of those wives, would you! Bridge and household and babies!

PERRY: Well, why not! What's the matter with that!

GWEN: Because I can't do that sort of thing any more than you can do the other. I'm an actress, Perry. An actress!

PERRY: Oh, what does that mean! Suppose you turn out to be as good as your mother—or better! What is there to it when it's all over? Get your name up in electric lights, and a fuse blows out—and where are you!

GWEN: I won't let you belittle my work. It's just as important as yours. I suppose the world would go to pieces if you didn't sell a hundred shares of Consolidated Whatnot for ten cents more than somebody paid for it!

PERRY: You can't compare business with acting.

GWEN: Is that so! I can give you the names of actors and actresses of three hundred years ago—dozens of them! Name me two Seventeenth Century stock brokers.

PERRY: All right, I'll give up my work. That'll be dandy! And trail along behind you carrying your Pekinese, huh? . . . Not me!

GWEN: It's not a Pekinese! . . . Oh, Perry, what are we talking like this for! It's horrible. (*Goes to him.*) Forgive me! How could I talk like that to you!

PERRY: It's my fault. I didn't know what I was saying.

GWEN: Perry—dear! (*He takes her in his arms.*)

PERRY: Oh, what does anything matter!

GWEN: Weren't we a couple of idiots! We've never quarrelled before.

PERRY: And we won't again. There isn't anything that matters to me except you. Business and acting— We must have been crazy!

GWEN: And you're all that matters to me.

PERRY: Gwen darling! (*They kiss again.*) You're wonderful. . . . Now come on, honey. It's late.

GWEN: What?

PERRY: Why—you are coming with me, aren't you?

GWEN: Oh, Perry!

PERRY: Huh?

GWEN: You haven't heard a word I've said.

PERRY: I heard everything you said. You heard what I said, too, didn't you!

GWEN: Oh, Perry, we're not going to go all over this again, are we!

PERRY: No. We're not going all over it again. Not at all. We're not going over any of it again. It just comes down to one thing, that's all.

GWEN: It's like a bad dream! I can't go, Perry! Haven't I explained to you that I can't.

PERRY: Oh! . . . Yes . . . Well, I've got to get started, of course, if I'm going to get there. Good-bye. (*He has been making a confused withdrawal. Hurt. Angry. You hear the door bang.*)

> (*Gwen stands, her head up, defiantly. Then, as the realization of what has happened creeps over her, she becomes less confident. Even terrified.*)

> (*Julie appears on the balcony from centre door. She is in hat and coat. She is first heard talking over her shoulder to Dean and Kitty, who are unseen in the hallway off the balcony.*)

JULIE: If he'd only try persuasion now and then instead of knocking people down right away . . . (*Glances at her wrist watch.*) Good Lord! (*Moving swiftly along balcony, calls over the railing.*) Are you ready, Gwen?

DEAN: (*Entering.*) Well, I'll be on my way, too.

KITTY: Where are you going?

JULIE: (*Descending the stairs. Sees that Gwen is not dressed for the street.*) Good heavens, Gwen! Get your things on! What have you been doing? I must say you weren't much interested in Tony. (*Goes into library.*)

> (*Fanny comes onto the balcony. She is talking in a rather high-pitched voice to an unseen Tony in the room she has just left.*)

FANNY: Stay on the stage where you belong you wouldn't get mixed up with all that riff-raff! (*A mumble to herself as she*

stumps along the balcony and toward the stairs.) Moving
pictures!

JULIE: (*From library.*) Is the car downstairs?

DEAN: (*Has gone up to alcove. Starts to plunge into his coat.*)
Drop me at the Lambs', Julie?

KITTY: You're late, aren't you? Lackaye'll be worried. (*Into her
coat.*)

(*Tony appears on the balcony, singing a snatch of an aria,
he is wearing a gay silk bathrobe, monogrammed, embroi-
dered, tasseled. He advances with a romantic swing to the
balcony rail. Reaching it he strikes a magnificent pose,
aided by a high top-note. Fanny picks up the melody and
carries it a phrase further.*)

JULIE: (*Re-enters from library, pulling on her gloves.*) Lord,
we're terribly late!

TONY: (*Shouts toward servants' door.*) Jo, where the hell's my
lunch!

JULIE: (*Making a last dash.*) Gwen, *will* you get your things
out. . . . 'Bye, Mother! . . . Where do you want to go,
Bert? . . . See you later, Tony! . . . Gwen, what the devil's
the matter with you! Why don't you come?

GWEN: I'm not coming.

JULIE: (*Turns quickly.*) Now, Gwen, don't start all that again.
It's so silly.

GWEN: I'm not going, do you understand! I'm not ever going.
I'm not going to act in it at all.

JULIE: (*Impatiently.*) Oh, for heaven's sake!

FANNY: Don't be sulky.

DEAN: My dear Gwen!

KITTY: What's the matter with her?

JULIE: *Will* you put on your hat and coat? (*Turns again as if
to go.*)

GWEN: Listen to me! (*A note in her voice makes them realize
that here is something serious.*) I don't just mean I'm not
going to be in this play. I'm not going to be in any play.

JULIE: My offspring has gone mad.

GWEN: I mean it. I'm through with the stage. I'm never going
to act again.

JULIE: What are you talking about!

KITTY: She does mean it!

DEAN: Not act again! Why—why—brrrrr—why—

FANNY: The child's sick!

TONY: (*From the balcony.*) Don't go into pictures.

GWEN: Please! I've made up my mind, and all of you put together can't stop me. I'm through with the stage, and I'll
tell you why, if you want to know. I'm not going to have it
mess up my whole life!

> (*An hysterical jumble of attempted explanation. Her talk is
> pierced from time to time by exclamations from the others of
> the family.*)

. . . do you know what he did! He walked right out of the
room. . . . If you think I'm going to give him up for a
miserable little stage career just because we've always done it
. . . we'd never see each other . . . he'd get up in the
morning and I wouldn't go to work till night. . . . Look at
this afternoon with his mother waiting out there . . . it'll
be like that for years and years . . . only it's not going to
be! You're not going to ruin my life! I'm going to quit
now, while there's time! I'm going to marry Perry Stewart
and be a regular person! And nothing you can say is going
to stop me!

JULIE: I never heard such silly rot in all my life!

> (*From Dean, Fanny, Tony, Kitty such lines as: "Why, it's pre-
> posterous! Quit and get married!" [Tony.] "Who's Perry
> Stewart?" [Fanny.] "Never thought I'd live to see this day."*)

I don't know what you're talking about.

GWEN: Well, *I* know what I'm talking about. I'm sick of all
this. I'm sick of being a Cavendish! I want to be a human
being!

> (*From the others a shocked murmur.*)

FANNY: What's that!

DEAN: But you *are* a Cavendish!

JULIE: Of course you are.

GWEN: But I don't want to be!

JULIE: You've got to be! What do you think we've worked for
all these years!

FANNY: You can't do this to us!

JULIE: My God! What anyone else would give for your chance!

DEAN: Yes!

FANNY: It's absurd!

JULIE: You can be the greatest of us all. Aubrey and Fanny Cavendish have just been stepping stones for you!

FANNY: (*Rises. She is all dignity.*) What's that! What's that!

JULIE: Oh, Mother, please!

FANNY: I'll be a stepping stone for nobody! And as for Aubrey Cavendish, there's nobody since his day that can touch him!

DEAN: One minute, please!

GWEN: (*Taut. Defiant.*) Listen to them! *That's* what I mean.

DEAN: I believe my Macbeth still takes rank as the finest interpretation of its day and age.

JULIE: (*Cutting in on Dean's speech and topping it.*) For heaven's sake, you two! Telling how good you are! I'm pretty good myself, but you don't hear me talking about it!

KITTY: (*Very haughtily.*) Well, if you want *my* opinion—

JULIE: Well, we don't want your opinion.

(*From this spot on, Kitty and Julie are talking together at each other; and Dean and Fanny are talking together, combating each other. All this time Tony, on the stairs, has been viewing this family scene with a good deal of interest and enjoyment.*)

KITTY: No, I suppose not. Just because I'm not one of your precious Cavendishes I haven't the right to speak. But I want to tell you that Kitty LeMoyne can hold her head up with the best of them when it comes to acting. I may not have reached my present position by stepping on the heads of other people. I've won out by talent and hard work. It isn't always the people who have their names up in electric lights that are the best actors. I may not be a tradition in the theatre, but just the same—

JULIE: (*At the same time.*) This is purely a family matter and it seems to me that you'll save yourself a good deal of trouble if you'll just keep out of it. (*Turns her attention to Fanny and Dean, who, by now, have resumed their argument.*) Oh, who cares which of you was the best actor! If it comes to a show-down probably neither of you was so dog-goned good! And while you're about it, Herbert Dean, will you tell that wife of yours to stop talking. This is no concern of hers. Why doesn't she keep out of it! And why shouldn't Gwen be a greater actress than any of us! At least she's got intelligence on her side, and that's more than I can say of any of the rest of you. (*Turning again to Kitty.*) Oh, all right! You're Bernhardt! You're Modjeska! You're Duse!

DEAN: Role for role, my dear Fanny, I am a better actor than Aubrey Cavendish ever dreamed of being. You must remember that his was the day of the provinces, and while I have no doubt that he was a great favourite in the hamlets, it is quite another thing to win critical acclaim in London and New York. You may recall that on three successive nights I played Othello, Iago, and Petruchio, and that never under the historic roof of Wallack's Theatre have there been three such ovations. And a year later, at the old Vic I—

FANNY: You miserable upstart! Do you expect me to stand here and allow you to mention yourself and Aubrey Cavendish in the same breath! Aubrey Cavendish was an artist. He wouldn't have had you as his dresser! The greatest actors of his generation have sat at the feet of Aubrey Cavendish. Henry Irving, Beerbohm Tree, Richard Mansfield! And you have the presumption to fancy that your absurd struttings are comparable in any way with the histrionism of Aubrey Cavendish, the greatest actor that the English speaking stage has ever seen! You can stand there and tell me—

(*As the four voices approach a climax the telephone starts ringing. Simultaneously Della and Jo enter, each with a laden tray. Tony greets the trays.*)

TONY: Ah! Food! Right over here, Jo!

(*Gwen is standing a little apart from the others, intense. Della deposits her tray hurriedly. Goes to telephone.*)

DELLA: (*In phone.*) Hello! . . . She's on her way down, Mr. Wolfe! . . . Quite a while ago. . . .

(*The argument is still raging.*)

CURTAIN

ACT II

The scene is the same.

The time is about six o'clock on the following afternoon, Saturday.

There are fresh flowers in bowls and vases. Two of the lamps are lighted. The room is not yet fully lighted for the evening, however. The double doors, leading into the library, are closed.

AT RISE: *At the rise of the curtain there is heard the clash of fencing foils, the thud of feet, and male voices calling out occasional fencing terms, sometimes in earnest, sometimes mockingly. "Have at thee, varlet!" in Tony's voice.*

The library doors open. Fanny enters. She is carrying a newspaper in one hand. Walks with her cane.

FANNY: Jo! (*She glances toward the balcony, from which comes the sounds of combat.*) Jo! (*Goes toward right, turns up one lamp on her way. Shivers a little, draws about her a little shawl that hangs at her shoulders.*)
  (*Della enters.*)
Della, the fire's nearly out in the library.

DELLA: (*Over her shoulder.*) Jo! Bring some wood.
  (*A muffled answer from Jo, off.*)

FANNY: I must have dozed off. (*Another little shiver.*) What time is it, anyway?

DELLA: (*Lighting the remaining lamps, tidying the rooms, picking up the papers, plumping cushions.*) It's near six, I guess. Miss Julie's late. Said she was coming right home after the matinee. Course Saturday lot of young girls in the house, crowding back stage, taking her time up.

FANNY: More likely it's that passport of Tony's that keeping her. Europe! Got to sail for Europe! Huh!

DELLA: One of those reporters tried to get up in the service elevator a little while ago, but they got him.

FANNY: That crowd still standing around down there? In the wet snow?

DELLA: There certainly is a mob of 'em. Jo says since that piece in the paper to-night there's a bigger crowd than the time Mr. Tony got his first divorce.

(*Clash! Clash! from the balcony. The sounds of combat swell into an uproar as the battle grows hot. "Aha!" from Tony. A shouted speech or two, unintelligible but loud, from the panting combatants.*)

DELLA: I wish Mr. Tony'd stop that fencing. Poor Miss Gwen feeling the way she does.

FANNY: Tony! Hush that racket! . . . He's carved his way through every room in the house this afternoon. I had to lock the door of my bathroom.

(*Jo enters. He carries an armful of fireplace wood.*)

JO: Gee! Ought to see the crowd down there now! And they just rolled up one of those trucks with a lot of lights on it.

DELLA: Good grief! What for?

JO: Going to take movies, I guess. Catch everybody, going in and out.

DELLA: Gosh!

FANNY: They'll take no movies of me.

JO: And there's a fellow down there selling hot dogs and doing quite a business. . . . You want your tea, Mrs. Cavendish?

FANNY: Too near dinner time.

(*The clash of foils comes up again. McDermott and Tony, fencing, appear on the balcony, the former backing away from Tony's attack.*)

DELLA: (*Going up stairs.*) I brought a cup up to Miss Gwen, but she wouldn't take it again.

FANNY: Still in her room, is she?

DELLA: Hardly eaten a mouthful in twenty-four hours. (*Della goes on out, after successfully dodging the fencers.*)

(*The combat leads across the balcony and down the stairs, Tony maintaining the advantage, and keeping up at the same time a running combat, couched in a mixture of medieval and movie sub-title style.*)

TONY: Ha! He gives ground! Black Jennifer knows now the dark fate that soon is to o'ertake him! . . . Came the dawn, and yet they battled grimly upon the ancient parapet.

McDERMOTT: Je's! Go easy there!

TONY: Ha! He begs for quarter! Too late! Expect no mercy from Anthony the Elegant.

FANNY: "Ah, the immortal passado! the punto reverso! the hai!"

TONY: Ha, ha, varlet! Thou didst not know, what time thou didst dash a flagon of Burgundy from this hand, that thou hadst run smack up against the niftiest little swordsman in all of Gascony.

McDERMOTT: Heh!

TONY: And now, thou cur, prepare to meet thy end!

> Prince, call upon the Lord!
> I skirmish . . . feint a bit
> I lunge . . . I keep my word.
> At the last line, I hit.

(*He disarms McDermott.*)

JO: Hot dog!

TONY: Come, a kiss, my pretty wench!

(*Fanny falls into Tony's mood. Takes a few mincing steps to the victor's arms.*)

For have I not won thee fairly!

(*Tosses his sword to McDermott, who deftly catches it.*)

Here you are, Mac. I'll be up in a couple of minutes.

JO: I told you he was good. (*Disappears into library.*)

McDERMOTT: (*Goes up the stairs.*) Yah! Gee!

FANNY: You should have seen your father hold off eight of them—Aubrey and Fanny Cavendish in "A Gentleman of France." (*She works her way toward the stairs, her cane in one hand, the folded newspaper still in the other. She accompanies her next few lines with graphic illustration, in which both cane and newspaper become weapons.*) He'd send one head first right down the stairway, throw another one over the banister, quick as a wink he'd whirl and get one creeping up behind him—that scene alone took a full bottle of liniment every week.

TONY: (*Pats the withered cheek.*) Those were the days, Fanny.

(*Fanny, nodding her head in reminiscent confirmation, turns away. Tony rolls down the sleeves of his shirt; a realization of the hour disturbs him.*)

Say, where the devil is Julie? What time is it, anyhow? It's late!

FANNY: Maybe the weather's delaying her. She rings down quarter to five.

TONY: Well my God, is she getting my passport or isn't she? I've got to get out of here! I can't sail without a passport! She ought to know that!

FANNY: Now, now! Wolfe is helping her. You'll get it all right.

TONY: But when? The boat sails at midnight! I've got to get aboard early if I'm going to dodge that mob down there! (*A vague gesture toward the downstairs region.*) I ought to crack a couple of them in the jaw—that's what I ought to do!

FANNY: You've done enough jaw cracking. How are you ever going to get past them anyhow, even if Julie does get you a passport?

TONY: Lots of ways. They don't know I'm here—they're not sure at all.

FANNY: They've got a pretty good idea or they wouldn't be hanging around all day. Trying to get up in the elevator; calling up on the 'phone in funny voices.

TONY: Oh, the hell with them! I've got to get on that boat to-night! God! If Julie hasn't got that passport!

FANNY: (*With something of Tony's fire.*) Suppose she hasn't? Who says you've got to get on the boat? What for?

TONY: A million reasons! I feel like it! I want to get so far from Hollywood and sunshine—I never want to hear camera again! Or stage either, for that matter! You can have it! I'm through!

FANNY: Through! You've been saying that ever since "Fauntleroy."

TONY: I mean it this time! That's why I'm going abroad! Give me two years in Munich with my violin—under Ascher—and I'll show you what the stage means to me! I can be a great musician! . . . Or I may go away into India with Krishnamurti and study Hindu philosophy! It's the only real thing in the world! You wear just one garment—a long white robe—and you eat just one food! Rice!

FANNY: That'll be restful!

TONY: The stage! I'd rather spend ten minutes in the Cathedral at Chartres—I don't give a damn if I nev— (*In the course of making a sweeping gesture he encounters the huge*

pile of letters on the table.) What the hell is all this stuff?
They've been here all day! What are they?

FANNY: (*Shouting at him.*) They're for you! We've told you a
dozen times! It's your mail we've been saving!

TONY: Well, why didn't you say so? (*A second's calm while he
picks up a handful of letters. Then he dumps them all into the
waste basket. Turns away a few steps.*)

FANNY: (*Advancing on him.*) Don't think you're fooling me
about why you're going to Europe. Cathedrals, and violins,
and rice! It's this Dago woman you're running away from.
Else why was she on the train with you?

TONY: Oh, I'm not afraid of her. I gave her the slip at Chicago.

FANNY: Just the same, that's why you're going to Europe!
Don't lie to me, Tony Cavendish!

TONY: (*Reluctantly giving ground.*) Well, suppose I am! (*Flares
up again.*) Only I'm not afraid of her!

FANNY: Then what is it?

TONY: (*Paces a bit first.*) It's that God damned process server
she's got after me!

FANNY: What God damned process server?

TONY: (*It is being torn out of him.*) The breach of promise suit.

FANNY: Breach of promise?

TONY: (*Scornfully.*) Two hundred thousand dollars! She wants
two hun— (*On fire again.*) That's why I've got to stay
cooped up here! You don't think I'm afraid of reporters, do
you? But if they ever clap that paper on me I can't sail!

FANNY: Two hundred thousand for breach of promise. Assault
and battery on this director—probably another hundred
thousand. And breaking your contract with the picture
company—I guess half a million will cover it.

TONY: It's worth it, I tell you! God, that sunshine!

FANNY: (*Fiercely.*) What did you ever promise this movie actress that's worth two hundred thousand dollars?

TONY: Oh, she claims to have some letters—I didn't want her
in the first place! She was Deming's girl! That's why he got
sore!

FANNY: Who is she, anyhow? Where'd she come from?

TONY: Zeta Zaydak! She's a Pole.

FANNY: Look out for Poles!

(*The 'phone bell rings. Tony darts to the telephone, takes the receiver off the hook and listens for a second. Then he quietly puts the receiver down on the table; edges away.*)

FANNY: A woman's voice?

TONY: No, but I'm not taking chances. (*He goes back to the 'phone, a little furtiveness in his manner; takes up the receiver and listens again. Apparently he is satisfied that the caller is gone; he hangs up the receiver. Instantly the bell starts to ring again; Tony quickly takes the receiver off again. Puts it once more on the desk; slides away quickly from the instrument.*)

(*The sound of the outer door opening.*)

Who's that?

(*The slam of the door.*)

(*Julie enters. She has come in from the matinee. She is wearing smart winter street clothes—a luxurious fur coat and a costume to match. There is a bristling sort of vigour in the way she stations herself in the doorway.*)

JULIE: Damn your dear public, Tony!

TONY: Did you get it?

JULIE: The entire population of New York is standing on the doorstep, howling for a glimpse of America's foremost screen lover. In the meantime they take what Fortune sends, and it just so happened to be me.

FANNY: Your coat's ripped!

TONY: Julie! The passport! Have you got my passport?

JULIE: (*Calls.*) Della! . . . Oh! What a dandy day this has been!

(*Della appears on balcony.*)

Della, my slippers are soaking! Bring me some mules. . . . I had to get out at the corner—you don't dare drive up. And my dear Mrs. Cavendish, have you ever played to an audience made up entirely of sea lions!

(*She is energetically tearing off hat, coat, probably standing on one leg to unstrap her slipper which she kicks off across the room. Della, meantime, comes down with mules and fresh stockings. During Julie's speech she kneels and assists her with stockings, slippers, etc.*)

JULIE: They came in wet to the knees and never did dry off. They spent the first act taking galoshes off and the last act putting them on. *You* know . . . (*Stoops to pull imaginary zippers.*) . . . I looked out once during the last act and couldn't see a face. And cough! I think they had a cheer leader. Lincoln couldn't have held them with the Gettysburg address. How's Gwen, mother? Is she better?

TONY: Now, look here, Julie!

JULIE: Shut up, Tony! . . . Has she eaten anything? What's she doing?

FANNY: No. Wouldn't take her tea.

JULIE: I'll go up.

DELLA: Dinner at the usual time, Miss Julie?

JULIE: No, hold it a while, Della.

DELLA: (*Edging toward the door as she talks, delivering the day's messages in a sort of monotone.*) Mr. Cartwright 'phoned, and Mrs. Blair's dinner's postponed till a week from Sunday, and—

JULIE: Not now, Della, please.

DELLA: And the La Boheme shop says your dress is all ready. (*Goes.*)

TONY: Dress be damned! My boat sails at midnight. What have you done about my passport!

JULIE: Tony, my love, Wolfe is bringing it.

TONY: He is? Why didn't you say so? Thank God!

JULIE: He's been pulling all sorts of wires. He's been in and out of my dressing room all afternoon. *Everybody's* been in and out of my dressing room all afternoon. Compared to my dressing room Grand Central Terminal was a rustic retreat. And all on account of you, my baby. Reporters, and process servers, and sob sisters. . . . I'm going up to Gwen.

FANNY: Gwen's all right. You lie down and take it easy—with another show to play.

TONY: Listen, Julie—how soon'll he get here?

JULIE: Oh, I don't know. Right away. And he's bringing the money for you, too. They kept your reservation, and I've paid for it. You neglected to tell me that you were roughing it across in the royal suite.

TONY: I can't travel like a stowaway.

JULIE: Hire a battleship for all I care! But remember I'm a working girl. What do you do with all your money, anyway? You go out to Hollywood with a billion dollar contract and you buy a pink plaster palace for one hundred and fifty thousand, an Isotta Fraschini for twenty thousand, an Hispano Suiza for twenty-five, a camp in the Sierras for another fifty—good God, you were sunk a quarter of a million before they ever turned a crank on you! . . . And as soon as they start to take a picture you knock out the director and quit.

TONY: It'll all blow over in a month. That's why I want to get away.

JULIE: But why does it have to be Europe! What are you going to do when you get there!

FANNY: He's going to eat rice and play the violin.

TONY: I'm going to bathe in the pure beauty of Athens! I want to lose myself in the Black Forests of Bavaria!

FANNY: Mm! Switched your bookings.

TONY: I don't know where I'm going! Any place where it rains all the time!

JULIE: All right. Go to Pago-Pago. But attend to your own passport. I got my Art to look after.

(*Doorbell rings. Tony dashes for the stairs; turns.*)

Keep calm! They can't get up here.

TONY: Think we'd better open it?

JULIE: You'll have to go out to catch the boat, won't you? They can't back the Aquitania up to the door.

TONY: I'll get out, all right, when the time comes.

(*Jo enters. Starts toward the outer door.*)

Wait, Jo! . . . (*To Julie.*) Maybe it's Wolfe, huh?

JULIE: Shoot from the hip, Jo.

JO: (*Genially.*) Reminds me of the time the Grand Jury was after you. Remember that sheriff? (*In the alcove.*) When you took his gun away!

TONY: Keep a foot against the door!

JO: Who's out there!

DEAN: (*A muffled voice, off.*) What, what! This is Herbert Dean!

JO: (*Opening door.*) Oh, come right in, Mr. Dean.

(*Herbert Dean enters, with Jo following him on. His entrance is marked by relieved sighs from Julie, Fanny, and Tony.*)

DEAN: They ought to be arrested, those fellows. (*Flicking from his garments the contaminating touch of those who had waylaid him on the sidewalk. This finished, he starts to remove*

his coat. Jo takes it, with hat and stick.) Pushing me all
around.

TONY: You didn't tell them I was here?

DEAN: Of course not. But I hope, Anthony, that your next director will prove more congenial to you.

TONY: There isn't going to be any next director, old socks. . . .
Come on, Jo—I've got to pack and get out of here— (*Leaps
up the stairs, followed by Jo.*) —Tell you what I want you to
do. Want you to sneak out and get me three taxis exactly
alike—

    (*By this time they are both gone.*)

DEAN: What the devil's he up to!

JULIE: Mother'll tell you. I'm going up to see Gwen.

DEAN: Well—wait!

FANNY: I'm going in by the fire, Bertie, if you want to talk to
me.

DEAN: No—Julie—I want to talk to you. I've had a devil of a
day. In the first place, where's Oscar? I gave him my play to
read last night and I haven't been able to find him since.

FANNY: Isn't that funny! (*Goes into the library.*)

JULIE: He's coming here, Bert. Nail him.

DEAN: Really! Oh, fine! Ah—just one thing more! (*Detaining
her.*) And this is what I really came about.

JULIE: Not now. Please!

DEAN: Now, hold on, Julie. I've got to talk to you. It's vital.

JULIE: Bert, can't it be some other time? I've simply got to see
Gwen.

DEAN: No, no. I never needed you worse than I do now. I
wouldn't tell this to anyone else, but I know you'll understand. Give me just a minute. Please!

JULIE: Why—what is it? What's the matter?

DEAN: You see, it's this way. These last five or six years I
haven't—things haven't exactly—damn it all, it's youth!
Youth! They write all the plays for young whipper-snappers!
You've got to be built like a—uh—greyhound! Now mind
you, I'm just as youthful as anybody. I keep in good condition. Try to. Walk. But it's impossible to get a good massage
nowadays.

JULIE: Your figure's grand, darling.

DEAN: Not bad. But you see, with my position—I can't go

round—sit in offices—they've got to come to me! I sit and wait for letters, rush to the telephone—think each time— first thing you know it's months and months— What am I to do!

JULIE: Oh, you're just a little down. Something may come along any minute.

DEAN: That's just it! I've got it! This play! It's a Godsend! Just what I need! It'll put me on my feet again. I can easily get in condition for it. Diet! Exercise!

JULIE: Yes, I know. I read it. It struck me then, that if instead of trying—if you'd be willing to play one of those attractive—uh—slightly greyed parts—

DEAN: Oh, I can get around that. Pink lights—and I don't look over thirty. But here is the real difficulty. It's the girl. She's got to be young—beautiful! A vision! I can't have— (*Very confidentially.*) To tell you the truth, Kitty will ruin it. She'll ruin *me*! She'll kill the first real chance I've had in years.

JULIE: But you know I can't do anything with her.

DEAN: But you can! That's just it. For God's sake, Julie, say you'll do it.

JULIE: Do what!

DEAN: Take her off my hands. Give her that part in your play—you know—the Colonel's wife. She'd be very good in that.

JULIE: But Bert, I've got a—

DEAN: Yes, yes—I know. But you could let that woman out. The point is, you're big enough, Julie. It wouldn't hurt your play. You're so admired, and popular—nothing can stop you. Now, I've never asked a favor before—little things, maybe—but we've always stood by each other—the family. Let me go and tell Kitty you suggested it.

JULIE: But I had Kitty once before, and—

DEAN: I know. But this will be different. She'll be very good in that part. . . . I'm sure to have a hit. I could pay back everything I owe you—you, and different people—

JULIE: Oh, that's all right. Don't think of that now.

DEAN: (*Pats her hand, gratefully.*) You're a brick, Julie. . . . You've been very kind—I hadn't meant to come to you again—but you're the only one—I wonder—I was going to

ask if you could spare another five hundred—just a few
weeks—

(*Outer door bell rings sharply, three times.*)

JULIE: That's Oscar!

DEAN: Oh! Splendid! Now, what do you say, Julie? Will you do
that for me? Will you?

JULIE: (*Weakly.*) Bert, I'll try to dig it up. I don't know—

(*Della enters, heading for outer door.*)

Della, that's Mr. Wolfe. Tell him I'll be right down. I've got
Gwen up here.

DELLA: (*Pausing on her way to the door.*) How about dinner,
Miss Julie? It's getting late.

JULIE: Oh, I can't right now, Della.

(*Della continues toward door. Julie is going up the stairs by
this time.*)

I don't know what to say about Kitty, Bert. You've given me
an awful problem. Fortunately I've got so many that one
more doesn't matter.

DEAN: Then you will do it, huh? Good!

JULIE: Good! Hell, it's perfect! (*She goes.*)

WOLFE: (*As Della opens the door for him.*) Say, what a mob
scene you got down there!

DELLA: It certainly is terrible, all right.

WOLFE: (*Entering.*) Terrible, and what's more it's bad publicity. (*Sees Dean. Breaks off. From his look in Dean's direction
he is plainly far from delighted.*)

(*Della follows. Waits to receive Wolfe's coat.*)

DEAN: Ah, Oscar, my boy!

WOLFE: Hello.

DEAN: This is fortunate!

DELLA: Miss Julie'll be right down. Shall I take your coat?

WOLFE: No, thanks. I don't stay. (*Fanny appears.*)

FANNY: Hello, Wolfe! I thought it was your voice.

(*Della goes.*)

WOLFE: Your gifted daughter, Mrs. Cavendish, certainly gave a
fine ham performance this afternoon.

FANNY: Did you get his passport?

WOLFE: Well, I want to talk to Julie about it. Where is she?

FANNY: She's up with Gwen.

WOLFE: Yah? How is Gwen? Come to her senses yet?

FANNY: Stubborn as ever.

WOLFE: She'll come around.

DEAN: Now, Oscar, I've got a dinner engagement. (*His watch.*) Tell me how the play impressed you. Wonderful, isn't it? Tremendous!

WOLFE: (*Hesitatingly.*) M-m-m, yes, b—

DEAN: I knew you'd be crazy about it! Now I'll start lining up a cast and come in to see you to-morrow. About what time, say?

WOLFE: Oh—uh—any time. I don't know—

DEAN: (*A dignified scamper up to the alcove, throws his coat over his arm, claps on his hat, takes his stick.*) That's fine! Fine! We can start rehearsals in about ten days, eh?

WOLFE: (*Strolls uneasily up toward alcove.*) Now, not so fast, Dean. Pretty heavy show you got there. Take a pile of money to put that on.

DEAN: (*In protest.*) Oh, no, no, no, no.

WOLFE: Say! Fourteen scenes. Grand Central Terminal, Garden of Eden, Court of King Solomon, Battle of Waterloo—

DEAN: We can do it all with drapes. (*He hurries out.*)

(*Wolfe walks slowly across the room, puffing out his cheeks in rather stunned perplexity. His eye roves to Fanny, a grim figure in her chair. The two are in accord.*)

FANNY: I think Bertie has retired and doesn't know it.

WOLFE: I wish they were all like you, Fanny. (*Comes over to pat her shoulder.*) What d'you think? Going to be able to troupe again after the holidays?

FANNY: Tried to tell you yesterday, but you were so busy with your English playwrights.

WOLFE: Say, if I had to pick one actress out of the whole caboodle of 'em you know who it'd be. Come on, tell me. Think you can start out again? Sure enough?

FANNY: You can dust off the "Castlemaine" scenery, and I'd just as soon you'd route me to the Coast.

WOLFE: 'At a girl! You're worth a dozen of these New-York-run actresses. No foolishness about you. No private cars, and maids in the contract, and telegrams from the company manager you won't go on because the theatre's cold. No, sir! You're the girl that does twenty-eight hundred in Boise

City, Idaho, and catches the six-fourteen next morning for Pocatello.

FANNY: I did twenty-nine hundred in Boise City.

WOLFE: Chairs in the aisles, h'm? I tell you— (*A gesture toward the departed figure.*) —if Bert had taken his hits out on the road he wouldn't be in this jam to-day. But by nature Bertie is a Lamb's Club actor, and look what happens! In a couple more years he'll own six toupees, and be playing Baron Stein in an all-star revival of "Diplomacy."

FANNY: (*Getting to her feet to take the oath.*) May God strike me dead if I ever appear in an all-star revival! (*She sits again.*)

(*Julie appears on the balcony. Starts downstairs.*)

JULIE: Well, she's promised to dress and come out of that room, anyhow. That's more than she's done all day.

WOLFE: Say, what kind of a show are you going to give to-night, with all this hullabaloo!

JULIE: Once Tony goes, things will be a little better. It's so restful to think that at midnight he'll be rounding Sandy Hook.

WOLFE: M-m—that's what I came to talk about.

JULIE: (*Alarmed.*) What!

WOLFE: It don't go so quick. These fellows—

JULIE: You mean you can't get a passport! Oh!

WOLFE: Well, now, hold on. I don't say I can't yet exactly. There seems to be some sort of monkey business going on. Maybe they got wind of something and don't want him to get away.

JULIE: Oscar, another twenty-four hours with this caged lunatic and you can order strait-jackets for two. He's impossible to live with—and those terrible people on the street! If you think I gave a rotten matinee just wait till you see the night show!

WOLFE: Now, now, now! Did Oscar ever fail you? We'll get it all right—I hope. Anyhow, here's his money. That's that much.

FANNY: *How* much?

JULIE: What's the difference, Mother? He has to have it. (*To Wolfe. Her hand on his arm.*) Oscar, I owe you a ghastly lot of money, don't I? How much?

WOLFE: The money you're welcome to, Julie. But it oughtn't to be that you got to come to me like this. You make as much money as any woman in the business. Forty-one weeks you've had in this show alone—ten per cent of the gross—over fifteen hundred a week you've averaged. What the devil do you do with all your money, anyhow!

JULIE: Why—I don't know. What do you mean—do with it?

FANNY: What does anybody do with it?

WOLFE: Well, just for argument's sake, let me ask you once. Forty-one weeks, you've made sixty thousand since you opened in this play, and that says nothing about all the other ones. In the past twenty years I bet you you made a million dollars. Now how much of it have you actually got?

JULIE: Let's see—where's my bag? I've got over three dollars in that, and Della owes me seventy-five cents—
    (*Jo enters on balcony; starts to descend stairs.*)
—Oh, I don't know, Oscar. It just goes. (*To Jo, who is crossing to the door.*) Jo, tell Della caviar for Miss Gwen's dinner.

JO: Yes, Miss Julie. (*Goes.*)

JULIE: (*To Wolfe and Fanny.*) Perhaps that'll tempt her.

WOLFE: Well— (*Quick little gesture and a squeeze of Fanny's hand.*) I stayed longer than I meant to. (*Starts up to alcove.*) I let you know the minute I see this fellow, huh?

JULIE: (*Following him up a step or two.*) You're a dear, Oscar. Would it interest you to know that you are adored by the most beautiful actress on the American stage?

WOLFE: (*Airily.*) Nope!

JULIE: My Galahad!

FANNY: Good-bye, Wolfe.
    (*Wolfe goes.*)

JULIE: (*The slam of the door.*) Gwen! . . . Oh, I hope he gets that passport! I don't dare tell Tony there's any doubt of it—let's just hope he gets it—Gwen! (*A second's vain pause for an answer.*) She promised she'd come down.

FANNY: I thought she'd get tired of moping in her room like Elsie Dinsmore.

JULIE: Gwen, dear!

GWEN: (*Heard upstairs.*) Yes, Mother.

JULIE: Aren't you coming down, dear? I wish you would.

GWEN: (*Off.*) Yes, Mother.

FANNY: Who is this What's-his-name of hers, anyway? Doesn't seem to me like anything but an average young man.

JULIE: They're all average young men, except to the girl who thinks they're wonderful.

FANNY: Speaking of average, how's Mr. Gilbert Marshall? Have you seen him yet?

JULIE: No.

FANNY: Didn't he come to see the play?

JULIE: You know he always hated the theatre.

FANNY: (*Meaningly.*) Oh, yes.

JULIE: I suppose when he telephoned yesterday, and they told him I was out, he just thought I didn't want to see him. Perhaps it's just as well. It's a long time ago, and he's probably bald, and fat, and talks about conferences.

(*Gwen appears on the balcony. She is in one of those chiffon and velvet negligees; there is something of the Ophelia about her appearance. She has been cooped up with her resolution for twenty-four hours, and it is beginning to wear her down.*)

GWEN: (*Advancing to the rail.*) Nobody else there, is there? (*Gwen comes slowly, pensively down the stairs.*)

JULIE: Only your aged relatives.

FANNY: Speak for yourself.

(*Gwen has come down.*)

JULIE: Do you want to sit here, dear? Or shall we go in by the fire?

GWEN: (*Sits.*) Oh, this is all right. . . . (*Glances up with a rather wan smile.*) I don't mean to act like a prima donna. I just feel like hell, that's all.

JULIE: (*Standing over her.*) I know you do, dear. I hate to see you unhappy like this. (*Leans over, kisses the top of her head lightly.*) But you have so little sense.

GWEN: (*Her lips quivering. Very low.*) He didn't even telephone. He might at least have telephoned.

FANNY: How do you know he didn't? Tony had the receiver off most of the day.

JULIE: (*Puts the receiver back on hook.*) Yes!

GWEN: (*Eagerly.*) Do you think so! He might have, mightn't he? Oh! (*A little whimper of dismay. She even weeps, weakly.*)

JULIE: (*Pats her shoulder tenderly.*) Now, Gwen.

GWEN: Oh, Mother, I love him so!

JULIE: But that's nothing to cry about. (*A hand on her shoulder, patting her into calm.*) There!

(*A moment's pause while Gwen grows quieter.*)

FANNY: You can love him and marry him too, can't you?

JULIE: Of course you can marry him, Gwen, and live happy ever after.

FANNY: Only why you think you have to quit the stage to do it is more than I can figure out.

JULIE: It's hard for us to realize that you wouldn't want to keep on, Gwen.

FANNY: Your mother and I both got married. But we didn't drop more important things to do it.

GWEN: There isn't anything more important.

FANNY: Fiddlesticks! Marriage isn't a career—it's an incident. Aubrey Cavendish and I were married in the Church of St. Mary Redcliffe, in Bristol, England, just before the matinee. The wedding supper was served on the stage of the Theatre Royale between the matinee and the night performance—we played "She Stoops to Conquer" in the afternoon, and "A Scrap of Paper" was the night bill. They sent the supper in from the George and Lion next door, and very nice it was, too, but I remember they'd gone and put nutmeg in the gooseberry tarts, and Aubrey never could abide nutmeg. It must have been that that upset him, for he gave the only bad performance that night that I ever saw him give.

GWEN: I know, Grandma. But that's got nothing to do with me. You married an actor and— (*Turning to her mother, swiftly.*) —so did you. You lived the same sort of lives. Don't you see that this is different!

JULIE: Oh, I knew some rather nice men who weren't actors— didn't I, Fanny?

(*A gesture from Fanny of utter dismissal of this subject as being too vast and agonizing to go into.*)

There were lots of times when I thought that being a wife and mother was all that mattered in the world. And then each time I'd learn all over again that that wasn't enough for me.

FANNY: I should say not.

JULIE: Earthquakes, and cyclones, and fire and flood, and somehow you still give the show. I know it says in the contract that you stop for acts of God, but I can't remember that I ever did.

FANNY: Nor I. Nor your grandfather. Nobody ever knew what a sick man Aubrey Cavendish was, those last months. But he played a full season of thirty-five weeks. Dropped dead on the stage of Macauley's in Louisville two minutes after the curtain fell on Saturday night, the week we closed. Not only that, but he waited to take four calls.

GWEN: I know, I know. (*Rises.*) But—I'm not like that, that's all.

JULIE: (*Rises.*) You think you're not, but you are! Marry him if you love him, Gwen, but don't give up everything to do it! The day might come when you'd hate him for it.

GWEN: Hate Perry! (*A little bitter scornful laugh.*) You just don't know what you're talking about.

JULIE: Gwen, do you think it's going to be any fun for me to have them see you step out—acting with me in my play, and for all I know, walking away with it! You'll be so fresh, and such a surprise! And it'll be your night. I'll be proud and happy of course. (*A very little pause, and then, almost as though to convince herself.*) . . . of course. They'll say, "That's her daughter." But ten years from now it'll be, "That's her mother."

GWEN: I'll never be half the actress you are.

JULIE: Gwen, if I could only make you realize that the thrill you get out of doing your work is bigger than any other single thing in the world!

(*A little gesture of protest from Gwen.*)

Oh, I know! There's love. But you can be the most fortunate person in the world, Gwen. You can have both. But for God's sake don't make the mistake of giving up one for the other.

FANNY: No, child!

GWEN: Work! Acting isn't anything. What's acting compared to—

FANNY: It's everything! They'll tell you it isn't—your fancy friends—but it's a lie! And they know it's a lie! They'd give their ears to be in your place! Don't make any mistake about that!

JULIE: They'll say, "Come on and play," and you'll say, "I have
to work," and they'll say, "Oh, work!" There'll be plenty of
things that you'll have to give up—gay things and amusing
things—

(*Della appears in the doorway, evidently meaning to get
Julie's attention.*)

I've missed parties and dinners and rides and walks! All my
life I've had to get up just before dessert was served and just
when conversation was most entertaining!

FANNY: What is it, Della?

DELLA: How about dinner?

FANNY: Don't bother us!

(*Della goes, puzzled.*)

(*Stealing Julie's thunder.*)

You've got to leave, and go down to a stuffy dressing room
and smear paint on your face and go out on the stage and
speak a lot of fool lines, and you love it! You couldn't live
without it! Do you suppose I could have stood these two
years, hobbling around with this thing— (*Brandishing her
cane.*) —if I hadn't known I was going back to it!

JULIE: Long as I've been on the stage there isn't a night when
I stand in the wings waiting for my cue that I don't get that
sick feeling at the pit of my stomach! And my hands are cold
and my cheeks are hot, and you'd think I'd never seen a
stage before!

FANNY: Yes, yes! That's it! (*Struggling to her feet in her excitement.*) Every night when I'm sitting here alone I'm really
down there at the theatre! Seven-thirty, and they're going in
at the stage door! Good evening to the door man. Taking
down their keys and looking in the mail racks. Eight o'clock!
The stage hands are setting up. (*Raps with her cane.*) Half
hour, Miss Cavendish! Grease paint, rouge, mascara! Fifteen
minutes, Miss Cavendish! My costume! . . . More rouge!
. . . Where's the rabbit's foot! . . . Overture! . . . How's
the house to-night? . . . The curtain's up! . . . Props! . . .
Cue! . . . Enter! . . . That's all that's kept me alive these
two years. If you weren't down there for me, I wouldn't
want to live. . . . I couldn't live. You . . . down there . . .
for me . . . going on . . . going on . . . going on. . . .

(*The excitement and the strain are too much for her. Suddenly she goes limp, topples, crumples. Julie and Gwen, standing near her, catch her as she is about to fall, and place her in the chair from which she has risen. She is briefly unconscious.*)

JULIE: Mother! Mother, what's the matter!

GWEN: Grandma! Grandma!

JULIE: Mother! Tony! Della! Quick!

GWEN: (*At Fanny's side, frantic and remorseful.*) It's all right, grandma. I'll do it. I will. I will! Grandma! I'll do it!

(*Julie rushes to door, right. Calls, "Della! Jo!" Tony appears on the balcony, followed by McDermott.*)

TONY: What's the matter! What is it!

(*Tony dashes down the stairs, followed by McDermott in a surprising descent.*)

JULIE: She fainted! We were talking!

TONY: Do something! For God's sake do something! What are you all standing around for! Where is everybody?

GWEN: It's all my fault! Grandma! Grandma!

(*Jo and Della enter swiftly.*)

JULIE: Get some water! Whiskey! Quick!

(*Jo exits hurriedly.*)

(*Exclamations, suggestions, broken speeches from the group. "She's coming round." "She's better." "There, Mother." "It's me, Mother. It's Julie." "Telephone the doctor!" "You're all right. You're all right, Mother." "You're all right now."*)

(*Jo returns carrying water and flask. "There, take that, Mother. Just a sip. You'll be fine in a minute. There. She's taking it. Moisten her forehead with it," etc.*)

TONY: Mother! Mother! It's me—Tony!

(*The confused murmur of talk slowly dies. "There. We'll take her upstairs. You're all right now. There, there. Yes, it's all right, Mother dear."*)

GWEN: I'm going to do it, grandma. I didn't mean it. I will! Of course I will!

JULIE: Did you hear? It's all right! Everything's going to be all right!

TONY: She's better now! Aren't you, Mother?

FANNY: (*Struggles rather feebly to rise; to assert her indepen-*

dence. Her voice is little more than a whisper.) I'm all right.
There's nothing the matter. But I think I'll go up and lie
down.

(*They gather round to assist her.*)

TONY: Shall I carry her?

JULIE: Della, run ahead and turn the bed down. Jo, get a hot
water bag.

(*Jo and Della run up the stairs ahead of the others.*)

McDERMOTT: That's the stuff. Just lean on me. You're doing
swell.

TONY: Here we go! Now!

JULIE: Careful, Tony. Slow.

(*They move cautiously up the stairway.*)

FANNY: (*They are halfway up the stairs.*) Wait a minute. . . .
Wait. . . .

JULIE: What is it! Mother, do you feel faint again!

FANNY: I just want to rest a minute. . . . Just a minute. . . .
(*A long sigh.*) No use. . . . No use fooling myself. . . . I'm
through. . . . I'll never go back again. . . . It's finished.

JULIE: Oh, Mother, what nonsense!

TONY: (*Starting her on up the stairs again, gently.*) You'll be as
good as new to-morrow.

McDERMOTT: Sure you will.

(*Jo comes hurrying out of the centre door carrying a hot
water bag, goes swiftly into Fanny's room.*)

(*They are now at the head of the stairs.*)

JULIE: Now you're all right, mother. Now you go right to bed.
(*They stream into the bedroom, urging her on, reassuring
her. Here we are! Now everything'll be fine. Take it easy!
There! Now!*)

(*The door closes.*)

(*Gwen, during the latter part of this scene, has taken a few
slow steps up the stairs, so that she is by now about halfway
up. The moment of the door's closing finds her quite still on
the stairs. She brings her hands together in a little gesture of
desperation. You hear the impact of her closed fist against
her palm. Stumbles on up, heavily. Exits.*)

(*There is a moment of silence. Jo bursts out of the door of
Fanny's room, bent on an errand. Between his opening and
shutting of the door the sound of voices in Fanny's room*

comes up confused and high. A voice is heard above the others. Probably Julie's voice.)

JULIE: Spirits of ammonia. Bring the whole thing.

(*Jo goes hurriedly into Julie's room. A moment's pause. McDermott dashes out of Fanny's room; the voices come up as before. A moment's pause. Della comes out of Fanny's room, goes toward Julie's room. Jo enters from Julie's room, goes towards Fanny's room, carrying a heavy medicine case. As Della and Jo meet on the balcony the front door bell rings. Jo, laden with the case, obviously cannot answer it. Della, after a second's hesitation, turns, goes toward stairway.*)

DELLA: I'll go.

(*Descends stairs quickly. Jo goes on into Fanny's room. Della goes to outer door.*)

GILBERT MARSHALL: (*Off.*) Miss Cavendish in? Miss Julie Cavendish?

DELLA: Yes, sir.

GIL: Will you tell her—Mr. Gilbert Marshall?

(*Della reappears from the alcove, a little ahead of Gil.*)

DELLA: Yes sir, if you'll just— (*Della comes quickly around to the stairs, starts to ascend, with a somewhat indefinite continuation of her speech.*) I'll ask her if she can see you. (*Goes up and into Fanny's room.*)

(*Gilbert Marshall is forty-seven, quiet, dominant, successful. He gives the effect of power and control. Hair slightly greying. Very well dressed. He is in top-coat now as he stands surveying the empty room. His hat and stick in his hand.*)

(*As Della opens the door to enter Fanny's room, there comes from it a chorus of high-pitched voices. At the sound of what evidently is a scene upstairs Marshall turns and surveys the balcony. There is something of recognition in his glance and manner as he hears this.*)

(*After a moment McDermott rushes hurriedly out of centre door, balcony. He is carrying a bottle containing a white liquid. Probably medicated alcohol. He goes quickly into Fanny's room. Again the babel as the door opens and closes. Instantly it re-opens and Jo comes out. He comes down the stairs. A glance of inquiry at Gil.*)

GIL: Is there something the matter? Is Miss Cavendish—?

JO: It's Mrs. Cavendish, sir.

GIL: Oh, I'm sorry.

(*The sound of voices is heard again as Fanny's door is opened.*)

Maybe I'd better not wait.

JO: Oh, she's all right. Just a kind of fainting spell.

GIL: I won't intrude now. Just say I'll telephone.

JO: I'm sure Miss Julie'll be right down.

GIL: (*Doubtfully.*) Well—

JO: Just be seated, sir. (*Jo exits.*)

(*Gil stands a moment, uncertainly. Then he picks up his gloves from the table where he has laid them, puts on his hat, starts toward outer door.*)

(*Julie comes out of Fanny's room, quickly. A small towel is pinned across the front of her gown. Her hair is somewhat dishevelled. One sleeve is rolled up. She sees Gil about to depart.*)

JULIE: (*Down the stairs, swiftly.*) Gil! Gil! Don't go!

GIL: Julie! (*Comes quickly to foot of stairs.*) Can I help? What's wrong?

JULIE: It's nothing. I'm—it's just— (*Begins to cry, suddenly. She covers her face with one end of the towel, helplessly.*)

GIL: Julie, dear! (*His hand on her shoulder, reassuringly.*)

JULIE: Oh, Gil! (*Clings to him, a refuge.*)

GIL: I'm so sorry. Is she very ill? I shouldn't have come, should I?

JULIE: I'm so ashamed. I don't know why I— She's all right now. She's perfectly all right. It's been such a hellish day. Everything in the world that could happen—Gil, you're still sane, aren't you?—and solid, and reliable and sure!

GIL: I hope so.

JULIE: How nice! . . . (*Suddenly aware of her appearance. Glances down at towel.*) And I was going to be so ravishing on our first meeting. I had it all planned. (*Unpins towel. Throws it aside.*) Let me make another entrance, will you? I'll say, wistfully, "It's really you, Gil! After all these years!" and you'll say—

GIL: (*One stride. Takes her hand.*) I'll say—

(*Della appears on the balcony from Fanny's room. The sound of the door interrupts Gil. Both glance up quickly.*)

JULIE: Do you want me, Della?

DELLA: (*Comes swiftly down the stairs.*) No, she's fine, Miss Julie. Mr. Tony's telling her stories about Hollywood to quiet her.

GIL: Julie, I know I'm in the way. I—

JULIE: Oh, please stay, Gil. This is the first peaceful moment I've had to-day.

GIL: No wonder, with the mob downstairs.

JULIE: You've seen the papers, of course.

DELLA: Pardon me, Miss Julie, but it's twenty minutes after seven. I thought perhaps— (*An apprehensive glance at Gil. Dinner is on Della's mind.*)

JULIE: It's all right, Della. Never mind. I'll let you know.

DELLA: Yes, ma'am. (*Goes.*)
   (*A moment's silence as the two are alone. They look at each other. Then they speak together.*)

GIL AND JULIE: You haven't changed a bit. (*A light laugh as they realize the absurdity of this.*)

GIL: (*Draws up a chair near hers.*) Do you know, Julie, I haven't gone to see you once in all these years.

JULIE: I think I'd have felt it if you'd been out front. And you never were? Not once?

GIL: No. I've only been in New York a few times since then. South America's a long way off. But I kept track of you. I took the New York Times and—the Theatre Magazine, is it?

JULIE: You haven't been exactly hidden from the public gaze, Gil. What was it you found down there? Radium? Lying around in chunks?

GIL: Oh, no, not radium. Platinum.

JULIE: Anyhow, you've got millions and millions.

GIL: I've done—pretty well. But say! You're certainly top of the heap in your line.

JULIE: Oh, the zenith!

GIL: And you have a daughter, haven't you? Seventeen.

JULIE: That was last year's paper. Gwen's eighteen.

GIL: I want so much to see her.

JULIE: We're going to be in a play together for the first time. Think of it!

GIL: That ought to be exciting.

JULIE: It's been exciting enough. Gwen got a sudden horrible idea that— (*The telephone rings. Julie glances quickly toward door right, as though expecting Della to answer.*) Sorry. (*Goes to telephone.*)

Hello! . . . Yes. . . . Oh, Oscar! . . . Oh, dear! . . . Yes, I'm sure you did, but—oh, Oscar!

(*Tony comes onto the balcony from Fanny's room, carefully closing door behind him, his attention all on the telephone below.*)

Well, of course, if you can't there's no use. . . . There's nothing to be. . . . Yes, I know it is. I'm leaving right away. . . . Don't worry. I'll give a swell performance. (*Hangs up.*)

TONY: Was that Wolfe?

JULIE: Oh, Tony! . . . How's mother? All right?

TONY: Asleep. . . . Who was that on the 'phone? Wolfe, wasn't it?

JULIE: Now, Tony, I don't want you to hit the ceiling—

TONY: (*With a snarl.*) He hasn't got it!

JULIE: It's not so vital. You haven't done anything so terrible—

TONY: You don't know what you're talking about! You'll find out if it's vital! Why, my God! If this woman—

JULIE: Oh, don't be childish, Tony! What can she do to you! You talk like somebody in a melodrama! Now calm down and shut up. . . . Gil, this is my brother Tony. Tony—Mr. Gilbert Marshall.

TONY: (*Through his teeth.*) Charmed! . . . (*Turns again to Julie.*) What the hell kind of a jam do you think I'm in, anyway? (*During the following speech he is down the stairs, up and down the room furiously, and up the stairs again.*) What do you think I blew all the way from California for! The ride! I've got to get out of here, I tell you! Zaydak's in town by this time. Do you know what that means! You don't know that Polecat! Why I've seen her pick up a— (*Snatches a fragile glass ash tray off the table, which he uses to accent his gestures as he goes on, forgetting meanwhile that he has it.*) She's a killer! She'll do anything! She'd just as soon shoot as look at you! She's a Pole, she's cuckoo about me, and she knows I'm through with her! Now if you don't want to do anything to help me, why, all right! (*Turns, starts up stairs.*) You're a hell of a sister! I'm only your brother and why should you bother about me! But I'm telling you now if

they get me I'll be all over the front page and so will you
and so will Gwen, and the whole damned family! Now, if
that's what you want, believe me, you're going to get it!
(*On the balcony, discovers ornament still in his hand. A smoth-
ered exclamation of disgust at finding it. Smashes it to the
floor.*) . . . Pleased to have met you, Mr. Gilson. (*He is
gone.*)

(*A moment's pregnant pause. Gil stands looking up after
the departed whirlwind. His gaze comes back to Julie.*)

GIL: Is he always like that?

JULIE: Oh, no. That's the brighter side.

GIL: But what is it he wants? What didn't you do for him?

JULIE: He wants to sail to-night on the Aquitania, and we
can't get a passport.

GIL: A passport? And he's putting you through all this for a—
well, no wonder you're upset.

JULIE: This! What you've seen is practically the rest hour.
We've had Gwen deciding to leave the stage forever—

GIL: What!

JULIE: —Mother having a little collapse, Uncle Herbert—you
remember Uncle Herbert, don't you?—well, we won't go
into that.

GIL: Look here, Julie. When does Tony want to sail?

JULIE: Midnight. The Aquitania.

(*Gil goes directly to the telephone, takes up the receiver.*)
Why?

GIL: Bowling Green ten-five-one-six. . . . How soon can he
get down there?—Tony, I mean.

JULIE: To the boat? Why—right away, I guess, if he can slip by
the reception committee.

GIL: Tell him to get ready—no, wait a minute—Hello! John?
. . . let me talk to Moran. . . .

JULIE: Gil, do you mean you can get it? Oh, if you only could!

GIL: Don't you know there isn't anything in the world that I
wouldn't . . . hello! . . . Why, if I thought you needed me,
Julie, I'd go to the ends of the . . . Hello! Moran? This is
Marshall. . . . Now get this. . . . I want an emergency
passport . . . Aquitania to-night. . . . That's right. . . . I
want you to meet me on the Cunard dock in half an hour.
. . . (*To Julie.*) Can he make it in half an hour?

JULIE: (*Eagerly.*) Yes, yes!

GIL: (*In 'phone.*) Now, no slip-up on this.

JULIE: (*Sotto voce.*) Twenty minutes.

GIL: I'll give you the detail when I see you. . . . Right. (*Hangs up.*)

JULIE: Oh, Gil!

GIL: I'll meet Tony and smuggle him on board. Moran will do the rest.

JULIE: Tony! Tony! (*Turns to Marshall.*) It's wonderful of you, Gil. Why, you're one of these strong silent men, aren't you!
   (*Tony appears.*)
   Tony, we've got it! Hurry up! Get ready!

TONY: What! You mean the passport!

JULIE: Yes! Yes! Gil got it for you! He's going to meet you there and fix—

TONY: (*Racing down the stairs.*) Whee! (*A leap.*) That's the stuff! (*Bounds over to Julie.*) You're a swell sister!— Jo! Jo!

JULIE: Now Tony, you understand you're to go right down there. Gil will meet you on the dock. He'll have the pass-port.
   (*Jo's head is seen in doorway.*)

JO: Yes, sir?

TONY: Jo, I'm going to leave in five minutes! You got every-thing ready?

JO: Yes, sir. It will be.

TONY: All right. Go to it. (*Leaps for the stairs as Jo exits.*) Sis, you're a grand kid! I knew I could count on you. Old reli-able. (*To Gil.*) Much obliged, old fellow! (*To Julie, in the same breath.*) Who is he, anyway? (*And off.*)

JULIE: (*Groping uncertainly for a chair. Rather mockingly ut-ters the trite phrase of the theatre to cover her own shaken con-dition.*) Won't you—sit down? (*Sits.*)

GIL: Why do you stand for all this?

JULIE: Oh, Tony doesn't mean anything. He's always like that.

GIL: What do you mean! That you have this kind of thing all the time, and that you go ahead and put up with it!

JULIE: Oh, sometimes families are. . . . It just happens to-day that blood is thicker than usual.

GIL: But these other things that you were talking about. You oughtn't to allow them to do that! You're a successful actress. Head of your profession. You ought to be the one they're running around for. And look! Everybody dumping their troubles on you.

JULIE: Oh, it isn't always like this.

GIL: You know, Julie, the reason I went away was so that you could go ahead and be an actress. All that stuff about Cavendish, and the stage being your real life, and the only way you could be happy. Well, here you are. You've got everything you went after. And how about it? Are you happy?

JULIE: Happy! I don't know.

GIL: Of course you're not. Julie, I've stayed away all these years because I thought at least you were living the life you wanted most. And then I come back and find this. You ought to have everything in the world. You ought to have everything done for you—done for you by some one who loves you . . . and I do love you, Julie, still.

JULIE: Oh, don't, Gil—don't say things that will make us both—

GIL: Don't you know what you ought to be doing instead of this! The way you ought to be living! Why, you ought to be in a country house somewhere, with a garden around it, and trees. Julie, if you could see the place I've got in England. Wyckhamshire. An old stone house, and the river's right down here, and a rose garden that's famous. People come from miles around. It's a beautiful place, Julie; and there it stands, empty.

JULIE: Oh, Gil!

GIL: And I've got a villa at Como—with the lake! (*A gesture.*) —I don't know why I bought all these places—it must have been for you. Or we can go any place else you want—Cairo, St. Moritz—anywhere you say. Don't you know that's the way you ought to be living! Don't you? Don't you! Don't you!

JULIE: I don't know! I don't know!

GIL: Julie! (*Takes her in his arms.*) What fools we've been! What fools!

JULIE: Gil—wait! Let me think a minute. Let me get my breath.

GIL: You've had too long to think. It's settled. (*Again he takes her in his arms.*)

JULIE: (*As she gently frees herself.*) No—please! I'm not quite sure what's happened. I can't think very clearly—

GIL: I'll tell you what's happened. Something that should have happened twenty years ago. That's what's happened.

JULIE: Well, perhaps if—maybe—Gil, you'd better go now. I think you'd better go. It's late.

GIL: All right. . . . Must I?

JULIE: Please.

GIL: I—I can't take you to the theatre?

JULIE: No—please. I must get Tony away, and—I couldn't give a performance if—just a minute alone—

GIL: (*Going up into alcove; getting hat and coat.*) It'll only be for a few hours—this time.

JULIE: You'll call for me at the theatre?

GIL: At eleven? Is that all right?

JULIE: At eleven.

GIL: I'll be waiting.

JULIE: That'll be wonderful.

GIL: Good-bye.

JULIE: (*Gayly.*) Good-bye!

(*Gil goes.*)

(*Julie stands a moment. A step toward him as he departs. Then a slow turn. A second's absolute silence.*)

(*Tony leaps out on balcony, clad in his B.V.D.'s and a bathrobe of silk worn open and billowing away behind him.*)

TONY: (*Very loud.*) Jo! Jo! Where's that bastard!

JULIE: Tony, be quiet! You'll wake mother!

TONY: Well, God damn it, I've got to get out! Jo!

(*Della enters, carrying a covered cup of hot soup on a small tray.*)

JULIE: Tony, will you shut up!

DELLA: Miss Julie, you'll have to be going. You've just got to have something hot in your stomach. Now, you drink this soup.

TONY: (*Simultaneous with Della's speech, above. Starting down the stairs, his robe ballooning behind him.*) Della, where the hell is Jo!

(*Jo enters, followed by hall-boy in uniform.*)

Jo, where the hell have you been! Come on! Bring that boy and come up here. I've got to get out!

JO: (*Crossing on a little flat-footed dog-trot.*) Yes, sir. On the job. Got it all fixed.

JULIE: What time is it? . . . Good heavens! . . . I can't stop to eat, Della. . . . No, I can't! . . . Get my things. . . . I've got to run. . . . Look after mother, won't you? . . . Bring her some hot soup. . . . Tony, what's all this hullabaloo! Oh, if you were only out of this! *What* I wouldn't give for a little peace and quiet!

TONY: (*Toward stairs. Talks through last part of Julie's speech.*) I'm not making any racket! You're making all the racket. Nobody'll be gladder than I am—

DELLA: (*Has placed tray on table. Up to alcove for Julie's hat and coat.*) You know very well you can't give a performance on an empty stomach. Go fainting in the wings, and then what! You wouldn't even have to sit down to it. You could swallow this cup of good hot broth.

> (*As the three voices climax, speaking together, Fanny appears on the balcony, from her room. She wears a rich and handsome dark silk dressing gown, voluminous and enveloping.*)
> (*Jo and the hall-boy have gone up the stairs meanwhile and have disappeared.*)

FANNY: Hush that clatter! Person can't get a wink!

JULIE: (*Goes toward her.*) Mother! What are you doing up!

TONY: (*Leaps up stairs.*) Hi there, Fanny! All right again! (*Stops as he reaches her. Pats her shoulder.*)

DELLA: Why, Mrs. Cavendish!

JULIE: Go back into your room this minute, Fanny Cavendish! Go back to bed!

FANNY: (*Starts down, assisted a step or two by Tony, who leaves her to Julie, who has come up part way.*)

> (*Della, hat and coat in hand, has trotted over to foot of stairs to assist when Fanny shall have got that far.*)

What's going on here! What's the excitement!

TONY: There you are! You're the comeback kid!

JULIE: Mother, I wish you hadn't done this. I've got to go to the theatre. . . . Gwen!

FANNY: I know. I know. Run along.

JULIE: I will not run along until you go back to bed. I want you to go back to bed.

FANNY: But I want to see Tony go! I can't stay in bed with
    Tony going!

JULIE: Tony, for heaven's sake hurry up! How soon will you be
    ready?

TONY: All set! I'll be gone in thirty seconds! . . . All aboard
    for Europe! (*As he turns to go he passes Gwen coming in.*)
    Hello, there! (*Tony exits.*)

GWEN: Mother, did you call me?

JULIE: Oh—yes, Gwen. I want you to look after mother.
    (*Gwen starts down stairs. Julie is descending with Fanny.*)
    I'm terribly late. Mother, lean on me. Gwen, take her other
    arm.

FANNY: I don't need any arms.

JULIE: Yes, but you do, though. You oughtn't to be up at all.
    Now Gwen's going to look after you—and Della, if you
    need me you're to telephone the box-office, you under-
    stand, and ask for Mr. Freidman—*you* know. I'll come right
    home after the performance— No! Yes, I will! There! (*She
    has settled Fanny in her chair.*) Now Della'll bring in your
    dinner, and Gwen'll get anything you want, and—Gwen,
    what makes—you've been crying.

GWEN: No, I haven't.

DELLA: (*Still with Julie's hat and coat.*) Miss Julie, it's quarter
    to eight. You know what the traffic is.

JULIE: (*Has gone over to the table on which the soup stands. Starts
    to drink a mouthful of it during this speech.*) Oh, I've got to
    go through that crowd downstairs again! . . . Whew! this is
    hot! . . . And how Tony's ever going to manage it. (*Calls.*)
    . . . Tony, are you ready!

TONY: (*Voice from balcony.*) Right!

JULIE: I've got to know he's on that boat or I won't be able to
    play. . . . Mother, I want you to promise me to go back to
    bed the minute Tony's gone. Have your dinner in bed.

FANNY: Don't you fuss about me.

JULIE: But don't wait up for me, will you? Della, I can't take
    this. I'm not hungry. I haven't got time for it anyhow. . . .
    (*Calls.*) Tony! Are you coming! . . . (*To Della.*) Hat! (*With
    a quick movement she seizes the hat from Della's hand and
    pulls it down on her head.*)

TONY: (*Heard off.*) All right! Go!

(*Out of the balcony entrance and down the steps sweeps the procession. It consists of Jo and Mac, laden with all the luggage that Tony arrived with on the preceding day. Then comes the hall-boy, disguised in Tony's hat and coat—the up-turned fur collar, the pulled-down slouch hat, just as Tony entered in the first act. His face is concealed almost entirely by the coat collar and the hat.*)

(*Julie and Gwen follow the group on up into the alcove, shouting their good-byes and last-minute instructions. Fanny rises, her arms out, as though expecting Tony to come to her before he goes out.*)

JULIE: Here he is! Thank goodness! How he's going to do it I don't know. I ought to go down with him.

GWEN: No, don't, Mother!

FANNY: Good-bye, Tony! Good-bye, my boy!

JULIE: Take care of your sinus. Keep out of Russia. . . . Why do you have to have golf clubs!

(*From this point the voices of Fanny, Julie and Gwen are heard simultaneously.*)

Don't start anything rough with anyone downstairs for Heaven's sake! Jo, make him behave himself. Mac, I'm trusting you too. They're sure to know him in those clothes. Why do you have to go to Europe! Well, anyhow, good-bye! Good-bye!

GWEN: Tony, take care of yourself. Send us a radio. Be sure! I think it's absurd to take all that stuff. He could buy it all over there. Good-bye! Good-bye!

FANNY: Tony! Tony! What are they going to do to him! I wish somebody was going along. Wolfe ought to be here. Don't stay away long, Tony. Come and kiss me. Good-bye, good-bye. Aren't you going to say good-bye!

(*The three figures have swept down the stairs, been joined by Della, have moved quickly across the room, and are now in the alcove on their way out. Julie, Fanny, and Gwen stand aghast as they realize that Tony is not stopping to say good-bye.*)

JULIE: Tony, aren't you saying good-bye to us? He isn't saying good-bye.

GWEN: Tony! Wait a minute! Say good-bye to us all. Why, he isn't stopping! He's going! He's gone!

FANNY: Tony, my boy! Don't let him go! Say good-bye to me!
He's never gone like that! Come back and say good-bye! He
didn't even talk to me! He didn't look at me! Tony! . . .
Tony! . . . Tony! (*Growing weaker.*)

JULIE: (*Rushing back to her.*) Now, Mother! He's all right! You
wouldn't want him to stop! He'll send you a radio. Now
don't! You'll only make yourself sick!

GWEN: Never mind, Grandma—it'll be all right. . . . I think
it's a rotten shame.

JULIE: (*Darting toward the alcove, then realizing that her
mother needs her more.*) Tony! Tony! . . . No, I guess I'd
better not! (*Runs back to her mother.*) Mother, you're all
right, aren't you? Don't worry. I've got to go to the theatre!
(*Through the outer door Kitty and Dean enter, Kitty
leading.*)

KITTY: (*Off.*) Why, the door's open.

DEAN: (*As he and Kitty enter.*) What was that? Tony?

GWEN: Are you all right, Grandma?

JULIE: Oh, good heavens! I wish I didn't have to go. Gwen,
do you think she's all right?

DEAN: What's the matter? Fanny sick?

KITTY: Listen, Julie Cavendish! I've got something to say to
you.

JULIE: What? . . . Don't—
(*Tony, in hall-boy's uniform, darts out onto the balcony. He
does not pause, but skims the balcony and down the stairs.*)

TONY: Hello, folks! Farewell appearance!

JULIE: (*In a sort of squawk that dies in her throat.*) Oh! . . .
Oh! . . . Oh, for . . .

FANNY: Tony!

GWEN: Oh!

DEAN: What *is* this?

KITTY: What's he doing?

TONY: (*Glances down at himself.*) How do you like it? Good on
me? Isn't it?

JULIE: Tony! What are you going to do!

TONY: Going to the boat, of course.

FANNY: Like that!

TONY: Sure! They'll make a dash for the taxi—the crowd will
all swarm after them—give 'em a nice run up Fifth Avenue.

Then I go down, cab at the door, ten minutes I'm on the dock. Voila!

DEAN: What's it all about?

FANNY: Tony, my boy!

JULIE: Oh, don't. . . . Oh! Tony!

TONY: (*A swift leap across the room.*) Good-bye everybody! (*Takes Fanny's head in his two hands. Kisses her.*) Good-bye, Mother! (*A pose.*)
> The open sea! the salt spray!
> The Arctic wind! . . . I'm on my way! . . .
> Remember it's the Guaranty Trust.

(*He goes.*)

FANNY: (*Rather feebly.*) Tony! Tony! (*Sits, weakly.*)

DEAN: Why! What! . . . What!

JULIE: (*Sinks into a chair.*) Ooooooh!

KITTY: (*Comes to Julie; stands over her.*) And now I want to ask you a question.

DEAN: Kitty!

KITTY: Did you offer me that part of your own accord, or did Bert put you up to it?

DEAN: Oh!

JULIE: (*From the position into which she slumped in the chair Julie begins to uncoil. Her eye is baleful. She rises slowly. Her whole attitude is so sinister and desperate that Kitty shrinks back a little.*) No! No, it isn't possible! You! You come to me with your miserable little— Your part! Bert's. . . . (*A little high hysterical laugh.*) After all that I've . . . it's too . . . I can't . . .

GWEN: Mother! Don't!

(*Perry enters.*)

Perry!

PERRY: What's the matter! What's going on?

JULIE: Well—what else! What else! Come on! What else! Perry! for God's sake take her out of this! Take her away before it's too late. Take her where she'll never hear stage again! Take her away! Take her away! Take her away!

FANNY: Julie! Julie!

GWEN: No! No! I won't do it! I'm not going to marry him!

JULIE: (*Pushes her hair back from her forehead with her open palm—a gesture of desperation.*) Not going to marry him!

Not going to ma— You mean because we said to you— (*A finger pointing to the spot where Julie, Gwen and Fanny have talked earlier.*)

GWEN: I'm not going to marry him and spoil his life! I love him too much for that!

PERRY: Gwen!

GWEN: No, no!

JULIE: Oh, no you won't! If you think I'm going to let you throw away your whole life! . . . And for what! . . . *This!* . . . So that nineteen years from now you can be standing here as I am, a mad woman in a family of maniacs! Money for this one, jobs for that one, rehearsals and readings and Graphics and tickets for God knows where! I'm damned if you're going to! You're going to get out of it now! You're going to marry Perry Stewart—

GWEN: No, no!

JULIE: Oh, yes, you are! You're going to do what I didn't do. They told me I had to be a Cavendish. (*A movement from her mother.*) Oh, yes, you did! (*Wheeling to Gwen again.*) Well, you're not going to be one! You're going to marry him now—to-night—to-morrow. And I'm going to be there with you, and stand up beside you, and cry for happiness, and wish to God it was me! (*Her voice suddenly low, thoughtful.*) Of course. . . . Of course. . . . There isn't any reason why not. . . . I'm not dead yet. I've got some of my life left. And I'm going to live it to suit *me!* You've all had your turn. Who's crazy *now!* I can walk out of this, and nobody can stop me. I can still have peace and serenity and beauty for the rest of my life. And I'm going to have it.

(*Exclamations from the others.*)

You don't believe it, h'm? I'll show you! I'm going to marry Gil Marshall and go to Egypt and Venice and Constantinople—and what do you know about that! As far as the stage is concerned—I make you a present of it. It's yours! I'm through with it! It doesn't exist! The whole silly business doesn't exist! From this time on I'm going to live life, and leave imitation behind me! I'm through! Cavendish! To hell with Cavendish! I'm never going to act again! I'm

never going to set foot on another stage as long as I live!
I'm never going inside a theatre! I'm ne—
DELLA: (*Rushing on.*) Miss Julie! It's eight o'clock!
JULIE: (*Grabs her coat. Rushes, in a panic, toward the outer
door.*) Oh, my God!

CURTAIN

ACT III

The scene is the same. The time, a year later. November. As always, flowers are everywhere. A small table is decked with a rich lace tea cloth. The doors to the library are open.

At the rise Della enters. She is carrying a laden tea tray—gleaming with cups and silver pitchers. She puts it down on the lace-covered table; starts to arrange the cups. Julie strolls casually out onto the balcony, from her room. She wears a costume slip of gold or silver, with only straps over the shoulder. Obviously a tea coat is presently to be slipped over this. She is polishing her nails with a buffer. She throws a careless glance toward Fanny's room; her gaze takes in the room below.

JULIE: Oh, Della.

DELLA: Yes, Miss Julie.

JULIE: Let's have tea in the library. I think it'd be cosier.

DELLA: All right. (*Starts to pile up the cups again.*)

FANNY: (*Her voice through the open door of her room.*) What's that smells so good?

JULIE: (*Sniffs.*) Gingerbread, I guess, for tea. (*Goes into her room. You get a glimpse of her slipping into her tea gown.*)
   (*Jo enters, carrying a little stack of plates.*)

DELLA: Library, Jo.

JO: Oh! . . . How many there going to be?

DELLA: Half a dozen, she said. Better count on twelve.
   (*Jo puts his plates on the tray. Picks up the whole thing and starts for library. Julie re-enters on balcony, putting some last touches to the adjustment of her costume.*)

JULIE: Jo, did you start a fire in the library?

JO: Yes, Miss Julie. Nice bright one. (*Into library.*)

DELLA: I told him to build one soon's I heard Miss Gwen was bringing the baby over.

JULIE: Coming down, Mother?

FANNY: (*From her room.*) Minute.

JULIE: (*Descending.*) Got on your plum silk?

FANNY: Yes, *sir!*

DELLA: (*Indicating a vase of roses.*) I brought Mr. Marshall's

80

roses out into this room. I thought you'd want 'em where he'd be sure to see them.

JULIE: Oh! Yes.

DELLA: Certainly been wonderful, him sending 'em to you every day, all the time he was gone.

JULIE: Yes. Hasn't it?

DELLA: Maybe now he's coming back again you can get him to stop them.

(*Jo comes back from the library.*)

Wonder what Mr. Marshall will say to Miss Gwen's baby. He knows about him, doesn't he?

JULIE: I wrote him, Della—let's hope he approves. (*Gathers up a few letters from the table.*) You might shake up a few cocktails, Jo. Somebody'll want them.

JO: Right. (*He goes.*)

DELLA: He'd better approve. I never saw a grander baby in all my life. Two months old, and you'd think he was twice that.

JULIE: (*Absorbed in a letter. Absently.*) You must tell that to Miss Gwen.

DELLA: I bet he don't see babies like that down in South America. Anyhow, they're black, ain't they?

JULIE: M-m— Well, maybe cafe au lait.

DELLA: (*A moment's hesitation. Then, with determination to know.*) Miss Julie, are you going to live down there in South America when you marry Mr. Marshall?

JULIE: (*Looks up.*) Mr. Marshall doesn't live there, Della.

DELLA: Well, he's been there twice this year, and this last time about six months. That's living there, ain't it?

JULIE: Oh, he won't be there as much, next year. (*Again turns her attention to her mail.*)

DELLA: You see, I'm only asking you on account—excuse me, Miss Julie, but I don't know if you're going to give up the apartment or what. You see, with Miss Gwen with her own place now, and you going to get married and go travelling—

JULIE: (*Absently holding a letter in her hand.*) Well, I wouldn't worry about that, Della. We may not give up the apartment after all.

DELLA: But who's going to live in it? With Mrs. Cavendish going touring on the road—

JULIE: I don't know about that, Della. The doctor doesn't think she ought to go on the road.

DELLA: But she was telling me only five minutes ago—

JULIE: Yes, yes, I know. (*She speaks dispassionately, but she is picking her words with care.*) But mother is not going to be able to travel again, Della.

DELLA: What?

(*Julie turns slowly and looks at her. A meaningful gaze.*)

Oh, my God!

(*Instantly Fanny comes out onto the balcony. She wears the plum silk gown, very proud, and is in a particularly gay mood.*)

FANNY: "And purple her habiliments and scarlet was her soul." (*She leans over the balcony.*) "Romeo, wherefore art thou, Romeo?" (*Starts down the stairs.*) Well, where's your young man? You'd think he'd come bounding right up from the dock after being away so long.

(*Della, in the light of the news she has just received, is hardly able to take her eyes from Fanny. She goes out slowly, looking back.*)

JULIE: He'll be along presently. He 'phoned from the hotel.

FANNY: Expect he's brought you another quart of emeralds. Got 'em piled up now like coal in a cellar.

JULIE: Mother, I wish you were fonder of Gil.

FANNY: I'm just as fond of him now as I ever was.

JULIE: You don't understand Gil, Mother. He's different from us.

FANNY: I understand him, all right. He's what they call steady-going. Regular habits. Look at those two dozen American beauties— (*A gesture in their direction.*) —that have been arriving every morning, like the milk.

JULIE: I think it was very sweet of him to leave an order like that.

FANNY: If there's one way to take the romance out of roses it's knowing that you're going to get them every day. We've been wading through rose petals ever since he went away. There was a whole week when you couldn't see the rug.

JULIE: But the very qualities he's got are the ones I need. I've had enough of temperamental people.

FANNY: I'll bet he's worked out your honeymoon by algebra.
Arrive Constantinople January twelfth, arrive Cairo February twenty-fourth. He'll tell you that the next Sahara sunset
is at 6:49, and it had better be. And while you're sitting on
the hill at Fiesole he'll know to the minute when you'll be in
Copenhagen.

JULIE: Even that'll be restful. After twenty years of checking
my own trunk.

FANNY: If you wanted to marry him why didn't you do it a
year ago? Yelled about it at the top of your lungs. Why
didn't you marry him then?

JULIE: You know why I didn't. There was Wolfe with the the-
atre all built—a new production on his hands—and then
Gwen dropping out of it. I had to agree to play the New
York run. How did I know it was going to be a whole year!

FANNY: Where are you going on your wedding trip? Made up
your mind yet?

JULIE: Why, I don't know. It'll depend on what Gil says, a
good deal. I'm not keen about these faraway places.

FANNY: Since when! Why, it's been Baghdad and Venice and
the Vale of Kashmir every day of the past year! What's
changed you all of a sudden!

JULIE: Why, nothing. I love the sound of the names, but they
are awfully far away.

FANNY: If you're going to marry him at all you might as well
see the world. You'll need it.

JULIE: I just thought I'd like to be around in case you needed
me—you or Gwen.

FANNY: What for? Gwen certainly doesn't need you. Settled
and through with the stage.

JULIE: Yes . . . still . . .

FANNY: And as for me, while you're drifting down the Nile I'll
be playing Ogden, Utah, and doing pretty well. I sold out
there in 1924.

JULIE: Now look here, Mother. I've been thinking it over—
your going on this tour—and I'd ever so much rather you
wouldn't go.

FANNY: What!

JULIE: You haven't been well. I wouldn't have any peace if I
had to think of you galloping around those terrible towns—

Tulsa, Albuquerque, Oklahoma City. I know I couldn't stand a tour like that.

FANNY: I'm tougher than you are. When I quit it'll be for the same reason that Aubrey did. And no other.

JULIE: Well, I don't think you ought to go. Besides, there's Gwen. She's awfully young. . . . I'd feel so much better if you were here to look after her.

FANNY: What's the matter with her husband!

JULIE: Besides, there's this place—Della was just asking if you were going to give it up—and then there's Bert—

FANNY: And Kitty. (*The doorbell rings.*)

JULIE: You see, if you stay here, all comfortable, it'll mean I'll have some place to come back to when I'm in New York.

FANNY: Oh! So as to make you comfortable I'm to give up my whole career!

JULIE: No, no. It isn't me. It's you. You must admit it's a hard trip, and—

(*Jo enters; goes toward outer door.*)

FANNY: (*Rising slowly.*) This'll be your Emerald King, I imagine.

JULIE: Oh . . . yes. . . .

FANNY: I'll run in by the fire as soon as I've said hello to him.

JULIE: Oh, no. Don't go.

DEAN: (*His voice heard off as Jo opens the door.*) Good afternoon!

JO: Afternoon, Mr. Dean.

FANNY: It's Bert.

JULIE: Oh, mother!

(*Bert and Kitty enter from the alcove, followed by Jo. During the next few speeches Jo takes their coats and Dean's hat; hangs them in alcove closet. Kitty is dressed with some expensiveness—a fur coat. Dean, who has been quite grey and nearly bald in the preceding acts, displays, when he removes his hat, a fine and unexpected crop of coal black hair.*)

DEAN: Ah! Here we are!

KITTY: Isn't it a marvellous day?

FANNY: Hello, there, Bertie. Kitty.

JULIE: (*Weakly.*) Why, hello.

DEAN: Just thought we'd drop in and see how you all were.

KITTY: Mm, what a smart tea coat, Julie!

JULIE: Do you like it?

KITTY: Oh, yes. I think the color's a little trying.

DEAN: Thanks, Jo. (*As he helps him with his coat.*) Marshall's boat get in? I see he's due.

JULIE: Yes, it did. He'll be here very soon.

KITTY: Oh, won't that be nice? We'll be here to greet him.

JULIE: That's—lovely.

DEAN: Queer fellow, Marshall. Always talking about the Panama Canal. . . . Well, Fanny, still determined to go out into the hinterland?

FANNY: Why not?

DEAN: No reason. Just be careful, that's all. You're not as young as you were, you know.

FANNY: Who is?

KITTY: Won't be many more chances for family gatherings, will there, Mother Cavendish?
    (*A bitter look of resentment from Fanny.*)
You won't be keeping this great big place when the family breaks up.

FANNY: I was not aware that the Cavendish family is breaking up.
    (*As Jo goes out, Della enters with a tray of tea, hot water, and cake.*)

KITTY: Well, after all, with you on the road, and Julie God knows where, and Gwen married—I don't see that you'll have any use for it. You can't count on Tony. It looks as if he's going to stay in Europe forever.

DEAN: (*Intercepting Della as she passes him with her laden tray, he gathers up a rich and crumbly piece of cake, which he negotiates with some difficulty through the following lines.*) Just what are your plans, Fanny? (*Pauses, cake in hand, ready for a bite.*) How about all this stuff? (*A huge bite.*) What are you going to do with everything? (*A gesture that indicates the room about him, but which does not disturb the precarious business in hand.*)
    (*Della takes the tea into the library.*)

FANNY: It'll all go to the storehouse, I suppose. And Aubrey there along with it. . . . But we're held together by something more than tables and chairs.

KITTY: It occurred to me this morning—remember I was

saying to you, Bert—that aside from Fanny on the road, it will be Bert and I who'll be carrying on the family tradition.

FANNY: Thanks for including me, anyhow.

KITTY: Has Bert told you what we're planning to do?

FANNY: Why, no.

JULIE: No.

DEAN: (*As all eyes go to him.*) Well, I was keeping it as a sort of surprise, but—ah—I have become more and more impressed, in recent months, with the opportunities offered by the so-called vaudeville field.

FANNY: Vaudeville?

DEAN: Why not? Why not? They don't want good plays any more—they proved that in the way they received "The Conqueror." Finest play of my career, and what happened?

FANNY: It closed.

DEAN: Now here comes this opportunity to reach a wide public, to create an audience for the finer things.

KITTY: We're getting eighteen hundred dollars a week, together.

DEAN: Ah—yes, and twenty weeks right in New York, and around it. They've got up a very neat little act for us. Amusing. Human. Now here's the plot.

JULIE: Oh, yes. Tell us.

FANNY: I'm all of a twitter.

DEAN: Well, I'm supposed to be a sort of bachelor chap—thirty-five or thereabouts—very rich, and have had an unhappy love affair that I tell the butler about.

KITTY: Ever since then he's been a woman hater.

DEAN: Yes. Then comes this letter from Australia. It seems that an old college friend has died out there, and it was his last wish that I should take care of his little girl—be her guardian.

JULIE: The letter is delayed in transit, so that it happens to arrive just before the little girl herself.

DEAN: You've read it!

JULIE: Oh, no. No.

DEAN: All events, presently there's a lot of noise outside—automobile horn, so on—the door opens, and instead of the little child they were expecting, there stands an ex-quisite young girl of eighteen.

FANNY: Kitty. (*She rises and starts for the library.*)

DEAN: Hold on, Fanny—I'm not through. (*Door bell rings.*)

FANNY: Oh, yes, you are. Besides, that's probably Marshall. Why don't you two come in here with me for a while?
(*Della enters from library. Goes toward front door.*)

DELLA: Tea's all ready, Mrs. Cavendish.

FANNY: Come on. Have some tea.
(*A step or two toward library door. A feeling of general movement of the group.*)

KITTY: I come in with my little dog Rags, that my father gave me— (*As she talks she is walking in what evidently is meant to be the way in which Bert's ward will walk. Toes in, and is pretty cute.*) —and I'm sort of a pathetic figure.

FANNY: You don't say!

WOLFE: (*Heard as Della opens the door.*) Well, Della! The whole family here?

JULIE: (*At sound of his voice.*) Oh, Oscar!

DEAN: AH!

KITTY: Well!

WOLFE: (*Entering.*) Yes! (*To Julie.*) "Oh, Oscar!" Don't Oscar me, you renegade!
(*Della goes.*)
Hello, folks! Fanny, my girl! (*Turns again to Julie.*) A lot you care about Oscar. All you're thinking about is this Whozis. The boat gets in to-day, huh? It couldn't sink or anything?

JULIE: Your own fault, Oscar. Why didn't you marry me?

WOLFE: Say, it's bad enough to manage you. . . . Well, Fanny, how are you? Good as ever?

FANNY: Certainly am. Come on—I want my tea.

WOLFE: Don't you go back on me like these other loafers. With Julie a millionaire's bride, and Gwen a society matron, all I need is you should marry John D. Rockefeller and my season is over.

FANNY: About time you had to concentrate on me. I want a brand new play for next season, and none of your cold storage tidbits.

WOLFE: (*To Julie.*) You hear that? There's a trouper for you!

JULIE: Anyhow, Oscar, I was a good fellow when I had it.

DEAN: And I'll come back to you, old fellow. This little flyer in vaudeville.

WOLFE: Mm. . . . Oh, Fanny! I knew there was something. Can you open a week earlier, do you think? Toledo on the 14th—all right with you?

FANNY: Full week in Toledo?

WOLFE: Well, maybe we should split it with Columbus, huh? Toledo ain't so good this year.

FANNY: (*With asperity.*) I can play the full week. (*She goes into the library.*)

KITTY: (*Following her as all drift toward library doors.*) So then comes this scene between guardy and I, where I perch on the arm of his chair.

   (*Kitty and Bert enter the library. Wolfe is about to follow.*)

JULIE: Oscar, wait a minute. (*Lays a hand on Wolfe's arm.*)

WOLFE: Huh?

   (*Julie quietly closes the library doors.*)

   What's going on?

JULIE: I've got to talk to you. (*She stands listening a brief moment to make sure that the others cannot hear.*)

WOLFE: What's the matter?

JULIE: It's about Fanny.

WOLFE: Yeh? What's up?

JULIE: (*Pause.*) Oscar, she can't go on this tour.

WOLFE: Why not?

JULIE: I don't know how you're going to do it, but some way or other you've got to keep her from going. Without her knowing it.

WOLFE: (*His keen gaze on her.*) What are you trying to tell me, Julie?

JULIE: I went to see Randall yesterday.

WOLFE: Yes?

JULIE: She's through, Oscar.

WOLFE: (*Dully.*) What!

JULIE: She can't go on this tour. She can't do anything.

WOLFE: What do you mean?

JULIE: She's got to have absolute quiet and rest. The least strain or exertion, and she's likely to go—like that.

WOLFE: He told you this? . . . Fanny?

JULIE: She never can play again—anywhere. She may never even leave this house.

WOLFE: Let me—let me realize this. Fanny Cavendish—in
there—it's all over?

(*Julie nods.*)

I don't know why I'm so—after all, she's been sick now a
long time, she ain't young any more—but she never seemed
sick—always going on again—busy with plans—sweeping us
all along—enough energy for six. It doesn't seem possible
that—

(*Julie's warning hand halts Wolfe's speech. Fanny appears
in the library doorway.*)

FANNY: Della! Della! No more mind than a rabbit.

WOLFE: (*Elaborately casual.*) So I says to him, that's one way
of looking at it. Everybody's got his own ideas—

JULIE: Yes—uh—

FANNY: Don't you two ever talk anything but business! . . .
Della!

(*Della appears.*)

DELLA: Yes, Mrs. Cavendish.

FANNY: Where's that gingerbread?

DELLA: We tried to cut it and it crumbled.

FANNY: Bring it in anyhow.

(*Della goes.*)

Don't you two want your tea?

JULIE: Right away, mother.

FANNY: Kitty's reached the love interest. (*With a wicked elabo-
ration of Kitty's manner she returns to the library, her walk
mincing, her expression a simper.*)

JULIE: (*Talking for Fanny's benefit as she goes quietly up to close
the library doors.*) Of course, Oscar, I think in a way you're
right, but there's still another— (*Closes door. Turns to Oscar.*)
What are you going to tell her, Oscar? How are we going to
manage it?

WOLFE: It's all right. First I tell her on account of booking
troubles we can't open just yet—make it March, say, instead
of January. Then when March comes along, it's late in the
season, the road ain't so good any more—maybe we ought
to wait till next year. And I guarantee you, the way I do it,
she won't suspect a thing.

JULIE: Oscar, what a grand person you are.

WOLFE: I wish I could really do something. Thirty-five years we been together. They don't make them like her any more. . . . I wish you could have seen her the first time I did, Julie. Her face. Young, and gay, and beautiful—but so much more than beautiful. And how she treated me that first meeting. Me—a beginner, a nobody. I went in there, I tried not to show how I was shaking. I came out, I could have been Sir Charles Wyndham.

JULIE: Oscar, if I could only tell you what you've meant to all of us! But you wouldn't listen.

WOLFE: And—you, Julie?

JULIE: What?

WOLFE: What about your plans, with this news? Still Egypt and India?

JULIE: Oh, no. But—what am I going to do, Oscar? Gil's got his heart set on the ends of the earth—he hates New York; I don't dare go far away.

WOLFE: Well, say. You tell him how things stand, what the situation is. After all, he can't be quite a— I mean, in the face of something like this, surely now—

JULIE: Oscar, why don't you like Gil? I wish you did.

WOLFE: Marshall? I like him all right. He ain't just my kind, but maybe I ain't his, either.

JULIE: Oscar, do you think if I asked him he'd be willing to take a house here in town for a while? Then I could look after her—be here if—anything happened.

WOLFE: How could he say no—a time like this?

JULIE: I'd feel so relieved.

WOLFE: Only what would you do with yourself all the time? New York—you've seen New York. Running a house—what's that for you? What are you going to do?

JULIE: Why, I don't know. It's all so sudden—I hadn't thought about it yet.

WOLFE: Well, then, say! You're living in New York anyhow; you haven't got anything to do; what's the difference if—

JULIE: No, no! I'm through with it, Oscar. Through with it forever.

WOLFE: So. You—Gwen—Fanny—that ends it, huh? And for you there's no excuse.

JULIE: I'm going to be married, Oscar. That's a pretty good excuse.

WOLFE: Tell me, what do you talk about when you're with this fellow? The theatre he says he don't care about. Imagine!

JULIE: There are other things in the world beside the theatre.

WOLFE: Sure! But not for you.

JULIE: I want to relax, and play around, and have some fun.

WOLFE: Fun! Fun is work! It's work that's fun. You've had more fun in the last twenty years than any woman in America. And let me tell you, Julie, the theatre is just beginning in this country. It used to be London—Paris—Berlin. Now it's New York. I tell you, a fine actress to-day—there's nothing she can't do. And the finest one of them all, that could do the biggest things of them all, she says she wants to have fun.

JULIE: Oh, Oscar, there are lots of actresses, and so many good ones.

WOLFE: Yes, good, but not for this play.

JULIE: What play?

WOLFE: Not even any of these smart young ones that are coming up. Gwen, maybe. A little young, but she could do this play. Only— (*A gesture of hopelessness.*) —she's gone too.

JULIE: Oscar, what play? What are you talking about?

WOLFE: Julie, I've never been one of these artistic producers— *you* know—The Theatre of the Future. Way back when I was a call boy at Daly's Theatre for two dollars a week I made up my mind show business was a good place to make money in, and so I went into it, and I been in it forty years, and I haven't got a nickel. Mind you, I've done a few good plays too, but always I had an idea they would also make a few dollars. But this time it's different. I have got, I tell you, a play I am so crazy to produce it I don't care how much I lose on it.

JULIE: Really, Oscar! What is it? Who wrote it!

WOLFE: A new fellow you never heard of. Gunther his name is—a college professor out in Idaho. You wouldn't believe a college professor could know so much. He sits out there in that desert, mind you, and he writes this play and he doesn't know himself how good it is.

JULIE: What's it about?

WOLFE: That doesn't matter—it's how he does it. It's going to revolutionize the theatre—bring in a whole new kind of playwriting. They've never seen anything like this! God, what a play!

JULIE: Oscar! How exciting!

WOLFE: Exciting, yes. If I can do it right. But how am I going to do it. You gone. Gwen gone.

JULIE: You'll find someone. You're sure to.

WOLFE: All right. Never mind. Go ahead and relax, when you could be making history. I do the play anyhow. Not so perfect maybe—but I do it. I do it because I want to be known as the man who produced this play.

JULIE: But if it's as good as that it would run years and years, wouldn't it?

WOLFE: No. A month—two months—I don't give it more than that. The first ones like this—they got to get used to them.

JULIE: I couldn't, Oscar. I couldn't.

WOLFE: All right. Get married and be a bazaar patroness. Mark my words, you'll come back again.

JULIE: They don't always come back. Look at Gwen. And Tony. He's been away a year.

(*The sound of the opening of the outer door, and a gay call from Gwen.*)

GWEN: (*Off.*) Yoo-hoo!

JULIE: Gwen!

(*Gwen and Perry enter.*)

GWEN: Oh, how nice! Hello, there!

WOLFE: Hello, children! And how's the mamma?

JULIE: (*A line shot through the greetings.*) Where's the baby?

PERRY: Hello, everybody!

(*Attracted by the sound of Gwen's voice, Fanny, Dean and Kitty enter from library.*)

(*Dean pops a final bite of cake into his mouth. Dusts his hands briskly.*)

FANNY: So it is . . . Hello, there . . . And Perry.

DEAN: How are you! How are you!

KITTY: Hello! Hardly ever see you people.

GWEN: How are you, Grandma, dear? You look wonderful! . . . Hello, Kitty.

(*Perry, a little aloof from the others, nods his greeting, or conveys it with a little wave of the hand.*)

FANNY: I'm fine. How's Aubrey?

KITTY: Where is he? Where's the baby?

JULIE: Don't tell me he isn't coming!

GWEN: Oh, yes, Miss Peake's bringing him. She makes him rest two minutes before his bottle or three minutes after—I never can remember. We didn't wait. . . . Where's Gil? I thought he'd be here.

(*Perry, still with an air of detachment from the group, is at the piano, leaning over it, his back partly turned to the others. He is glancing idly at the pages of a book, without seeming really to be interested in it.*)

JULIE: He'll be here soon.

GWEN: Oh, fine!

WOLFE: Soon enough he'll be here. All the way from South America he's got to come to ruin my business. And Perry here—he couldn't marry a nice girl from Park Avenue some place. It's got to be a Cavendish.

PERRY: How's that? (*Emerges briefly from his book.*)

WOLFE: I say you couldn't have picked a good Junior League actress, huh? Instead of my Gwen.

PERRY: Oh . . . uh . . . yeh.

GWEN: Now, Perry!

JULIE: The boy friend's a little upstage to-day, isn't he?

GWEN: No, he isn't. Are you, Perry?

PERRY: I didn't think I was. Gosh, I want to do whatever . . . (*Slowly.*) Why don't you tell them about it? See what they think.

JULIE: Why, what's up?

FANNY: What is it?

GWEN: Well—it's me. Now this is the way it is. The baby's two months old, and he's the darlingest baby that ever lived, but he doesn't do anything but sleep all the time, and according to Miss Peake's schedule you can only play with him about four minutes a day. Of course when he gets older it'll be different, but just now he doesn't need me at all. I'm in the way.

PERRY: How can you be in the way!

GWEN: I *am* in the way. (*Turns to the others.*) She glares whenever I pick him up. I thought there'd be all kinds of things to do for him, but there aren't. So here I am with absolutely nothing to do until he gets so he kind of knows me. And on top of that here's Perry going away on a business trip. He'll be gone about four weeks, anyway.

PERRY: I may be back in three.

GWEN: The whole thing's only five. . . . Now this is what's happened. They've got this Hungarian play and they've offered me a simply marvellous part—

JULIE: Who has?

GWEN: The Theatre Guild.

FANNY: Theatre Guild!

DEAN: What? What?

GWEN: It only means every other week because they're going to alternate with Shaw's play.

FANNY: You're going on again!

GWEN: No! It's only for the subscription period, unless it turns out to be a great hit, and this can't.

KITTY: Well!

(*On Julie's face there is a look which is not altogether happy. There is something of shock in Gwen's news, and, for her, something of apprehension. Somehow, this makes Julie's leaving the stage a little less agreeable.*)

WOLFE: Hold on a minute. Let me understand this. You're going back to the stage? Is that it?

GWEN: No! Nothing like that. It's only for these few weeks, and just because it's a marvellous part. She's a slavey in this Budapest household—the kind of thing I've always been crazy to play—apron and cotton stockings and my hair pulled back tight. . . . Oh, Perry, it would be such fun!

KITTY: Well, that *is* news.

FANNY: And about time!

DEAN: Nice little organization—the Theatre Guild.

PERRY: Gosh, Gwen! I don't mind a few weeks if it's going to make you as happy as that.

GWEN: Oh, Perry! (*Throws her arms about him. Kisses him.*) Isn't he a darling!

KITTY: It's really thrilling, to think of Gwen going back. Aren't you thrilled, Julie?

JULIE: Why—I should say I am! (*Goes to Gwen.*) Gwen, darling, I'm very happy.

GWEN: I'm as excited as if I'd never been on the stage before! My, it'll be funny to see my picture in the papers again. To tell the truth, I've sort of missed it.

FANNY: How soon are you going to open?

GWEN: About a month, I guess. We go into rehearsal next week.

DEAN: That'll be a first night!

KITTY: I should say so.

GWEN: It's really a terrific part. She carries the whole play. I'm scared pink, but of course if I can do it it'll put me where I can—it'll be dandy! (*A little embarrassed laugh.*)
    (*The outer doorbell rings.*)

JULIE: Yes. Won't it!

WOLFE: Five weeks, eh? (*Thoughtfully.*) That means you are through with it early in January.

GWEN: (*Puzzled.*) What?
    (*Della enters; goes to answer door. Jo follows almost immediately, carrying tray of cocktail shaker and glasses.*)

DEAN: Ah!

GWEN: Perry, you do feel all right about it, don't you? Because if you don't, I just won't do it, that's all.

PERRY: Why, of course you'll do it. What do a few weeks matter!
    (*Dean strolls toward the cocktails. Jo, at his approach, begins to shake them, genially. He pours one for Dean.*)

DELLA: (*At door, off.*) Welcome back, Mr. Marshall.

GIL: (*Also heard off.*) Thank you, Della. How are you?

JULIE: It's Gil.
    (*Echoes of, "It's Gil." "Well, well!" "Ah!" "Fine!"*)
    (*Gil enters from the alcove. He pauses a moment on the threshold. Seeing that others are present he contents himself with kissing Julie's hand. Then he greets the others.*)

GIL: Julie, dear!

JULIE: Gil!

GIL: It's good to see you—to be back.
    (*There is a general handshaking—greeting—business of welcome, with, perhaps, two shaking his hands at the same time.*)

DEAN: Hello, there, old fellow!

KITTY: Welcome back, Mr. Marshall!

GWEN: Hello, there! How brown you are!

GIL: Think so? And how's the little mother?

PERRY: Hello, Marshall. Glad to see you.

WOLFE: Mr. Marshall.

GIL: (*To Fanny.*) How well you're looking.

FANNY: Never was better. How are you, Gil?

GIL: Fine, thanks. Well! It's nice to find you all gathered here like this. I'm going to assume it's all in my honour, too.

KITTY: Indeed, yes!

DEAN: Cocktail, Marshall?

GIL: Uh—no, I don't believe I will. I'm used to a different kind of stuff, down there. I'm a little afraid of the New York brand.

FANNY: I'll take one, Bertie.

(*Dean hands Fanny a cocktail.*)

JULIE: How was the trip, Gil? How many knots an hour, and all that sort of thing?

GIL: Oh, about as usual. Pretty hot when we started, but cooled off as we came up north.

DEAN: How long does that trip take, anyhow? Three weeks, isn't it?

GIL: Eighteen and a half days, as a rule, with fair weather. Let me see—yes, we made it in eighteen and a half days, this time.

GWEN: Oh, what a trip! I'd be bored to death, wouldn't you? (*To Julie.*)

JULIE: Why—I don't know. No. The boat might be full of dashing young Brazilians, or one or two of the Horsemen of the Apocalypse. . . .

GIL: As a matter of fact, there was a very representative crowd on board on this trip. Some of the biggest planters in South America. Zamaco. Manolo Berlanga.

FANNY: Really?

GIL: (*A sudden recollection.*) Oh, here's something that'll interest you folks. There was a theatrical troupe on board. American. They'd been down in Buenos Aires trying to play in English. Ridiculous, of course! Poor devils! Didn't even have money enough to pay their passage. There they all were, on the dock. Of course we couldn't see them stranded. So we got together enough to see them home. I guess I felt a little sentimental about them on account of you people.

JULIE: Oh!
> (*A second's rather terrible pause.*)

FANNY: Really!

GIL: Seems the manager had skipped out with the money—
you know how those fellows are. You'd think they'd be
down-hearted, but they were carefree enough, once they
got on the boat. I talked to some of them; turned out to be
a very decent lot. Couple of them were married—uh—lived
in Jersey some place—had—uh—
> (*This speech of Gil's had been received with a mannerly but
> stony silence on the part of the Cavendish family.*)

FANNY: I'll go in and finish my tea. (*To Julie and Gil.*) . . .
Jo, some hot water. Put a log on the fire. (*She goes into the
library.*)
> (*Dean and Kitty leave in Fanny's wake.*)

GWEN: (*Rather breathlessly—an attempt to find something to
say.*) Is it true that it's winter in South America when it's
summer in New York?

GIL: Yes. The seasons are just the opposite from yours.

GWEN: How funny! But then I suppose they think *we're* funny.

GIL: No. You see, they travel a great deal—understand how it is.

GWEN: Oh.

GIL: Well! And so you've got a family now, h'm? How is she?
Am I going to see her?

PERRY: He's a boy.

GIL: Well, that *was* a boner, wasn't it! Anyhow, I imagine
you're the busy little wife and mother nowadays. No more
of this theatrical business, h'm?

GWEN: Well—

JULIE: Gwen is going into a new play.

GIL: A new play! Why, how old is your child!

GWEN: Not old enough to miss me—is he, Perry? . . . Come
on, let's have some tea.
> (*Gwen and Perry escape into library.*)

WOLFE: (*With great dignity.*) I hope to see you again, Mr.
Gilbert Marshall.
> (*Into library. The door closes part way as he draws it behind
> him on leaving.*)
> (*Gil acknowledges this with a little formal nod. He waits for
> the library door to close partly. Turns eagerly to her.*)

GIL: Julie! Julie! How I've missed you! (*Goes to her.*)

JULIE: Gil! How could you!

GIL: What!

JULIE: How could you talk like that! Didn't you see how they —Oh, Gil!

GIL: What do you mean! What did I do?

JULIE: You— Oh, never mind. It doesn't matter.

GIL: But, Julie, if you'd just tell me. What was it!

JULIE: No. . . . Tell me about your . . . trip, Gil. Did you have a nice time?

GIL: The trip didn't matter. It just meant reaching you.

JULIE: Oh, that's so nice—I—

GIL: You're looking just lovely, Julie. I've never seen you so beautiful. Kiss me, dear.

(*She turns a cheek to him, coldly. There is nothing else she can do.*)

It's been the longest six months of my life. When you finally wired that the end was in sight—that the play was actually closing—do you know what I did? I gave everybody on the place a holiday with double pay. It took them all next day to sober up enough to come back to work.

JULIE: I'm very—honoured.

GIL: They're like a lot of children down there. It's a great country, Julie.

JULIE: It must be.

GIL: It's as different from the life up here as you can imagine. At Cordoba I was in bed every night at ten o'clock, for four months. Up at six, in the saddle eight hours a day.

JULIE: Oh! Yes?

GIL: You'll love it there, Julie. It's so beautiful—and peaceful —and big! And you'll meet real people. None of your . . . Solid! Substantial! The kind that make a country what it is. This man Zamaco who was on the boat. He's my nearest neighbour, you know. Has the next estancia.

JULIE: Oh, yes. You told me.

GIL: Yes, indeed. You'll see a lot of the Zamacos. He's a Spaniard of the highest type—very big cattle man. She was a Kansas City girl—Krantz—you know—daughter of Julius Krantz—packer.

JULIE: Oh! Julius Krantz.

GIL: Very fine woman, and most entertaining.

JULIE: I'm sure.

GIL: They're stopping at the Ritz. I thought we'd dine together Sunday night—the four of us—they're getting tickets
for a concert some place—she used to be a harpist, you
know.

JULIE: No, I didn't.

GIL: Of course, it'll be wonderful for you down at Cordoba—
having her only thirty miles from us. She'll be company for
you while I'm off at the mines.

JULIE: Mines?

GIL: Though for that matter you'd be perfectly safe alone.
There are fifteen house servants and most of them have
been there for years. Old Sebastian, for example. Do you
know what he'll do, if necessary? He'll sleep on the floor
outside your door all night.

JULIE: Oh, no—really, I'd rather he didn't. You see, I'd start
getting sorry for him, and I'd give him one of my pillows,
and then a blanket, and pretty soon I'd be out there and
he'd be in the bed.

GIL: (*A mirthless laugh.*) But England's the place you'll love,
Julie. The absolute quiet of it—you know English people—
they never intrude. I don't see any of the county people
except Hubert Randolph. He and Lady Randolph have the
Wyckhamshire place—they drop around evenings, as a rule,
or I go over there. Isn't a finer man in England, to my way
of thinking. And very amusing. Anybody who says the English haven't got a sense of humour doesn't know Randolph. He'll stand there, sober as a judge—you won't think
he's going to say a word—suddenly he'll get off something
that'll make you laugh every time you think of it.

JULIE: Such as what?

GIL: Oh, I don't know. It isn't what he says, so much, as the
way he says it. He's a great fellow. One thing I've found,
Julie, is that for real people you've got to go to the men
who've done something in the world, gone out and made
names for themselves. I tell you—

(*The door bell rings.*)

JULIE: (*Relieved at the interruption.*) Oh, that's the baby, I
guess. Gwen! I guess this is the baby!

GIL: Huh? Oh! Gwen's baby?

(*Jo goes to outer door.*)

JULIE: (*Going toward library doors.*) Where do you want him, you people? Here's the baby!

(*Wolfe and Gwen enter, the former with his arm about Gwen's shoulder. She is smiling up at him, he looking down at her. They have evidently been having a chummy conversation.*)

WOLFE: (*On the entrance.*) . . . and I know what I'm talking about.

JULIE: Say, what are you two so chummy about?

WOLFE: We two? We got our secrets. (*To Gwen.*) Ain't we?

GWEN: Big guilty ones.

WOLFE: You bet we have! You go ahead—relax. We get along.

(*Jo has opened the outer door. There is heard a bedlam of barking—more than one dog, certainly. Sounds of voices— "Quiet there! Down! Shut up! What's the matter with you!"*)

JO: (*A voice off.*) Well, who'd of thought!—What!—

JULIE: Good heavens! What's that! What is it!

(*There appears in the doorway alcove the tall sinister figure of Gunga. He is an East Indian, wearing his native costume, with turban. In one hand he carries a cage in which there is a brilliant-hued bird as large as a parrot. On his shoulder is a monkey. He stands silent after his entrance. This figure is greeted with a little involuntary shriek of terror from Julie.*)

Oh! What's that!

GWEN: Oh, look at him!

WOLFE: Say, what in God's name! . . .

GIL: What's going on?

(*Tony enters. Ahead of him, straining at the leash, are two huge police dogs. Tony wears a dashing top coat of camel's-hair, and a light felt hat with a brush or feather in it, of the sort one sees in the Austrian Tyrol. On his entrance he is admonishing the dogs.*)

TONY: Here, here! Where're you going! Not so fast!

JULIE: Tony! Tony!

WOLFE: Tony! Is it you!

GWEN: Why, Tony!

(*In the background, following close on Tony, are Jo and the hall-boy. They are laden with luggage of surprising size,*

*quantity and richness. The hall-boy carries an artificial
sunlight machine, hooded.*)

TONY: (*Casually.*) Hello, Sis! How've you been? . . . Hi,
Gwen. . . . Oscar. . . . Say, Jo, got any beefsteak? (*Indicates the dogs.*)

JULIE: Tony, where have you come from? Why didn't you let
us know?

(*At the end of Tony's speech about the beefsteak there enter
from the library Fanny, Kitty, Dean, Perry. Jo takes the dogs
from Tony and goes off with them. Della comes running on.*)
(*There now follows a babel of greetings, exclamation. Tony
kisses Julie, Fanny, Gwen. "Tony! For God's sake! . . . How
did you get here! . . . Of all the surprises! . . . Why didn't
you radio!"*)

TONY: Hush, my pretties! Tell you all about it in a minute. All
the fascinating facts. (*Throws off his coat as he speaks. His hat
sails through the air to the nearest hand that may catch it.
Then he turns to the Indian servant.*) Gunga!

GUNGA: Waguha!

TONY: Mem singha salah ronhamar. Pondero mulah giva.
Salah singha ronhamar. Gahlef! Della, show him where to
go, will you?

DELLA: (*Awed.*) Yes, sir.

(*Jo re-enters at right. Helps with the luggage. During the
next few speeches Jo, Della, Gunga and the hall-boy carry
everything upstairs.*)

FANNY: Is he going to stay in the house?

TONY: Gunga? He saved my life over in India. Another minute
and the tiger'd have had me. (*A quick clutch at this throat by
way of illustration.*)

JULIE: Tony, what do you mean by doing a thing like this!
Bursting in on us this way! Why didn't you let us know!

DEAN: I should say so.

TONY: I was afraid to let you know. That's why I came by way
of Canada. I landed in Canada.

FANNY: Canada!

JULIE: Why?

TONY: Because Albania and Schlesingen were going to declare
war on each other. I knew if I got out she'd marry him and
everything would be all right.

JULIE: Who'd marry whom!

FANNY: What's that?!

DEAN: What's he talking about?

GWEN: He's making it up!

TONY: It's been in the papers! Natalia broke off her engagement with Rupert of Schlesingen. Then the Albanians—

JULIE: Wait a minute!

GWEN: Hold on!

WOLFE: Natalia! Natalia!

FANNY: Who's Natalia?

TONY: (*Patiently*) Natalia's the Princess of Albania. She's a nice kid, but God! I didn't mean anything serious. That's the trouble with those princesses. Sheltered lives. Dance with 'em a couple of times and they want to elope with you. Of course when she broke off with Rupert, and the Prime Minister sent for me—

JULIE: Oh! I'm beginning to understand. You've started a European war.

TONY: Oh, I don't think they'll fight. I'm gone. She'll get over it. . . . Anyhow, that isn't why I came home. Oscar, listen! I was cruising around the Bayerstrasse in Koenigsberg one night, and I happened to pass a little theatre. Stuck away in a courtyard. There was a poster of this thing outside. I started to read it—I don't know, I got a hunch about it, and went in.

> (*Gil and Perry find their interest in this narrative flagging. They stand a little apart from the group, hands in pockets, thoughtful.*)

Well, say!

WOLFE: Good, huh?

TONY: Good? It's the God-damnedest play I ever saw in my life, and I bought it. You're to wire 'em three hundred dollars to-morrow. American money.

WOLFE: You bought it.

FANNY: What for?

JULIE: Yes. What for?

TONY: What for? I'm going to act in it, of course.

GWEN: Really?

FANNY: Well, that's fine.

DEAN: I'm glad of that, Tony.

WOLFE: You don't say. (*He turns to see the effect of this revelation on Julie. She is mildly stunned.*)

JULIE: Tony, you don't mean pictures? You're going back on the stage?

KITTY: Of course. (*To Tony.*) Don't you?

TONY: Do I? Wait till you see this play, Oscar. Reinhardt's going to do it in Berlin, and Pitoeff's got the French rights.

WOLFE: Well, what's it all about? What's so wonderful?

TONY: Look! I'll show you!

(*As this account gets under way Gil and Perry withdraw even a little further from the group. Presently their eyes meet; there is a flash of understanding between them. In a moment they are deep in conversation. For the present, however, they are drowned by Tony's voice.*)

If this doesn't bowl you over I'll go back to the Ganges. (*He is pulling a pile of assorted papers out of his pocket. Quickly selects the one that he wants; lets the others drop to the ground.*) Where the devil—oh, yes. (*Spreads one of them out on the table. They all crowd around.*) Now here's the scene plan. Of course you can't make anything out of this, but I'll show you how it works.

KITTY: What's that there?

TONY: In the first place they use this new constructivist scenery —grouping the actors on different levels, and playing one scene up there and another one down here.

DEAN: Oh, my God!

GWEN: That new German stuff!

TONY: You don't enter or exit in the ordinary sense—you just slide, or you're let down by wires. Schwenger, the fellow that does it in Koenigsberg, fainted six times the first night. When they want to show a different scene all they do is switch off the lights down here, switch them on up here. In goes this level, out goes that! It's got every trick of the motion pictures, plus another dimension. Now here's the big kick. See that? Where my finger is?

DEAN: Yes!

KITTY: Yes!

(*As they all crane their necks there is just an instant's complete silence. The voice of Gil, talking to Perry, comes up.*)

GIL: . . . but by shipping through the canal, of course, we cut our overhead fourteen per cent.

TONY: (*As he picks up again, the voice of Gil is once more drowned. Gil, in another second, ends his talk with Perry; waits with some impatience for a chance to have a word with Julie.*) That swings the whole thing around—the audience becomes the actors and the actors become the audience.

JULIE: Serve 'em right.

TONY: I tell you it's a knock-out. It's been running a year in this hole, mind you, and nobody ever heard of it. Then all of a sudden—you know the way those things are—I looked around one night and there was Hopkins in the second row. I knew what that meant, so I streaked it up the aisle, found Meyerhoff, and settled it then and there. Of course the great thing about this play is it takes two nights to do it.

FANNY: Two nights!

DEAN: Tony, my boy!

KITTY: I never heard of such a thing!

WOLFE: Only two?

GWEN: You're cuckoo, Tony! Two nights!

TONY: Now wait a minute! You don't understand what this thing is. It's a modern version of the Passion Play.

WOLFE: (*Fearfully.*) And you play—what?

TONY: The lead, of course. It's pure blank verse, and the incidental music—listen. (*He dashes to the piano, followed by the eager group. Seats himself.*) There's a sacrificial motif runs right through—tear your heart out— (*He strikes a single chord. Is about to proceed when Gil breaks in.*)

GIL: Ah—Tony—Julie, before you start—

JULIE: Huh? . . . Wait a minute, Tony . . . Yes, Gil?

  (*Tony stops playing. They all pay polite but impatient attention.*)

GIL: If you people don't mind—I'm awfully sorry—I've got to break away, Julie. . . . Glad you're back, Tony. But I've got about an hour's business.

JULIE: Oh, must you go, Gil? I—

GIL: Well, I'll be right back. Later, I thought, perhaps we could . . .

PERRY: Gwen, I think I'll have to go too . . . seeing this fellow . . . you'll be home, huh?

GWEN: Of course, Perry.

PERRY: Well then, I'll—

GIL: Good-bye, everybody. Good-bye.

(*A chorus of heedless good-byes from the group.*)

GIL: Good-bye. . . . Oh, Julie. Where would you like to dine?

JULIE: What? Oh, Gil, I don't think I'll go out to dinner tonight. I think I'd better—Tony here—if you don't mind—

GIL: I understand. That's all right. I'll call for you at the theatre at eleven.

(*Gil and Perry depart.*)

JULIE: (*As he goes.*) Oh . . . yes . . . (*She stands apart from the rest; thoughtful, silent.*)

TONY: (*Picking it up on high.*) Now! Here's the way this thing goes. (*He plays a few impressive chords.*) Then when he comes down from the mountain there's a stunning passage— (*He goes into something subdued and wistful.*)

(*He plays for a moment. Fanny, Dean, Kitty and Gwen are leaning over the piano. Wolfe stands a little apart from the others, but his head is turned toward Tony, and his attention is on him. Julie comes to Wolfe, puts a hand on his arm to attract his attention. Wolfe turns to Julie, slowly.*)

WOLFE: (*Rather absently.*) Huh?

(*Doorbell rings.*)

JULIE: Why don't you let me read the play?

WOLFE: What?

JULIE: That play by your college professor. Why don't you let me read it?

WOLFE: What do you mean read it? What for?

JULIE: Why, I just thought I'd like to, that's all. To sort of get an idea of the part.

WOLFE: (*A hand briefly on her shoulder.*) I send you up the manuscript this evening.

(*Della enters; goes to outer door.*)

(*The music ceases; there is a chorus of exclamation and admiration from the group.*)

GWEN: Oh, that's thrilling!

FANNY: Gives me goose-flesh!

DEAN: Very nice—very nice indeed!

KITTY: Goes right through you!

TONY: But the biggest kick of all comes in the fire-worship scene in the eighth act. They've got a religious procession there, lasts twelve minutes— (*Strikes a chord or two. Sings "BOOM! Boom!"*) and believe me it's pretty pagan! Oscar, if you can get by with that and not be padlocked—

(*Miss Peake, the nurse, enters with the baby in her arms. Della follows, admiring the baby.*)

JULIE: It's the baby! Look! It's the baby!

(*The group breaks. They leave Tony and the piano and surround the baby. There is a good deal of clucking and kitzakitzing and those strange noises with which adults seek to divert the helpless infant. "Look at him! . . . Isn't he darling! . . . Tony, look! You've never seen him before. . . . Well, what do you think of him. . . . Here, let me take him. . . . He's going to cry . . . no, he isn't. . . . Is him frightened of all the big bad grown up people, yes he is!"*)

FANNY: Give him to me. Give him to me. (*He is passed over to her.*) Well! There you are!

KITTY: He *is* cute!

TONY: I think he's terrible.

FANNY: (*Standing the baby in one arm. Indicates the portrait of Aubrey Cavendish on the wall.*) Do you know who that is, young man! You were named for him, Aubrey Cavendish Stewart, and see that you live up to it. . . .

JULIE: Mother, do you think you ought to hold him?

FANNY: Now, now! I guess I can hold a baby!

TONY: Here you are. Sit down.

(*A deep chair is quickly pulled around to meet her. The back of the chair is toward the audience.*)

KITTY: Oooooooo! Who you staring at, oo big eyes! Ooo great big eyes sing!

GWEN: Miss Peake, don't you want to take his coat off?

MISS PEAKE: I think it's a bit chill in here, Mrs. Stewart.

KITTY: Oh, he can't keep his coat on.

JULIE: Let's take him in by the fire.

DELLA: (*At tea table.*) Another cocktail, Mr. Dean?

(*Dean takes cocktail. Della goes to Wolfe. He takes a cocktail.*)

GWEN: We've got to take him in by the fire, people.

WOLFE: (*Stooping to survey the baby, his hands on his knees.*) Say, that young fellow is a Cavendish, all right! He can't deny that!

DEAN: By Jove, Fanny! He does look like Aubrey!

KITTY: Do you think he'll be an actor?

WOLFE: Say, *he* shouldn't be an actor! Look at him! (*A sudden thought. A snap of the fingers.*) Here's an idea!

GWEN: (*Who is fluffing the baby's hair a little after removing his hood.*) Yes? What?

WOLFE: Listen, show folks! I got a great new play I'm going to produce— (*A side look at Julie.*) —and in it they talk all the time about a baby. Why shouldn't we have a scene where the baby is carried on, and— (*A gesture toward the baby.*)

GWEN: You're crazy, Wolfey! Perry wouldn't hear of it.

JULIE: Gwen, he'll have to start *some* time.

FANNY: Certainly will!

DEAN: (*Holding up his cocktail glass, and signalling the others to join him.*) Here's to Aubrey Cavendish Stewart!
    (*A chorus of assent from the others. A little rush for the cocktails.*)

ALL: Yes! Yes! Aubrey!

TONY: (*Gives a glass to Fanny.*) Here you are, Fanny! (*Holds aloft his glass.*) To the kid!

FANNY: (*The child in her arm. Takes the glass in her hand. Holds it aloft.*) To Aubrey Cavendish!

GWEN: Stewart!

FANNY: That won't stop him! He's a Cavendish, and he's going to carry on. We always have, and we always will. When one drops out there's always another one to take his place. (*A pause. She starts to repeat the last phrase, but in a different tone.*) When one drops out, there's always another—

JULIE: (*A hand on Fanny's arm.*) Now, Mother—

FANNY: (*Gathering herself together with a great effort . . . Raises her glass.*) To the future greatest actor of his day! Aubrey Cavendish Second!
    (*They all drink.*)

MISS PEAKE: I really think, Mrs. Stewart—

GWEN: (*Takes the child from Fanny.*) Yes. All right, Miss Peake. Come on, everybody. He's got to go in where it's warm.

(*A general movement toward the library door. More clucking and hubbub over the child. "Look! He's laughing! . . .
Here we go! . . . He knows what it's all about. . . . Can't
fool this bimbo!"*)

TONY: Wait till you hear the ballet music, you people! How's
this piano?

JULIE: Come on, Mother dear.

(*All except Fanny go into the library. The noise goes on from
there, fainter, of course, but still heard, very merry. Tony is
playing some gay strains on library piano.*)

(*Fanny has remained in her chair. As the others have passed
into the next room she has slowly and unobtrusively sunk back
in the deep chair so that she is almost entirely lost to the audience. Now her hand, holding the glass with which she has
drunk the toast, is seen groping rather aimlessly for the table
at the side of the chair. The hand reaches, wavers, the glass
drops from the fingers, the hand drops to the side. Della comes
on carrying the gingerbread; crosses to library door. She
speaks as she crosses, scarcely looking at the figure in the chair.*)

DELLA: Isn't he the cute one, though? (*Goes into the library.*)

(*There is a moment's pause. The voices from the next room
come up, high and gay, and there is laughter, and chirping
to the baby.*)

GWEN: (*Voice from the library.*) Where's Fanny?

JULIE: Where's Mother? . . . Mother, come on in! See what
he's doing now! Mother, where are you? (*Appears in library
doorway.*) Mother, come on in! He just did the cutest . . .
(*Stops, startled, at something queer in the figure huddled in
the chair. Comes quickly, fearfully, goes to the chair, one hand
outstretched. Comes around in front of chair. Touches Fanny.
Calls.*) Gwen! Tony! Quick! Quick!

GWEN: (*Rather gaily.*) What? What is it?

JULIE: Come! Quick! Oscar!

(*At the note in her voice they come, streaming in slowly,
talking a little, perhaps, in a subdued tone, and rather apprehensive. At the look in Julie's face they are warned. Their
faces take on a stricken look. Awed, fearful, they tiptoe toward the still form in the chair.*)

CURTAIN

ANIMAL CRACKERS

by
George S. Kaufman
and
Morrie Ryskind

Music and Lyrics by
Bert Kalmar
and
Harry Ruby

ACT ONE

MAJOR-DOMO:
>You must do your best tonight
>Be on your toes tonight
>There's an honored guest tonight
>He's one of those men
>Who is being feted by the smart set

BUTLERS:
>We'll see that he gets what he deserves

MAJOR-DOMO:
>Again I mention
>Be on your toes men
>He craves attention
>He's one of those men

BUTLERS:
>Yes sir, we will give him just what he deserves
>(*Exit Major-Domo.*)
>Before we all begin our duty
>We'll let you in on a thing or two
>It's on the Q.T.
>We're telling you
>The people that we work for are below us
>The side they show us
>Don't mean a thing
>We have to swallow all the bull they throw us
>The dough they owe us
>Would keep a King
>While we are pouring wine into their glasses
>And list'ning to the trash that they discuss
>We're looking down upon the upper classes
>While they are looking down on us
>But far be it from us to criticize
>Or knock their reputation flat

Far be it from us to do a dirty thing like that.
(*Exit Butlers—enter Maids.*)

MAIDS:

When guests remain we put them in the spare rooms
But none of them are good on mem'ry tests
Somehow they can't remember which are their rooms
It's awfully hard to separate the guests.
We put them in the pink room or the blue room
But when it's time for bed we always find
That they're all color blind.
Among the married folks there's no commotion
We never saw the equal in our lives
The married men are models of devotion
They're devoted to the other fellows' wives.
But far be it from us to scandalize
Or drag someone across the mat
Far be it from us to do a lousy thing like that.
(*Dance. Enter Guests.*)

GUESTS:

We are dying for a drink
We're getting nervous

MAIDS:

We will gladly pour a drink
We're at your service.

GUESTS:

Mix it with a kick and serve it quickly

MAIDS:

You will get the kick where you deserve.
(*Maids exit.*)

GUESTS:

Pep the place up—don't let the party slow down
Keep the pace up—to music fast and low down
Let's begin to get hot and do a trot
Snappy and not too tame
It's the style and—you might as well, get in it
On Long Island we're right up to the minute
We were asked by a friend
To spend a week end
And we're glad we came.
(*Dance and exit.*)

MRS. RITTENHOUSE (*enters*): Oh, Hives.

HIVES (*enters*): Yes, Madam.

MRS. RITTENHOUSE: I'd like to make a few changes in the assignment of the rooms.

HIVES: Very good, Madam.

MRS. RITTENHOUSE: Suppose you put Mr. Chandler in the blue suite? That will leave the yellow for Mr. Winston.

HIVES: The yellow for Mr. Winston.

MRS. RITTENHOUSE: And of course Captain Spaulding as the guest of honor will have the Green Duplex with the two baths.

HIVES: Two baths.

MRS. RITTENHOUSE: The Captain, the Archbishop, would you care to hear the names of those who are invited?

HIVES: I think not, Madam.

MRS. RITTENHOUSE: Some very nice names, Hives.

HIVES: Not today, thank you. (*Bows and exits.*)

DOUCET (*enters with painting*): Ah, Madam.

MRS. RITTENHOUSE: Ah, Monsieur Doucet. I was just thinking of you.

DOUCET: I am always thinking of Madam.

MRS. RITTENHOUSE: So that's the famous painting? I can't tell you how much I appreciate your kindness. (*Sits.*)

DOUCET: It is nothing. But it is all I have in the world. And so I lend it to you. For six weeks I have lived with it. I have slept with it.

MRS. RITTENHOUSE: My, how peculiar.

DOUCET: Tell me, Madam. What time do you expect Captain Spaulding?

MRS. RITTENHOUSE: He'll be here shortly. That's why I was so anxious to have the Beaugard here. Now I had an idea. (*Rises.*) It ought to be hung in the music room.

DOUCET (*stopping her with gesture*): If Madam does not mind, I would like first to lose myself in the mood of the room alone. A great painting— (*He picks it up.*) is not just hung, it is— (*He gropes for the right word.*) hung.

    (*He is near the door, holding the picture at arm's length and talking back to Mrs. R. Arabella enters. The painting is being extended toward her. She falls into a gracious mood of acceptance.*)

ARABELLA: For me? Why how did you know my size?

MRS. RITTENHOUSE: Arabella.

ARABELLA: Yes, Mother.

MRS. RITTENHOUSE: Shut up.

ARABELLA: Well, mother knows best. (*Gives painting to Doucet.*)
Go, and sin no more.
    (*Exit Doucet.*)
Well, Mother, how is it going?

MRS. RITTENHOUSE: Very well, my dear. After this week, I
    don't think there'll be any doubt about who's who on Long
    Island. And it wouldn't surprise me if Mrs. Whitehead
    moved to Staten Island.

ARABELLA: Yes, and that Fanny Ward sister of hers gives me a
    pain in the instep.

MRS. RITTENHOUSE: I do wish you'd take this more seriously.
    Here you are a debutante. You've been out two months and
    you aren't engaged to a single person.

ARABELLA: What would you suggest, suicide?

MRS. RITTENHOUSE: I would suggest that you begin to make
    something of yourself. When I was a girl all that a debutante
    had to do was to come out, but nowadays you must do
    something out of the ordinary. Something that will defi-
    nitely mark you apart from the other girls.

ARABELLA: I'll tell you what, I'll give up smoking.

MRS. RITTENHOUSE: Mr. Winston.

ARABELLA: Huh?

MRS. RITTENHOUSE: Mr. Wally Winston. He's coming here to-
    day. Why not?

ARABELLA: Why not, what?

MRS. RITTENHOUSE: You know Mr. Winston's column in the
    Morning Traffic, the flaming forties, all about Broadway,
    42nd Street and 43rd Street?

ARABELLA (*sits*): And 44th Street and 45th Street. I get the idea.

MRS. RITTENHOUSE: Everybody reads it, and everybody who
    is anybody is in it, and that's where you've got to get.

ARABELLA: Oh, I'd love that.

MRS. RITTENHOUSE: Cultivate him a little. Furnish him with
    some gossip. You know the kind of thing he prints.

ARABELLA: Making whoopee.

MRS. RITTENHOUSE: Exactly. All about who makes whoopee with whom, and who's expecting what.

(*Hives enters.*)

HIVES: Mrs. Whitehead is here, Madam, and her sister, Miss Carpenter.

(*Mrs. Whitehead and Miss Grace Carpenter enter. Hives exits.*)

MRS. WHITEHEAD: My dear Mrs. Rittenhouse.

MRS. RITTENHOUSE: My dear Mrs. Whitehead, and Grace. So good of you both to come.

GRACE: Thank you.

ARABELLA: Yes, and it was pretty nice of us to ask you.

GRACE: Where are all the distinguished guests?

MRS. WHITEHEAD: Yes, where is Captain Spaulding? Hasn't he arrived?

MRS. RITTENHOUSE: Not yet. He'll be here presently.

MRS. WHITEHEAD: You're quite sure he's coming?

ARABELLA: Oh yes, he doesn't know you're here.

MRS. RITTENHOUSE: He asked me to tell you, he's so sorry he can't get out your way. But of course with only one weekend at his disposal, naturally we can understand.

GRACE: A likely story. (*Grace stands right of chair. Hives enters.*)

HIVES: Monsieur Doucet is ready, Madam, to hang the painting.

MRS. RITTENHOUSE: Thank you.

(*Hives exits. Mrs. Rittenhouse starts toward left.*)

I hope you will pardon me. I am exhibiting a painting you know.

GRACE: Really.

MRS. WHITEHEAD: A painting?

MRS. RITTENHOUSE: Oh nothing important. Just Beaugard's little masterpiece, "After the Hunt."

(*Mrs. Rittenhouse exits.*)

ARABELLA: You'll have to pardon me too. Nothing important. George Bernard Shaw wants me to help him with his new play.

(*Arabella exits. Mrs. Whitehead and Grace center.*)

GRACE: Beaugard's "After the Hunt." Now where in the world did she get hold of that?

MRS. WHITEHEAD: Is it very valuable?

GRACE: Is it? One of the most famous in the world. When it was shown in Paris, it was unveiled by Marion Davies.

MRS. WHITEHEAD: Sis, it looks as though we're licked for the season.

GRACE: It certainly does.

MRS. WHITEHEAD: Unless we can put this party on the fritz.

GRACE: There's an idea.

MRS. WHITEHEAD: What has she got down here, anyhow? Spaulding, Chandler and that painting. Who's Spaulding? An African explorer. Hasn't seen a white woman in two years. No wonder Mrs. Rittenhouse looks good to him.

GRACE: Cat.

MRS. WHITEHEAD: Now between us we can get him.

GRACE: What about Chandler?

MRS. WHITEHEAD: Oh, he can be had too. You know these Wall Street men.

GRACE: I've got it.

MRS. WHITEHEAD: What?

GRACE: That painting she's got here, the "Beaugard."

MRS. WHITEHEAD: What are you going to do? Retouch it?

GRACE: No, swipe it.

MRS. WHITEHEAD: Great, where is it?

GRACE: Not so fast. (*Takes Mrs. W. by the hand. Both go toward exit.*) Come over to the house with me, there's something I want to get.

(*Enter Winston.*)

MRS. WHITEHEAD: But sis, I don't understand.

GRACE: Never mind. I'll tell you later.

WINSTON: Mrs. Whitehead, I believe.

MRS. WHITEHEAD: You believe? Come on home with me and I'll show you the certificate.

(*Exit Grace and Mrs. W. Enter two girls.*)

FIRST GIRL: Hello, Wally.

WINSTON: Hello.

FIRST GIRL: What's the news in town?

SECOND GIRL: Got any dirt for us?

WINSTON: What's the matter, didn't you read the column this morning?

FIRST GIRL: But that's old stuff now.

SECOND GIRL: Yeah, we want the latest.

FIRST GIRL: What's happened today?

WINSTON: Read tomorrow's column; knows all, sees all, and tells all.

GIRLS:
> We read ev'ry single column that you write
> It gives us great delight
> We think it's swell

WINSTON:
> I am writing for a sheet that only takes
> That kind of stuff that makes
> The paper sell

GIRLS:
> Maybe you can give us some publicity

WINSTON:
> That depends a lot on what you can do

GIRLS:
> You'll do us a favor that you won't regret
> If you will help us get
> A line or two

WINSTON:
> It isn't up to me it's up to you.
>
> Give me a scandal that I can handle
> And get your name in the dailies

GIRLS:
> We would like to drop you a hint
> Tell us what you can use

WINSTON:
> Something thrilling
> Will get you billing
> As big as Barnum and Bailey's
> We don't care if it's fit to print
> Just as long as it's news

GIRLS:
> Give him scandal
> That he can handle
> And get your name in the dailies
> To the paper it's worth a mint
> If it's what they can use
> Something thrilling

Will get you billing
As big as Barnum and Bailey's
They don't care if it's fit to print
Just as long as it's news.
(*All off after number.*)
(*John Parker enters, carries a bag and a portfolio of paintings. He puts the hand bag down. His hat in hand. Hives enters.*)

HIVES (*looks at John. John looks at Hives*): Someone you wish to see?

JOHN: Yes, is Mrs. Rittenhouse in?

HIVES: I'll see. (*Hives takes up gold salver; extends it to John.*)

JOHN (*looks at salver*): That's very nice. Yours?

HIVES: May I have your name?

JOHN: Parker. John Parker.

HIVES: Of the Massachusetts Parkers?

JOHN: No.

HIVES: Then, the Southern Parkers.

JOHN: No. The Central Parkers. You know the Benches.

HIVES: I see.

JOHN: You don't mind my being here, do you?

HIVES: I'll tell Mrs. Rittenhouse you're here. (*Exits.*)

JOHN: Thank you.
(*John puts portfolio of paintings right of center stairs. Mrs. Rittenhouse enters.*)

MRS. RITTENHOUSE: Mr. Hoffman?

JOHN: Parker.

MRS. RITTENHOUSE: Oh, Parker. What is it I can do for you?

JOHN: I guess it's my mistake. I thought you invited me here.

MRS. RITTENHOUSE: I invited you?

JOHN: I'm sorry, but I guess—
(*He starts to get his things, and is about to leave.*)

MRS. RITTENHOUSE: Oh, of course. You're the young man who paints.

JOHN: Yes.
(*Hives walks past center entrance and exits.*)

MRS. RITTENHOUSE: I met you at Mrs. Potter's. We had that perfectly lovely talk about art.

JOHN: Yes, I remember.

MRS. RITTENHOUSE: So nice of you to come, Mr. Harper.

JOHN: Parker.

MRS. RITTENHOUSE: And did you bring those wonderful paintings of yours? Where are they?

JOHN: Please, if you don't mind, I'd a little rather—
(*Hives enters.*)

HIVES: Mr. Roscoe W. Chandler.

MRS. RITTENHOUSE: The very person I want you to meet.
(*Two footmen enter with luggage, golf clubs, etc. They stand at attention, while Chandler enters.*)

CHANDLER: Mrs. Rittenhouse.

MRS. RITTENHOUSE: Mr. Chandler.

CHANDLER: Well, I'm certainly glad to see—
(*Comes down stairs with outstretched hands. The splendid formality of this entrance is slightly marred at this point by the fact that Chandler trips over John's bag, which has been left center. He falls flat. The Footmen and Hives help pick Chandler up. Mrs. Rittenhouse and John also are about to help. Chandler gets to his feet, and starts to brush himself off.*)
Who put that there?

JOHN: I'm awfully sorry, I—
(*Hives and Footmen exit upstairs.*)

MRS. RITTENHOUSE: This is Mr. Parker, a young protégé of mine, and a perfectly gorgeous painter. I've been so anxious for you two to meet.

JOHN (*his hand extended*): I'm pleased to meet you.

CHANDLER (*brushing his clothes at the time*): It is a pleasure.

MRS. RITTENHOUSE: Of course I don't have to tell you about Mr. Chandler. Busy as he is in the financial world, he still finds time to lend a hand to the struggling young artists—

CHANDLER: I am just a lover of art, that is all. What the people have given to me, I give back to them, in the form of beautiful things.

MRS. RITTENHOUSE: I do hope you'll be interested in Mr. Parker's work. He gave that exhibition last week—Didn't you?

JOHN: Why no, I—

MRS. RITTENHOUSE: Oh no, of course not. That was Rembrandt. Why don't you let Mr. Chandler see some of your paintings now? Where are they?

CHANDLER: I would like very much to, some other time.
(*Chandler crosses behind table, stands left of table. Hives and Footmen are descending stairs. Footmen exit.*)

JOHN: That's very kind of you.

MRS. RITTENHOUSE: Hives.

HIVES: Yes, Madam.

MRS. RITTENHOUSE: Show Mr. Parker to his room.

HIVES: Certainly, Madam. (*Speaking to Mrs. R. quietly.*) Which room shall I put Mr. Parker in?
(*Mrs. Rittenhouse whispers to Hives. Hives beckons John to follow him. John points to his luggage, but Hives leads the way out, leaving John to pick up his own luggage and follow him off.*)

MRS. RITTENHOUSE (*sitting*): Mr. Chandler, I think it's wonderful of you to give so much of your time to art. It must mean a great financial sacrifice.

CHANDLER (*sitting opposite Mrs. R.*): Ah, but after all, money isn't everything. Suppose a man works hard, and makes eighty million dollars a year, after he has paid his income tax, what has he left, seventy million.

MRS. RITTENHOUSE: That's life.

CHANDLER: Anyhow if it is in you to be artistic, then it comes out of you no matter what. Only this morning at a conference with young Rockefeller, young Morgan and myself, what did we do? With 62 corporations waiting in the hall, young Rockefeller took out his fiddle, young Morgan his harmonica, and the three of us played. (*A gesture.*) Beautiful music.

MRS. RITTENHOUSE: What instrument do you play?

CHANDLER: I vistle. For an hour we played. We all felt good, so we decided that the stock market should go up ten points. And what did it, music.

MRS. RITTENHOUSE: What, in your opinion, has done the most for music in the past year?

CHANDLER: Unquestionably, the Movietone. You see I am a lover of all kinds of art. The good and the bad kinds. So long as it is art I love it. I love it because it is beautiful. I love everything that is beautiful. And that brings me to my point. You are beautiful.

MRS. RITTENHOUSE (*rises*): Oh, no, Mr. Chandler.

CHANDLER: Well, maybe I'm wrong.

MRS. RITTENHOUSE (*quietly spoken*): What?

CHANDLER: Mrs. Rittenhouse, I love— No, no, do not take away your hand. (*Kisses her hand.*) I love you.

(*Arabella enters.*)

ARABELLA: Hello, Ma, playing house?

CHANDLER: Well, two is company, but three is a corporation. (*Exits.*)

ARABELLA: Isn't that what Dr. Freud calls "sex"?

MRS. RITTENHOUSE: How are you getting on with Mr. Winston?

ARABELLA: Fine, I haven't seen him yet.

(*Hives enters.*)

MRS. RITTENHOUSE: Haven't seen him? Hives, where's Mr. Winston?

HIVES: I think he was talking to some of the young ladies, Mrs. Rittenhouse.

(*Enter Winston.*)

WINSTON: Hello, and how are the Dolly Sisters?

MRS. RITTENHOUSE: Did Hives take your things, Mr. Winston?

WINSTON (*throwing his cap to Hives*): Here you are, Hives. My shirt's out in the hall.

HIVES: Very good, sir. I'll tuck it in.

(*Exit Hives.*)

WINSTON: Tuck it in— (*Making a note.*) Say, that's not bad. I think I'll use that in my column.

ARABELLA: In your Monday column?

WINSTON: No, Monday special.

MRS. RITTENHOUSE: Tell me, what would Arabella have to do to get in the Monday column.

WINSTON: Well, she could make whoopee with some prominent person, like Mr. Coolidge.

ARABELLA: Coolidge?

MRS. RITTENHOUSE: What Coolidge?

WINSTON: The ex-President.

ARABELLA: Ex-President of what?

WINSTON: The United States.

ARABELLA: Oh, the insurance agent. (*To Mrs. R.*) You remember. We met him when he was Governor of Massachusetts.

WINSTON: Was he Governor of Massachusetts?

MRS. RITTENHOUSE: Well, I should say so.

WINSTON: That's more like it. That's the kind of stuff I run on Monday. (*Writes.*) "What White House resident began life as Governor of the Bay State."

MRS. RITTENHOUSE: If there's anything you're interested in, just ask Arabella. You'd be surprised how much she knows. (*Exits.*)

ARABELLA (*calling after her*): And so would you.

WINSTON: Say, what about this party. Anything in it for me?

ARABELLA: Oh, you know. It's in honor of Captain Spaulding. He's just back from Africa. (*Sits on table.*)

WINSTON (*writes. Rests left foot on chair*): "Captain Spaulding, the African Trail Tramper, is Long Islanding over the week-end." Now, all I need is about five more items.

ARABELLA: What have you got? Let's hear some of them.

WINSTON: Well, the Sultan of Turkey is expecting eight blessed events.

ARABELLA: Eight? I'll say that's a record.

WINSTON: Have you got any news like that?

ARABELLA: Did you know that Edgar Allan Poe used to drink a lot?

WINSTON: He did? Great. (*Writes.*) "Eddy Poe, the big raven and nevermore man, was keen for his giggle-water."

ARABELLA: And did you know that Christopher Columbus, who discovered America, was a foreigner?

(*The Crowd comes running on. Cries of: "He's here. Spaulding is here." "Here comes Captain Spaulding." The music strikes up.*)

1ST GIRL: Captain Spaulding is here. He just drove up.

1ST BOY: He's here. Captain Spaulding. I just saw him.

(*All on stage become quiet.*)

MRS. RITTENHOUSE (*enters*): My friends, Captain Spaulding has arrived.

OMNES:

> At last we are to meet him,
> The famous Captain Spaulding
> From climates hot and scalding
> The Captain has arrived.
> Most heartily we'll greet him
> With plain and fancy cheering
> Until he's hard of hearing

The Captain has arrived.

At last, the Captain has arrived.

HIVES (*enters, stands at entrance*): Horatio Jamison, Field Secretary to Captain Spaulding.

(*Exits. Enter Jamison.*)

JAMISON:

I represent the Captain who

Insists on my informing you

Of these conditions under which he comes here.

In one thing he is very strict

He wants the women young and picked

And as for men, he won't have any bums here.

OMNES:

As for me he won't have any bums here

There must be no bums.

JAMISON:

The men must all be very old

The women hot, the champagne cold

It's under those conditions that he comes here.

(*Enter Hives.*)

HIVES: I'm announcing Captain Jeffrey Spaulding.

(*Enter two footmen carrying Captain's luggage. Enter two footmen carrying gun rack; with guns and revolver walk right center.*)

OMNES:

He's announcing Captain Jeffrey Spaulding

Oh dear he is coming

At last he's here.

(*Captain Spaulding, wearing pith helmet, white hunting pants, leather boots, etc., is carried in sedan chair borne by four Nubians. He gets out of chair.*)

SPAULDING (*to one of the Nubians*): Well, how much do I owe you? (*He gets an unintelligible reply.*) What, from Africa to here $1.35? It's an outrage. I told you not to bring me through Australia. That it was all torn up. You should have come right up Eighth Avenue. Where do you come with stuff? Pull over on the side there. Let me see your driving license.

MRS. RITTENHOUSE (*beginning a formal speech*): Captain Spaulding—

SPAULDING (*to Mrs. R.*): I'll attend to you later.

MRS. RITTENHOUSE: Good heavens. What in the world is the matter?

SPAULDING (*calling after the departing Nubians as they exit*): Don't try to put that stuff over on me.

MRS. RITTENHOUSE: Captain Spaulding.

SPAULDING (*finally greeting her*): Well, you're one of the most beautiful women I've ever seen and that's not saying much for you.

MRS. RITTENHOUSE: Captain Spaulding, Rittenhouse Manor is entirely at your disposal.

SPAULDING: Well, I'm certainly grateful, for this magnificent wash-out, I mean turn-out. And now I want to say a few words.

SPAULDING:
>Hello—I must be going
>I cannot stay
>I came to say
>I must be going
>I'm glad I came
>But just the same
>I must be going.

MRS. RITTENHOUSE:
>For my sake you must stay
>If you should go away
>You'd spoil this party I am throwing.

SPAULDING:
>I'll stay a week or two
>I'll stay all summer through
>But I am telling you
>I must be going.

OMNES:
>Before you go will you oblige us
>And tell us of your deeds so glowing?

SPAULDING:
>I'll do anything you say
>In fact I'll even stay.

OMNES:
>Good!

SPAULDING (*bass*):
>But I must be going.

JAMISON:

    There's something that I'd like to state.

    That's he's too modest to relate

    The Captain is a moral man

    Sometimes he finds it trying.

SPAULDING:

    This fact I'll emphasize with stress

    I never take a drink unless—

    Somebody's buying.

OMNES:

    The Captain is a very moral man.

JAMISON:

    If he hears anything obscene

    He'll natch-rally repel it.

SPAULDING:

    I hate a dirty joke I do

    Unless it's told by someone who

    Knows how to tell it.

OMNES:

    The Captain is a very moral man.

    Hooray for Captain Spaulding,

    The African Explorer.

SPAULDING:

    Did someone call me schnorrer?

OMNES:

    Hurray, hurray, hurray.

    (*Dance by Spaulding from side to side.*)

JAMISON:

    He went into the jungle

    Where all the monkeys throw nuts.

SPAULDING:

    If I stay here I'll go nuts.

OMNES:

    Hurrah, hurrah, hurrah.

    (*Dance Mechanical Man and Hula-Hula by Spaulding.*)

    He put all his reliance,

    In courage and defiance,

    And risked his life for science.

SPAULDING:

    Hey, hey. (*Charleston.*)

MRS. RITTENHOUSE:
> He is the only white man
> Who covered every acre.

SPAULDING:
> I think I'll try and make her.

OMNES:
> Hurrah, hurrah, hurrah.
> (*Dance by Spaulding. Finger and toe step. Egyptian—Whirl—Hornpipe.*)
> He put all his reliance,
> In courage and defiance,
> And risked his life for science.

SPAULDING:
> Hey, hey. (*Dance—Charleston.*)

OMNES:
> Hurrah for Captain Spaulding
> The African Explorer
> He brought his name,
> Undying fame
> And that is why we say,
> Hurrah hurrah hurrah.

SPAULDING (*spoken*): My friends I want to thank you for this wonderful reception you have given in my honor—

OMNES (*sing*):
> Hooray for Captain Spaulding
> The African Explorer
> He brought his name,
> Undying fame
> And that is why we say,
> Hooray, Hooray, Hooray.

SPAULDING (*spoken*): My friends, I want to thank you for this wonderful reception you have given in my honor—

OMNES (*sing*):
> Hooray for Captain Spaulding
> The African Explorer
> He brought his name,
> Undying fame
> And that is why we say,
> Hooray, Hooray, Hooray.

SPAULDING (*spoken*): My friends, I want to thank you for this wonderful reception you have given in my honor— (*Sings.*)
> Hooray for Captain Spaulding
> The African explorer—
Well, somebody's got to do it.

MRS. RITTENHOUSE: Captain Spaulding, it is indeed a great honor to welcome you to my poor home.

SPAULDING: Oh, it isn't so bad. (*Starts looking around.*)

MRS. RITTENHOUSE: Needless to say, I—

SPAULDING: Wait a minute, I think you're right. It is pretty bad, as a matter of fact, it's one of the frowziest looking places I've ever seen.

MRS. RITTENHOUSE: Why, Captain.

SPAULDING: Where did you get your wall paper?

MRS. RITTENHOUSE: Why, I—

SPAULDING: You're letting the place run down, and what's the result? You're not getting the class of people that you used to. You're beginning to get people like you here now. Now I'll tell you what we'll do. We'll put a sign outside "Place under new management." We'll set up a seventy-five cent meal that'll knock their eyes out and after we knock their eyes out, we can charge them anything we want. (*Takes paper and pen from pocket.*) Now sign here and give me your check for fifteen hundred dollars. And I want to tell you, Madam, that with this insurance policy you have provided for your little ones and for your old age, which will be here any day now, if I'm any judge of horseflesh. And now, I'll tell you what we'll do. We'll allow you $250 in trade on a brand new Buick—

MRS. RITTENHOUSE: Captain Spaulding, you stand before me as one of the bravest men of all times—

SPAULDING: Alright, I'll do that. (*Stands in front of Mrs. R.*)

MRS. RITTENHOUSE: In the dark forests of Africa there has been no danger you have not dared.

SPAULDING: Do you mind if I don't smoke?

MRS. RITTENHOUSE: Fearlessly, you have blazed new trails—

SPAULDING: Quack, quack.

MRS. RITTENHOUSE: Scornful of the lion's roar and the cannibal's tom-tom—

SPAULDING: Sez you. (*Spaulding has assumed by this time an heroic posture. Two footmen enter with bottle of champagne, glass, and tray.*)

MRS. RITTENHOUSE: Never once, in all these weary months, did your footsteps falter. Cowardice is unknown to you, fear is not in you.

(*Footman has been opening a bottle of champagne at Spaulding's side. The cork comes out with a pop. Spaulding swoons. Chandler catches him, and takes him to chair. And with Mrs. R. and Winston they try to revive him. Footmen exit. General cries of "Whiskey. Get some whiskey."*)

CHANDLER: Where is the whiskey?

(*Noise from the crowd subsides.*)

MRS. RITTENHOUSE: He's fainted. Give him some whiskey, get the whiskey.

CHANDLER: Where is the whiskey?

SPAULDING: It's in my little black bag. In the right hand corner.

(*The scene is broken by the sound of a trumpet.*)

MRS. RITTENHOUSE: What is that?

HIVES (*enters and announces*): Signor Emanuel Ravelli.

(*Orchestra plays. Ravelli enters carrying long trumpet.*)

RAVELLI: How do you do?

MRS. RITTENHOUSE: How do you do?

RAVELLI: Where is the dining-room?

SPAULDING: Say, I used to know a fellow that looked exactly like you by the name of Emanuel Ravelli. Are you his brother?

RAVELLI: I am Emanuel Ravelli.

SPAULDING: You're Emanuel Ravelli?

RAVELLI: I am Emanuel Ravelli.

SPAULDING: Well, no wonder you look like him. But I still insist there is a resemblance.

RAVELLI: He thinks I look alike.

MRS. RITTENHOUSE: You are one of the musicians? But you were not due until tomorrow.

RAVELLI: We couldn't come tomorrow. It was too quick.

SPAULDING: Say, you're lucky they didn't come yesterday.

RAVELLI: We were busy yesterday, but we charge you just the same.

SPAULDING: This is better than exploring. What do you fellows get an hour?

RAVELLI: For playing we get ten dollars an hour.

SPAULDING: I see. What do you get for not playing?

RAVELLI: Twelve dollars an hour.

SPAULDING: Well, cut me off a piece of that, will you?

RAVELLI: Now, for rehearsing we make a special rate, fifteen dollars an hour.

SPAULDING: That's for rehearsing? What do you get for not rehearsing?

RAVELLI: You couldn't afford it. You see if we don't rehearse we don't play, and if we don't play that runs into money.

SPAULDING: How much do you want to run into an open man-hole?

RAVELLI: Just the cover charge.

SPAULDING: Well, if you're ever in the neighborhood, drop in.

RAVELLI: Sewer. Looks like he's got me in a hole. Now let's see how we stand—

SPAULDING: Flat-footed.

RAVELLI: Yesterday we didn't come—that's three hundred dollars.

SPAULDING: Let's get this straight now—yesterday you didn't come that's $300?

RAVELLI: That's right.

SPAULDING: Well that's reasonable. I can see that.

RAVELLI: Today we did come—

SPAULDING: That's a hundred you owe us.

RAVELLI: I bet I'm gonna lose on the deal. Now tomorrow we leave, that's worth about—

SPAULDING: A million dollars.

RAVELLI: That's alright for me. But I got a partner.

SPAULDING: What?

MRS. RITTENHOUSE: A partner?

(*The trumpet is heard off stage again. The Professor is announced four times off stage.*)

HIVES (*enters, announces*): The Professor.

SPAULDING: It's probably the Professor.

(*Music plays. Professor enters dressed in opera hat, cape, white stiff shirt, collar, tie, etc. Carrying umbrella. Smoking cigarette.*)

The gate swung open, and a fig newton entered.

(*Professor does smoke-bubble business. About three times.*)

You haven't got strawberry, have you?

(*Professor makes red bubble—by blowing up red balloon in mouth.*)

MRS. RITTENHOUSE (*to Hives*): Hives.

HIVES: Yes, Madam.

MRS. RITTENHOUSE: Take the Professor's hat and coat.

SPAULDING: And ring for the wagon.

(*Hives takes hold of Professor's cape at the collar to remove it and all the Professor's clothes come off, leaving the Professor in red trunks, opera hat, and umbrella. The guests scream as they turn their backs and start towards the various exits. The Professor takes a piece of chamois from the gun-rack and covers himself with it.*)

With all these ladies present here, chamois on you.

(*The Professor puts his foot in Spaulding's hat. Ravelli shoves the Professor and starts to quarrel with him. The Professor turns to gun-rack and reaches for a revolver.*)

Put that gun down. I'm loaded.

(*Professor shoots several times as all scream and exit. Professor shoots his own foot. Business. Professor takes gun from rack and shoots at pendulum of large clock as it sways. He shoots at pendulum the second time. Pendulum revolves rapidly. Bird starts to sing. Professor shoots at bird. Bird stops singing. Professor puts down gun. Bird starts to sing again. Professor takes another gun from rack and shoots at bird the second time. Razz business. Man enters. Professor shoots his hat off. Man exits. Woman enters. Professor shoots her hat off. Woman exits. Hives crosses with tray and bottle of champagne. Professor shoots bottle off tray. Hives exits. Professor shoots at statue. Statue shoots at Professor. Professor shoots at statue again. Professor exits as music plays. Enter Grace and Mrs. Whitehead.*)

MRS. WHITEHEAD: Sis, that's a perfectly marvelous idea. Believe me, if this little scheme works, it's the last party Mrs. Rittenhouse will ever give.

GRACE: Yes, and who gave you the idea?

MRS. WHITEHEAD: Yes, and who took it? Now be a nice little

girl, and run along and let your big sister handle the dirty work.

GRACE: Aw, no, that's my department.

MRS. WHITEHEAD: Nothing doing. I'm the boss.

(*Hives enters. Starts to pick up guns and put them on gun-rack.*)

Oh, Hives, you're just the person I want to see. (*To Grace.*) Run along, my dear. I'll see you later.

GRACE: Alright sis, good luck.

(*Exit Grace.*)

MRS. WHITEHEAD: You know Hives, it seems strange to see you any place but in our own home.

HIVES: I miss you too, Mrs. Whitehead.

MRS. WHITEHEAD: It's too bad you left. I always felt, Hives, that you and I understood each other.

HIVES (*with a touch of emotion*): So did I.

MRS. WHITEHEAD: Tell me, Hives. This painting that Mrs. Rittenhouse is showing, where will it be exhibited?

HIVES: In the Music Room. It's to be unveiled this evening.

MRS. WHITEHEAD: Oh, I see.

(*John enters.*)

Oh, hello.

JOHN: How do you do? (*Starts to withdraw but stops at chair.*)

MRS. WHITEHEAD: That will be all, Hives.

(*Hives bows, takes gun rack and exits. Mrs. W. walks toward John.*)

Well, how do you like the party?

JOHN: Is it a party?

MRS. WHITEHEAD: You don't seem to be having a very good time.

JOHN: Oh, it's alright.

MRS. WHITEHEAD: Oh, come now. There's no good reason why two young people shouldn't have a good time. Do you dance?

JOHN: Why no, I don't.

MRS. WHITEHEAD: Well, that's good. Couldn't we sit down and sort of talk it over. They tell me I talk it over pretty well.

(*Mary Stewart enters.*)

MARY: Hello, John.

JOHN (*he crosses to Mary*): Mary— (*He catches himself.*)

MRS. WHITEHEAD (*taking it in*): I see. The love interest, and about time too. Well if things don't turn out alright, look me up. (*Exits.*)

　　(*John and Mary, as soon as they're alone, go immediately into each other's arms.*)

JOHN: Gee, Mary, I'm glad to see you. Where have you been?

MARY: Oh, the City Editor sent me on one of those fool assignments, but now everything is alright. Everything that happens here I can phone in.

JOHN: Anything?

　　(*Mary nods yes.*)

JOHN (*kissing Mary*): Phone that in.

MARY: Alright. "Among those present were—"

JOHN: Another ten minutes and I'd have been among those absent.

MARY: I know—these Rittenhouse parties—I've covered a dozen of them. I wonder where is she? I ought to say hello.

JOHN: Don't. She probably won't remember you.

MARY: She'll remember me alright. I'm the little girl that puts her picture in the paper.

JOHN: Gee, I wish I hadn't let you talk me into coming here. (*Walks.*)

MARY: Just the same, if you want to be a successful artist, these are the people you've got to meet.

JOHN: But it isn't worth it. (*Walks and Mary follows him.*) I'd rather not have a career.

MARY: But John, dear, how can you—

JOHN (*sitting*): What does Chandler know about Art? Yet, I'm no good unless he says so.

MARY (*walks behind table and stands there*): Listen, dear, let's be fair about this. You don't think I'm enjoying it, do you?

JOHN: Mary, you know I love you, and I'd do anything for you. But even if I do go through with it, and Chandler gives me all the chance in the world, suppose then that I don't make good?

MARY: If you don't, alright. But we'll have had our chance.

JOHN: Last year I sold two paintings, one brought me a hundred dollars, and the other fifty. We've got to have a little common sense about it.

MARY (*sitting*): If you love me I don't care how much money you make.

JOHN (*walks to her*): If I love you?
    It is needless to tell you
    That I love but you
    For I know very well you are sure that I do.

MARY:
    I have kept our secret

JOHN:
    I have kept it too.

MARY:
    You and I concealed it

JOHN:
    But who revealed it?

    It seems to me the whole world knows I love you
    Who's been listening to my heart?
    Somehow they seem to know I'm dreaming of you
    Who's been listening to my heart?
    My eyes have said it
    The flowers read it
    The breezes spread it
    That's how it started
    Everything shows the whole world knows I love you
    Who's been listening to my heart?

(*After number enter Ravelli and Chandler.*)

CHANDLER: Yes, my boy, Chandler is the name, Roscoe W. Chandler.

RAVELLI: Still I got a feeling some place I have met you before. I don't care what your name is, I know your face.

CHANDLER: After all, I am one of the most well known men in America. The newspapers will keep on running my photographs.

RAVELLI: You're not Abe Kabibble? Let me see, were you ever in Sing-Sing, Joliet—

CHANDLER: Please—

RAVELLI: Don't tell me, let me guess. San Quentin—Leaven-worth—

CHANDLER: No, no you are entirely wrong. I spent most of my time in Europe.

RAVELLI: Europe? Ah, Czecho-Slovakia.

CHANDLER: No, no you are mistaken I tell you, I've never been there before.

RAVELLI: Yes, Czecho-Slovakia.

(*Girl enters, walks fast, then runs and exits. Professor enters chasing her, but stops at top of stairs, as Ravelli calls him, and comes downstairs.*)

Hey, Byzon. You remember him, who was he?

(*Professor shakes his head—No.*)

He comes from Czecho-Slovakia.

CHANDLER: You are wrong, I was never there. You are mistaken.

RAVELLI: I tell you he came from Czecho-Slovakia.

CHANDLER: No, no, no, no.

(*Professor takes Chandler's hands and turns them palm up, and starts to whistle Yiddish song. Chandler unconsciously starts to dance.*)

RAVELLI: Ah, Ivan Pidulski, the Fish-Peddler.

CHANDLER: I am not Ivan Pidulski!

RAVELLI: Yes, Ivan Pidulski. Wait, the birth mark. Ivan Pidulski had a birth mark.

(*Professor and Ravelli take hold of Chandler, as Professor pulls up Chandler's right sleeve showing birth mark.*)

CHANDLER (*while birth mark business is going on*): Please, what are you trying to do to me. Gut in Himmel.

RAVELLI: You see, I was right—the birth mark.

CHANDLER: Alright, boys, I confess. I was Ivan Pidulski.

RAVELLI: How did you get to be Roscoe W. Chandler?

CHANDLER: Say, how did you get to be an Italian?

RAVELLI: Never mind, whose confession is this?

CHANDLER: Now listen, boys, don't tell anyone. For God's sake don't tell anyone. I am sure we can come to some agreement. Some agreement that will be mutually satisfactory, yes? Shall we say five hundred dollars? (*Takes out money.*)

RAVELLI: Piker. Five hundred dollars?

(*Chandler attempting to put the money back into his pocket, puts it in the Professor's pocket instead.*)

CHANDLER: That is all the cash I have with me.

RAVELLI: Alright, we take your I.O.U.

CHANDLER: I am sorry but that is positively my best offer. That is all you will get.

RAVELLI: He's Ivan, the Horse-thief. He's Ivan, the Fish-Peddler.

> (*Professor whistles. Business of Ravelli and Professor running around. Chandler tries to quiet them. Ad lib.*)

CHANDLER: Keep quiet. Please. Please. Boys, just a minute. I have a check with me for five thousand dollars. Here, I will give it to you. Yes? (*Gives check to Professor.*)

RAVELLI: Is it good?

CHANDLER: Of course it is good. Who would give me a bad check?

RAVELLI: I would.

> (*Professor looks at check and drops it on the floor, and the check bounces back in his hand. Professor gives check back to Chandler shaking his head "No." Chandler puts check in pocket.*)

CHANDLER: Alright, if you won't take this check, then that is all you will get.

RAVELLI: He's Ivan the Fish-Peddler. He's Ivan the Fish-Peddler.

> (*Professor whistles. Business of Ravelli and Professor running around. Chandler tries to quiet them. Ad lib. Business. Professor shakes hands with statue. Chandler takes his tie off and puts it in his pocket.*)

CHANDLER: Please, please, boys. What are you trying to do to me?

> (*Business with handkerchief, as Chandler wipes his forehead and puts handkerchief in his pocket. He then discovers that his tie is missing.*)

My tie, where is my tie? What happened to my tie?

> (*Professor hands Chandler a tie.*)

RAVELLI: Ha, ha, ha. That looks like—that is my tie.

> (*Ravelli grabs tie from Chandler.*)

CHANDLER: Well where is my—

> (*Professor hands Chandler his own tie. Chandler then discovers his teeth are missing.*)

My teeth! Where are my teeth?

(*Professor gives Chandler his teeth. Chandler storms off, and exits. Ravelli takes Chandler's tie as Chandler is making his exit. Ravelli laughs. Then Professor gives Ravelli his tie, and then shows Ravelli by rolling up his left sleeve—the birth mark. Both exit. Enter Grace and Winston and stand behind table.*)

WINSTON (*taking notes*): Did you know that Priscilla Alden was that way about Captain Miles Standish?

GRACE: No, I didn't.

WINSTON: Oh, there was one more thing I wanted to ask you, Miss Carpenter. How many children did you say Mrs. Fletcher had?

GRACE: She had four children. Two by her first marriage and two before that.

WINSTON: Gee. That's interesting. You know I get a great kick coming down here to find out how the other half lives.

(*Grace sits in chair. Winston stands.*)

GRACE: Oh, this is nothing. You must come to Paris with us some time.

WINSTON: Thanks. You know I can get the low-down on Broadway alright, but this society stuff is hard to crash.

GRACE: Why, it's the easiest racket in the world if you know how. What do you think society is anyhow? Just Texas Guinan's without the cover charge.

> When you are invited out among the who is who
> You'll hear the band begin to play a melody blue
> You'll see them do a dance, and you must learn it too
> Be in the swim
> Then everyone dances, till the sun comes peeping thru
> And stars grow dim
>
> Follow the style and
> Do the Long Island Low-down
> Take off your spats
> And throw your high hats away
> Learn how to tap
> Your hip while you slap your toe down
> Come from below
> Get into the social sway.
> You should see the feet start to fly

When all the high-brows get hot
That upper crust kicks up a dust and how
Follow the style and
Do the Long Island Low-down
People high up are doing the Low-down now.

CURTAIN

SCENE TWO

SCENE: *Before the curtains.*

(*Enter Spaulding and Chandler. Chandler enters first,
Spaulding follows him on.*)

CHANDLER: Yah, Mein lieber Herr.

SPAULDING: Yes, I've heard about you for a great many years,
Mr. Chandler, and I'm getting damn sick of it too.

CHANDLER: And quite naturally I've also heard of the great
Captain Spaulding.

SPAULDING: Well, that's fine. I've heard of you, and you've
heard of me. Now have you ever heard the one about the
two Irishmen?

CHANDLER (*laughing heartily*): Yes, yes.

SPAULDING: Well, now that I've got you in hysterics, let's get
down to business. My name's Spaulding, Captain Spaulding.

CHANDLER: And I am Roscoe W. Chandler.

SPAULDING: I am Jeffrey T. Spaulding. I'll bet you don't know
what the T. stands for.

CHANDLER: Thomas?

SPAULDING: Edgar. You were close though, you still are I'll
bet. Now, Mr. Chandler, this is what I wanted to talk to you
about. How would you like to finance a scientific expedition?

CHANDLER: Well, that's a question.

SPAULDING: Yes, that is a question. You certainly know a question when you see it. I congratulate you, Mr. Chandler. And
that brings us right back to where we were. How would you
like to finance a scientific expedition?

CHANDLER: Well, is there any particular kind of an expedition
that you have in mind?

SPAULDING: Well, I'll tell you, I'm getting along in years now,
and there's one thing I've always wanted to do before I quit.

CHANDLER: What is that?

SPAULDING: Retire. Now would you be interested in a proposition of that kind? I've always felt that my retirement would be the greatest contribution to science that the world has ever known. This is your chance, Mr. Chandler. When I think of what you've done for this country. And when my baby smiles at me.

CHANDLER: Well, I've always tried to do what I could. Especially in the world of art.

SPAULDING: Well, I don't know how we got around to it, but what is your opinion of art?

CHANDLER: I'm very glad you asked me.

SPAULDING: I withdraw the question. (*To audience.*) This fellow takes things seriously. It isn't safe to ask him a simple question. Tell me, Mr. Chandler, where are you planning on putting your new Opera House?

CHANDLER: I thought I would put it somewhere near Central Park.

SPAULDING: Why not put it right in Central Park?

CHANDLER: Could we do that?

SPAULDING: Sure, do it at night when no one is looking. Why not put it in the reservoir and get the whole thing over with. Of course that would interfere with the water supply. But after all, we must remember that art is art. Still, on the other hand, water is water, isn't it? And East is East and West is West. And if you take cranberries and stew them like applesauce they taste much more like prunes than rhubarb does. Now you tell me what you know.

CHANDLER: Well, I would be very glad to give you my opinions.

SPAULDING: That's fine. I'll ask you for them sometime. Remind me, will you? I'll tell you what, can you come to my office at ten o'clock tomorrow morning? If I'm not there, ask for Mr. Jamison, that's my secretary, and if he sees you I'll discharge him. That's a date now, Saturday at three. No, you'd better make it Tuesday. I'm going to Europe Monday. Pardon me, my name is Spaulding. I've always wanted to meet you Mr. Chandler. Tell me, Mr. Chandler, what do you think of the stock market?

CHANDLER: Well, you see, last year, after all, was a Presidential year.

SPAULDING: Wasn't it though. Everybody was complaining. Remember the year we had the locusts, I voted for them too. And what did I get? A lot of promises before election, and a lot of locusts after. What do you think of the traffic problem? What do you think of the marriage problem? What do you think of at night when you go to bed, you beast?

CHANDLER: Well, I'll tell you—

SPAULDING: I'd rather not hear any more about it. Remember, there are traveling men present.

CHANDLER: Well, Captain, in the last analysis, it is a question of money. You see, the nickel today, is not what it used to be ten years ago.

SPAULDING: I'll go further than that. I'll get off at Mt. Vernon. It's not what it was fifteen years ago. Do you know what this country needs today?

CHANDLER: What?

SPAULDING: A seven-cent nickel. We've been using the five-cent nickel in this country since 1492. That's pretty near a hundred years daylight savings time. Why not give the seven-cent nickel a chance? If that works out, next year we can have an eight-cent nickel. Think what that would mean, you could go to a news-stand, buy a three-cent newspaper and get the same nickel back again. One nickel carefully used would last a family a lifetime.

CHANDLER: Captain Spaulding, I think that is a wonderful idea.

SPAULDING: You do, eh?

CHANDLER: Yes.

SPAULDING: Well then there can't be much to it. Forget about it.

CHANDLER: Tell me, Captain Chandler—er—er—Spaulding.
   (*Business.*)

SPAULDING: Yes, Spaulding. You're Chandler. You're Chandler and I'm Spaulding. It's the switching from the light to the heavy underwear. You're Chandler and I'm Spaulding. Let's have no more of that either. Weren't you on the daisy chain at Vassar years ago? I've seen you on some chain, I don't know where it was.

CHANDLER: Tell me, Captain—er—er—

SPAULDING: Spaulding. You're Chandler and I'm Spaulding.

(*To audience.*) Could I look at a program for a minute? I might be intermission for all he knows.

CHANDLER: Tell me, Captain Spaulding, you've been quite a traveler, what do you think about South America? I'm going down there very soon you know.

SPAULDING: Is that so, where are you going?

CHANDLER: Uruguay.

SPAULDING: Uruguay? Well, you go Uruguay and I'll go mine. Say how did this ever start anyhow? Let's talk about something else. Take the foreign situation. Take Abyssinia. I'll tell you, you take Abyssinia and I'll take a butterscotch sundae on rye bread.

(*Exit Chandler and Spaulding.*)

CURTAIN

SCENE THREE

SCENE: *The Drawing Room. The same evening. Beaugard's "After the Hunt," veiled, hangs against the rear wall.*

DANCE TEAM AND CHORUS:
We go places, like one who chases a butterfly
That's just what you should try
Here's all that you need
Just follow your leader
It's the racket and you should pack it with fun and
    cheer
If you'll gather near we'll tell you how to use our
    system
You're waiting to hear.

Don't sit around
Just flit around
Go places and do things
Don't stop at a few things
You must—keep things a-going
Just gad about
Go mad about
New faces and new things

Go places and do things
Keep doing the town
(*After exit of Dance Team, enter Ravelli and Professor.*)

RAVELLI: Hey, come here. Everybody play cards. (*Professor does leg business.*) They no ask us. Here we are, waste all the time. We been here all day. How much we make? The first thing we know we got to live on charity, then we have to go to the old ladies' home. How would you like that? (*Professor indicates "Yes."*) No, that's no good.
(*Professor does leg business.*)
Everybody here got plenty of money. We got to make some money. We got to get somebody to play with us. We play anything: Poker, polo, tag—
(*Enter Mrs. Rittenhouse.*)

MRS. RITTENHOUSE (*to Ravelli*): Just the person I want to see.
(*Leg business.*)
I want to speak to you about the musical program.
(*Leg business.*)
What is the matter with him?
(*Leg business.*)
Get away from me.
(*Ravelli does leg business with Mrs. Rittenhouse.*)
Go away from me.
(*Professor touches Mrs. R. and indicates for her to do leg business. Mrs. R. raises left leg.*)
Oh!
(*Mrs. R. walks right. Mrs. Whitehead enters.*)

MRS. WHITEHEAD: Hello, Professor.
(*Professor does leg business with Mrs. Whitehead.*)
(*Professor pulls out a chemise from Mrs. W's bosom with his teeth. Mrs. W. screams as Professor shows chemise to audience and then puts it in his pocket.*)

RAVELLI: We play all kinds of games, we play blackjack, soccer—
(*Professor takes blackjack from his pocket and attempts to hit Mrs. W. but Ravelli stops him.*)

MRS. RITTENHOUSE: Here, here, what are you doing?
(*Mrs. R. and Mrs. W. start toward couch. Mrs. R. is about to sit down. Professor is under her and she sits in Professor's lap. She screams and rises. Professor moves to left of couch. Mrs. W. sits on couch right. Professor throws his right leg over*)

on Mrs. W.'s lap. She throws it back. He repeats it. He then throws both legs over on Mrs. W.'s lap. She throws them back. He repeats it. He then throws one leg over shoulder and one leg on lap. The Professor and Ravelli intertwine legs and arms. Professor then raises Mrs. W.'s legs. She screams and rises. Professor does fight business with Mrs. Rittenhouse.)

MRS. RITTENHOUSE: Hives, where are you? Oh, Hives, where are you? (*Ad lib.*)

(*Gong rings off stage as Professor falls in chair. Ravelli fans him. Mrs. R. and Mrs. W. ad lib. Gong rings again. Professor again goes into fight scene with Mrs. R.*)

Here he comes again. Oh, Hives. Hives.

(*Professor tries to embrace Mrs. R. She pushes him away.*)

RAVELLI: Well, why don't you leave him alone?

(*Professor does leg business with Ravelli.*)

Now that that game is over, how about playing some bridge? You play bridge?

MRS. RITTENHOUSE: Well, I play bridge a little.

RAVELLI: How much you play for?

MRS. RITTENHOUSE: Oh, we just play for small stakes.

RAVELLI: And french fried potatoes?

(*Enter Hives with folding card table.*)

MRS. RITTENHOUSE: Set it up right over there, Hives.

(*Hives begins opening table. As he opens each leg of table the Professor standing at his right pushes leg closed again with his foot. This business is repeated until center of table falls out. Hives exits with table. Mrs. R., Mrs. W., and Ravelli sit at table. Professor pulls table away from them. All follow Professor with chairs and put them at table. Professor does barber business.*)

Now, just a moment, you're not in a barber shop.

(*They all sit at table. Positions for a card game.*)

RAVELLI: Now, how do you want to play, honest?

MRS. RITTENHOUSE: I hope so. Come along now, we'll all cut for partners.

RAVELLI: He's my partner, that's the only way we play.

MRS. RITTENHOUSE: I'm sorry but it's against the rules. We'll have to cut for partners.

RAVELLI: Alright, we'll cut for partners.

(*Mrs. Rittenhouse spreads the cards. They all pick one.*)

I got ace of spades.

(*Professor shows them his card.*)

He's got ace of spades.

MRS. RITTENHOUSE: Two aces of spades?

RAVELLI: Two? He's got thousands of them.

MRS. RITTENHOUSE: Well, I suppose that gives him the choice of seats. (*To Professor*) You have the choice of seats. (*Professor attempts to sit on Mrs. R.'s lap.*) Not over here, not on my lap.

RAVELLI: He likes to play contact bridge.

(*Professor looks at a few cards on top of the deck, puts them back and starts to deal.*)

MRS. WHITEHEAD: Just a minute, shuffle the cards.

RAVELLI: Scrumble 'em up.

(*Professor does fake shuffle and passes the deck to Ravelli to cut. Ravelli raps on table, indicating that he doesn't want to cut the cards. Professor takes cards and starts to deal again. Mrs. R. stops him, extending her left hand. He kisses her hand.*)

MRS. RITTENHOUSE: Just a moment. I want to cut the cards, please.

(*Professor passes cards to Mrs. R. to cut. Mrs. R. cuts the cards, but Professor puts the two halves back as they were originally. He then starts to deal. He wets the thumb of his left hand, as he deals a card to each player with his right hand. Professor deals cards slowly and occasionally exposes a card to Ravelli's view. Ravelli indicates whether or not he wishes the card. Professor finally throws one card away. They are about to begin playing.*)

RAVELLI: Alright, you bid, partner.

(*Professor passes.*)

You pass? Misdeal.

(*Ravelli and Professor change cards.*)

MRS. WHITEHEAD: You pass? I bid one spade.

RAVELLI: I pass.

MRS. RITTENHOUSE: Three spades.

(*Professor passes.*)

MRS. WHITEHEAD: Four spades.

RAVELLI: One club.

MRS. RITTENHOUSE: I don't understand this kind of bidding.

(*Mrs. R. slams her cards on the table. Professor slams his cards on the table and at the same time exchanges cards with Mrs. Rittenhouse. Mrs. R. picks up the Professor's cards instead of her own. She looks at the cards and realizes that they are not the cards she laid down. Professor takes black-jack from pocket and lays it on table. During the above action Mrs. Whitehead and the Professor exchange shoes.*)

These are not my cards.

RAVELLI: You bid four spades, eh?

MRS. RITTENHOUSE: I haven't a spade in my hand.

RAVELLI: Alright, we double.

MRS. WHITEHEAD: I want a resume. I want you to go over the bidding.

RAVELLI (*to Professor*): Hey, she wants you to start 'em up again. (*Professor indicates one.*) He bids one.

MRS. WHITEHEAD: One. One what?

RAVELLI: That's alright, you'll find out.

MRS. RITTENHOUSE: But we have to know what he's bidding.

RAVELLI: We tell you later. I bid two.

MRS. RITTENHOUSE: Two what?

RAVELLI: Two the same as he's bidding. Now the bidding is over. (*To Mrs. W.*) It's your lead. (*Mrs. Whitehead leads a card.*) You can't lead that.

MRS. WHITEHEAD: Why not?

RAVELLI: We can't take it.

MRS. WHITEHEAD: Well, what should I lead? (*Professor leans over, looks at her hand, selects a card, and leads it for her.*)

RAVELLI: Ace of clubs.

(*Professor plays one of Ravelli's cards.*)

Deuce of clubs.

(*Professor plays one of Mrs. Rittenhouse's cards.*)

King of clubs.

(*Professor trumps the trick.*)

You trump it, eh? Ha, ha, ha.

(*Professor nods yes.*)

See, that's what you call a finesse.

(*Professor starts to lead a card.*)

No clubs, partner?

(*Professor tears up a card. Professor leads a card.*)

Ace of diamonds. Looks like a big slam.

(*Professor leads another card.*)
Ace of hearts. Dummy leads.
   (*Professor indicates that Mrs. R. should lead.*)
MRS. RITTENHOUSE: I'm not the dummy.
   (*Professor leads another card.*)
RAVELLI: Ace of spades, a hundred aces, eh?
   (*Professor indicates two.*)
Two hundred aces.
   (*Professor leads another ace. Mrs. R. and Mrs. W. realize that there is something wrong with the game. They rise and start to exit. Talking ad lib. Mrs. W. discloses to the audience that her shoes are missing. It then becomes evident that the Professor has stolen Mrs. W.'s shoes during the course of the game. All exit.*)

———

GRACE: You've never met anyone like me before, have you?
CHANDLER: The very words I was about to say.
GRACE: You know, we were fated to meet. I knew it the minute I read about your income.
CHANDLER: Oh, you know about my income, eh?
GRACE: I know about all your various interests. I mean, finance, painting, music, and art.
CHANDLER: Ah, but you have left one out. One that will surprise you, literature.
GRACE: Literature? I didn't know about that.
CHANDLER: Well, I am the owner of the *Morning Traffic.*
GRACE: You—the owner of the *Morning Traffic*?
CHANDLER: Yes. But nobody knows about it, not even Mr. Winston.
GRACE: Lovely.
CHANDLER: Imagine, he works on the *Traffic* and doesn't even know that I am his boss.
GRACE: So, a newspaper owner too. Tell me, don't you ever find time for anything except—work?
CHANDLER (*about to embrace Grace*): Well, sometimes I—
   (*Enter Winston.*)
WINSTON: Ah, something for the column. (*Writes.*) "Financial Wizard in Sex Orgy." Do you mind?
GRACE: Mind, I love it.
CHANDLER: Very well said, my dear.

(*Exit Grace and Chandler, arm in arm. Winston walks right. Enter Arabella, running on.*)

ARABELLA: Oh, Wally, Wally! I just learned something wonderful.

WINSTON: Really, what?

ARABELLA: I overheard that Italian talking to his partner. It's about Chandler.

WINSTON: Yeah?

ARABELLA: His name isn't Chandler at all. He comes from Czecho-Slovakia and he used to be Ivan Pidulski, the Fish-Peddler.

WINSTON: He? What? Come here.

(*He glances in the direction of Chandler's exit. Turns to Arabella and impulsively folds her into his arms and kisses her until she is breathless.*)

ARABELLA: Wally, what are you doing?

WINSTON: Don't you know?

ARABELLA: No.

(*He kisses her again.*)

WINSTON: Imagine, Roscoe W. Chandler a Fish-Peddler. That's the kind of stuff they're crazy about at the paper. Do you know what they'll do, they'll probably give me a raise.

ARABELLA: Oh, Wally, and I did it all.

WINSTON: You bet you did. Where is the phone? (*Arabella indicates that the phone is off right.*) I can get it in tomorrow's *Traffic* if I hurry up. Say, wait until that big bum reads this.

(*Winston and Arabella exit. Enter Mary and John.*)

MARY (*indicating the painting*): Well, so this is the famous Beaugard. You've seen it, haven't you?

JOHN: Seen it? I sat in front of it three days copying it.

MARY: You did?

JOHN: Me and a couple hundred other promising young artists.

MARY: Well, I'll bet your copy was better than any of them.

JOHN: It wasn't bad at that. I've got it with me. I'll show it to you later.

MARY: John.

JOHN: What?

MARY: I've got an idea.

JOHN: Well?

MARY: They're going to unveil the Beaugard tonight, aren't they?

JOHN: Yes.

MARY: Suppose—suppose when they unveil it, they don't find the Beaugard there, at all. But find yours.

JOHN: You mean put mine in place of the Beaugard?

MARY: Exactly.

JOHN: Mary, we couldn't do that.

MARY: Yes, we could. It's our big chance. Don't you see? The painting is unveiled, they all admire it, and then after they've hailed the artist, we'll tell them who he really is.

JOHN: Gee, that'd be great. But wait a minute. Suppose they don't hail the artist.

MARY: But they will.

JOHN: But suppose they don't. Suppose they say the painting is no good.

MARY: Isn't the chance worth taking? Think what it means if it works.

JOHN: Gosh, Mary, I'm scared.

MARY: What are you scared of? Marrying me? That's what it means if it works.

JOHN: Gee, that'd be wonderful. That'd change everything. All those nights of worry and care—

MARY (*taking John's hand, reading the palm*): John, dear, that's all over. Look, you're going to have a wonderful future.

> Nearly ev'ry new day
> For me was a blue day
> My life was just one blue Monday
> How the days would drag on
> If they had no tag on
> I couldn't tell which was Sunday.
> I kept my eyes on
> The horizon, but only clouds were there
> Nothing could move them, nobody seemed to care.
> Suddenly you stepped in
> And happiness crept in
> And everything changed in one day
> Now you and I
> Can clear the sky.

Looking for the sun,
Two loving hearts are better than one
We'll have lots of fun
Watching the clouds roll by.
Cares don't mean a thing
Whether it's Winter, whether it's Spring.
While two hearts can sing
Watching the clouds roll by.
We'll be as near like love birds
What are a few April showers
When it's dark or fair
What does it matter, what do we care
If we both are there
Watching the clouds roll by.

Life to me was boredom
Each hour was more dumb
Than every one that preceded
Time would slowly tick off
I wanted to kick off
The hours could not be speeded
I counted all days
Spring and Fall days
Just like so many sheep
Even the night through
I'd go right through
Counting them in my sleep
Suddenly I woke up
And all the clouds broke up
For you were all that I needed
My clouds I find
Are silver-lined.

(*After number, girl enters walking fast and exits followed by Ravelli, as she slams door in his face. He stops at door. Mary enters. Has painting hidden under her large fan.*)

MARY: Oh, Mr. Ravelli.
RAVELLI: (*Greets her, with an Italian speech.*)
MARY: There is something I want you to do for me.
RAVELLI: I'd do anything you want.
MARY: Do you mean that?

RAVELLI: What do you think? I just talk to hear myself say nothing?

MARY (*indicating painting*): Do you see that painting?

RAVELLI: You mean this picture?

MARY: Yes, I want you to take that out of there and put another in its place.

RAVELLI: I don't know what you mean, but I do it.

MARY: I mean, I want you to take that picture out of there, and put this one in its place.

RAVELLI: You want me to take that picture down, and put this picture upstairs?

MARY: Yes.

RAVELLI: You want I should steal.

MARY: Oh no, it's not stealing.

RAVELLI: Then I couldn't do it.

> (*Ravelli and Mary exit. Ad lib as she follows him off.*)
> (*Storm effect off stage. Hives enters and draws the curtains closed. Mrs. Whitehead enters.*)

MRS. WHITEHEAD: Well, Hives, it looks as though we're in for a storm, doesn't it? (*Walking behind her.*) So that's the big painting, is it?

HIVES: Yes, Mrs. Whitehead.

MRS. WHITEHEAD: Oh, Hives, do you still feel that there is a strong bond between us?

HIVES: Indeed I do.

MRS. WHITEHEAD: Strong enough for you to do me a big favor?

HIVES: Anything at all.

MRS. WHITEHEAD: Suppose I were to ask you to take away the Beaugard. Oh just temporarily, and substitute a little thing of my own.

HIVES: I should consider it rather extraordinary.

MRS. WHITEHEAD: It is, Hives. But somehow I still think of you as one of the Whiteheads.

HIVES: Thank you. It's hard for a man to serve two mistresses.

MRS. WHITEHEAD: It's been done. (*Takes his arm, and they start to walk toward exit.*)

HIVES: My soul is yours, Mrs. Whitehead. Even though my body may belong to Mrs. Rittenhouse.

MRS. WHITEHEAD: Why, Hives. (*Mrs. Whitehead and Hives exit.*)
> (*Thunder and lightning off stage.*)

(*Ravelli enters with painting under his arm. Ad lib. There is a loud burst of thunder and lightning, as Professor enters, carrying a step ladder, pick, and a shovel and umbrella.*)

RAVELLI: Hurry up. You want to get wet? Now listen, we got to be very quiet.

(*Professor drops tools and umbrella and pushes ladder over to the mantel, underneath the painting.*)

(*A loud noise off stage.*)

Somebody come. Hide.

(*Professor stands on his head. Ravelli hides behind couch.*)

Never mind it's a mistake, nobody come.

(*Ravelli shows Professor duplicate painting.*)

Now listen, we got to take this picture out (*indicating painting on wall.*) and put this one in. You got everything, the shovel, the axe, the dynamite, the pineapples. Where you got the flash? The flash.

(*Professor indicates his own flesh by pinching his own cheek.*)

No, no. The flash. The flash.

(*Professor takes out fish from pocket.*)

That's a fish. I no wanna a fish. Flash. When you go out in the night time you gotta have a flash.

(*Professor takes out a large silver flask.*)

That's a flisk.

(*Professor takes out flute and plays it.*)

That's a flutes. I no wanna the flutes. Flash. When you wanna see somebody, you gotta have the flash.

(*Professor takes out five playing cards.*)

That's a flush. When it's light and you wanna make it dark, you gotta have the flash.

(*Professor takes out blackjack.*)

No, I make a mistake. When it's dark and you wanna make a light then you gotta have the flash.

(*Professor finally brings out a flashlight.*)

That's fine. That's what I want.

(*Professor flashes light in his own face. Then covers his eyes with his hand.*)

Now we getta da picture.

(*There is a loud crash of thunder and lightning. All stage lights out.*)

That's fine. The storm put the lights out. Now nobody can see what we do. Where's the flash? Where's the flash? I no wanna the fish. The flash.

(*The Professor plays the flute.*)

No flutes. Where you got the flash? What's the matter, you lose it? You lose it, eh? Well you gotta find it. Look for it.

(*Professor then lights flash and looks around the stage lifting up parts of the couch, evidently looking for the flashlight that he has in his hand.*)

You can't find it, eh? Alright we work without it. Come on.

(*There is a long flash of lightning and thunder as they both start up center. The Professor climbs up the ladder. As he nears the top of the ladder there is a loud knock off-stage. The lightning ceases.*)

Quick, somebody come. Hide.

(*Ravelli pulls the ladder away from under the Professor leaving him hanging on to the mantel. The Professor whistles loudly as Ravelli occasionally flashes the light on the Professor.*)

That's alright. I know where you are.

(*Enter Mrs. Rittenhouse followed by Spaulding.*)

MRS. RITTENHOUSE: Captain Spaulding, oh Captain Spaulding, where are you?

SPAULDING: Well? What's the trouble?

MRS. RITTENHOUSE: Captain Spaulding, the lights are out all over the place. You can't see your hand before your face.

SPAULDING: Well, you wouldn't get much enjoyment out of that. I don't know what you're going to do but I'm going to take a nap. Leave me a call for three o'clock.

RAVELLI: Cuckoo, cuckoo, cuckoo.

SPAULDING: Make it three thirty.

RAVELLI: Cuck——

SPAULDING: You certainly get service around here. Mrs. Rittenhouse, did you see a fish?

(*Ravelli and Professor make a noise.*)

MRS. RITTENHOUSE: Oh—did you hear that? There's somebody over there.

(*Another noise.*)

I say, there's somebody over there.

SPAULDING: Nonsense, the place is just settling, that's all. Anybody over there?

RAVELLI: I don't see anybody.

(*Ravelli and Professor make a terrific noise.*)

MRS. RITTENHOUSE: Oh . . . Good heavens, what's that? What is it?

SPAULDING: You know what I think? I think you've got roaches.

(*Ravelli and Professor make another loud noise.*)

Yes, you've got roaches. You've got roaches and the biggest one has got asthma.

(*There is a tremendous burst of thunder and lightning. Mrs. Rittenhouse screams and exits followed by Spaulding.*)

RAVELLI: Well, that's fine. We got the picture and we no make one sound.

(*They start to exit but there is a tremendous crash of thunder and lightning which drives them back.*)

Oh boy, that's some storm. That's a regular tomato. We'd better go this way. It's shorter.

(*They start to exit. As they draw the shades and open the doors, there is a burst of sunshine, birds singing, etc. Both exit.*)

(*Hives enters carrying a painting. He draws the curtains that conceal the "Beaugard," places a chair under the mantel, then switches the lights and steals the painting, apparently replacing it with the one presumably given to him by Mrs. Whitehead. He switches lights on again, replaces chair, draws the curtains on the "Beaugard" and, with the painting under his arm, he casually strolls off. Spaulding and Mrs. Rittenhouse enter.*)

SPAULDING: So there was only one bedroom in the farm house and the farmer had three daughters and only one traveling salesman—

MRS. RITTENHOUSE: Captain Spaulding, what kind of a story do you call that?

(*All guests enter in various entrances.*)

Come right in, everybody. Captain Spaulding has kindly consented to tell us about his African adventures.

(*Spaulding's business with flask and fish.*)

Now before we start the musical program, Captain Spaulding

has kindly consented to tell us all about his trip to Africa.
Captain Spaulding.

(*All applaud. Laugh.*)

SPAULDING: My friends, I am here to tell you about that great
and mysterious continent known as Africa. Africa is God's
country, and he can have it. We left New York drunk and
early on the morning of February 2nd. After fifteen days on
the water and six on the boat, we arrived in Africa. We at
once proceeded into the heart of the jungle, where I shot a
polar bear. . . .

MRS. RITTENHOUSE: But Captain, I thought polar bears lived
in the frozen north?

SPAULDING: They do. But this one was anemic and he couldn't
stand the cold climate. Besides, he was a rich bear and could
afford to go away in the winter. You takes care of your animals and I'll take care of mine. And don't bring Lulu.

From the day of our arrival we led an active life. The first
morning saw us up at six, breakfasted and back in bed at
seven. This was our routine for the first three months. Then
we finally got so we were back in bed by six-thirty.

MRS. RITTENHOUSE: But Captain, you promised to tell us
about the wild life of Africa.

SPAULDING: Oh yes. One day while standing in front of the
cabin, I bagged six tigers. I bagged six of the biggest
tigers. . . .

MRS. RITTENHOUSE: Oh Captain, did you catch six tigers?

SPAULDING: No, I bagged them to go away but they kept
hanging around all day. . . .

The principal animals inhabiting the African jungle are
Moose, Elks, and Knights of Pythias. Of course you all
know what a moose is. That's big game. The first day I shot
two bucks. That was the biggest game we had. Of course,
you all know what a moose is. A moose runs around the
floor, eats cheese, and is chased by the cat. The Elks, however, stay up in the hills, most of the year. But in the spring
they come down for their annual convention. It is very interesting to watch them come to the water hole, and you
should see them when they find it is only a water hole. What
those Elks are looking for is an Elka-hole.

One morning I shot an elephant in my pajamas. How he

got in my pajamas I don't know. Then we tried to remove the tusks, we tried to remove the tusks. Tusks. That's not so easy to say. You try that some time.

CHANDLER: Oh, simple. Tusks.

SPAULDING (*to Chandler*): Pardon me, my name is Spaulding. . . .

(*Business.*)

We tried to remove the tusks, but they were embedded in so firmly we couldn't budge them. Of course in Alabama, the tusks are looser. However that is entirely ir-elephant to what I was saying. We took some pictures of the native girls but they weren't developed. But we're going back again.

MRS. RITTENHOUSE: A very enlightening speech, Captain.

(*All applaud.*)

CHANDLER: Hooray for Captain Spaulding. Three cheers for Captain Spaulding.

(*Professor enters with three chairs. Business. Mrs. R. and Chandler ad lib. Professor exits with chair.*)

MRS. RITTENHOUSE: And now Signor Ravelli has kindly consented to play for us. Signor Ravelli.

(*Four footmen bring piano down-stage. All applaud.*)

SPAULDING: Signor Ravelli's first selection will be "Somewhere My Love Lies Sleeping," with a male chorus.

(*Ravelli begins to play, always repeating the same notes.*)

Say, if you get near a song, play it.

(*Ravelli continues playing.*)

RAVELLI: I can't think of the finish.

SPAULDING: That's funny, that's all I can think of.

RAVELLI: I think I went past it.

SPAULDING: The next time you come around, jump off.

(*Song title.*)

RAVELLI: I'll play one of my compositions by Victor Herbert.

(*Ravelli plays "Gypsy Love Song." At the finish of piano specialty, Ravelli exits. Professor enters, walks to piano and spins the stool. Professor plays a few bars. Spits on hands. Spins stool. Business with Chandler. Professor plays again and hurts fingers. Business with fingers. Chandler sneezes. Professor whistles—"He's Ivan the horse-thief." Business with fingers. Spaulding starts toward piano and trips. Professor plays "Some of these Days." Business.*)

SPAULDING: He plays them both well . . .
> (*Ravelli enters. Basketball game. Professor does leg business with girl. Ravelli plays same notes as before.*)
I was afraid of that.
> (*Ravelli plays chorus of song. Professor whistles song. Near last few bars "He's Ivan the Horse-thief." Anvil Chorus. Song title. "Cow-Slips." Ravelli plays "Collegiate," exits.*)
And now, Mrs. Rittenhouse, I have a big surprise for you.
> (*Chest is brought by footmen.*)
When I departed from Africa, I was presented with a little gift. And that gift, Mrs. Rittenhouse, I'm going to give to you, at a very low figure.

MRS. RITTENHOUSE: Well, what is it Captain, what is it?

SPAULDING: It's a match box for an elephant. This magnificent chest . . . (*Indicating his own chest.*) No, this magnificent chest . . . (*Indicating the gift.*) I was probably right the first time. This magnificent chest I take pleasure in presenting to you with my compliments.

MRS. RITTENHOUSE: Captain, this leaves me speechless.

SPAULDING: Well, see that you remain that way.
> (*Enter Hives. He stands left of painting.*)

MRS. RITTENHOUSE: And now through the graciousness of Monsieur Doucet.
> (*All applaud.*)
It is my privilege to reveal the masterpiece of François Jacques Dubois Guilbert Beaugard.

SPAULDING: On track twenty-four. No trains will be sold after the magazines leave the station. The Mexican weather report is chilly today and hot tamale.

MRS. RITTENHOUSE: "After the Hunt."
> (*Hives draws curtains displaying the painting. Exclamations by all, "Wonderful, bravo," etc. Applause. Finaletto. Professor enters with small flag on top of long pole, waving it, then exits.*)

MARY: My dear, you're great as Beaugard. I'm happy for you'll be as great as Beaugard, there'll be no more April showers.

CHANDLER: Stop! There must be some mistake! This painting is not a "Beaugard."

DOUCET (*forces his way through*): What? Stop! This picture is a fake! My "Beaugard" is stolen.

CHORUS: A fake?

MRS. WHITEHEAD: That's what I call a pretty rotten break.

DOUCET: This painting spurious will drive me furious. This imitation means ruination.

CHORUS: Doucet is furious, this is injurious, this news will cause a big sensation.

WINSTON (*stepping downstage*): This is scandal that I can handle, I'll get it into the *Traffic*.

MRS. WHITEHEAD: I wonder how the crime was done, and who can be the guilty one?

CHORUS: We'd like to know the guilty one.

SPAULDING (*walks with dance step*): Maybe I did it.

ALL: You?

JAMISON: No. The Captain is a moral man, he wouldn't stoop to crooking.

SPAULDING: This fact I'll emphasize with stress, I never steal a thing, unless nobody's looking. (*Spaulding walks with a dance step.*)

CHANDLER (*seeing painting gone*): Look! That one is gone too.

(*Shots off stage. Auto klaxon.*)

The crooks! They are escaping! Come with me.

(*All exit with exclamations of "The crooks are escaping, there they go," etc.*)

(*After all are off, music plays. The lid of the chest, which has been left, stage center, slowly opens. The Professor appears. He scratches his head. He puts his finger in his ear. He scratches his foot, then scratches the chest. He emerges from the chest and sits on the edge of it. Wrist watch business. He gets his finger caught in the sleeves of his coat. He then takes first one picture and then another out of the chest. Cowboy business. He then takes the third picture out of the chest. Newsboy business. Counting papers. Warming up. "Extra." Change business. He then puts the paintings back into the chest. He goes to the couch, takes a cushion from the couch, and puts it in the chest. He then takes a second cushion and puts that into the chest. He then tries to lift the couch and put it into the chest. He then takes a vase of flowers from a table, starts toward chest, attempts to lift couch again, but*) *being unable to do so, proceeds to chest, and closes the lid. He then attaches the rope to the handle of the chest and starts to exit. Simultaneously the chest is drawn off-stage in the opposite direction.*)

CURTAIN

ACT TWO

Scene One

SCENE: *The breakfast room. The next morning.*
AT RISE: *Opening Chorus.*

GUESTS:
>
> We are mystified
> We're all a-flutter
> But no one will heed us
> Though there's been a crime
> We want something to eat
> Where's our ham and eggs
> The bread and butter
> They forgot to feed us
> We hate to be rude
> But we must have food
> Far be it from us to criticize the hostess
> But we'd like to know
> When do we eat
> Although it's very seldom that we mind a thing
> This is the kind o' thing—we always dread
> We're sorry for the Madam
> And we sympathize with her—but
> Just the same we must be fed
> Oh here comes Hives—and maybe he can save our lives.

HIVES:
>
> The Madam's in an awful state
> All morning she's been fainting
> Each time we bring her to—she says
> Who stole the painting.

GUESTS:
>
> We're sorry that the Madam's low
> But we would like to know .
> When do we eat.

HIVES:
>
> She's in the arms of Spaulding—
> The African Explorer.

GUESTS:

> Hooray for Captain Spaulding.

HIVES:

> He's trying to restore her.

GUESTS:

> The Captain is a very moral man—but we repeat
> When do we eat?

HIVES:

> I'll do the best I can—
> Although my nerves are quite unsteady
> I'll put the breakfast in the pan and get it ready.

GUESTS:

> Even tho' we fail to get a plateful
> Keep the party going
> Let's forget the food
> Strike a happy mood
> Till the breakfast arrives.
> We appear to be a bit ungrateful
> We must make a showing
> Now that we've begun
> Let's keep up the fun.

(*After musical opening . . . enter Mrs. Whitehead.*)

MRS. WHITEHEAD: Well?

HIVES: Good morning, my lady.

MRS. WHITEHEAD: Good morning my eye! Where have you been all night?

HIVES: I hardly know. I've been so worried. I don't know how to tell you.

MRS. WHITEHEAD: Tell me what?

HIVES: The picture. They got it away from me. I don't know what happened, I was hit on the head.

MRS. WHITEHEAD: Which picture? What are you talking about?

HIVES: When the lights were put out somebody stole the "Beaugard."

MRS. WHITEHEAD: Good God! Hives, then it wasn't you that put the lights out?

HIVES: No, no, Mrs. Whitehead.

MRS. WHITEHEAD: And it wasn't you that took my painting? (*Hives shakes his head, "No."*) Who did?

HIVES: I don't know.

MRS. WHITEHEAD: Hives, everything was fixed. Wait a minute
 . . . when the lights were put on again I happened to notice
 that there was one person missing—the Professor.

HIVES: The Professor?

MRS. WHITEHEAD: Hives, I do feel better already. Now I'll tell
 you what we'll do . . .
  (*Grace enters. She is carrying a copy of the* Morning Traffic,
  open at Winston's column. Walks to table.)

GRACE: Hello, Sis.

MRS. WHITEHEAD: Hello.

GRACE: 'Morning, Hives.

HIVES: Good morning, Miss Grace.

GRACE: Oh, Hives, has that windbag Chandler come down yet?

HIVES: Not yet, Miss Grace.

GRACE: Well, where is he going to sit?

HIVES (*points to the chair*): Right here, Miss Grace.

GRACE (*looking at chair*): I wouldn't think he could make it.
  (*Grace sits at table. Grace props up paper on table, so that
  Chandler can't help seeing it when he sits at table. Hives
  laughs . . . and exits.*)

MRS. WHITEHEAD (*standing back of table*): What's the big idea?

GRACE: Wally Winston's column in the *Morning Traffic* cross
 marks spot.

MRS. WHITEHEAD (*picks up the paper and reads*): "Roscoe W.
 Chandler the big coupon clipper was once Ivan Pidulski the
 Fish-Peddler, of Czecho Slovakia." Whoopee, there goes
 one of her pet celebrities.

GRACE: You don't know the half of it. Because Mr. Chandler
 owns the paper.

MRS. WHITEHEAD: No.

GRACE: Yes . . . (*Rises and comes down in front of the table, followed by Mrs. Whitehead.*) And that means Mr. Winston will
 be canned.

MRS. WHITEHEAD: Isn't that great!

GRACE: Haven't we a couple of nasty dispositions?

MRS. WHITEHEAD: Haven't we though. But remember, when
 this party started there were a lot of important people
 around here.

GRACE: By the time the pageant arrives, there'll be nobody left
 to act in it.

MRS. WHITEHEAD: They'll have to send to the Lambs.

GRACE: God works in a mysterious . . .

> (*Mrs. Rittenhouse enters, stands near table. Grace crosses to stage center.*) Good morning, Mrs. Rittenhouse.

MRS. RITTENHOUSE: Good morning.

GRACE: And how are you this morning? You look charming.

MRS. WHITEHEAD: Did you sleep well? Beautiful morning, isn't it?

MRS. RITTENHOUSE: Yes. Yes.

MRS. WHITEHEAD: I think I'll go in for a swim. Coming, Grace?

GRACE: Why yes, I'd love to.

MRS. WHITEHEAD: It's a beautiful party, Mrs. Rittenhouse.

GRACE: I wouldn't have missed it for the world.

MRS. WHITEHEAD: It's just full of surprises. (*Exit.*)

> (*Mrs. Rittenhouse stands looking after them. Enter Doucet.*)

DOUCET: Madam, I cannot wait any longer. We must send for the police.

MRS. RITTENHOUSE: But, Monsieur, that will spoil the whole week-end. My guests will leave, what will become of the pageant?

DOUCET: The pageant? I have something more important on my mind than pageants.

MRS. RITTENHOUSE: But, Monsieur, you promised last night.

DOUCET: Ah—last night, Madame—the moon was out—the stars were shining—you were beautiful, and I was soused to the gill.

MRS. RITTENHOUSE: But, Monsieur, if you really love me . . .

DOUCET: Yes, yes, I do love you. But I want the police. I want my painting—$100,000. I want the police.

MRS. RITTENHOUSE (*crosses to table*): I can't stand it any longer. I can't stand it.

> (*Chandler enters in the middle of this outburst.*)

CHANDLER: What is the matter? What is the matter?

DOUCET: Mr. Chandler, my painting has been stolen. I insist on having the police.

CHANDLER: Alright, very well—but quietly—calmly.

DOUCET: A $100,000!

CHANDLER: But, is this something to get excited about?

DOUCET: Mon Dieu!

CHANDLER: Have you no philosophy?

DOUCET: Philosophy?

CHANDLER: Look at me, here are two of my very best friends in trouble, am I excited? No.

(*Hives enters.*)

MRS. RITTENHOUSE: But, Mr. Chandler, you don't understand.

CHANDLER: I understand perfectly. (*To Mrs. Rittenhouse.*) Now sit down right here, quietly—calmly.

MRS. RITTENHOUSE: I don't want to sit down. I've already had my breakfast.

CHANDLER: Nevertheless sit down right here quietly and calmly.

(*Mrs. Rittenhouse sits behind table.*)

(*To Doucet*) And you my friend, I'm surprised at you. Sit right over here.

(*Doucet sits right of table.*)

(*Hives is standing left of table.*)

Olzo, Hives, what have we this morning? a bisschen orange juice?

HIVES: Certainly, sir.

CHANDLER (*to Doucet*): Very good for the nerves—orange juice.

DOUCET: I want the police.

CHANDLER: And a couple of lamb chops, Hives. A couple of soft boiled eggs—one hard boiled egg—three fried eggs— some toast and some coffee.

HIVES: Yes, sir. Nothing solid, sir. (*Exits.*)

DOUCET (*rises*): But, madame . . . I cannot wait any longer. (*Doucet sits down.*)

CHANDLER: Now, now, no matter what happens, a man should never lose his temper. He should eat his breakfast and read his morning paper. (*Chandler walks around back of table.*) No matter what happens, one must always be happy, satisfied, contented, at peace with the world . . . (*Chandler sits, and as he sees item in newspaper—he springs up in a furious rage.*) It's a lie. It's not true. It's not true I tell you. (*Walking from left of table to right.*)

(*Doucet and Mrs. Rittenhouse rise.*)

Gott, verdamte schwein!

(*His outburst is punctuated by excited inquiries from Mrs. Rittenhouse and Doucet: "What's the matter?" "What is it?" "What has happened?"*)

I never was.

MRS. RITTENHOUSE: You never were what?

CHANDLER: They will suffer for this.

(*Hives enters with tray.*)

HIVES: Your orange juice, sir.

CHANDLER: Orange juice! Throw away your orange juice.

DOUCET: But, Mr. Chandler!

CHANDLER: He talks to me of orange juice. Orange juice.

(*Exits, storming. As Chandler exits, Mrs. Rittenhouse walks right.*)

DOUCET (*picking up where Chandler left off*): Orange juice! and he was preaching to me. My painting, police! I've got to have my painting, I want the police!

MRS. RITTENHOUSE: Shut up, shut up. Very well then—we shall send for the police.

(*Mrs. Rittenhouse exits and Doucet follows her off, saying: "I want the police!" "My painting, a hundred thousand dollars!"*)

HIVES (*drinking the orange juice*): Good for the nerves.

(*Winston enters with* Traffic *in hand, dressed in bright sport clothes, whistling.*)

WINSTON: Hello, old socks! And how are you this morning?

HIVES: Lousy.

WINSTON: Well, I've got a little tonic here that will put you dead to rights. Ever read the *Morning Traffic*?

HIVES: Heaven forbid, sir. Oh, I have a telegram for you, sir. (*Handing him the telegram.*)

WINSTON: Thank you, Hives. (*Opening telegram.*) And if this is what I think it is, and I think it is, yes, it is. Here you are, Hives. Take this and buy yourself some giggle water. (*Hands Hives a bill.*)

HIVES: Thank you very much, sir. (*Exits.*)

(*Arabella enters—sees Winston hand Hives a bill.*)

ARABELLA: That's right. Squander your money on butlers—while I stand over a hot stove.

WINSTON: Baby, you can throw the hot stove out. I'm going to buy you a Frigidaire. Drop your mascara on this. (*Handing her telegram.*)

ARABELLA (*reading part of telegram*): "Your brilliant work in unearthing the Roscoe W. Chandler item"—A fifty dollar raise! Oh, Wally, that's wonderful!

WINSTON: You're wonderful—if it hadn't been for you, this whole thing never would have happened. A fifty dollar raise! (*Glancing at telegram.*) Let me see—is that every week? . . . Yes. Why you're practically Mrs. Wally Winston this minute.

ARABELLA: Oh, you're going to do the right thing, are you?

WINSTON: I always do the right thing.

ARABELLA: You don't say. How many right things have you done?

WINSTON: I take it back. I never did the right thing before.

ARABELLA: I got some more news for you. Beautiful society queen accepts tabloid dirt disher.

WINSTON (*embracing her*): Whoopee! and what do we do now?

ARABELLA (*starting right, Winston follows her*): We'll break the news to mother . . . Wait a minute . . . We'd better not bother her until this painting business is over.

WINSTON: What do you think she'll say?

ARABELLA: She'll give three cheers . . . She's a sucker for that column of yours.

WINSTON: That makes it clear sailing.

ARABELLA: Then we're both in the same boat.

WINSTON:

> Now that everything is jake
> We'll hit the high spots
> Baby we'll get a thrill

ARABELLA:

> You bet we will.

WINSTON AND ARABELLA:

> When things look bright and rosy
> When all your castles are rising high
> You're sitting pretty, everything is coy
> And there is not a cloud up in the sky
> When fortune looms before you
> And at the core you are feeling right
> The world's full of mirth
> It's just like Heaven on Earth
> When everything looks rosy and bright.

CHORUS:

> What's the meaning of this joy
> This gay abandon

WINSTON:

    We're full of happiness

ARABELLA:

    From head to toe

CHORUS:

    You're a very lucky boy

WINSTON:

    Which end I stand on—I really do not know

ARABELLA:

    The world's aglow.

    (*After Chorus has gone off Winston and Arabella re-enter and start to sing another chorus. Hives enters with another telegram.*)

HIVES: A telegram, sir. (*Winston does not notice him.*) A telegram, sir.

ARABELLA: Wally, a telegram.

HIVES: A telegram for you, sir. (*Handing it over.*)

ARABELLA: Another raise.

WINSTON: It wouldn't surprise me. (*Hands Hives a bill.*) Here you are, Hives, go out and buy yourself some more laughing soup.

HIVES: Thank you very much, sir. (*Exits.*)

WINSTON (*opening telegram*): When good luck comes, it comes in bunches. It never rains luck, but what it pours luck . . . (*He has scanned the wire, and his smile slowly fades away.*)

ARABELLA: What's the matter?

WINSTON (*hands telegram to Arabella*): What do you think that says?

ARABELLA (*reads telegram . . . a pause*): You're fired.

WINSTON (*reading telegram*): While you were finding out things about Chandler, why didn't you find out that he owns the paper? (*Weakly.*) Chandler is the owner of the paper.

ARABELLA: Yeah . . .

WINSTON: Did you know that?

ARABELLA: No, I didn't.

WINSTON: I didn't either. Oh, well, live and learn . . . (*Tears up telegram.*) Let's see . . . where were we? (*Both start to sing . . . weakly.*)

WINSTON AND ARABELLA: When things are bright and rosy . . .

WINSTON: Oh yeah.

> (*They start to sing, when they get to middle of chorus, they both break down and start to cry . . . Winston takes out handkerchief . . . Arabella takes it out of his hand. They cry on each other's shoulders.*)
>
> (*Hives enters.*)

HIVES: Is anything the matter, sir? (*No answer.*) Is anything the matter, sir? (*Taps Winston light on shoulder.*)

WINSTON: Is anything the matter? (*Throws torn telegram on "sir."*) Read that.

> (*Winston and Arabella start singing last half of chorus of "Bright and Rosy." They break down and start to cry . . . Hives also cries . . . as they all exit.*)
>
> (*Mrs. Rittenhouse enters. Jamison enters.*)

MRS. RITTENHOUSE: Good morning, Jamison. And how is Captain Spaulding this morning?

JAMISON: Oh, he was out horseback riding.

MRS. RITTENHOUSE: I'm sorry, but of course we've all been pretty well upset.

> (*Captain Spaulding enters. He is wearing riding costume and carrying whip. He begins looking around the room for something he has obviously lost.*)

Good morning Captain Spaulding. Did you enjoy your ride? What in the world are you looking for?

SPAULDING: I lost my horse, yes. He slipped right out from between me. I had my feet in the syrups too . . . I don't know how he got away. I didn't care about that. But I lost the bit you loaned me.

MRS. RITTENHOUSE: Oh, that's alright. I'll get you another bit.

SPAULDING: That'll be two bits I owe you then.

MRS. RITTENHOUSE: Captain, I hope you've not been distressed by last night's unfortunate occurrence.

SPAULDING: You mean the dinner you served?

MRS. RITTENHOUSE: No, the painting that was stolen.

SPAULDING: Was there a painting stolen? I haven't seen a paper in three weeks. Are you sure you're in the right house? Jamison, as my secretary, why didn't you inform me that there was a painting stolen? What do you think I hired you for?

JAMISON: Why, Captain, I didn't know it.

SPAULDING: You should have asked me. I didn't know it.

JAMISON: Well, I'm sorry.

SPAULDING: You're sorry, you're a contemptible cur. I repeat, Sir, you're a contemptible cur. Oh, if I were a man, you'd resent that. (*To Mrs. Rittenhouse.*) Please don't interfere. (*To Jamison.*) I can get along without you, you know. I got along without your father, didn't I? Yes, and your grandfather, yes, and your uncle. (*To Mrs. Rittenhouse.*) Yes, and your uncle. Yes, and my uncle.

MRS. RITTENHOUSE: But Captain . . .

SPAULDING: I didn't come here to be distributed.

(*Hives enters.*)

HIVES: I beg pardon, Mrs. Rittenhouse . . .

SPAULDING: Oh, you do, eh? Well, I'd like to see you crawl out of a rumble seat.

HIVES: The police are here, Madam.

MRS. RITTENHOUSE: The police? Have them come in.

(*Hives bows and exits.*)

SPAULDING: Oh, so that's your game, is it? Well, you can't shut me up.

MRS. RITTENHOUSE: But Captain . . .

SPAULDING: No, no, you can talk to my attorney. Jamison, take dictation . . .

(*Jamison sits in chair. Takes out note-book and pencil. Mrs. Rittenhouse stands behind table.*)

I'll show you a thing or three. Jamison, take dictation.

JAMISON: I'm taking it.

SPAULDING: Well, read me what you have . . . verbatim. "Hon. Charles D. Vasserschlogel, c/o Vasserschlagel, Vasserschlegel, Vasserschlugel and McCormick, semi-colon."

JAMISON: How do you spell semi-colon?

SPAULDING: Make it a comma. Dear Elsie. No, never mind . . . No, never mind Elsie.

JAMISON: You want me to scratch Elsie?

SPAULDING: Well, if you enjoy that sort of thing, it's quite alright with me. However, you'd better take it up with Elsie. Begin this way, Jamison. Let's get off with a bang. "Hon. Charles D. Vasserschlogel, c/o Vasserschlagel, Vasserschlegel, Vasserschlugel and McCormick. Gentlemen, question-mark. I re yours of the fifth inst. your to hand and in reply, I wish to state that the judiciary expenditures of this year, i.e. has not exceeded the fiscal year—brackets—this procedure is problematic and with nullification will give us a subsidiary indictment and priority. Quotes, unquotes, and quotes. Hoping this finds you, I beg to remain . . . "

JAMISON: Hoping this finds him where?

SPAULDING: We'll let him worry about that. Damn it all, don't be insolent, Jamison. Sneak. Hoping this finds you, I beg to remain as of June 9th, cordially respectfully regards. That's all, Jamison. (*To Mrs. Rittenhouse.*) I'll show you where I get off. (*To Jamison.*) Now read me what you have, Jamison.

JAMISON (*reading*): Hon. Charles D. Vasserschlogel, c/o Vasserschlagel, Vasserschlegel and McCormick. . . .

SPAULDING: Thought you could slip one over on me, didn't you, eh? Alright, leave it out and put in a windshield wiper instead. No, make it three windshield wipers and one Vasserschlegel.

JAMISON (*reading*): Dear Elsie, scratch . . .

SPAULDING: That won't do at all, Jamison. The way you've got it, you've got McCormick scratching Elsie. Turn that around, and have Elsie scratch McCormick. You'd better turn McCormick around too, Jamison. And see what you can do for me.

JAMISON (*reading*): Gentlemen, question-mark . . .

SPAULDING: Gentlemen, question-mark . . . put it on the diphthong, not on the penultimate.

JAMISON (*reading*): In re yours of the fifth inst. . . . Now you said a lot of things here that I didn't think were important, so I just omitted them.

SPAULDING: So, you just omitted them, eh? (*Business with crop.*) You just omitted them, eh? You left out the body of the letter. Alright, send it that way, and tell them the body will follow. Closely followed by yours.

JAMISON: Want the body in brackets?

SPAULDING: No, it'll never get there in brackets. Put it in a box. Put it in a box and mark it F–r–a–g–i–l–e–.

JAMISON: Mark it what?

SPAULDING: Mark it Fragile. F–r–a–g——look it up, Jamison. Look up under Fragile.

JAMISON (*reading*): Quotes, unquotes and quotes.

SPAULDING: That's three quotes?

JAMISON: Yes, sir.

SPAULDING: Add another quote and make it a gallon.

JAMISON (*reading*): Regards.

SPAULDING: That's fine. That's going to make a dandy letter,
Jamison. Now I want you to make two carbon copies of
that, and throw the original away . . . And when you get
through with that, throw the carbon copies away. Just send
a stamp, air-mail. That's all. You may go, Jamison.

(*Six policemen enter and line up. They are the Filipino
Band, in police uniforms, carrying their instruments.*)

I'm sorry, Mrs. Rittenhouse, but we . . .

MRS. RITTENHOUSE: But I don't understand, you are musicians. I sent for the police.

FIRST POLICEMAN: We are the police band, the regular police,
they are busy.

SPAULDING: Now listen, you boys, I don't care what you do
with those instruments, but don't be scratching them
around here.

(*Jamison exits. Policemen exit.*)

MRS. RITTENHOUSE: Oh, but Captain, we ought to have them
play, then nobody will suspect them of being police.

SPAULDING: You bet they wouldn't, or musicians either. He
said with an ugly leer.

MRS. RITTENHOUSE: I know, I'll have them play an overture to
the pageant.

SPAULDING: That's fine. That means there'll be no pageant.

MRS. RITTENHOUSE: Oh, but there must. Everything must
proceed just as planned. I don't want anything to interfere
with your week-end.

SPAULDING: Nothing interferes with my week-end. And I'll
thank you not to get personal, Mrs. Rittenhouse. Jamison,
where's my secretary, Jamison. A more dastardly crack I've
never heard. I wish I was back in the jungle where men are
women.

MRS. RITTENHOUSE: Captain, I'm sorry you feel that way.

SPAULDING: I'm feeling more that way every minute, Mrs.
Rittenhouse. (*Business.*) Mrs. Rittenhouse . . . are you
alone? (*Takes her hand.*)

MRS. RITTENHOUSE: Why, Captain, I don't understand.

SPAULDING: Don't understand being alone? Don't give me
that innocent stuff or you'll be alone. (*Drops her hand.
Walks right.*) A big cluck like you turning cute on me.
(*Comedy run.*) I'm giving you a whiff of old Japan. (*Taking
her hand.*) Mrs. Rittenhouse, ever since I met I've swept you
off my feet. There's something on my mind. Something
that's burning in my brain, like a red hot steed. Something
that I must ask you.

MRS. RITTENHOUSE: What is it, Captain?

SPAULDING: Will you wash out a pair of socks for me?

MRS. RITTENHOUSE (*crossing in front of Captain*): Why, Captain, I'm surprised.

SPAULDING: It may be a surprise to you, but it's been on my
mind for months. It's just my way of telling you that I love
you, Mrs. Rittenhouse, I love you.

   (*Mrs. Whitehead enters unnoticed by Spaulding.*)

MRS. RITTENHOUSE: Captain, please. Mrs. Whitehead is here.
Please keep quiet.

MRS. WHITEHEAD: I beg your pardon. Am I intruding?

SPAULDING: What a question, are you intruding? I should say
you were—I should say you are. Pardon me, I was using the
subjunctive instead of the past tense. Yes, we're way past
tents now, we're living in bungalows . . . This is a mechanical age . . .

MRS. RITTENHOUSE: You're not intruding, Mrs. Whitehead.

MRS. WHITEHEAD: I'm afraid you're being just a bit selfish,
Mrs. Rittenhouse. We haven't seen very much of the Captain lately.

SPAULDING (*to Mrs. Whitehead*): That's what I was telling her.
We haven't seen much of you either, lately. And how are
you?

MRS. WHITEHEAD: Fine, thank you. And how are you?

SPAULDING: And how are you? That leaves you one up. Did
any one ever tell you, you had beautiful eyes.

MRS. WHITEHEAD: No.

SPAULDING: Well, you have. (*To Mrs. R.*) And so have you. He
shot her a glance. A smile played around his lips. I don't
think I've seen four more beautiful eyes in my life. Well,
three anyway. You know you two grisettes have everything.
You're tall and short, and slim, and stout, and blond and

brunette, and that's just the kind of girl I crave. Why, you two, and Texas Guinan and I could be perfectly happy. You've got beauty, charm, money . . . (*To Mrs. R.*) You've got money, haven't you. Because if you haven't we can quit right now.

MRS. WHITEHEAD: The Captain is charming, isn't he?

MRS. RITTENHOUSE: I'm fascinated.

SPAULDING: Maybe you think I'm not. Right on the arm. If I were Eugene O'Neill I could tell you what I really think of you two. You know, you're very fortunate the Theater Guild isn't putting this on. So is the Guild. (*Walks down-stage, strikes frozen pose.*) Why you couple of baboons, what makes you think I'd marry either one of you? Strange how the wind blows tonight. It has a thin eerie voice. Reminds me of poor old Marsden. How happy I could be with either of these two if both of them just went away. (*Walks back to Mrs. R. and Mrs. W.*) Well, what do you say girls? Will you marry me?

MRS. RITTENHOUSE: But Captain, which one of us?

SPAULDING: Both of you. Let's get married. This is my party. (*Walks down stage. Strikes frozen pose.*) Party, party. Here I am talking of parties. I came down here for a party. What happens? They show me a painting. They don't even show it to me. They steal it. The gods look down and laugh. This would be a better world for children if the parents had to eat the spinach. (*Walks back to Mrs. R. and Mrs. W.*) Well, what do you say, girls? Are we all going to get married?

MRS. WHITEHEAD: All of us?

SPAULDING: All of us.

MRS. WHITEHEAD: But that's bigamy.

SPAULDING: Yes, and it's big o' me too. It's big of all of us. Let's be big for a change. I'm sick of these conventional marriages. One woman and one man was good enough for your grandmother, but who wants to marry your grandmother? Nobody, not even your grandfather. Not even DeWolf Hopper. Not even his brother, Grass. (*To audience.*) Well, don't hang on to it. Either laugh at it, or don't laugh at it. (*To Mrs. R. and Mrs. W.*) Think, girls, think of the honeymoon. Strictly private. I wouldn't let another woman in on this. Well, maybe one or two. But no men. I may not even go myself.

MRS. RITTENHOUSE: Are you suggesting companionate marriage?

SPAULDING: Well, it's got its advantages. You could live with your folks and I could live with your folks. (*To Mrs. W.*) And you, you could sell Fuller brushes. (*Walks down-stage. Strikes frozen pose.*) Living with your folks, the beginning of the end . . . drab dead yesterdays shutting beautiful tomorrows—hideous stumbling footsteps creaking along the misty corridors of time—and in those corridors I see figures—strange figures—Steel 181—Anaconda 74—Simmons Beds. (*Walks back to Mrs. R. and Mrs. W.*) Let's see, where were we? Oh yes, we were about to get married. Well, what do you think girls? Do you think we really ought to get married?

(*Mrs. Whitehead & Mrs. Rittenhouse take Spaulding's arms, and all three start toward exit.*)

MRS. RITTENHOUSE: I think marriage is a very noble institution.

MRS. WHITEHEAD: It's the foundation of the American home.

SPAULDING: But the trouble is you can't enforce it. It was put over on the American people while our boys were over there.

(*Mrs. Whitehead & Mrs. Rittenhouse & Spaulding exit. Doucet and Policemen enter.*)

DOUCET: Allez! We have searched that room—the painting is not there, come with me.

(*Doucet and Policemen cross stage and exit. Girl enters dressed in bathing suit, walking fast, then breaks into a run and exits. Professor enters on a run. Chasing a girl. He gives it up. He is carrying three paintings stuck in the front of his trousers. He spreads one painting on table, examines it . . . Police whistle blows off stage. Professor stands on head. Another police whistle blows off-stage. Professor runs to table, takes bowl of fruit, stands right of table. Doucet and policemen enter. Policemen exit. Doucet does not recognize the Professor. As he starts to exit, the Professor throws a piece of fruit at him. Mrs. Whitehead enters. Professor picks up newspaper from table, puts it up with paintings under his arm, so as to indicate newsboy.*)

MRS. WHITEHEAD: Oh hello, I've been looking all over for you. Where have you been?

(*Professor does leg business with Mrs. W.*)

Let me see what you have there? The morning papers?

(*He offers her a newspaper.*)
No, that isn't the one I want. Let me see one of the others.
(*He offers her another newspaper.*)
That still isn't the one I want.
(*He slaps her with paper.*)
You know what I want.
(*He smiles very shyly. Baseball business.*)
Come over here and sit down. I want to talk to you.
(*They both sit on chair. Professor puts paintings under them.*)
Don't you like me?
(*He shakes his head "No."*)
You don't? Well, I like you. I like little boys like you.
(*He whistles.*)
By the way, how old are you?
(*He indicates that he is five years old.*)
Five years old. Why you're just a baby, aren't you?
(*They both laugh. Mrs. W. tries to take the painting from under the Professor but he stops her by holding her wrist. He slaps her hand. Then kisses her hand. Then attempts to break her arm. Ad lib by Mrs. W.*)
Now all joking aside, tell me, isn't there somebody you like?
(*Professor shakes his head, "No."*)
Isn't there someone you love?
(*Professor shakes his head "No."*)
Now think again, isn't there someone you really and truly love?
(*Professor nods "yes."*)
There is? Tell me, who?
(*Professor takes photo from his pocket and hands it to Mrs. W. She looks at it.*)
Why that's a horse.
(*They both laugh.*)
You love a horse.
(*Hives enters unseen by the Professor. He takes a bottle of chloroform, saturates a handkerchief with it, and proceeds to chloroform the Professor. When the Professor is chloroformed, Hives lifts him up from the chair and Mrs. Whitehead takes the paintings from beneath him. Hives and Mrs. W. exit. Girl dressed in bathing suit enters and exits followed by the Professor. Mary and John enter.*)

JOHN: Do you know what I'm going to do . . . I saw an ad in this morning's paper. "Wanted, a bright young man to make himself generally useful. Salary $25.00 a week with a big chance for advancement."

MARY: But John, you can't quit like that . . .

(*John discovers painting lying on table, left there by Professor.*)

JOHN: Mary! Look! This isn't mine and it isn't the Beaugard either.

MARY: A third one? I don't understand.

JOHN: Wait a minute—somebody else had the same brilliant idea that you did—don't you see?

MARY: All I know is—that the musicians took the Beaugard and put yours in its place.

JOHN: Then somebody stole mine thinking it was the Beaugard, and this is what they left. Say, they certainly got the better of the bargain, alright.

MARY: Let me see . . .

(*Examining painting. Then puzzled she looks at John.*)

John, this is the picture that was unveiled—Chandler and Doucet never saw your painting.

JOHN: That's right.

MARY: We'll show them yet.

JOHN: I know I'm better than this, anyhow.

MARY: Better than this. Why, you're better than Beaugard.

(*Show Girls enter dressed in bathing suits.*)

1ST GIRL: Hello.

2ND GIRL: Aren't you coming in for a swim?

JOHN: Oh not now, thanks.

2ND GIRL: Why not?

MARY: I'm sorry, we can't now . . . (*To John.*) Come on dear, let's find Captain Spaulding.

(*Exit John and Mary taking painting with them.*)

1ST GIRL: Where is Grace, isn't she coming?

2ND GIRL: She said she'd be here in a minute.

3RD GIRL: She'd better hurry.

(*Grace enters dressed in bathing suit.*)

GRACE: Oh—there you are.

GIRLS: Hello.

4TH GIRL: Grace, are you going to teach me that new stroke?
GRACE: No, I've changed my mind about that. I'm going to
let one of the boys teach me.

> I always say
> When things are away off
> It's time to play
> So I take a day off.

CHORUS:

> Pack up the grip
> And take a trip
> Down to the shore.

GRACE:

> I couldn't stand for
> Living a blue life
> Down on the sand you're
> Living a new life.

CHORUS:

> Leave where you are
> Hop in your car
> Come to the shore
> No room for care
> Give it the air
> Down at the shore

GRACE (*with Chorus*):

> When things begin to get hot
> Here's all that you've got to do
> Just follow me
> Hop into the sea, and cool off
> You'll find your worries will go
> When you're in the ocean blue
> Wash 'em away
> Hop into the spray, and cool off
> Put your cares asleep in the deep
> Out where the waves keep rolling
> They'll decide the turn of the tide for you
> Pack up the troubles you've got
> If you have a lot or a few
> Just follow me
> Hop into the sea and cool off

(*Spaulding and Mary enter.*)

SPAULDING: Well, that's very interesting—fairly interesting anyhow. All we have to do is keep a short look out.

MARY: But, Captain, I feel so guilty, if it hadn't of been for me the painting would never have been stolen.

SPAULDING: Now, don't worry, everything's going to be alright. You just let me work on this case for twenty-four hours and then we'll call in somebody else. You think it's a mystery now—wait till you see it tomorrow. Remember the Charles Ross disappearance? I worked on that case for twenty-four hours and they never did find him. They couldn't find me for five years. That's me—Captain Spaulding of the Royal Mounted, I always get my woman—or painting.

(*Enter John excitedly.*)

JOHN: Mary—what do you think happened. You know that painting—the one we found here—

MARY: Yes—?

JOHN: It's been stolen from my room.

MARY: Why, John.

SPAULDING: What did I tell you, I haven't been on the case five minutes and there's another painting gone. It's not even five, I'll bet it's not more than three . . .

(*Fumbles in pocket for his watch.*)

JOHN: This is it, alright.

SPAULDING: Yes, this is it, but which one is it?

MARY: The third one that they put in place of John's.

SPAULDING: Well, we got that back. Maybe I got my watch back. (*Reaching for it.*) Now the fob is gone. Well, I've still got the pocket. Anything I retain now is velvet, except the coat, that's Prince Albert. (*To audience.*) Well, all the jokes can't be good. You've got to expect that once in a while.

JOHN: Say, you know if you could find the person who painted this we'd have a pretty good clue.

SPAULDING: What did you say?

JOHN: I said, if we could find the person who painted this, we'd have a pretty good clue.

SPAULDING: Why, you just said that. What a dull conversationalist you turned out to be. You want to be careful or you'll wind up in a Rotary Club. Let's see it a minute. (*Takes*

painting from John and examines it.) It's signed Beaugard.
There's the criminal, Beaugard.

JOHN: No, Beaugard is dead.

SPAULDING: Beaugard is dead. Then it's murder. (*Ravelli enters.*) Now, we've got something.

RAVELLI: Whatta you got, Cap.?

SPAULDING: I've got Jacks and Eights. What have you got?

RAVELLI: That's good. I was bluffing.

SPAULDING (*holding painting*): Look at this, Ravelli. Isn't there something that strikes you very funny about this picture. (*Ravelli laughs heartily.*) Come, come, it isn't as funny as all that. Did you ever see a tree like that?

RAVELLI: That's no tree. That's spinach.

SPAULDING: It can't be spinach. Where's the egg?

RAVELLI: That could be spinach. Look at all the sand around there. Nope, you're right, Cap., that's coleslaw.

SPAULDING: Coleslaw? Did you ever see coleslaw like that?

RAVELLI (*indicating his own lip*): Sure. Here.

SPAULDING: I don't want none of your lip, now. Did you ever see anything like that? Do you know what this is? This is a left-handed painting.

JOHN: You're right. Look at the signature.

RAVELLI: It's in the right-hand corner.

SPAULDING: This is either a left-handed painting or a vegetable dinner. Now, all we've got to do is find the left-handed person who painted this and we'll have the trial of Mary Dugan, with sound.

RAVELLI: Well, I saw that. Good-bye.

SPAULDING: No—you stay here. I need you. (*To John and Mary.*) Now, we mustn't lose this again. This is evidence. Take this to your room and leave the door open this time. We'll try that. (*Spaulding gives painting to John.*)

JOHN: Right-o, Captain.

(*John and Mary exit. Ravelli sits. Spaulding paces back and forth in front of him.*)

SPAULDING: Ravelli, there's dirty work around here. We've got to find the left-handed painter. In a case like this, the first thing you've got to do is to find the motive. Now what could've been the motive of the guys that swiped the Beaugard?

RAVELLI: I got it Captain. Robbery!

SPAULDING: Say, would you mind going out and crossing the boulevard when the lights are against you? (*Spaulding sits.*)

RAVELLI: Sit down, Cap. Now I got an idea how to find this painting. Of course, in a case like this, what's so mysterious —you gotta to do lika Sherlock Holmes. You gotta get whatta they calla da clues. Now you go about it lika this— you say to yourself, what have you—and the answer come right back, something was stolen. Then you say to yourself, what was stolen? and the answer come right back, a painting.

SPAULDING: Say, what are you, a ventriloquist?

RAVELLI: Now, you say to yourself, who stola da painting? And the answer come back, somebody in this house. So far I'm right, eh?

SPAULDING: Well it's pretty hard to be wrong if you keep answering yourself all the time.

RAVELLI: Now, you take da clue, and you put 'em together. And whata we got? A painting was stolen. Where was it stolen? In this house. Who stole it? Somebody in this house. Now, to find the painting, all we got to do is to go to everybody in this house, and ask them if they took it. That's what you call a brain, eh Captain?

SPAULDING: You know I could rent you out as a decoy for duck hunting. You say you're going to go to everybody in this house and ask them if they took it, eh? Suppose nobody in the house took the painting?

RAVELLI: Then we go to the house next door.

SPAULDING: Well, suppose there isn't any house next door?

RAVELLI: Well, then of course, we got to build one.

SPAULDING: Well, now you're talking. What kind of house do you think we ought to put up?

RAVELLI: Now look, I tell you what my idea is. I think we build something nice and small and comfortable.

SPAULDING: That's the way I feel about it. I don't want anything elaborate. Just a little place that I can call home and tell the wife I won't be there for dinner.

RAVELLI: I see, you just want a telephone booth.

SPAULDING: No, if I did, I'd get in touch with Chic Sales.

RAVELLI: Now what do you say, Cap., we build right about here (*indicating spot on table*).

SPAULDING: No, I think I'd like something over here, if I could get it. I don't like Junior crossing the tracks on his way to the reform school. I don't like Junior at all as a matter of fact.

RAVELLI (*indicating another spot on table*): Alright, we got something over here. And believe me that's very convenient. All you have to do is to open the door, step outside and there you are.

SPAULDING: There you are? There you are where?

RAVELLI: Outside.

SPAULDING: Well, suppose you want to get back in again?

RAVELLI: You had no right to go out.

SPAULDING: Don't do anything till I hear from you, will you? Now all we've got to do is find the painting.

RAVELLI: Ah, that's where my detective brain comes in. We got to hurry up and build the house because I think the painting is inside.

SPAULDING: Maybe it's me. Maybe I'm not getting enough sleep these days. (*Pointing to spot on table.*) Say, maybe that's the painting down in the cellar.

RAVELLI: That's no cellar. That's the roof.

SPAULDING: That's the roof, way down there?

RAVELLI: Sure, you see we keep the roof in the basement, so when the rain comes, the chimney he's no get wet.

SPAULDING (*rises*): Well, I'm going out and getting X-rayed. I'll be back later. I may be wonderful but I think you're wrong.

RAVELLI: Now, look, here are the rooms. (*Ravelli points to spots on the table.*) This is your room—this is my room—and this is the maid's room.

SPAULDING: Oh! I'd have to go through your room?

RAVELLI (*laughing*): That's alright. I won't be in it.

SPAULDING: Say, Ravelli, you couldn't put the maid in your room, eh?

RAVELLI: What makes you think I couldn't?

SPAULDING: There's going to be a lot of traffic in there, I can see that.

RAVELLI: Now what do you say? Are you ready to sign the lease?

SPAULDING: Well, it's a little abrupt. I'd like to discuss it with my husband. Could you come back this evening?

RAVELLI: Are you married?

SPAULDING: Didn't you see me sewing on little things? Why, I've got a girl as big as you are.

RAVELLI: Well, get me one.

SPAULDING: How about the painting, Ravelli?

RAVELLI: Oh, we take care of that. I think the kitchen should be white, the dining room should be green . . .

SPAULDING: No, no, the painting. The painting.

RAVELLI: That's what I say—the painting. The kitchen should be white, the dining room . . .

SPAULDING: No, I'm not talking about the kitchen. I mean the painting. The painting that was stolen. Don't you remember there was a painting stolen? A valuable oil painting? Don't you remember that?

RAVELLI: No, I'm a stranger around here.

SPAULDING: What do you think I am, one of the early settlers around here? Don't you remember that Mrs. Rittenhouse lost a valuable Beaugard oil painting worth $100,000. Don't you remember that?

RAVELLI: No. But I've seen you someplace before.

SPAULDING: Well, I don't know where I was, but I won't go there again.

RAVELLI: Hey Cap, it come to me like a flash. You know what happened to this painting? This painting wasn't stolen. This painting disappear. And do you know what make it disappear? Moths. Moths eat it. Left-handed moths. That's my solution.

SPAULDING: I wish you were in it. (*Cramp business.*) Go away. I'll be alright in a minute. You say that left-handed moths ate the painting, eh? You know I'd buy you a parachute if I thought it wouldn't open.

RAVELLI: I got pair of shoes.

SPAULDING: Well, let's get out of here. I've taken an awful licking here tonight. (*Spaulding starts left followed by Ravelli.*) We solved it. You solved it. Let's go and get the reward. The painting was eaten by a left-handed moth. I don't know how I overlooked it.

RAVELLI: You know we did a good day's work.

SPAULDING: How do you feel, tired? Maybe you ought to lie down for a couple of years?

RAVELLI: No, I stick it out.

SPAULDING: I'll tell you how we can get the painting. We'll go to court and we'll get out a writ of habeas corpus.

RAVELLI: Get a rid of what?

SPAULDING: I should never have started that way, I can see that. I said, we'll go to court and get out a writ of habeas corpus. Didn't you ever see a habeas corpus?

RAVELLI: No, but I see "Habie's Irish Rose."

(Both exit. Mrs. Rittenhouse and Chandler enter.)

MRS. RITTENHOUSE: Mr. Chandler, I feel sure that after we've had a swim, we'll both feel better.

CHANDLER: Well, I'll try it. I couldn't feel any worse.

(Enter Doucet excitedly. He is carrying a painting. Hives follows him on.)

DOUCET: Madame . . . Madame . . .

MRS. RITTENHOUSE: The painting . . . thank God.

DOUCET: No, not the Beaugard, the imitation. But where do you think I find it? In the room occupied by the young man—Monsieur—What is his name . . . ? The police find it in his room.

HIVES: In Mr. Parker's room, Madame.

CHANDLER: Parker.

MRS. RITTENHOUSE: Mr. Parker.

DOUCET: And where you find the imitation . . . That is the person who steal the Beaugard.

MRS. RITTENHOUSE: Hives, find Mr. Parker and ask him to come here immediately.

HIVES: Certainly, Madam.

(Hives exits.)

CHANDLER: What do you know about this young man? Where did he come from?

MRS. RITTENHOUSE: He seemed alright enough. I met him at Mrs. Potter's at tea.

CHANDLER: I don't think he is a painter at all. It sounds fishy to me.

(Enter John with a few guests. Mary enters with a few guests. Other guests enter.)

JOHN: Pardon—did you want to see me, Mrs. Rittenhouse?

DOUCET: We certainly do.

MRS. RITTENHOUSE: Why yes, something has come up, Mr. Parker, and we thought you might be able to help us out.

JOHN: Certainly. Anything at all.

DOUCET (*shakes painting under John's nose*): We find this imitation in your room. What have you done with my Beaugard?

CHANDLER: Well, speak! Where is the Beaugard?

JOHN: There's nothing I can say, I didn't steal it.

DOUCET: Sacre bleu! Where is my Beaugard?

CHANDLER: What do you mean you didn't steal it?

MRS. RITTENHOUSE: Really I think it would be wise of you—

JOHN: I have nothing to say, except that I did not steal the Beaugard.

MARY: I'm the one you can arrest.

JOHN: If you think I did, go ahead.

DOUCET: We go ahead—we turn you over to the police.

> (*Song "Old Kentucky Home" is heard being sung off-stage. Just before the end of it, in time to sing the last line on stage, they enter . . . Spaulding, Jamison, Ravelli and Professor, who is hidden, with only his head showing . . . All have bathing suits and robes on. There is a second of harmonizing the last line, with arms around each other's shoulders.*)

SPAULDING: This program is coming to you from the House of David.

> (*The Professor wearing a bathing suit up side down and white canvas gloves, with Chandler's tie around his neck. He comes out from behind Spaulding, Jamison, and Ravelli.*)

I still don't believe it. He's either got that suit on up side down or there is no law of gravity.

> (*Chandler walks to Professor and takes his tie away from him.*)

MARY (*crosses to Spaulding*): Captain, what are we going to do? They're going to arrest us.

SPAULDING: Who's going to arrest you?

DOUCET: I am.

MRS. RITTENHOUSE: I'm sorry to say that it looks very bad for them.

SPAULDING: Nonsense. In a case like this it's never the first person suspected. You're old enough to know that. Older. (*To Ravelli.*) How old is Mrs. Rittenhouse?

RAVELLI: Fifty.

SPAULDING: Correct, who's fifty?

RAVELLI: Mrs. Rittenhouse.

SPAULDING: How old is Mrs. Rittenhouse?

RAVELLI: Fifty-five.

SPAULDING: What's the number of my watch?

RAVELLI: Mrs. Rittenhouse.

SPAULDING: He never fails. The great Ravelli. We will now saw a woman in half. Did you ever saw a woman in half?

RAVELLI: No, but I saw a woman in strange quarters.

SPAULDING: Well, that's another section. Now, Mrs. Rittenhouse, if you'll kindly step this way, we will proceed to sever you from head to toe.

(*Business of Professor sawing Mrs. Rittenhouse's hand. In doing so, he removes an artificial hand that is concealed from audience while he is imitating a saw. And doing sawing business.*)

(*Professor does business. Scratching himself with artificial hand, then shakes hands with Spaulding.*)

Give me your hand, sugar-foot.

(*Spaulding takes the artificial hand, as he shakes hands with Professor.*)

Give the little girl a great big hand.

(*Offers hand to Mrs. Rittenhouse.*)

MRS. RITTENHOUSE: I don't want it.

(*Spaulding throws the hand to one of the male guests.*)

DOUCET: I demand that the police be called—these two must be placed under arrest.

CHANDLER: By all means, or nobody will be safe here.

SPAULDING: What? Those two? Why, you can't arrest them. That's the hero and the heroine.

MRS. RITTENHOUSE: Good heavens no. We must have them or there can't be any pageant.

SPAULDING: Imagine not having a pageant. What would the neighbors say? I'm surprised at you, Mr. Chandler. How would you like to walk around without a pageant?

DOUCET: I demand that the painting be returned this minute or they be placed under arrest. Do you understand? I demand that the police be called. This instant! I demand that they be put in jail. I demand . . .

(*The Professor has shaken some chloroform on a handkerchief from bottle. And supplies the handkerchief to Doucet's nose. Doucet grows weaker. Continues . . .*)

I demand that they be arrested . . . I demand . . .

(*Doucet drops . . . then the Professor takes flight with chloroform can and starts to administer same to the various Guests that crowd around him. One by one they all topple over. He waves to John and Mary, and John and Mary exit. Professor administers the chloroform to Spaulding.*)

SPAULDING: Oh, to think that I've to go so young.

(*Spaulding after falling keeps left foot up, and Professor makes it go down by spraying it with chloroform.*)

(*After all are lying on floor, the Professor raises one of the young ladies by the hand. Looks at her face, and chloroforms himself and lies down beside her.*)

BLACKOUT

SCENE TWO

SCENE: *Before the curtains.*

(*Specialty . . . the Band . . . and Harp Specialty.*)

SCENE THREE

SCENE: *The Garden. That night.*

(*A French garden of the period of Louis XV. Ballet. After the Ballet, Hives as Major Domo enters.*)

HIVES (*announces*): The Countess Felice is D'Aragon.

(*Grace enters as the Countess escorted by two Ladies-in-waiting.*)

The Princess Milane.

(*Mary enters as the Princess, escorted by two Ladies-in-waiting.*)

Her Majesty the Queen.

(*Mrs. Rittenhouse enters as Queen escorted by four Ladies-in-waiting.*)

MRS. RITTENHOUSE: We thank the citizens of Burgundy for their gracious tributes on this our Birthday and in recognition thereof, you are invited to attend the festivities of the Royal Court.

(*Music plays as all exit, and until bedroom scene is set, by attendants . . . it is to represent the bedroom of Louis the XV. Hives enters through swinging doors and announces.*)

HIVES: His Majesty the King.

(*Four attendants enter and stand at attention. Jamison enters dressed as a Musketeer. Spaulding enters dressed as the King. Hives exits.*)

SPAULDING: Is this the Palace?

JAMISON: Yes, Sire.

SPAULDING: And I'm the King?

JAMISON: Yes, Sire.

SPAULDING: France is in a hell of a fix.

(*Four attendants exit. Spaulding stands watching the swinging doors.*)

I certainly get homesick when I see those swinging doors.

JAMISON: Sire, the Queen presents her compliments to your Majesty, and begs that you will attend the Musicale to be given in her honor.

SPAULDING: You give the Queen my compliments and tell her I won't be there.

JAMISON: Yes, Sire.

SPAULDING: Tell the Queen to lay off my razor blades. She'll understand.

JAMISON: Her Majesty also wishes to inform you that in honor of her birthday, Monsieur Jean Beaugard will present Her Royal Highness with his latest painting.

SPAULDING: He will, eh? Well, that means I've got to do the right thing. Run down to Woolworth's and get the Queen some candy.

JAMISON: Yes, Sire.

SPAULDING: Get her a pound.

JAMISON: Yes, Sire.

SPAULDING: Get her two pounds. Get her a dime's worth.

JAMISON: Yes, Sire.

SPAULDING: And while you're about it, get her a new glass top for the percolator.

JAMISON: Yes, Sire.

SPAULDING: And Jamison, run over to Tiffany's and pick out a nice pearl necklace for Du Barry.

JAMISON: Yes, Sire.

SPAULDING: Get her the best one obtainable. And have it charged to the Queen.

JAMISON: Yes, Sire.

(*Exits. Enter Hives.*)

HIVES: His Excellency, the Premier.

(*Doucet enters. Hives exits.*)

DOUCET (*bowing*): My compliments, your Majesty.

SPAULDING: Oh yeah?

DOUCET: The people, the people are at the gate. They want bread.

SPAULDING: Give 'em the gate.

(*Hives enters. Doucet exits.*)

HIVES: The Ambassador from America. Mr. Benjamin Franklin.

(*Chandler enters. Hives exits.*)

CHANDLER (*bowing*): Your Majesty.

SPAULDING (*bowing*): Your Benjamin Franklin.

CHANDLER: Yes, your Majesty.

SPAULDING: Well, you're just the man I want to see. How is it I didn't get my *Saturday Evening Post* until Friday last week?

(*Winston enters.*)

WINSTON: Hey, King.

SPAULDING: Mr. King, and cut out the hey, hey.

WINSTON: I've got to speak to you a minute.

SPAULDING: What's up?

WINSTON: It's about—you know.

SPAULDING: Oh, I see. (*To Chandler.*) Well so long, Ben. Go fly a kite. (*Chandler exits.*) (*To Winston.*) Well?

WINSTON: Du Barry is down-stairs.

SPAULDING: Du Barry is down-stairs?

WINSTON: In a taxi.

SPAULDING: Is the meter running? You say she's down there in a taxi, eh? Where's her husband?

WINSTON: He's on a trip.

SPAULDING: You're sure this time? You know it doesn't look right for a King to keep jumping out of the window at three o'clock in the morning. The last window I jumped out of, I forgot to open. I'd show you the scars but I know you don't smoke. I can still feel the pane. I'll tell you what, you go down-stairs and tell Du Barry to come on up. (*Winston exits.*) Tell her to come on up. It's her turn to jump. (*Calls.*) Oh, Jamison. (*Jamison enters.*) I've got a little affair of state to attend to tonight and I don't wish to be disturbed.

JAMISON: Yes, Sire.

SPAULDING: You keep the Queen out of here and I'll make you master of the hounds. I know it's a dog's fight but you won't know the difference.

JAMISON: Yes, Sire. (*Exits.*)

SPAULDING (*walking and singing "Old man river, the old man river, the old man river." Keeps repeating the old man river. Speaks.*): Must be more than that to that song. That's the longest river I've ever seen. (*Looks at wrist-watch.*) I wonder what's keeping Du Barry? Grammatical error? I wonder who's keeping Du Barry. Well, today is the old Queen's birthday. It's her Sesqui-centennial. Fifteen years and I'm going to tear her down. I ought to give her something for her birthday. I think I'll give her a divorce.

(*There's a knock at the door. Spaulding sits at table.*)
Filet mignon.

(*Mrs. Whitehead enters as Du Barry.*)

MRS. WHITEHEAD (*after stately curtsy*): Your Majesty.

SPAULDING (*rises, walks to her, and kisses her hand*): Du Barry, did you bring my galoshes? I was in a hurry when I left.

MRS. WHITEHEAD: Sire, I fear for me to come here is indiscreet.

SPAULDING: Nonsense, you'll be in the street sooner or later. You come from good stock. You'll probably be on the curb. Ah, Du Barry, you look wonderful in that French dressing.

(*Mrs. Whitehead sits left of table, Spaulding right of table.*)
How about a nice little drink?

MRS. WHITEHEAD: Fine.

SPAULDING (*calling off-stage*): Garçon.

(*Enter Jamison. Business.*)
You want to get tightened up. You sound like last year's Essex. Yes, and this year's too. Yes, and next year's. And so

on, ad nauseam. Garçon, bring in some of that rare old champagne right off the boat.

JAMISON: Yes, Sire. (*Starts to go.*)

SPAULDING: Hey, better bring the boat. I'm getting suspicious. (*Exit Jamison.*)

You drink, I quiver.

MRS. WHITEHEAD: If your Majesty wishes.

SPAULDING (*hits table*): You're darn tootin' his Majesty wishes. What do you think I got you up here for? To show you my magic lantern? Well, we'll slide over that.

(*Business—lies across table.*)

Du Barry . . .

MRS. WHITEHEAD: Yes?

SPAULDING: May I call you Du, Du?

MRS. WHITEHEAD: As you will, milord.

SPAULDING: No, as you were. Well, as you will. Let's get down to cases.

(*Jamison enters with tray containing two bottles of champagne, glasses, and bucket of ice. He sets it on table.*)

No, let's make it quarts. What do you think, do you think we'll ever get the saloon back?

MRS. WHITEHEAD: I don't know.

SPAULDING: And if we do, what's going to become of the bellboys in the Hotel Astor. Now there's a question . . .

JAMISON (*extending slip of paper*): Check, Sire.

SPAULDING: What?

JAMISON: Check, Sire, check.

SPAULDING: Jack the Giant-killer?

JAMISON: Check.

SPAULDING (*looking at check*): $350.60? Say, what do you think I am, an out-of-towner? I'm the King.

JAMISON: Sorry, Sire, but those are the prices.

SPAULDING (*rises*): Is this the Royal Palace or the Palais-Royal? (*Sits again, and looks at check.*) $350.60. That's an outrage. Cover charge $37.50 . . . War tax $40.00. Well, that's reasonable. What war was that? Roast terrapin $30.00. Baked squab $1.25 . . . Arithmetic A.—Spelling B.—Deportment C.—changing one rear tire and five gallons of gas—exemption for three children under Budget A $1200.00—Say, you forgot to charge me for the wine.

JAMISON: Zat is wizz ze compliments of ze house, Sire. (*Starts to exit.*)

SPAULDING (*Negro dialect*): Well, that's mighty nice of you people. (*Rises and does negro walk.*) I'se a-coming in again sometime. I'se a-gonna tell all my friends too.

JAMISON (*Negro dialect*): How come?

SPAULDING: And the police. You certainly ain't the man what I am, you is. That's what I was. You certainly is. I never seen a boy like that. (*To audience.*) This is the southern part of France. (*Sits and starts rubbing leg of table.*) Du Barr, I've never seen you looking so lovely . . . (*Sees his mistake.*) My judgment of distance is not what it used to be. Well, pour yourself a load of schnapps, Du Barr. And don't forget your old Louis.

MRS. WHITEHEAD (*pours wine in glasses*): Your health, Sire.

SPAULDING: Your health. (*There is a knock at the door. Both rise.*) We're raided. Tell them you're an engineer.

(*Enter Professor and Ravelli. Professor does leg business with Ravelli.*)

Who's there? Friend or foe?

RAVELLI: One of each.

SPAULDING: Just as I thought. A pair of French heels. You may advance, friend, and greet your Majesty.

(*The Professor embraces the King, at the same time taking a bottle of champagne from the table. Professor and Ravelli start to exit.*)

Just a minute, have a little drink before you go, eh?

(*Professor reveals the bottle of champagne he has taken from the table. He and Ravelli exit.*)

That was a swell bottle of wine we nearly had.

MRS. WHITEHEAD: What does it matter, Sire? After all we have each other, haven't we?

SPAULDING: Well you have me there, and I have you here. Having you here tonight, Du Barry, makes me feel that you love me. Call me Louie. Not because it's me, but I want you to call me Louie.

(*Ravelli enters with sandwich in hand.*)

RAVELLI: You got any mustard, Louie?

SPAULDING: Look in the library.

RAVELLI: Where's the library?

SPAULDING: Fifth Ave. and 42nd St.

> (*Ravelli exits.*)

He certainly picked out a hot time to be asking me for mustard. There's nothing in the whole world I need less right now than mustard. Well, let's see, where were we? Oh yes, I had you here, and you had me there. (*Runs and jumps on Du Barry's lap.*) Well, that's neither here nor there.

> (*Girl enters and exits, followed by Professor. On his way out the Professor stops at the table and exchanges an empty bottle for a full one. He starts to exit.*)

Say, just a minute. You've got a nickel coming for the empty bottle.

> (*Professor exits.*)

You know that's the second bottle of wine I had, and I don't even feel it yet. You don't get the wine you used to. At least, I don't. Let's see. Where were we? (*Sits in Du Barry's lap.*) Oh yes, we were down to cases. How about brass tacks? This can't go on indefinitely, Du Barry. Sooner or later, you've got to say yes or no.

MRS. WHITEHEAD: Your Majesty has but to command, and all France will obey.

SPAULDING: All France? Well, that's a little more than I had planned on. You want to remember I'm Louie, not Montgomery Ward.

> (*Professor enters, runs, and exits, followed by girl in her chemise. Spaulding runs to doors as they exit. He tries to peek through the cracks of the door. Mrs. W. stands left.*)

You see that? You don't seem to get into the spirit of the thing. Now there's a man that's getting somewhere. Yes, and on my liquor too. I'm nothing but a royal Kibitzer around here. Oh, I get terribly discouraged at times, Du Barry. Fits of melancholy assail me—I feel morose and run-down—tired and worn out—and then I took Konjola. I could take some lessons from that fellow. It might improve my game. Oh I don't know, Du Barry. I'm all wrong. All wrong.

MRS. WHITEHEAD: Ah Sire, the King can do no wrong.

SPAULDING: You bet I can't. Not with all these people running in and out I can't.

> (*Du Barry starts to sit on couch and Spaulding slides under her.*)

Ah, it's good to be alone. It's no time to be good though.
Anyhow we're alone.

(*Ravelli enters.*)

RAVELLI: Hey, I can't find the mustard.

SPAULDING: You don't think I'm trying to hide it, do you?

RAVELLI: My partner, maybe he's got it. Did you see him?

SPAULDING: He's due along any minute now. He runs on the
hour and the half hour.

RAVELLI: He said he'd meet me here. Move over. I'll wait.

(*Ravelli sits on couch beside Mrs. Whitehead. Spaulding rises.*)

SPAULDING: If there's anybody you're looking for, just wait
right here. This used to be my private bedroom . . .

(*Professor enters and sits right of Mrs. Whitehead. Spaulding sees him.*)

Oh, so that's your game, is it, going to outnumber me, eh?
Whose girl do you think Du Barry is? You boys better read
up on your history.

RAVELLI: You read history. We'll make it.

SPAULDING: You're the King's Musketeers, aren't you? Well
the King orders you to stand up.

(*Professor and Ravelli stand. Professor stands on couch . . .
Ravelli on floor.*)

Attention.

(*Business with Ravelli and Professor.*)

Salute.

(*Ravelli and Professor salute.*)

Left face.

(*Business with Ravelli and Professor.*)

Forward march.

(*Professor walks over Mrs. Whitehead and Ravelli walks on
floor.*)

Halt—

(*Business with Ravelli and Professor.*)

Company rest.

(*Ravelli and Professor and Mrs. Whitehead lie across couch
and, unseen by audience, change wigs.*)

Well, you'll never get any rest that way. I'd like to get them
out of here, but I can't think of the right command. I can't
even think of one that'll get me over there. This is a crisis I
have never encountered. Company attention!

(*Professor and Mrs. Whitehead and Ravelli sit up straight. Professor has on a white wig, Ravelli a white wig, and Mrs. Whitehead has on a red wig.*)

My gosh! I've now got two Martha Washingtons and a water spaniel. Company attention. Left face.

(*Business with Ravelli and Professor.*)

Forward march.

(*Ravelli and Professor walk left.*)

Halt.

(*Spaulding makes a run for couch, also Professor and Ravelli do the same. Now Ravelli, Spaulding, Professor and Mrs. Whitehead are still lying across couch, changing wigs, etc., unseen by audience. All have on red wigs, moustaches and glasses, as they sit up straight. Spaulding runs and gets a tray, and uses it as a mirror. He rubs it on trousers and looks into it.*)

One of those three guys is me. But I don't know which one it is.

(*Jamison enters excitedly.*)

JAMISON: Jiggers. The Queen is coming.

(*Mrs. Whitehead exits in a hurry. Mrs. Rittenhouse as the Queen enters. Ravelli changes back to white wig and stands left. Spaulding with ice pail on his head stands right of Ravelli. Professor with wine glass on his head stands right of Spaulding, and Jamison stands right of Professor.*)

MRS. RITTENHOUSE: May I inquire what has been going on here? Where is the King? I asked where is the King?

RAVELLI: Somebody trumped him.

MRS. RITTENHOUSE: His presence is urgently required by the Prime Minister. Attention, left face, forward march.

(*Ravelli, Spaulding, Jamison and the Professor start toward center. A girl in chemise enters. Ravelli, Spaulding, Jamison and the Professor follow her.*)

BLACK OUT

(*Screens and props are cleared. All guests enter.*)

LIGHTS UP

(*Orchestra plays incidental music during above business. Hives enters.*)

HIVES (*announcing*): Monsieur Jean Jacques Beaugard.

(*John enters as Beaugard carrying a painting. He drops on one knee before the Queen.*)

JOHN: Your Majesty, as a humble representative of the artists of France, I beg that you will accept this my latest effort. (*He hands the Queen the painting.*)

MRS. RITTENHOUSE: We do indeed accept. (*She looks at painting and is apparently shocked.*)

Monsieur, this is the Beaugard, *the* Beaugard.

CHANDLER: Well, young man, so you've decided to return it, eh?

JOHN: Yes, I have, and here it is.

(*Professor enters. He turns to Professor who hands him another painting. Ravelli and Jamison enter with Spaulding.*)

DOUCET (*looking at paintings with Chandler*): What? What is going on?

CHANDLER: I don't understand.

MRS. RITTENHOUSE: Good heavens! Another one!

DOUCET: Which is my Beaugard—I can't tell.

CHANDLER: Is this a trick?

SPAULDING: Yes, and a darn good one too. We will now saw Mrs. Rittenhouse in half.

RAVELLI: Mrs. Rittenhouse.

MRS. RITTENHOUSE: But, what does it mean?

MARY: I'll tell you. It means that the one Mr. Chandler has is the real Beaugard, and the other was painted by John.

DOUCET: What?

CHANDLER: Why, young man you are a great painter.

DOUCET (*to John*): But if you did not steal it, where did you get it?

JOHN: From the Professor.

DOUCET (*to Professor*): Then you stole it?

JOHN: No, he didn't. He found it in the room of . . .

(*Turns to Professor, the Professor stops him from finishing sentence. The Professor points to Hives. All exclaim . . . "Hives!" Hives bows.*)

DOUCET: But, then who painted the imitation—the bad one?

(*Mary points to Grace who stands, applying lip stick with her left hand.*)

MARY: Look.

SPAULDING: The left-handed painter.

GRACE: I knew it all the time.

(*Prof. jumps on Mrs. Rittenhouse's dress. Messenger Boy enters.*)

MESSENGER BOY: Telegram! Telegram for Mr. Chandler.

CHANDLER: Here you are, boy. (*Takes telegram and opens it.*) Whoopee! It is from the President!

(*Professor whistles "He's Ivan the Fish-Peddler," wiggles hand like a fish.*)

SPAULDING: When I was in the jungles of Africa . . .

(*Music . . .*)

CURTAIN

JUNE MOON

A Comedy
in a Prologue and Three Acts
by
Ring Lardner
and
George S. Kaufman

FOREWORD

In the year 1898 there were 201 fatal street accidents in the city of New York. Of these, eighty-eight were caused by horse vehicles and 113 by street-cars. In the latter total are included people who died of old age while waiting for cars that were not labelled "Car Barn Only." The following year brought the automobile to America's metropolis and the statistics attribute one fatality to its arrival, as against 103 deaths by horse vehicles and 167 by street-cars. It was not until 1913 that the automobile forged to the front as a lethal weapon, never again to be headed. After 1918 the horses and street-cars virtually gave up trying, and the figures for last year show that the thing has ceased to be a contest and become a joke—1,075 deaths by autos, 64 by street-cars and 14 by horse vehicles.

It is estimated that if the horse vehicles and street-cars had kept on fighting and maintained their early leadership over automobiles, by the year 1970 the entire population of New York City would have been wiped out and no harm done.

The *World Almanac*, from which this information was gleaned, gives us only one ray of hope. In New York's biggest borough, Brooklyn, there were a thousand fewer births and thirteen hundred more deaths in 1928 than in 1927. It may also comfort some folks to know that only fifty thousand more New Yorkers speak Yiddish and Hebrew than English and Celtic.

THE SCENES

PROLOGUE
In a parlor car.

ACT I
Paul Sears' place.
Ten days later.

ACT II
A room at Goebel's.
A few weeks later.

ACT III
Still at Goebel's.
About a month later.

PROLOGUE

*The scene is a section of a parlor car speeding toward New York,
and not so very far from it when the curtain rises. We see only two
chairs clearly; the ends of the car dissolve in shadows. On these less
visible chairs are tossed vague overcoats and magazines; the racks
above them are filled with baggage. There is a bag or two overhead; on the floor are quantities of Sunday newspapers, along
with plenty of rotogravure sections, curling carelessly against the
bottoms of the chairs. It is night, and the shades are down.*

*In the two vital chairs sit a boy and a girl. The name of the boy,
as we presently find out, is Fred Stevens. The girl is Edna Baker.
She sits with her back to him, and is absorbed in a magazine
when the curtain goes up. The boy, who is not exactly a literary
type, is a bit restless. He wriggles in his seat, sighs, peers discreetly
at the girl, who pays no attention. With a bit too much of a
flourish, as though he thus hoped to attract her attention, he
whips out a time table and studies it. Consults his watch; swings
and peers out of the window, hand cupped over eyes to exclude the
light. Then he swings back, relaxes—and looks toward the girl
again. She swings her chair around for a second; peers down the
aisle, but swings back without having permitted the boy to catch
her eye. He rattles his newspaper a trifle obviously; indulges in a
bit of bad whistling; hums a little. She swings around again; another look down the aisle. Fred girds up his courage to break the
ice. The girl, who has the situation well in hand, gives sudden
and demure attention to an imaginary spot on her dress. She
chips at it with a fingernail.*

FRED (*diffidently extending his newspaper*): Would you—care
to look at the paper?

EDNA (*ever so properly, in the manner of a young woman who
never has been spoken to on a train before*): Oh, thank you
very much. I don't think so, thank you. (*By turning away
from him again she indicates that she is not encouraging a
continuation of the interview.*)

FRED: I thought maybe you might want to read.

EDNA: No, thank you. (*She gives him a small smile.*)

FRED (*trying desperately to keep things going*): We're due in New York at ten-three.

EDNA: Yes, I know.

FRED: You got on at Hudson, didn't you?

EDNA: Yes.

FRED: I seen you. (*A pause after this momentous remark.*) I been on ever since Schenectady.

EDNA: Really?

FRED: That's where I work. I mean, where I did work. At the G.E.

EDNA: G.E.?

FRED: General Electric. They call it the G.E. That's where their plant is, Schenectady.

EDNA (*feeling that it's all right to help along*): I've got a girl friend from Schenectady.

FRED: Is that so?

EDNA: She's in New York now, or at least she was the last time I heard of her. Working at Saks'. Grace Crowell.

FRED: I used to know a Mildred Crowell, but her name wasn't Grace.

EDNA (*refusing to give in*): This was Grace. I haven't seen her for years, and I never did know her very well.

FRED: Mildred Crowell's brother was quite a billiard player. Three cushions. Eddie, his name was.

EDNA: That's my name, too. (*Laughs.*) Of course it isn't my real name. It's just my nickname. My real name's Edna.

FRED: Oh! (*He comes back to vital matters.*) Eddie Crowell used to pretty near live on the billiard table. Then finally his health broke down and he went out West somewheres. I couldn't tell you now if he's dead or alive.

EDNA: It's funny how we lose track of people. Some of the girls I used to go with, they still live there yet, but I never look any of them up, except Gertie Hutton. I guess it's terrible of me not to, because if a person's got good friends, they ought to keep them.

FRED: I certainly got good ones. They showed that last night, at the banquet. (*He has finally managed to bring that up.*)

EDNA: Were you at a banquet?

FRED: I had to be. It was me they give it for. I mean, I was the guest of honor.

EDNA: How exciting!

FRED: It was a farewell testimonial on account of me going to New York. And then this afternoon ten or eleven of them come down to the station, and Ernie Butler had a hangover and bought me this seat in the parlor car; he said it would be a disgrace for me to ride in the day coach with this new bag. (*He indicates a shining yellow suitcase at his side.*)

EDNA: It's a beautiful bag!

FRED: They give it to me at the banquet. It's got my initials. See? F.M.S. Frederick M. Stevens.

EDNA: What's the M for?

FRED: Martin.

EDNA: I like a man to have a middle name. Girls don't usually have them. I'm just plain Edna.

FRED (*pretty daring, for him*): I wouldn't say "plain."

EDNA: You know how to make pretty speeches.

FRED: I bet you're used to them.

EDNA: There's another one. I'm not so used to them that I don't like to hear them, especially from people whom I think they're sincere.

FRED: I don't say things unless I mean them.

EDNA: I'm glad of that.

FRED: Talking about speeches, you ought to heard the speech Carl Williams made when he give me this bag. At the banquet, I mean. I guess I blushed, the things he said about me. A lot more than I deserve.

EDNA: I bet they were sorry to see you go. You look like the kind of a man men would like. And girls, too.

FRED: I don't go around much with girls.

EDNA: I don't go much with men, either.

FRED: Neither do I. (*A pause;* that *subject's cleaned up.*) It's comfortable in here, ain't it? Like being home. I never been in a parlor car before.

EDNA: My brother always insists on me riding in it. He says the day coach is generally dirty, for one thing—and another thing, the men that ride in the day coach are the kind that try and make up to pretty girls. That sounds like I was throwing a bouquet at myself, but I'm just repeating what Dick said. That's my brother's name, Dick. I guess a brother always thinks their sister is good-looking.

FRED: I believe in a man sticking up for their sister, or any woman. I got no use for a man that don't respect woman's hood. Where would a man be if it wasn't for their mothers and sisters and wives?

EDNA: Some men haven't got wives.

FRED: I haven't got one myself—yet. I ain't been lucky enough to meet a woman who would be a good pal as well as a sweetheart. I want my wife to be like mother used to be.

EDNA: I love to have a man love their mother.

FRED: I wished mine was still here. Like Carl Williams said in his speech last night—if she was still here, maybe she would be a little proud of me.

EDNA: I'll bet she would.

FRED: He made quite a speech, all right. He said the boys expected me to make Irving Berlin jealous. I said I didn't want to make nobody jealous, but I wanted to make my friends proud. I said my only regret in going to New York was on account of leaving so many good friends behind, and as soon as my songs begun to sell up in the hundred thousands, and my dreams came true, I would invite them all down to visit me on Broadway and show them the sights.

EDNA (*a bit too eagerly*): Is that what you are? A song-writer?

FRED (*nods*): Not the music part; just the words. Lyrics, they're called.

EDNA: It must be wonderful to have a gift like that.

FRED: That's what Benny Davis called it—a gift. I guess you've heard of him—he's turned out a hundred smash hits.

EDNA: I guess I must have.

FRED: He wrote, "Oh, How I Miss You To-night!" It was a song about how he missed his mother—he called her his "Old Pal."

EDNA: That's sweet!

FRED: Well, he happened to be playing in Schenectady in vaudeville, and I happened to meet him and I happened to show him some of my lyrics. And he said a man like I with the song-writing gift was a sucker not to go to New York, because that's where they have the Mecca for a man if you got the song-writing gift. So he give me a letter to the Friars' Club, asking them to give me a two weeks' card, they call it. The Friars' Club is where they have the Mecca for song-writers. And he give me a letter of introduction to Paul Sears, the composer. He wrote "Paprika." You remember "Paprika"? (*He sings a strain of it.*) "Paprika, Paprika, the spice of my life——"

EDNA (*with quick concurrence*): I think so.

FRED: When you write a song like "Paprika" you don't ever have to worry again. He's one of the most successful composers there is, Paul Sears. I bet you I and he will turn out some hits together.

EDNA: Are you going to be partners with him?

FRED: If he wants me to, and I guess he will when I show him Benny Davis's letter. That's the hard part, getting acquainted. I'd have broke away a long while ago only for my sister. I couldn't leave her alone.

EDNA: Is she in Schenectady?

FRED (*nods*): She got married a week ago Saturday. A fella I been working with in the shipping department—Bob Gifford.

EDNA: She'll miss you just the same. I know how sisters feel, especially when their brother is like you or Dick.

FRED: Well, anyway, she got married, and I give them a pair of book-ends.

EDNA: She'll love them!

FRED: She always done everything for me—I mean, cooked my meals and sewed things for me. Look! (*Dives for his bag and starts opening it.*) She made me a half a dozen shirts before I left. Different colors. Here's one of the blue ones. I bet if you was to buy a shirt like that, you couldn't buy a shirt like that under a dollar seventy-five.

EDNA: I'll bet it would cost more than that.

FRED: Marion can sew, all right. My mother used to say she was a born seamstress.

EDNA: I love to sew. (*Looks at the shirt.*) Has it got your monogram, your initials?

FRED: No. She was going to put a "F" on the sleeve, but she was too busy.

EDNA: It's too bad you're not my brother and I'd embroider your whole initials.

FRED: You don't have to be a man's sister to embroider their shirt.

EDNA: I don't want you to misjudge me, Mr. Stevens. I'm not the kind of a girl that talks to strangers. My friends would die if they knew I was talking to a man whom I had not been properly introduced.

FRED: You don't need to be scared of me, girlie. I treat all women like they was my sister. Till I find out different.

EDNA: A girl alone in New York can't be too careful, especially a girl in my position. You take at Dr. Quinn's, where I work—he's one of the best dentists there is, and he has lots of men patients that would be only too glad to start a little flirtation. Why even Doctor himself was fresh, the first day I met him. It turned out he wasn't really, but it seemed that way. He put his arm around my shoulders and I jumped away from him like he was a leopard or something, and I told him, I said, "Doctor, I guess I don't care to work here after all." Then he laughed and said forget it, that he was just testing me. He said he didn't want an assistant who was inclined to flirt. And from that day he's never made any advances, except once or twice.

FRED: He'd keep his distance if I was around.

EDNA: I wish you could be.

FRED: I got plenty of excuses for being there. I got a cavity as big as the Grand Canyon.

EDNA (*laughing a little harder than is necessary*): You must forgive me laughing. Caroline used to tell me I had the keenest sense of humor of any person she ever met.

FRED: First thing you know I'll be in to see Dr. What's-His-Name myself.

EDNA: He'll fix it for you. He's a wonderful dentist.

FRED: If I come, it'll probably be when he's out to lunch.

EDNA: Then what would you come for?

FRED: I'll let you guess.

EDNA: I'd rather you told me. I'm a bad guesser.

FRED: I might come to see you. Would you let me?

EDNA: I'd love it, if you wanted to.

FRED: I wouldn't say so if I didn't.

EDNA: You'll forget all about it.

FRED: No, I won't. Your smile will always haunt me.

EDNA: I'll bet you're a wonderful song-writer. No wonder your friends gave you that big dinner.

FRED: It certainly was quite a banquet. I bet some of my pals got a headache to-day, all right.

EDNA: I hope you haven't got one.

FRED: No. Liquor don't afflict me like most people.

EDNA: I hardly ever touch it myself, only once in a great while, at a party.

FRED: Girls ought to lay off it entirely.

EDNA (*quickly covering her slip*): I never touch it.

FRED: Take some of those women in Schenectady and they want to go out somewhere every night and guzzle. Married women, too.

EDNA: I don't see how they can, with a home to take care of.

FRED: Either they get all dressed up and drag their husband to a dance or a card party every night, or either they lay around the house in a wrapper.

EDNA: When I marry I'll be just as careful of my appearance as I am now. I believe a husband appreciates a wife dressing up for him.

FRED (*ever the practical soul*): If it ain't too expensive.

EDNA: The man I marry won't have any complaints. I make practically all my own clothes. Caroline—she's the girl I used to live with—she used to say I always looked like I had just stepped out of a bandbox, even if we were only sitting in our room. We hardly ever went out evenings; personally I prefer to stay home and read, or else just sit and dream. But still I always bathe and change my clothes even when I'm only going to cook dinner.

FRED: I think I'll take a room with a bathroom when I get to the hotel.

EDNA: Where are you going to stay?

FRED: The Hotel Somerset. They got rooms with a bathroom right in the room, so you don't have to go out of the room. And it's close to the music publishing houses and the Friars' Club—any place I want to go, I can walk. Except to Paul Sears' place. He probably lives in some swell apartment, or maybe a country place in Great Neck or Jamaica.

EDNA: A successful man like he wouldn't live in Jamaica.

FRED: Well, some place. I don't know much about New York; I only been there once before, with Carl Williams. He's the fella that made the speech last night. It was the first time he's been away from home in the evening since he was married. He's got a wife and baby now.

EDNA (*so impulsively*): Oh, I'm dying to have a baby! (*She catches herself.*) Heavens! I didn't mean to say that. I love them so.

FRED: It's nothing against a woman to like babies. Carl's wife certainly likes hers. She's made him a nice home, too. He didn't have to buy hardly anything in the way of furniture; her grandmother gave her a bedroom suit and she bought some herself with money she saved while she was working at Berger's.

EDNA: She must be a good deal like myself. I could almost start housekeeping with the things I've got. I suppose I'm silly and old-fashioned, but I always thought a girl should bring her husband something besides herself. I even wouldn't mind going on working after I was married, till my husband established himself.

FRED: The girl I marry won't never have to work. I don't believe God ever meant for a woman to endure a life of druggery.

EDNA: Oh, Mr. Stevens, if only all men felt the same way!

FRED (*a look at his watch*): My, it's nine twenty-six already.

EDNA: It's been a shorter trip than usual, for some reason.

FRED (*trying to peer out the window*): I wonder where we're at now?

EDNA (*also peering*): Pretty near Yonkers, I guess.

FRED: If we was on the other side we could see the Hudson River.

EDNA: My, but it's dark!

FRED: There's a moon out.

EDNA: Yes, I love it.

FRED: June—moon.

EDNA: What?

FRED: I just said June moon.

EDNA: It isn't June. It's October.

FRED: I know, but June and moon go together. They rhyme. I'm always thinking of words that rhyme, even when I ain't working.

EDNA: That'd be a catchy name, June Moon. For a song, I mean.

FRED: Yes, you could get words to go with it. Spoon, and croon, and soon. Marry soon, or something.

EDNA: And macaroon.

FRED: Yeah. I wish I had some. I'm hungry.

EDNA: I am, too, kind of. (*After a pause.*) Some day when that song is published and people are singing it everywhere, I'll say to my friends, "I knew the man that wrote that. We were riding on a train and he looked out and saw the moon, and he thought of this song, and then the train got to New York and he never saw poor little me again."

FRED: You won't be telling the truth, because I'm going to see you again.

EDNA: You say that now. But you'll forget all about me.

FRED: No, I won't. Are you going right home when we get in?

EDNA: Why—I intended to. (*She sits up, expectantly.*)

FRED: I thought I'd go and get something to eat some place, only I wouldn't know where to go if I didn't have somebody with me that knowed where to go.

EDNA: I can tell you a place where I go once in a while, the Little Venice. Though most of the time I stay home and cook my own dinner, just because I love to cook.

FRED: It'll be a little late to cook to-night. I was wondering if you wouldn't go along to this place, and maybe we could eat together.

EDNA: I'd love to.

FRED: It ain't a very expensive place, is it?

EDNA: Oh, no. The last time I went, there was two of us and we had hot roast beef sandwiches, and peas, and coffee, and it only came to a dollar-twenty.

FRED (*with vast relief*): All right. I guess we can each afford sixty cents.

(THAT WINDS UP THE PROLOGUE)

ACT I

The scene is one of those Riverside Drive apartments, in a place called New York City. It is up in the neighborhood of One Hundred and Sixteenth Street, and once it was pretty good. It's a bit run down now, and since people began moving to the East Side the neighborhood has become somewhat declassee—not more so, however, than Paul Sears, the tenant of this particular apartment.

We see the living-room, if you can call it living. There is a piano, because Paul Sears is a composer. The rest of the furniture is what you might imagine, or worse.

Paul, a commonplace-looking man in his middle thirties, is at the piano when the curtain rises. He is in his shirt sleeves and is alternately hitting a few discouraged keys and making probably meaningless notations on the music sheet in front of him. He lacks one finger of being a two-fingered piano player. He is laboriously going over the same phrase again and again. And if you had never even heard it once, it would be too often.

Lucille, his wife, comes on from the rear rooms of the apartment. A spare but still attractive woman, on whom three years of marriage with Paul Sears have left their mark. She looks around for something. Finds it. It turns out to be a copy of the "Graphic." She drops listlessly into a chair and starts to read. Paul continues torturing the piano.

LUCILLE (*addressing herself more than Paul, as she scans her paper*): What do you know about that! Myra Vale's engaged!

PAUL: I read it. Automobile man. Probably drives a truck.

LUCILLE: If he does, at least she'll have something to go places in.

PAUL: I got Myra her first job; I introduced her to Dillingham.

LUCILLE: Yes, you did! She was in "Nanette" with Eileen and me before you ever saw her.

PAUL (*belligerently*): Who says so?

LUCILLE: Ask the doorman down at the Globe. He used to have to carry her in.

PAUL: She never took a drink when I knew her.

209

LUCILLE: I can vouch for that.

PAUL (*jumping up from the piano*): This is the last time I'll work with Fagan! I rewrite two whole bars of the melody for him, and when I ask him to change one word of his lyric, he squawks. He's got it "as a rose in June," and I want him to make it "as roses in June." Listen—here's his way (*he plays and sings*): "As a rose in June." And here's the way I want it: "As roses in June." All the difference in the world.

LUCILLE (*wearily*): It sounds just the same to me.

PAUL: My way gives me a triplet and makes it twice as effective! Listen! (*Starts hitting the same old notes.*)

LUCILLE: Oh, isn't that enough? (*Paul stops.*) Must I sit around all night listening to that?

PAUL: Why don't you go out? You could go out if you want to.

LUCILLE: Who with?

PAUL: You could go out with Eileen. You and *her* could go somewhere.

LUCILLE: You know she's got a date with Hart. I suppose you want me trailing along.

PAUL: Well, I explained to you *I* can't go no place, with this fella coming up. I told you a dozen times.

LUCILLE: I don't expect you to take me anywhere, except maybe for a walk around the block. That's free.

PAUL: I don't enjoy laying around here no more than you do. I'm not a nun.

LUCILLE: That's the first I've heard about it.

PAUL: You wait till this number gets over. We'll go everywhere then.

LUCILLE (*tiredly*): Oh, sure!

PAUL: You haven't heard it played yet. It'll be another "Paprika." Did I tell you what Dave Stamper said about it?

LUCILLE (*quickly*): Yes!

PAUL (*just as though she'd said "No"*): He said it was another "Paprika." You wait till you hear it played. Dave Stamper says it's sure fire. (*Back to his "playing" again.*)

LUCILLE: The silliest thing in the world to me is a man trying to be a composer when he can't even play "Chopsticks."

PAUL: I can play as good as I need to. I can play as good as Berlin, and he's turned out twice as many hits as anybody.

LUCILLE: He knows what people want. He appeals to the women.

PAUL: It ruins a composer to play the piano too good. They depend on fancy harmony and tempo, instead of pretty melodies.

LUCILLE (*giving up*): All right.

PAUL (*his eye drawn to the newspaper*): Did you read that thing from that Boston paper about "Pretty Polly"? They say Gershwin hasn't given them one tune. (*He's pretty pleased about it, too.*) Ten years from now, nobody'll know there *was* a Gershwin. He won't live.

LUCILLE: At least he won't starve to death.

PAUL: It was me that was responsible for Gershwin getting his start. I brought him and Georgie White together.

LUCILLE (*simply not listening*): Why can't you see this man in the daytime instead of asking him up here?

PAUL: Because I don't want him to come in the office yet, that's why. I'm keeping him under cover till I get rid of Fagan.

LUCILLE: If there's one thing that'll round out my day, it's entertaining a lyric-writer.

PAUL: This fella ain't like the rest of them. He's got a fresh slant. Take fellas like Fagan, that's been around Broadway all their life, and all their lyrics sound just alike. If Fagan gave me a new idea, I'd drop dead. But this fella's got a fresh slant.

LUCILLE: Fagan would drop even deader if you gave him a new tune.

PAUL: I gave him "Paprika," didn't I?

LUCILLE: That's so long ago I don't see how you remember it.

PAUL: Old man Goebel remembers it, and so does Hart. They made enough money out of it.

LUCILLE (*the eternal wife*): Everybody makes money but you.

PAUL: Yes, they do! There's plenty fellas around the club that's just as flat as I am.

LUCILLE (*ever so brightly*): That makes everything all right.

PAUL: I'll tell you who's got money, if you want to know, and that's Stevens.

LUCILLE: Who?

PAUL: This lyric-writer, Stevens. He's got money.

LUCILLE: A lot of good that'll do me.

PAUL: He's a nice kid, too. (*His eye falls on his watch.*) If Eileen's got a date with Hart, why don't she keep it? It's half past eight.

LUCILLE: Don't you worry about that.

PAUL: What about him and her, anyway? If she's engaged to him, aren't they ever going to get married?

LUCILLE: You'll know as soon as there's anything to know.

PAUL: He'll wriggle off the hook some way. If you ask me he's getting tired of her already.

LUCILLE (*with sudden interest*): What makes you think so?

PAUL: Just the luck I'm running in. If I ever marry again, it'll be a woman without a sister.

LUCILLE: She don't cost you much, and she's company for me.

PAUL: What's the matter with her getting a job somewheres?
(*The telephone rings.*)

LUCILLE: Yeah. You ought to be able to place her, with your influence.

PAUL (*at the telephone*): Hello. . . . Oh, hello, Maxie!
(*There enters, from the rear rooms, Eileen. She has been drawn by the ring of the telephone, and comes on eagerly, expectantly. She is a young woman in her late twenties, and has plenty of good old-fashioned sex appeal. But with it she is a bit hard, a trifle worldly. She wears a good-looking and rather revealing negligée, and is carrying what seems to be an evening dress, on which she has been sewing, or trying to sew. She stops short as she senses that the phone call is not for her; relaxes. From her mouth comes a cloud of cigarette smoke. Paul, of course, has kept right on with his phone conversation.*)
Sure—going to be here all evening. . . . All right. . . . Fine! (*He hangs up; turns to Lucille.*) Maxie's coming over. Wait till you hear him play it— (*a gesture toward his music*) —then you'll see!

EILEEN (*drifting over to Lucille*): What time is it?

PAUL (*going right on*): It's going to be another "Paprika."

LUCILLE (*reaching for the dress that Eileen has brought along*): Want me to do that?

EILEEN: I'll go crazy, waiting around here!

PAUL (*you can't stop him*): If I team up with this new fella you'll hear some hits.

LUCILLE (*handing over the paper to Eileen*): Did you see this? Myra Vale's announced her engagement.

EILEEN: Who to, for God's sake?

LUCILLE: Nobody we know.

EILEEN (*reading*): No. And nobody that knows her, you can bet on that.

LUCILLE: Paul was trying to tell me he got her her first job; introduced her to Dillingham.

EILEEN: Oh, sure. He introduced Rogers to Peet, didn't he?

LUCILLE (*indicating the dress*): This isn't going to last much longer.

EILEEN: I know it.

LUCILLE: Why don't you look around Monday? See what you can find.

EILEEN: Maybe I will. I've just been putting it off. I'm lazy, I guess.

LUCILLE: I'd never be too lazy to shop, if I had anything to shop with.

PAUL: You wait till this number gets over.

LUCILLE (*quite pleasantly*): By that time I'll only want a shawl.

PAUL (*finally flaring up*): There's nothing helps a man like being married to a woman that always encourages you and looks on the bright side. I'm going to write an article for the *American Magazine*, saying I attribute my success to my wife.

EILEEN: Why don't you try writing articles? They might be pretty near as good as your tunes.

PAUL: You don't have to worry about my tunes. Anyhow, I was talking to Lucille.

EILEEN: It's time you did something more for Lucille besides talk to her!

PAUL: If I was in your place, I'd keep pretty still in this house. That is, unless I was paying board.

EILEEN (*it's a good battle, by this time*): Don't you dare say I'm dependent on you, because I'm not!

PAUL: Only for your meals and a place to sleep!

EILEEN: You wouldn't even have a job if it wasn't for me! Do you think Hart is keeping you on the staff because you wrote a hit three years ago?

LUCILLE: Now!

EILEEN: Well, make him lay off me, if he knows what's good for him. If he keeps riding me, he'll be looking for a new job!

PAUL: Swell chance of them letting me out when I've got a number like "Montana." I'd run right to Harms with it.

EILEEN: Harms wouldn't let you in their elevator!

PAUL (*as he goes proudly into the next room*): I was in it this afternoon!

EILEEN (*a long, long sigh*): Is Hart going to phone or isn't he? It gets me crazy, this waiting.

LUCILLE: I wouldn't mind waiting if there was something to wait for. I nearly go out of my mind, just sitting. You hear women brag about the nice, cozy evenings they spend at home with their husband. They're not married to a piano tuner with ten thumbs.

EILEEN (*hoping against hope*): Maybe he didn't get back from Philadelphia. He might still be over there.

LUCILLE: What time was he going to call up?

EILEEN: Six o'clock. He said he'd call me the minute he got in. Maybe the train was late.

LUCILLE: They aren't late very often, from Philadelphia.

EILEEN: It's the only evening we'll *have* for three weeks, with him going away again to-morrow. (*Restlessly pacing.*) If he was going to be late you'd think he'd try to reach me.

LUCILLE: Of course, you know him better than I do, but when a man's really crazy about a girl, he calls her up, I don't care what he's doing. It's only when he begins cooling off that he finds excuses, like being in Philadelphia.

EILEEN: But he was in Philadelphia.

LUCILLE: I know, but they've got phones there now, too.

EILEEN: If you think he's cooling off you're crazy! He's insanely jealous. When I told him I was thinking of going out with Bert Livingston he was sore as hell. He said, "All right, go ahead and go out with him." I asked him if he meant it, and he said, "Sure! Go out with the whole Lambs Club!" He's insanely jealous and tries to hide it.

LUCILLE: I'd go out with the janitor if he asked me. God, I'm sick of this place!

EILEEN: Why don't you go to a picture?

LUCILLE: They charge admission. (*A little sardonic laugh.*) Remember the way I used to figure when Paul first came
along? I thought marrying a song-writer meant going to all
the first nights, meeting everybody that was worthwhile,
going down to Palm Beach—

EILEEN: You would, too, if Paul was any good.

LUCILLE: I wonder what it'd be like if we'd stayed in Strouds-
burg. I'd probably be married to Will Broderick, and we'd
have a car—

EILEEN: To drive over to Scranton in.

LUCILLE (*a sigh*): I suppose I ought to get consolation out of
one thing. I never expect a phone call or a mash note or an
invitation or even a half pound box of candy. Whatever happens is velvet.

EILEEN: You're a fool if you keep it up. You ought to break
away while there's still time.

LUCILLE: That's an easy thing to say. I haven't got any
grounds, in the first place.

EILEEN: You wouldn't need grounds. Just get him up in court
and let the judge look at him.

LUCILLE: And even if I did get free, where am I? I'm not
young any more. No man under sixty would look at me.

EILEEN: Well, men over sixty are more liable to have money
than boy scouts.

LUCILLE: I don't like old men.

EILEEN: Who does? Just the same, they've got their good
points. They sleep eighteen hours a day. And they're like
little kids—they believe everything you tell them.

LUCILLE: I never could fool anybody. That's why I've been
afraid to try anything, with Paul. He knows when I'm lying
to him, every time.

EILEEN: Him! He isn't even listening to you! You could have
callers right in this room and he wouldn't hear them come
in—not with all those God-given melodies ringing in his
ears.

LUCILLE: What's the use of talking about it? There haven't
been any volunteers. Women can't go wrong if they're not
invited.

EILEEN: All I can say is, if you don't break away from him,
you're crazy!

LUCILLE: And if I did, do you know what would happen? He'd write ten smash hits in a week. That's my luck. . . . God! It would be wonderful to have some clothes and hold up my head again!

EILEEN: I'm through arguing with you. You're hopeless.

LUCILLE: You'd better be thinking about Mr. Hart. You may be as bad off as I am.

EILEEN: Don't you worry about me! If he wasn't crazy about me, why would he be so insanely jealous? He's insanely jealous!

LUCILLE: Has he ever said anything half-way definite? About marrying, I mean?

EILEEN: Not in words, exactly.

LUCILLE: What did he say it in?

EILEEN: He must be thinking of it. He doesn't ever go out with anybody else.

LUCILLE (*trying to recall what Eileen had said*): How long's he going to be gone this time—three weeks?

EILEEN: Yeah—about. He's got to go to Chicago, and—a lot of places.

LUCILLE: What are you going to do with yourself all that time—just sit around?

EILEEN: Maybe he'll treat us to some shows—I'll ask him to-night. Maybe he'll get us seats for some shows.

LUCILLE: Do they still have seats at shows?

EILEEN (*restless again*): Only I wish that thing would ring!

LUCILLE: Why *don't* you go out with Bert or somebody, while he's gone? It might be a good thing for him.

EILEEN: Do you want to get me murdered? I tell you he's insanely jealous. (*The door bell rings.*) Who's that?

LUCILLE: Maxie, I guess. (*Starting for the door.*) Or maybe that lyric-writer.

EILEEN: Who?

LUCILLE (*disappearing into the hallway, talking as she goes*): *You* know, that's coming to see Paul. From Albany or some place.

EILEEN: Oh!

LUCILLE: Of course he couldn't meet him in the daytime. He has to bring him up here in the middle of the night—(*Having opened the outside door.*) Oh, it's you!

MAXIE (*outside*): Hello, there!
    (*Paul comes back into the room.*)

PAUL: Who is it? Maxie?

MAXIE: Yah, Maxie. (*He is a man in his late forties, easy-going, kindly. Wears a dinner coat. He is an arranger for Goebel's, and he knows the popular song business backwards.*)

PAUL: Hello!

MAXIE: Well! All staying home on a Saturday night?

LUCILLE: All nights are alike up here.

EILEEN: You didn't come right up from the office, did you?

MAXIE (*indicates his dinner coat*): Do I look it? I'm playing down at the Orchard this week. Pounding the piano for a lot of morons. I envy you people that can spend an evening at home.

LUCILLE (*with emphasis*): Yes. It's a great treat.

PAUL: I want the girls to hear the "Montana" number, the way it sounds when it's really played.
    (*Eileen starts to go.*)

MAXIE: O.K.

PAUL (*stopping Eileen*): Hey! He's going to play the "Montana" number.

EILEEN: That's all right. I'll close the door. (*She leaves.*)

PAUL: Go ahead, Maxie. She don't know anything.

MAXIE: Think of me slaving down at the Orchard while you people enjoy all the comforts of home.
    (*An impatient movement from Lucille.*)

PAUL: Go ahead with "Montana."

MAXIE: It certainly was a tough day for me when Edison invented the piano. Fixing up other people's tunes—there's a life work for you.

PAUL: Go on.

MAXIE (*his fingers rambling over the keys*): You know, I might have been a song-writer myself but I got stuck on my own stuff. I wrote tunes nobody ever heard before—they wouldn't stand for it.

PAUL (*prompting with a gesture*): "Montana."

MAXIE (*about to start, but resumes talking instead*): That was a great idea of Fagan's, writing a lyric about Montana. I've often wondered why lyric writers stayed out of the Northwest.

PAUL: Maybe Fagan was born there.

MAXIE: Naw! Shamokin, Pennsylvania. If song-writers always wrote about their home state, what a big Jewish population Tennessee must have. (*He starts playing a popular tune—the telephone rings. Paul takes it up.*)

PAUL: Hello. . . . This is him. . . . Oh, hello! . . . Where are you at now? . . . Well, you better hop in a taxi—it's quite a ways yet. (*Eileen makes another expectant appearance in the doorway—departs in disappointment as she learns that it still isn't her call.*) 448 Riverside Drive. Tell him just above 116th Street. . . . That's it. (*He hangs up; addresses Maxie, who continues to drum.*) That's Stevens, the lyric writer I was telling you about. From Schenectady.

MAXIE: Thank God he can't get that in a lyric.

PAUL: He had the phone number, but he didn't know the address.

LUCILLE: How'd he get the phone number?

PAUL: Telephone book, I guess.

LUCILLE: And then he called up for the address? (*She shakes her head—it's too much for her.*) I want to meet him.

PAUL (*to Maxie*): You'll like this fella. He's young yet. He's got a fresh slant.

MAXIE: What does he do—write about counties instead of states?

PAUL: I've been thinking maybe he and I could do something together, if I can get rid of Fagan.

MAXIE: Fagan isn't so bad. Only he's using up his ideas too fast. "Montana Moon." He puts a state and a moon all in one song.

PAUL: Are you going to play it? (*Maxie plunges into the preliminary chords; Paul comes to life and sets himself to sing. Raises a warning finger in the direction of Lucille.*) Now listen!

"Golden West that seems so far away,
    Golden girl for whom I'm always pining,
    Don't you know I love you night and day,
    But chiefly when the full bright moon is shining!"

(*He takes new breath for the chorus. Lucille, meanwhile, is listening intently, but hardly enthusiastically. In fact, you might almost think she didn't like it so much.*)

"Montana moonlight,

As bright as noon light,
Oh, may it soon light
   My way to you!
I know you're lonely,
My one and only,
For I am lonely,
   Yes, lonely, too."

(*At this point Lucille simply goes back to her sewing. Paul's tone grows sharper as he sings, and she resigns herself to further listening.*)

"My heart is yearning
For kisses burning,
For lips as sweet as a rose in June.
I'm always dreaming
Of your eyes gleaming,
Beneath the beaming
   Montana Moon!"

(*Maxie plunges into a second chorus as Paul presses Lucille for an opinion.*) Don't it sound great? The way Maxie plays it?

LUCILLE (*delivering the verdict*): I don't think Berlin will kill himself.

PAUL: It's nothing like Berlin. Play it in two-four and it's a great dance tune. (*Maxie is obliging. Paul sings a strain of it and dances.*)

LUCILLE: You don't get Berlin's songs to dance to. You get them to cry to.

PAUL: All right. You can cry to this, too. "My heart is yearning for kisses burning." That's sad.

LUCILLE: Yes, but there's something behind his songs. (*Sighs.*) They're sympathetic.

PAUL: Do you want to know why? Because he gets a little sympathy now and then! He's appreciated at home! He don't sit around here night after night with you yapping your head off at him, telling him he's all through!

MAXIE: Now, now! You're going to write plenty of hits.

PAUL (*sits*): Well, it makes a fellow lose confidence in himself.

LUCILLE: I'm trying to help you, not hurt you.

PAUL: You go about it in a funny way.

(*Eileen comes back; is lighting a cigarette.*)

MAXIE: She doesn't mean anything. Of course she wants to

help you. But this number—I wouldn't count on it too much if I were you.

LUCILLE: What do you mean?

PAUL: Why not?

MAXIE: I just wouldn't—that's all. You can't tell which way they're going to jump these days.

PAUL: They'll snap this one up. Unless they're crazy.

LUCILLE: Keep still a minute. (*To Maxie*) What's happened?

MAXIE (*reluctant*): Nothing definite. Only they were talking about it—Hart and Goebel.

PAUL: When were they?

EILEEN (*has heard just enough*): What did you say?

MAXIE: Huh? I said Hart and Goebel were talking about Paul's new number.

EILEEN: When?

PAUL: What did they say about it?

EILEEN: You mean they were talking about it to-day?

MAXIE: Sort of.

EILEEN: In the office, you mean?

MAXIE: Yah. Sure.

EILEEN: What time?

MAXIE: I don't know. Five o'clock.

EILEEN: Goebel and—Hart both?

MAXIE: Yah. Why? (*Eileen takes a moment to digest this bit of information; her eyes meet Lucille's. Then, with a sudden movement, she turns and leaves the room. Lucille, after a thoughtful second, follows her out. Maxie looks after them, un-comprehending. Then he turns back to Paul.*) Did I say something dirty?

PAUL: That don't matter. What did they say about the song?

MAXIE: But I don't understand—

PAUL: Listen—what did they do? Turn it down?

MAXIE (*he has to say it*): Right now they don't want it.

PAUL (*hotly*): When did they hear it? After I left?

MAXIE: They asked me, so there was nothing for me to do but give it to them. I had Nate sing it.

PAUL: It's the lyric kills it! The melody's sure fire! Even if it don't sell over the counter it'd get a good mechanical break.

MAXIE (*brightly*): Maybe you could sell it outside.

PAUL: It makes a man look like a fool, working for one house and selling your stuff to another. (*He drops into a chair, discouraged.*)

MAXIE: You mustn't let it worry you. The next one'll be great, and you'll forget all about this.

PAUL: What else did they say—when they heard it? Anything about me?

MAXIE: What could they say about you?

PAUL: If I don't deliver pretty soon they'll let me out. I'll be like all those fellows that come around every day with another tune. (*The door bell sounds.*) I guess this is Stevens.

MAXIE: Who?

PAUL: Stevens—that lyric writer.

MAXIE: Maybe he's just what you need. Maybe he'll make all the difference in the world.

PAUL: His stuff's pretty good—what I've seen of it. (*Disappears into the vestibule.*)

MAXIE (*cheerily*): There you are! Everything'll be fine! You see! (*He is playing the piano again.*)

PAUL (*in the hallway*): Hello, Stevens! Glad to see you!

FRED: Hello, Mr. Sears!

PAUL: Put your hat and coat on the chair. Come right in! This is Maxie—Mr. Schwartz. Shake hands with Mr. Stevens.

FRED: Glad to meet you, Mr. Schwartz.

MAXIE (*playing with one hand and shaking hands with the other*): Hello, Stevens.

(*Lucille strolls back, eyeing the new arrival.*)

PAUL: And this is my wife. Dear, this is Mr. Stevens.

LUCILLE: How are you?

FRED (*right there with an answer*): I'm all right.

LUCILLE: Paul tells me you're a song-writer yourself.

FRED (*modestly*): Just the words.

LUCILLE: Well, that's all Paul needs—that and the music.

FRED: I've always been one of Mr. Sears' greatest admirers. I've admired Mr. Sears ever since he wrote "Paprika."

LUCILLE: You've got a good memory.

PAUL: Maybe Stevens and I will turn out another "Paprika."

FRED: I'm anxious to get started, all right. Since I got to town, all I've done so far is spend money.

LUCILLE (*expansively*): Well, you're quite a stranger!

PAUL: Sit down.

FRED: Thanks. I guess I'm a little late. I got off the wrong sub-
way station and there was an old woman there selling papers, and I stopped and talked to her because I knew she
must be somebody's mother.

MAXIE (*who has never stopped playing*): A fresh slant.

FRED: I was right too, because she told me she has six sons. I
feel sorry for old women that has to earn their living.

LUCILLE: What do the boys do—rent her the stand?

FRED: No, most of them are in a hospital and two of them had
their foot cut off. She told me all about it and I give her a
dollar.

PAUL: You want to be careful in a place like New York. There's
all kinds of people waiting to take your money away from
you.

FRED: It's a great city, all right. To-day I took the ferry-boat
over to Staten's Island and back. (*He explains it to Lucille.*)
It's an island and you have to take a ferry-boat. But I suppose you been there.

LUCILLE: I go there a lot—just for the trip.

FRED: I seen the Goddest of Liberty, too—I mean the statue.
It cost a million dollars and weighs 225 ton.

MAXIE (*gently*): She ought to cut out sweets. (*He indulges in a
fancy run.*)

FRED (*a gesture in the direction of Maxie*): He can play the
piano! . . . And I seen some of the big ocean liner steam-
boats. I seen the *President Harding* just coming in from
London or Europe or somewheres, and the other day I seen
the *Majestic* tied up to the dock. She's pretty near twicet as
long as the *President Harding* and weighs 56,000 ton. The
President Harding only weighs 14,000 ton.

LUCILLE: Imagine.

FRED (*to Lucille*): Have you been through the Holland Tunnel?

LUCILLE: No, I haven't.

FRED (*to Paul*): Have you been through the Holland Tunnel?

PAUL: No.

FRED (*not for a minute giving up*): Have you been through the
Holland Tunnel, Mr. Schwartz?

MAXIE: I've been waiting for somebody to go with.

FRED: I'll go with you!

MAXIE: Fine!

FRED: I want to go every place so as to get ideas for songs. I was telling Mr. Sears about one idea—I haven't got it written yet—it's a song about the traffic lights. Green for "Come ahead!" and red for "Stop!" Maybe a comical song with a girl signaling her sweetheart with different colored lights in the window; a green light when it's all right for him to call—

LUCILLE: And a red one when her husband's home.

FRED (*shocked*): No, I was thinking about her father. I wouldn't write about those kind of women—I got no sympathy for them.

LUCILLE: I guess you're right.

FRED: I was thinking of another idea on the way up here. Maybe a song about the melting pots—all the immigrants from overseas who've come to the Land of Liberty. Take the Jews—do you know there's nearly two million Jews in New York City alone?

MAXIE: What do you mean alone?

FRED: And then there's the Hall of Fame, up to Washington Heights. They got everybody up there. Washington, Lincoln, Longfellow. They got two dozen—what do you call 'em—busts?

LUCILLE (*sweetly, to Paul*): That's the place for you, dear.

FRED: No. A man's got to be dead for twenty-five years.

LUCILLE: Well, that fits in.

MAXIE (*it's too much for him*): I've got to be going along.

PAUL: Wait! I want Stevens to show you one of his lyrics—have you got that one with you? About the game?

MAXIE: I've got to be downtown at ten.

PAUL: This won't take a minute. (*To Fred.*) Go ahead.

FRED: I'll have to explain first, so you'll understand. The idea came to me at a football game between Syracuse and Colgate. They beat them, and they felt pretty bad, so the idea come to me for this little song. I call it "Life Is a Game."

MAXIE: A novelty!

FRED: Here's the verse. Are you ready?

PAUL: Yeah.

FRED:

"I don't know why some people cry
When things appear to go wrong;

I always say 'Laugh and be gay!'
Things cannot always go wrong!
No use to pine, no use to whine,
Things will come right if you just give them time."
That's the verse.

LUCILLE: Uh-huh!

FRED: Then here's the refrain:
"Life is a game; we are but players—"

MAXIE: Hey, bring it here! Maybe we can put some music to it.

FRED: Just play some chords.

MAXIE: I'll see if I know any.

MAXIE (*sings as well as he can to Maxie's improvisation*):
"Life is a game; we are but players
Playing the best we know how.
If you are beat, don't let it wrangle;
No one can win all the time.
Sometimes the odds seem dead against you;
What has to be, has to be,
But smile just the same, for life is a game,
And God is a fine referee."

(*Maxie picks up the last line and sings it again, tacking on a rousing musical finale to fit. It is really the finish of "All Those Endearing Young Charms," but so far as Fred is concerned it has been composed especially for his lyric. He is beaming with pleasure.*)
I haven't got the second verse yet.

MAXIE: You won't need one.

LUCILLE: I like a song with love interest.

FRED: Well, I got an idea and a title for another one—I mean, of course I got lots of ideas, but this one, I told it to a party and she— (*he catches himself, embarrassed*) —I mean, this party seemed to think it was pretty good.

PAUL: Let's hear it.

FRED: It's just a title. You told me you'd rather have just a title and then write the tune first.

PAUL: What's the title?

FRED: "June Moon." That's the title—"June Moon."

MAXIE: A war song.

FRED: No, no. The verse will be about a fella that's met a girl in June, when there was a moon shining, and then

something happened so that she went away, or maybe he
went away, and then whenever he looks up at the moon
after that, he thinks of her. In the second verse, she'll be
doing the same thing for him.

LUCILLE: That's fair enough.

PAUL: I don't know—another moon song.

MAXIE (*dashing to the piano*): "June Moon"—I've got it!

>   (*He ad-libs a melody; Fred chimes in with some extempo-
>   rized words.*)

FRED (*singing*): June Moon, how I wish you so-and-so, how I
miss my so-and-so, spoon! (*He comes out strong on the
"spoon"—that's right, anyhow.*)

>   (*Meanwhile the phone has rung again, and under cover of
>   the music Lucille has answered it.*)

LUCILLE: Hello. . . . No, this is Lucille. Just a minute. (*She
puts down the receiver.*) Eileen!

PAUL (*who has managed, despite the confusion, to make mental
note of Maxie's melody*): Well, I might be able to dig up
something for that.

FRED (*plunging expansively into explanation*): I got the idea
coming in on the train. I happened to look out of the
window—

>   (*He stops abruptly as Eileen comes back on. She has put on a
>   dress, but, in view of the news that Maxie had brought, not
>   the evening dress. She looks smart, however, and Fred is im-
>   pressed, to say the least. Paying no attention to any one, she
>   heads straight for the telephone.*)

EILEEN: Hello! . . . Oh, no, not at all. (*To say that the lady is
sarcastic is putting it mildly.*) What train? . . . You're sure of
that, are you? . . . Nothing, only I thought you might be
mistaken. Everybody makes mistakes, you know. (*It's a good
chance for Maxie to escape, and he leaps up. While Eileen is
still talking he manages to get out—"Good-by everybody! I'm
due at the Orchard! Glad to have met you, Stevens," etc. Paul
follows him out with: "Now look! Don't say anything to Fagan,
because I don't want him to know until—" The voices die out.
Fred, a bit embarrassed, is left alone with the two girls, while
Eileen continues her phone talk.*) Yes, I can imagine. It must
have been terribly tiresome in Philadelphia all day. . . .
What? . . . Oh, really? (*Her tone indicates that this is the*

body blow.) I thought you were leaving to-morrow. . . . What time to-night? . . . My, it must be important! . . . Then—I won't have a chance to say good-by before you go. . . . Oh, no, don't trouble yourself—it's quite all right. . . . Yes, I'm sure you are. . . . No, I don't mind a bit. I'm just sorry you have to spend the night on a train, that's all. . . . Oh, perfectly! . . . Have a pleasant trip. (*But she doesn't mean "pleasant trip." She hangs up; a look flashes between her and Lucille.*)

LUCILLE (*coming back to the present*): Mr. Stevens, this is my sister, Miss Fletcher. Eileen—Mr. Stevens. (*She gives a broad wave of the hand, as if to say, "And if you want him, he's yours."*)

EILEEN (*her mind on the telephone*): Hello.

FRED: I'm glad to meet you, Miss Fletcher.

EILEEN: Thanks.

LUCILLE: Mr. Stevens is a lyric writer. He's from Schenectady.

EILEEN: Oh, yes. Have you been in New York long?

FRED: Just a couple of weeks. I'm from Schenectady.

EILEEN (*a lot she cares*): Schenectady, eh?

LUCILLE (*with the air of a person who is washing* that *up*): Schenectady.

FRED: I was with the General Electric Company, but I left them.

EILEEN: I suppose they've closed down?

FRED (*who knows better than that*): No. I had a post-card to-day from a fella that works there.

LUCILLE: Mr. Stevens has been all over New York, getting ideas for songs.

EILEEN: Do you like it?

FRED: Yes, I like it fine, but it costs money to live here. For instance, I had breakfast in the hotel this morning and it was ninety cents for salt mackerel and mashed potatoes and a cup of Instant Postum.

LUCILLE: No wonder you think New York's expensive! A few more breakfasts like that and you won't have any money left.

FRED: I still got plenty.

LUCILLE: Really? (*She flashes a look to Eileen.*) I'll bet you haven't been to any of the real places, have you? It takes a New Yorker to find those.

FRED: I seen the Goddest of Liberty.

LUCILLE: Oh, I mean the night places!

FRED: I seen it at night.

LUCILLE: Oh, no! Restaurants!

FRED: Huh?

LUCILLE: Mr. Stevens would love those. (*To Eileen.*) Wouldn't he?

EILEEN (*slowly coming to*): Yah.

LUCILLE: I'll tell you what! Why don't we make up a party— the four of us—and show Mr. Stevens the town!

FRED: You mean to-night?

LUCILLE: What do you say, Eileen? How about it?

EILEEN (*thinking hard; her eyes go involuntarily to the telephone*): Why—sure! I don't know why not! Sure!

FRED: Well, wait! It'd be great to go, all right, only the trouble is I got another engagement!

LUCILLE: Oh, but you could put that off!

EILEEN: Of course you could!

LUCILLE (*as Paul re-enters*): Paul had another engagement, too. He broke it on your account, didn't you, dear?

PAUL (*to whom this is news*): What?

LUCILLE: We thought it would be fun for the four of us to go out some place, but Mr. Stevens doesn't want to.

FRED: It ain't that I don't want to, but—

LUCILLE: You know, you really ought to. Paul was just saying that what you needed was to go places where they do the latest numbers and hear what kind of songs are getting over! That's true, isn't it, Paul?

PAUL: Ah, yes! Sure!

LUCILLE: Of course it is! Are we all set?

FRED: Well, I want to go all right. It's only I don't know on account of this other engagement.

EILEEN: But you could do something about that. You could go if you really wanted to. (*So close to him that he is groggy.*) Don't you—want to?

FRED (*hesitating*): Well, I ain't dressed to go out. I mean, to some swell place.

EILEEN: We'll go where we don't have to dress.

LUCILLE: How about the Orchard? Wouldn't Maxie be surprised to see the four of us stroll in?

EILEEN: Lucille and I'll go right in and get our things on. (*A movement.*)

PAUL: Well, wait a minute! It's just that I didn't happen to bring much money with me—

LUCILLE: Oh, that's all right. Mr. Stevens can be the treasurer to-night and you can fix it up with him later!

EILEEN: As long as you're going to be partners!

LUCILLE: Come on! Let's hurry!

(*The Girls rush off.*)

PAUL: Is that all right with you?

FRED (*looking after the pair*): Say, she's quite a girl, isn't she?

PAUL: Who? Eileen?

FRED: Does she live here with you all the time?

PAUL: Yah. She does.

FRED: She's a regular New York girlie.

PAUL: Maybe it wouldn't be a bad notion for you to knock around a few nights—I mean, before we start working. Might give you some ideas.

FRED: I'm willing.

PAUL: Great!

FRED: Say, can I use your phone a minute?

PAUL: Sure. Do you want the book?

FRED: No, I know the number. (*Takes receiver off.*) Rhine-lander 4160.

PAUL: I'd better clean up a bit.

FRED: Look! They was talking about this Orchard. That ain't one of them expensive places, is it?

PAUL: No. Just about average.

FRED: Hello. . . . I want to speak to Miss Edna Baker, please. . . . Yes. (*To Paul.*) I mean, what do you think it would be likely to come to for the four of us? More than ten dollars?

PAUL (*vaguely*): No—not unless we go on to some other place. You've got more with you, haven't you?

FRED: What other place?

PAUL: One of the other clubs.

FRED: But I don't—hello. . . . Hello. . . . Eddie? . . . . I want to tell you something.

PAUL: I'll go and wash up. (*Departs.*)

FRED: Well, I'm up here now, but that isn't— Sure. . . . Yeah, it looks all right. . . . No, I'm still here. There was a piano

player here from Goebel's. He liked my stuff and made up a
tune to some of it. . . . Yeah. . . . He said it was all right.
But that isn't . . . what I called up to say was I can't get
around there till late. . . . No, it'll be later than that. There's
no telling what time it'll be. . . . We got to study some
songs. . . . Paul Sears and his wife. . . . No, no, don't
think that. It's a business proposition. They're taking me to
a place where we'll get some ideas. . . . Just the three of us.
. . . But you know I'd rather be with you. (*Eileen comes
back, coat over arm.*) But I can't. . . . I can't. . . . *They're*
taking *me*. I'll tell you all about it in the morning. . . .
That's all I can say now. . . . I can't. . . . In the morning.
. . . Good night. (*Hangs up.*)

EILEEN: You seem to be having your troubles.

FRED: No, that wasn't anything. Just a—friend of mine.

EILEEN: Is she nice?

FRED: It isn't anybody. Just a little girl I happened to meet.

EILEEN: I understand.

FRED: She's just a—a girl from a little town.

    (*Lucille comes back, full of life. Pulling on gloves, etc.*)

LUCILLE: Listen—it's kind of early for the Orchard anyhow. So
why don't we take in the second show at the Capitol?

    (*Paul is on again.*)

PAUL: Is everybody ready?

EILEEN: Oh, that's fine! And I know what you'd love! After
the Orchard what do you say we go to the Cotton Club?
(*She throws a quick explanation to Fred.*) That's Harlem!

LUCILLE: Great!

EILEEN: They've got a wonderful tap dancer up there! Better
than Bill Robinson!

PAUL: But say, the Cotton Club don't get hot till three!

FRED (*who has never heard of that hour*): What time?

EILEEN: Oh, that's all right! We can go to the Madrid or Richman's in between!

LUCILLE: Oh, great!

PAUL: But say, Richman's burned down the other night!

FRED: Let's not go there!

LUCILLE: I'll tell you where I haven't been for a long while!
The St. Regis Roof!

EILEEN: Grand!

LUCILLE: They've a wonderful view!
FRED: Where?
LUCILLE: The St. Regis Roof.
FRED: I get dizzy if I climb a ladder!
   (The voices of the others pick up in a confused jumble as

THE CURTAIN FALLS

ACT II

The scene is a room at Goebel's music publishing house. A piano, a few chairs, some shelves, and you have it. Three or four weeks have gone by since Act I.

Maxie is at the piano just amusing himself when the curtain rises. He is playing "La Boheme" and cutting loose a trifle. There enters, from one of the adjacent offices, a young woman (an employee) known as Goldie. She may have got her name because of the color of her hair or from the fact that she is really a Miss Goldberg. That point is never brought up in this play, but may some day be the subject of a musical comedy. Anyway, she comes on and busies herself looking over songs at the music shelves, on which the hits of these and other days are piled high.

GOLDIE (*busy with her songs*): "There Never Was a Girl Like Mother."

MAXIE: Maybe it's all for the best. . . . How's the boss? Did he have a good trip?

GOLDIE: He says not. He says in the Middle West they're still wild over "The Rosary."

MAXIE: That looks like a hit.

GOLDIE: Did Benny find you? He was looking for you.

MAXIE: Not yet.

GOLDIE: He's got a new song.

MAXIE: That's good. I was afraid he was written out.

GOLDIE: You'd better hide if you don't want to hear it.

MAXIE: No use—he always gets his man. Besides, I've got to stick around and play Paul's new one, "June Moon."

GOLDIE: Is it any good?

MAXIE: It's got a chance. It's a tune that's easy to remember, but if you should forget it it wouldn't make any difference.
  (*Fred plunges in.*)

FRED: Ain't Mr. Hart back yet?

GOLDIE: Not yet.

FRED: Don't you even know what time he's coming?

GOLDIE: Can't tell. His first day back in town—he's probably

231

got a lot of things to do. (*She goes—and pretty disrespectfully, too.*)

FRED: It's half past four. He said he was coming back at two o'clock.

MAXIE: You get used to waiting in this game. I've been in it twenty-two years and nothing's happened yet.

FRED: Paul's coming right in. We want to play the song once before Mr. Hart hears it. I made a change.

MAXIE: Whereabouts.

FRED: In the refrain. We had it "Sweet night-bird, hovering above," now it's "winging aloft." You see, "aloft" means the same like "above."

MAXIE: Only higher.

FRED: I wish I'd known Mr. Hart was going to be late. I could have slept some more. I had to get up at twelve.

MAXIE: That must be tough after working for the General Electric, where a man's hours are practically his own.

FRED: No. I had to be on the job at eight, every morning. But I went to bed about ten, except Saturday nights, when I seen a picture or something. I didn't know what life was, in Schenectady.

MAXIE: I bet it's an open book to you now.

FRED: Imagine—only going out one night a week and then just to a moving picture show! Down here it's like as if every night was a special night—there's always new places to go to. Miss Fletcher—she's always locating new ones! We was in three last night! Wound up at half past seven this morning, in the Bucket of Blood! There's a lively place! We was the last ones there. Paul and Lucille, they went home at seven, but I and Miss Fletcher stayed and she made the proprietor sell me six bottles of his gin. It's real gin; what they call pro-war. You got to have good gin. It's one of the things they put into what they call a Bronx cocktail.

MAXIE: Is that so?

FRED: Didn't you ever have one?

MAXIE: I don't drink. After I listen to songs all day I don't want liquor. I just go home and take a general anæsthetic.

FRED: I like Bronxes best. They're nothing but gin and orange juice. I don't know why they call it a Bronx.

MAXIE: It's great orange country, up there.

FRED: Anyway, I got a bargain—six bottles for sixty bucks. I give Miss Fletcher three bottles for a present, because if it hadn't been for her I wouldn't have got them. She made the man do it. When you're around with her you just can't resist doing things.

MAXIE: I know. That's why I don't carry a gun.

FRED: She's a great sport, all right. She'd make a wonderful wife—she's such a good pal. I think a man's wife ought to be their pal as well as their sweetheart.

MAXIE: You ought to patent that.

FRED: Say—how much money do you think a fella ought to be making before he could get married? In New York, I mean?

MAXIE: It depends on the girl.

FRED: Buddy De Sylva makes pretty near half a million dollars a year out of just writing lyrics. I guess a man could support a wife on that!

MAXIE: If she was satisfied to ride a bicycle.

FRED: Well, suppose "June Moon" is a big smash? What's the most we could make out of it?

MAXIE: It's hard to say. Take a song like "Swanee River" and it's still going big.

FRED: Yeah, but that's because it was in a big production like "Show Boat."

MAXIE: How's that?

FRED: And with that girl to sing it, that sits on the piano.

MAXIE: You're thinking of Ruby Keeler in "The Wild Duck."

FRED: Well, whoever it was. (*Turns away; suddenly remembers.*) Oh, say! I was over to the tailor's to-day. I'm getting a new suit. Miss Fletcher took me.

MAXIE: That so?

FRED: It's a blue search, with a hair-bone strip. He took my measures all over. Like I was a fighter. I'm thirty-eight inches around my chest, and thirty-three around my stomach, and—I forget my thigh. Anyway, he's got it all wrote down.

MAXIE: I must get a copy.

FRED: If they like "June Moon" I'm going to have an evening dinner coat made, with a Tuxedo. I been wearing an old suit of Paul's, but it's too big. Miss Fletcher says it would hold two like me.

MAXIE: There couldn't be two.

FRED: She was just joking.

MAXIE: I see.

FRED: They've given me a wonderful time, all right. They've introduced me to all the big stars! Gil Boag, and Earl Carroll, and Texas Guinan! I met Texas Guinan!

MAXIE: She's kind of hard to meet, isn't she?

FRED: No. She's one of the friendliest women I ever seen. When the girls told her who I was she said it was a big night in her life—she said she'd always wanted to meet a lyric writer. I wonder what my friends in Schenectady would say if they knew I sat around and talked to Texas Guinan! I didn't know nothing when I lived there. Even the first few weeks I was in New York, I was kind of a sap.

MAXIE: That sounds incredible.

FRED: I went sightseeing to places like the Aquarium, and Grant's Tomb, and the Central Park animal zoo, and thought I was having a great time. A little friend of mine, she took me around places she'd been to and I thought I was seeing New York because I didn't know no better. She was from a small town, too—she didn't know no better either. Only now I've learned.

MAXIE: What's become of her? Did she go home?

FRED: No, she lives here. She works for a dentist. I must call her up some time and see how she's getting along. (*A Window Cleaner enters. He looks a great deal like a window cleaner.*) What are you going to do?

WINDOW CLEANER: Wash the windows.

FRED: But we're going to try a song here. Can't you go somewheres else first?

WINDOW CLEANER: First! I'm pretty near through for the day. Besides, they're singing songs all over the building. That don't bother me.

FRED: But we're going to sing a new one for Mr. Hart.

WINDOW CLEANER: How much does a man get for writing songs?

FRED: It depends on the song.

WINDOW CLEANER: Say a big hit like "Nearer My God To Thee"?

(*Just before Maxie can brain him, Paul comes on.*)

PAUL: Are you ready?

FRED: Yah. (*To Maxie.*) Let's do the song now.

MAXIE: Plenty of time.

FRED: I wish Hart would come, so I can get my advance royalty check. Say, where will I get it cashed? At the American
Express Company?

MAXIE: Or the 59th Street Bridge.

> (*Benny Fox bounds on. He's a song-writer of the dangerous
> type.*)

BENNY: Where's Hart?

FRED: He ain't back yet.

BENNY (*buttonholing Maxie*): I've got it this time! "Hello,
Tokio!" How's that for a title? They wanted a novelty number! I guess I'll give it to them!

FRED: I and Paul have got a hit!

PAUL: Yeah!

FRED: We think so, anyway.

BENNY (*paying no attention to them*): In the verse I've got a
fella here in New York that sees a pitcher of a Japanese
princess and he's nuts over her, but he can't afford a trip to
Japan just on a chance. So he calls her up—get it? "Hello,
Tokio!" Get this! Here's the refrain! After he calls her up!
(*He plays and sings it, the chorus being as follows*):

> "Hello, hello, Tokio!
> Girlie, you'll excuse it, please,
> If I no spik Japanese.
> This little call will leave me broke-o,
> But I simply had to say, 'I love you so.'
> Believe me, dearie, it's no joke-o;
> I'd gladly fly through fire and smoke-o
> To share with you the marriage yok-o,
> Fairest flower of Tokio-oki-okio!"

> (*But that isn't all. Paul and Fred start expectantly toward
> the piano as the finish approaches, but Benny double-crosses
> them by plunging quickly into a second chorus. This time the
> Window Cleaner, who has been entranced by the whole
> thing, starts to beat time with his sponge. He holds the sponge
> directly over Benny's head, and the resulting drips do not
> help the second chorus any. By way of good measure, he then
> chimes in on the finish, winding up with one "Okio" left over*)

after Benny is through playing. Benny glares at him, and he turns back to his window-washing.)

BENNY (*to Maxie, when it's all over*): Well, what do you think?

MAXIE: It would sound better in Japanese.

BENNY: How about it, Paul?

PAUL: It's a pretty good number.

BENNY: It's a great number! Here's another one—just come to me last night!

(*He starts to play a refrain—a melody so familiar that Maxie calmly pushes him off the bench and finishes it himself.*)

BENNY (*a bit discouraged*): Oh, you're too wise! (*He goes.*)

MAXIE (*starting to play*): All right, boys!

(*The Window Cleaner decides that he doesn't want to hear this one. He opens the window, and a good gale of wind blows most of the papers off the piano.*)

PAUL: Hey!

FRED: What are you trying to do?

WINDOW CLEANER: I'm sorry. I didn't realize it was blowing so hard. I'm glad I ain't out in a boat.

MAXIE: I wish you'd been on the Hesperus. (*The Window Cleaner climbs out the window, and presently disappears from view. Maxie and the boys plunge into "June Moon," with Fred leading the singing.*)

"Summer winds are sighing in the trees, my dear;
   I am sure I know what makes them sigh:
   They are sad on moonlight nights like these, my dear;
   They are lonely for you, same as I.
   Sweetheart, how can you resist their plea,
   And the moon you used to share with me?

     June Moon, shining above,
     Will my true love come soon?
     June Moon, I am so blue;
     I know that you long for her, too.
     Sweet night-bird, winging aloft,
     Singing a soft love tune,
     Tell her to come to me here,
     To me and her dear June Moon."

(*As the song finishes, Edna, the girl of the prologue, quietly enters. Maxie is the first to see her.*)

MAXIE: You got an audience.

FRED (*none too pleased*): Hello there, girlie!

EDNA (*ill at ease*): Hello.

FRED: I wasn't expecting to see you. Ah—this is—you met Mr. Sears. This is Miss Baker, everybody. And this is Mr. Schwartz.

MAXIE: How do you do, Miss Baker?

EDNA: Hello. They told me to come in, but I'm afraid you're busy.

MAXIE: Not a bit.

FRED: We were just polishing off our number. "June Moon."

EDNA: You've finished it, haven't you? It's beautiful.

PAUL (*eagerly*): Did you like the melody?

(*Goldie enters; she has work to do at the music shelves.*)

EDNA: I loved it. And I love Fred's words. I think everybody will.

MAXIE: Are you fond of music?

EDNA: I love it.

MAXIE: We'll send you some good stuff. Goldie! Get Miss Baker's address before she leaves—we'll send her some music.

GOLDIE (*visions of more work*): Oh, yeah? (*She goes.*)

EDNA (*an embarrassed pause*): I don't want to interrupt. Maybe I'd better be going.

MAXIE: No, no! We'll go. You stay right here!

FRED: But look, if Mr. Hart comes in—

MAXIE: We'll be in Benny's room. Good-by, Miss Baker.

EDNA: Good-by, Mr.—

MAXIE: Schwartz. Maxie Schwartz. It's a Greek name.

(*Paul and Maxie go. Fred and Edna are alone.*)

EDNA: Hello.

FRED: I'm fine. Are you?

EDNA: We're all alone, Fred.

FRED: Huh?

EDNA: Nobody's looking.

FRED: Oh! (*He kisses her—a kiss that would easily get by the censors.*)

EDNA: My, it seems nice again!

FRED: You bet!

EDNA: Fred, what's been the matter?

FRED: Nothing. I just been busy, that's all. I was going to call you as soon as I wasn't busy.

EDNA: I thought maybe you were sick or something. I tried to call you up two mornings—I mean, at your hotel—and they said you couldn't be waked up before one o'clock, I think it was.

FRED: That's only because I been up late the night before, working. We got the song all finished.

EDNA: It's beautiful! I had no idea it would turn out so beautiful! It's beautiful!

FRED: We're going to sing it for Mr. Hart as soon as he gets here.

EDNA: It's a beautiful song. Up to now I felt it was sort of ours together. I mean, the way it started when we were on the train, and then you telling me how it was getting along every day, and now all of a sudden it's finished and I haven't got anything to do with it any more.

FRED: Yes, you have. When it's published I'll make them put your name on the cover—"Dictated to Miss Edna Baker."

EDNA: Oh, Fred, I'd love that! But I'd love something else better.

FRED: What's that?

EDNA: It's been two Sundays since we went anywhere together. Remember the day we took our lunch, and went over on the Palisades all day, and then in the evening we went to the amusement park and went on all the rides! We didn't get home till pretty near twelve o'clock! And then we were going again the next Sunday, only—we didn't.

FRED: But that's because I've been working. I told you.

EDNA: You don't have to work days and nights both.

FRED (*trying to wriggle out*): I have to work when Paul feels like it. Music writers don't keep no hours—they work when they're inspired. And it ain't just writing the songs that takes time. You have to go around places, and keep in contact with the other boys, so you get new notions. You got to keep getting new notions in this game.

EDNA: What kind of places do you have to go to?

FRED: You know—places where they have music.

EDNA: You mean—night clubs?

FRED: Some of them.

EDNA: Just you and Mr. Sears?

FRED: Well, generally we all go together.

EDNA: Who else?

FRED: Paul's wife. Lucille, her name is.

(*Benny starts to come on; stops as he sees them.*)

BENNY (so *graciously, as though the interruption had been the other way around*): That's all right. (*Withdraws.*)

EDNA: Doesn't anybody else go along, to sort of even up the party?

FRED (*a second's hesitation; then he blurts it out*): Nobody you know! I hardly know her myself. She just comes along because she's Lucille's sister and lives there.

EDNA: Oh!

FRED: You can't leave her home by herself. She's timid.

EDNA: Does she know about—me, Fred?

FRED: Huh?

EDNA: Didn't you ever tell her about—me?

FRED: Well, you see, we just—it's only business, and there hasn't nothing like that come up.

EDNA: What's she like, Fred?

FRED: I don't know. She—

EDNA (*hard at work*): A girl like she has probably got lots of beautiful clothes. She probably makes little me look like nothing.

FRED: That part don't matter. It wouldn't make no difference to me if she had all the clothes in the world. Or if she was bare, either.

EDNA: Is she—very pretty?

FRED: Yah, she—I hardly ever noticed if she was pretty or not.

EDNA: What's her name?

FRED: Miss Fletcher.

EDNA: I mean her first name.

FRED: I think they call her Eileen.

EDNA: That's a beautiful name. It's a lot nicer than mine, don't you think?

FRED: It's just a different name.

EDNA: Is she blonde or brunette?

FRED: Both—I mean she's red-headed. That is, I never paid much attention.

EDNA: How old is she?

FRED: I don't know.

EDNA: Older than I am?

FRED: A little bit, I guess. I guess she must be. She's been on the stage.

EDNA (*putting across a little mild horror*): Honestly, Fred?

FRED: Yah, but don't think—I mean, that don't mean anything.

EDNA: Oh, Fred, you want to be careful! Because you take a woman like she, that's close to forty or more—

FRED: She ain't forty.

EDNA (*conceding two years*): Well, thirty-eight. And she sees a young boy who almost any woman would be proud to win your affection, and there isn't anything she might not stoop to, to entangle you.

FRED: There won't no woman untangle me.

EDNA: You can't tell, Fred—the most terrible things can happen. There was a near friend of mine, a man, and he was acquainted with a count, an international count, and he came here to New York and one night they went on a wild party and he fell in love with a beautiful chorus girl from the Metropolitan Opera Company—I forgot the name of the opera. And he bought her pearls and diamonds, and in less than a week's time he found out they was both married. That's just what could happen to you, dear.

FRED: Who found out who was married?

EDNA: Both of them were married—the count and the girl.

FRED: He must have been a fine count, not to know he was married.

EDNA: Fred, doesn't it cost an awful lot of money when you go around to all these places—or do they take you?

FRED: Well, that part's going to be all right, because as soon as they take our song I'll get what they call an advance royalties. And of course after it's a big hit I'll have plenty of money.

EDNA: I see.

FRED: Only the first thing I'm going to do—I mean, when I get my advance royalties—I'm going to pay you back that little loan.

EDNA: That doesn't matter, Fred.

FRED: But I don't like owing money to a girl. Especially a girl.

EDNA: But it's all right when two people are like you and I.

That makes it all right. I'd give you everything I've got, only I'm afraid I'm not going to have very much from now on.

FRED: What do you mean?

EDNA: I wasn't going to tell you, but I haven't got my position any more. I mean, with Doctor.

FRED: You mean you quit?

EDNA: He discharged me.

FRED: What for?

EDNA: I made a mistake. I gave Mr. Mowrey's appointment to Mr. Treadwell, and Doctor scraped Mr. Treadwell's bones instead of Mr. Mowrey's.

FRED: I'm terrible sorry, Eddie. Gosh, I wish there was something I could do about it.

EDNA (*snapping him up*): There is, Fred, if you felt like doing it.

FRED: What?

EDNA: Are you going to be busy—after they hear the song?

FRED: Well, I'm afraid so—to-night. I got to work with Paul.

EDNA: Well, then, before that. After Mr. Hart hears it. Oh, Fred, couldn't I stay and hear it too?

FRED: Oh, no, Eddie. When Mr. Hart's hearing a new number he can't have nobody around. He's got to concentrate.

EDNA: Oh!

FRED: I'll tell you what. You can wait in the reception room or somewheres, and the minute he's heard it I'll come and tell you what he says.

EDNA: Oh, Fred, that's grand! Then can we go somewhere together for a little while? Have a soda or something?

FRED: Yah, I guess so.

EDNA: Oh, Fred, I'm so glad! You do care a little, then? I mean, you do care whether you—see me?

FRED: Of course I do. Sure. Certainly.

EDNA: Oh, Fred! (*She presents herself impulsively. He kisses her.*) Everything seems all right again now. I don't care about losing my position any more.

FRED: Yah, but— (*Mr. Hart finally arrives. A big man, and important-looking. He crosses the room enroute to his own office.*) Oh, Mr. Hart! Mr. Hart!

HART: What?

FRED: We've been waiting for you! We're all ready!

HART: Ready with what?

FRED: The new number. We'll go through it for you if you'll just wait a minute.

HART: What number?

FRED: "June Moon." The number I wrote with Paul Sears.

HART: Oh! (*Starts away.*)

FRED: I'll get he and Maxie and we'll run it through for you.

HART: That's very thoughtful. (*But he goes.*)

FRED: Yes, sir. Paul! Maxie! All right, Eddie, you go in there and as soon as the song's over I'll come and tell you.

EDNA: All right, dear.

PAUL (*coming in*): Did Hart get back?

FRED: Yah! He went in there! I told him we was ready! Where's Maxie?

PAUL: He's coming. (*And so he does.*)

MAXIE: Well! Are we all set?

FRED: He's here, but he went in there! He came in, and I talked to him, and he went out!

PAUL: What do you think we better do?

MAXIE: How about throwing a cordon around the building? (*He goes into Hart's office.*)

PAUL: Maxie'll bring him.

FRED (*trying his voice*): "June Moon"— (*Suddenly sees Edna again.*) All right, Eddie, we're going to sing it now.

EDNA: All right, dear. I can wait happy now. (*She goes.*)
    (*The Window Cleaner climbs through the window again.*)

FRED: Hey! You can't work here now!

WINDOW CLEANER: What?
    (*Maxie comes back, bringing Hart.*)

MAXIE: Here we are!

HART: All right—let's have it. What's the name of this song? (*Benny bounds on, following Hart.*)

BENNY: Are you ready, Boss?

HART: What?

BENNY: For "Tokio!"

MAXIE: Listen, Joe—these boys have been waiting since two o'clock.

HART: All right, all right. Let's have it. What's the name of it?

FRED: "June Moon."

BENNY (*bitingly*): Great idea!
    (*Goldie enters.*)

GOLDIE: Pardon me, Mr. Hart. Mr. Wayburn's on the wire.

HART: Can't talk to him now. Go ahead, boys! What's this song called?

GOLDIE: He wants to know if he can use the "Java" number to-night. It's a benefit.

HART: Who for? Him?

GOLDIE: I think he said the Widows of Long Island Commuters.

HART: Oh, sure. Tell him he can have it if he pays for it.

GOLDIE: Yes, sir! (*Goes.*)

HART: That's a great number, "Java." Great number.

BENNY: Yes, sir.

HART (*very much the big man*): Do you boys want a sure-fire idea?

PAUL: Yes.

BENNY: Yes.

FRED: Yes, sir.

WINDOW CLEANER (just one of the boys): Yeah!

HART: Write a war song. Just have it ready—in case.

FRED: Is there going to be a war?

HART (*taking them all in*): I won't say yes and I won't say no. But in this little swing around the West I had a chance to sort of feel out the common people. (*Grows very confidential.*) I'll tell you something. I'm not a bit comfortable about the Mexican situation.

WINDOW CLEANER: Me neither.

HART: It's a dangerous situation. I don't like it. I don't like it a bit. (*A long, low whistle from Benny.*) Wouldn't surprise me at all if something happened and happened soon. And when it does, the first fellow in the field is going to clean up. You boys want to watch the papers—be ready for an emergency. Not only war, but these aeroplane flights all over the place—television—all the big inventions. (*A man named Brainard comes in—just a stranger.*) What is it?

BRAINARD: Have you seen a couple of men?

HART: What?

BRAINARD: Have you seen a couple of men? There's two of them.

HART: What men?

BRAINARD: From our office. One of them's had his appendix out.

HART: What office? Where are you from?

BRAINARD: Devlin, Devlin, Stewart and Devlin.

MAXIE: How did Stewart crash in? Marry one of the Devlin girls?

BRAINARD: No. Only one of the Devlins has got a daughter. She's Mrs. Carl Bishop, the architect.

HART: For God's sake! Get out of here, will you?

BRAINARD: But I got to find them.

HART: Well, they're not here. What would they be doing here?

BRAINARD: This is their day in this building.

HART: We're busy now. Come in to-morrow.

BRAINARD: They won't be here to-morrow.

HART: Listen to me; I don't know who you are or where you're from—

(Goldie enters.)

GOLDIE: Beg pardon, Mr. Hart!

HART: Now what?

GOLDIE: George Gershwin's out there.

HART: George Gershwin!

GOLDIE: Yes, sir.

HART: My God! *(He hurries out.)*

FRED: Who is it?

WINDOW CLEANER: George Gershwin. *(He also hurries out.)*

BRAINARD: Yeah! *(Brainard, after a second's hesitation, also goes, hurrying a little. Benny is next to go.)*

PAUL *(to Fred)*: Did you ever see him?

FRED: No.

PAUL: He stole my rhapsody. *(He and Fred go.)*

(Maxie runs a careless scale; gets up from the piano.)

GOLDIE: Aren't you going out to see him?

MAXIE: Make him come to me. *(Goes off the other way.)*

(Eileen and Lucille come on—Eileen leads the way and seems thoroughly at home.)

EILEEN: Where's everybody?

LUCILLE: Hello, Goldie.

GOLDIE: Good afternoon, Mrs. Sears.

EILEEN *(to Goldie)*: I see you've moved the piano.

GOLDIE *(with vast impertinence)*: Not me! *(She goes; the women are alone.)*

LUCILLE: Well, here we are! Why don't you go in and say hello to Hart?

EILEEN: I'd rather run into him accidentally. It looks better.

LUCILLE: You're not as sure of him as you let on.

EILEEN: Yes, I am! Why shouldn't I be?

LUCILLE: Well, the way he went away, in the first place. And he didn't exactly keep the wires hot while he was gone.

EILEEN: He wrote to me, every place he went.

LUCILLE: Yah, if you call picture post-cards writing.

EILEEN: He was busy most of the time. It was a business trip.

LUCILLE: He certainly sent you a beautiful view of the Detroit Athletic Club. (*Eileen glares at her.*) And that new water-works in Cleveland. A man that didn't care about you would have sent a picture of the *old* water-works. He's kind of a Latin type. Hot-blooded.

EILEEN: You can say all you want to. Just the same, when he finds I've been going out with Stevens he's going to be insanely jealous. You watch him.

LUCILLE: Well, maybe. But he didn't even wire you for a date to-night. It's the first time he hasn't done that.

EILEEN: He's taking it for granted. That's even better.

(*Any prospective reply is cut short by the return of Benny.*)

BENNY: Hello, there!

LUCILLE: Hello!

BENNY: George Gershwin's outside.

LUCILLE: Yeah?

BENNY: Don't you want to meet him?

LUCILLE: It's too late now.

BENNY: No—he's still there.

LUCILLE: Yah, but I'm not.

BENNY: I was telling him about my new number—"Hello, Tokio!" He said it was a great idea. But I forgot—you ain't heard of it. (*He dashes for the piano.*)

LUCILLE: It's all right. I'll take Gershwin's word.

BENNY: He said it would make the nuckelus of a great musical show. It's about a fella that falls in love with a pitcher of a Japanese princess, and he calls her up on the long distance phone.

LUCILLE: Is she sitting home?

BENNY: Yah. Why?

LUCILLE: I just wondered if things were the same over there.

BENNY (*thinking hard*): Of course in a musical show he and she have got to get together. (*Gets a sudden idea; a snap of the fingers.*) I got it—he flies there! That's what he does—he flies there! (*Now working as if in a trance.*) And he arrives in cherry blossom time!

LUCILLE: Is that a record?

BENNY: What a part for Lindbergh, if he could sing! (*He goes.*)

LUCILLE: We'd better be moving. We're kind of exposed here.
    (*Paul and Fred return.*)

FRED: Hello, there! Gee, I'm glad to see you!

PAUL (*not so glad*): Oh, hello!

EILEEN: Hello!

PAUL: You two can't stay here. We're going to do the song.

FRED: Mr. Hart ain't heard the song yet. Gee, I hope he likes it.

EILEEN: He'll like it all right. Lucille and I have brought you luck.

LUCILLE: Yah. I'm a born rabbit's foot.

PAUL: We don't need luck, with this number.

FRED (*to Eileen*): If they take it we'll have some celebration tonight! Won't we!

EILEEN: We can decide that later. I don't know—I may not want to go out to-night.
    (*Mr. Hart comes back. Apparently Gershwin didn't stay long.*)

PAUL: Here we are!

FRED: Oh, Mr. Hart!

HART (*a little flustered; he had not counted on running into Eileen this way*): Well! I didn't know we had visitors. Hello, Lucille.

LUCILLE: Hello.
    (*Hart turns slowly to Eileen.*)

FRED (*coming to the rescue*): This is Miss Fletcher, Mr. Hart. Miss Fletcher's Paul's sister-in-law.

HART: Yes. I've already met Miss Fletcher.

FRED (*still helping*): Mr. Hart's been off on a trip.

EILEEN: That's very interesting.

FRED: He's been in all the big cities. Chicago, and Cincinnati, and Cleveland—

LUCILLE: I understand Cleveland's got a new water-works.
(*Hart looks at her, dumbly.*)

FRED: Are you ready for our song now, Mr. Hart? I mean "June Moon"?

HART: In a minute. I've a little work to do.

EILEEN (*quickly*): Fred's been trying very hard to learn the business.

HART (*arrested*): Yes?

EILEEN: I guess we've been pretty nearly every place, haven't we, hearing the new songs?

FRED: You bet! Miss Fletcher's taken me every place. I think I know now what people want, all right.

HART (*looking at Fred with new interest*): Oh! So you are a friend of Miss Fletcher's?

FRED: We ain't been acquainted long, but—well, we're pretty good friends. (*To Eileen*) Aren't we?

EILEEN: Yah!

HART (*has a thought*): Suppose you boys come into my office and we'll run this song over.

FRED: You mean right away!

HART: Yes, of course.

FRED: That's fine. (*Rushing to the piano.*) Where's the lead sheet and the lyrics?

PAUL: Here they are!

FRED: Shall we go right in?

HART: Yes, of course.

FRED: But where's Maxie? We got to have Maxie.

HART: I'll send for him. Now then, who wrote this song?

FRED AND PAUL (*together, as they go through the door*): I did!
(*The women are once more alone.*)

EILEEN: Did you see that? He's insanely jealous.

LUCILLE: Well, if that's jealousy I'll take a plain lemon-ade.

EILEEN: You don't know him the way I do! He's burning up!

LUCILLE: He controlled it pretty well. He didn't say anything about a date to-night.

EILEEN: How could he, with Stevens here?
(*Maxie crosses the stage, enroute to Hart's office.*)

MAXIE: Well, it won't be long now. He's going to hear it at last.

LUCILLE: Yah. We're waiting for the verdict.

MAXIE: It's Stevens' first offense. They'll acquit him on the grounds of insanity. (*He is gone.*)

LUCILLE: You know, if they buy that limerick, Stevens'll be getting up a party for to-night. He was talking about it already.

EILEEN: I know.

LUCILLE: What are you going to do about him, anyhow? He's going to be kind of a nuisance with Hart back.

EILEEN: I can handle him. He's so far gone you can tell him anything.

LUCILLE: We certainly do attract song-writers, we Fletcher girls. It's a curse.

EILEEN: He's not a bad kid. I kind of like him. And he might make a lot of money in this game. Plenty of others have done it.

LUCILLE (*slowly*): I wonder if that damned song *is* any good. All of Paul's stuff sounds just alike to me.

EILEEN: Maybe Stevens' lyrics are just silly enough to get over. I've got kind of a hunch that they are.

LUCILLE: Even if they buy it it won't mean anything to us. Paul's so far ahead of his royalties they'll never catch up. He could write "Madame Butterfly" and it wouldn't even get me a new girdle.

EILEEN: Anyway, I've got Stevens broken in right, whoever gets him. You've got to give me credit for changing some of his ideas. I imagine every week was Thrift Week in Schenectady.

LUCILLE: It's Thrift Year for me. Year after year. (*She drops into a chair.*) And I'm getting pretty sick of it.

EILEEN: Why don't you do something?

LUCILLE: Well, maybe I am.

EILEEN: You are? What?

LUCILLE (*shakes her head*): That's all right.

EILEEN: Don't be a fool! What's happened?

LUCILLE: Nothing exactly yet.

EILEEN: Well, what's going to happen?

LUCILLE: I don't know. Nothing.

EILEEN (*pleading*): Will you tell me?

LUCILLE (*makes up her mind*): Remember—Ed Knowlton?

EILEEN: Yes. What about him?

LUCILLE: I ran into him Friday, on Madison Avenue.

EILEEN: Why didn't you tell me?

LUCILLE: Because I knew what you'd say and I wanted to think it out for myself.

EILEEN: What's it all about? What's he doing here?

LUCILLE: He's left Chicago for good. They're living on East Fifty-seventh—he and his wife and the two kids.

EILEEN: Well?

LUCILLE: He still likes me, and I like him.

EILEEN: Has he got any money?

LUCILLE: He makes a lot, but he spends it.

EILEEN: If he likes you that's not a fatal drawback.

LUCILLE: He likes me all right.

EILEEN: Can he get rid of her?

LUCILLE (*shakes her head*): No, it's her uncle or something owns the business. But he saw I wasn't happy, and—well, we had a couple of drinks and talked. He kept saying I ought to have nice things,—and that he was willing to give them to me.

EILEEN: Don't tell me you aren't going to do it?

LUCILLE: I'm kind of afraid. Suppose Paul gets inquisitive?

EILEEN: Paul! He doesn't know silk from asbestos. To hell with him anyway! It's time you had some luck!

LUCILLE: I don't know what to do. You and I look at things different. But Ed's so nice. The things he says—they make me feel young again. And it's such a relief to just talk to a man that hates music!

EILEEN: Listen, if you don't do this—

(*Fred runs on, all excitement.*)

FRED: They're going to take it! They've took it! They're crazy about it!

EILEEN: Well, that's fine! I knew they'd like it!

FRED: It's my first song! My first one to be published!

EILEEN: That's wonderful.

LUCILLE (*wildly unenthusiastic*): It's quite thrilling.

FRED: They're making me out a check for two hundred and fifty dollars! That's just what they call an advance royalties!

(*Paul returns.*)

PAUL: They took it all right!

LUCILLE: So Fred said.

EILEEN: Yes!

PAUL: You should have heard what Hart said about the melody.

FRED (*to Eileen*): Aren't you glad about the song? Aren't you excited?

EILEEN (*her mind beyond the door*): I should say so.
(*Hart comes in.*)

HART (*expansively*): Well, what do you think of this young man? Making good in his first attempt!

EILEEN: It's wonderful!

LUCILLE: Yes, indeed.

HART: And Paul, too. He's written a nice little melody. Did you get your check, Stevens?

FRED: No, sir. Not yet.

HART: Goldie'll bring it to you.

MAXIE (*crossing to his own office*): Well, thought you people would be on your way by this time.

EILEEN: We are waiting for Fred's check!

MAXIE: I'll bet you are! (*He's gone.*)

FRED: Mr. Hart! We were all planning on going some place to-night, to celebrate the success of the song. We'd love to have you come along with us, if you can.
(*A moment of embarrassment. Eileen just waits.*)

HART: Well, now, I'd like to do that, but I'm very sorry. (*Hart starts talking to Fred, but shifts his gaze to Eileen.*) You see, I just got back from this trip, and I'm tied up with Mr. Goebel to-night.

FRED: Oh, that's too bad.

EILEEN (*with more meaning*): Yes, it is.

HART: I'm sure you'll have a wonderful time. Can't tell you how much I'd like to be along. But of course, business comes first.
(*A very beautiful young lady enters. Her name is Miss Rixey.*)

MISS RIXEY: Hello, Joe. Am I late?

HART (*after clearing his throat*): Miss Rixey, isn't it?

MISS RIXEY (*puzzled at this reception*): What?

HART: Ah—they told me you were coming.

MISS RIXEY (*coming right to him*): You knew damn well I was coming!

HART (*still trying to cover up*): Did you bring those orchestrations?

MISS RIXEY (*holding up a bundle which obviously contains two bottles of liquor*): You mean this?

HART (*sunk by this time; grabs her by arm and rushes her into his office*): Ah—just step into my office and we'll talk business.

MISS RIXEY: Listen, Joe, that driver of yours is so damn dumb—

HART (*loudly*): Yes, we publish that! Right this way!

LUCILLE (*airily, when they are gone*): Well, well, well!

FRED: It's too bad he can't go, but the four of us can have a good time.

EILEEN (*recklessly*): Have a good time! You bet we can! We're going to have the best time any crowd ever had! Aren't we, Freddy boy? (*Throws her arms around him and kisses him.*)

FRED: We sure are, girlie!

 (*Goldie comes on.*)

GOLDIE: Here's your check, Mr. Stevens.

PAUL: Great!

EILEEN: Hooray! Here's the check! (*She takes it.*)

FRED: Just in time!

EILEEN: Two hundred and fifty dollars! You've just got to give me a great big kiss!

LUCILLE: Oh, you two!

EILEEN: Do you love me?

FRED: You bet I do!

LUCILLE: Where'll we go for dinner?

PAUL: I want a good steak.

EILEEN: How about the Park Casino?

LUCILLE: Oh, fine! I've never been there! I hear it's marvellous!

EILEEN: They've got the most wonderful band! You'll love it, Freddie boy!

FRED: I will if you're along!

EILEEN: I'm going to be, don't you worry about that! Wherever you are, that's where I'm going to be!

FRED: That suits me all right!

EILEEN: Come on, everybody!

PAUL: Don't forget we got to cash the check.

EILEEN (*waving the check*): I should say not! We're not going to forget that, are we, Freddie boy?

FRED: You bet we aren't!

(*They are gone; Goldie alone is left. She picks out some songs from the shelves. Edna, the girl he left behind him, peeps in, then enters.*)

EDNA: Do you know if they've heard Mr. Stevens's song yet? I mean "June Moon"?

GOLDIE (*pretty hard-boiled*): Yah. They did.

EDNA (*starting brightly forward*): Was it all right? Did they like it?

GOLDIE (*surveying her*): They took it.

EDNA (*in pleased excitement*): Really! Where are they? Still in there?

GOLDIE: Not any more. They've all gone.

EDNA: What?

GOLDIE: They went out just a couple of minutes ago.

EDNA: Mr.—Stevens, too?

GOLDIE: Yah. With Mr. Sears and the two girls.

EDNA: Oh! . . . Thank you very much.

(*Goldie takes a moment to look her up and down, then goes. Edna stands stock still for a moment, stunned. The door opens and the Window Cleaner returns, sponge still in hand. He looks at Edna a bit curiously; the scrutiny is more than she can stand. All she can do is rush out.*)

(*The room belongs to the Window Cleaner, and maybe he doesn't realize it. He scampers over to the piano and hits a few tentative notes. Resigning himself to a musical career, he drops his sponge on the window sill and starts picking out the notes of "Hello, Tokio!" Encouraged by his success with the first phrase, he starts again, this time singing it. Then he takes a long breath and starts again, louder this time. He is plunging recklessly into it, and oblivious of his surroundings, when Maxie comes in behind him. Maxie stands perfectly still for a second, taking in the situation. Then he makes up his mind. Turn about, he decides, is fair play. He picks up the sponge and starts feverishly washing the window.*)

THE CURTAIN FALLS

ACT III

The scene is still at Goebel's—the time about a month later. Goldie comes on and goes to the music racks. While she is searching for songs, Benny enters. Except that Benny never just enters— he shoots on.

BENNY: Where's Hart?

GOLDIE: He's out somewhere.

BENNY: Did you tell him I wanted to see him?

GOLDIE: Yes, but he was on his way out.

BENNY: What did he say?

GOLDIE: Nothing. He just hurried.

BENNY: I've got to see him. I've got a number that will knock his eye out.

GOLDIE: Like "Tokio?"

BENNY: Don't kid me about "Tokio." If ever a man got a crooked deal! Listen—

GOLDIE: I've heard it.

BENNY: You ain't heard it all because I didn't know it myself till last night. Harry Ruby told me at the Friars. It seems that the night I played it there, there was a fella named Stein hanging around.

GOLDIE (*incredulous*): At the Friars?

BENNY: Well, he hears my number, and he tells these other fellas, and they turn out their damn "Hello, Shanghai!" and beat me to it. It's increditable, but that's what happened. And on top of that Maxie says their number is better than mine because Shanghai's further away than Tokio. I'll kill the two of them the first time I get them alone together, I don't care if they got a thousand friends with them. And that ain't all. They stole my song and I'm going to sue them for perjury.

GOLDIE: I think you'll get it.

BENNY: And it wasn't only a song they stole—it was a whole production. A musical comedy. That's where the big money is. And that's what I'm going to get into. I'll tell you something. (*Confidentially.*) I'm not going to be with Goebel's much longer.

GOLDIE: I heard that.

BENNY: Who from?

GOLDIE: Mr. Goebel.

BENNY: You couldn't—he doesn't know it yet.

GOLDIE: Oh!

BENNY: I'm quitting and they can see how they like that. They can get along with Stevens and his brilliant ideas. "June Moon!" The lucky saphead!

GOLDIE: It was on at five different stations last night.

BENNY: The oldest idea in the world! And I write a great novelty number and it's stole off me!

  (*Paul arrives.*)

PAUL (*to Goldie*): Have you seen Stevens?

BENNY: Want to hear a great song?

PAUL (*still to Goldie*): Have you?

GOLDIE: He hasn't come in.

BENNY: Get this, Paul! Tell me if you don't think it'll slaughter them! (*Benny hits one chord; Hart enters.*) Hello, Boss! You're just in time!

HART (*a wave of the hand that takes care of Benny for the moment*): Where's Stevens? Is he in yet?

PAUL: I'm waiting for him myself.

HART (*to Goldie*): Call his hotel. See if he's there.

GOLDIE: I did a while ago. He was out.

HART: See if they know where to get a hold of him. (*Goldie goes. She loves her work, this girl.*) How are you coming with the new numbers?

PAUL (*uncomfortably*): Pretty good, only Fred don't seem to want to work lately. He was going to meet me here at eleven.

HART: He ought to be getting busy. He's not going to work on his honeymoon.

PAUL: No, sir.

HART: When he comes in, tell him I'd like to see him.

PAUL: Yes, sir. (*He goes out.*)

BENNY (*stopping Hart before he can escape*): Listen, Mr. Hart! It won't take me two minutes to show you this number. It's sure to hit you.

HART: Anything like "Tokio"?

BENNY: I had a tough break on that, Mr. Hart—that "Hello, Shanghai." Why, do you know what? There ain't even a telephone between New York and Shanghai!

HART: Well, we'll have one put in. (*Maxie comes on.*) Oh, Maxie, I was just going to send for you. There's a young fellow outside who has written a song.

MAXIE: Who is it?

HART: That's just the point. Somebody my sister-in-law sent, so do whatever you can for him. He's only sixteen years old.

MAXIE: And still grinding them out?

HART: It's probably one of those things, but *you* know—you never can tell. Anything can happen, after "June Moon."

MAXIE: As long as you've brought that up, would you mind answering me a riddle?

HART: What is it?

MAXIE: Did you have any idea that was going to be a hit? Honestly, now?

HART (*hesitantly*): Well, I'll tell you, Maxie—

MAXIE (*starts to leave*): That's all I wanted to know.

HART: Do whatever you can for the lad, Maxie. He came all the way from Plainfield.

MAXIE: He'll get home safe. (*He goes.*)

BENNY (*still trying*): Listen, Mr. Hart, won't you hear this?

HART: Hear what?

BENNY: This number. The title is "Give Our Child A Name." It'll make "June Moon" sound like a dirge. It's a couple that give birth to a little one in two-four tempo.

HART: It won't do you any good knocking Stevens's number.

BENNY: I ain't knocking his lousy number, but get this, Mr. Hart! (*He jumps to the piano.*)

> "Should a father's carnal sins
>   Blight the life of babykins?
>   All I ask is give our child a—"

(*His hands descend on the keyboard in an annoyed discord as Fred and Eileen enter.*)

HART: Well! Here's the groom at last!

(*Benny goes, banging the door behind him.*)

EILEEN: You can blame it on me. I've been making him get some new clothes.

HART: Well, you two are certainly to be congratulated.

EILEEN: Thanks.

FRED: Much obliged.

HART: But don't forget your work. When do you sail?

EILEEN: Saturday.

FRED: We sail Saturday.

HART (*having his bit of fun*): I certainly envy you. I wish I could go along.

FRED: There's no chance, I suppose?

HART: Not at this time of year. (*Visibly enjoying the situation.*) If you could postpone it a month—

FRED (*brightening*): Yah, that might be a good idea!

EILEEN: Don't be silly!

FRED: I forgot. Eileen wants to be on the Riveeria in the season.

HART: I see. Well, I hope they don't take you at Monte Carlo.

FRED: If they don't take us there we can go somewheres else.

HART: Anyhow, be sure to get your work done. (*He starts to go.*)

EILEEN: Oh, Mr. Hart!

HART: Yes?

EILEEN: Fred wants to speak to you about something else.

FRED (*quickly*): No, I don't.

EILEEN: But you do, dear.

FRED: I'll ask you later.

HART: Is anything the matter?

FRED: No, no! It wasn't— I just—

HART: Well, I'll be in my office, if you want me. (*He leaves.*)

EILEEN: Why didn't you ask him when you had a chance?

FRED (*weakly*): They've advanced me so much already.

EILEEN: But sweetheart, you promised me. You said you'd ask him to-day.

FRED: I will after while. I got to find Paul now—I got to go to work.

EILEEN: Oh, don't go to work yet. You never have any time for me. You don't realize I want to be loved once in a while.

FRED: I held your hand in the taxi.

EILEEN: Just think! Only three more days till we belong to each other. Isn't it marvellous!

FRED: It's four, ain't it?

EILEEN: Four till we sail. Only three till we get married.

FRED: I wished it wasn't quite so soon.

EILEEN: What?

FRED: I mean, on account of those two numbers.

EILEEN: Don't forget—you're to ask him for a thousand dollars advance on each of them.

FRED: But that's too much! I've borrowed thirty-five hundred dollars off them already on "June Moon"—maybe more than my royalties will amount to altogether.

EILEEN: Don't be ridiculous! That number will still be selling when you're dead.

FRED: I won't care so much then.

EILEEN: Your children will. (*Fred is embarrassed.*) Don't you want children, dear?

FRED: I don't get along with them very good.

EILEEN: You would with your own.

FRED: No. I figure I'd get along better with other people's, because they'd go home once in a while.

EILEEN: We needn't think of that now. Let's just think of you and me, all alone on that big boat.

FRED: We won't be alone. The fella said it would be pretty near full.

EILEEN: But we don't have to see anybody. A bride and groom don't generally go around much—they're supposed to be so awfully in love.

FRED: I'll want to eat once in a while.

EILEEN: They'll serve us in our cabin.

FRED: It'll be kind of close quarters. Maybe I could go in the dining-room and order you a meal sent up.

EILEEN: And leave me all alone? I'd be scared to death.

FRED: It's just as dangerous in the dining-room as the bedroom. If the ship sinks, pretty near all the rooms will be under water.

EILEEN: Let's not think about such things. Just think of the pleasant side. London and Paris—I'm glad we're going to Paris first, so I can get some clothes.

FRED: Clothes? What have you been buying?

EILEEN: They're all right for the ship, dear, but not the Riviera. Don't you want to be proud of me—the way I look?

FRED: But if you're going to stay in your cabin all the time you won't need nothing but a Mother Hubbard.

(*Maxie comes back; Eileen automatically starts to go.*)

MAXIE: Well! All ready for the big trip?

FRED: Pretty near. The boat sails Saturday.

MAXIE: I don't know what you want to go to Europe for.

EILEEN (*bristling*): Why not?

MAXIE: Because he's never been there. A song-writer never goes anywhere for the first time—they're always going back to places. Back to Indiana—back, back to Baltimore.

EILEEN (*annoyed*): Fred, are you going to talk to Mr. Hart?

FRED: Yes, ma'am.

EILEEN: Well, this would be a good time. (*She goes, in about medium dudgeon.*)

FRED: I'd like to be going back, back to Schenectady, but Eileen's got her heart set on Europe.

MAXIE: I hear it's quite a place.

FRED: Yes, I guess so. I was kind of excited about it at first, but now I don't know—I don't want to go so bad. I'm kind of tired, I guess—the way we been going it lately. I'm kind of behind on my sleep.

MAXIE (*appraisingly*): But you've been having a lot of fun. All those night clubs.

FRED: I did at first—dancing and everything—but now my feet's so sore I have to take a bath every day. You might as well take a whole bath as just your feet. And they ache so I can't sleep in them. Gosh, I'm so tired all the time. I don't have time to sleep, anyway. We shop till the stores is closed, and then we get dressed up for dinner and the evening. If I don't get some rest soon I'll have a nervous break-up. And everything costs so much. Eileen wants a taxi if she's only going in the other room.

MAXIE: This trip to Europe—that's going to be kind of expensive, too, ain't it?

FRED: Yes. I always thought I'd save my money, if I ever got any.

MAXIE: You picked out a thrifty girl, all right.

FRED: I kind of get thinking sometimes, maybe a man like I that's just breaking in, maybe he shouldn't get married so soon, especially a woman that's got to have so many clothes. Sometimes I think it would be better if I hadn't got engaged.

MAXIE (*feeling his way*): I read of a case once, in Michigan, where a man was engaged to a girl and didn't marry her.

FRED: I didn't read that. Have you got the clippings?

MAXIE: No. But my memory's pretty good. For instance, I remember a mighty nice little girl that was here to see you one time. I even remember her name—Miss Baker.

FRED (*nervously*): Maxie, you haven't seen her or anything, have you?

MAXIE (*the picture of innocence*): Me? No. Why?

FRED (*uneasily*): I guess I shouldn't be thinking of her at a time like this—

MAXIE: Are you?

FRED: I don't know. Sometimes I—

(*Goldie enters, bound for those same old music shelves. It is a welcome interruption so far as Fred is concerned.*)

FRED: I got to find Paul. I got to do some work. (*He withdraws.*)

MAXIE (*looking after him*): Just one of the Happiness boys—he and Pagliacco.

GOLDIE (*with her songs*): Mother song and mother song—why don't they ever write about their uncle?

MAXIE (*thoughtfully*): Suppose I told you I was thinking of doing something about him?

GOLDIE: What?

MAXIE: Suppose I went even further and told you I'd already done it?

GOLDIE: What are you talking about?

MAXIE: I'm talking about a little girl that came in here to see Stevens about a month ago. The one you sent the music to.

GOLDIE: Oh!

MAXIE: She's the one he ought to be marrying, instead of this whatever-she-is.

GOLDIE (*with monumental indifference*): My God, what's the difference who marries a lyric writer? (*She goes.*)

(*Maxie stands a moment, deep in thought. He drifts to the piano—aimlessly, instinctively. Drops onto the bench; his fingers slide over the keys. But he is not thinking about his music.*)

(*And then Lucille enters. A new Lucille, patently. She wears a gorgeous red dress, topped off with a coat of the same material, trimmed in white fur. But it's not only the clothes. She has that note of assurance that only the perfectly dressed woman can have. She comes into the room slowly, confidently.*)

MAXIE (*as he looks her over*): Hello.

LUCILLE: Where's everybody?

MAXIE: Paul's outside somewhere. I think he's working.

LUCILLE: Has Eileen been here?

MAXIE: She's around.

LUCILLE: Thanks.

MAXIE: All dressed up to-day.

LUCILLE: Not especially.

MAXIE: You look like a bride yourself.

    (*Lucille gives a visible start; the situation is saved by the entrance of Eileen.*)

EILEEN: Hello! I thought I saw you!

MAXIE: Well, I've got to get busy, if you'll excuse me. (*He goes.*)

EILEEN (*observing the dress*): Oh, say, it's a peach!

LUCILLE: Do you like it?

EILEEN: You bet! (*She lowers her voice.*) Have you got a date?

LUCILLE: I think so. I'm to phone his office later on. (*She is not at ease.*)

EILEEN (*a look at her watch*): What do you say we have lunch?

LUCILLE: Wait a minute.

EILEEN: What's the matter?

LUCILLE: I don't want to go out there yet.

EILEEN: Why not?

LUCILLE: I don't feel like running into Paul.

EILEEN: Aren't you ever going to get over that? What is there to be afraid of?

LUCILLE: I don't know. I'm just nervous.

EILEEN: He'll never guess anything. He's blind and always has been.

LUCILLE: Thanks!

EILEEN: You know what I mean. All he thinks about's his tunes. We've got a chance to be happy, you and I—for a while, anyhow. Let's take it!

LUCILLE: You're a funny one to figure out.

EILEEN: Why?

LUCILLE: Taking up with Stevens this way. You always lectured

me about Paul—his being a song-writer. And now you're
going to go and do the same thing.

EILEEN: Stevens is different. He's a nice kid. Of course, he's
not exactly what you'd call—bright.

LUCILLE: Bright? He's not even born yet.
(*Paul enters.*)

PAUL: Oh, hello.

LUCILLE: Hello.

PAUL: What's that—a new dress?

LUCILLE (*a silly question*): This?

EILEEN (*sensing a storm*): I'll meet you outside, Lucille.

LUCILLE: Wait a minute—I'll go with you.

PAUL: No, I want to talk to you.

LUCILLE (*scared*): What?

PAUL (*a look at Eileen*): Stay in here a minute.

LUCILLE: What for?

EILEEN: I'll go on out. I want to talk to Fred. (*She escapes, and
glad of the chance.*)

LUCILLE: What's the matter?

PAUL (*on the dress again*): That *is* new, isn't it?

LUCILLE: Don't you think it's about time?

PAUL: How much was it?

LUCILLE: It won't come due for a while. I may take care of it
myself.

PAUL: I can take care of it, if it ain't too soon.

LUCILLE: I've got to go on out. Eileen's waiting.

PAUL: Hold on! (*Lucille turns, not knowing what to expect.*)
That's what I want to talk to you about.

LUCILLE: What?

PAUL: About her and Fred.

LUCILLE (*in vast relief*): Oh!

PAUL: She's got him so he can't hardly work at all. I don't
know when we're going to finish the new numbers.

LUCILLE: Of course you can finish them.

PAUL: But taking him off on this trip! It's going to cost him a
million dollars. And just when we're beginning to work
good together!

LUCILLE: You can write other numbers while he's gone.

PAUL: But that ain't the point. I mean—do you think they
ought to do it?

LUCILLE: Do what?

PAUL: Do you think they ought to go ahead and get married? He's a hell of a nice guy—I've kind of got to like him.

LUCILLE: What of it? Eileen's a nice girl.

PAUL: But—you know what I mean. Isn't it kind of a dirty trick—I mean, after the way Eileen— (*Lucille gives him a sharp look.*) Well, Hart and everything?

LUCILLE (*in a low tone*): You ought to have more sense.

PAUL: Just the same, I don't feel right about it. And the way she's throwing his money around—like it was confetti. Spending every nickel she can get on herself! Clothes, clothes—

LUCILLE: You can't go to Europe in a life belt.

PAUL: Do you know what she spent in one afternoon, yesterday? Close to four hundred dollars. He pretty near cried when he told me. And I don't blame him. He's too nice a kid.

LUCILLE: She doesn't spend that every day.

PAUL: She shouldn't have spent it at all. You should have had more sense than to let her.

LUCILLE (*flaring a little*): How could I stop her? I wasn't there!

PAUL: Yes, you were! You were with her all afternoon.

LUCILLE (*quickly covering herself*): Oh, yes. I thought you meant the day before.

PAUL: It was Sunday, the day before.

LUCILLE: Yah—I just mixed up, that's all.

PAUL: Anyhow, something ought to be done about it. She's got him in debt enough.

LUCILLE (*nervously*): I'll talk to her about it. (*Starts out.*) Don't you say anything to her. Don't say anything about—I mean, what she spent yesterday afternoon. I'll go and talk to her. (*She gets away.*)

(*Paul stands in thought for a moment; then he starts to go. Benny catches him in the act.*)

BENNY: Can you listen to that number?

PAUL: What?

BENNY: Can you hear that number now?

PAUL: Aw—I got to work, Benny. (*Goes.*)

(*Goldie immediately enters.*)

BENNY: Where's Hart?

GOLDIE: Can't you think up a new question?

BENNY: Where is he?

GOLDIE: He's out getting a permanent. (*And she goes.*)

> (*Benny almost gives up; is about to leave. But then there arrives the beautiful young woman known as Miss Rixey. She heads for Hart's door.*)

BENNY (*without much hope*): Say, do you want to hear a new song?

MISS RIXEY: Sure!

BENNY (*bowled over by this answer*): What?

MISS RIXEY: I said sure.

BENNY (*darts to the piano and starts*):

> "Should a father's carnal sins
>> Blight the life of babykins?
>>> All I ask is give our child—"

> (*But Miss Rixey has not waited. Something about the rhythm has caught her ear, and she has simply gone into her dance. It has expressed itself in the form of a neat Off-to-Buffalo, right through the door and into Hart's office. And perhaps further.*)

> (*Benny sits looking after her, stunned. As he does so Edna enters—a bit uncertainly, as is her wont, but she enters.*)

BENNY (*willing to take anything*): Hello, kid.

EDNA: Hello.

BENNY: Want to see somebody?

EDNA: I'll be going.

BENNY: Wait—you want to hear a great song? You know who I am, don't you? I'm Benny Fox, the hit-writer. I write words and music both. I'm like Berlin, only more pathetic. Now I got a new one. It's about a couple that have a baby without benefit to a clergyman, and you can dance to it. (*He plays it.*)

> "Should a father's carnal sins
>> Blight the life of babykins?
>>> All I ask is give our child a name—I mean a last name.
>>> I don't ask to share your life,
>>> Live with you as man and wife;
>>> All I ask is give our child a name—
>>> Not just a first name."

(*Maxie comes on.*) Hello, Maxie. I'll start over so you can get this.

      "Should a father's carnal sins—"

MAXIE (*looking at Edna*): Wait a minute! Isn't this—Miss Baker?

EDNA: And you're Mr. Schwartz.

MAXIE: Correct!

BENNY: Come on, Maxie! Get a load of this!

      "Should a father's carnal sins—"

MAXIE: Go back to your cell! We want to talk!

BENNY: But she wants to hear this number!

MAXIE (*gets an idea*): Listen! You don't know who she is.

BENNY: No.

MAXIE: Well! Remember what happened to "Tokio." (*It's a case of the burnt child. Benny scoots out, throwing a look back at Edna as he goes.*) My, but I'm glad to see you!

EDNA: It's nice of you to say so, anyway.

MAXIE: I guess it was kind of nervy of me, calling you up that way. Hope you don't mind.

EDNA: Why—no. I—I thought it was very friendly.

MAXIE: Of course it isn't really any of my business exactly, but —nobody else was doing anything, so I thought I would. Probably you can guess who it's about.

EDNA: Tell me about him! What's happened? What's happened to him?

MAXIE: Do you mind if I ask a question? I think I know the answer.

EDNA: What?

MAXIE: You're in love with him, aren't you? (*Edna turns away.*) You know, you can tell me. I'm for you—I want to help you. You do—love him? (*Edna nods.*) Enough to keep him from—ruining himself?

EDNA: How do you mean?

MAXIE: He's engaged to be married. You know that?

EDNA: I—supposed that was it.

MAXIE: But he's not happy. He's not in love with her.

EDNA (*breaking out*): I can't do anything! He doesn't love me! He never did!

MAXIE: Somebody's got to do something. He's not a fellow that can think for himself. They left that out.

EDNA: Oh, why did you make me come here? I shouldn't have

done it—I don't know why I did! I've been trying every way
to forget him—I went away, and I didn't see anybody, and
then I went around with lots of people—it only made it
worse. I kept wanting to call him up, and once I did, only—
I hung up before he could come to the telephone.

MAXIE: Let me bring him in here.

EDNA: No, no! I don't want to talk to him! I mustn't!

MAXIE: But he's in trouble. And you're the only one that can
help him.

EDNA: He don't want to see *me*!

MAXIE: Let me tell him you're here. It can't do any harm.
(*Edna is silent.*) You needn't answer. Only promise me one
thing.

EDNA: What?

MAXIE: No matter what happens, come and see me afterward.
Will you? (*Edna nods.*) The second door on the left, down
that hall. (*Maxie goes. Edna is alone for a moment. Two moments, even. Then a pretty excited Fred comes on.*)

FRED: Hello, Eddie.

EDNA: Hello.

FRED: I'm awful glad to see you, Eddie! Gee, but I'm glad to
see you!

EDNA: I didn't really come to—I mean, it was Mr. Schwartz
that made me talk to you.

FRED: My, but it's great to see you again! I didn't know how
great it would be.

EDNA: I'm glad to see you, too, Fred. I'm glad you're well and
that you're going to be—happy.

FRED: I been thinking about you, Eddie—an awful lot, lately. I
been waking up in the morning, thinking about you.

EDNA: Are you waking up in the morning again, Fred?

FRED: I been going to call you up and tell you about it. We
used to have a lot of fun together. (*Eagerly.*) Remember that
day in Van Cortlandt Park when I lost my watch and that
little boy found it?

EDNA: You gave him a nickel.

FRED: It was a dime. And he said, "Keep it and buy your wife
a raddio set." He thought we was married. (*He laughs, as
though trying to induce a mood of merriment in Edna.*)

EDNA: I remember.

FRED: You was embarrassed, all right. You got red.

EDNA: Any girl would.

FRED: And then coming back we forgot to change at Seventy-second Street. That is, you forgot. I didn't know any better.

EDNA: I just wasn't thinking.

FRED: We had to go all the way down to Times Square. That's when we saw the flea circus.

EDNA: You said one of the fleas reminded you of a man in Schenectady.

FRED: Yeah. Perry Robinson. He always walked like he'd just picked up a nail. (*Fred drops the pretense and comes out with it.*) Eddie, did Maxie say anything to you? About me.

EDNA (*in agony*): He said you were going to be married, Fred. I should have congratulated you.

FRED (*suddenly*): I don't want to any more, Eddie! I know it now! I don't want to!

EDNA: Don't say that, Fred! Don't! Don't say it unless you mean it! I couldn't stand it!

FRED: But I do mean it, Eddie! I mean it more than anything in the—

(*Eileen comes on. You knew she would.*)

EILEEN (*rather gaily*): I'm sorry.

FRED (*as Edna shows signs of bolting*): No—don't go away. This is—Miss Fletcher.

EILEEN (*appraisingly*): Hello.

FRED: And this is Miss Baker. She's the little girl—I mean, I used to know her when—

EDNA (*who can't stand it*): I'll be going if you don't mind. Good-by, Fred.

FRED: No—look! Don't go away!

EDNA: Yes, I must! I—good-by, Miss Fletcher! (*She rushes off. Fred hesitates for a second; then starts out after her.*)

EILEEN: Fred!

FRED (*stopping short*): Huh?

EILEEN: Why, what's the matter with you? One would almost think it was her you were going to marry instead of me.

FRED (*facing her*): I got to tell you something.

EILEEN: Why, what is it?

FRED: I don't want to get married! I mean—you and I!

EILEEN: Do you know what you're saying?

FRED: I can't help it. I shouldn't ever have done it! I didn't realize!

EILEEN: Well! This is a fine time to tell me! Why didn't you wait till Friday!

FRED: I just now realized it!

EILEEN: I see! And you think all you have to do is tell me and that settles it. Well, it doesn't work quite that way!

FRED: What?

EILEEN: You think I'm going to stand by and let you throw me over for that little snip!

FRED: She is not!

EILEEN: Not by a damned sight! I'll sue her for alienation—that's what I'll do.

FRED: You can't. She was born right here in New York State!

EILEEN: You seem to have forgotten something! Did you beg me to marry you or didn't you?

FRED: But I didn't know then.

EILEEN: You seem to have forgotten that I was engaged to another man, and that you took me away from him! What about that?

FRED: I can't help it.

EILEEN (*a change of method*): But that isn't the main thing. I love you, Freddy. You made me love you. I didn't at first, but you made me. And now you want to leave me.

FRED: But you don't want me to marry you, if I feel that way.

EILEEN: What would you think of a man that made a girl love him, when she was already engaged, and then threw her over? Do you think that would be quite—honorable?

FRED (*with sudden inspiration*): Honorable! That's just what I got to be! That's why I can't marry you!

EILEEN: What do you mean?

FRED: I mean I got to marry another girl, to save her from—from worse than death.

EILEEN: That little kid? (*A gesture.*)

FRED: Yes!

EILEEN: You mean you've got her in trouble?

FRED: Yes! That's it!

EILEEN: I don't believe you! I'm going to call her back!

FRED (*stopping her*): No, no! You mustn't tell her that!

EILEEN: Why not?

FRED: I—I want to surprise her.

EILEEN (*a scornful surveying*): Did you think I was going to fall for any story like that? (*Fred turns away.*) I'm the one you're engaged to, and I'm the one you're going to marry. (*Paul comes in.*)

PAUL: Not interrupting, am I?

EILEEN (*slowly, and narrowly observing Fred*): No, I was just going. (*With great deliberation.*) We understand each other. Don't we? (*She watches Fred; gets no response; goes out.*)

PAUL: What's the matter?

FRED (*dully*): Huh?

PAUL: You haven't had a fight, have you?

FRED (*shakes his head*): There ain't anything the matter.

PAUL: I thought maybe we might get after one of those numbers.

FRED: I don't feel much like working.

PAUL: I'm sorry if anything's happened.

FRED: It ain't nothing. I'll be all right soon.

PAUL: The only thing is—there isn't much time left if we're going to finish before you go. Here it is Tuesday.

FRED: How about starting in early to-morrow morning?

PAUL: What are you doing this afternoon?

FRED: I got to go to the French passport place.

PAUL: I thought you went there yesterday.

FRED: I couldn't. I told you I went with Eileen while she was shopping.

PAUL: Oh, yah. Four hundred dollars.

FRED: She certainly knows how to spend.

PAUL (*lightly*): You must have had a swell time, running around with two women all afternoon.

FRED: No, I wasn't. What two women?

PAUL: Her and Lucille.

FRED: Lucille wasn't along. Just I and Eileen.

PAUL: Yesterday?

FRED (*nods*): We was together from one till five-thirty. Why?

PAUL (*trying to fit things together*): Nothing, only—and it was yesterday she spent the four hundred?

FRED: It was three eighty-seven.

PAUL: That's funny.

FRED: What's the matter?

PAUL (*slowly*): I don't know. I guess I got things kind of mixed up.

FRED: What things?

PAUL: Didn't Lucille ever meet you, during the afternoon?

FRED: No. Why?

(*Eileen and Lucille look in.*)

LUCILLE: We're going out to lunch. Want to come along?

PAUL (*almost too casually*): I want to talk to you.

LUCILLE: What?

PAUL: I said I want to talk to you.

LUCILLE: What about?

EILEEN (*catching a note of something in Paul's manner*): What's the matter with *him*?

PAUL: Where were you yesterday afternoon?

LUCILLE (*trying to do some quick thinking*): I was—out.

PAUL (*quiet, but terrifying*): I said, where were you?

LUCILLE: Do I have to report all my movements?

PAUL: You do when I catch you lying! Where were you?

(*Fred is following this with wide but uncomprehending eyes. Eileen is scared but wary, waiting to go to the defense if she can.*)

LUCILLE: I had an engagement! It was—with an old friend of mine, and I thought you might not want me to do it, and so I told you I was with Eileen.

FRED (*beginning to understand*): Oh!

LUCILLE: I know it was foolish of me! I was going to tell you later.

EILEEN: She was going to tell you to-night! She told me so.

LUCILLE: Yah!

PAUL: Yah? (*After another terrible pause.*) Where'd you get that dress?

LUCILLE: What? I bought it.

EILEEN: I treated her to it, if you want to know.

PAUL: Is that so? That wasn't what you told me.

LUCILLE: I was afraid you wouldn't let me take it.

PAUL (*after a bit of thinking*): Where'd you go, yesterday after-noon? With this fellow?

LUCILLE: We went to a matinée.

PAUL: On a Monday?

LUCILLE: It was at the Palace. We went to the Palace.

PAUL (*taking plenty of time*): Who was there?

LUCILLE: What?

PAUL: On the bill. Who were the headliners?

LUCILLE (*panic in her voice*): I don't see what difference that makes.

PAUL (*not raising his tone*): You—dirty—lying—double-crosser!

EILEEN: That's not true!

LUCILLE (*stopping Eileen*): Keep still! I'm sick of the whole thing! (*She faces Paul.*) Yes! . . . Yes, if you want to know! . . . Yes and to hell with you! Did you think I was going to wait around forever for you to give me the things I wanted? God knows I waited long enough! And then—I just didn't wait any longer, that's all. What do you know about that? Huh? What do you know about that? (*Paul is stunned. Turns slowly away.*) So—that's the way that stands! (*She takes a step toward the door; breaks into sobs. Eileen goes to her; puts her arm around her.*)

FRED: But—but you mean to say that when you were married to him— (*He takes a moment, trying to realize it. Then, to Eileen.*) But *you* must have known she was doing it!

EILEEN: What? Why—no, I didn't.

FRED: Yes. You said you bought her the dress.

PAUL (*a scornful laugh*): Known she was doing it! She put her up to it!

EILEEN: That's not true!

PAUL: No? Well, then I'll tell you something that is true!

EILEEN: Don't you believe him, Fred!

PAUL: And thank God I've got the courage to tell you at last!

EILEEN: He's a liar, that's what he is! I tell you he's a liar!

FRED: Why, what is it?

PAUL: You didn't know your fiancée had a lover, did you?

FRED: What?

EILEEN: I tell you it's a lie. He's just trying to separate us!

PAUL: Am I?

EILEEN: He's just making it up!

PAUL: She told you she was engaged to be married! Well, she wasn't! He was her lover, and he kicked her out, and that's why she took up with you! I'd have told you long ago, if I hadn't been a coward!

FRED (*staggered. Turns to Eileen*): Is this true?

EILEEN (*in final realization that the game is up*): Of course it is, you little fool!

FRED: Gosh!

EILEEN: That's probably a pretty big shock to those fine up-state morals of yours.

FRED: Then I been going around all this time with a—bad woman?

EILEEN: And now have we both got permission to go, or does somebody else want to speak? (*Spotting Edna, who has been brought on the scene by Maxie.*) Maybe your little girl friend would like to say a few words?

FRED: If she does, she'll say them to me. And I'll know I can believe them, too.

EILEEN: I'm sure you'll understand each other. What's more, you're probably the only two people in the world that would. Come on, Lucille. (*She surveys the lovers.*) I want to come and visit that child of yours—next month. (*Lucille and Eileen go.*)

(*Paul has dropped into a chair, his head buried in his hands.*)

FRED (*turning to where Edna and Maxie stand*): Eddie, I—I don't have to marry her.

EDNA: I'm so happy, Fred.

FRED: I'm sorry, Paul, about—everything.

PAUL: That's all right. I'm glad if I helped to fix things for you. I should have told you long ago. (*He goes.*)

FRED: Only look! I've still got the tickets for the boat, and it says "Frederick M. Stevens and Wife." And I wonder if the steamship people allow you to change your wife?

MAXIE: Yes. If you don't do it in midstream.

EDNA: If your wife is the right kind she won't let you take her on an expensive trip. She'll make you put everything into a home. I don't mean a big home—just a little bungalow would do.

FRED: Bungalow! A bungalow for two! That'd be a great title!

MAXIE: And I've got a great tune! (*Maxie goes into "Button Up Your Overcoat." Fred is enchanted—to him it is something*

that Maxie has composed on the spur of the moment. He starts
improvising words.)

FRED:

"In a bungalow for two,
    Where we can bill and coo—"
(*Mercifully, the curtain is down.*)

CURTAIN

ONCE IN A LIFETIME

A Comedy
by
Moss Hart
and
George S. Kaufman

SCENES

Act One

Act Two

Act Three

ACT ONE

Scene i

A room in the West Forties, New York City. It is a replica of the countless other furnished rooms in the district—cheerless and utterly uninviting. There is a bed, a washstand, an easy chair, two faded pictures on the walls. A pretty dismal place, all in all—yet George Lewis, seated in the easy chair, seems completely content. George is about twenty-eight, a clean-cut, nice-looking young fellow, with the most disarmingly naïve countenance it is possible to imagine. Completely without guile. He is the sort of person insurance men and book agents instinctively head for, and in the case of George, it might be noted, usually succeed in selling. Withal, there is a quiet sincerity about George and a certain youthful ardor and genuineness that make him a decidedly likeable person.

He is sunk deep down in the easy chair, at the moment, immersed to the exclusion of all else in that Bible of show business, VARIETY. *He has a large plate of Indian nuts on the arm of the easy chair, and these he proceeds to crack and eat with a methodical thoroughness, stopping only to turn a page of the paper or to brush some of the shells off his trousers. It is a picture of a man thoroughly content and blissfully happy in the moment. There is a sharp knock at the door. George murmurs a "Come in" and May Daniels enters. She is quite a person, this May Daniels. It is evident from the moment she enters the room. There is a sharp, biting incisiveness about everything she says and does—a quick mind, and a hearty, earthy sense of humor. Tall and slender, she carries herself with the conscious ease and grace of a person who has always been thoroughly sure of herself, and her blonde good looks are a bit clouded just now by a tired line between the eyes and a discouraged droop at the corners of the mouth. With one glance she takes in George,* VARIETY, *and the Indian nuts—then sits dejectedly on the edge of the bed.*

MAY: Jerry not back yet, huh?
GEORGE: No.

MAY: Anything new since this afternoon? You haven't heard anything, have you?

GEORGE: No. Are you going to stay and talk, May? I'm reading.

MAY: What time's Jerry coming back, do you know?

GEORGE: He went to a show.

MAY: It's wonderful how you two take it. You off to ball games every day, Jerry going to shows! What about the old vaudeville act? Are we gonna get some bookings or aren't we?

GEORGE: I don't know anything about it, May. I'm reading.

MAY: Still "Variety"?

GEORGE: Uh-huh.

MAY: One of these days you'll pick up a paper that's written in English, and you'll have to send out for an interpreter.

GEORGE: What do you mean, May? "Variety" is in English.

MAY: All right.

GEORGE: It has news of the show world from different countries, but it's all in English.

MAY: (*Willing to call the whole thing off.*) I said all right, George.

GEORGE: Want some Indian nuts?

MAY: No, thanks. (*He cracks a nut—and a good sturdy crack it is. May surveys him.*) Don't your teeth ever bother you?

GEORGE: No. Why?

MAY: I dunno—after all those damn things you've eaten. Do you realize, George, that you've left a trail of Indian nuts clean across the United States? If you ever commit a crime they could go right *to* you.

GEORGE: (*Going back to his reading.*) Aw!

MAY: You've thrown them shells under radiators in every dollar and a half hotel from here to Seattle. I can visualize hundreds of chambermaids, the country over, coming in the morning you check out and murmuring a blessing on your head. Don't you ever have bad dreams, George, with that on your mind?

GEORGE: Listen, May, are you gonna keep talking till Jerry gets here?

MAY: (*Nervously.*) What's Jerry up to, George? Is he going to land us something or isn't he? How much longer are we going to lay around here?

GEORGE: Don't ask me—ask Jerry.

MAY: I'm gonna—and we'll have a showdown to-night. The Automat don't spell home to me.

GEORGE: (*Just a literal boy.*) We don't live there.

MAY: We do everything but sleep there, and we'd be doing that if they could get beds into them slots.

GEORGE: You oughta have patience, May. We've only been here four weeks.

MAY: George, listen. Dumb as you are, you ought to be able to get this: the bank-book says there's just one hundred and twenty-eight dollars left. One hundred and twenty-eight dollars. Get that?

GEORGE: Sure.

MAY: Well, how long do you think three people can live on that, with Jerry going to opening nights and you taking in the world series?

GEORGE: Something'll turn up. It always does. (*And for good luck he cracks another nut.*)

MAY: Well, I'm glad you like those goddam things—you're certainly a lucky fellow. Because the way things are going you may have to live on 'em in another week.

GEORGE: Go on, May—nobody could live on Indian nuts. There isn't enough to 'em. Look—that's all they are. (*He cracks another; exhibits the contents.*)

MAY: All right, George. (*A moment's restless pacing.*) Well, I suppose it's another week of hanging around offices, and another series of those nickel-plated dinners. I'm so sick of the whole business I could yell.

GEORGE: You're just blue, May.

MAY: I wouldn't wonder. Living alone in that hall bedroom—without even the crack of an Indian nut to cheer me up. . . . Well! I wanted to do it, and here I am. I guess it's better than selling ninety-cent perfume to the feminine population of Connellsville, Pa., but there's times when I wish I was back there.

GEORGE: (*Brightly.*) Maybe we'll play there some day.

MAY: (*That's all she needs yet.*) It wouldn't surprise me.

GEORGE: I wonder if we'll ever play Medallion—I haven't been back for four years.

MAY: Has it got an Automat?

GEORGE: I don't think so.

MAY: We'll never play it.

GEORGE: Jerry played it once—that's where he discovered me. He played the theatre I was working in—I was an usher.

MAY: Yah, I remember. Too bad that was pre-Roxy, George— you'd have had a career.

GEORGE: If I'd have stayed I might have been a lieutenant. One of the boys I started with is a major.

MAY: Do you think they'll ever have conscription for ushers?

GEORGE: Then Jerry came along and offered me this job. He said I was just right for it.

MAY: He had a good eye. As far as I'm concerned you're best dead pan feeder in all show business.

GEORGE: Don't the audiences like me, too?

MAY: No one ever gave birth in the aisle, George, but you're all right.

GEORGE: I love doing it, too. The longer we play the act the more I like it.

MAY: (*Suddenly looking at him.*) George, you and Jerry have been bunking together for four years. Isn't Jerry a swell guy?

GEORGE: He's been a wonderful friend to me.

MAY: I wouldn't tell this to him, George, but I'll never forget what I owe Jerry Hyland. (*Quickly.*) And don't you go telling him, either.

GEORGE: I won't tell him. How much do you owe him?

MAY: (*Nearly ready to give up.*) George, please stop eating those things—they're going to your head. I don't mean I owe him any money. But he's never made me feel that we were anything but good friends, or that I'd have to feel any-ways else to keep the job.

GEORGE: (*Not to be outdone.*) He never made me feel anything, either.

MAY: Well, that's just dandy.

GEORGE: Shall I tell you something, May?

MAY: I wish you would.

GEORGE: I think Jerry likes you.

MAY: All right, George.

GEORGE: No—I mean he *really* likes you—a whole lot.

MAY: O.K., George. The question is: What do we do about bookings? Are we going to crash the big time or aren't we?

GEORGE: We were doing all right on the small time. We could be working right along—you know what the Booking Office told us.

MAY: And you know where the Booking Office books us. Bellows Falls, Vermont.

GEORGE: I liked it there.

MAY: What?

GEORGE: We had a good dinner there. With jello.

MAY: Look, George. Don't you want to do anything else all your life but knock about all over the map as a small-time vaudeville actor?

GEORGE: No.

MAY: You don't?

GEORGE: No.

MAY: Well, I guess that settles that, doesn't it? You might as well go ahead and read.

GEORGE: No, I feel like talking now.

MAY: I feel like reading now.

(*At which the door is flung rather violently open and Jerry Hyland enters the room. Jerry Hyland is your idea of the complete bond salesman. Looking like one of those slick Men's Clothing Advertisements in "Vanity Fair," he completes the illusion by talking as if he had just stepped out of the picture. It is almost impossible not to like Jerry immediately, and, if his talent for salesmanship has been submerged by that for second-rate acting, he makes up for it by being the first to tell you what a bum actor he really is and outlining a project to merge Ford and General Motors. Jerry is in the early thirties, and the major part of his late twenties have been spent in concocting one scheme or another to get them out of Vaudeville and into the Big Money. Just at the moment he is laboring under the stress of some tremendous piece of news, and it is a moment or two before he can find the breath to tell them.*)*

MAY: Well, here we are! When do we play the Palace?

GEORGE: Hello, Jerry!

MAY: Or did you settle for the last half in Bridgeport?

JERRY: May, it's here!

MAY: You got bookings?

GEORGE: Is it the Palace?

JERRY: Never mind about that! I've got some news for you! I saw history made to-night!

MAY: What are you talking about?

GEORGE: You saw what?

JERRY: I've just been to the opening of Al Jolson's talking picture, "The Jazz Singer."

MAY: Well, what of it?

JERRY: And I'm telling you it's the greatest thing in all the world!

MAY: There've been good pictures before, Jerry—

JERRY: I'm not talking about the pictures! I mean the Vitaphone!

MAY: The what?

JERRY: The Vitaphone—the talkies!

GEORGE: They talk.

MAY: Oh, that!

JERRY: That! You ought to hear them cheering, May! Everybody went nuts! I tell you, May, it's going to revolutionize the entire industry. It's something so big I bet even the Vitaphone people don't know what they've got yet. You've got to hear it, May, to realize what it means. Why, in six months from now—

MAY: Come out of it, Jerry! What are *you* getting so het up about? It's no money in *your* pocket, even if it *is* good!

GEORGE: No!

JERRY: (*Pretty calmly, for him.*) No? (*He takes in the pair of them.*) Well, we're leaving for Los Angeles in the morning.

MAY: What did you say?

JERRY: We're leaving for Los Angeles in the morning.

GEORGE: (*All he wants are the facts.*) What time?

MAY: Are you out of your mind?

JERRY: Don't you understand, May? For the next six months they won't know which way to turn! All the old standbys are going to find themselves out in the cold, and somebody with brains and sense enough to use them is going to get into the big dough! The movies are back where they were when the De Milles and the Laskys first saw what they were going to amount to! Can't you see what it would mean to get in *now*?

MAY: What do you mean get in, Jerry? What would *we* do there—act, or what?

JERRY: No, no! Acting is small potatoes from now on! You can't tell what we'll do—direct, give orders, tell 'em how to do things! There's no limit to where we can go!

MAY: (*Vaguely groping.*) Yah, but what do we know about—

JERRY: Good Lord, May! We've been doing nothing but playing the act in all the small-time houses in the country. Suppose we *do* cut loose and go out there? What have we got to lose?

GEORGE: A hundred and twenty-eight dollars.

MAY: Shut up, George! I don't know, Jerry—

JERRY: We gotta get out there, May! Before this Broadway bunch climbs on the bandwagon. There's going to be a gold rush, May. There's going to be a trek out to Hollywood that'll make the '49ers look sick.

MAY: Y'mean thar's gold in them hills, Jerry?

JERRY: Gold and a black marble swimming pool, with the Jap chauffeur waiting outside the iron-grilled gate—all that and more, May, if we can work it right and get in *now*! They're panic-stricken out there! They'll fall on the neck of the first guy that seems to know what it's all about! And that's why we gotta get there quick!

MAY: Yah, but give me time to think, Jerry. (*A hand to her head.*) Suppose we don't catch on right away—how are we going to live? You heard what the boy wonder said—a hundred and twenty-eight dollars.

JERRY: (*Exploding the bombshell.*) I've got five hundred more!

MAY: What!

JERRY: I've got five hundred more! Right here!

MAY: Where'd you get it?

JERRY: Now don't yell, May! I sold the act!

MAY: You did what?

JERRY: I sold the act! I took one look at that picture and sold the act outright to Eddie Garvey and the Sherman Sisters for five hundred cash. Now don't get sore, May! It was the only thing to do!

MAY: (*Slowly.*) No, I'm not getting sore, Jerry, but—

GEORGE: (*Coming to life.*) You sold the act to the Sherman Sisters?

JERRY: My God, if people once took a mule and a covered wagon, just because they heard of some mud that looked yellow, and endured hardships and went all the way across the country with their families—fought Indians, even—think what it'll mean, May, if we win out! No more traveling all over the country—living in one place instead of—

MAY: (*Catching some of his excitement.*) Okay, Jerry—I'm with you! You had some helluva nerve, but count me in!

JERRY: Good for you! How about you, George?

GEORGE: What?

JERRY: Are you willing to take a chance with us—leave all this behind and cut loose for Hollywood?

GEORGE: Well, but look—if you sold the act—

JERRY: Sure I sold the act! We're going out and try this new game! Now what do you say?

MAY: Come on, George!

JERRY: It's the chance of a lifetime!

GEORGE: But what'll we do there?

JERRY: We can talk that over on the train! The important thing is to get out there and to get there fast!

GEORGE: But if you've sold the act—

(*Jerry gives up; May leaps into the breach. They are working in relays now.*)

MAY: (*As to a child of ten.*) George, listen. We're giving up the act. We're not going to do the act any more. Don't you understand that?

GEORGE: Yah, but he sold the act—

(*It seems that they sold the act.*)

MAY: I *understand* that he sold the act. Look, George. There is a new invention called talking pictures. In these pictures the actors will not only be seen, but will also talk. For the first time in the history of pictures they will use their voices. (*And in that moment a notion comes to her. Slowly she turns to Jerry.*) I've got an idea.

JERRY: What?

MAY: I think I know what we're going to do out there.

JERRY: Well?

MAY: Most of these bozoes haven't ever talked on a stage! They've never spoken lines before!

JERRY: They gotta learn, that's all!

MAY: You bet they do! And who's going to teach them? We'll open a school of elocution and voice culture!

JERRY: What?

MAY: We'll open a school, Jerry—teach 'em how to talk! They're sure to fall for it, because they'll be scared stiff! We'll have them coming to us instead of our going to them!

JERRY: Yah, but—but *us* with a school, May! We don't know anything about it!

MAY: Maybe *you* don't, but *I* went to one once, and it's easy!

JERRY: But what do you have to do? Can I learn it?

MAY: Sure! Anyhow, I'll do all that!

GEORGE: (*Five minutes behind, as usual.*) *What* are you going to do?

MAY: I tell you it's a natural, Jerry!

JERRY: (*Quieting both of them.*) Shut up a minute, will you? Let me think! Maybe you got hold of something! A school of elocution—it might not be a bad idea.

GEORGE: (*Getting right down to the root of it.*) What's elocution?

MAY: It's a swell idea! And if I know actors, Jerry, they'll come running! Why, between you and I and the lamp-post here— (*She takes in George, and it's really the best notice he's had from her in some time.*) —it's the best idea anybody ever had! How soon we gonna leave?

JERRY: To-morrow! I want you to see the picture first!

MAY: O.K.! Twenty-five of that five hundred goes for books on elocution first thing in the morning! I'll learn this racket or know the reason why!

GEORGE: But what'll *I* do? I don't know anything about elocution!

MAY: George, you don't know anything about anything, and if what they say about the movies is true, you'll go far! (*Swinging to Jerry.*) So help me, Jerry, it'll work out like a charm—you watch if it doesn't! It's coming back to me already—I remember Lesson No. 1.

JERRY: Well, if you're sure you can get away with it, May—

MAY: It's a cinch! Just watch! Come here, George!

GEORGE: What?

MAY: Say "California, here I come."

GEORGE: Huh?

MAY: Don't argue—say it!

GEORGE: "California, here I come."

MAY: Now, then—stomach in, chest out! Wait a minute—

maybe it's the other way around! No, that's right—stomach in, chest out! Now say it again!

GEORGE: (*Better this time.*) "California, here I come."

MAY: (*Working him up to a pitch.*) Now this time with feeling! You are about to start on a great adventure—the covered wagon is slowly moving across the plains to a marble swimming pool!

JERRY: Come on, George—give it everything!

GEORGE: (*With feeling plus.*) "California, here I come."

JERRY: Yay!

MAY: It works, Jerry—it works!

JERRY: And if it works on George it'll work on anybody!

MAY: California, here we come!

CURTAIN

SCENE 2

The corner of a Pullman car, on a train Los Angeles bound. The regulation Pullman, with May, Jerry, and George slumped down in their seats in various attitudes. Jerry is in the middle of his hundredth cross-word puzzle, George is busy with VARIETY *and the inevitable Indian nuts, while May gazes straight ahead, a troubled expression in her eyes. There is a silence, broken only by the cracking of the shells.*

MAY: This dust is about an inch thick on me.

(*There is a pause, and, as usual in any pause, George cracks an Indian nut.*)

George!

GEORGE: Yeah?

MAY: Do those things come without shells on them?

GEORGE: I don't think so. Why?

MAY: A few more days of hearing you crack them and I'll go bugs.

GEORGE: I didn't know they were bothering you, May.

MAY: I was keeping it secret. (*Opens the book on her lap. Reads with venom.*) "To teachers of the culture of the human voice—"

JERRY: (*Busy over his puzzle.*) What's a four-letter word for actor?

MAY: (*She knows that one.*) Dope. (*Reading again.*) "We strongly urge the use of abdominal breathing as a fundamental principle in elocutionary training. This is a very simple operation and the following methods may be used."

(*There enters, pillow in hand, a negro Porter.*)

PORTER: You ready to have your berth made up?

MAY: No!

PORTER: Yes, ma'am.

MAY: All you people know is make up berths. The minute it gets dark you want to make up berths.

PORTER: Lots of time folks wants 'em made up.

MAY: Where are we now—pretty near out of this desert?

PORTER: No'm, I guess we're still in it. Pretty dusty, all right.

MAY: It is, huh?

PORTER: Yes, ma'am, it's dusty, all right. Dust all over. See here? (*He shows her.*)

MAY: Thanks.

PORTER: (*Blandly wiping the dust off on the pillow.*) You welcome. Anything else you want?

MAY: No, that's all, thank you. I just wanted to know if it was dusty.

PORTER: Yes, ma'am, it is.

MAY: I'm ever so much obliged.

PORTER: I guess this your first trip out, ain't it, ma'am?

MAY: How did you know?

PORTER: 'Count of your noticing the dust that way. I've taken out lots of folks—I mean that was going out for the moving pictures, like you folks—and they always notices the dust.

MAY: They do, huh?

PORTER: Yes, ma'am. But coming back they don't generally care so much. (*And having planted this sweet thought he departs.*)

MAY: Did you hear that? Coming back they don't generally care so much.

JERRY: Oh, come out of it, May! If we don't put up a front like a million dollars, we're lost!

MAY: You know how much of a bankroll we've got, Jerry, and how long it's going to last. And this elocution idea—how do we know it's going to work?

JERRY: It's just around the corner, if we keep our nerve! Think what it'll mean, May, if we put it over!

MAY: Well, I mustn't go out there this way—it's aging me. But my God, wouldn't you think the railroad would put a couple of mountains in here somewhere? I'm so sick of looking at wheat and corn—

(*A nut cracks.*)

—and those nuts cracking are beginning to sound like cannons going off.

GEORGE: Why, May—

MAY: Oh—go ahead and crack two at a time and see if I care. I'm going out to the ladies' smoker—maybe I'll hear a good dirty story.

(*She goes. In the distance the train whistle is heard.*)

JERRY: George!

GEORGE: (*Deep in* VARIETY.) Uh-huh.

JERRY: You and I have got to pull May out of this. Y'understand?

GEORGE: Sure.

JERRY: We've got to keep her spirits up—keep telling her we're going to get away with it.

GEORGE: All right.

JERRY: If she starts anything with you, come right back at her. We can't fail. We're pioneers in a new field. The talkies are the thing of the future and there's going to be no stopping them. Got that?

GEORGE: (*Glibly.*) The legitimate stage had better look to its laurels.

JERRY: (*Somewhat bowled over.*) What?

GEORGE: The legitimate stage had better look to its laurels. It's in "Variety."

JERRY: Sure! That's the idea.

GEORGE: Here is a medium that combines the wide scope of the motion picture with the finer qualities of the stage proper. It's an interview with Mr. Katzenstein.

JERRY: Let me see it.

GEORGE: (*Wound up.*) It affords opportunities for entertainment—

JERRY: All right, all right.

(*May returns.*)

MAY: Say, what do you think?

GEORGE: What?

MAY: I just saw somebody I know—anyhow, I *used* to know her.

JERRY: Who is it?

MAY: This may mean something, Jerry—maybe the luck's changing.

JERRY: It's Gloria Swanson and she wants to take lessons.

MAY: Gloria Swanson nothing! It's Helen Hobart!

GEORGE: Helen Hobart! I read her stuff.

MAY: Sure you do, and a million like you. America's foremost movie critic.

GEORGE: And she's on this train?

JERRY: How well do you know her?

MAY: We used to troupe together. I knew her well enough to tell her she was a rotten actress.

JERRY: What'll we do? Can we get her in here?

MAY: We've got nothing to lose.

JERRY: Ring the bell, George!

GEORGE: (*Pressing the buzzer.*) Helen Hobart!

JERRY: Say, if she ever sponsored us we'd have all Hollywood begging to get in. She's a powerful important lady, and don't you forget it.

MAY: I don't know whether she'll remember me or not—I didn't dare stop and say hello. The way I feel to-day I'd break down and cry if anybody ritzed me.

JERRY: (*As the Porter appears.*) There's a woman named Miss Helen Hobart in the next car—

MAY: Talking to a young girl. You page her and tell her Miss May Daniels would like to see her.

PORTER: Yes, ma'am.

MAY: And come right back and tell me what she says.

(*The Porter goes.*)

I'd like to talk to the old battleship again, if only to see her strut her stuff. She's the original iron horse, all right.

JERRY: How long is it since you knew her?

MAY: Plenty. Now listen. If you ever let her know we're just a small-time vaudeville act you'll get the prettiest freeze-out you ever saw. Unless she thinks you're somebody she won't even notice you.

JERRY: Well, what'll we tell her? Let's get together on a story!

MAY: Leave it to me. This is my party.

GEORGE: Don't make up any lies about me.

JERRY: Say, if we could ever get her interested! Her stuff is syndicated all over the country.

GEORGE: It's in two hundred and three newspapers. I was just reading it. (*He produces the paper.*)

MAY: Yah. It's an awful thought, Jerry, but there must be thousands of guys like George reading that stuff every day.

GEORGE: But it's good.

MAY: And thinking it's good, too. (*She takes the paper from George.*) Get this, Jerry. "Hollywood Happenings, by Helen Hobart. Well, movie fans, Wednesday night was just a furore of excitement—the Gold Room at the Stilton just buzzed with the news. But your Helen has managed to get it to you first of all. What do you think? Tina Fair is having her swimming pool done over in egg-shell blue." How do you like that?

GEORGE: Nice color.

JERRY: They've *all* got swimming pools!

MAY: And if I know Helen she lives and acts just like this column of hers. Did I hear that door? I did. (*She has taken a quick peep.*) Here she comes!

(*Making quite an entrance of it, Helen Hobart comes in. Helen is an important figure in The Fourth Largest Industry, and she looks and acts pretty much like an important figure in The Fourth Largest Industry. She positively glitters. Jewels stud her person from the smart diamond arrow in her hat to the buckles of her shoes, and her entire ensemble is the Hollywood idea of next year's style à la Metro-Goldwyn.*)

HELEN: My dear! How perfectly lovely! How nice to think of your being on this train!

MAY: Helen, you look marvelous!

HELEN: Thank you dear, you haven't changed at all.

MAY: Really? I expected living abroad would change me somewhat.

HELEN: What?

MAY: But let me introduce you to my business manager, Mr. Jerome Hyland—

HELEN: How do you do?

MAY: And my technical advisor, Doctor Lewis.

HELEN: How do you do, Doctor?

(*Jerry murmurs an acknowledgment, but George is too stunned to speak.*)

MAY: Please sit down, Helen, and chat awhile.

HELEN: Thanks, I will. There's some little girl back in my car who discovered I was Helen Hobart, and she simply won't let me be. That's why I was so glad to get away. She's been reading my column, and she just can't believe I'm human like herself— (*A modest little laugh.*) —thinks I'm some sort of goddess. If you *knew* how much of that sort of thing I get!

MAY: (*Innocently.*) You're doing some sort of newspaper work, aren't you?

HELEN: (*Amazed.*) My dear—didn't you *know*?

MAY: Don't tell me you're a film actress?

HELEN: (*With measured definiteness—from a great height.*) I write the most widely syndicated column in the United States. Anybody who reads the newspapers—but where on earth have you *been*, my dear, that you haven't heard about *me*?

MAY: I've been living in England for the last eight years, Helen. That's probably why I didn't know. But go on and tell me. I'm frightfully interested.

HELEN: Well—! (*She settles herself—after all, this is quite a chance.*) If you don't *know*, my dear, I can't quite tell you *all*! But I think I can say in all modesty that I am one of the most important figures in the industry. You know, it was I who gave America Gary Cooper and Rex the Wonder Horse. Yes, I've done very well for myself. You know I always *could* write, May, but I never expected to be *the* Helen Hobart! Oh, I can't tell you *everything*, one-two-three, but movie-goers all over the country take my word as law. Of course I earn a perfectly fabulous salary—but I'm hardly allowed to *buy anything*—I'm simply *deluged* with gifts. At Christmas, my dear—well, you'll hardly believe it, but just before I came East they presented me with a home in Beverly Hills!

MAY: (*In spite of herself.*) No kidding!

HELEN: They said I deserved it—that I simply *lived* in the

studios. I always take an interest in new pictures in production, you know, and suggest things to them—and they said that I ought to have a home I could go to and get away from the studios for a while. Wasn't that marvelous?

MAY: Marvelous!

HELEN: I call it Parwarmet. I have a penchant for titles.

MAY: You call it *what*?

HELEN: Parwarmet. You see, I always call my gifts after the people who give them to me—rather a nice thought, you know. And I didn't want to offend anybody in this case, so I called it after the three of them—Paramount, Warner, Metro-Goldwyn—the first syllable of each. Parwarmet.

GEORGE: Won't Fox be sore?

HELEN: Oh, no, Doctor. Because the Fox Studios gave me a wonderful kennel, and I have twelve magnificent dogs, all named after Fox executives. But listen to me rattling on and not asking a word about *you*! Tell me what you've been doing. And what in the world took you abroad for eight years? The last I heard of you—

MAY: (*Quickly.*) Yes, I know. Well, of course, I never expected to stay in the theatre—that is, as an actress. I always felt that I was better equipped to teach.

HELEN: Teach?

MAY: Voice culture. I began with a few private pupils, and then when I was abroad Lady Tree persuaded me to take her on for a while, and from that I drifted into opening a school, and it's been very successful. Of course I accept only the very best people. Mr. Hyland and Dr. Lewis are both associated with me, as I told you—

HELEN: And now you're going to open a school in Hollywood!

MAY: What? Why, no—we hadn't expected—

JERRY: Hollywood? We hadn't thought about it.

HELEN: *Wait* till I tell you! Of course you don't know, but something is happening at the present time that is simply going to revolutionize the entire industry. They've finally perfected *talking pictures*!

MAY: No!

HELEN: Yes! And you can't imagine what it's going to *mean*! But here's the point! Every actor and actress in the industry will have to learn to talk, understand? And if *we* were to open the first school—my dear!

MAY: But Helen, we couldn't *think* of such a thing!

JERRY: Oh, no, Miss Hobart!

GEORGE: Sure! That's why we— (*Jerry silences him.*)

HELEN: I simply won't take No for an answer!

MAY: But what about our school in London?

JERRY: We've got a good deal of money tied up in London, Miss Hobart.

HELEN: May—America needs you. You're still, I hope, a loyal American?

MAY: Oh, yes, yes. But—

HELEN: Then it's settled. This is Fate, May—our meeting— and in the industry Fate is the only thing we bow to.

MAY: But—

HELEN: Now please—not another word! Oh, but this is mar- velous—right at this time! Of course, it'll take a certain amount of money to get started, but I know just the man we'll take it to—Herman Glogauer! You know—the Glo- gauer Studios!

MAY: Well, I'm not sure—

JERRY: Oh, yes, of course!

GEORGE: Yah!

HELEN: I'll send him a telegram right away, and ask for an ap- pointment.

JERRY: That's a good idea! George! (*George presses the buzzer.*)

MAY: Is he important?

HELEN: Oh, my dear!

JERRY: *Is* he important?

GEORGE: You bet!

HELEN: One of the biggest! And he's the man who first turned down the Vitaphone!

MAY: He did?

HELEN: So he buys *everything* now! Why, he just signed that famous playwright—you know, May—that Armenian who writes all those wonderful plays and things.

MAY: Noel Coward.

HELEN: That's right! Of course you people can't realize, but a school of voice culture, opening up at this time—well! I should say my half interest alone would bring me in I just don't know how much! (*It seems that Helen is declaring herself in.*) Because there's absolutely no limit to where the talkies are going—just no limit! Tell me, Doctor—

(*George fails to respond.*)

Doctor—

(*George, spurred on by Jerry, pays attention.*)

What do you think of this marvelous development in the motion pictures? Just what is your opinion?

MAY: (*Trying to save the day.*) Well, the Doctor hasn't had much time—

JERRY: He looks after the scientific end.

GEORGE: (*Coming right through with it.*) I think the legitimate stage had better look to its laurels.

HELEN: My words exactly! Just what I've been saying in my column!

GEORGE: (*Blossoming.*) It combines the wide scope of the motion picture with the finer qualities of the stage proper.

HELEN: That's *very* true. May, you've got a great brain here. (*To George again.*) I *do* want to talk to you sometime, Doctor. I want to discuss voice and body control with you.

GEORGE: It affords opportunities for entertainment—

(*There arrives, at this point, Miss Susan Walker. The first glimpse of Susan makes it obvious that she and George have been "made for each other." Susan Walker, to give you the idea immediately, is the female counterpart of George, very young, very pretty, very charming, and, as you must have guessed by this time, very dumb. She has a number of cute little mannerisms of the sort that intrigue the stronger sex, and a complete and unshakeable belief in her powers as an actress. She flutters about a good deal, and her anxiety not to lose her contact with Helen makes her positively twitter.*)

SUSAN: (*Who is not at all bashful.*) Oh, hello, Miss Hobart! You said you were coming back, and I waited—

HELEN: Yes, dear, but this is very important. I can't talk to you now.

SUSAN: When *can* you talk to me?

HELEN: I'm sure I don't know. Later.

SUSAN: I only want to ask you some questions.

HELEN: I understand, but I'm busy, dear.

SUSAN: Because you could be of such help to me.

HELEN: *Yes*, dear.

GEORGE: (*Who has been showing a growing interest.*) Wouldn't you like to sit down?

SUSAN: Oh, thank you. I—

HELEN: (*Compelled to introduce her.*) This is little Miss—

SUSAN: Susan Walker.

HELEN: Susan Walker. She's the little girl I was telling you about.

GEORGE: (*To Susan.*) Are you going to act in the pictures?

HELEN: She wants to—yes. Tell, me, Doctor—

SUSAN: I'm going to try to, if I can get started. I don't know very much about it.

HELEN: She doesn't know very much about it.

GEORGE: You could go to our school! May!

SUSAN: What?

HELEN: Yes, yes, of course. Now run along, dear, and read the Book of the Month or something. We're very busy.

SUSAN: Well, but you *will* let me talk to you later, won't you?

HELEN: Yes, of course, dear.

SUSAN: Good-bye. (*Her glance sweeps the others; rests timidly on George for a second.*)

GEORGE: Are you right in the next car?

SUSAN: No, I'm in Number 20—with my mother.

HELEN: She's with her mother.

GEORGE: I'll take you back, if you want.

MAY: Yes, you do that, George. That'll be fine.

SUSAN: Oh, thank you very much.

HELEN: You won't stay long, will you Doctor? Because I want to hear more of your ideas. I can see that you've given it thought.

GEORGE: (*Piloting Susan out.*) No, I'll be right—that is, unless— (*He takes refuge in turning to Susan.*) —what's your mother's name? Mrs. Walker? (*They go.*)

HELEN: What a man! He must have been enormous in England!

MAY: Very big! Wasn't he?

JERRY: Yes, indeed!

HELEN: May, *do* you think we can keep him in America?

MAY: Jerry, can we keep him in America?

JERRY: I think we can keep him in America.

MAY: I guess we can keep him in America—

HELEN: Marvelous! How much would it cost, May, to start things going?

JERRY: Fifty thousand!

MAY: A hundred thousand!

HELEN: Oh, that's more like it. Now we get to Hollywood Tuesday! On Wednesday everybody gathers at the Stilton—

(*The falling curtain cuts them off.*)

SCENE 3

The gold room of the Hotel Stilton, in Los Angeles. Early de Mille. Gold-encrusted walls, heavy diamond-cut chandelier, gold brocade hangings and simply impossible settees and chairs. There is an air of such complete phoneyness about the room that an innocent observer, unused to the ways of Hollywood, rather expects a director suddenly to appear from behind a door and yell: "All right, boys! Take it away!"

This particular room, for all its gaudiness, is little more than a passage to the room where Hollywood really congregates—so you can imagine what THAT *is like. The evening's function is approaching its height, and through the room, as the curtain rises, there pass various gorgeous couples—one woman more magnificently dressed than another, all swathed in ermine and so hung with orchids that it's sometimes a little difficult to see the girl. The women, of course, are all stunningly beautiful. They are babbling of this and that phase of Hollywood life as they cross the room— "This new thing, dialogue"—"Why didn't you introduce me to him—I just stood there like a fool"—"It wasn't the right time— I'll take you to him when they're ready to cast the picture." Through it all an unseen orchestra is grinding out "Sonny Boy," and it keeps right on playing "Sonny Boy" all evening. Because it seems there was a man named Jolson.*

Weaving through the guests is a Cigarette Girl—but not just an ordinary cigarette girl. Like every other girl in Hollywood, she is beautiful enough to take your breath away. Moreover, she looks like Greta Garbo, and knows it. Hers is not a mere invitation to buy her wares: on the contrary, her "Cigars! Cigarettes!" is

*charged with emotion. You never can tell, of course, when a di-
rector is going to come along.*

*The Coat Check Girl, certainly the most beautiful girl in the
world, buttonholes the Cigarette Girl as the crowd thins out.*

COAT CHECK GIRL: Say, I got a tip for you, Kate.

CIGARETTE GIRL: Yah?

COAT CHECK GIRL: I was out to Universal to-day—I heard
they was going to do a shipwreck picture.

CIGARETTE GIRL: Not enough sound. They're making it a college picture—glee clubs.

COAT CHECK GIRL: That was this morning. It's French Revolution now.

CIGARETTE GIRL: Yah? There ought to be something in that
for me.

COAT CHECK GIRL: Sure! There's a call out for prostitutes for
Wednesday.

CIGARETTE GIRL: Say, I'm going out there! Remember that
prostitute I did for Paramount?

COAT CHECK GIRL: Yah, but that was silent. This is for talking
prostitutes.

(*She drops into a respectful silence as a great procession enters the room. It is headed by Phyllis Fontaine and Florabel
Leigh, two of filmdom's brightest and most gorgeous lights—
or at least they were until yesterday, when Sound hit the industry. They are dressed to the hilt and beyond it—ermines,
orchids, jewels. Behind each of them walks a Maid, and the
Maids are hardly less beautiful than their mistresses. Next
come a pair of Chauffeurs—tall, handsome men, who were
clearly cut out to be great lovers, and who will be just as soon
as the right director comes along. Each of the Chauffeurs
leads a Russian wolfhound—smartly jacketed animals who
are doing their respective bits to celebrate the fame of their
mistresses. For on one jacket is lettered: "Phyllis Fontaine in
'Diamond Dust and Rouge'," and on the other: "Florabel
Leigh in 'Naked Souls'." All in all, it is an imposing procession. Led by its haughty stars, it advances and prepares for
the Grand Entrance. The maids remove their mistresses' ermine coats; perform those last little powdering rites.*)

MISS LEIGH'S CHAUFFEUR: Is the staircase clear?

COAT CHECK GIRL: Yes, it is.

MISS LEIGH'S CHAUFFEUR: The staircase is clear.

MISS LEIGH'S MAID: The staircase is clear, Miss Leigh.

MISS FONTAINE'S MAID: The staircase is clear, Miss Fontaine.

MISS LEIGH'S MAID: (*Signalling to a Chauffeur.*) Boris, please.

    (*One of the great dogs is passed over to his mistress.*)

MISS FONTAINE'S MAID: (*Repeating the operation.*) Katrina,
    please.

    (*Dogs on leash, they are posed for their moment of triumph.
    As they sweep out of the room you hear their voices for the
    first time. May they be charitably described as Pretty Bad?*)

FLORABEL: (*From the depths of her bower of orchids.*) If they put
    us at that back table I'm going to raise an awful stink.

PHYLLIS: Yes, God damn it, they ought to know by this
    time. . . .

    (*They are gone. There is a moment's relaxation on the part
    of the Other Half.*)

A CHAUFFEUR: You girls working this week?

CIGARETTE GIRL: No, we ain't.

THE OTHER CHAUFFEUR: Universal's doing a college picture.

    (*A Bellboy bounds in.*)

BELLBOY: Say, I hear you boys are all set out at Universal!
    French Revolution picture.

CHAUFFEUR: No, they changed it. It's a college picture.

BELLBOY: It's Revolution again—they just changed it back,
    down in the Men's Room.

CIGARETTE GIRL: Oh, that's good!

BELLBOY: Yah, on account of the sound. They're going to be
    playing the guillotine all through. (*He strums an imaginary
    banjo.*)

MAID: That means I'm out of it. I don't know one note from
    another.

CHAUFFEUR: You can't tell. Let's see what it is in the morning.
    (*The Maids and Chauffeurs are gone.*)

BELLBOY: What do you think happened about five minutes
    ago? I was down in the Men's Room, singing, and Mr.
    Katzenstein came in.

COAT CHECK GIRL: That's a break!

CIGARETTE GIRL: Did he hear you?

BELLBOY: You bet he heard me! Said I had a great voice and told me to come and see him! What do you think of that?

COAT CHECK GIRL: Gosh, I wish he'd come into the ladies' room. (*They go.*)

(*There runs on, in great excitement, Miss Susan Walker. She is followed by her mother.*)

SUSAN: Mother! Come on! Hurry up!

MRS. WALKER: Yes, dear.

SUSAN: This is wonderful here! Look! (*Peers into the next room.*) There's where they're all going to eat!

MRS. WALKER: Yes, dear. Don't over-excite yourself.

SUSAN: But mother, imagine! Practically every big star in Hollywood will be here.

MRS. WALKER: Yes, I know, dear.

SUSAN: This is where they come every Wednesday. They're all over the place now. Look! Can you recognize anyone?

MRS. WALKER: (*Peering.*) Isn't that John Gilbert?

SUSAN: Where? Where?

MRS. WALKER: Over there! Right near that post!

SUSAN: Mother! That's a waiter!

MRS. WALKER: Well, I'm sure I don't know how one is to tell. Every man we see looks more and more like John Gilbert.

SUSAN: Well, we'll see some of the real ones to-night, mother. Dr. Lewis said we're sure to see everyone.

MRS. WALKER: If there's so many people trying to be picture actors, I'm afraid they'll never give *you* a chance.

SUSAN: Oh, but it's different now—

(*And right now John Gilbert himself enters the room. Anyhow it looks like him. It is a careful, measured entrance— obviously designed to impress. With a good deal of deliberation he slowly turns his head, revealing the profile of an Apollo. Susan and her mother are terrifically impressed. At this moment a new couple enter the room—a dashingly handsome couple, of course.*)

THE MAN: (*Chatting as he enters.*) I just saw her downstairs. Wouldn't you think, after the preview of that last picture, that she'd stay home and hide?

THE GIRL: They've no shame, some of them.

THE MAN: (*Sighting the handsome stranger.*) Oh, Ernest!

ERNEST: (*For that is indeed his name.*) Yes, Mr. Weisskopf?

THE MAN: I'm expecting some guests—two gentlemen and a lady. Will you see that they're brought to my table?

ERNEST: (*Bowing much too low for John Gilbert.*) Yes, sir. Very good, sir.

(*The couple continue their stroll as Susan and her mother relax in disappointment.*)

THE GIRL: Who was that man that came over to Diane's table —must have been one of her new ones, eh?

THE MAN: Must have been.

THE GIRL: I give him about three weeks.

(*They go. The late John Gilbert addresses Susan and Mrs. Walker.*)

ERNEST: Anything I can do for you, Madam?

MRS. WALKER: Why, no, I guess not.

SUSAN: Have any of the stars arrived yet?

ERNEST: Very few, Miss. It's only nine-thirty. There are one or two cowboy stars here, but I don't suppose you'd be interested in them.

SUSAN: Oh, no.

MRS. WALKER: I don't like Westerns very much.

ERNEST: Of course no one of any consequence gets here before ten. You get a smattering of First National and Pathé about nine-thirty, but you don't get United Artists until ten-fifteen.

SUSAN: But they'll all *be* here, won't they?

ERNEST: Oh, yes. Everyone who is of any importance in the industry comes here every Wednesday night.

MRS. WALKER: My, you must find it interesting!

ERNEST: Yes, you get *life* out here. In fact, I get most of the ideas for my scenarios right here in the hotel.

SUSAN: Scenarios? Mother, he's a scenario writer!

MRS. WALKER: Really?

ERNEST: (*Modestly.*) I dabble a bit, that's all.

SUSAN: Have you had any produced? Who was in them?

ERNEST: Well, Paramount is dickering for something of mine right now.

MRS. WALKER: It is?

SUSAN: How proud you must feel!

ERNEST: Well, of course, one never knows.

MRS. WALKER: But to have Paramount dickering!

SUSAN: Who is the story for? I hope it's Greta Garbo.

ERNEST: Well, Miss Garbo's all right, but— (*He breaks off, apparently sighting someone in the next room. The women excitedly follow his gaze.*)

SUSAN: Who is it?

ERNEST: I *think*—yes, it is! It's Buddy Rogers!

SUSAN: It is?

MRS. WALKER: Really? Where?

ERNEST: You're very lucky, ladies! Only nine-forty-five and you've got Buddy Rogers!

(*The women rush off, gurgling in their excitement. As Ernest follows them another couple crosses the room, talking as they go.*)

THE MAN: So I said to Katzenstein, "Why don't we buy it? It's the biggest thing in New York to-day—'Strange Interlude.' And look at the name you get! Eugene O'Neill!"

THE GIRL: Well, did he write the music too?

THE MAN: No, he just did the libretto. But if we can get him out here I've got a great guy to team him up with. He's a little Jewish fellow—

(*They are gone. But already another couple is present.*)

THE MAN: What's the use of your meeting him? The part isn't your type. The girl is eighteen years old and a virgin.

THE GIRL: Well, I look eighteen under lights, and I can talk like a virgin.

(*They too depart. On their heels enters George—rather a bewildered George, a good deal impressed by everything that is going on around him. His eyes take in the room. The Cigarette Girl glides on; finding someone present, she at once drops into character.*)

CIGARETTE GIRL: (*In the well-known Garbo manner.*) Will— you—have—some—cigarettes?

GEORGE: (*Scared.*) Why—no. No.

CIGARETTE GIRL: (*And from her tone you gather that George is really the father of her child.*) Very well. I'm—sorry—I— intruded.

(*She goes. George weighs his decision for a moment, then decides that he had better get out of there. Before he can do so, however, Susan rushes in.*)

SUSAN: Hello, George. Isn't it exciting? Seeing all the stars and everything!

GEORGE: I should say so!

SUSAN: I left mother at the staircase, watching them all walk down. Hollywood is even better than I dreamed it would be! Aren't you crazy about it?

GEORGE: It's wonderful, all right. It kinda reminds me of the first time I went to the circus—only there's no elephants.

SUSAN: I can hardly wait till I become a star—when I can do the things they do, and have myself pointed out to tourists.

GEORGE: I'll tell you something, Susan, if you promise not to breathe it. Who do you think we're going to meet here to-night?

SUSAN: Who?

GEORGE: Herman Glogauer, one of the biggest motion picture producers in the country.

SUSAN: Really? Oh, George, will you tell him about me—see if he'll give me a part?

GEORGE: Sure. That's what I'm meeting him for.

SUSAN: Oh, George!

(*Mrs. Walker enters in excitement.*)

MRS. WALKER: Susan, I just saw—

SUSAN: Mother, what do you think? Dr. Lewis is meeting Herman Glogauer here to-night and he's going to tell him all about me!

MRS. WALKER: Well, isn't that fine? A big man like that coming here to talk about Susan!

SUSAN: Where's he going to be? Right here? Will you introduce me to him?

MRS. WALKER: You just leave it to Dr. Lewis, dear.

GEORGE: I think you'd be just great in talkies—the way you recite and everything. I told May all about those poems you recited. Especially that one—what was it?

MRS. WALKER: "Boots"? By Rudyard Kipling?

GEORGE: Yes, that's it.

SUSAN: (*To a pedal accompaniment.*) "Boots, boots, boots, boots, movin' up and down again—Five, seven, nine, eleven, four and twenty miles to-day—"

GEORGE: (*Trying to stop her.*) Yeah, yeah, that's the one. She told me she sort of felt Susan recited "Boots" from the minute she laid eyes on her. Does she do that one about "It Takes a Heap of Loving to—"

SUSAN: "To Make a House a Home"? Oh, yes.

MRS. WALKER: That's one of her best.

GEORGE: Miss Daniels said you probably did. She felt a lot more things about you, too. I guess she's pretty interested.

MRS. WALKER: Would she want to give her an audition?

GEORGE: I don't think she'll have to. I told her how Susan made me feel—when that man in the poem goes crazy how I felt sort of weak myself—and she said she wouldn't want to take a chance.

MRS. WALKER: You've been wonderful to us, Doctor. I'd just trust Susan anywhere with you—I told her to-day I thought you were the most harmless motion picture man in the business.

GEORGE: Say, I'm going to try to live up to that.

(*May comes in. She's followed by Jerry.*)

MAY: Good evening! What's going on here?

MRS. WALKER: Hello, Miss Daniels. Mr. Hyland.

GEORGE: Oh, May! Susan does know that poem, about living in a house or something.

MAY: Sure she does. She knows "Ring Out, Wild Bells," too, don't you, Susan?

MRS. WALKER: That was one of her first ones.

MAY: (*To Jerry.*) That's five you owe me.

JERRY: O.K.

MRS. WALKER: Well, come on, Susan. We'll get on out. We know you're going to meet Mr. Glogauer.

MAY: Oh, did George tell you we're going to meet Mr. Glogauer?

SUSAN: Oh, yes.

JERRY: Isn't that fine?

GEORGE: I just mentioned it.

MRS. WALKER: I think it's just wonderful, what Dr. Lewis has accomplished.

MAY: How's that?

MRS. WALKER: Just wonderful!

SUSAN: Good-bye.

GEORGE: Good-bye.

MAY: Take care of yourselves.

(*Susan and Mrs. Walker go.*)

Jerry!

JERRY: Huh?

MAY: (*A look at George.*) Would there be some way of making him silent as well as dumb?

GEORGE: I didn't hurt anything.

JERRY: (*Peering into the next room.*) Well, kid, here it is! Hollywood! And was I right? Did you hear 'em downstairs? Scared stiff!

MAY: Not nearly as scared as I am.

JERRY: All we got to do is play our cards right! This is the time and place! Chance to make a million or lose a million!

MAY: Which do you think we ought to do?

JERRY: If things go right for us, May, it won't be long now. And we'll do it in style, too.

GEORGE: What do you mean, Jerry—that you and May are going to get married? Are you, May?

MAY: Look, George, we've got all kinds of things on our mind. You'll be the first to know.

JERRY: Yes, sir, it's all up to how we click with Glogauer—and we'll click with him, too!

GEORGE: He's pretty lucky we came out here.

MAY: (*In measured tones.*) George, when Mr. Glogauer gets here and you're introduced to him, just say, "Hello." See? In a pinch, "Hello, Mr. Glogauer." Then from that time on —nothing.

GEORGE: But suppose I have a good idea?

MAY: We'll take a chance on that.

JERRY: Say, Glogauer ought to be getting here. Where's Helen?

MAY: Down talking terms with a couple of hundred movie stars. I was out at Parwarmet to-day. Only twenty-two rooms —just a shack, really.

JERRY: *That* part's all right. She's been damned nice to us.

MAY: Sure. For fifty per cent of the gross she'd be damned nice to Mae West.

(*Outside the door you hear a little crescendo of voices. It is topped by Helen Hobart, bidding her public be patient. She will talk to them all later, the dears. She enters, on the crest of the wave.*)

HELEN: My dear, *everyone* is here to-night! And such excitement! Nobody knows where they're at!

(*There are greetings from the three, which Helen, in her excitement, rides right over.*)

And of course, wherever you turn all you hear is Sound!
Sound! One has to be very careful whom one insults these
days—they may be the very ones to survive!

MAY: Things are pretty well topsy-turvy, aren't they?

HELEN: I should say so! What do you think I just heard? You
know that tremendous spectacle the Schlepkin Brothers are
putting on—"The Old Testament." Well, Mr. Schlepkin—I
mean the oldest of the twelve brothers—the real brains of
the business—he used to have the cloak room privilege in all
the West Coast theatres—he just told me that they've
stopped work on the picture and they're scrapping the
whole thing. They're not going to make anything but talkies
from now on!

JERRY: Big people, the Schlepkins. I'd like to meet them.

MAY: Are they all here to-night?

HELEN: Oh, all twelve of them. That shows you what they
think of the talkies—it's the first time in years that they've all
been in Hollywood at the same time. They generally keep
two with their mother—she lives in Brooklyn and they fly
back and forth. Such a lovely thought! Why, their aeroplane
bill alone is ten thousand dollars a month.

(*The Bellboy enters, followed by two uniformed policemen.*)

HELEN: Oh, Mr. Glogauer must be coming now. Is that for
Mr. Glogauer?

BELLBOY: Yes, Miss Hobart. His car just drew up.

(*They march out.*)

HELEN: They always give him an escort, so he can get through
the lobby. If he says "yes" to our little proposition we can
turn this into a celebration.

MAY: It's marvelous you were able to get him to come.

JERRY: Yes, indeed.

HELEN: Oh, they'll all come running now. Even the big ones.
Besides, Glogauer is scared stiff. He's the man who first
turned down the Vitaphone—I told you.

MAY: Oh, yes.

HELEN: Anyhow, that's the story. Of course, he's never admitted it, and no one's ever *dared* mention it to him.

JERRY: I wouldn't think so.

GEORGE: (*Ever literal.*) What did he turn it down for?

HELEN: He just didn't know, Doctor, what it was going to amount to. He didn't have enough vision.

(*As a young girl enters, pleading.*)

No, dear, not now. Later on, maybe. (*She waves the girl out.*) Someone wanted to meet the Doctor.

GEORGE: What?

HELEN: Oh, I lost no time, Doctor, in telling them about you. Isn't it marvelous, May—

(*From outside the door comes a rising tide of voices, presently mounting into a roar. Fighting its way into the room comes a streaming and screaming mob, which the Bellboy and the Policemen are trying to hold in check. You hear "Mr. Glogauer!" . . . "Mr. Glogauer!" . . . "Mr. Glogauer, can I have just a minute?" And then the voice of Glogauer— "No, no, no! See me at my office! Write me a letter!" The attendants beat back the mob; Glogauer finally disentangles himself.*)

GLOGAUER: I can't see anyone now! Close the doors! Let's have a little peace here!

(*With no difficulty the Bellboy and the two Policemen get the doors closed. Herman Glogauer, who now stands brushing himself off, emerges as a nervous little man who probably has a bad stomach. You can't go through that kind of thing every day without it's having some effect.*)

HELEN: (*As the noise subsides.*) Well, here's the great man himself—and on time, too! Mr. Glogauer, this is Miss Daniels, Mr. Hyland, and Dr. Lewis.

GLOGAUER: How are you?

BELLBOY: (*Who has been biding his time.*) Mr. Glogauer, are you in the market for a great trio?

GLOGAUER: What?

(*For answer the Bellboy and the Policemen burst loudly into "Pale hands I love!"*)

No, no, no! Go away! Go away!

(*They go.*)

MAY: What's all that about?

GLOGAUER: These people!

HELEN: You see, they all know Mr. Glogauer, and they try to show him they can act.

GLOGAUER: It's terrible! Terrible! Everywhere I go, they act at me! Everyone acts at me! If I only go to have my shoes shined, I look down and someone is having a love scene with my pants.

HELEN: That's the penalty of being so big a man.

GLOGAUER: All over the hotel they come at me. Ordinarily I would say, "Let's go out to my house," where we got some peace. But Mrs. Glogauer is having new fountains put in the entrance hall.

HELEN: It's the most gorgeous house, May. You remember— we saw it from the train.

MAY: Oh, yes. With the illuminated dome.

HELEN: And the turrets.

GLOGAUER: In gold leaf.

HELEN: But the *inside*, May! I want you to see his bathroom!

MAY: I can hardly wait.

HELEN: It's the show place of Hollywood! But they can see it some other time—can't they, Mr. Glogauer?

GLOGAUER: Any Wednesday. There is a guide there from two to five. I tell you what you do. Phone my secretary—I send my car for you.

MAY: Why, that'll be wonderful.

HELEN: Yes, and what a car it is! It's a Rolls-Royce!

MAY: You don't say?

GEORGE: What year?

(*It is, to say the least, an awkward moment.*)

JERRY: (*Coming to the rescue.*) Well, Mr. Glogauer, we understand that you're in the midst of quite a revolution out here.

HELEN: I should say he is!

GLOGAUER: Is it a revolution? And who have we got to thank for it. The Schlepkin Brothers. What did they have to go and make pictures talk for? Things were going along fine. You couldn't stop making money—even if you turned out a *good* picture you made money.

JERRY: There is no doubt about it—the entire motion picture is on the verge of a new era.

HELEN: Mr. Glogauer, I tell you the talkies are here to stay.

GEORGE: (*Who knows a cue when he hears one.*) The legitimate stage had better—

MAY: All right, George.

GLOGAUER: Sure, sure! It's colossal! A fellow sings a couple of songs at 'em and everybody goes crazy! Those lucky bums!

HELEN: He means the Schlepkin Brothers.

GLOGAUER: Four times already they were on their last legs and every time they got new ones. Everything comes to those Schlepkin Brothers! This fellow Lou Jackson—sings these mammies or whatever it is—he comes all the way across the country and goes right to the Schlepkin Brothers.

(*The Bellboy enters.*)

BELLBOY: I beg your pardon, Mr. Glogauer?

GLOGAUER: Yes, yes? What is it?

BELLBOY: The twelve Schlepkin Brothers would like to talk to you. They're downstairs.

GLOGAUER: Tell 'em later on. I come down later.

BELLBOY: Yes, sir. (*Goes.*)

GLOGAUER: Schlepkin Brothers! I know what they want! They're sitting on top of the world now—with their Lou Jackson—so they try to gobble up everybody! All my life they been trying to get me! Way back in the fur business already, when I had nickelodeons and they only had penny-lodeons. Always wanting to merge, merge! And because there's twelve of them they want odds yet!

JERRY: But you can teach your own people to talk! Why not let us take them in hand and give them back to you perfect in the use of the English language?

HELEN: I told you about their school in London—Lady Tree!

MAY: It's entirely a matter of correct breathing, Mr. Glogauer. Abdominal respiration is the keynote of elocutionary training.

JERRY: We'll not only teach your people to talk, Mr. Glogauer, but we'll have them talking as well as you do.

GLOGAUER: Well, I don't ask miracles.

(*Again the Bellboy enters.*)

BELLBOY: Mr. Glogauer!

GLOGAUER: Well? Well? What now?

BELLBOY: The Schlepkin Brothers are flying to Brooklyn in half an hour. They say they've got to see you right away.

GLOGAUER: Tell 'em in a minute. And tell Phyllis Fontaine and Florabel Leigh I want to see 'em up here right away. (*To the others.*) Two of my biggest stars. (*To the Bellboy.*) Tell 'em to come up alone—without any of the Schlepkin Brothers.

BELLBOY: Yes, sir. (*Goes.*)

GEORGE: Excuse me—I'll be right back. (*He dashes out.*)

GLOGAUER: Phyllis Fontaine—$7500 a week she draws down. And in the old days she was worth it! Every time she undressed in a picture it was sure-fire!

HELEN: The most beautiful legs in America!

GLOGAUER: But you can't hear 'em! That's just the trouble. They're beautiful girls, but unspeakable. You know what I do now? The biggest stage actress in America I am bringing out—from New York. Ten thousand a week I'm paying her! What's her name, anyhow?

HELEN: Dorothy Dodd.

GLOGAUER: That's it! All day I was trying to remember.
    (*Phyllis and Florabel return.*)

PHYLLIS AND FLORABEL: (*In those awful voices.*) Hello, Hermie!

GLOGAUER: Ah, here we are, girls! This is the ladies I was telling you about. Phyllis Fontaine and Florabel Leigh.

HELEN: Hello, darlings!

FLORABEL: Hello, Helen!

GLOGAUER: Listen, girls—this is Miss Daniels and Mr. Hyland —voice specialists from England.

PHYLLIS: Voice specialists!

FLORABEL: Whaddye know?

GLOGAUER: Well, here they are, Miss Daniels. This is what I'm up against.

MAY: I'd like to listen to their breathing, if I may, Mr. Glogauer.

HELEN: You know, it's all a question of breathing.

JERRY: That's the whole story!

MAY: May I ask if you ladies have ever breathed rhythmically?

PHYLLIS: What?

FLORABEL: Why, not that I know of.

MAY: You see, rhythmic breathing is the basis of all tonal quality.

JERRY: It's the keynote.

MAY: If you are able to breathe rhythmically then there is every reason to believe that you will be able to talk correctly.

HELEN: That's right!

GLOGAUER: Well—what about it? (*To the girls.*) Can you do it?

MAY: (*As the girls look blank.*) If you'll permit me, I think I can tell you.

GLOGAUER: (*Impressed.*) Sure, sure.

(*There is a momentous silence as May goes to Phyllis and puts her head to her chest.*)

MAY: Will you breathe please?

(*She listens a moment; then raises her head. They expect some word; the suspense is terrific.*)

GLOGAUER: Well?

HELEN: Sssh!

(*May passes on to Florabel.*)

MAY: Please breathe.

(*She repeats the operation. Glogauer is on edge.*)

GLOGAUER: (*When it is over.*) Well? How about it?

(*May nods, sagely.*)

GLOGAUER: We got something?

MAY: (*Quietly.*) Absolutely.

HELEN: Isn't that wonderful?

PHYLLIS: We can do it?

GLOGAUER: Keep still, girls! We got something, huh? We ain't licked yet? What's next? What do they do now?

MAY: For the present they should just keep breathing.

GLOGAUER: Hear that, girls? Wait around—don't go home. Now I tell you how we handle this! I give you rooms right in the studio and as fast as you turn 'em out put 'em right to work! We got to work fast, remember?

JERRY: Right!

MAY: Right!

GLOGAUER: You teach these people to talk and it's worth all the money in the world!

JERRY: We'll teach 'em.

GLOGAUER: You people came just at the right time! We'll show 'em—with their Lou Jackson! This is a life saver! To hell with the Schlepkin Brothers!

(*George, breathless, runs back into the room, dragging Susan after him. You begin to understand what he went out for.*)

GEORGE: (*Indicating Glogauer.*) There he is, Susan! Right there!

SUSAN: (*Rushing right up to him and starting in.*) "Boots," by Rudyard Kipling.

GLOGAUER: What?

SUSAN: (*Making the most of her opportunity.*) "Boots, boots, boots, boots—"

GLOGAUER: What? What? I don't want any boots!

SUSAN: "Marchin' up and down again . . ."

(*The Bellboy again returns.*)

BELLBOY: The Schlepkin Brothers!

(*As Susan continues her recitation the Schlepkin Brothers march in. And when the Schlepkin Brothers march in they march in. There are twelve of them—all shapes and sizes. Two abreast, they head for Glogauer.*)

MOE SCHELPKIN: (*At the head of the line.*) Listen, Herman, we're flying back to New York to-night—

GLOGAUER: No, sir! I wouldn't merge! I got something better! I wouldn't merge!

SUSAN: "Five, seven, nine, eleven, four and twenty miles to-day . . ."

THE CURTAIN IS DOWN

ACT TWO

The scene is the reception room at the Glogauer studio, and it may be briefly described as the God-damnedest room you ever saw. Ultra-modernistic in its decor, the room is meant to impress visitors, and it seldom falls short of its purpose. The walls are draped in heavy grey plush, the lighting fixtures are fantastic, and the furniture is nobody's business. It is the sort of room that could happen only as the reception room of a motion picture studio. In addition to a semi-circle of chairs, designed for those who are hopefully waiting, the furniture includes one desk—modernistic as hell, but a desk. It belongs to the reception secretary, who is seated there at the moment, languidly examining this paper and that. She is pretty much like the furniture. She wears a flowing black evening gown, although it is morning, fondles a long string of pearls, and behaves very much like Elinor Glyn.

Also present is Lawrence Vail—a nervous young man who is waiting, none too comfortably, in one of the modernistic chairs. He wears the hunted look of a man who has been waiting for days and days, and is still waiting.

Things are buzzing—the telephone is ringing; an office girl is crossing the room with papers.

MISS LEIGHTON: (*For that is the name of the Reception Secretary.*) Miss Leighton at this end. (*She is answering the 'phone, it might be explained.*)

OFFICE GIRL: (*Putting papers on desk.*) Requisition Department! (*She goes.*)

MISS LEIGHTON: Requisition right!

    (*Two men, named Meterstein and Weisskopf, cross the room.*)

WEISSKOPF: But the important thing is your retakes.

METERSTEIN: That's it—your retakes.

WEISSKOPF: You take your retakes, and if they aren't good you've got no picture.

METERSTEIN: Oh, it's the retakes.

FIRST MAN: Yeh, it's the retakes, all right.

    (*They are gone.*)

MISS LEIGHTON: (*On 'phone through all this.*) I shall have to consult the option department . . . Oh, no, all options are taken care of by the option department . . . That would be Mr. Fleming of the option department . . . Correct! (*Hangs up.*)

> (*There is quiet for a second. Then a Page enters, wearing a simply incredible uniform—all gold braid and tassels. He carries an illuminated sign, on which is lettered:* MR. GLO-GAUER IS ON NUMBER FOUR. *He shows the sign to Miss Leighton, who acknowledges it with a little nod, then to Vail, whose nod is a shade more vicious. A nasty fellow, this Vail. As the Page goes the telephone rings again.*)

MISS LEIGHTON: Miss Leighton at this end . . . Who . . . Oh, yes. Yes, he knows you're waiting . . . How many days? . . . Well, I'm afraid you'll just have to wait . . . What? . . . Oh, no, you couldn't possibly see Mr. Glogauer . . . No, I can't make an appointment for you. Mr. Weisskopf makes all Mr. Glogauer's appointments. . . . Oh, no, you can't see Mr. Weisskopf . . . You can only see Mr. Weisskopf through Mr. Meterstein . . . Oh no, no one *ever* sees Mr. Meterstein. (*She hangs up.*)

> (*Another Page enters with a sign reading:* MR. WEISSKOPF IS ON NUMBER EIGHT. *Clicks his heels in military fashion; Vail must again nod a response.*)
>
> (*A third Page enters, with some papers, which he gives to Miss Leighton.*)

PAGE: Waiting to see Miss Daniels.

MISS LEIGHTON: Miss Daniels is still busy with the ten o'clock class. Take them into Number Six. I will be there in three minutes.

PAGE: Number Six in three minutes. Yes, Miss Leighton. (*He goes.*)

> (*A couple of men come in—Sullivan and Moulton, their names are.*)

SULLIVAN: Get it? She makes believe she's falling for this rich bozo—to save her sister, do you see?—*and the show goes on!* Plenty of spots for numbers in the revue scenes—are they ready for us, sister?

MISS LEIGHTON: Waiting for you, Mr. Sullivan. Number Ten.

SULLIVAN: (*Hardly stopping.*) And the kid sister thinks she's double-crossing her. Of course she sees her kissing this fellow—

(*Another man comes on. The name, if it matters, is Oliver Fulton.*)

FULTON: Hello, boys.

SULLIVAN: Hello, Ollie—you're just in time. They're waiting to hear it.

FULTON: O.K.

SULLIVAN: Wait till I tell you the new twist. She makes believe she's falling for the rich guy—for her sister's sake, get it?

FULTON: And the show goes on! For God's sake, Art, I told you that at lunch yesterday.

SULLIVAN: Did you?

FULTON: I don't mind your stealing from Fox or Metro— that's legitimate—but if we steal our own stuff we'll never know where we are.

(*They go. The 'phone again.*)

MISS LEIGHTON: Miss Leighton at this end . . . No, Miss Daniels is still with the ten o'clock class . . . Oh, no, the lisp and nasal throat toners are at one . . . Didn't you receive the notification? . . . I'll have Miss Daniels' secretary send you one. . . . You're welcome.

(*Another Page. Another sign.*)

(*Miss Leighton finally notices Vail.*)

I beg your pardon, but I forgot whom you're waiting to see.

VAIL: I don't wonder.

MISS LEIGHTON: I beg your pardon?

VAIL: I am waiting to see Mr. Glogauer.

MISS LEIGHTON: Mr. Glogauer is on Number Nine.

VAIL: Napoleon just informed me.

MISS LEIGHTON: How's that?

VAIL: I said Lord Nelson just came in here with a sign.

MISS LEIGHTON: Have you an appointment with Mr. Glogauer?

VAIL: Yes, ma'am—direct. Right through Mr. Meterstein to Mr. Weisskopf to Mr. Glogauer.

MISS LEIGHTON: If you'll give me your name I'll tell Mr. Weisskopf.

VAIL: My name is Lawrence Vail. I gave it to you yesterday, and the day before that, and the day—I would like to see Mr. Glogauer.

MISS LEIGHTON: I'll tell Mr. Weisskopf.

VAIL: I'm ever so much obliged.

MISS LEIGHTON: (*As the 'phone rings again.*) Miss Leighton at this end . . . Yes . . . Yes . . . Very well—holding the line for thirty seconds.

> (*A Page enters with a sign reading:* MR. WEISSKOPF IS ON NUMBER SIX. *Shows it.*)

VAIL: Thank you so much.

FIRST PAGE: You're welcome, sir.

VAIL: Wait a minute. Now I'll give you a piece of news. I'm going to the Men's Room and if anybody wants me I'll be in Number Three.

> (*He goes. So does the Page.*)

MISS LEIGHTON: (*Continuing into telephone.*) Miss Leighton at this end. . . . You will receive yesterday's equipment slips in seven minutes. Kindly have Mr. Weisskopf O.K. them. Thank you. (*Hangs up.*)

> (*Phyllis and Florabel come in.*)

PHYLLIS: (*As she enters.*) . . . by the seashore. She sells sea-shells by the seashore.

FLORABEL: Sixty simple supple sirens, slick and smiling, svelte and suave.

PHYLLIS: Ain't it wonderful, Miss Leighton? We can talk now.

MISS LEIGHTON: Really?

FLORABEL: Yes, and a damn sight better than most of them.

MISS LEIGHTON: I think your progression has been just marvelous. I can't see why they keep bringing people from New York.

FLORABEL: Yeh—people from the "legitimate" stage, whatever that is.

PHYLLIS: Yes, Miss Leighton, we've been wondering about that. What the hell *is* the legitimate stage, anyway?

MISS LEIGHTON: It's what Al Jolson used to be on before he got famous in pictures. He worked for some real estate people—the Shuberts.

FLORABEL: Do you know what someone told me at a party the other day? They said John Barrymore used to be on the legitimate stage.

PHYLLIS: I heard the same thing and I didn't believe it.

MISS LEIGHTON: My, you'd never know it from his acting, would you?

FLORABEL: And that ain't all. I heard that since *he's* made good some sister of his is trying to get out here.

MISS LEIGHTON: Yes, Elsie Barrymore. . . . It must have been kind of interesting, the legitimate stage. Of course, it was before my time, but my grandfather used to go to it. He was in the Civil War, too.

PHYLLIS: The Civil War—didn't D. W. Griffith make that?
   (*May enters.*)

MAY: Got a cigarette, Miss Leighton?

MISS LEIGHTON: Right here, Miss Daniels.

PHYLLIS: Oh, Miss Daniels! I got the seashells.

FLORABEL: And I got the supple sirens.

MAY: Well, that's fine. But I won't be happy till you get the rigor mortis.

PHYLLIS: Oh, that'll be wonderful!

FLORABEL: I can hardly wait!
   (*They go.*)

MISS LEIGHTON: There are some people outside for the ten o'clock class, Miss Daniels. Are you ready for them? They're the stomach muscles and abdominal breathing people.

MAY: You heard the girls' voices just now, Miss Leighton.

MISS LEIGHTON: Yes, Miss Daniels.

MAY: How did they sound to you?

MISS LEIGHTON: Oh, wonderful, Miss Daniels.

MAY: You didn't hear anything about their tests, did you? Whether Mr. Glogauer has seen 'em yet?

MISS LEIGHTON: No, I haven't. But I'm sure they'll be all right.

MAY: Thanks.

MISS LEIGHTON: Miss Daniels, I know you're very busy, but sometime I'd like you to hear me in a little poem I've prepared. "Boots" by Rudyard Kipling.

MAY: (*Smiling weakly.*) Fine. I've never heard "Boots."

MISS LEIGHTON: I've been having some trouble with the sibilant sounds, but my vowels are open all right.

MAY: Any fever?
   (*A Page enters.*)

PAGE: Miss Leighton, please!

MISS LEIGHTON: Excuse me. (*Her eyes sweep the message.*) Oh, dear! Some of the nasal throat toners are out there with the abdominal breathers. What shall I do about it?

MAY: Tell 'em to pick out two good ones and drown the rest.

MISS LEIGHTON: How's that?

MAY: Oh, send 'em in. I'll make one job of it.

MISS LEIGHTON: Yes, ma'am. (*To Page.*) Understand?

(The Page goes.)

(Jerry comes briskly in.)

JERRY: Say, May! (*His watch.*) You've got a class waiting, haven't you?

MAY: I know.

JERRY: Oh, Miss Leighton—Mr. Glogauer busy? I want to see him.

MISS LEIGHTON: Afraid he is, Mr. Hyland.

JERRY: Tell him I've got some figures on the school—just take a minute.

MISS LEIGHTON: I'll tell him. But he has conference after conference all morning. In fact, at 11:57 two of his conferences overlap. I'm so ashamed. (*Goes.*)

JERRY: Well, the old school is working on high, isn't it?

MAY: Jerry, are you busy for lunch?

JERRY: Afraid I am, May. Booked up pretty solid for the next two days.

MAY: Oh, I see.

JERRY: Kinda hard finding time for everything.

MAY: Isn't it, though?

JERRY: This school's a pretty big thing. You don't realize, just with the classes. But the business end keeps a fellow tied down.

MAY: Of course, Jerry. I suppose you're busy to-night?

JERRY: (*Nods.*) Party up at Jack Young's.

MAY: Ah, yes. Still I—I would like to have a little chat with you—sometime.

JERRY: Why? Anything special?

MAY: We haven't really had a talk for—of course, I kinda expected to see you last night—

JERRY: Oh, yes. Sorry about that, May, but I knew you'd understand. Got to trot with the right people out here. I'm meeting everybody, May. I was sorry I had to break that date with you, but—

MAY: Oh, that's all right about the date, Jerry. I wouldn't bother you, but I do think it's kind of important.

JERRY: Why? What's happened?

MAY: Oh, nothing's happened, but—Glogauer was supposed to hear those tests last night, wasn't he?

JERRY: Sure—you mean Leigh and Fontaine?

MAY: Well, what about them? We haven't heard anything yet.

JERRY: How do you mean—you're not nervous, are you? He just hasn't got round to it.

MAY: He was pretty anxious to get 'em—calling up all afternoon.

JERRY: Say! He's probably heard 'em already and buying up stories—that's more like it! Stop worrying, May! We haven't got a thing in the world to worry about. We're sitting pretty. (*Goes.*)

    (*May stands looking after him a moment. She is worrying, just the same. George appears, brightly. He carries a single book.*)

GEORGE: May!

MAY: What is it?

GEORGE: Is it stomach in and chest out or stomach out and chest in or the other way around?

MAY: Huh?

GEORGE: I've got the class all in there with their chests out and now I don't know what to do about it.

MAY: George, are you fooling with that class again?

GEORGE: I was just talking to them till you got ready.

MAY: Look, George. You know that big comfortable chair over in the corner of my office?

GEORGE: You mean the blue one?

MAY: That's right. Will you go and just sit in that, until about Thursday?

GEORGE: Huh?

MAY: You know, I'm only one lesson ahead of that class myself. That's all we need yet—your fine Italian hand.

GEORGE: My what?

MAY: That's all right.

GEORGE: May!

MAY: Yes?

GEORGE: Susan's doing all right in the school, isn't she?

MAY: Sure—great.

GEORGE: She's got a new poem that would be fine for a voice test.

MAY: All right, George.

GEORGE: "Yes, I'm a tramp—what of it? Folks say we ain't no good—"

MAY: Yes, George!

GEORGE: "Once I was strong and handsome—"

MAY: George, will you go on in there?

GEORGE: She does it wonderful, May. Susan's a wonderful girl, don't you think?

MAY: Yes, George.

GEORGE: She's the kind of girl I've always been looking for. And she says *I* am, too.

MAY: George, it isn't serious between you two, is it?

GEORGE: Well, Susan says she won't get married until she's carved out her career.

MAY: Oh, that's all right, then.

GEORGE: She likes me—*that* part of it's all right—but she says look at Eleanora Duse—her career almost ruined by love. Suppose I turned out to be another D'Annunzio?

MAY: She's certainly careful, that girl.

GEORGE: May, now that the school's a success, what about you?

MAY: What?

GEORGE: What about you and Jerry?

MAY: Jerry's a busy man these days, George. We've decided to wait.

GEORGE: Oh!

MAY: Just the minute there's any news, I'll let you know.

GEORGE: Thanks, May.

MAY: Before *you* tell *me*.

GEORGE: It was a wonderful idea of Jerry's—coming out here. I guess you must be pretty proud of him.

MAY: (*Nods.*) I'm working on a laurel wreath for Jerry, evenings.

GEORGE: I won't say anything about it—it'll be a surprise.

MAY: Look, George. Even when Susan has carved out her career —and I want to be there for the carving—you just do a good deal of figuring before you get married. And you come to me before you take any steps. Understand?

GEORGE: Why? I love Susan, May.

MAY: I understand, but of course all kinds of things can happen. You never can tell.

GEORGE: Can happen to Susan, you mean?

MAY: I'll tell you what might happen to Susan. She's going to be reciting "Boots" some day, and a whole crowd of people is going to start moving toward her.

GEORGE: With contracts?

MAY: Well, contracts and—

(*A Page enters.*)

PAGE: There's a lady asking for Miss Susan Walker.

MRS. WALKER: (*Entering on the heels of the Page.*) Oh, Miss Daniels, can Susan get away for a little while? Hello, Doctor! You won't mind if Susan goes away for a little while, will you?

MAY: No, no.

GEORGE: Is anything the matter?

MRS. WALKER: It's nothing to worry about—Susan's father is going to call us up—long distance. Down at the hotel in ten minutes—that really leaves us nine minutes. He sent a telegram and says he wants to talk to us.

GEORGE: Well, I'll get Susan. Will it be all right if I went along with you, while you telephoned?

MRS. WALKER: Why, I'd love to.

GEORGE: You don't care, do you, May?

MAY: No, indeed.

GEORGE: (*Calling.*) Susan! (*He hurries off.*)

MAY: (*About to withdraw.*) I'm awfully sorry, but—

MRS. WALKER: Oh, Miss Daniels! Please don't go! I wonder if I could talk to you about Susan? I mean about how she's getting along in the school?

MAY: (*Hooked.*) Of course.

MRS. WALKER: I've been kind of worried about her lately. You do think she's doing all right?

MAY: Oh, sure. I—ah—I think she's got Garbo licked a dozen ways.

MRS. WALKER: Really, Miss Daniels? What at?

MAY: Oh, pretty near everything. Crocheting—

MRS. WALKER: Oh, I'm so happy to hear you say that, because her father gets so impatient. I've tried to explain to him that it isn't so easy out here, even if you're the kind of an actress Susan is.

MAY: It's even harder if you're the kind of an actress Susan is.

MRS. WALKER: Of course. Then last week I wrote and told him what you said about her—you know—that you thought Technicolor would help? And he said for me to say to you— that you are doing the most courageous work out here since the earthquake. I couldn't understand what he was driving at.

MAY: Thanks. Just tell Mr. Walker for me that the next time I'm in Columbus I want to drop in and shake him by the hand.

MRS. WALKER: Oh, yes, you must come and see us.

(*George and Susan run in.*)

SUSAN: Mother, what does father want?

GEORGE: We've got six minutes!

MRS. WALKER: I don't know, dear. My, we've got to hurry. Six minutes. We mustn't keep Mr. Walker waiting.

GEORGE: What kind of a man is he, Mrs. Walker? Do you know him very well?

(*They are gone. May alone is left. Back comes Vail—a nod to May, who returns it in kind. Immediately Vail sinks into his chair again.*)

MAY: (*Surveying him.*) Isn't there some disease you get from sitting?

VAIL: If there is, I've got it.

MAY: What do you do about your meals—have them sent in?

VAIL: What's the record for these chairs—do you happen to know?

MAY: I'm not sure—I think it was a man named Wentworth. He sat right through Coolidge's administration.

(*A Girl peeps in through one of the doors.*)

GIRL: Oh, Miss Daniels, we're waiting for you.

MAY: What?

GIRL: We're still breathing in here.

MAY: (*Rolling up a sleeve.*) Yah? Well, I'll put a stop to that. (*She goes.*)

(*Vail is alone. He rises; goes to the table and inspects a magazine. He gives it up for another, which he also glances idly through. Takes it back to his seat, drops it onto the chair and sits on it.*)

(*Miss Leighton enters. Sees Vail. It is as though she had never seen him before.*)

MISS LEIGHTON: Yes?

VAIL: Don't you remember me, Princess? I'm the Marathon chair warmer.

MISS LEIGHTON: What is the name, please?

VAIL: Lawrence Vail. I am waiting to see Mr. Glogauer.

MISS LEIGHTON: O, yes. I gave him your name, but he doesn't seem to remember you. What was it about, please?

VAIL: It's about a pain in a strictly localized section.

MISS LEIGHTON: How's that?

> (*Rudolph Kammerling, a German director, enters. He is in a mood.*)

KAMMERLING: Where is Mr. Glogauer, Miss Leighton? Get hold of him for me right away.

MISS LEIGHTON: He's on Number Eight, Mr. Kammerling.

KAMMERLING: I just come from Number Eight—he is not there.

MISS LEIGHTON: Then he must be in conference with the exploitation people, Mr. Kammerling.

KAMMERLING: Maybe he is just through. Try his office.

MISS LEIGHTON: I've just come by there. He isn't in his office.

KAMMERLING: Gott in Himmel, he must be *some* place. Try number eight again.

MISS LEIGHTON: Yes, sir.

KAMMERLING: (*Pacing nervously up and down.*) For two cents I would go back to Germany and Ufa!

MISS LEIGHTON: (*At 'phone.*) Number Eight! Mr. Kammerling calling Mr. Glogauer! Imperative!

KAMMERLING: America! Reinhardt begged me not to come! On his knees in the Schauspielhaus he begged me!

MISS LEIGHTON: Hello? Mr. Glogauer not there? Just a moment. . . . He isn't there, Mr. Kammerling. Any message?

KAMMERLING: (*Beside himself—shouting.*) Yes! Tell them I take the next boat back to Germany! Wait! Who is it on the phone?

MISS LEIGHTON: Mr. Weisskopf.

KAMMERLING: Give it to me! (*Takes the phone; Miss Leighton leaves.*) Hello! This is Kammerling . . . How much publicity is there sent out on Dorothy Dodd? . . . What? . . . We are lost! . . . Why? I tell you why! Because I have just seen her and she is impossible! I will not ruin my American career! . . . (*Hangs up.*) What a country! Oh, to be in Russia with Eisenstein! (*He storms out.*)

(*Two Electricians enter. They carry work kits, and they're
tough specimens.*)

1ST ELECTRICIAN: You take all this studio equipment—they
don't know what they're getting when they buy this stuff.

2ND ELECTRICIAN: They certainly pick up a lot of junk.

1ST ELECTRICIAN: Look at that base plug—torn half way out of
the socket. Socket all wrenched out of shape, too. Haven't
got a new one in your bag, have you?

2ND ELECTRICIAN: Don't think so. Wait a minute. (*He looks
through his tools, whistling as he does so.*) No. Nothing doing.

1ST ELECTRICIAN: No use till we get one—it's all torn out.

(*The other man, while packing up his tools, shakes his head.
Still whistling.*)

Say, what *is* that?

(*The 2nd Electrician whistles a bit further—interrogatively,
as if to inquire if he was referring to the melody.*)

Yah—is it yours?

(*Still whistling, the other man nods.*)

Start it again.

(*He does so; whistles a phrase.*)

I think I got the lyric.

(*He improvises to the other man's whistling.*)

    "By a babbling brook at twilight,
      Once there sat a loving twain—"

2ND ELECTRICIAN: That's great!

1ST ELECTRICIAN: (*Hotly.*) And this one doesn't go to Paramount, after the way they treated us.

(*They go, whistling and singing.*)

(*Miss Leighton enters; notices Vail. As usual, she never saw
him before.*)

MISS LEIGHTON: Yes?

VAIL: (*Ready to commit murder.*) Say it ain't true, Duchess—
say you remember?

MISS LEIGHTON: Oh, yes. An appointment, wasn't it?

VAIL: That's it—an appointment. I got it through a speculator.
Listen, maybe this will help. I work here. I have an office—a
room with my name on the door. It's a big room, see? In
that long hall where the authors work? The people that
write. Authors! It's a room—a room with my name in gold
letters on the door.

MISS LEIGHTON: (*Visibly frightened by all this.*) What was the name again?

VAIL: Lawrence Vail.

MISS LEIGHTON: Oh, you're Lawrence *Vail*. Well, I'll tell Mr. Weisskopf—

VAIL: (*Stopping her.*) No, no! Nothing would come of it. Just let the whole thing drop. Life will go on. Only tell me something—they make talking pictures here, is that right?

MISS LEIGHTON: What?

VAIL: This is a picture studio? They make pictures here—pictures that talk? They do *some*thing here, don't they?

MISS LEIGHTON: (*Edging away.*) I'll tell Mr. Weisskopf—

VAIL: Don't be afraid of me, little girl. I'll not harm you. It's just that I've been in that room—my office—the place with my name on the door—for months and months—nobody ever noticed me—alone in there—the strain of it—it's been too much. And so I came out. I don't expect to see Mr. Glo-gauer any more—I just want to go in and wander around. Because to-morrow I'm going home, and I want to tell them I saw 'em made. Who knows—maybe I'll run into Mr. Glogauer—I'd love to know what God looks like before I die. (*He goes.*)

MISS LEIGHTON: Yes—yes—I'll tell Mr. Weisskopf. (*Sinks into her chair.*)

(*Helen Hobart bustles in.*)

HELEN: Good morning, Miss Leighton!

MISS LEIGHTON: (*Weakly.*) Good morning.

HELEN: My dear, what *is* the matter? You're shaking.

MISS LEIGHTON: There was a drunken man in here just now.

HELEN: You poor child. Well, they'll soon be weeded out— Will Hays is working as fast as he can.

MISS LEIGHTON: Yes, I know.

HELEN: Dorothy Dodd get here, Miss Leighton?

MISS LEIGHTON: Yes, she got in this morning.

HELEN: I do want to meet her. You know, more people have told me I look like her. . . . Tell me, Miss Leighton. My paper wants me to try to find— (*Delving into bag.*) What *is* his name? He works here. (*Finds slip of paper.*) Lawrence Vail.

MISS LEIGHTON: Lawrence Vail? No, I don't think I ever heard of him. Is he a director?

HELEN: No, no, he's a playwright. From New York. He's supposed to have come out here a long time ago and nothing's been heard of him. He seems to have just disappeared.

MISS LEIGHTON: Why, isn't that terrible? Have you tried Paramount?

HELEN: No, he's not at Paramount. They've lost six playwrights of their own in the past month. Once they get out of their rooms nobody knows what becomes of them. You'd think they'd lock the doors, wouldn't you?

MISS LEIGHTON: (*Going to her desk and taking a stack of cards from a drawer.*) Yes—that's what we do. (*Looking through cards.*) Lawrence Vail. I'm sure he isn't one of our playwrights, because if he was I'd be sure to— (*Finds the card.*) —well, isn't that strange? He *is* one of our playwrights. (*Reads.*) "Lawrence Vail."

HELEN: (*Looking over her shoulder.*) That's the man.

MISS LEIGHTON: (*Eyes on card.*) Yes—he came out here on Oct. 18. "From New York City." He was one of a shipment of sixteen playwrights.

HELEN: (*Reading.*) "Dark hair, brown eyes—"
    (*May returns.*)

MAY: Oh, hello, Helen.

HELEN: (*With no warmth whatever.*) May, dear.

MISS LEIGHTON: Suppose I look in the playwrights' room. Maybe he's there.

HELEN: Oh, thanks, Miss Leighton. Shall I come along with you?

MISS LEIGHTON: No, if he's there I'll find him. Though I hate to go into the playwrights' room. It always scares me—those padded walls, and the bars over the windows. (*She goes.*)

HELEN: (*Plainly anxious to slide out.*) My, nearly twelve o'clock! I'd no idea!

MAY: Oh, must you go? You're quite a stranger these days.

HELEN: Yes—the mad, mad pace of Hollywood! I have two luncheons to go to—the Timken Ball Bearing people are having a convention here and it's also the fifth anniversary of Golden Bear cookies.

MAY: Well, if you have just a minute—

HELEN: The cookie people are so prompt—

MAY: I just wondered how you thought everything was going, Helen.

HELEN: Oh, wonderful, wonderful! You know, my column is being translated into Spanish now—they'll be reading it way over in Rome.

MAY: Yes, that's fine. But what I was going to ask you was— have you heard anything about the school lately?—how everybody thinks it's going?

HELEN: (*Evasively.*) Well, of course you'd know more than I do about that—after all, it's *your* enterprise. Naturally I'd be the last person to—

MAY: Then you *have* heard something, haven't you, Helen? Who from—Glogauer?

HELEN: Why, of course not, May—whatever gave you such an idea? Of course you never can tell about things out here— sometimes something will just happen to catch on, and then again—*well!* (*The final "Well!" is a sort of grand dismissal of the subject, coupled with relief at having got that far. She is on the verge of departure.*)

MAY: (*With quiet dignity.*) Thanks, Helen. I'm very grateful.

HELEN: Well, I—ah— (*Turning to her.*) I don't imagine you've made any plans?

MAY: Not yet.

HELEN: After all, I suppose you've got all of your friends in England—it's only natural that—

MAY: Oh, yes. All of them.

HELEN: Well, I may be coming over in the spring—and if I do we must get together.

MAY: By all means.

HELEN: Well! (*She beams on her.*) Bon voyage!

> (*She goes. May stands looking after her. A gentleman named Mr. Flick, carrying various strange boxes, looms in the doorway.*)

FLICK: Pardon me, but can you tell me where I am?

MAY: What?

FLICK: I'm looking for the office of— (*Takes out paper.*) —Miss May Daniels.

MAY: Huh?

FLICK: (*Reading.*) Miss May Daniels, Mr. Jerome Hyland, Dr. George Lewis.

MAY: I'm Miss Daniels. What do you want?

FLICK: Oh, I don't want you. I just want to know where your office is.

MAY: (*A gesture.*) Right through there.

FLICK: Thanks. (*Starts.*)

MAY: You won't find anybody in there.

FLICK: Oh, that's all right. I've only got to do some work on the door.

MAY: Oh! On the door?

FLICK: I just gotta take the names off.

MAY: You mean Daniels, Hyland and Lewis are coming off the door?

FLICK: That's right.

MAY: So that's your business, is it—taking names off doors?

FLICK: Well, I put 'em on too. I do more door work than anybody else in Hollywood. Out at Fox the other day I went right through the studio—every door. Why, some of the people didn't even know they were out till they saw me taking their names off.

MAY: Must have been a nice surprise.

FLICK: Yes, sometimes they leave their office and go out to lunch and by the time they get back it says Chief Engineer.

MAY: We aren't even out to lunch.

FLICK: Well, if you'll excuse me—

MAY: Yes, you've got your work to do. Well, it's been very nice to have met you.

FLICK: Much obliged.

MAY: You're sure you know where it is? Right at the end of the corridor—see?

FLICK: Oh, yes. Miss May Daniels, Mr. Jerome Hyland— (*He is gone.*)

> (*May stands at the door a moment. A few office workers come in and go again—things are pretty busy. And then Jerry. Brisk, businesslike, whistling gayly.*)

MAY: (*Quietly.*) Jerry.

JERRY: Huh?

MAY: Have you got a minute?

JERRY: Gosh, May—afraid I haven't.

MAY: Yes, you have.

JERRY: I've got to see Weisskopf right away.

MAY: No, you don't.

JERRY: What?

MAY: You don't have to see Weisskopf.

JERRY: Yah, but I do.

MAY: No, you don't.

JERRY: What are you talking about?

MAY: (*Very lightly.*) Did you ever hear the story of the three bears?

JERRY: Huh!

MAY: There was the Papa Bear, and the Mama Bear, and the Camembert. They came out to Hollywood to start a voice school—remember? A couple of them were engaged to be married or something—that's right, they were engaged—whatever happened to that?

JERRY: Wha-at?

MAY: Well, anyway, they *did* start a voice school—what do you think of that? They started a voice school, and had a big office, and everything was lovely. And then suddenly they came to work one morning, and where their office had been there was a beautiful fountain instead. And the Mama Bear said to the Papa Bear, What the hell do you know about that?

JERRY: May, stop clowning! What is it?

MAY: And this came as a great big surprise to the Papa Bear, because *he* thought that everything that glittered just *had* to be gold.

JERRY: Say, if you're going to talk in circles—

MAY: All right—I'll stop talking in circles. We're washed up, Jerry.

JERRY: What are you talking about?

MAY: I said we're washed up. Through, finished, and out!

JERRY: What do you mean we're out? Why—who said we were out?

MAY: I knew it myself when we didn't hear about those tests—I felt it. And then ten minutes ago Helen Hobart walked in here.

JERRY: What did she say?

MAY: She handed the school right back to us—it seems she had nothing to do with it. That tells the story!

JERRY: That doesn't mean anything! You can't tell from what she says!

MAY: Oh, you can't, eh? Then I'll show you something that does mean something, and see if you can answer this one! (*She starts for the door through which Mr. Flick has vanished. The arrival of George stops her.*)

GEORGE: May! May, something terrible has happened!

MAY: I know it!

GEORGE: You can't! It's Mr. Walker! Susan has to go back home—they're leaving to-morrow!

JERRY: May, what were you starting to tell me?

GEORGE: Did you hear what I said, May? Susan has got to go back home!

JERRY: Shut up, George! (*To May.*) What were you going to tell me?

MAY: (*Breaking in.*) For God's sake, stop a minute! George, we've got more important things!

GEORGE: There couldn't be more important things!

JERRY: Oh, for the love of—

MAY: Well, there are! We're fired, George—we haven't got jobs any more!

GEORGE: What?

JERRY: How do you know, May? How do you know we're fired?

MAY: I'll show you how I know! (*She goes to the door and opens it. In a trance, they follow her and look off.*)

JERRY: (*In a hushed tone.*) Gosh!

GEORGE: You mean the window washer?

JERRY: (*Stunned.*) Why—why, I was talking to Glogauer only yesterday—

MAY: Well, there you are, Jerry. So you see it's true.

GEORGE: You mean—you mean there isn't any school any more?

MAY: That's the idea, George.

GEORGE: But—but—why? Then—what about Susan?

MAY: Oh, let up on Susan! Besides, I thought you said she was going home.

GEORGE: Yah, but if we could get her a job right away!

(*Mr. Flick returns with scraper and tool-kit in hand. Crosses cheerfully, with a nod to all.*)

MAY: Well, that was quick work.

FLICK: Oh, it don't take long. You see, I never use permanent paint on those doors.

(*A pause after his departure.*)

MAY: Well, I suppose we might as well get our things together. (*She looks at the disconsolate figure of Jerry.*) Don't take it so hard, Jerry. We've been up against it before.

JERRY: But everything was so—I don't know which way to turn, May. It's kind of knocked me all of a heap.

MAY: Don't let it lick you, Jerry—we'll pull out of it some way. We always have.

JERRY: Yah, but—not this. A thing like this sort of—what are we going to do?

MAY: What do you say we go to Hollywood? I hear they're panic-stricken out there. They'll fall on the necks of the first people—

(*They go.*)

(*George is alone. The two studio men, Meterstein and Weisskopf, come in with their interminable chatter.*)

WEISSKOPF: But the important thing is your retakes.

METERSTEIN: That's it—your retakes.

WEISSKOPF: You take your retakes and if they aren't good you've got no picture.

METERSTEIN: Oh, it's the retakes.

WEISSKOPF: Yah, it's the retakes, all right.

(*They go.*)

(*Susan comes in. Pretty low.*)

GEORGE: (*Eagerly.*) Susan! Anything happen? After I left?

SUSAN: (*Forlornly.*) I just came back to get my books and things. (*In his arms.*) Oh, George!

GEORGE: Susan, you can't go back like this—it isn't fair! Why, you were just made for the talkies—you and I both! Did you tell your father we were waiting for Technicolor?

SUSAN: He just said stop being a goddam fool and come on home.

GEORGE: But giving up with your career only half carved!

SUSAN: He wants mother home, too. He says eating all his meals in restaurants that it's ruining his stomach.

GEORGE: But you've got your own life to live—you can't give up your career on account of your father's stomach!

SUSAN: It's no use, George. You don't know father. Why, when the first talking picture came to Columbus he stood up and talked right back to it.

GEORGE: I guess your father's a pretty hard man to get on with.

SUSAN: Oh, you don't know, George. It's going to be terrible, going back to Columbus, after all this.

GEORGE: I'm not going to let you go back, Susan. Something's got to be done about it.

SUSAN: But it's so hopeless, George. (*She leaves him.*)

(*George stands a moment, puzzled. Miss Leighton enters, still carrying the Lawrence Vail card.*)

GEORGE: Could you find Mr. Glogauer for me?

MISS LEIGHTON: Sorry, Doctor—I'm terribly worried. I'm looking for a playwright, and there's a drunken man following me all around.

(*As she goes Lawrence Vail immediately enters. Goes to chair for his coat. George watches him as he brings his magazine back to the table.*)

GEORGE: Excuse me, but have you seen Mr. Glogauer?

(*Vail, his eyes on George, drops the magazine onto the table.*) I've been trying to find him, but nobody knows where he is.

VAIL: You one of the chosen people?

GEORGE: What?

VAIL: Do you work here?

GEORGE: Oh! I thought you meant was I—yah. I'm Dr. Lewis.

VAIL: Oh, yes. About Mr. Glogauer. Tell me something—it won't go any further. Have you ever seen Mr. Glogauer?

GEORGE: Oh, yes. Lots of times.

VAIL: Is that so? Actually seen him, huh? I suppose you've been here a good many years.

GEORGE: (*Shakes his head.*) No. Only about six weeks.

VAIL: Only six weeks. I wouldn't have thought it possible.

GEORGE: Do you work here too?

VAIL: Yes. Yes. You see, Doctor, I'm supposed to be a playwright. Probably it doesn't mean anything to you, but my name is Lawrence Vail. (*George's face is a complete blank.*) It *doesn't* mean anything to you, does it?

GEORGE: No.

VAIL: No, I wouldn't have thought so.

GEORGE: Well, is that what you're doing here—writing plays?

VAIL: Not so far I'm not.

GEORGE: Well then, what are you doing?

VAIL: (*Sadly.*) Don't ask me that. I don't know. I don't know anything about it. I didn't want to come out to this God-forsaken country. I have a beautiful apartment in New York—and friends. But they hounded me, and belabored me, and hammered at me, till you would have thought if I didn't get out here by the fifteenth of October every camera in Hollywood would stop clicking.

GEORGE: You don't say?

VAIL: And so I came. In a moment of weakness I came. That was six months ago. I have an office, and a secretary, and I draw my check every week, but so far no one has taken the slightest notice of me. I haven't received an assignment, I haven't met anybody outside of the girl in the auditor's office who hands me my check, and in short, Dr. Lewis, I haven't done a single thing.

GEORGE: Why do you suppose they were so anxious to have you come out, then?

VAIL: Who knows? Why do you suppose they have these pages dressed the way they are, and those signs, and that woman at the desk, or this room, or a thousand other things?

GEORGE: Don't you like it out here?

VAIL: Dr. Lewis, I think Hollywood and this darling industry of yours is the most God-awful thing I've ever run into. Everybody behaving in the most fantastic fashion—nobody acting like a human being. I'm brought out here, like a hundred others, paid a fat salary—nobody notices me. Not that I might be any good—it's just an indication. Thousands of dollars thrown away every day. Why do they do that, do you know?

GEORGE: No, sir.

VAIL: There you are. Plenty of good minds have come out here. Why aren't they used? Why must everything be dressed up in this goddam hokum—waiting in a room like this, and having those morons thrust a placard under your nose every minute. Why is that?

GEORGE: I don't know.

VAIL: Me neither. The whole business is in the hands of incompetents, that's all. But I don't have to stay here, and I'm not going to. I've tried to see Mr. Glogauer—God knows I've tried to see him. But it can't be done. So just tell him for me that he can take his contract and put it where it will do the most good. I'm going home, and thank you very much for listening to me.

GEORGE: There's a lot in what you say, Mr. Vail. I've been having a good deal of trouble myself.

VAIL: You bet there's a lot in what I say. Only somebody ought to tell it to Glogauer.

GEORGE: That's right. Well, look—why don't you make an appointment with Mr. Glogauer and tell him?

(*It is too much for Vail. He goes.*)

GEORGE: (*George is alone. He thinks it over, then decides that action of some sort has to be taken. He goes to the telephone.*) Hello . . . This is Dr. Lewis . . . Dr. Lewis . . . Well, I work here. That is, I—ah—I've got to get in touch with Mr. Glogauer.

(*Glogauer and Kammerling enter, in the middle of a hot argument. George, of course, hangs up the receiver immediately.*)

GLOGAUER: What can I do about it now? Miss Leighton! Where is Miss Leighton? You know just how we are fixed! What can I do about it at a time like this? You know just who we've got available—what do you want me to do about it?

GEORGE: Mr. Glogauer, could I talk to you for a minute?

KAMMERLING: There is no use of going on! Dorothy Dodd will not do! I will go back to Germany and Ufa before I shoot a foot!

GLOGAUER: (*Into the 'phone.*) Get Miss Leighton for me—right away.

GEORGE: Mr. Glogauer—

GLOGAUER: Do you realize that I brought that woman from New York, took her out of a show, and she's on a play or pay contract for the next three months? Besides, she's got a big legit name! Take her out, he says!

(*George, a little bowled over by the momentum of all this, is between the two fires.*)

KAMMERLING: But I will not have my work ruined! She will be terrible—she is not the type!

GLOGAUER: Then go to work on her! What are you a director for?

KAMMERLING: No, no—she is a good actress, but it is the wrong part. The part is a country girl—a girl from the country!

GLOGAUER: Don't I know that?

KAMMERLING: But Dorothy Dodd is not a country girl! She is a woman—a woman who has lived with a dozen men—and looks it! Can I make her over? I am just a director—not God!

GLOGAUER: But if it was explained to her! How long would it take to explain a country girl?

KAMMERLING: But everyone knows about her—it's been in the newspapers,—every time they break a door down they find *her*!

GLOGAUER: But what am I to do at a time like this?

KAMMERLING: Get somebody else! Somebody that looks it!

GEORGE: Mr. Glogauer—

KAMMERLING: My work would go for nothing! My work would be ruined!

GLOGAUER: Let me get this straight—you mean she *positively* won't do?

KAMMERLING: *Positively.*

GLOGAUER: Well, if it's positively I suppose there's nothing for it.

KAMMERLING: Ah!

GLOGAUER: We got to get somebody then, and quick!

KAMMERLING: Now you're again the artist! Somebody like Janet Gaynor—she would be fine! Maybe Fox would lend her to you!

GEORGE: (*Weakly.*) I know who could do it.

GLOGAUER: Maybe Warners would lend me John Barrymore! Don't talk foolish, Kammerling! I went over our list of people with you and you know just who we've got available.

GEORGE: (*Stronger this time.*) I know somebody could do it.

GLOGAUER: I can't do a magician act—take somebody out of my pocket! You know just who we've got!

GEORGE: (*Making himself heard.*) But I know exactly the person!

GLOGAUER: You what?

GEORGE: (*Excited.*) I know an actress who would fit the part perfectly.

KAMMERLING: Who?

GLOGAUER: What's her name? Who is she?

GEORGE: Her name is Susan Walker.

KAMMERLING: Who?

GLOGAUER: I never heard of her. What's she done?

GEORGE: She hasn't done anything.

GLOGAUER: Hasn't done anything! Taking up our time with a girl—we must have a name! Don't you understand? We must have a name!

GEORGE: Why?

GLOGAUER: What's that?

GEORGE: Why must you have a name?

GLOGAUER: Why must we have—go away, go away! Why must we have a name? I spend three hundred thousand dollars on a picture and he asks me—because Susan Walker as a name wouldn't draw flies—that's why! Not flies!

GEORGE: But she could play the part.

GLOGAUER: So what? Who would come to see her? Why do you argue on such a foolish subject? Everybody knows you can't do a picture without a name. What are you talking about?

GEORGE: (*His big moment.*) Mr. Glogauer, there's something you ought to know.

GLOGAUER: What?

GEORGE: This darling industry of yours is the most God-awful thing I've ever run into.

GLOGAUER: Huh! (*Stares at him.*)

GEORGE: Why don't people act human, anyhow? Why are you so fantastic? Why do you go and bring all these people out here, whoever they are, and give them all this money, and then you don't do anything about it. Thousands of dollars —right under your nose. Why is that?

GLOGAUER: Huh?

GEORGE: Can you tell me why in the world you can't make pictures without having the stars playing parts they don't fit, just because she's got a good name or something? How about a girl that hasn't got a good name? And how about all these signs, and this room, and that girl, and everything? And everything else? It's the most God-awful—all kinds of people have come out here—why don't you do something about it? Why don't you do something about a person like Miss Walker, and give her a chance? Why, she'd be wonderful. The whole business is in the hands of incompetents, that's what's the trouble! Afraid to give anybody a chance! And you turned the Vitaphone down!

(*Glogauer gives him a startled look.*)

Yes, you did! They're all afraid to tell it to you! That's what's the matter with this business. It's in the hands of— you turned the Vitaphone down!

GLOGAUER: (*Stunned; slowly thinking it over.*) By God, he's right!

GEORGE: (*Not expecting this.*) Huh?

GLOGAUER: He's right! And to stand up there and tell me that—that's colossal!

GEORGE: You mean what I said?

GLOGAUER: That's what we need in this business—a man who can come into it, and when he sees mistakes being made, talk out about them. Yes, sir—it's colossal.

GEORGE: (*If it's as easy as that.*) Why, it's the most God-awful thing—

KAMMERLING: Who is this man? Where did he come from?

GLOGAUER: Yes, who are you? Didn't I sign you up or something?

GEORGE: I'm Dr. Lewis.

GLOGAUER: Who?

GEORGE: You know—the school.

GLOGAUER: You are with the school? But that school isn't any good.

GEORGE: (*Moved to an accidental assertiveness.*) It *is* good!

GLOGAUER: Is it?

GEORGE: (*With sudden realization that an emphatic manner can carry the day.*) Why, of course it is. You people go around here turning things down—doing this and that—

GLOGAUER: (*To Kammerling.*) He's right! Look—I pretty near fired him! I did fire him.

GEORGE: You see? And here's Susan Walker—just made for the talkies.

GLOGAUER: Say, who is this girl?

KAMMERLING: Where is she?

GLOGAUER: Tell us about her.

GEORGE: Well—Mr. Kammerling knows her—I introduced her.

GLOGAUER: She's here in Hollywood?

GEORGE: Oh, sure! She just went—

KAMMERLING: I remember! She might be able to do it! She is dumb enough.

GEORGE: Shall I bring her in?

GLOGAUER: Yes, yes—let's see her!

GEORGE: She's right out here. (*Rushing out.*)

GLOGAUER: Fine, fine! There is a big man, Kammerling! I can tell! Suddenly it comes out—that's the way it always is!

KAMMERLING: In Germany, too!

GLOGAUER: Turned the Vitaphone down—no one ever dared say that to me! I got to hang on to this fellow—take options. (*Miss Leighton enters.*)

MISS LEIGHTON: Did you send for me, Mr. Glogauer?

GLOGAUER: Yes! Where's my coffee? I want my coffee!

MISS LEIGHTON: Yes, Mr. Glogauer—where will you have it?

GLOGAUER: Where will I have it? Where *am* I? Answer me that! Where am I?

MISS LEIGHTON: Why—right here, Mr. Glogauer.

GLOGAUER: All right—then that's where I want my coffee.

MISS LEIGHTON: Yes, sir.

GLOGAUER: And tell Meterstein I want him—right away! And Miss Chasen, with her notebook.

MISS LEIGHTON: Yes, sir. (*Goes.*)

GLOGAUER: Now I show you how we handle this! We'll have her and a name too! We'll create a name for her! I've done it before and I do it again!

KAMMERLING: If only she looks like it—

GEORGE: (*Rushes in with Susan.*) Here she is, Mr. Glogauer— here she is!

GLOGAUER: Yes! Yes! She can do it! He's right!

KAMMERLING: Ya, ya! Wunderbar!

GEORGE: Of course I'm right.

KAMMERLING: Say "I love you."

SUSAN: "I love you."

KAMMERLING: Ya! Sie kann es thuen!

GLOGAUER: That's wonderful!

GEORGE: Sure it is!

GLOGAUER: No time to talk salary now, Miss Walker—but you don't have to worry!

SUSAN: Oh, George!

GEORGE: Susan!

KAMMERLING: (*To Susan.*) "I hate you!"

SUSAN: "I hate you!"

KAMMERLING: Ya, ya!

> (*Miss Chasen enters.*)

MISS CHASEN: Yes, Mr. Glogauer?

GLOGAUER: Ah, Miss Chasen! Where Meterstein? I want Meterstein!

> (*Meterstein rushes in.*)

METERSTEIN: Here I am, Mr. Glogauer!

GLOGAUER: Listen to this, Meterstein! Miss Chasen, take this down! Tell the office to drop everything they're doing and concentrate on this! Drop everything, no matter what it is!

MISS CHASEN: (*Over her notes.*) Drop everything.

GLOGAUER: Wire the New York office that Susan Walker, a new English actress we've just signed, will arrive in New York next week— (*A quick aside to George.*) I want her to go to New York first!

GEORGE: Yes, sir.

SUSAN: Does he mean me?

KAMMERLING: Yes, yes!

GLOGAUER: Have them arrange a reception at the Savoy-Plaza—get her pictures in every paper! Tell them I want her photographed with Mayor Walker!

METERSTEIN: Mayor Walker.

GLOGAUER: I want everybody in the studio to get busy on this right away! Everybody! And get hold of Davis for me right away!

MISS CHASEN: Get Davis!

METERSTEIN: (*Calling out the door.*) Get Davis!

VOICE IN THE DISTANCE: Get Davis!

VOICE STILL FURTHER AWAY: Get Davis!

GLOGAUER: Get hold of Photoplay and Motion Picture Magazine and the trade papers—I want them all! Send for Helen Hobart and tell her I want to see her personally! And I want Baker to handle this—not Davis! Don't get Davis!

METERSTEIN: Don't get Davis!

VOICE IN THE DISTANCE: Don't get Davis!

VOICE STILL FURTHER AWAY: Don't get Davis!

GLOGAUER: I want national publicity on this—outdoor advertising, twenty-four sheets, everything! Meterstein, arrange a conference for me with the whole publicity department this afternoon! That's all!

METERSTEIN: Yes, sir. (*Goes.*)

SUSAN: Oh, George! What'll father say now?

GLOGAUER: Miss Chasen, shoot those wires right off!

MISS CHASEN: Yes, sir.

GLOGAUER: I'll be in my office in ten minutes, and no appointments for me for the rest of the day! That clear?

MISS CHASEN: Yes, sir. (*Goes.*)

GLOGAUER: Now then, Doctor, tear up your old contract!

GEORGE: I haven't got one!

GLOGAUER: You are in charge of this whole thing—understand? What you say goes!

GEORGE: Yes, sir.

SUSAN: George, does that mean—

GLOGAUER: When I have faith in a man the sky's the limit! You know what I do with you, Doctor? I make you supervisor in full charge—over all productions of the Glogauer Studio!

SUSAN: George—!

GEORGE: (*Very matter-of-factly.*) All right.

(*May and Jerry enter—Jerry carrying a brief case, May with her hat on, both obviously ready to leave.*)

GEORGE: May! Jerry! What do you think! I've just been made supervisor!

SUSAN: Yes!

JERRY: Huh!

MAY: What!

GEORGE: I told him about the Vitaphone!

MAY: You did what?

GLOGAUER: The one man! (*To George.*) To-morrow morning you get your office—with a full staff!

GEORGE: (*To May and Jerry.*) Hear that?

GLOGAUER: That's the way we do things out here—no time wasted on thinking! I give you all the people you need—anybody you want! All you got to do is say so!

GEORGE: I know who I want, Mr. Glogauer!

GLOGAUER: Already he knows—see, Kammerling?

KAMMERLING: Wonderful!

GLOGAUER: All right! Name 'em—name 'em!

GEORGE: I want Miss Daniels and Mr. Hyland!

JERRY: What is this?

GLOGAUER: What? Those people? (*A deprecatory wave of the hand.*) You don't want them! They're fired!

GEORGE: Mr. Glogauer, I know who I want!

GLOGAUER: But you could have Weisskopf, Meterstein—

GEORGE: No, sir. I have to have Miss Daniels and Mr. Hyland or I can't do anything. And if I can't have them— (*In a very small voice.*) —I walk right out.

SUSAN: George, you mustn't!

MAY: California, here we go!

(*But it doesn't seem to be true. Glogauer fairly throws his arms around George, pleading with him to stay.*)

GLOGAUER: No! No! . . . Miss Daniels! Mr. Hyland!

MISS LEIGHTON: (*Entering, followed by two Pages bearing an enormous silver coffee service.*) Here you are, Mr. Glogauer. (*The phone rings.*) Miss Leighton at this end—

THE CURTAIN IS DOWN.

ACT THREE

A set on the Glogauer lot. The curtain rises on a scene of tremendous but rather vague activity. Set against a background of church wall and stained glass windows, are pews, altar, wedding bell, and all the other paraphernalia that go to make up the filming of a movie wedding. In and out of this, all talking, all shouting, all rushing, weave cameramen, assistant directors, electricians, routine studio workers, and actors. In this particular instance the players are costumed to represent bridesmaids and ushers, and above a hammering and sawing and shouting, bits of: "Hey, Weber—we're taking the truck shot with your camera!" "Use your soft lights for the altar shots, Butch" are heard from the cameramen, etc., and snatches of: "Where are you going, Lily?" "Oh, I don't know—get a soda." "You just had one." "Say, I hear Paramount sent a call out." "What for?" "Dunno—just heard they had a call out," come from the bridesmaids and ushers. Sitting a little apart from the rest of the actors is a gentleman dressed in the gorgeous robes of a Bishop, peacefully snoozing away until it is time to play his part.

It is the last day of shooting on Susan Walker's picture, "Gingham and Orchids," and all these incredible goings-on are nothing more than the usual "getting set" of camera and lights, the usual yelling and the usual standing about, the inevitable waiting that is part and parcel of the whole business of taking pictures.

(*A Page Boy, in the regular studio page uniform, enters, calling for Mr. Meterstein. He arouses, for the first time, The Bishop.*)

THE BISHOP: (*Who is a shade less spiritual than you might expect.*) Oh, Boy! Can you go out and get me a copy of "Racing Form"?

PAGE: I'll try.

LIGHT MAN: Hey, Spike!

BISHOP: Yeh?

LIGHT MAN: What are you playing?

BISHOP: I've got one in the fourth at Caliente, looks good. Princess Fanny.

LIGHT MAN: Whose?

BISHOP: Princess Fanny.

(*A wandering Bridesmaid strolls on.*)

BRIDESMAID: Where the hell's the Bishop? Oh, there you are.

BISHOP: What's up?

BRIDESMAID: Send me up a case of gin, will you—same as last time.

BISHOP: O.K.

(*In the distance a voice is heard: "Oh, Butch! When we get through here we go over on twenty-eight." And hammering and sawing. Endless hammering and sawing.*)

BISHOP: (*Seating himself in a pew.*) You know, these pews are damned comfortable. I should have gone to church long ago.

A BRIDESMAID: Good-night.

BISHOP: There's nothing like a good Simmons pew.

1ST ELECTRICIAN: Hey, Mixer! Mixer!

MIXER: (*In the distance.*) What do you want?

ELECTRICIAN: How are we on sound?

MIXER: O.K.

(*Mrs. Walker bustles on, carrying Susan's bridal bouquet.*)

MRS. WALKER: (*To the Bridesmaids.*) Well, I've just had the most exciting news! Susan's father is coming on for the wedding. Isn't that just too lovely?

A BRIDESMAID: I'm all choked up inside.

MRS. WALKER: He wasn't coming at first—it looked as if he'd have to go to Bermuda with the Elks. You know, the Elks are in Bermuda.

BRIDESMAID: (*To another Bridesmaid.*) The Elks are in Bermuda.

THE OTHER BRIDESMAID: (*Telling still another.*) The Elks are in Bermuda.

NEXT BRIDESMAID: (*Singing it.*) The Elks are in Bermuda.

FINAL BRIDESMAID: (*Singing, of course.*) The farmer's in the dell.

BISHOP: There's a horse named Elk's Tooth running at Tia Juana. I think just on a hunch I'll—

(*Miss Chasen hurries on.*)

MISS CHASEN: Is Dr. Lewis on the set?

(*They tell her he isn't.*)

MRS. WALKER: He's at the architect's.

MISS CHASEN: Well, Mr. Glogauer wants to know the minute he gets here. Will you have somebody let me know?

(*She goes. Kammerling comes on—a great show of activity. The actors leap to their feet. The script girl enters; various actors stroll back onto the set.*)

KAMMERLING: Good morning, everybody! Good morning! Is Dr. Lewis here yet?

MRS. WALKER: He's at the architect's. I'll get Susan for you. (*She dashes off.*)

KAMMERLING: Now listen, everybody! We take first the scene on the church steps—

(*Along comes Jerry—so busy.*)

JERRY: Well, we're on the home stretch, eh?

KAMMERLING: That is right. We do first the retake on the steps.

(*Susan enters in full bridal regalia.*)

SUSAN: Oh. Mr. Kammerling, I'm ready to be shot!

KAMMERLING: Fine! We take the scene on the church steps.

SUSAN: The what?

KAMMERLING: The scene on the church steps.

SUSAN: But I don't think I know that scene.

JERRY: Didn't May rehearse you in that this morning?

SUSAN: No—she didn't.

KAMMERLING: Miss Daniels! Where is Miss Daniels!

VOICE OFF: Miss Daniels on the set!

KAMMERLING: She knew we were going to take it. (*Calling.*) Miss Daniels!

SUSAN: Jerry, did mother tell you—we just had a telegram from father?

JERRY: No. What's up?

THAT BRIDESMAID: He's joined the Elks.

(*May arrives.*)

MAY: Does there seem to be some trouble?

JERRY: May, what about the church steps? Susan says you didn't rehearse her.

MAY: Susan, I know your memory isn't very good, but I want

you to think way back to—Oh, pretty near five minutes ago. We were sitting in your dressing room—remember?—and we rehearsed that scene?

SUSAN: But that isn't the scene he means.

MAY: (*To Kammerling.*) Outside the church, is that right?

KAMMERLING: Yes, yes!

SUSAN: Outside the church— Oh, yes, we did *that*! You said the church steps.

KAMMERLING: That's right! That's right!

MAY: Susan—we feel that it's time you were told this. Outside the church and the church steps are really the same scene.

SUSAN: Are they?

MAY: Yes. In practically all churches now they put the steps on the outside.

SUSAN: Oh, I see.

KAMMERLING: Then are we ready?

MAY: I doubt it. Do you remember the scene as we just rehearsed it, Susan? You remember that you ascend four steps —then turn and wave to the crowd—

SUSAN: Oh, yes— Now I remember! (*She waves her hand—a violent gesture.*)

MAY: No, no—you do not launch a battleship. You see, they'd have to get a lot of water for that.

KAMMERLING: Is it then settled what you are doing?

SUSAN: Well, I think I understand. . . . The steps are outside the church. . . .

A BRIDESMAID: Lily, want to make a date to-night? Those exhibitors are in town again.

LILY: Who?

BRIDESMAID: Those two exhibitors.

LILY: Oh, Mr. Hyland, do you want us to-night?

JERRY: Can't tell till later.

LILY: Well, I've got a chance to go out with an exhibitionist.

(*The crowd is all gone by this time. May and Jerry are alone.*)

JERRY: May, I just came from Glogauer and he's tickled pink.

MAY: He must look lovely.

JERRY: Picture finished right on schedule, advancing the opening date—it's the first time it ever happened!

MAY: Yah.

JERRY: You don't seem very excited about it! Picture opening in three days—and it's going to be a knockout too!

MAY: (*Who has heard all this before.*) Now, Jerry.

JERRY: Well, it is, and I don't care what you think.

MAY: But Jerry, use a little common sense. You've seen the rushes. What's the use of kidding yourself?

JERRY: All right. Everybody's wrong but you.

MAY: I can't help what I see, Jerry. The lighting, for example. Those big scenes where you can't see anything—everybody in shadow—what about those?

JERRY: That's only a few scenes. You know that—George forgot to tell them to turn the lights on, and they thought he meant it that way. Nobody'll notice it.

MAY: All right. But I caught something new yesterday. That knocking that goes on—did you get that?

JERRY: Well, we're trying to find out about that. The sound engineers are working on it.

MAY: Don't you know what that was?

JERRY: No. What?

MAY: That was George cracking his goddam Indian nuts.

JERRY: Is that what it was?

MAY: I suppose nobody's going to notice that, either.

(*There is a great hubbub outside—cries of "Dr. Lewis is coming!" "Here comes the Doctor!" And presently he does come—preceded by a pair of pages bearing a silver coffee service and the inevitable box of Indian nuts, and followed by his secretary and a stream of actors. There come along, too, the three scenario writers—pressing for his attention.*)

GEORGE: Good morning! Good morning! Good morning! (*He sights Susan.*) Good morning, darling. Well, Kammerling? What have I done this morning?

KAMMERLING: We have taken the retake on the church steps.

GEORGE: Well, what have I got to decide?

KAMMERLING: There is only the last scene—the wedding ceremony.

JERRY: Right on schedule.

GEORGE: There's just the one scene left to take?

KAMMERLING: That is all.

GEORGE: (*A snap of the fingers; the decision has been reached.*) We'll take that scene.

KAMMERLING: Everybody on the set, please! Everybody on the set!

GEORGE: I'll decide everything else at two o'clock.

SECRETARY: Yes, sir.

MAY: (*Coming to George.*) Dr. Lewis, I met you in New York. I'm Miss Daniels.

GEORGE: Hello, May.

KAMMERLING: Are we then ready? Ready, Dr. Lewis?

ONE OF THE SCENARIO WRITERS: Dr. Lewis, we left a scenario in your office—

SECRETARY: No answers on scenarios until two o'clock.

GEORGE: That's right.

WRITER: But it's five weeks now.

GEORGE: All right. We'll take the scene from wherever we left off.

KAMMERLING: We will take the end of the wedding ceremony, where we left off! Places, please! We are going to take the end of the wedding ceremony. Everybody in their places.
    (*The wedding party takes its place at the altar.*)

KAMMERLING: (*To the Bishop.*) Oh, Mr. Jackson, have you got this straight?

GEORGE: (*Sternly.*) Get this straight, Mr. Jackson.

BISHOP: What?

GEORGE: (*To Kammerling.*) Yes—what?

KAMMERLING: About the ceremony. You understand that when she says "I do," you release the pigeons.

BISHOP: Oh, sure.

KAMMERLING: They are in that little cottage up there. When Miss Walker says "I do," you pull that ribbon and the pigeons will fly out.

BISHOP: They ain't gonna fly down on me again, are they?

KAMMERLING: No, no, they have been rehearsed.

GEORGE: Those pigeons know what to do. They were with Cecil DeMille for two years.

BISHOP: Oh, that's where I met 'em.

GEORGE: Oh! I forgot! There aren't any pigeons.

KAMMERLING: What?

GEORGE: Well, they had to stay up in there so long, and I felt kinda sorry for them, so I had them sent back to the man.

KAMMERLING: Well, what shall we do?

GEORGE: I know! Let's not have any. That's what we'll do—we won't use them.

KAMMERLING: Very well, Doctor.

MAY: He certainly meets emergencies.

SUSAN: Oh, George! Is that all I say during the entire ceremony—just "I do"?

GEORGE: Is that all she says, May?

MAY: That's all. That's the part she knows, too.

SUSAN: But that's so short.

GEORGE: Yes!

MAY: Well, maybe the ceremony could be rewritten so she could have more to say.

GEORGE: Yes! That's it!

(*In the distance comes the cry that signals the approach of the great. "Mr. Glogauer is coming!" "Mr. Glogauer is coming!" He arrives all bustle and importance. He is followed by one page who carries a portable desk and a telephone, by a second page who brings a small folding chair, and by the ubiquitous Miss Chasen and her notebook. Immediately the Page puts together the desk and plugs in the telephone; Miss Chasen settles herself, and in the twinkling of an eye the place is open for business.*)

GLOGAUER: Well! Here is the happy family!

(*A general greeting.*)

Well, everything going fine, huh?

JERRY: Right on schedule, Mr. Glogauer.

GEORGE: That's what it is.

GLOGAUER: Well, that's wonderful—wonderful. What's going on now?

GEORGE: We're taking the last scene.

GLOGAUER: That's fine—fine! I congratulate everybody.

MISS CHASEN: (*Into the telephone.*) Miss Chasen speaking. Mr. Glogauer is on Number Nine.

GLOGAUER: Tell 'em I'll lay that cornerstone at three fifteen.

MISS CHASEN: Mr. Glogauer will lay that cornerstone at three fifteen.

GLOGAUER: The reason I came down—you don't mind if I interrupt you for a minute for a very special reason?

GEORGE: Why, no.

> (*There is a general movement. Some of the Bridesmaids are about to depart.*)

GLOGAUER: Everybody stay here, please! I want everybody to hear this!

GEORGE: Everybody listen to Mr. Glogauer! Mr. Glogauer is probably going to say something.

KAMMERLING: Attention, everybody!

GLOGAUER: Boys and girls, as you know this is the last day of the shooting. Many of you have worked for me before, but never under such happy circumstances, and so I want you all to be here while I say something. Seventeen years ago—

> (*The Bishop, who is no fool, sits down.*)

—when I went into the movie business, I made up my mind it should be run like a business, as a business, and for a business. And that is what I have tried to do. But never before have I been able to do it until to-day. Never since I started to make Glogauer Super-Jewels has a picture of mine been finished exactly on the schedule. And what is the reason for that? Because now for the first time we have a man who is able to make decisions, and to make them like *that*—Dr. George Lewis.

GEORGE: (*As the applause dies.*) Ladies and Gentlemen—

GLOGAUER: Wait a minute—I am not through yet.

> (*George apologetically steps back.*)

And so in recognition of his remarkable achievement, I take great pleasure in presenting him with a very small token of my regard.

> (*He gives a signal. Immediately Two Men enter, carrying a huge table on which is spread out a golden dinner set— something absolutely staggering. It is met with a chorus of delighted little gasps. Susan scampers down to gurgle over it.*)

A solid gold dinner set, a hundred and six pieces, and with his initials in diamonds on every piece.

MAY: What's the first prize?

> (*There are calls of "Speech," and "Dr. Lewis."*)

GEORGE: Ladies and gentlemen—and Mr. Glogauer—this is the first solid gold dinner set I have ever received. I hardly know what to say, because this is the first solid gold dinner

set I have ever received, and I hardly know what to say. All I
can say is it's wonderful, Mr. Glogauer, and now let's show
Mr. Glogauer the finish of the picture, and take the last scene.

KAMMERLING: (*Pushing the Bridesmaids away.*) All right, all
right! Look at it afterwards!

GLOGAUER: (*As Miss Chasen starts to leave.*) I will address the
new playwrights on Number Eight.

MISS CHASEN: Yes, Mr. Glogauer.

KAMMERLING: Everybody take their places! Mr. Glogauer is
waiting!

GEORGE: Everybody take their places!

LIGHT MAN: Hey, Spike!

BISHOP: Yah?

LIGHT MAN: They're off at Caliente. Fourth race.

BISHOP: O.K. Let me know the minute you hear.

LIGHT MAN: O.K.

KAMMERLING: All right. We are taking the scene now, Mr.
Jackson. Horses come later.

GEORGE: We are taking the scene now, Mr. Glogauer.

GLOGAUER: Fine!

KAMMERLING: Are we lined?
    (*Cameramen assent.*)
Phased?
    (*Another assent.*)
Red light. How are we for sound?

MIXER: (*Through his phone.*) O.K.

KAMMERLING: All right. Are we up to speed?

VOICE: Right.

KAMMERLING: Four bells!
    (*Four bells sound. There is complete silence.*)

VOICE: (*Off.*) Taking on upper stage! Everybody quiet!

KAMMERLING: Hit your lights!
    (*Lights on.*)
Camera!

BISHOP: Cyril Fonsdale, dost thou take this woman to be thy
wedded wife, to live together in the holy state of matri-
mony? Dost thou promise within sacred sight of this altar to
love her, comfort her, honor and keep her in sickness and in
health, and, forsaking all others, keep true only unto her, so
long as ye both shall live?

THE GROOM: I do.

BISHOP: Mildred Martin, dost thou take this man to be thy wedded husband? Dost thou promise to obey him and serve him, love, honor and keep him in sickness and in health, so long as ye both shall live?

SUSAN: I do.

BISHOP: Forasmuch as these two have consented together in holy wedlock, and have witnessed the same before this company and have given and pledged their troth each to the other, I hereby pronounce them man and wife.

(*Susan and The Groom embrace, as camera on truck is moved up for close-up.*)

KAMMERLING: Cut! One bell!

(*One bell sounds. Hammering and sawing instantly spring up all over the place again.*)

LIGHT MAN: Spike! That horse ran sixth.

BISHOP: God damn it! I knew that would happen.

GEORGE: There you are, Mr. Glogauer—embrace, fade-out, the end.

GLOGAUER: I see, I see. Wait a minute—I don't understand. You said what?

GEORGE: Embrace, fade-out, the end.

GLOGAUER: End? You mean you take this scene last. But it's not really the end.

GEORGE: Sure it is. (*To Kammerling and the others.*) Isn't it?

KAMMERLING: Certainly it's the end.

GLOGAUER: But how can it be? What about the backstage scene?

KAMMERLING: What?

GLOGAUER: (*Slightly frenzied.*) On the opening night! Where her mother is dying, and she has to act anyhow!

GEORGE: That wasn't in it, Mr. Glogauer.

KAMMERLING: Why, no.

GLOGAUER: Wasn't in it! I had twelve playwrights working on that.

GEORGE: But it wasn't in it.

GLOGAUER: (*Dangerously calm.*) This is a picture about a little country girl?

GEORGE: Yes, sir.

GLOGAUER: Who gets a job in a Broadway cabaret?

GEORGE: There isn't any Broadway cabaret.

GLOGAUER: No Broadway cabaret?

GEORGE: She doesn't come to New York in this.

GLOGAUER: Doesn't come—you mean the cabaret owner doesn't make her go out with this bootlegger?

GEORGE: Why, no, Mr. Glogauer.

GLOGAUER: Well, what happens to her? What *does* she do?

GEORGE: Why, this rich woman stops off at the farmhouse and she takes her to Florida and dresses her all up.

GLOGAUER: And there is no backstage scene? Any place?

GEORGE: No. She goes out swimming and gets too far out and then Cyril Fonsdale—

GLOGAUER: Let me see that script, please.

GEORGE: It's all there, Mr. Glogauer.

(*Glogauer looks through the script.*)

See? There's where she goes swimming.

GLOGAUER: (*Closing the script with a bang.*) Do you know what you have done, Doctor Lewis? You have made the wrong picture!

(*Consternation, of course.*)

GEORGE: Huh?

KAMMERLING: What is that?

GLOGAUER: That is all you have done! Made the wrong picture?

GEORGE: But—but—

JERRY: Are you sure, Mr. Glogauer?

GLOGAUER: (*Looking at the thing in his hand.*) Where did you get such a script?

GEORGE: Why, it's the one you gave me.

GLOGAUER: I never gave you such a script. She goes swimming! Swimming! Do you know who made this picture? Biograph, in 1910! Florence Lawrence, and Maurice Costello —and even then it was no good!

JERRY: But look, Mr. Glogauer—

GLOGAUER: Sixty thousand dollars I paid for a scenario, and where is it? In swimming!

GEORGE: Well, everybody was here while we were making it.

GLOGAUER: Everybody was here! Where were their minds? Kammerling! Kammerling!

KAMMERLING: It is not my fault. Dr. Lewis gave us the script.

GLOGAUER: I had to bring you all the way from Germany for

this! Miss Newton! You held the script in your hands! Where were your eyes?

MISS NEWTON: I got it from Dr. Lewis—right in his office. I'm sure I couldn't—

GLOGAUER: So, Doctor! On Wednesday night we open and we have *got* to open! And after that it goes to four hundred exhibitors and we got signed contracts! So tell me what to do, please!

GEORGE: Well—well, what do you think we ought to do?

GLOGAUER: Never in my life have I known such a thing! After this I make a ruling—every scenario we produce, somebody has got to read it!

JERRY: Yes, Mr. Glogauer.

GLOGAUER: You know what this does to *you*, Miss Walker! You are through! Swimming! This kills your career! And you know who you got to thank for it? Dr. Lewis!

(*Susan meets the situation by bursting into tears.*)

A fine supervisor! The business is in the hands of incompetents, he says! So what do I do? I give him everything the way he wants it—his own star—his own staff— (*It is a new thought. He fixes May and Jerry with a malignant eye.*) Oh, yes. And where were *you people* while all this was going on?

JERRY: Mr. Glogauer, I was on the cost end. I didn't have anything to do with the script. Dr. Lewis was the—

GLOGAUER: But Miss Daniels was here—all the time! Right with Dr. Lewis! What about *that*?

MAY: (*Not frightened.*) Yes. I was here.

GLOGAUER: Well! Where was your mind?

MAY: To tell you the truth, Mr. Glogauer, I thought it was just another Super-Jewel.

GLOGAUER: Oh, you did?

MAY: I couldn't see any difference.

GLOGAUER: You couldn't, huh?

MAY: And while we're on the subject, Mr. Glogauer, just why is it all Dr. Lewis's fault?

GLOGAUER: Why is it his fault? Who did this thing? Who else is to blame?

MAY: Well, if I'm not too inquisitive, what do *you* do with yourself all the time? Play marbles?

GLOGAUER: What's that?

MAY: Where were *you* while all this was going on? Out to lunch?

GLOGAUER: (*Drawing himself up with dignity.*) I go to my office. That will be all. (*About to say something else, but changes his mind.*) I go to my office. (*Notices the script still in his hand.*) Mr. Supervisor, I make you a present.

GEORGE: (*Weakly, as he takes it.*) Thank you.

GLOGAUER: (*To the company.*) And will you all please understand that nothing about this is to get out of the studio. That is official. Come, Hyland! Seventeen years and this is the worst thing that has ever happened to me!

JERRY: (*Following him.*) Mr. Glogauer, if I'd been on the set this never would have happened. I didn't have anything to do with the script—

(*They are gone.*)

KAMMERLING: (*After a moment's embarrassed pause.*) That is all for to-day. You will be notified.

BISHOP: Well—the wrong picture and the wrong horse!

(*A babble of talk springs up as everyone starts to go. Susan has a fresh outburst of tears.*)

GEORGE: Susan, don't cry like that.

SUSAN: (*Through sobs.*) You heard what Mr. Glogauer said— my career is ruined. I'm—through.

MRS. WALKER: Now, darling, you mustn't take on that way. Everything'll turn out all right.

GEORGE: But, Susan, it wasn't my fault. I didn't know it was the wrong picture.

(*All are now gone except May and Kammerling.*)

KAMMERLING: It is too bad, Miss Daniels.

MAY: Yah. Isn't it?

KAMMERLING: But after all it is the movie business. It is just the same in Germany.

MAY: It is, huh?

KAMMERLING: Even worse. Oh, it is terrible over there. I think I go back.

(*He leaves. Jerry returns, at white heat.*)

JERRY: Well, you fixed everything fine, didn't you? On top of everything else you had to go and get smart!

MAY: It was time somebody got smart, Jerry.

JERRY: Well, you *did* it! And maybe you think Glogauer isn't sore!

MAY: Well, you don't have to worry, do you, Jerry?

JERRY: What?

MAY: (*Very calmly.*) You don't have to worry. You crawled out from under. You gave as pretty an exhibition as *I've* ever seen.

JERRY: What do you mean?

MAY: Oh, nothing. Just the way you stood up for George.

JERRY: Well, somebody's got to keep his feet on the ground around here!

MAY: (*So quietly.*) Yours are all right—aren't they, Jerry? Yah. Right deep in the soil of California!

JERRY: I was trying to fix things up—that's what I was trying to do.

MAY: No, Jerry. No. It's been coming on ever since you got out here, and now it's here. You've gone Hollywood, Jerry. And as far as I'm concerned, that's that.

(*It has been said very quietly, but its very quietness gives it a definiteness. Jerry looks at her; senses that she means it. He turns on his heel and goes.*)

(*May is alone for a moment. Then, in the offing, a man's voice is heard, singing, "I wanna be loved by you-ou-ou, and nobody else but you,—I wanna be kissed by you, a-lone." At the end of the song the singer comes into sight. It is the Bishop. He disappears again.*)

(*George comes back.*)

GEORGE: She wouldn't talk to me, May! Shut the door right in my face and wouldn't talk to me!

MAY: (*Abstracted.*) What?

GEORGE: She just keeps on crying and won't even talk to me.

MAY: That's all right. Everything is all right. It is for me, any-how. Just fine and dandy.

GEORGE: Fine and dandy?

MAY: Just swell.

GEORGE: Susan ought to know I didn't do it on purpose. I tried to tell her. Look, May, do you think the picture's so bad?

MAY: Bad as what, George?

GEORGE: Bad as he thinks it is?

MAY: Well, I think it's got a good chance.

GEORGE: Chance of what, May?

MAY: Of being as bad as he thinks it is.

GEORGE: Oh!

MAY: By the way, George—just to keep the record straight—how'd you come to *make* the wrong picture. Or don't you know?

GEORGE: Well, I've been trying to think. I remember there were a whole lot of scenarios lying on my desk, and I had the right one in my hand, and then suddenly I felt a draft right on my back—and I got up to close the window, and—you know it's awfully hard for me to do two things at once, May—

MAY: (*A wave of the hand that takes in the set.*) So you did this.

GEORGE: You know what I think must have happened, May? I put down the right picture—

MISS CHASEN: (*In the distance.*) Paging Dr. Lewis! Miss Daniels!

MAY: Ah, here we are! Right in here. I thought it was taking a long time.

(*Miss Chasen enters.*)

You're late.

MISS CHASEN: (*Giving her two envelopes.*) Executive office! No answer! (*Turns to go.*)

MAY: Wait a minute. Who else have you got? (*Examining remaining envelopes.*) Kammerling, Weisskopf, Meterstein—Ah, yes.

(*Miss Chasen goes.*)

(*May turns back to George.*) Do you want yours?

GEORGE: Do you mean we're—fired, May?

MAY: Good and fired!

GEORGE: (*In a daze, opening his letter.*) Yah.

MAY: (*Looking at hers.*) Me too. Well, George—we've got a solid gold dinner set, anyway. A hundred and six pieces, and every piece with your initials in diamonds. That's not bad for two months' work.

(*Two Pages enter and carry off the dinner set.*)

No, George—you *haven't* got a solid gold dinner set.

CURTAIN

Scene 2

It is the Pullman car again, and, by a strange coincidence, the same car on which May and her companions went West. But it is May alone who is traveling back East—at all events, she is seated alone when we first behold the car. The Porter enters—and, since it is the same car, it is also the same porter. He is right there with the same question, too.

PORTER: You ready to have your berth made up?

MAY: No, thanks.

PORTER: I been meaning to ask you, Miss Daniels—how's come those two gentlemen ain't going back?

MAY: Well, that's a long story.

PORTER: Yes, ma'am.

MAY: But I wouldn't be surprised if at least one of them was with you pretty soon.
      (*The train whistle blows.*)

PORTER: We makes a two-minute stop here. Anything you want?

MAY: No, thanks. Where are we?

PORTER: We makes a stop at Needle's Point. That's where they got that sanitarium.

MAY: Look—is there a news stand?

PORTER: Yes, ma'am.

MAY: See if you can get hold of Thursday's Los Angeles papers, will you?

PORTER: Yes, ma'am. (*Starts off.*)

MAY: (*Calls after him.*) They've got to be Thursday's or I don't want 'em. (*May is left alone. There is a single blast of the whistle; the lights no longer fly past outside the window. May tries to look out. Then she settles herself again; takes up a book; tries to read; throws it down.*)
      (*The Porter re-enters with luggage.*)

PORTER: Right this way, sir. You need any help? Just a gentleman from the sanitarium.
      (*Lawrence Vail enters. Instantly of course, he recognizes May.*)

MAY: Why, Mr. Vail!

VAIL: Hello, Miss Daniels.

MAY: So you're the gentleman from the sanitarium?

VAIL: That's right. Well, this is a good deal of a surprise!

MAY: Well—please sit down.

VAIL: Thanks. Well!

MAY: You're certainly the last person I—I hadn't heard you were ill. Nothing serious, I hope?

VAIL: (*Shakes his head.*) Just a kind of breakdown. Underwork.

MAY: I can't quite picture that reception room without you.

VAIL: Then I heard about this place—sanitarium here. Sounded pretty good, so I came out. Fellow named Jenkins runs it. Playwright. Seems he came out here under contract, but he couldn't stand the gaff. Went mad in the eighth month. So he started this place. Doesn't take anything but playwrights.

MAY: Good, is it?

VAIL: Great. First three days they put you in a room without a chair in it. Then they have a big art gallery—life-sized portraits of all the studio executives. You see, for an hour every day you go in there and say whatever you want to any picture.

MAY: (*Nods.*) I see.

PORTER: (*Passing through.*) I'll get your papers right now.

VAIL: And now what's all this about? Going home on a visit?

MAY: Well—going home.

VAIL: All washed up?

MAY: Scrubbed.

VAIL: Really? I'm kind of surprised. I never quite got the hang of what you people did out there, but I had the idea you were in pretty solid. Something happen?

MAY: (*Taking a moment.*) Did you ever meet Dr. Lewis?

VAIL: I had quite a talk with Dr. Lewis.

MAY: Well, Dr. Lewis did something that no one had ever done before. He reminded Mr. Glogauer about turning the Vitaphone down. That made him supervisor.

VAIL: Only supervisor?

MAY: And there was also Miss Susan Walker. Miss Walker is a young woman who has a chance of becoming the world's worst actress. I should say a very good chance. She's young yet—has plenty of time.

VAIL: I see.

MAY: With that to start with, the Doctor cinched things by working from the wrong scenario. Some little thing from

1910. The picture opened Wednesday. And how is *your* uncle, Mr. Vail?

VAIL: My recollection of the 1910 pictures is that they weren't so bad.

MAY: They didn't have the Doctor in those days. Most of it you can't see because the Doctor forgot to tell them to turn the lights on; Miss Walker has a set of gestures that would do credit to a travelling derrick—and did you ever happen to hear about the Doctor's bright particular weakness?

VAIL: There's something else?

MAY: It's called Indian nuts. (*A glance around.*) There must be one around here somewhere. Anyhow, he eats them. With sound. He kept cracking them right through the picture, and they recorded swell.

VAIL: That, I take it, decided you?

MAY: That, and—other things.

VAIL: Funny—I should think there would be a great field out there for a man who could turn out the wrong picture.

MAY: Yes, if he could do it regularly. But sooner or later Dr. Lewis would make the right one.

VAIL: Not the Doctor.

MAY: Well, maybe you're right.

PORTER: (*Re-entering with newspapers and a pillow.*) Here your papers, Miss Daniels.

MAY: (*Taking them.*) Thanks.

PORTER: (*To Vail.*) I brought you a pillow.

VAIL: Thank you.
    (*Porter goes.*)

MAY: (*Scanning the date line.*) Yah. These have probably got the notices.

VAIL: (*Reaching for one.*) Oh, you mean the picture?

MAY: It wouldn't surprise me.
    (*They each open a paper. May is in no hurry.*)

VAIL: You're a pretty brave girl, actually sending out for these.

MAY: Well, I might as well know the worst.

VAIL: (*Finding the place.*) Here we are, I guess. "Gingham and Orchids"—that the name of it?

MAY: That's it.

VAIL: (*Scanning the headlines as he folds the paper.*) An all-talking, all-singing—

MAY: All-lousy picture.

(*She takes the paper, Vail meanwhile opening the other one.*)

VAIL: (*As May reads.*) I guess that must be what they mean by a hundred per cent.

(*May's eyes slide quickly down the column, then she looks blankly up at Vail.*)

What is it?

(*May hands the paper over to him, indicating the spot. Vail reads.*)

"Never in the history of Hollywood has so tumultuous an ovation been accorded to any picture—"

MAY: (*Not quite able to speak; indicates a spot further on in the review.*) No. Down there.

VAIL: (*Reads.*) "Herman Glogauer's 'Gingham and Orchids' is a welcome relief from the avalanche of backstage pictures. It marks a turning point in the motion picture industry— a return to the sweet simplicity and tender wistfulness of yesteryear."

MAY: It *does* say that?

VAIL: Indeed it does.

MAY: (*As if in a daze, takes the paper from Vail and reads further.*) "A new star twinkled across the cinema heavens last night and the audience took her at once to its heart. Here at last is an actress who is not afraid to appear awkward and un- graceful." That word is "afraid," isn't it?

VAIL: That's right.

MAY: "In the scene on the church steps, where she waved to the onlookers below, her hands revealed a positively Duse- like quality." I'll tell you about that some day.

VAIL: I'll be there.

MAY: (*Still reading.*) "And here is one wedding, by the way, that sets a new mark for originality and freshness. It does not use pigeons." Remind me about that one, too.

VAIL: I will.

MAY: (*Reads.*) "Then too, the lighting of the picture is superb. Dr. Lewis has wisely seen the value of leaving the climaxes to the imagination of the audience. In the big scenes almost nothing was visible." (*She indicates the other paper.*) I'm afraid I haven't got strength enough to reach for that one.

VAIL: I beg your pardon. (*He changes papers with her.*) The whole thing couldn't be a typographical error, could it?

MAY: (*Looks the new paper quickly over, then looks up at Vail with a weak smile.*) I want you to settle yourself for this.

VAIL: I'm ready.

MAY: Put the pillow right back of you.

VAIL: All right. (*Does so.*)

MAY: "In the opening sequences the audience was puzzled by a constant knocking, and it seemed to many of us that something might be wrong with the sound apparatus. Then suddenly we realized that what was being done was what Eugene O'Neill did with the constant beating of the tom-tom in 'The Emperor Jones.' It was the beat of the hail on the roof." (*She looks up at Vail, who nods.*) "It is another of the masterly touches brought to the picture by that new genius of the films, Dr. George Lewis." (*She lowers the paper, then, as if she cannot quite believe it, raises it and reads again.*) "That new genius of the films, Dr. George Lewis."

(*For a moment, May and Vail merely look at each other. Then Vail leans back, crosses his legs, sighs.*)

VAIL: I hear the boll weevil is getting into the cottoncrop again.

(*The Porter returns.*)

PORTER: Here's a telegram for you, Miss Daniels. Caught us right here at Needle's Point.

MAY: Oh, thanks.

(*The Porter goes.*)

My guess is that this is from that new genius of the films.

VAIL: I wouldn't wonder.

MAY: Oh, yes. (*Reads.*) "The picture is colossal. It has put the movies back where they were ten years ago. I am the Wonder Man of the Talkies. They keep coming at me to decide things. Please take next train back—Jerry is gone and I am all alone here. They have made me an Elk and Susan is an Eastern Star. Please take next train back—I need you. Where is Jerry? I am also a Shriner."

VAIL: Well, what are you going to do about that?

MAY: (*Looking at the telegram.*) "Jerry is gone and I am all alone here." (*Letting the telegram slowly fall.*) Well, it looks as if I'm going back.

VAIL: I think you have to.

MAY: Because if George is alone out there— (*She breaks off.*) And then there's another thing. As long as George owns Hollywood now, there are two or three reforms that I'd like to put into effect. Do you know what I'm going to do?

VAIL: What?

MAY: I'm going to get all those page boys together and take their signs away from them—then nobody will know where anybody is. I'm going to pack up the Schlepkins and send 'em back to Brooklyn, and then I'm going to bring their mother out *here*. I'm going to take Miss Leighton out of that reception room—

VAIL: Put cushions on those chairs—

MAY: And make her ask for an appointment to get back in!

VAIL: Great!

MAY: And when I get that done, I'm going out to Mr. Glogauer's house, put the illuminated dome where the bathroom is, and then I'm going to take the bathroom and drop it into the Pacific Ocean. . . .

THE CURTAIN IS DOWN.

SCENE 3

It is again Mr. Glogauer's reception room, but altered, as you see at first glance, in one vital particular. Over every door, and the room is fairly fringed with doors, there is a sizeable picture of Dr. George Lewis. And that isn't all. The thoughtful Glogauer has so arranged matters that these pictures light up whenever the corresponding door is opened—every last one of them. When there is plenty of dashing in and out—and that is one of the things that there is an abundance of in Mr. Glogauer's place of business— you see a George whose beaming countenance is being constantly ringed with incandescents.

It is a busy place at the moment. Half a dozen people are talking at once, all pressing the great Dr. Lewis about this matter or that. A man at an easel is sketching the Doctor's portrait. There are two or three newspapermen. Miss Newton is there with her eternal scripts. There is a man who wants an indorsement for somebody's neckties, and still another man who seems, believe it or not, to be taking down the Doctor's autobiography. A Page stands waiting with a gold box filled with Indian nuts, and occasionally the Doctor dips a hand in. Presiding over the whole thing is the Doctor's able secretary, who stands with watch in hand and arm upraised, as though about to bring everything to halt at any second.

As for the Doctor, he is pacing busily up and down, and handling all comers.

GEORGE: So far as my plans for Mr. Glogauer are concerned, I can only say that the coming year will be a Glogauer year. And by the time all of our plans have been carried into effect, why, the legitimate stage had better look to its laurels.
　(*Meterstein dashes in.*)
METERSTEIN: They're waiting for you on No. 8, Dr. Lewis!
SECRETARY: Dr. Lewis on No. 8 at three-twenty.
METERSTEIN: Right! (*Dashes out again.*)
PAINTER: Dr. Lewis, will you turn your head just a little this way?
BIOGRAPHER: Dr. Lewis, we were up to Chapter 7. September, 1910.
GEORGE: Oh, yes. My biography. I was still living in Medallion then. I was but a boy, and one day an idea came to me. I decided to be an usher.
TIE MAN: Dr. Lewis, your indorsement will have a hundred thousand men wearing Non-Wrinkable Ties inside of three months.
REPORTER: Dr. Lewis, can I have the rest of that statement?
SECRETARY: (*Watch in hand.*) One minute more, Doctor!
MISS NEWTON: Dr. Lewis, I have to have a decision on these scenarios.
PAINTER: Dr. Lewis, please!
REPORTER: Doctor, it's getting late.
WEISSKOPF: (*Dashing in and out.*) O.K. on those contracts, Doctor!
GEORGE: O.K.
REPORTER: How about a statement from Miss Walker?
GEORGE: Miss Walker is making a personal appearance in San Francisco. She'll be here pretty soon.

SECRETARY: Time! Time's up!

(*Miss Newton goes out as Miss Leighton comes in.*)

MISS LEIGHTON: Dr. Lewis, the Knights of Columbus are downstairs.

SECRETARY: Your time is up, gentlemen! Sorry!

REPORTER: Well, can we see him again later?

PAINTER: I'm only half finished here.

TIE MAN: If I could have just one minute—

SECRETARY: (*Shepherding them out.*) The Doctor has no free time this month. All requests must be submitted in writing.

MISS LEIGHTON: What about the Knights of Columbus, Dr. Lewis? Shall I tell them to come up?

GEORGE: Tell them I'll join later.

MISS LEIGHTON: Yes, sir. (*Goes.*)

GEORGE: Now, where were we?

BIOGRAPHER: You decided to be an usher.

GEORGE: Oh, yes. I became an usher and pretty soon I was put in charge of the last two rows of the mezzanine.

(*Susan enters.*)

GEORGE: Hello, darling! (*Dismissing the others.*) All right, everybody!

SECRETARY: You are due on No. 8 in two minutes, Doctor.

GEORGE: All right.

SECRETARY: The Doctor will start Chapter 8 on Tuesday at twelve-fifteen.

(*They all go out—George and Susan are alone.*)

GEORGE: How was it, Susan?

SUSAN: Oh, wonderful, George! Thousands of people, and arc lights, and my name on top of everything! Oh, it was wonderful, George!

GEORGE: It's been wonderful here, too. I'm up to Chapter 8 in my biography, and there's a man painting my portrait, and— Oh, what do you think? I've got a surprise for you, Susan.

SUSAN: George, what is it? Tell me quick!

GEORGE: Three guesses.

SUSAN: A swimming pool?

GEORGE: No.

SUSAN: Two swimming pools?

GEORGE: It's an aeroplane.

SUSAN: George!

GEORGE: The man gave it to me for nothing. All I had to do was buy a few aeroplanes for Mr. Glogauer.

SUSAN: That's wonderful, George! Just what we needed!

GEORGE: First I was only going to buy a couple, but the man kept talking to me, and it worked out that if I bought a few more I'd get one free.

SUSAN: George, you're so clever! You couldn't have given me a nicer surprise! Isn't everything wonderful, George?

GEORGE: Yes, only I wish May and Jerry would get here. They always know what to do in case things come up.

SUSAN: George, you mustn't worry about it. They got your telegrams.

GEORGE: Yes, but you see, Susan, we've always been together. This is the first time in years I haven't been together, and— did you see my pictures, Susan? They light up! (*He points to one of them, and at that moment it does light up.*) See? (*Through the door comes a pretty annoyed Glogauer, followed by Miss Chasen.*)

GLOGAUER: Dr. Lewis, I want to talk to you. How do you do, Miss Walker? Dr. Lewis, did you order four hundred and sixty aeroplanes?

GEORGE: How's that?

GLOGAUER: Four hundred and sixty aeroplanes have just arrived in front of the studio. They say you ordered them.

GEORGE: (*Uneasily.*) Well, don't you believe in aviation, Mr. Glogauer?

GLOGAUER: The question is, Dr. Lewis; why did you buy four hundred and sixty aeroplanes? (*Enter Miss Leighton.*)

MISS LEIGHTON: Mr. Glogauer! Another hundred aeroplanes just arrived and there's more coming every minute!

GLOGAUER: WHAT?

MISS LEIGHTON: They're arriving in groups of fifty, Mr. Glogauer.

GLOGAUER: What is this, Doctor! Don't tell me you bought *more* than four hundred and sixty aeroplanes!

MISS LEIGHTON: The man from the aeroplane company says the order calls for two thousand!

GLOGAUER: Two thousand!

MISS LEIGHTON: That's what he said!

GLOGAUER: Is this *true*, Doctor? Can such a thing be possible?

GEORGE: Well, the man from the aeroplane company—

GLOGAUER: Two thousand! Two thousand aeroplanes! Where's Meterstein—Weisskopf!

MISS CHASEN: Mr. Weisskopf! Mr. Meterstein!

GLOGAUER: Two thousand aeroplanes! Seventeen years and never in my life—

(*He storms out, followed by the others.*)

MISS LEIGHTON: I told them you weren't in and that you couldn't see anybody.

SUSAN: George, is anything the matter? Shouldn't you have bought the aeroplanes?

GEORGE: (*Bringing up the rear of the procession.*) But Mr. Glogauer, I don't see what you're so angry about! All I did was buy a few aeroplanes!

(*All are gone. A pause; then May enters. She at once becomes conscious of the pictures of George; looks at the lighted picture over the door through which she has entered. Closes the door, then opens and closes it again. Miss Leighton returns.*)

MISS LEIGHTON: Hello, Miss Daniels.

MAY: Hello, Miss Leighton.

MISS LEIGHTON: Have you been away?

MAY: (*Indicating the pictures.*) I see you've got some new decorations.

MISS LEIGHTON: How's that?

MAY: (*Trying another door.*) Is that all they do? No fireworks?

MISS LEIGHTON: Aren't they lovely? Mr. Glogauer had them put up all over the building the day after the picture opened. When Dr. Lewis came into the studio, everything lit up.

MAY: Mr. Glogauer, too?

MISS LEIGHTON: How's that?

MAY: (*A change of manner.*) Miss Leighton—is Mr. Hyland around?

MISS LEIGHTON: Mr. Hyland? Oh, Mr. Hyland isn't with us any more.

MAY: He isn't? Where is he?

MISS LEIGHTON: I don't know, Miss Daniels. I only know he isn't with the company. I think he went back East.

MAY: Went back East? When did he leave, Miss Leighton?

MISS LEIGHTON: Well, I really don't know, Miss Daniels—

MISS CHASEN: (*Entering.*) Miss Leighton, Mr. Glogauer wants his coffee. He's going crazy.

MISS LEIGHTON: But he's had it twice this morning.

MISS CHASEN: He wants it over again—he's raving.

MISS LEIGHTON: Oh, dear. That's the second time this week he's raved.

(*She departs with Miss Chasen. Immediately George sticks his head in; then, seeing May, literally falls on her neck.*)

GEORGE: May!

MAY: Well, if it isn't Dr. Lewis!

GEORGE: Gosh, but I'm glad to see you, May! Did you—did you get my telegrams? I've been wiring you and wiring you!

MAY: Where's Jerry, George?

GEORGE: Why—why, I don't know. Isn't he with *you*, May?— he went to find *you*.

MAY: Went where? When?

GEORGE: Why—why, right after you did. He had a big fight with Mr. Glogauer—he told him all kinds of things—and then he went looking for you, but you were gone already.

MAY: Wait a minute, George. You mean Jerry got fired?

GEORGE: (*Nods.*) He didn't even get a letter.

MAY: Well, where is he now, George? Where did he go? Haven't you heard from him?

GEORGE: I don't know. Look, May, something terrible has happened. I bought a lot of aeroplanes—

MAY: George, where would Jerry be likely to go to? What did he say when he left here?

GEORGE: He didn't say anything, May. He just said he was going to find you and nothing else mattered.

MAY: (*A smile.*) Oh, he didn't say anything, eh? Just that?

GEORGE: He'll come back, May—he'll come back when he knows you're here. But May, what am I going to do about the aeroplanes?

(*He breaks off as Jerry enters. May and Jerry stand looking at each other.*)

Hello, Jerry! Why—here's Jerry now, May!

JERRY: May, you've got to listen to me. You were right. I knew you were right the minute I walked off that set. And I went straight up to Glogauer and told him so.

GEORGE: I told her, Jerry. I told her all about it.

JERRY: And so the answer is—here I am.

GEORGE: Here he is, May. We're all together again.

JERRY: Are we together, May? What about it, May? Are we together?

MAY: (*Landing into him.*) What the hell do you mean by leaving George alone here?

JERRY: Well, I wasn't going to stay here without you!

MAY: Then why didn't you come after me?

JERRY: I did!

MAY: All right, then!

GEORGE: Yes, sir, we're all together again.

(*Suddenly May turns away from them—averts her face.*)

JERRY: What is it, kid—what's the matter?

GEORGE: Why, May!

MAY: (*Coming out of it.*) I'm all right, gentlemen. Let a lady have her moment, for God's sake. It's just that we're together again, I guess. It's seemed so long.

JERRY: May, I can't ever forgive myself—

MAY: Don't, Jerry—you make me feel like a second act climax. Well, from now on it's the Army with Banners, no matter what happens! George is the biggest man in Hollywood and we're riding the high wave!

GEORGE: No, we aren't, May.

MAY: What?

GEORGE: Mr. Glogauer is awful mad. I bought two thousand aeroplanes.

JERRY: You did what?

GEORGE: I bought two thousand aeroplanes.

MAY: What for?

GEORGE: I don't know. The man must have been a salesman.

MAY: Let me get this straight—you bought two thousand aeroplanes?

GEORGE: That's right.

MAY: For Mr. Glogauer?

GEORGE: (*Nods.*) I got one free.

JERRY: What! In God's name, George, what did you do it for?

GEORGE: Can't we do something with them? There ought to be some way to use two thousand aeroplanes!

MAY: Sure—make applesauce!

JERRY: Well, you can't lick that! It's all over but the shouting, May. For God's sake, George, how could you do such a thing?

MAY: Well, there you are, Jerry, and what are you going to do about it?

JERRY: Why did you do it, George?

GEORGE: Well, if somebody offered you an aeroplane—
(*And back comes Mr. Glogauer, followed by Susan and about half the studio force.*)

GLOGAUER: (*Who seems to be beaming.*) Well, Doctor, we have done it again! Isn't it wonderful?

SUSAN: George!

GEORGE: Huh?

GLOGAUER: We've done it again! What a man you are, Doctor—what a man you are!

JERRY: What is this?

GLOGAUER: Miss Daniels! Mr. Hyland! Did you hear what the Doctor did? He went out and bought two thousand aeroplanes! Wasn't that wonderful?

MAY: (*Trying to get her bearings.*) Wonderful!

JERRY: Wonderful!

GLOGAUER: The trend is changing, Miss Daniels—they just been telephoning me! Everybody wants to make aeroplane pictures, but they can't make 'em because the Doctor bought up all the aeroplanes! Every company is phoning me —offering me any amount!

GEORGE: Yes, I thought they would.

SUSAN: Isn't it wonderful?

GLOGAUER: So, Doctor, you saw the trend coming! You saw the trend!

MAY: Saw it? He *is* the trend!

JERRY: You don't realize the kind of man you've got here!

GLOGAUER: Yes, I do! Doctor—this is the way you work— always you make believe you are doing the wrong thing— and *then*! Doctor, I bow to you!

SUSAN: Oh, George!

MAY: George, you don't need us. You just go ahead and be yourself.

GEORGE: Mr. Glogauer, there's something we've got to take up.

GLOGAUER: (*Anxiously.*) What?

GEORGE: (*Pointing to the door through which Glogauer has just entered.*) One of my pictures doesn't light up!

GLOGAUER: (*Greatly upset.*) What! Meterstein! Weisskopf! (*Meterstein and Weisskopf hurry off, to rectify the error.*) Doctor, you're not angry! Tell me you're not angry!

MISS LEIGHTON: (*Entering.*) Mr. Glogauer—

GLOGAUER: Yes?

MISS LEIGHTON: Do you know the studio's being torn down?

GLOGAUER: What?

MISS LEIGHTON: There's a lot of workmen downstairs. They have orders to tear down the studio!

GLOGAUER: Tear down the studio!

MISS LEIGHTON: Yes, sir!

GLOGAUER: (*Looks slowly to George to see if he is the man who gave the order. George wears a broad grin of perfect confidence. He nods. Glogauer turns back to Miss Leighton.*) Tell 'em to go ahead! Tell 'em to go ahead! I don't know what it is, but it'll turn out all right! (*Meterstein and Weisskopf dash in, indicating the relit picture.*)

METERSTEIN: O.K. now, Mr. Glogauer!

GEORGE: We're putting up a bigger one, Mr. Glogauer.

JERRY: Say, that's a good idea!

GLOGAUER: Wonderful! There's another trend coming, eh, Doctor?

GEORGE: Sure, sure!

SUSAN: Isn't he wonderful, May?

MISS LEIGHTON: (*At 'phone.*) Construction department, please.

THE CURTAIN IS DOWN.

OF THEE I SING

A Musical Play
by
George S. Kaufman
and
Morrie Ryskind

Music and Lyrics
by
George and Ira Gershwin

THE SCENES

ACT I

SCENE 1: *Any city in America—with a political parade in progress. The marchers, with their torchlights and banners, move against a shadowy background of skyscrapers, churches, and— almost certainly—speakeasies. Across this background is flung a huge election banner, on which are gargantuan reproductions of the faces of the party's candidates. Highlit and prominent is the party battlecry:*

FOR PRESIDENT: JOHN P. WINTERGREEN

The name of the vice-presidential candidate, however, is lost in shadow. As for the countenances of the candidates, it is a little hard to pick them out in the general blur, and the chances are that that's a break for the party.

The procession shambles across the scene, singing as it goes. The song is a combination of all the campaign tunes of the past, into most of which the recurrent phrase, "Wintergreen for President," seems mysteriously to fit. This brilliant slogan is repeated on many of the banners, with "Win With Wintergreen" another favorite. On other banners are such sentiments as:

"Vote for Prosperity and See What You Get."
"A Vote for Wintergreen Is a Vote for Wintergreen."
"Hawaii Wants Wintergreen."
"Turn the Reformers Out."
"Wintergreen—A Man's Man's Man."
"Wintergreen—The Flavor Lasts."
"He Kept Us Out of Jail."
"Even Your Dog Loves John P. Wintergreen."
"The Full Dinner Jacket."

As the procession wends its way a few lines of lyric emerge from the general singing:

WINTERGREEN FOR PRESIDENT

Wintergreen for President!
Wintergreen for President!
He's the man the people choose;
Loves the Irish and the Jews.

It passes on into darkness, band playing, banners flying, torches flaring.

SCENE 2: *A room in a hotel, and a pretty shabby room it is. It is, however, the temporary headquarters of those mysterious politicians who make up the National Campaign Committee. It's not that they couldn't afford a better hotel, for the party is notoriously rich, but somehow this room seems thoroughly in keeping with the men who occupy it.*

Two of the committeemen are present when the curtain goes up. Their names are Francis X. Gilhooley and Louis Lippman, and they are, of course, representatives of those two races which the candidate so loves. Mr. Gilhooley sits in his shirtsleeves at a small table, and between drinks of White Rock—well, maybe not White Rock—he is trying to work out a game of solitaire. Mr. Lippman, also coatless, sprawls on the bed with a newspaper.

The room is thick with cigar smoke.

Mr. Lippman yawns, stretches, and puts down his newspaper. There comes a knock on the door.

LIPPMAN: Come in.
    (*A Chambermaid enters, carrying towels*)
CHAMBERMAID: I brought you some towels. (*To Gilhooley, as she passes him*) I'm just going to the bathroom.
GILHOOLEY: First door to the left.
    (*The Maid disappears into the bathroom as the telephone rings*)
LIPPMAN: (*At the 'phone*) So what? . . . Who? . . . What's his name? . . . Throttle *what*? . . . Must have the wrong room. This is the National Committee . . . I say this is the National Campaign Committee. (*Hangs up*) Some fellow downstairs.
    (*The Chambermaid re-enters*)
GILHOOLEY: Did you find it?
CHAMBERMAID: Shall I turn the bed down now?
LIPPMAN: Sure. Go ahead.
CHAMBERMAID: I can't turn it down unless you get off it.

LIPPMAN: Oh, then the hell with it!

CHAMBERMAID: Yes, sir. Shall I come back later?

LIPPMAN: Why not?

CHAMBERMAID: Yes, sir. (*She goes*)

LIPPMAN: Nice girl.

GILHOOLEY: (*Rising and stretching*) Ho-hum! Certainly is great to take it easy for a while.

LIPPMAN: Yep. It was a tough convention, all right.

GILHOOLEY: I'll say it was tough. Sixty-three ballots.

LIPPMAN: But we put the ticket over. That's the big thing.

GILHOOLEY: Well, there's still the election. I don't mind telling you I'm a little bit worried.

LIPPMAN: Say, we never lost an election yet, and we've had a lot worse candidates.

GILHOOLEY: It ain't just the candidates—it's the whole party.

LIPPMAN: What do you mean the whole party?

GILHOOLEY: Mm. I think maybe they're kind of getting wise to us.

LIPPMAN: Say! If they haven't got wise to us in forty years they'll never get wise.

GILHOOLEY: Yah, but I don't like the way they've been acting lately. You know, we never should have sold Rhode Island.

LIPPMAN: We've got a great ticket, haven't we? For President: John P. Wintergreen. He even *sounds* like a President.

GILHOOLEY: That's why we picked him.

LIPPMAN: And for vice-president— (*Hesitates*) —what's the name of that fellow we nominated for vice-president?

GILHOOLEY: Ah—Pitts, wasn't it?

LIPPMAN: No, no—it was a longer name.

GILHOOLEY: Barbinelli?

LIPPMAN: No.

GILHOOLEY: Well, that's longer.

LIPPMAN: You're a hell of a National Committeeman. Don't even know the name of the vice-president we nominated.

(*Matthew Arnold Fulton enters. Mr. Fulton owns a string of newspapers, and he is not without power in this land of ours*)

(*There are the customary greetings*)

LIPPMAN: Hey, Fulton! To decide a bet: what's the name of that fellow we nominated for vice-president?

FULTON: What? Oh—Schaeffer, wasn't it?

GILHOOLEY: That's right!

LIPPMAN: No, no! Schaeffer turned it down.

FULTON: Oh, yes.

GILHOOLEY: Wait a minute! Wait a minute! Are you sure we nominated a vice-president?

FULTON: Of course. Didn't I make the nominating speech?

GILHOOLEY: Oh, yeah.

FULTON: (*Thoughtful*) What was his name again?

GILHOOLEY: Well, think a minute. How did you come to nominate him?

LIPPMAN: Who introduced him to you?

FULTON: Nobody introduced him. I picked his name out of a hat. We put a lot of names in a hat, and this fellow lost. (*The telephone again*)

LIPPMAN: Hello . . . No, no, you've got the wrong room. . . . What's his name again? . . . Gotabottle? . . . Oh, Throttle-bottom. Wait a minute. (*To the others*) Guy named Bottle-throttle says he has an appointment with somebody here.

FULTON: Never heard of him.

GILHOOLEY: Not me.

LIPPMAN: (*Into 'phone*) Must have the wrong room. Tell him this is the National Committee . . . Well, then tell him it *isn't* the National Committee. . . . Hello. And give me room service, will you?

GILHOOLEY: (*Lighting a cigar*) What do you know, Matty?

FULTON: I know I'm thirsty.

GILHOOLEY: (*Producing a bottle*) Got just the ticket.

FULTON: Had it analyzed?

GILHOOLEY: Had it psycho-analyzed.

LIPPMAN: Room Service? This is 413. Listen—send up a half a dozen bottles of White Rock, a couple of ginger ales— (*To others*) Who's paying for this?

GILHOOLEY: General party expense.

LIPPMAN: (*Into 'phone*) Make that a dozen White Rock. And some dill pickles. (*Hangs up*) Well, Matty, how's the news-paper king?

FULTON: Well, if you want to know, a little bit worried.

LIPPMAN: What's the matter?

FULTON: Well, I've just been over to the office doing some

long distance 'phoning. Called up about twenty of my editors all over the country, and it's not going to be the cinch
we figured on.

GILHOOLEY: (*To Lippman*) What did I tell you?

LIPPMAN: What did you find out?

FULTON: Just that. It isn't going to be cinch we—

(*Enter Senators Carver Jones and Robert E. Lyons. Senator
Jones is from the West, and Senator Lyons is from the South.
And maybe you don't think they know it*)

JONES: Ah, gentlemen, good evening!

LYONS: Gentlemen!

GILHOOLEY: Hello, Senator!

LIPPMAN: Senator!

FULTON: How about Wintergreen? Is he coming over?

JONES: (*Right up on the rostrum*) My friends, I am informed
on excellent authority that John P. Wintergreen will shortly
honor us with his presence.

FULTON: Fine! Gentlemen, you probably wonder why I asked
you over here.

LYONS: (*Sighting the liquor and pouring himself a good one*)
Something about a drink, wasn't it?

FULTON: Senator Jones—

JONES: (*Bounding to his feet*) My friends—

FULTON: Senator Jones—

JONES: My good friends—

FULTON: You're a man that keeps his ear close to the ground.
What do they think about the ticket in the West?

JONES: My very good friends. (*He clears his throat*) John P.
Wintergreen is a great man—one of the greatest that the
party has nominated since Alexander Franklin. . . .

LYONS: And Robert E. Lee.

JONES: Unfortunately, however, while the people of the West
admire our party, and love our party, and respect our party,
they do not trust our party. And so, gentlemen, in the name
of those gallant boys who fought overseas, and the brave
mothers who sent them, we must not, we cannot, we dare
not allow Russian Bolshevism to dump cheap Chinese labor
on these free American shores! Gentlemen, I thank you.
(*He finishes his drink, and sits*)

FULTON: Thank *you*, sir. And now, Senator Lyons, tell us about the South.

LYONS: (*Who doesn't need to be asked twice*) Gentlemen, you ask me about the South. It is the land of romance, of roses and honeysuckle, of Southern chivalry and hospitality, fried chicken and waffles, salad and coffee.

LIPPMAN: No dessert?

FULTON: Thank you, gentlemen. That just about confirms what my editors have been telling me. The people of this country demand John P. Wintergreen for president, and they're going to get him whether they like it or not. And between you and me, gentlemen, I don't think they like it.

(*There is a knock on the door*)

Come in.

(*The door is slowly opened. Enter a timid little man—hopefully smiling. His name, believe it or not, is Alexander Throttlebottom*)

THROTTLEBOTTOM: Hi, gentlemen!

FULTON: Yes, sir. What can we do for you?

THROTTLEBOTTOM: (*All smiles*) Hello, Mr. Fulton.

FULTON: I'm afraid I don't quite place you. Your face is familiar, but—

THROTTLEBOTTOM: I'm Throttlebottom.

FULTON: What?

THROTTLEBOTTOM: Alexander Throttlebottom.

JONES: (*Pushing him right out*) We're very busy, my good man. If you'll just—

THROTTLEBOTTOM: But I'm Throttlebottom.

FULTON: I understand, Mr. Teitelbaum, but just at present—

GILHOOLEY: You come back later on.

LIPPMAN: After we're gone.

THROTTLEBOTTOM: (*Insistent about it*) But I'm Throttlebottom. I'm the candidate for vice-president.

FULTON: That's the fellow!

GILHOOLEY: Of course!

LIPPMAN: Sure!

FULTON: What's your name again?

THROTTLEBOTTOM: Alexander—

FULTON: Of course! I nominated you! Alexander! Boys, this is— What's your first name, Mr. Alexander?

THROTTLEBOTTOM: That's my first name. Alexander.

FULTON: Well, well, Alexander Alexander.

GILHOOLEY: Well, that certainly is a coincidence.

(*A Waiter has arrived with accessories. Check in hand, he looks uncertainly around for the victim*)

THROTTLEBOTTOM: But that isn't my last name. It's Throttle-bottom.

LIPPMAN: Throttle what?

THROTTLEBOTTOM: Bottom.

LIPPMAN: How do you spell it?

THROTTLEBOTTOM: (*As he starts to spell Lippman takes the check from the Waiter and writes*) "T-h-r-o-t-t-l-e-b-o-t-t-o-m."

LIPPMAN: Right! And thank you very much.

(*The Waiter goes, and with him the signed check*)

FULTON: Well, sir, we're very glad indeed to see you, and very proud to have you on our ticket. Sit down.

(*They all sit, leaving no place for Throttlebottom*)

THROTTLEBOTTOM: Thanks. I won't sit. I'm only going to stay a minute. There's something I came up to see you about.

FULTON: What's that?

THROTTLEBOTTOM: Being vice-president. I want to know if you won't let me off.

FULTON: What!

GILHOOLEY: What do you mean?

THROTTLEBOTTOM: I don't want to be vice-president. I want to resign.

FULTON: Why, you can't do that!

JONES: That's treason!

LYONS: Absurd, suh!

LIPPMAN: Why don't you want to be vice-president? That's a good job.

THROTTLEBOTTOM: It's—it's on account of my mother. Suppose she found out?

FULTON: You've got a mother?

GILHOOLEY: He's got a mother.

LIPPMAN: This is a fine time to tell us!

FULTON: Yes, why didn't you tell us? You can't back out now. Everything's printed.

GILHOOLEY: Listen—she'll never hear about it.

JONES: Of course not.

THROTTLEBOTTOM: But maybe she will. Somebody may tell her.

LIPPMAN: Who'll tell her?

FULTON: Nobody'll know!

GILHOOLEY: You'll forget it yourself in three months.

FULTON: Of course!

LIPPMAN: (*Ever the salesman*) Besides, suppose something should happen to the president?

THROTTLEBOTTOM: What?

LIPPMAN: Suppose something should happen to the president? Then you become president.

THROTTLEBOTTOM: Me?

LIPPMAN: Sure.

THROTTLEBOTTOM: President! Say!

LIPPMAN: Let's drink to that! To our next president!

> (*There is a great passing of glasses, and Throttlebottom comes out of it without one. He dashes into the bathroom, and emerges with one of those green tumblers*)

GILHOOLEY: Our next president!

JONES: Our next president!

> (*And he enters. John P. Wintergreen himself*)

WINTERGREEN: I'll drink to that! (*Takes the glass from the extended arm of Jones and drinks*)

JONES: (*As the others greet him*) You dirty crook!

WINTERGREEN: I'll drink to that too!

LIPPMAN: Well, how's the candidate?

WINTERGREEN: Thirsty. Say, doesn't a fellow get a drink? (*He sees the drink Throttlebottom has just poured for himself, and takes it from his hand*) Ah! Thank you, waiter. And get me one of those dill pickles, will you?

THROTTLEBOTTOM: But I'm not—

WINTERGREEN: There they are—right over there.

> (*Throttlebottom obediently goes for the pickle*)

Well, gentlemen, it certainly was a great convention. I never expected to get the nomination. Didn't *want* the nomination. Never was so surprised as when my name came up. (*Takes pickle from Throttlebottom, and gives him the empty glass*)

GILHOOLEY: Who brought it up, anyway?

FULTON: Yah. Who was that in the back calling "Wintergreen!"

WINTERGREEN: That was me. Most spontaneous thing you ever saw. So here I am, gentlemen—nominated by the people, absolutely my own master, and ready to do any dirty work the committee suggests. (*In one quick movement he takes the full glass Throttlebottom has finally succeeded in getting for himself, and replaces it with the pickle*)

LYONS: *Mr.* President—

WINTERGREEN: I'll drink to that too! Anything else, gentlemen? Anything at all!

(*Fulton, meanwhile, is nervously pacing*)

What's the matter, Fulton? Something wrong? You're not sober, are you?

FULTON: (*His tone belying the words*) No, no! I'm all right.

WINTERGREEN: Must be something up. (*A look at the others*) What's the matter?

LIPPMAN: (*Deprecatingly*) A lot of schmoos.

FULTON: Well, it's this way. Begins to look as though there may be a little trouble ahead.

WINTERGREEN: Trouble?

FULTON: I don't think the people are quite satisfied with the party record.

WINTERGREEN: Who said they *were*?

FULTON: Well, you know what Lincoln said.

WINTERGREEN: Who?

FULTON: Lincoln.

GILHOOLEY: What did he say?

WINTERGREEN: Was it funny?

FULTON: "You can fool some of the people all the time, and you can fool all of the people some of the time, but you can't fool all of the people all of the time."

WINTERGREEN: Was that Lincoln?

THROTTLEBOTTOM: Abraham J. Lincoln.

WINTERGREEN: It's different nowadays. People are bigger suckers.

GILHOOLEY: We made one bad mistake. Never should have sold Rhode Island.

WINTERGREEN: Rhode Island! Nobody missed it! (*A gesture indicating its size*) Where is Rhode Island now? Anybody know?

FULTON: New York some place. Never get it back.

WINTERGREEN: (*A slap of the hands*) I'll tell you what! We'll leave it out of the campaign—not mention it!

(*There is a chorus of approval*)

Yes, sir, that's the idea—we won't mention it!

THROTTLEBOTTOM: But suppose somebody else brings it up?

WINTERGREEN: Don't answer 'em! It takes two to make an argument. (*Gazes curiously at Throttlebottom*) I thought this was a closed meeting.

FULTON: Sure it is. Why?

WINTERGREEN: (*Whispering*) Who's that?

FULTON: (*Also whispering*) Vice-president.

WINTERGREEN: (*Whispers*) What?

FULTON: This is Mr. Wintergreen. Mr.—ah—ah—

THROTTLEBOTTOM: (*Who has also forgotten it*) Ah—ah—Throttlebottom.

(*They shake hands*)

WINTERGREEN: Haven't I seen you before some place?

THROTTLEBOTTOM: I gave you that dill pickle.

WINTERGREEN: Of course!

FULTON: But look here, Mr. President—it's not only Rhode Island. There've been a whole lot of things the last four years.

GILHOOLEY: How about the four years before that?

WINTERGREEN: I'll tell you what—let's stick to the party record of 1776. That was a good year.

LIPPMAN: What's the matter with 1492?

WINTERGREEN: We can use that year too. We won't mention anything before 1492, or after 1776. That gives us pretty nearly three hundred years.

FULTON: Say, that's great!

LYONS: Just a minute, suh! Down South the people want to hear about the Civil War.

WINTERGREEN: What year was that?

LYONS: (*Exploring his pockets*) I haven't got the exact figures with me, but it was around 1812.

WINTERGREEN: 1812—let's see. . . .

THROTTLEBOTTOM: What year was 1812?

WINTERGREEN: Well, how about putting the Civil War back in 1776?

LYONS: Perfectly satisfactory, suh. Perfectly satisfactory.

JONES: Eminently fair.

FULTON: Yah, but it isn't enough.

GILHOOLEY: No! What we need is a good live issue!

FULTON: Yes! That's what we need—an issue. Something that everybody is interested in, and that doesn't matter a damn. Something the party can stand on.

THROTTLEBOTTOM: (*Who has to know everything*) Excuse me, gentlemen, but what party are we?

WINTERGREEN: We've got plenty of time for that. The important thing is to get elected.

JONES: You see, we're Republicans in most states.

LYONS: But the South is Democratic.

JONES: Oh, sure! We're Democrats down there.

THROTTLEBOTTOM: (*To Wintergreen*) I had a dog that was bitten by a Democrat.

WINTERGREEN: (*Whispers to Jones*) Who the hell is that?

JONES: (*Whispers*) Vice-president.
    (*The Chambermaid returns*)

CHAMBERMAID: Excuse me. (*She goes through the bathroom door*)

FULTON: Boys, I tell you this is serious. We've got to get something that'll take hold of the popular imagination—sweep the country.

LIPPMAN: The country could stand a good sweeping.

JONES: Mr. Fulton is quite correct.

CHAMBERMAID: (*Emerging from the bathroom*) Can I turn the bed down now?

FULTON: What?

CHAMBERMAID: Can I turn the bed down now?

FULTON: Say—come here a minute.
    (*The Maid and Throttlebottom both start toward Fulton*)
    (*To Throttlebottom*)
No, not you!
    (*To the Maid*)
You're an American citizen?

CHAMBERMAID: Yes, sir.

FULTON: Ever vote?

CHAMBERMAID: (*What an idea!*) Oh, no, sir.

FULTON: What do you care more about than anything else in the world?

CHAMBERMAID: I don't know. Money, I guess.

GILHOOLEY: That's no good.

WINTERGREEN: Brings up Rhode Island.

FULTON: Of course, money. We all want money. But there must be something else, isn't there?

CHAMBERMAID: (*Thinks*) No—I like money.

FULTON: (*Exasperated*) But after money, what?

CHAMBERMAID: Well, maybe love.

FULTON: Love?

CHAMBERMAID: Yeh. *You* know, to meet a nice young fellow that's crazy about you, and you're crazy about him, and you get engaged, and then you get married, and—*you* know—love.

THROTTLEBOTTOM: (*A trifle fussed*) Sure.

FULTON: (*Rather thoughtful*) Oh, yes. Thank you. Thank you very much.

CHAMBERMAID: Shall I turn the bed down now, sir?

FULTON: Not now. Come back later on.

CHAMBERMAID: Yes, sir. (*Starts to go*)

FULTON: Ah—here you are. (*Starts to give her a coin. Throttle-bottom reaches for it*) No, not you.

CHAMBERMAID: Thank you, sir. (*Goes*)

LIPPMAN: Well, you got a lot out of that.

WINTERGREEN: Put women into politics and that's what you get. Love.

GILHOOLEY: Love!

FULTON: (*Slowly*) What's the matter with love?

THROTTLEBOTTOM: I like love!

FULTON: People *do* care more about love than anything else. Why, they steal for it, they even kill for it.

WINTERGREEN: But will they vote for it?

FULTON: You bet they will! If we could find some way to put it over—why, we could get every vote. Everybody loves a lover; the whole world loves a— (*Stops as he gets an idea; looks fixedly at Wintergreen*)

WINTERGREEN: What's the matter?

FULTON: I've got it!

THROTTLEBOTTOM: He's got it!

FULTON: You've got to fall in love!

WINTERGREEN: You're crazy!

FULTON: You've got to fall in love with a typical American girl!

WINTERGREEN: Huh?

LIPPMAN: What good's that?

GILHOOLEY: What are you talking about?

JONES: What for?

FULTON: Wait a minute! You make love to her from now till Election Day as no girl was ever made love to before!

WINTERGREEN: What's the gag?

GILHOOLEY: Yeah!

LIPPMAN: So what?

FULTON: My God, are you blind? You do this right and you'll get elected by the greatest majority that the American people ever gave a candidate! You'll get every vote!

WINTERGREEN: But wait a minute—

GILHOOLEY: I think there's something in it.

JONES: It sounds good!

LYONS: Certainly does!

LIPPMAN: Say!

FULTON: I tell you it's great!

WINTERGREEN: But look here—

FULTON: You'll go down in history as the greatest lover this country has ever known! You'll be the romantic ideal of every man, woman and child in America!

WINTERGREEN: Oh, no! I don't want anything like that!

FULTON: But man, it's the biggest thing in the world! A hundred million hearts will beat as one; they'll follow your courtship in every State in the Union! You meet the girl, you fall in love with her, you propose, you're accepted, and you're swept into the White House on a tidal wave of love!

WINTERGREEN: But there's nobody I'm in love with! I'm not in love with anybody!

FULTON: We'll get the girl! That'll be easy!

LIPPMAN: My wife's sister!

FULTON: I've got the idea! We'll have a contest—a nationwide contest to select Miss White House—choose the most beautiful girl from every State—get them all together at Atlantic City, pick the winner and you fall in love with her!

(*Chorus:* "*Yah!*" "*Great!*" "*That's it!*")

WINTERGREEN: But suppose I *don't* fall in love with her!

THROTTLEBOTTOM: Then *I* get her!

FULTON: You can't *help* falling in love with her! The most beautiful girl in America! I tell you this is wonderful! (*Into the telephone*) Give me Beekman 5000.

WINTERGREEN: Give me another drink!

LIPPMAN: Let's all have another drink! Scotch or rye, Jack?

WINTERGREEN: Both!

FULTON: Give me Jenkins! Hello!

LIPPMAN: Say when!

FULTON: That's what I said—Jenkins!

WINTERGREEN: That's enough! (*Takes the bottle instead of the glass*)

FULTON: Jenkins? Fulton! Stop the presses! John P. Wintergreen will run for President on a one-word platform: Love! National beauty contest in Atlantic City to select Miss White House! Now listen! I want a love cartoon on the front page of every one of my papers from now till Election Day! Right! And call up Coolidge and tell him I want a thousand words on love tomorrow morning!

CURTAIN

SCENE 3: *Atlantic City—with the beauty contest in full swing. The scene is a section of the boardwalk, and the various candidates for First Lady are in about three-quarter-piece bathing suits. For it is notorious, of course, that the prime requisite for a First Lady is that she should look well in a bathing suit.*

To music and lyric the candidates introduce themselves.

WHO IS THE LUCKY GIRL TO BE?

GIRLS:

>Who is the lucky girl to be?
>Who is to leave the bourgeoisie?
>Who is to be the blushing bride?
>Who will sleep at the President's side?
>Strike up the cymbals, drum, and fife!
>One of us is the President's future wife!

FOUR GIRLS:

> We're in Atlantic City
> To meet with the committee.

FOUR OTHERS:

> And when they've made their mind up
> The winner will be signed up.

FOUR OTHERS:

> The prize is consequential—
> Presidential!
> Our bodies will bear witness
> To our fitness.

ALL:

> If a girl is sexy
> She may be Mrs. Prexy!
> One of us is the President's future wife!
> (*Enter the Gentlemen of the Press, cameras in hand*)

The Dimple on My Knee

PHOTOGRAPHERS:

> More important than a photograph of Parliament
> Or a shipwreck on the sea—
> What'll raise the circulation
> Of our paper through the nation
> Is the dimple on your knee.

> More important than a photograph of Parliament
> Or a western spelling bee
> Or the latest thing in science
> For our pleasure-loving clients
> Is the dimple on your knee.

> What our readers love to see
> Is the dimple on your knee;
> What our readers love to see
> Is the dimple on your knee.

GIRLS:

> More important than a photograph of Parliament
> Is the dimple on my knee.
> But supposing I am losing
> When the judges are a-choosing—
> What will my poor future be?

Do I have to go back to the cafeteria
With my lovely dimpled knee?
Does a girl who's so ambitious
Have to work at washing dishes?
I'm afraid that worries me.

Oh, what will the future be
Of my lovely dimpled knee?
Oh, what will the future be
Of my lovely dimpled knee?

BECAUSE, BECAUSE

PHOTOGRAPHERS:

Don't worry, little girl,
For even if you lose the prize—
Don't worry, little girl,
Myself, I can't resist your eyes.

GIRLS:

I'll worry, little boy,
Until you tell what's on your mind.

PHOTOGRAPHERS:

Don't worry, little girl,
I've asked my heart and this is what I find—
Don't worry, little girl;
Don't worry, little girl.

GIRLS:

Why shouldn't I worry?

PHOTOGRAPHERS:

Because, because, because, because,
Because you're in the money
With a smile that's sweet and sunny,
I could fall for you myself.

Because, because, because, because
Your looks are so appealing
They have given me a feeling
I could fall for you myself.

The thrills you're sending through me
All prove that you will do me;

And so I'm giving you me—
If *they* don't want you, *I* want you!

Because, because, because, because,
Because your ways are simple
And your knee can show a dimple,
I could fall for you myself.

Next: The Committee headquarters in one of the grander Board-walk hostelries. A few banners on the walls proclaim the fact that this is no longer just a hotel parlor, but the center of national interest. A few dozen girls, still in bathing suits, are scattered around the room.

Enter Mr. Fulton, followed by the faithful Gilhooley and a handful of newspapermen and newsreelers

GILHOOLEY: (*To the movie men*) Come on, boys! Set 'em up right here—that'll give you a good angle! Hello, ladies!

FULTON: Well, well! What a crowd! How are you, ladies? This certainly is a big day, all right! Must be ten thousand people outside this hotel! Never saw so much excitement in all my life!

ONE OF THE GIRLS: Say! What does a President's wife have to do, anyhow?

GILHOOLEY: That depends on the President.

(*A young woman comes forward to greet Mr. Fulton. She is chiefly distinguished from the other girls by the fact that she is dressed. Her name is Mary Turner*)

MARY: Good morning, Mr. Fulton.

FULTON: Well, Miss Turner! Having quite a day, huh?

MARY: Quite a day, Mr. Fulton.

FULTON: Heard some very nice things about the way you've been handling this. Afraid I'll have to give you a raise.

MARY: Well, I'm afraid I'll have to take it.

(*Enter those two pillars of the government—Senators Jones and Lyons*)

LYONS: Afternoon, gentlemen! Ladies!

FULTON: Ah, here's some of the committee now! Good afternoon, gentlemen!

JONES: Mr. Fulton! Good afternoon, ladies! Good afternoon.

(*Beams on the Photographers*) Well! Quite a battery you have here—quite a battery!

LYONS: Gentlemen of the press!

JONES: Very glad to see you, gentlemen! Always glad to meet the newspaper boys!

> (*Enter a lad named Jenkins, who is one of Fulton's various assistants*)

JENKINS: Good morning, Chief!

FULTON: Oh, hello, Jenkins!

JONES: Hello, there! I've met you before! Never forget a face! Just tell me—we've met before? Am I right?

JENKINS: Right you are, Senator!

JONES: (*SO pleased with himself*) Right! Where was it?

JENKINS: San Francisco. That opium joint on 4th Street.

JONES: (*Not so pleased*) Well, I guess I got the wrong man. Remarkable resemblance, though, remarkable resemblance.

> (*Throttlebottom enters. Still hoping*)

THROTTLEBOTTOM: Hello, everybody! Hello, Mr. Fulton!

GILHOOLEY: Hello, there!

JONES: How are you?

LYONS: Good morning, suh!

FULTON: Who is that guy?

GILHOOLEY: Vice-president.

FULTON: Oh, yes. Hello! How are you?

THROTTLEBOTTOM: Are these the girls? I'm Mr. Throttlebottom. (*Sights a promising girl*) Hello! How are you?

THE GIRL: Fine!

THROTTLEBOTTOM: Is your mother down here with you?

THE GIRL: (*She's no fool*) Yes, sir.

THROTTLEBOTTOM: Oh! Well! Never mind!

FULTON: (*Goes to Throttlebottom*) Say, look here a minute. You know, vice-presidents don't usually go around in public. They're not supposed to be seen.

THROTTLEBOTTOM: But I'm not vice-president yet. Couldn't I go around a little longer?

GILHOOLEY: That isn't the point. If you're going to be vice-president you've got to practice up for it. You've got to go in hiding.

THROTTLEBOTTOM: But I came up the back way.

FULTON: You shouldn't have come at all. Suppose somebody sees you?

GILHOOLEY: We'd lose the election.

THROTTLEBOTTOM: You mean you want me to hide from everybody?

JONES: That's it!

FULTON: Right!

THROTTLEBOTTOM: (*Gets an idea*) I could go back to my old business.

FULTON: What's that?

THROTTLEBOTTOM: I used to be a hermit.

FULTON: Great!

GILHOOLEY: That's the idea!

THROTTLEBOTTOM: The only thing is, I thought you might want me to make some speeches.

FULTON: No, no!

GILHOOLEY: You just go and sit in your cave.

THROTTLEBOTTOM: (*Thinks it over*) I know. I could go back to the cave and write my speeches there.

FULTON: That's the idea!

JONES: Perfect!

GILHOOLEY: And make 'em there, too!

JONES: Don't let anybody find you—don't let anybody see you.

THROTTLEBOTTOM: I won't. I won't even come out in February to cast my shadow. (*He goes.*)

> (*Enter, then, a particularly beauteous girl named Diana Devereaux. She is from the South, as one speedily discovers when she speaks*)

DIANA: Mo'nin', Senator Lyons.

LYONS: Well, Miss Devereaux! And how is the fairest flower of the South?

DIANA: Senator Lyons, that's the prettiest thing been said to me since I left Louisiana. I sure been gettin' pow'ful homesick.

ONE OF THE GIRLS: (*Who seems to be a little embittered*) She sure is getting pow'ful Southern.

LYONS: You're just a breath of the old Southland.

DIANA: Senator, you keep sayin' sweet things like that and I'm just going to throw my arms right around your neck.

FULTON: You never made me an offer like that, Miss Devereaux.

DIANA: Why, Mr. Fulton!

FULTON: Yes, sir, when I look around I'm sorry I didn't run for President myself.

DIANA: You'd make a mighty nice consolation prize. Wouldn't he, girls?

FULTON: Now, now! Matter of fact, we're getting up some consolation prizes. Got that list, Jenkins?

JENKINS: Here you are, sir.

FULTON: Of course the first prize, as you all know, is Mr. Wintergreen himself. The second prize is a season pass to Coney Island. And the third prize is an autographed photograph of Clara Bow, or ten cents in gold.

> (*There is a burst of cheering in the distance. Enter Wintergreen, followed by Lippman and practically all the reporters in the world*)

Well, well! The candidate himself! Hello, Jack!

WINTERGREEN: Hello, there!

FULTON: Ladies, permit me to introduce your future husband, John P. Wintergreen! Here they are, Jack. How do you like 'em?

WINTERGREEN: (*A trifle nervously*) Why, they're wonderful. Hello! How are you?

FULTON: Say something to them.

WINTERGREEN: Well, ladies, this certainly is a pleasure. All I can say is I love you, and you're the only girls I have ever loved. (*With growing nervousness*) And after we're married, I hope you'll all be happy, and—listen, Fulton, I can't go through with this.

FULTON: You've got to go through with it.

WINTERGREEN: But I don't know any of these girls! How can I marry them? If it was only somebody I knew, like—Lippman, whatever became of your wife's sister?

LIPPMAN: (*With a shake of the head*) Not in a bathing suit.

FULTON: By the way, Jack, I want you to meet Miss Diana Devereaux.

LYONS: Miss Devereaux, may I have the honor—

DIANA: Mr. President, I'm mighty happy to meet you! I hope we're going to see a lot of each other.

WINTERGREEN: Any hope of yours, Miss Devereaux, is a hope of mine, I hope.

DIANA: You keep on saying sweet things like that and I'm just going to throw my arms right around your neck.
    (*The Girls chime in when she is halfway through the sentence and finish it right with her, Southern accent and all*)

WINTERGREEN: Seems to be quite an echo here.

DIANA: (*Playing with his lapel*) Have you-all got a fraternity pin?

WINTERGREEN: Well, would a safety pin do?

DIANA: Mr. Wintergreen, you've got the grandest sense of humor.

MARY: All right, Mr. Fulton.

FULTON: And now, ladies—attention, please! The time has come for the final test.
    (*The Girls start a general primping and there is an excited buzz*)

It has been a grueling contest—you have been under a great strain. And we of the committee want to thank you—and through you the three million others who took part in this contest, only ninety-eight per cent of whom had to be sent home for misbehavior. And now, ladies, the judges await you. And may the best girl win.

WHO IS THE LUCKY GIRL TO BE? (*Reprise*)

GIRLS:

    Who is the lucky girl to be?
    Who is to leave the bourgeoisie?

DIANA:

    Bye-bye, Mister President—
    I'm a-prayin'
    I'm the little lady
    You're obeyin'.

DIANA AND GIRLS:

    Strike up the cymbal, drum, and fife—
    One of us is to be the President's wife.

COMMITTEE:

    We'll get you Mrs. Wintergreen.

WINTERGREEN:

    Oh!

COMMITTEE:
> We'll get you Mrs. Wintergreen.

WINTERGREEN:
> Oh!

COMMITTEE:
> We'll present you with a bride.
> She will be the nation's pride.
> Ta ta ta ta ta ta ta.

(*They go. Wintergreen, his nervousness mounting, is left alone in the room. But not quite alone, for at her desk in the corner Mary Turner is quietly working*)

WINTERGREEN: (*As he sees her*) Oh! (*Takes a moment*) Say! (*She turns*)
> You haven't got a drink on you, have you?

MARY: Why, no. I'm sorry.

WINTERGREEN: That's all right. Didn't want it anyhow. (*Pacing*)

MARY: Little bit nervous?

WINTERGREEN: (*Whirling*) Who? Me? What have I got to be nervous about?

MARY: That's what I was wondering. Twenty-four of the most beautiful girls in the country—and you get the winner. Lot of men would like to be in your shoes.

WINTERGREEN: Yeah, but it's my bedroom slippers I'm worrying about. . . . Say, you've been watching them—who do you think it's going to be?

MARY: I couldn't say. Likely to be any one of them.

WINTERGREEN: That's what I was afraid of. But which one? What's your guess?

MARY: Well, don't hold me to it, but I shouldn't be surprised if it were Miss Devereaux.

WINTERGREEN: Devereaux! I thought so! That's the one with the Southern exposure?

MARY: That's Miss Devereaux. She's a good-looking girl, don't you think?

WINTERGREEN: (*In heavy Southern accent*) Yes, she's a good-looking gal, all right.

MARY: (*Falling right into line*) Don't you-all like good-looking gals?

WINTERGREEN: Down Carolina way we're all a-crazy about

good looking gals, but we-all don't like 'em talking that-a-way.

MARY: How do you-all like 'em to talk, sure enough?

WINTERGREEN: (*Abandons the dialect*) Say, that's terrible, isn't it? If she wins would I have to listen to that all the time?

MARY: But she does it charmingly. And she's very beautiful.

WINTERGREEN: Beautiful, yeah—I like a beautiful girl— they're all right, but— (*He stumbles*) —when a fellow gets married he wants a home, a mother for his children.

MARY: You've got children?

WINTERGREEN: No, no, I mean if I was married. You see, when you're married—well, *you* know.

MARY: Well, I think Miss Devereaux might listen to reason. And she'd make a very beautiful mother for your children.

WINTERGREEN: Will you stop saying beautiful? I don't know anything about these girls, any of them. What kind of wives they'd make—whether they could sew, or make a bed, or cook. They don't look as though they'd ever had a skillet in their hands. Say, what *is* a skillet?

MARY: You wouldn't have to worry about that in the White House. They have plenty of servants there.

WINTERGREEN: The White House—yeah, but some day we'll have to move out of the White House. Then what? The Old Presidents' Home? There'll be no servants there. She'll *have* to cook.

MARY: Then she'll cook. And like it.

WINTERGREEN: But will *I* like it? Why, the average girl today can't cook—she can't even broil an egg.

MARY: Nonsense! Every girl can cook.

WINTERGREEN: (*Scornfully*) Every girl can cook—can *you*?

MARY: I certainly can!

WINTERGREEN: Then what are you doing here?

MARY: (*Right back at him*) I'm holding down a job! And I can cook, and sew, and make lace curtains, and bake the best darned corn muffins you ever ate! And what do you know about that?

WINTERGREEN: Did you say corn muffins?

MARY: Yes, corn muffins!

WINTERGREEN: Corn muffins! You haven't got one on you, have you?

MARY: I haven't far to go. (*Opens a drawer in her desk*) It's lunch, but you can have it.

WINTERGREEN: Oh, I couldn't do that!

MARY: Please! (*As he reaches*) The second from the left is a corn muffin. That's an apple.

WINTERGREEN: (*Taking muffin*) Well! You must let me take *you* to lunch some day. (*Samples it*) Why—it melts in the mouth! It's—it's marvelous.

MARY: And I'm the only person in the world who can make them without corn.

WINTERGREEN: What a muffin! Say, I don't even know your name.

MARY: That's right—you don't.

WINTERGREEN: Mine's Wintergreen.

MARY: I know. Mine's Turner.

WINTERGREEN: Just Turner?

MARY: Mary Turner.

WINTERGREEN: (*Suddenly*) Say, why in God's name didn't you get into this contest?

MARY: One of the three million?

WINTERGREEN: Well, you know what the first prize is?

MARY: Yeah, can you imagine?

WINTERGREEN: And you get your picture in the paper.

MARY: Having tea on the lawn with the Filipino delegation. And you throwing the medicine ball at the cabinet.

WINTERGREEN: Oh, do we have to have a cabinet?

MARY: What would you throw the medicine ball at? Me?

WINTERGREEN: (*Suddenly sober*) Gosh, it'd be fun with you. We could have a grand time.

MARY: (*The Southern accent*) Why, Mr. Wintergreen—

WINTERGREEN: No, I mean it! Listen—I've only got a minute—maybe less than that! I love you! I know it's awful sudden, but in a minute it'll be too late! Let's elope—let's get out of here!

MARY: But—but wait a minute! You don't know me!

WINTERGREEN: I know you better than those girls! (*A gesture*) You can make corn muffins, and—you're darned cute-looking, and—I love you!

MARY: But I don't know *you*!

WINTERGREEN: What's there to know? I'm young, I'm a swell

conversationalist, and I've got a chance to be President! And besides that you love me!

MARY: But it's absurd! Why, you can't—

WINTERGREEN: The hell I can't! (*He seizes her and starts kissing her*) It's fate, Mary, that's what it is—fate! (*Kisses her again*) Why, we were meant for each other—you and me!

MARY: You and *I*!

WINTERGREEN: All right, you and I!

>(*A burst of music. The sound of many voices as the doors are thrown open. Enter Fulton and the Committee, full of importance*)

AS THE CHAIRMAN OF THE COMMITTEE

FULTON:

>As the chairman of the committee,
>I announce we've made our choice;
>Ev'ry lover from Dubuque to Jersey City
>Should rejoice!

ALL:

>We rejoice!
>When the angels up there designed her
>They designed a thoroughbred;
>And on March the fourth the President will find her
>Worthy of his board and bed.

FULTON: (*spoken*) And now it thrills me to introduce the rarest of American beauties, the future First Lady of the land—a fit consort for the ruler of 122 million freeborn. Ladies and gentlemen—Miss Diana Devereaux!

>(*Diana appears, a golden crown on her head, followed by all the other Girls*)

HOW BEAUTIFUL

ALL: (*Sing*)

>How beautiful, beautiful, beautiful!
>How utterly, utterly so!
>The charming, the gracious, the dutiful
>Diana Devereaux.

FULTON: (*spoken*) The committee will now state its reasons—with music!

Never Was There a Girl So Fair

COMMITTEE:
>   Never was there a girl so fair;
>   Never was there a form so rare;

DIANA: (*spoken*) Ah could throw mah arms right around your neck!

COMMITTEE:
>   A voice so lyrical
>   Is given few;
>   Her eyes a miracle
>   Of Prussian blue;
>   Ruby lips and a foot so small;
>   As for hips—she has none at all!

GILHOOLEY:
>   Did you ever see such footsies
>   Or a more enticing limb?

LIPPMAN:
>   And the ankles of her tootsies
>   Are so slim!

LYONS:
>   What a charming epiglottis!
>   What a lovely coat of tan!
>   Oh, the man who isn't hot is
>   Not a man!

COMMITTEE:
>   She's a bargain to whom she's wed;
>   More than worthy his board and bed!

FULTON:
>   Says the chairman of the committee,
>   Let the newsmen now come in.

>   (*to Diana*)
>   For the sound reels you must look your best, my
>   pretty.

>   (*to guards*)
>   Have the interviews begin!

WINTERGREEN:
>   Stop! No!
>   Though this may be a blow,
>   I simply cannot marry
>   Diana Devereaux!

COMMITTEE:

    What's this? What's this?

ALL:

    He says he cannot marry
    Diana Devereaux!

COMMITTEE: (*to Wintergreen*)

    You mean you will not marry
    Diana Devereaux!

WINTERGREEN:

    Please understand—It isn't that I would jilt or
        spurn 'er;
    It's just that I love someone else—

ALL:

    Who?

WINTERGREEN: (*reprovingly*)

    Whom! Mary Turner.

COMMITTEE:

    The man is mad!
    Or else a cad!
    He'll have to take her—
    He can't forsake her!

DIANA:

    This jilting me—
    It cannot be!
    This lousy action
    Calls for retraction!

COMMITTEE:

    We must know why
    You should prefer
    Instead of Di
  (*pointing to Diana*)
    A girl like her.
  (*pointing to Mary*)

ALL:

    Yes, tell us why
    You should prefer
    Instead of Di
    A girl like her.

WINTERGREEN:

    All that I can say of Mary Turner

Is that I love Mary Turner.

COMMITTEE:

What's to be done?
Though she has won,
(*indicating Diana*)
Though she is signed up,
He's made his mind up!
His love he'd ruther
Give to the other.
(*indicating Mary*)
What shall we do now?
What is our cue now?

DIANA: (*to Committee*)

He will do nothing of the sort;
First we'll settle this thing in court.
(*to Wintergreen*)
You seem to think Miss Turner hits the spot;
But what has she got that I haven't got?

ALL:

Yes, what has *she* got
(*pointing to Mary*)
That *she*
(*pointing to Diana*)
hasn't got?

WINTERGREEN:

My Mary makes corn muffins.
(*to Diana*)
Can you make corn muffins?

DIANA:

I can't make corn muffins.

ALL:

She can't make corn muffins!

WINTERGREEN:

Well, there you are!

SOME GIRLS CAN BAKE A PIE

WINTERGREEN:

Some girls can bake a pie
Made up of prunes and quinces;

Some make an oyster fry—
Others are good at blintzes.
Some lovely girls have done
Wonders with turkey stuffin's,
But I have found the one
Who can really make corn muffins.
(*He passes muffins to the Committee*)
DIANA:
Who cares about corn muffins?
All I demand is justice.
(*Wintergreen repeats "Some girls . . ." Mary joins in, as
Committee and Ensemble, sold on the idea, sing obligato*)
COMMITTEE AND ENSEMBLE:
Corn muffins—
Though other girls are good at turkey stuffin's,
She takes the cake—for she can bake—corn muffins;
Corn muffins—
He's not to blame for falling if she's able
To serve them at his table.
(*Committee starts to sample muffins*)
They should be happy night and day;
They'll make a couple so delightful
When two agree on corn muffins,
Their marriage is only rightful.
DIANA: (*against the above*)
Don't surrender!
Don't be tender!
I'm the winner.
She is a little sinner.
Come! Make your mind up!
I, not she
Is the one who's really signed up!
COMMITTEE: (*holding up muffins*)
Great, great!
It really must be fate!
We must declare these muffins
The best we ever ate!

There's none but Mary Turner
Could ever be his mate!

ALL:

> There's none but Mary Turner
> Could ever be his mate!
> (*Half the voices keep repeating this, other half sing:*)
> She can make corn muffins!
> She can make corn muffins!
> (*Together*)
> Let's all rejoice!
> (*One and all, with the exception of Diana, they burst into a joyous dance, expressing the ecstasy that is theirs at the very existence of so remarkable a young woman. On this pæan of joy the curtain falls*)

SCENE 4: *Madison Square Garden—the height of the campaign. One sees first the outside of the Garden, and across it a great banner bearing the pictures of Wintergreen and Mary Turner. WOO WITH WINTERGREEN, the slogan now runs, and beneath it: LOVERS! VOTE FOR JOHN AND MARY! Of Mr. Throttlebottom, or whatever his name is, there is just no mention at all.*
A band plays. Drawn by the ballyhoo, a crowd gathers and goes gayly into the Garden, singing and cheering.

> (*Jenkins and Miss Benson enter.*)

LOVE IS SWEEPING THE COUNTRY

> Why are people gay
> All the night and day,
> Feeling as they never felt before?
> What is the thing
> That makes them sing?
>
> Rich man, poor man, thief,
> Doctor, lawyer, chief,
> Feel a feeling that they can't ignore;
> It plays a part
> In ev'ry heart,
> And ev'ry heart is shouting "Encore!"
>
> Love is sweeping the country;
> Waves are hugging the shore;

All the sexes
From Maine to Texas
Have never known such love before.

See them billing and cooing
Like the birdies above!
Each girl and boy alike,
Sharing joy alike,
Feels that passion'll
Soon be national.
Love is sweeping the country—
There never was so much love!

Spring is in the air—
Each mortal loves his neighbor.
Who's that loving pair?
That's Capital and Labor.

Chevrolet and Ford
Have felt this cosmic urging;
They, with one accord,
Have kissed and now are merging.

Florida and Cal-
Ifornia get together
In a festi*val*
Of oranges and weather.

Boston's upper zones
Are changing all their habits,
And I hear the Cohns
Are taking up the Cabots.

Taximen take dimes
And never curse the traffic,
While the New York *Times*
Adores the New York *Graphic*.

   (*Repeat refrain*)

Inside the Garden, then, with the proceedings in full swing. A Garden that is packed to the rafters with cheering humanity, alive with cold-drink vendors, and hot dog salesmen, and everything that goes with so great an occasion. Over the rostrum there hangs the inevitable loud speaker, set in a cluster of lights that send a concentrated glow down on the platform. The various committeemen occupy the platform seats, and the two centre chairs are conspicuously empty, obviously waiting for the stellar pair. When the scene starts Fulton is in the midst of an impassioned address.

FULTON: . . . seventeen hundred and seventy-six, eighteen hundred and twelve, eighteen hundred and sixty-one, eighteen hundred and ninety-eight, and nineteen hundred and seventeen!

(*There is loud applause as he stops for a sip of water*)

And so, my friends, on Tuesday next yours is a great privilege. You will cast your ballots for the greatest cause and the greatest emotion known to the heart of mankind! Love!

(*Applause*)

Yes, my good friends, for love! For love and for the greatest of all lovers! John P. Wintergreen!

(*He sits down to great applause*)

LOUD SPEAKER: (*Through the cluster of megaphones that hangs overhead*) Attention, please! Next Wednesday night: Jack Sharkey, American champion of the world, versus Max Schmeling, German champion of the world, for the championship of the world!

(*Applause*)

FULTON: (*Again to his feet*) And, my friends, as a good American, I believe that Jack Sharkey will win!

(*Applause; he sits*)

LOUD SPEAKER: Attention, please! Message for Dr. Hugo Kristmacher! Dr. Kristmacher! Your wife just telephoned the box-office and says not to come home to-night.

(*Applause*)

FULTON: And now, my good people, it is my great pleasure and privilege to introduce a man who has served his country long and gloriously, a man who has for many years waged a great and single-handed fight for what he considered his own interests. The silver-tongued orator of the golden West, Senator Carver Crockett Jones!

(*Applause*)

(*Senator Jones rises*)

LOUD SPEAKER: Attention, please! While Senator Jones is speaking you will be entertained by the world's greatest wrestlers. Vladimir Vidovitch, the Harlem Heaver, and Yussef Yussevitch, the Terrible Turk, in a match for the world's championship.

(*Two Attendants dash out and quickly unroll a mat. Then enter, from opposite sides, Vidovitch and Yussevitch. As they reach the arena they drop their bathrobes and stand revealed as great three-hundred pounders, with arms like tree trunks. There is the sound of a gong. Simultaneously the Wrestlers go into action and Senator Jones starts his speech*)

JONES: My friends! We have arrived at a great moment in our history. Magnificent though our past has been, it dwindles into utter insignificance beside the brilliance of our future destiny. Gaze into that future, my friends, and what do you see? What do you see?

(*At this moment what one chiefly sees is the rear elevation of Vidovitch, which is being stared at by something akin to admiration by Yussevitch*)

There it is, my friends, for all the world to envy.

(*The Wrestlers reverse, and it is now Yussevitch that is starred. They break, and resume wrestling as Jones resumes talking*)

Not for us the entangling alliances of Europe, not for us the allying entanglances of Asia.

(*A burst of applause. The Wrestlers, at the moment, have a complicated double scissors hold on each other, but their arms are free. Pausing in their labors, they join in the applause*)

Here then we stand, alone in our strength, solitary in our splendor, the greatest and most glorious country that God Almighty put upon earth—the United States of AMERICA!!!

(*The Wrestlers, relinquishing a complicated hold, jump to their feet and salute. The Crowd bursts into applause.*)

And so, my friends—

(*One of the Wrestlers makes a sensational dive for the other's legs, throwing him to the mat with a crash. The Crowd sets up a cheering and yelling, egging on the Wrestlers. The Committeemen sitting behind Jones crowd to the edge of the rail to look on; the whole Crowd is on its feet. Jones tries bravely to talk against this for a moment, but his own*) *interest in the Wrestlers finally gets the better of him. He joins the cheerers. It all comes to a climax as one of the men finally gets the other down. Cheers. Applause. Bows. The Wrestlers exit; the Attendants roll up the mat; the Crowd settles back)*

FULTON: And now, my friends, while we are waiting for our beloved candidate—

(There is a hullabaloo at the entrance—the sound of a scuffle, voices, etc. The Crowd gets to its feet as the noise mounts. Enter Throttlebottom, trying to fight off four Policemen and a couple of Garden Attendants. As he comes into view it is seen that he is practically in tatters, his coat off, his collar askew. He struggles to the foot of the platform stairs)

Here, here, here! What's all this? Who is this man? Stop that noise! What is this?

(The noise quiets down. The Policemen stand holding tightly onto Throttlebottom, two to each arm. Behind him stand the Garden Attendants, one of whom has picked up a huge iron bar somewhere)

What is all this? What do you want here?

THROTTLEBOTTOM: *(Tears himself loose and gets half-way up the steps)* But wait, wait! I'm Throttlebottom! I'm the vice-president. Here—look! I'm Throttlebottom! *(Takes a banner from his pocket and unrolls it. Sure enough, it reads: For Vice-President: Alexander Throttlebottom)*

FULTON: Oh, yes! Yes! It's all right, officers. This man is all right!

(Throttlebottom gets up on the platform. The other Committeemen come forward to greet him, but not too cordially. Throttlebottom, meanwhile, is trying to get his clothes together, stuffing his shirt into his trousers, getting his collar back on)

FULTON: What are you doing here? Why didn't you stay in your cave?

THROTTLEBOTTOM: The other hermits objected.

FULTON: *(At the rostrum, reluctantly)* My friends, we have an unexpected surprise for you. It is your great and rare privilege to hear a few words from—

(*Throttlebottom prompts him*)

Alexander Throttlebottom— (*He pronounces the name with great care*) candidate for—

> (*Throttlebottom prompts him again, first looking at the banner himself*)

vice-president. (*Then, as an afterthought*) Of the United States of America.

> (*The Crowd is silent*)

> (*Throttlebottom advances to the rostrum; takes his speech from his pocket. It unrolls all the way to the ground, turning out to be about ten feet long. A pleased expression spreads over his face; recognition is his at last*)

LOUD SPEAKER: (*Just as Throttlebottom opens his mouth to speak*) Attention, please! At the end of the first period in Montreal: Boston Bruins, 3; Chicago White Sox, 1.

> (*The machine clanks off; Throttlebottom again gets ready to speak. Once more a slow smile comes over his face*)

Attention, please! There will now be an intermission of fifteen minutes.

> (*There is a great pushing back of chairs; everybody gets up and starts to leave*)

THROTTLEBOTTOM: No, no, no! No!

> (*The various noises merge into a greater and growing noise. Cries of "Wintergreen!" "Here comes Wintergreen!" Flashlights. Cheering. Music. Enter Wintergreen and Mary Turner, preceded by Policemen. To the accompaniment of cheers and handshaking they advance to the platform and go up the stairs. There is a great shaking of hands with the Committeemen. Throttlebottom, as the presidential procession gets up onto the platform, is simply pushed right out of the way by the Policemen, and practically falls down the stairs on the other side. Here he is met by other Policemen, and is ignominiously dragged out of the place, kicking and protesting. Meanwhile, as the noise subsides, Wintergreen and Mary take their seats, and Fulton advances to the rostrum to introduce them*)

FULTON: (*Stilling the tumult with upraised hand*) No need to tell you who the next speakers will be. They are the most beloved couple in America to-day, the most beloved couple that have ever run for the highest office in the gift of the American people. There have been many great lovers in history. But Romeo never loved Juliet, Dante never loved Beatrice, Damon never loved Pythias, as John P. Wintergreen loves Mary Turner.

(*Applause*)

My friends, the issue of this campaign is a simple one. We do not talk to you about war debts or wheat or immigration—we appeal to your hearts, not your intelligence. It is the old, old story, yet ever new—the sweetest story ever told. John P. Wintergreen, candidate for President of the United States of America, loves Mary Turner. Mary Turner, the most beautiful, the loveliest example of typical American womanhood—and I defy our opponents to say otherwise—loves John P. Wintergreen. He has proposed to her in 47 States of the Union, and in 47 States she has accepted him. To-night she will give him her answer in the great Empire State of New York! John and Mary, stand up!

(*They do so*)

Can you look at them and not be thrilled by their youth, their charm, their passion? Ladies and gentlemen, I give you John P. Wintergreen and Mary Turner!

(*Fulton sits down as pandemonium breaks loose. Wintergreen and Mary come forward; the tumult slowly dies*)

WINTERGREEN: My friends, I come before you in this final rally of the campaign not as John P. Wintergreen the candidate, not as John P. Wintergreen the statesman, but as a simple man in love. So I beg you to bear with me for a moment, while I ask the girl of my dreams if she will be my heart's delight.

(*There is applause as he turns to Mary*)

Miss Turner, there has been something on my mind for a long, long time.

MARY: Yes, Mr. Wintergreen?

WINTERGREEN: (*The hesitant lover*) May I not call you—Mary?

MARY: I wish you would—John.

WINTERGREEN: Do you remember that night we first walked together, on the boardwalk in Atlantic City?

MARY: With the moon shining overhead?

WINTERGREEN: And the lights rippling on the water. Do you remember what I said to you, Mary, as I took your dear hand in mine?

MARY: You said— (*She drops her eyes*) that I reminded you of your mother, who had been dead these many years.

WINTERGREEN: And in the cornfields of Kansas, on the plains of Arizona, in the mountains of Nebraska, I whispered to you how much you were beginning to mean to me.

MARY: Our friendship has been a wonderful thing to me.

WINTERGREEN: And in the cave in Kentucky—

(*Two Photographers dash on. Wintergreen stops until picture is taken*)

—when you were frightened of the darkness, I put my arm around your trembling shoulder and drew you to me.

MARY: You were so brave, so strong.

WINTERGREEN: Mary, I can conceal it from you no longer. Look at me, darling. (*He tilts her face up*) I love you.

(*The Crowd breaks into great cheers and applause. Wintergreen stops them with a gesture*)

Yes, Mary, I love you.

(*A gesture to halt applause that has not come*)

MARY: Why, John! I hardly know what to say.

WINTERGREEN: Say that you love me, Mary, and that you will be mine.

MARY: I do love you, John.

(*Applause. The Crowd on its feet. Wintergreen again checks them*)

WINTERGREEN: And if I am elected President, will you marry me?

MARY: (*With simple determination*) I will.

WINTERGREEN: (*Turns quickly to the crowd, his arm still around Mary*) Citizens, it is up to you! Can you let this glorious romance end unhappily!

MARY: Can you tear asunder two loving hearts whom God hath joined together!

WINTERGREEN: I put my faith and trust in the American people! Go then to the polls on Tuesday and show the whole world that the United States of America stands first, last and always for Love! Are you with me?

ALL: (*On their feet*) YES!

FULTON: Sing 'em the campaign song, Jack! Sing the campaign love song!

OF THEE I SING

WINTERGREEN:

From the Island of Manhattan to the Coast of Gold,
From North to South, from East to West,
You are the love I love the best.
You're the dream girl of the sweetest story ever told;
A dream I've sought both night and day
For years through all the U.S.A.
The star I've hitched my wagon to
Is very obviously you.

Of thee I sing, baby—
Summer, autumn, winter, spring, baby.
You're my silver lining,
You're my sky of blue;
There's a love-light shining
Just because of you.

Of thee I sing, baby—
You have got that certain thing, baby!
Shining star and inspiration,
Worthy of a mighty nation—
Of thee I sing!

(*The Crowd yells itself blue in the face. When they are good and blue, the curtain falls*)

SCENE 5: *Election Night. The roar of the Crowd, the blowing of horns, the tooting of sirens. A band that plays furiously. The voice of a nation is speaking, and the results are being thrown upon a motion picture screen. Faster and faster they come—bulletins from here, there, and everywhere; photographs of the candidate, photographs of Mary Turner, photographs of people that have nothing to do with anything. And returns, returns, returns:*

WHITESIDE, VERMONT
Indications are that Wintergreen has swept the town by a
plurality of 154.

—

WATERVILLE, MASS.
Early returns show Wintergreen well ahead.
First election district gives:
Wintergreen 12
Scattering 1

—

A picture of John P. Wintergreen.

—

A picture of Mary Turner.

—

ATLANTA, GA.
16 election districts out of 184 give:
Wintergreen 12,736
Jefferson Davis 1,653

—

NEW YORK, N.Y.
126 election districts report:
Wintergreen 72,639
Bryan 128
Absent 4
Late 2

—

A Picture of Mary Turner.

—

A Picture of Wintergreen.

—

A Picture of George Washington, of all people.

—

LANDSLIDE, NEB.
John P. Wintergreen 12,538
A Man Named Wilkins 1

—

A Picture of Patrick Henry.

—

HOLLYWOOD, CAL.

Wintergreen 160,000
Mickey Mouse 159,000
Gloria Swanson's First Husband 84,638

—

John P. Wintergreen Casting Ballot No. 8 at Public School 63 at 6:05 o'clock this morning.
(And a picture of him doing so)

—

John P. Wintergreen Casting Ballot No. 168 at Public School 145 at 8:10 o'clock this morning and 2:25 this afternoon.

—

NEW YORK, N.Y.

Alexander Throttlebottom, vice-presidential candidate, gets his shoes shined preparatory to entering election booth.
(But one sees only the feet.)

—

A Picture of The White House.

—

Wintergreen again.

—

NEW YORK, N.Y.
8 Rubbers Out of 150 Give:

Culbertson 300
Lenz 200
Grand Slam 1000
Vulnerable 1500

—

More pictures:
Benjamin Franklin.
Babe Ruth. (*Just for good measure*)

—

NEW YORK, N.Y.
41 Election Districts give:

Wintergreen 46,572
Walter Hampden 136
Mae West 82

—

LEXINGTON, KENTUCKY.

Wintergreen 27,637
Light Wines and Beer 14
Straight Whiskey 1,850,827

—

Pictures again:

John P. Wintergreen.
Patrick Henry.
Primo Carnera.
Man O' War.

—

MANCHESTER, ENGLAND.

Wintergreen 14,653
King George 3
Queen Mary 1

—

ROME, ITALY.
127 Election Districts give:

Wintergreen 0
Mussolini 828,638

—

NEW YORK, N.Y.
Empire State gives Wintergreen plurality of
1,627,535, with only three counties missing.

—

LATER
Three missing New York counties located by
Pinkerton men in Northeast Nebraska.

—

More pictures:
George Washington.
The Marx Brothers.

—

NEW YORK, N.Y.
First Returns from Wall St. Give:

Wintergreen 192,000
Radio . . . . $5\frac{3}{4}$
Goldman, Sachs . . . . $2\frac{1}{8}$

—

And still more pictures:
The White House.
The Capitol.
The Roxy.
Roxy Himself.
A Friend of Roxy's.
An Unidentified Man.
(*Who looks suspiciously like the vice-presidential candidate*)

—

MACY'S BASEMENT.
Wintergreen ......~~$1.50~~............. 97¢
(Only one to a customer)

—

RICHMOND, VA.
Wintergreen 98,728
Mason............................ 499
Dixon 1
Mason & Dixon 500

—

ST. LOUIS, MO.

				R	H	E
Cardinals .	000	010	000	1	4	1
Giants . . .	000	000	002	2	5	0

—

All returns indicate that
Wintergreen is sweeping
Country!

—

Wintergreen lacks
only four votes
to win!

—

WINTERGREEN
CASTS LAST
FOUR VOTES!

—

WINTERGREEN
ELECTED!

—

Our Next President!
(*A beaming picture of Wintergreen*)

—

Our Next First Lady!
(*Miss Turner at her gayest*)

BULLETIN

At a late hour to-night the defeated candidate sent the following telegram to John P. Wintergreen, the winner:

"Heartily congratulate you on your splendid victory and charge fraud in Indiana, Illinois, Nebraska, Montana, Washington, Ohio and Massachusetts."

—

BULLETIN

At midnight to-night Alexander Throttlebottom refused to concede his election as Vice-President.

—

NEXT WEEK:
NORMA SHEARER
in
"THE LOVE GIRL"

—

And, to finish off, the Metro-Goldwyn lion.
It opens its mouth. It crows.

CURTAIN

SCENE 6: *On the steps of the Capitol, Washington, D.C. It is In-auguration Day, and the scene is one of flashing uniforms and surging crowds. Except for a cleared space in which the all-important ceremony is to take place—two ceremonies, as a matter of fact—the steps are packed with diplomats, Army and Navy attachés, Cabinet members, Senators, Congressmen, and anyone else who could get a ticket. As background for all this there looms the Capitol itself, with the great dome polishing it all off.*

A hush falls on the crowd. The proceedings are about to begin.

Enter, to music, the nine judges of the Supreme Court of the

United States—wrapped in their black robes, and all looking as-
tonishingly like a certain Chief Justice who shall be nameless.

The Judges sing.

ENTRANCE OF SUPREME COURT JUDGES

JUDGES:

We're the one, two, three, four, five, six, seven, eight,
nine Supreme Court Judges.
As the super Solomons of this great nation
We will supervise today's inauguration,
And we'll sup'rintend the wedding celebration
In a manner official and judicial.
One, two, three, four, five, six, seven, eight, nine
Supreme Court Judges!

We have powers that are positively regal;
Only we can take a law and make it legal.

ALL:

They're the A.K.s who give the O.K.s!
One, two, three, four, five, six, seven, eight, nine
Supreme Court Judges!

(*There is a great fanfare of trumpets in the distance—a*
swelling cheer)

Hail! Hail! The ruler of our gov'ment!
Hail! Hail! The man who taught what love meant!
Clear, clear the way
For his inaugural and wedding day!
Hail! Hail! The mighty ruler of love!
Hail! Hail! The man who made us love love!
Hip! Hip! Hooray!
For his inaugural and wedding day!

(*Enter to terrific cheering, Wintergreen and the Committee.*
High-hatted, frock-coated)

CHIEF JUSTICE: (*spoken*) And, now, Mr. President, if you don't
mind, we'd like your inaugural address.

WINTERGREEN: (*Sings*)

I have definite ideas about the Philippines
And the herring situation up in Bismarck;
I have notions on the salaries of movie queens
And the men who sign their signatures with *this* mark!

(*Makes cross*)

ALL:

He has definite ideas about the Philippines
And the herring situation up in Bismarck;
He has notions on the salaries of movie queens
And the men who sign their signatures with *this* mark!

(*Make cross*)

A KISS FOR CINDERELLA

WINTERGREEN:

But on this glorious day I find
I'm sentimentally inclined.
And so—
I sing this to the girls I used to know:

Here's a kiss for Cinderella
And a parting kiss for May;
Toodle-oo, good-bye, this is my wedding day.

Here's a parting smile for Della
And the lady known as Lou;
Toodle-oo, good-bye, with bach'lor days I'm through!

(*And the girls in question, believe it or not, parade tantalizingly by him*)

Tho' I really never knew them,
It's a rule I must obey;
So I'm saying good-bye to them
In the customary way.

My regards to Arabella
And to Emmaline and Kay!
Toodle-oo, dear girls, good-bye!
This is my wedding day.

(*Wintergreen repeats first six lines of above; all others sing against this:*)

ALL OTHERS:

He is toodle-ooing all his lady loves,
All the girls he didn't know so well,
All the innocent and all the shady loves,

> Oh, ding-a-dong-a-dell!
> Bride and groom, their future should be glorious—
> What a happy story they will tell;
> Let the welkin now become uproarious,
> Oh, ding-a-dong-a-dell!

(*On a platform at the head of the stairs, as if by magic, there appears Mary Turner, gorgeous in bridal attire*)

ALL:

> Clear the way!
> Hail the bride!
> Sweet and gay—
> Here comes the bride!

MARY:

> Is it true or am I dreaming?
> Do I go to Heav'n to stay?
> Never was a girl so happy on her wedding day!

CHIEF JUSTICE: (*spoken*) Do you, John P. Wintergreen, solemnly swear to uphold the Constitution of the United States of America and to love, honor, and cherish this woman so long as you two shall live?

WINTERGREEN: I do.

CHIEF JUSTICE: Do you, Mary Turner, promise to love, honor, and cherish this man so long as you two shall live?

MARY: I do.

CHIEF JUSTICE: Therefore, by virtue of the power that is vested in me as Chief Justice, I hereby pronounce you President of the United States, man and wife.

WINTERGREEN: Mary!

MARY: John!

(*They embrace; the crowd yells its head off*)

BOTH: (*Sing*)

> Is it true or am I dreaming?
> Do I go to Heav'n to stay?
> Never was a girl (man) so happy on her (his) wedding—

(*Enter, of all people, Diana Devereaux. And is she annoyed?*)

DIANA: Stop! Halt! Pause! Wait!

ALL:

> Who is this intruder?

There's no one could be ruder!
(*to Diana*)
>   What's your silly notion
>   In causing this commotion?

I WAS THE MOST BEAUTIFUL BLOSSOM

DIANA: (*recitative, and with highly operatic interludes*)
>   I was the most beautiful blossom
>   In all the Southland;
>   I was sent up North to enter the contest
>   With the understanding that the winner
>   Was to be the President's wife.
>   The Committee examined me.
>   My lily-white body fascinated them.
>   I was chosen.
>   It was the happiest moment of my life.

ENSEMBLE:
>   Yes, yes, go on!
>   Yes, yes, go on!

DIANA:
>   Suddenly, the sky fell.
>   Suddenly, for no reason at all,
>   No reason at all,
>   This man rejected me.

>   All my castles came tumbling down.
>   And so I am serving him with a summons
>   For breach of promise!

ENSEMBLE:
>   What! What!
>   The water's getting hot!
>   She says he made a promise,
>   A promise he forgot.

DIANA:
>   It's true! It's true!

JUDGES:
>   The day he's getting married,
>   You put him on the spot!
>   It's dirty work of Russia,
>   A communistic plot!

WINTERGREEN:
> Please understand,
> It wasn't that I would jilt or spurn 'er;
> It's just that there was someone else.

ENSEMBLE:
> Whom?

WINTERGREEN: (*correcting them*)
> *Who!*
> Mary Turner!

CHIEF JUSTICE:
> We're having fits!

ENSEMBLE:
> We're having fits!

CHIEF JUSTICE:
> The man admits . . .

ENSEMBLE:
> The man admits . . .

CHIEF JUSTICE:
> This little sinner . . .

ENSEMBLE:
> This little sinner . . .

CHIEF JUSTICE:
> Was really winner!

ENSEMBLE:
> Was really winner!

DIANA:
> I couldn't see . . .

ENSEMBLE:
> She couldn't see . . .

DIANA:
> His jilting me.

ENSEMBLE:
> His jilting she.

DIANA:
> And so I'm doing . . .

ENSEMBLE:
> And so I'm doing . . .

DIANA:
> A bit of suing.

ENSEMBLE:

    A bit of suing.

MEN:

    And if it's true she has a claim,
    You should be called a dirty name!

GIRLS:

    Yes, if it's true she has a claim,
    Then you're a dirty, dirty name!

MARY:

    John, no matter what they do to hurt you.
    The one you love won't desert you.

DIANA:

    I'm a queen who has lost her king!
    Why should she wear the wedding ring?

SOME GIRLS CAN BAKE A PIE (*Reprise*)

WINTERGREEN:

    Some girls can bake a pie
    Made up of prunes and quinces;
    Some make an oyster fry—
    Others are good at blinzes.
    Some lovely girls have done
    Wonders with turkey stuffin's,
    But I have found the one
    Who can really make corn muffins

DIANA:

    Who cares about corn muffins?
    All I demand is justice!

WINTERGREEN:

    Which is more important?
    Corn muffins or justice?

ENSEMBLE:

    Which is more important?
    Corn muffins or justice?

JUDGES:

    If you will wait a minute,
    You'll have our decision.

    (*The Justices leap into a football huddle. After a moment they resume their positions*)

The decision of the Supreme Court is—
Corn muffins!

ENSEMBLE:

Great! Great!
It's written on the slate!
There's none but Mary Turner
Could ever be his mate!

DIANA:

It's I, not Mary Turner,
Who should have been his mate.
I'm off to tell my story
In ev'ry single state.

ENSEMBLE:

Be off with you, young woman,
He's married to his mate.
There's none but Mary Turner
Could ever be his mate.

(*Repeat these lines*)

DIANA: (*spoken*) See you in court, y'all.

(*Diana goes, but she'll be heard from again*)

OF THEE I SING (*Reprise*)

WINTERGREEN:

Of thee I sing, baby—

ENSEMBLE:

Summer, autumn, winter, spring, baby!
Shining star and inspiration
Worthy of a mighty nation,
Of thee I sing!

CURTAIN

ACT II

SCENE 1: *The President's office, in the White House. And not only the President's office, but the President's wife's office, too. There are several indications of this joint occupancy. The Presidential desk, for example, is divided into two sections—one piled high with various state papers, and the other lined with perfumes, powders, and the other perquisites of femininity. Great portraits of George and Martha Washington look down from on high; the governmental eagle adorns the curtains.*

The same Jenkins who used to work for Mr. Fulton is now secretary to the President, and with Mrs. Wintergreen's secretary, Miss Benson, he is hard at work when the curtain rises. Enter, to music, about two dozen more secretaries. They all get together in a little song and dance—an old White House custom:

HELLO, GOOD MORNING

BOYS:
> Hello, good morning!

GIRLS:
> Good morning, hello!

BOYS:
> How are you this very lovely day?

GIRLS:
> I feel very well, sir.

BOYS:
> And I'm feeling swell.

BOTH:
> It's great to be alive
> And work from nine to five.

JENKINS AND BENSON:
> Hello, good morning!

GIRLS AND BOYS:
> Good morning, hello!
> Isn't this a moment that's divine?

JENKINS AND BENSON:
> I see it's almost nine.

421

ALL:

> And we only have one minute more to say:
> Hello, good morning!
> Isn't this a lovely day?
> Isn't this a lovely day?
>
> Oh, it's great to be a secret'ry
> In the White House, D.C.
> You get inside information on Algeria;
> You know ev'ry move they're making in Liberia.
> You learn what's what and what is not
> In the Land of the Free.
> Ev'ry corner that you turn you meet a notable
> With a statement that is eminently quotable.
> Oh, it's great to be a secret'ry
> In the White House, D.C.

(Jenkins and Benson dance. At conclusion, all exit, arm in arm, singing:)

> So long, good morning!
> Wasn't this a lovely day?
> Wasn't this a lovely day?

(They whistle as they exit)

(A White House Guide enters, followed by a crowd of Sightseers. They are plainly from the country—men with loosely wrapped umbrellas, women with waistlines not in the right place, and a terrible child or two)

GUIDE: And this, ladies and gentlemen, is the executive office. This is the room in which the President discharges his official duties, and has been occupied by every President since Hoover. On your right stands the famous double desk used by the President and Mrs. Wintergreen in administering the affairs of the country. During the 1912 coal shortage this room was used as a garage. Right this way, please. We are now entering the room from which, on an historic occasion, the Spanish Ambassador jumped out of the window, in the very nick of time. Here the diplomatic corps gathers once a month to pay its formal respects to the Chief Executive, and here too the cabinet assembles when—

(The last Sightseer is through the door)

(*The telephone on the desk rings*)

JENKINS: Hello. . . . Who? . . . No, the Coolidges don't live here any more!

MISS BENSON: (*Holding a perfume bottle up to the light*) Mrs. Wintergreen is running low on Chanel No. 5.

JENKINS: (*Consulting a schedule*) Looks like a pretty full day. (*Reads*) Delegation from South America—

MISS BENSON: What's eating them?

JENKINS: Usual thing. Want Hollywood cleaned up. (*Looking at list*) Delegation of Camisole Indians—they want scalping restored. Committee of cotton manufacturers—that's for Mrs. Wintergreen. They want her to bring back cotton stockings.

MISS BENSON: Oh, they do, eh?

JENKINS: Mayors of fourteen American cities—

(*Another Secretary enters with newspaper clippings*) Well?

SECRETARY: Morning editorials.

(*He goes. Jenkins looks the clippings over; shakes his head*)

MISS BENSON: What's the matter?

JENKINS: Same thing. They're still harping on it.

MISS BENSON: You mean Devereaux?

JENKINS: (*As he reads*) Mm.

MISS BENSON: What's it say?

JENKINS: Nothing new. They just think she got a raw deal.

MISS BENSON: A lot of people think that.

JENKINS: (*Crumpling a clipping*) Just as well if he doesn't see this one. You know, it wouldn't surprise me a bit—

(*Another Secretary enters*)

SECRETARY: Mr. Jenkins—

JENKINS: Yes?

SECRETARY: Those people are here now. Can you see them?

JENKINS: Show them into the Blue Room.

SECRETARY: Yes, sir. (*Goes*)

JENKINS: Want to come along? Delegation from the Virgin Islands.

MISS BENSON: Well, well! And what are they after?

JENKINS: They want their name changed. They claim it's hurting business.

(*They go, as another Guide enters with a sightseeing party. A Sailor or two. A Swede. A Dutchman*)

GUIDE: Right this way, please—follow me. This ladies and gentlemen, is the executive office. It is in this room that the President signs the many laws that govern your every-day life, and from which he controls the various departmental activities.

(*One of the Sightseers emerges a bit from the crowd, eagerly taking in the scene. He turns out to be, of all people, Alexander Throttlebottom*)

Here come the various heads of government for daily consultation with the Executive, and to receive from him the benefit of his wide experience. It is in this room— (*To Throttlebottom, who has strayed a little too far from the group*) I beg your pardon, sir, but would you please stay over there with the others? You see, we're personally responsible in case anything is stolen.

THROTTLEBOTTOM: (*Meekly rejoining the group*) Yes, sir.

GUIDE: (*Opens door*) Thank you. (*Resuming his formal tone*) Now, are there any questions?

A SIGHTSEER: Does the President live here all year round?

GUIDE: All year round. Except when Congress is in session.

SIGHTSEER: Where does the vice-president live?

GUIDE: Who?

SIGHTSEER: The vice-president. Where does he live?

GUIDE: (*Taking a little red book out of his pocket*) Just one moment, please. Vice regent, viceroy, vice societies—I'm sorry, but he doesn't seem to be in here.

THROTTLEBOTTOM: (*So mildly*) I can tell you about that.

GUIDE: What?

THROTTLEBOTTOM: I know where the vice-president lives.

GUIDE: Where?

THROTTLEBOTTOM: He lives at 1448 Z Street.

GUIDE: Well, that's very interesting. He has a house there, has he?

THROTTLEBOTTOM: Well, he lives there.

GUIDE: All by himself?

THROTTLEBOTTOM: No, with the other boarders. It's an awfully good place. Mrs. Spiegelbaum's. It's a great place, if you like Kosher cooking.

GUIDE: Think of your knowing all that! Are you a Washingtonian?

THROTTLEBOTTOM: Well, I've been here since March 4. I came down for the inauguration, but I lost my ticket.

GUIDE: You don't say? Well! First time you've been to the White House?

THROTTLEBOTTOM: (*Nods*) I didn't know people were allowed in.

GUIDE: You seem to know the vice-president pretty well. What kind of fellow is he?

THROTTLEBOTTOM: He's all right. He's a nice fellow when you get to know him, but nobody wants to know him.

GUIDE: What's the matter with him?

THROTTLEBOTTOM: There's nothing the matter with him. Just vice-president.

GUIDE: Well, what does he do all the time?

THROTTLEBOTTOM: He sits around in the parks, and feeds the pigeons, and takes walks, and goes to the movies. The other day he was going to join the library, but he had to have two references, so he couldn't get in.

GUIDE: But when does he do all his work?

THROTTLEBOTTOM: What work?

SIGHTSEER: Doesn't he preside over the Senate?

THROTTLEBOTTOM: What?

GUIDE: Sure he does! That's the vice-president's job.

THROTTLEBOTTOM: What is?

GUIDE: To preside over the Senate.

THROTTLEBOTTOM: Over what?

GUIDE: The Senate. You know what Senators are, don't you?

THROTTLEBOTTOM: Sure—I saw them play yesterday.

GUIDE: No, no! The vice-president presides over the Senate. It meets in the Capitol.

THROTTLEBOTTOM: When does it?

GUIDE: Right now! It's going on now!

THROTTLEBOTTOM: (*Frenzied*) How do you get there?

GUIDE: The Capitol?

THROTTLEBOTTOM: Yeah!

GUIDE: Street car at the door—right up Pennsylvania Avenue.

THROTTLEBOTTOM: (*Hurrying out*) Street car at the door—right up Pennsyl— (*Turns back*) —what's the name of that place?

GUIDE: The Senate!

THROTTLEBOTTOM: The Senate! (*He dashes out*)

GUIDE: Right this way, please. (*Opens door*) Here the diplomatic corps gathers monthly to pay its formal respects to the Chief Executive, and here too the cabinet assembles upon the occasion of its weekly meetings—

> (*They go. In the distance there is a fanfare of trumpets; Jenkins and Miss Benson enter and take their places at the Presidential chairs. Enter, then, the President and Mary*)

WINTERGREEN AND MARY: Good morning!

JENKINS AND MISS BENSON: Good morning!

> (*Wintergreen looks out the window, through which is visible the panorama of Washington, with Washington's Monument prominent in the foreground*)

WINTERGREEN: What a country—what a country! Jenkins, what monument is that?

JENKINS: (*Promptly*) Grant's Tomb.

WINTERGREEN: Oh, yes. Well, what's on the schedule this morning? Ah, here we are! (*Takes up some letters*) Tell the Secretary of the Navy to scrap two battleships.

JENKINS: What?

WINTERGREEN: Scrap two and build four. Disarmament.

JENKINS: Yes, sir.

WINTERGREEN: Cablegram to the President of San Domingo: "Congratulations on beginning your second day in office. That's five I owe you, and will bet you double or nothing on tomorrow."

JENKINS: Yes, sir.

WINTERGREEN: Tell the Secretary of War to stand ready to collect that bet.

JENKINS: Yes, sir.

WINTERGREEN: Letter to the Friars' Club, 48th St., New York City. "Dear Brother Friars: Regret very much I cannot take part in this year's minstrel show. Owing to conditions in the South, I do not think it would be wise for me to black up." (*Looks through the pile of letters*) I get the lousiest mail for a President!

MARY: Emily! Take a cablegram to the Queen of Roumania.

MISS BENSON: Yes, ma'am.

MARY: Queen of Roumania. "Dear Marie: I have been trying out that new soap you are selling, and I predict an even greater success for it than you had with the shaving cream.

Jack joins me in sending love. Do write and tell us all about Carol."

WINTERGREEN: And that French girl. . . . Jenkins!

JENKINS: Yes, sir.

WINTERGREEN: Take a memo to the Secretary of State: "Referring to last Tuesday night's poker game, please note that the Liberian minister's check for twelve dollars and forty-five cents has been returned for lack of funds. Kindly get a new minister for next Tuesday night's game, and add $12.45 to the Liberian National Debt."

JENKINS: Yes, sir.

WINTERGREEN: Get the Governor of Maryland on the phone and ask him what horse he likes in the fourth at Pimlico.

JENKINS: Yes, sir.

WINTERGREEN: (*Brandishing a telephone bill*) And tell the telephone company that this is not my bill. (*Hands it to secretary*) That long distance call was March 3rd.

JENKINS: Yes, sir.

WINTERGREEN: Anybody in the ante-room?

JENKINS: Yes, sir. Secretary of the Navy, Secretary of Agriculture, and four zebras.

WINTERGREEN: Zebras?

JENKINS: There's a man who wants to give them to you.

WINTERGREEN: (*Thinking it over*) Well, I could use two.

(*A Secretary enters with a wooden board, covered with electric buttons. A long wire is attached to it*)

JENKINS: All ready, Mr. President. Time to press a button.

WINTERGREEN: So early in the morning?

JENKINS: Opening of the International Corn Growing Exposition. Button No. 1. . . . Ready. . . . Press.

WINTERGREEN: (*Presses button, then laughs*) Say, Jenkins, I will never forget the time I reopened the Bank of United States by mistake.

(*Jenkins beats a hasty retreat*)

(*The telephone rings*)

Hello! (*Annoyed, hands the instrument to Mary*) For you!

MARY: Who is it?

WINTERGREEN: The butcher!

MARY: Hello! . . . Oh, good morning, Mr. Schneidermann. . . .

Fine, thank you. . . . Now, let me see. What have you got
that's good? . . . Well, we had lamb chops yesterday. . . .
They *are*? Well, wait a minute. (*To Wintergreen*) John, who's
coming to dinner to-night?

WINTERGREEN: What? Let me see—the Chief Justice, the Attorney General, Jackie Cooper, and those three judges that
got paroled. That's six.

MARY: (*As she returns to 'phone*) That's eight with us. . . .
Hello, Mr. Schneidermann. Make it sixteen lamb chops—

WINTERGREEN: Wait a minute! What about that dirigible?

MARY: What?

WINTERGREEN: That dirigible from Germany. If that gets in
we've got to have *them*.

MARY: Oh, dear! How many are there?

WINTERGREEN: Ah—sixty-four passengers, and of course two
stowaways—that's sixty-six.

MARY: That's seventy-four in all.

WINTERGREEN: But they may not get here.

MARY: But when'll we know? . . . Just a minute, Mr. Schneidermann. (*Back to Wintergreen, pretty testily*) I've got to
know whether they're going to get here.

WINTERGREEN: How do I know? Take a chance! You can always use lamb chops.

MARY: (*Back to 'phone, wearily*) Listen, Mr. Schneidermann. A
hundred and forty-eight lamb chops. . . . That's right. . . .
Now, how is your asparagus? . . . Well, make it a carload of
asparagus, and about seventy-five loaves of rye bread. That's
all, thank you.

JENKINS: (*Entering*) Beg pardon, sir. Another button.

WINTERGREEN: What's this? (*Reads*) Opening of a new speakeasy on 52nd Street, New York. Didn't I open that yesterday?

JENKINS: Yes, sir. This is the re-opening. They closed it last
night. (*He goes*)

MARY: (*Coming to Wintergreen with a stack of bills in her hand*)
John, look at these grocery bills!

WINTERGREEN: Well, what about it?

MARY: I've simply got to have a bigger allowance.

WINTERGREEN: Again! For God's sake, Mary!

MARY: Well, I can't help it. Fifty people to dinner every night.
And Senators to breakfast every morning. It mounts up.

WINTERGREEN: I've got to have them! It's business!

MARY: Then you've got to give me enough to feed them.

WINTERGREEN: Where am I going to get it from?

MARY: Get it from! If you had any gumption you'd ask Congress for a raise.

WINTERGREEN: Ask Congress for a raise! I'm lucky they don't lay me off!

(*Jenkins enters*)

JENKINS: I beg your pardon.

WINTERGREEN: It's all right. What is it?

JENKINS: The Secretary of Agriculture and the Secretary of the Navy are still waiting.

WINTERGREEN: I forgot. Have them come in.

SECRETARY: The Secretary of Agriculture!

(*He enters. It turns out to be our old friend Lippman*)

LIPPMAN: Hello, Jack! Hello, Mary!

WINTERGREEN: Hello, Secretary!

SECRETARY: The Secretary of the Navy!

(*Enter Gilhooley. It seems that Wintergreen took care of the boys*)

WINTERGREEN: Sit down, boys. Sorry I kept you waiting.

LIPPMAN: That's all right.

GILHOOLEY: O.K., Chief.

WINTERGREEN: Well, what's on your mind, Louis? How's agriculture?

LIPPMAN: That's what I came to talk to you about. Listen, Jack! I don't know anything about agriculture. I told you I wanted the Treasury.

WINTERGREEN: What's the matter with agriculture?

LIPPMAN: Agriculture's all right—it's those farmers. Wheat, wheat! All they know is raise wheat! And then they raise hell with me because nobody wants it.

WINTERGREEN: Why do you let them raise so much?

LIPPMAN: How can you stop 'em? I did all I could. I invited the seven-year-locusts, but they didn't come. Even the locusts don't want their lousy wheat. And they're always complaining about being in one place all the time—they want to travel.

GILHOOLEY: You call that trouble. How'd you like to have a lot of sailors on your neck?

WINTERGREEN: What do *they* want—*two* wives in every port?

GILHOOLEY: Yeah. And any port in a storm. And no storms. And they won't stand for those bells any more. They want to know what time it is the same as anybody else. But that's not the big thing.

WINTERGREEN: Well?

GILHOOLEY: It's the ocean. They don't like the ocean.

WINTERGREEN: Which ocean don't they like?

GILHOOLEY: All of them. They say it's a nice place to visit, but they don't want to live there. It's no place to bring up a family.

WINTERGREEN: (*Thinking it over*) The farmers want to travel and the sailors want to settle down. . . . I've got it! Have them change places!

LIPPMAN: What?

WINTERGREEN: It'll solve the whole problem! Sailors don't know anything about farming—in two years there won't *be* any wheat! You'll have a wheat shortage!

LIPPMAN: And I'll get hell again!

WINTERGREEN: And look what it does for business! You get the farmers on the boats; the traveling salesmen will come back to the farmhouses—*you* know, to stay over night! Why, I haven't heard a good story in years!

(*A Secretary enters*)

SECRETARY: The Secretary of State!

(*He comes in. It is Fulton*)

FULTON: Hello, boys. Everybody.

WINTERGREEN: How are you, Matty?

FULTON: (*All business*) What are you doing, Jack? Important?

WINTERGREEN: Just chinning.

FULTON: (*A look toward the doors*) Can you keep the room clear for a little while?

WINTERGREEN: Sure. What's up?

FULTON: (*Starts toward door*) Shall I tell 'em?

WINTERGREEN: No, here we are. (*Presses a buzzer*)

LIPPMAN: (*Starting off*) See you later.

FULTON: No, no. Want you fellows to stay.

(*Jenkins enters*)

WINTERGREEN: I don't want to be disturbed for a little while.

JENKINS: Yes, sir.

FULTON: Just a minute. When Senators Jones and Lyons get here, bring 'em in.

JENKINS: Yes, sir.

FULTON: And nobody else.

JENKINS: Yes, sir. What shall I do about the press conference?

FULTON: Have 'em wait!

(*Jenkins goes. Fulton waits for the doors to close*)

There's hell to pay!

WINTERGREEN: What's the matter?

FULTON: Devereaux!

MARY: John! (*He puts an arm around her*)

WINTERGREEN: What about her?

FULTON: The thing has been growing for weeks—*you* know that, boys— (*This to Lippman and Gilhooley*)

WINTERGREEN: What has?

FULTON: Well, you know there's always been a certain bunch that said Devereaux didn't get a square deal.

WINTERGREEN: A handful of Southerners!

FULTON: At the beginning, yes. But now it's spreading all over the country!

WINTERGREEN: What do you mean?

MARY: What's happened?

FULTON: I'll tell you what I mean. Yesterday the Federation of New Jersey Woman's Clubs came out solid for Devereaux.

MARY: John! (*A sob from Mary*)

FULTON: And this morning I got a petition from the Kansas City Elks—demanding Devereaux! And the same thing'll happen with the Moose and the Shriners!

(*Enter Senators Jones and Lyons*)

(*A nod or two from the others*)

FULTON: Good! I've just been telling the President how things stand!

JONES: Mr. President, I cannot overstate the case. The West is up in arms.

LYONS: The South, suh, is on fire!

JONES: Nebraska has just declared martial law! A posse has been formed!

LYONS: In Louisiana you have been hanged in effigy!

WINTERGREEN: (*Defiant*) How do the Philippines feel about it?

MARY: It's all my fault!

WINTERGREEN: No! I'd rather have you than Nebraska!

FULTON: It doesn't matter whose fault it is. We've got to do something! We've got to do something to counteract this Devereaux propaganda!

WINTERGREEN: I'll tell you what we'll do! (*Presses a buzzer*) We carried 48 States in the campaign, didn't we? Mary and I?

FULTON: Yeah!

WINTERGREEN: And there was Devereaux propaganda then! But we licked it before and we can do it again!

(*As Jenkins enters*)

Those newspaper men still out there?

JENKINS: Yes, sir.

WINTERGREEN: Bring 'em in when I ring!

JENKINS: Yes, sir. (*Goes*)

WINTERGREEN: The trouble with you boys is you're yellow!

FULTON: Now look here!

WINTERGREEN: One sock and you're ready to quit! We've got to fight, that's all! I'm as good as I ever was! And so's Mary! And we still love each other! (*Turning to her*) Don't we?

MARY: (*With spirit*) You bet we do!

WINTERGREEN: (*Swinging back onto the men*) There you are! We're not through! We haven't begun to fight! By God, we can tour again if we have to! I can still sing! Once a trouper always a trouper!

(*Mary is freshening the lip-stick and powdering the face*)

What do you say, boys? Are you with me?

ALL: Yes!

(*Wintergreen presses the buzzer*)

FULTON: You got to put it over, Jack!

WINTERGREEN: I'll put it over! I'll give them the best performance since Richard Mansfield! Are you ready, Mary?

MARY: (*Finishing the make-up job*) Ready!

WINTERGREEN: (*As a Secretary enters*) Bring in those newspapermen!

(*Music strikes up. Enter the Newspapermen*)

WINTERGREEN: Well, gentlemen, what's on your mind?

REPORTERS: (*Singing it, of course*)

WHO CARES?

REPORTERS:

> We don't want to know about the moratorium,
> Or how near we are to beer,
> Or about the League of Nations,
> Or the seventeen vacations
> You have had since you've been here.

> Here's the one thing that the people of America
> Are beside themselves to know:
> They would like to know what's doing
> On the lady who is suing
> You—Diana Devereaux!

> Ev'rybody wants to know:
> What about Miss Devereaux?
> From the highest to the low:
> What about Miss Devereaux?

WINTERGREEN:

> It's a pleasant day—
> That's all I can say!

MARY:

> Here's the one thing we'll announce:
> Love's the only thing that counts!

REPORTERS:

> People want to know:
> What of Devereaux?

WINTERGREEN:

> When the one you love is near,
> Nothing else can interfere.

ALL:

> When the one you love is near,
> Nothing else can interfere.

WINTERGREEN:

> Here's some information
> I will gladly give the nation:
> I am for the true love;
> Here's the only girl I do love.

MARY:

> I love him and he loves me,
> And that's how it will always be,

So what care we about Miss Devereaux?

BOTH:

Who cares what the public chatters?
Love's the only thing that matters.

Who cares
If the sky cares to fall in the sea?
Who cares what banks fail in Yonkers,
Long as you've got a kiss that conquers?
Why should I care?
Life is one long jubilee,
So long as I care for you—
And you care for me.

(*This argument being unanswerable, the Reporters go, completely convinced. The Committee, highly pleased, surrounds Wintergreen and congratulates him*)

WINTERGREEN: Nothing at all, boys! I owe it all to the little woman!

MARY: You were grand, John!

FULTON: I never heard you in better voice!

WINTERGREEN: Did you hear that F sharp I gave them?

GILHOOLEY: Great!

WINTERGREEN: (*Letting his voice loose for a second in a snatch of operatic aria*) Do you know what I'll do? I'll go on the radio every night! Mary and I!

FULTON: National Biscuit Co.! They've been after you!

JONES: National Biscuit! That's a very popular hour in the West!

WINTERGREEN: A new song every night! I'll even get a megaphone!

MARY: And we can make records!

WINTERGREEN: (*Ever practical*) No, dear. They don't sell any more!

FULTON: Well, every little helps!

MARY: And I can still bake!

WINTERGREEN: What!

MARY: Corn muffins! Corn muffins for the unemployed!

WINTERGREEN: That's my girl! You feed 'em and I'll sing to them! We'll get the country back! Give us a week and they'll forget that Devereaux ever lived!

(*A chorus of approval from the Committee*)
And you fellows wanted to quit! Why, we haven't begun to fight! This is a cinch! What would you do if a real fight came along!

(*Enter a dozen Secretaries*)
What's this?

SECRETARIES: The French Ambassador!

WINTERGREEN: I can't see him!

(*Enter another dozen Secretaries*)
And what's this?

SECRETARIES: The French Ambassador!

WINTERGREEN: I can't see him!

(*Enter half a dozen French Soldiers, in full uniforms and Oh! what beards. They line up and sing, it being an old rule that French Soldiers always sing when they line up*)

Garçon, S'il Vous Plaît

FRENCH SOLDIERS:

> Garçon, s'il vous plaît,
> Encore Chevrolet coupé;
> Papah, pooh, pooh, pooh!
> À vous tout dir vay à vous?
> Garçon, qu'est-ce que c'est?
> Tra la, Maurice Chevalier!
> J'adore crêpes Suzette
> Et aussi Lafayette!

(*They march, repeat this, come to attention*)

> And now we give the meaning of this song:
> We're six of the fifty million and we can't be wrong!

(*Enter the French Ambassador. You never saw so many medals*)

FRENCH SOLDIERS: Ze French Ambassador!

WINTERGREEN: I still can't see him!

Entrance of French Ambassador

FRENCH AMBASSADOR:

> I am the Ambassador of France,
> And I've come here to see
> A grievous wrong righted.
> My country is deeply hurt.
> Not since the days of Louis the Seventh,

> The Eighth, the Ninth, the Tenth,
> And possibly the Eleventh,
> Has such a thing happened.

ENSEMBLE:

> What's troubling you?

FRENCH AMBASSADOR:

> You have done a great injustice
> To a French descendant—
> A lovely girl
> Whose rights have been trampled in the dust.

ENSEMBLE:

> Who is she? What's her name?

FRENCH AMBASSADOR:

> Her name is Diana Devereaux.

ENSEMBLE:

> Diana Devereaux! Diana Devereaux!
> Since when is she of French descent?

FRENCH AMBASSADOR:

> I've been looking up her family tree
> And I have found a most important pedigree!

THE ILLEGITIMATE DAUGHTER

> She's the illegitimate daughter
> Of an illegitimate son
> Of an illegitimate nephew
> Of Napoléon.

ENSEMBLE:

> Napoléon?

FRENCH AMBASSADOR:

> She offers aristocracy
> To this bizarre democracy,
> Where naught is sacred but the old simoleon!
> I must know why
> You crucify
> My native country
> With this effront'ry
> To the illegitimate daughter
> Of an illegitimate son
> Of an illegitimate nephew
> Of Napoléon!

ENSEMBLE:

>To the illegitimate daughter
>Of an illegitimate son
>Of an illegitmate nephew
>Of Napoléon!

   (*Ensemble turns on Wintergreen*)

ENSEMBLE:

>You so-and-so!
>We didn't know
>She had a tie-up
>So very high up!
>She's the illegitimate daughter
>Of an illegitimate son
>Of an illegitimate nephew
>Of Napoléon!

   (*The voice of Diana is heard in the distance. A snatch of aria. She enters, singing*)

DIANA:

>Ah!
>I was the most beautiful blossom
>In all the Southland.

MARY AND WINTERGREEN:

>We know all that.

FRENCH AMBASSADOR:

>You know all that,
>But you *don't* know the misery
>Of this poor little girl who has suffered.
>Because . . .

ENSEMBLE:

>Because?

MARY AND WINTERGREEN:

>Because?

FRENCH AMBASSADOR:

>Because . . .

BECAUSE, BECAUSE (*Reprise*)

DIANA:

>Because, because, because, because
>I won the competition
>But I got no recognition

And because he broke my heart!

Because, because, because, because
The man who ought to love me
Tried to make a monkey of me,
Double-crossing from the start!

I might have been First Lady,
But now my past is shady.
Oh, pity this poor maidie!

FRENCH AMBASSADOR:
And there's the man who ought to pay!

ENSEMBLE:
Because, because, because, because
She won the prize for beauty,
But he didn't do his duty;
He has broken her poor heart!

FRENCH AMBASSADOR: (*to Wintergreen*)
You see this poor girl has suffered.
And so, on behalf of France,
I demand that your marriage be annulled
And that you marry Diana.

WINTERGREEN:
Never, never!

FRENCH AMBASSADOR:
Then you will arouse the anger of France,
And you must be prepared to face the consequences!
(*Soldiers line up with Ambassador and Diana. They march off, singing*)

FRENCH SOLDIERS:
Garçon, s'il vous plaît,
Encore Chevrolet coupé!
Papah, pooh, pooh, pooh,
À vous tout dir vay à vous?

FULTON:
Jack, you've got to do something about this.

WINTERGREEN:
Leave Mary? Never!

FULTON:
We are all in this together;
We are birdies of a feather.

          And if you don't change your thesis
          Then our party goes to pieces!

LYONS:
          All our jobs you'll be destroying
          With your attitude annoying.

GILHOOLEY:
          You will get us all in trouble!
          And in spades, sir, which is double!

WINTERGREEN:
          I will never leave my Mary!

LYONS:
          Since he's acting so contrary,
          Send him off on a vacation.

GILHOOLEY:
          I suggest his resignation.

WINTERGREEN:
          Resignation?

ENSEMBLE:
          Resignation?

FULTON:
          You've got to face it—This is a crisis!
          To leave your Mary you may decline;
          But to save us, my good advice is:
          You resign!

ENSEMBLE:
          Yes, resign.

WINTERGREEN:
          I assure you—though it's a crisis,
          To leave my Mary I must decline,
          And I don't care what your advice is;
          I decline to resign!

MARY:
          We decline to resign!

          WE'LL IMPEACH HIM

LYONS AND GILHOOLEY:
          He is stubborn—We must teach him;
          I'm afraid we must impeach him!

ENSEMBLE:
          He is stubborn—We must teach him;

                    He has forced us to impeach him!
COMMITTEE:
            You decline to resign.
            So we'll teach you!
            We'll impeach you!
SECRETARIES:
            You decline to resign—
            We don't envy you at all!
COMMITTEE:
            You decline to resign.
            So we'll teach you!
            We'll impeach you!
            You decline to resign—
            Humpty Dumpty has to fall!
        (*They go—leaving Wintergreen and Mary alone. In the cir-
        cumstances there is only one thing to do—and they do it.
        They sing a reprise*)

                    WHO CARES? (*Reprise*)
MARY:
            Who cares
            If the sky cares to fall in the sea?
WINTERGREEN:
            We two together can win out;
            Just remember to stick your chin out.
MARY:
            Why should we care?
            Life is one long jubilee—
BOTH:
            So long as I care for you—
            And you care for me!
        (*The lights dim; the curtains come together*)

SCENE 2: *A Capitol corridor, just outside the United States Senate. A smartly dressed page comes out of the Senate door; another
goes in.*

*Enter, then, the Committee—those same five boys. As they come in
Fulton is doing the talking.*

FULTON: Say, I'm just as sorry as anybody. I like Jack as much as you do, and I'd give my shirt not to have to do this.

JONES: We can't be sentimental at a time like this.

GILHOOLEY: Say! Wait a minute! If he's put out of office who becomes the President?

JONES: Why, the vice-president, of course.

LIPPMAN: Who's that?

FULTON: (*As it dawns on him*) We haven't got a vice-president.

GILHOOLEY: Sure we have! He came up to the room!

    (*Enter Alexander Throttlebottom. He is panting, having run all the way from the White House. The Committee continues its argument*)

FULTON: (*Suddenly remembering*) Pitts! I nominated him!

    (*A chorus of dissent. Lippman: "No, that wasn't his name!" Jones: "It was Schaeffer!" Lyons: "No, Pitts!" Gilhooley: "No, it was a longer name. Barbinelli!"*)

    (*Throttlebottom, who has been listening to all this in full expectation of imminent discovery, now comes over to them*)

THROTTLEBOTTOM: Hello, gentlemen!

FULTON: It was Alexander Something.

GILHOOLEY: Yah, that's it!

THROTTLEBOTTOM: Throttlebottom.

GILHOOLEY: That's right!

    (*A chorus from the others. "Yes, that's right!"*)

FULTON: (*Realizing that it is a stranger who has spoken*) Oh! Thank you. (*Hands him a cigar*)

THROTTLEBOTTOM: Oh, thank you, Mr. Fulton.

FULTON: (*Looking at him*) Haven't I seen you before some place?

THROTTLEBOTTOM: I'm Throttlebottom.

FULTON: Huh?

THROTTLEBOTTOM: Throttlebottom. The vice-president. That's how I knew the name.

    (*A chorus of greetings. "Well, hello!" "Where have you been?" "Well, for God's sake!" "Here! Have a light!"*)

FULTON: Well, for heaven's sake! Just the fellow we were looking for!

GILHOOLEY: Yes, *sir!*

FULTON: We want to talk to you!

THROTTLEBOTTOM: Me?

LYONS: That's what!

FULTON: We've got a surprise for you!

THROTTLEBOTTOM: (*Covering his eyes*) A surprise?

LIPPMAN: Sure! Remember I told you you had a chance to be President?

THROTTLEBOTTOM: Yeah!

FULTON: Well, we've been thinking it over and we're going to make you President!

GILHOOLEY: That's what we are!

THROTTLEBOTTOM: President! Say! You mean of the United States?

JONES: That's what we do!

THROTTLEBOTTOM: But what was the matter with the other fellow?

FULTON: We're going to impeach him!

GILHOOLEY: He wouldn't play ball with us!

THROTTLEBOTTOM: Well, I don't play very well—you see this finger—

FULTON: Come on! Let's get started!

GILHOOLEY: Yeah, we've got work to do!

THROTTLEBOTTOM: You really mean it? I'm not vice-president any more?

JONES: Not if we impeach the President!

THROTTLEBOTTOM: Well, when do we do that?

JONES: Right now! Come on!

FULTON: You've got to preside over the Senate!

THROTTLEBOTTOM: And after that I'll be President?

LYONS: That's what you will!

(*The Committee enters the Senate. Throttlebottom is about to follow when a Scrubwoman comes along the corridor*)

THROTTLEBOTTOM: President! Say! (*To the Scrubwoman*) How will that sound? President Alexander Bottlethrottom. (*Corrects himself*) Throttlebottom.

SCRUBWOMAN: Huh?

THROTTLEBOTTOM: (*He has to tell someone*) I'm going to be President!

SCRUBWOMAN: I'd rather have this job. It's steady.

(*She goes, just as Wintergreen and Jenkins arrive from the other side*)

JENKINS: Well, it's a dirty trick, Chief. That's all I've got to say.

WINTERGREEN: It's politics. They've got to eat, too.

JENKINS: Want me to go in with you?

WINTERGREEN: No. I want to handle this alone.

JENKINS: More power to you, Chief. (*Takes his hand; holds it during the following speech*) And I want you to know that if the worst comes to the worst, and they fire you out—

WINTERGREEN: I know—if they fire me out you want a job with the next President.

JENKINS: Right! (*He goes*)

(*Wintergreen starts for the door into the Senate*)

THROTTLEBOTTOM: Hello, Mr. President. Hey!

WINTERGREEN: Hey?

THROTTLEBOTTOM: I'll bet you don't remember me, do you?

WINTERGREEN: (*After a searching gaze*) You're the fellow that gave me that dill pickle.

THROTTLEBOTTOM: That's right.

WINTERGREEN: What are you doing now?

THROTTLEBOTTOM: I'm vice-president.

WINTERGREEN: You don't say? Lost your other job, huh?

THROTTLEBOTTOM: Well, I'm going to have a good job now, because I'm going to be President.

WINTERGREEN: (*Realizing it*) Say, that's right! If they kick me out that makes you President.

THROTTLEBOTTOM: Say, I wonder if you'd mind doing me a favor?

WINTERGREEN: Sure!

THROTTLEBOTTOM: You see, I don't know anything about being President. I just found out today how to be vice-president.

WINTERGREEN: Well, that's something.

THROTTLEBOTTOM: Isn't there some book I could read?

WINTERGREEN: Yes. I'm writing one. "What Every Young President Ought to Know."

THROTTLEBOTTOM: Has it got pictures?

WINTERGREEN: It's got everything! Tells you just what to do! Of course the first four years are easy. You don't do anything except try to get re-elected.

THROTTLEBOTTOM: That's pretty hard these days.

WINTERGREEN: It looks that way. The next four years you wonder why the hell you wanted to be re-elected. And after that you go into the insurance business and you're all set.

THROTTLEBOTTOM: Well, couldn't I save a lot of time and go right into the insurance business?

WINTERGREEN: No, you've got to work yourself up.

THROTTLEBOTTOM: Yeah, but it's a pretty hard job, being President. You've got to keep on writing those Thanksgiving proclamations, no matter what—and then there's that other bunch, Congress. I guess there isn't anything you can really do about Congress, is there?

WINTERGREEN: Take my advice and keep them out of Washington.

THROTTLEBOTTOM: Can you do that?

WINTERGREEN: St. Patrick did it. Keep them out if you have to quarantine the place. Get the measles.

THROTTLEBOTTOM: I had measles once.

WINTERGREEN: Yeah, but you never had Congress. That's worse.

THROTTLEBOTTOM: Oh! What about those messages that the President is always sending to Congress—who reads those, anyway?

WINTERGREEN: The fellow who prints 'em.

THROTTLEBOTTOM: Well, wouldn't everybody read them if you made 'em funnier?

WINTERGREEN: No, we've had some pretty funny ones.

THROTTLEBOTTOM: Couldn't you make a speech instead? Then they'd *have* to listen.

WINTERGREEN: No, no! You've got to be careful about speeches. You only make a speech when you want the stock market to go down.

THROTTLEBOTTOM: What do you do when you want the stock market to go up?

WINTERGREEN: (*Fairly falling on his neck*) Oh! wouldn't I like to know!

CURTAIN

SCENE 3: *Inside the Senate Chamber. The great desk of the presiding officer, mounted on a dais; in circles around him the desks of the Senators. Senators with Dundrearies, Senators with long white beards, Senators of all kinds and descriptions.*

When the curtain rises they are all in their places, and Throttle-bottom is on high. The roll is being called, to music, of course, and the Senators sway rhythmically back and forth in time to the music, humming as they do so.

THE SENATORIAL ROLL CALL

THROTTLEBOTTOM:

The Senator from Minnesota?

SENATOR:

Present.

THROTTLEBOTTOM:

Check!

The Senator from North Dakota?

SENATOR:

Present.

THROTTLEBOTTOM:

Check!

The Senator from Louisiana?

SENATOR:

Present.

THROTTLEBOTTOM:

Check!

The Senator who's from Montana?

SENATOR:

Present.

THROTTLEBOTTOM:

Check!

The Senator who's from Nebraska?

SENATOR:

Present.

THROTTLEBOTTOM:

Check!

The Senator who's from Alaska?

(*A new State, by the way*)

SENATOR:

Present.

THROTTLEBOTTOM:

Check!

The Senators from other states will have to bide their
time,
For I simply can't be bothered when the names don't
rhyme!

ENSEMBLE:

Oh, he simply can't be bothered when the names
don't rhyme!
The Senators from other states will have to bide their
time,
For he simply can't be bothered when the names don't
rhyme!

(*The Senators continue to hum and to sway; led by Throttlebottom, they now go into song*)

THROTTLEBOTTOM:

The country thinks it's got depression.

SENATORS:

Ha! Ha! Ha!

THROTTLEBOTTOM:

Just wait until we get in session!

SENATORS:

Ha! Ha! Ha!

THROTTLEBOTTOM:

The people want a lot of action.

SENATORS:

Ho! Ho! Ho!

THROTTLEBOTTOM:

We're here to give them satisfaction!

SENATORS:

Ho! Ho! Ho!

THROTTLEBOTTOM:

Today is really full of laughter.

SENATORS:

Ha! Ha! Ha!

THROTTLEBOTTOM:

Compared to what will follow after!

SENATORS:

Ha! Ha! Ha!

THROTTLEBOTTOM:

There's action ev'ry minute when this happy group
convenes:

ALL:

 To get business into tangles
 We can guarantee more angles
 Than the town of Boston guarantees in beans!
 If you think you've got depression,
 Wait until we get in session,
 And you'll find out what depression really means!
 Ha! Ha! Ha!
 Ha! Ha! Ha! Ha!
 Ha! Ha! Ha! Ha! Ha!

CLERK: It is now twelve o'clock noon and the Senate of the United States is hereby declared in session.

THROTTLEBOTTOM: Thanks. Gentlemen, when you hear the musical note it will be exactly twelve o'clock noon.

 (*And he brings the gavel down—right on his watch*)

Well, gentlemen, I'm glad to meet you all. You'll have to excuse me for not knowing much about this job. I see I made one mistake already—I went and got shaved. Now let's get at things—I'm only going to be with you one day, so let's make it a pip.

CLERK: The first thing before the Senate is unfinished business!

THROTTLEBOTTOM: But aren't we going to impeach the President?

CLERK: Unfinished business!

SENATOR FROM MASSACHUSETTS: Mr. Chairman! Mr. Chairman!

CLERK: (*To Throttlebottom*) That's you.

THROTTLEBOTTOM: Oh, I thought I was just vice-president.

CLERK: You must recognize the Senator from Massachusetts.

THROTTLEBOTTOM: Oh, hello! How's everything in Massachusetts?

SENATOR FROM MASSACHUSETTS: Mr. Chairman! I rise to protest against a great injustice! In seventeen hundred and seventy-five Paul Revere made the famous ride that saved this country from the greedy clutch of England.

THROTTLEBOTTOM: That's right—I read about that. (*Informally, to the Clerk*) He went from one house to another, and he knocked on the door, and by the time they came out he was at the next house.

SENATOR FROM MASSACHUSETTS: Paul Revere's name has been given the affectionate tribute of a grateful people. But what of that gallant figure who is even more responsible? Gentlemen: what about Jenny, Paul Revere's horse?

(*Applause*)

Surely, gentlemen, Jenny is entitled to the protection of a governmental pension. A bill providing such a pension was introduced into this body in the year 1804, and came up for its first reading in 1852.

THROTTLEBOTTOM: I wasn't here then.

SENATOR FROM MASSACHUSETTS: Gentlemen, in these hundred and fifty-five years Jenny has not been getting any younger. I ask you, gentlemen, what are we going to do about Jenny?

THROTTLEBOTTOM: Well, that's unfinished business if I ever heard it.

SENATOR JONES: May I point out to the Senator of Massachusetts that Jenny is dead?

THROTTLEBOTTOM: She is? What do you think of that? Good old Jenny! When did she die?

SENATOR JONES: She died in 1805.

THROTTLEBOTTOM: The Senate will rise for one minute in silent tribute to the departed horse from Massachusetts.

(*They rise; he bangs the gavel*)

Well, that finishes Jenny. Is there any other unfinished business?

SENATOR LYONS: Mr. Chairman! Gentlemen! I crave the indulgence of this august body while I say a few words in honor of my wife's birthday.

(*Applause*)

And I move you, Mr. Chairman, that the Senate appropriate $5,000 for flowers to be sent her on this historic occasion.

A SENATOR: Second the motion!

THROTTLEBOTTOM: All in favor say "Aye"!

(*A full-throated "Aye" from the assemblage*)

Motion carried! (*To the Clerk*) Put in my card. . . . Now, what comes next? How about impeaching the President?

CLERK: (*Handing him a sheet of paper*) Mr. Vice-President—

THROTTLEBOTTOM: What's this?

CLERK: The following committees are ready to report.

THROTTLEBOTTOM: (*Consulting the paper*) Committee on Aviation. . . . Airedales. . . . Bloomingdale's. . . . (*Closes his eyes, one finger suspended over the paper*) Eenie, meenie, minie, mo. Catch a committee by the toe. If they holler give 'em dough, eenie, meenie, minie, mo. (*Places his finger on the paper, looks to see which committee he has selected*) Committee on Unemployment.

SENATOR JONES: The Committee on Unemployment is gratified to report that due to its unremitting efforts there is now more unemployment in the United States than ever before.

THROTTLEBOTTOM: Now we're getting some place! Now let's impeach the President!

SENATOR FROM MASSACHUSETTS: Mr. Chairman! I would like to call the attention of the Senate to a matter that has been puzzling me for some time. It has to do with a very interesting bridge hand, in which the cards were distributed as follows: East held the four aces, West the four kings, North the four queens, and South—ah—nothing of any importance.

LYONS: (*Rising indignantly*) Mr. Chairman! The South will never be satisfied with a hand like that!

(*A fanfare of trumpets*)

PAGES: (*Announcing*) The President of the United States!

THROTTLEBOTTOM: Who?

CLERK: The President of the United States!

(*He enters*)

IMPEACHMENT PROCEEDING

CLERK:

> The next business before the Senate is the resolution on the impeachment of the President.

(*A fanfare of trumpets. Two pages enter*)

TWO PAGES:

> The President of the United States!

THROTTLEBOTTOM:

> Who?

CLERK:

> The President of the United States!

THROTTLEBOTTOM:

> Oh, Mr. President, won't you sit down while we kick you out?

FULTON, LIPPMAN, GILHOOLEY, AND LYONS: (*in harmony*)

> Whereas:

LYONS:

> At a meeting of the Senate at which a quorum was
> present a motion was made and it was proposed
> that—

FULTON, LIPPMAN, AND GILHOOLEY:

> Whereas:

LYONS:

> John. P. Wintergreen has undertaken to marry the
> winner of a beauty contest held in Atlantic City—

FULTON, LIPPMAN, AND GILHOOLEY:

> Whereas:

LYONS:

> His refusal to marry the winner Diana Devereaux will
> lead to international complications—

FULTON, LIPPMAN, AND GILHOOLEY:

> Now therefore be it resolved that John P. Wintergreen
> be, and hereby is, impeached from the said office
> of President of these United States.

SENATOR JONES:

> I second the resolution.

FULTON:

> Our first witness—the French Ambassador!

GARÇON, S'IL VOUS PLAÎT (*Reprise*)

FRENCH SOLDIERS: (*marching in*)

> Garçon, s'il vous plaît,
> Encore Chevrolet coupé,
> Papah, pooh, pooh, pooh!
> À vous tout dir vay à vous?

SENATORS:

> We say how-de-do—
> Which means that we welcome you:
> We're glad of the chance
> To say hello to France.

> (*Enter French Ambassador*)

FRENCH AMBASSADOR:

> You've dealt a lovely maid
> A blow that is injurious;
> A very dirty trick was played
> And France is simply furious!

SENATORS:

> He says a lovely maid
> Was dealt a blow injurious;
> He says a dirty trick was played
> And France is simply furious.

FULTON:

> Ambassador, please explain why France is so con-
> cerned about the plaintiff.

The Illegitimate Daughter (*Reprise*)

FRENCH AMBASSADOR:

> She's the illegitimate daughter
> Of an illegitimate son
> Of an illegitimate nephew
> Of Napoléon.

SENATORS:

> Napoléon?

FRENCH AMBASSADOR:

> She's contemplating suicide
> Because that man, he threw aside
> A lady with the blue blood of Napoléon.
> What sort of man
> Is this who can
> Insult my country
> With his effront'ry.

SENATORS:

> To the illegitimate daughter
> Of an illegitimate son
> Of an illegitimate nephew
> Of Napoléon?

FRENCH AMBASSADOR:

> The Atlantic City witnesses!
>
> (*Entrance of the Atlantic City bathing beauties and Diana Devereaux*)

DIANA:

> I have come all ze way from France to bring ze
> greetings.

FRENCH AMBASSADOR:

> Tell your story, little one!
> Commencez, s'il vous plaît.

JILTED

DIANA:

Jilted, jilted,
I'm a flow'r that's wilted;
Blighted, blighted,
Till the wrong is righted;

Broken, broken,
By a man soft-spoken;
Faded, faded—
Heaven knows why!

When men are deceivers, I'm afraid
'Tis sad to be a trusting maid.

Jilted, jilted, jilted am I.
Oh, what is there left but to die?

ENSEMBLE:

Jilted, jilted,
She's a flower that's wilted;
Blighted, blighted,
Till the wrong is righted;

Broken, broken,
By a man soft-spoken;
Faded, faded—
Heaven knows why!
Just as in the Frankie and Johnny song,
He done her wrong, he done her wrong.

ENSEMBLE:

Jilted, jilted, jilted is she!
Oh, what is there left but to dee?
Boo-hoo! Boo-hoo! Boo-hoo!
(*The Senate is visibly affected*)

THROTTLEBOTTOM:

And now, Mr. President, what have you to say for
yourself?

WINTERGREEN:

Impeach me! Fine me! Jail me! Sue me!
My Mary's love means much more to me!

THROTTLEBOTTOM:

Enough! Enough! We want no preachment!

It's time to vote on his impeachment!

ALL:

It's time to vote on his impeachment!

SENATORIAL ROLL CALL (*Continued*)

THROTTLEBOTTOM:

The Senator from Minnesota?

SENATOR:

Guilty!

THROTTLEBOTTOM:

Check!

The Senator from North Dakota?

SENATOR:

Guilty!

THROTTLEBOTTOM:

Check!

The Senator from Louisiana?

SENATOR:

Guilty!

THROTTLEBOTTOM:

Check!

The Senator who's from Montana?

(*And at this dramatic moment, in breaks Mary Turner Wintergreen*)

MARY:

Stop! Stop! Stop!
Before you go any further,
With your permission,
I must tell you of my husband's delicate condition.

ENSEMBLE:

Delicate condition! What do you mean?

I'M ABOUT TO BE A MOTHER

MARY: (*such a gay song*)

I'm about to be a mother;
He's about to be a father;
We're about to have a baby.
I must tell it;
These doings compel it!
Oh, I'm about to be a mother;

He's about to be a father;
We're about to have a baby.

ENSEMBLE:

A baby!

MARY:

A baby to love and adore—
Who could ask for anything more?

ENSEMBLE: (*dancing happily*)

She's about to be a mother;
He's about to be a father;
They're about to have a baby;
We can't bother
A budding young father!

WINTERGREEN: (*spoken*) Mary, is it true? Am I going to have a baby?

MARY: It's true, John, it's true.

WINTERGREEN: Water! (*He faints*)

ENSEMBLE: (*Sings*)

They're about to have a baby, a baby—

DIANA: (*spoken*) It eez a fine countree—I am compromised and she has ze baby!

THROTTLEBOTTOM: Gentlemen, gentlemen! This country has never yet impeached an expectant father. What do you say?

SENATORS: Not guilty!

THROTTLEBOTTOM: (*to Wintergreen*) You can still be President and I'll go back to Vice!

FRENCH AMBASSADOR:

Sacré! I go to the telegraph office to cable my report;
This is American trickery of the most reprehensible sort!

DIANA: (*Sings*)

I was the most beautiful blossom . . .

(*French Ambassador takes her by the hand, leads her off*)

In all the Southland.

ATLANTIC CITY GIRLS:

Strike up the cymbals, drum, and fife,
One of us was to be the President's wife.

CHIEF JUSTICE: (*Spoken*) Great work, Jack; you'll be reinstated in the hearts of the American people.

JONES:

You're doing your duty by posterity.

WINTERGREEN:

Posterity—why, posterity is just around the corner.

POSTERITY IS JUST AROUND THE CORNER

WINTERGREEN:

Posterity is just around the corner!

(*Senators bring out tambourines*)

ALL:

Posterity is just around the corner!

MARY:

It really doesn't pay to be a mourner.

ALL:

Posterity is just around the corner!

WINTERGREEN:

Posterity is here—I don't mean maybe!

ALL:

There's nothing guarantees it like a baby!

MARY:

Posterity is here and will continue!

ALL:

We really didn't know you had it in you!

Posterity is in its infancy!

WINTERGREEN:

I sing to ev'ry citizen and fore'gner

ALL:

Posterity is just around the corner!

(*Throttlebottom, with a bass drum, is leading a march around the room*)

COMMITTEE:

We'll soon be pulling plums like Jackie Horner!

ALL:

Posterity is just around the—

Oom-posterity, oom-posterity, oom-pah, oom-pah, oom-posterity!

Oom-posterity, oom-posterity, oom-pah, oom-pah, oom-posterity—

Is just around the corner!
Around the corner!

CURTAIN

SCENE 4: *A corridor in the White House.*

Enter Jenkins and Miss Benson.

JENKINS: It'll certainly be great to have a baby in the White House. I wonder when it'll be born.

MISS BENSON: Let's see—they were married March 4, weren't they?

JENKINS: That's right.

MISS BENSON: (*Counting on her fingers*) April, May, June, July, August, September, October, November, DECEMBER! It'll be born in December.

JENKINS: How do you know?

MISS BENSON: Well, it won't be born *before* December.

JENKINS: How do you know?

MISS BENSON: Oh, the President wouldn't do a thing like that. He'd never be re-elected.

JENKINS: You can't tell. Might be the very thing that would re-elect him.

MISS BENSON: It's certainly wonderful the way this has lined people up behind the President.

JENKINS: Yeah, but we don't know what France is going to do. She's still liable to make trouble.

MISS BENSON: My, you'd think a woman could have a baby without France butting in.

JENKINS: Well, fifty million Frenchmen—they've got to do something.

MISS BENSON: Let 'em do it in Paris. Why should they come over here and—

WINTERGREEN: (*Singing as he enters*) "Somebody's coming to our house; somebody's coming to stay—" Oh, hello.

JENKINS: Hi, Chief!

MISS BENSON: Good morning, Mr. President. And how is Mrs. Wintergreen this morning?

WINTERGREEN: (*Vaguely*) Who? Mrs. Wintergreen? (*Realizes that there is such a person*) Oh, she's fine! Fine! Yes, sir! (*Tapping his own chest*) Should have seen the breakfast I ate!

MISS BENSON: Tell me, Mr. President. Ah— (*Hesitantly*) —when is the baby expected?

WINTERGREEN: Well, of course you can't tell about such things, but we think sometime in Novem—December. (*Another quick correction*) December.

MISS BENSON: (*With a look at Jenkins*) Oh, December.

WINTERGREEN: Yes, we sort of thought December would be a nice month. End the old year right and all that sort of thing. Have a cigar? Oh, pardon me, the baby isn't born yet.

(*Enter Fulton*)

FULTON: Hello, Jack!

WINTERGREEN: Hello, there! Should have seen the breakfast I ate. (*To the Secretaries*) See you later.

MISS BENSON: (*To Jenkins*) I told you December.

JENKINS: Well, I'd still like to make a bet on it.

(*The Secretaries go*)

FULTON: Well, Jack, how are you? And how's the wife?

WINTERGREEN: Fine, fine! Never felt better.

FULTON: Mighty smart girl, Mary. She certainly saved the day for us.

WINTERGREEN: *She* saved the day? I suppose I was just an innocent bystander?

FULTON: I don't mean that, but I thought it sort of came as a surprise to you.

WINTERGREEN: Surprise? Why, I planned the whole thing. I foresaw the situation months ago.

FULTON: Anyway, it settled France. They're still yelling, but there's nothing they can do about it. The American people are behind you to a man. How'd you ever get the idea, Jack?

WINTERGREEN: Why, it wasn't anything. Nothing at all. Anybody in my place would have done the same.

FULTON: Yes, sir, it'll be a wonderful thing to have a baby in the White House.

WINTERGREEN: You mean instead of a President?

FULTON: No, no, Jack—I mean it. I tell you, there's something about the patter of baby feet, trickling down the stairs. . . .

(*Enter the French Ambassador*)

FRENCH AMBASSADOR: Gentlemen!

FULTON: (*With a bow*) Monsieur!

FRENCH AMBASSADOR: (*With an elaborate bow*) Monsieur President.

WINTERGREEN: You all alone?

FRENCH AMBASSADOR: But yes.

WINTERGREEN: Where are those six guys who used to march in ahead of you— (*His gesture carries out the idea of crossed bayonets, and even goes a bit further by bringing thumb and nose into close juxtaposition*) —*you* know.

FRENCH AMBASSADOR They could not come to-day. They have dancing lesson.

WINTERGREEN: You look kind of naked without them.

FRENCH AMBASSADOR: (*Acknowledges this with a bow*) You will pardon this intrusion, Monsieur, but I have received another note from my country.

WINTERGREEN: That's all right. We've got a lot of notes from your country, and some of them were due ten years ago.

FRENCH AMBASSADOR: But this is not a promise to pay—this is serious.

WINTERGREEN: Shoot!

FRENCH AMBASSADOR: (*Bows*) Monsieur, I have good news for you. France consents to your having the child.

FULTON: Ah!

WINTERGREEN: France consents?

FRENCH AMBASSADOR: Freely.

WINTERGREEN: Why, that's wonderful of her. Good old France! Do you mind if I tell my wife, so she can go ahead? (*Ambassador bows*) You've no idea how this will please her. Won't take me a minute—I'll be right back.

FRENCH AMBASSADOR: But one moment, Monsieur. (*Wintergreen pauses*) France consents, but on one condition.

WINTERGREEN: Yeah?

FRENCH AMBASSADOR: France must have the baby!

FULTON AND WINTERGREEN: WHAT?

FRENCH AMBASSADOR: Do not be hasty, Monsieur. You must understand the desperate situation of my country. For fifty years the birth rate of France has been declining, declining, declining.

WINTERGREEN: What's that got to do with me?

FRENCH AMBASSADOR: You must see, Monsieur. If you had married Mlle. Devereaux, as you have promise, the baby she is French. But now you have taken away from France one baby, and she demand replacement.

WINTERGREEN: Never!

FULTON: I should say not!

FRENCH AMBASSADOR: It is the old law, Monsieur; an eye for an eye, a tooth for a tooth, and a baby for a baby.

WINTERGREEN: You'll get no tooth from my baby!

FRENCH AMBASSADOR: The tooth, the whole tooth, and nothing but the tooth!

WINTERGREEN: Not one tooth!

FRENCH AMBASSADOR: That is your final word?

WINTERGREEN: It is! Good day, Monsieur!

FRENCH AMBASSADOR: Good day! (*Clicks his heels; salutes; turns and starts out*) Lafayette, we are coming! (*Goes*)

FULTON: What do you think France'll do?

WINTERGREEN: What's the worst she can do? Sue us for what she owes us?

FULTON: But that other thing! France is awful touchy about her birth rate!

WINTERGREEN: What are you worrying about? I fixed *this* up, didn't I?

FULTON: What?

WINTERGREEN: Well, Mary's going to have a baby, isn't she?

FULTON: Yes!

WINTERGREEN: Well! Next year I make a tour of France! Lafayette! (*He salutes*)

CURTAIN

SCENE 5: *The Yellow Room of the White House. And is it yellow? But it is also very beautiful—and endless. It extends as far as the eye can reach—a vista of hallway, and polished floor, and chandeliers, and ladies in evening clothes, and men in magnificent uniforms. White-wigged flunkies move in and out of the assemblage.*

*At the rise of the curtain an endless line of diplomats is presenting
the Wintergreens with an endless line of baby carriages. The
flunkies bellow the names as they accept the carriages—"Compliments of Ecuador," "Compliments of Bolivia," "Compliments of
Spain," "Compliments of Lithuania." And then, for finale, an
exceedingly small baby carriage. You've guessed it—"Compliments of Scotland."*

(*There is a burst of music*)

TRUMPETER, BLOW YOUR GOLDEN HORN

ALL:

Oh, trumpeter, trumpeter, blow your golden horn!
Oh, trumpeter, trumpeter, blow your golden horn!
A White House baby will very soon be born!
A White House baby will very soon be born!
Blow your horn!

FLUNKIES: (*stiffly*)

With a hey-nonny-nonny and a ha-cha-cha!
With a hey-nonny-nonny and a ha-cha-cha!

ALL:

There's something glorious happening today
For all the citizens of the U.S.A.
A White House baby will very soon be born!
Oh, trumpeter, blow your horn,
Oh, trumpeter, blow your horn,
Oh, trumpeter, blow your horn,
Your golden horn, your golden horn!

(*Doctor enters*)

Oh, doctor, doctor, what's the news, we pray?
We've waited for your bulletin all day.

DOCTOR:

The baby of the President and Frau
Will be here almost any minute now.

FLUNKIES:

With a hey-nonny-nonny and a ha-cha-cha!
With a hey-nonny-nonny and a ha-cha-cha!

ALL:

Oh, doctor, here is the one thing we must know—

We're all of us anxious and we've got to know:
The baby, is it to be a girl or boy?
A baby girl or boy?
A nation's pride and joy!
We must know whether it's a girl or boy,
A girl or boy!

DOCTOR:

On that point, nobody budges,
For all matters of the sort
Are decided by the judges
Of the Supreme Court.
(*All repeat*)

CHIEF FLUNKY:

The Supreme Court!

JUDGES: (*entering*)

We're the one, two, three, four, five, six, seven, eight,
nine Supreme Court Judges!

FLUNKIES:

With a hey-nonny-nonny and a ha-cha-cha!
With a hey-nonny-nonny and a ha-cha-cha!

ALL:

About the baby—Will it be
A boy or girl—a he or she?

JUDGES:

On that point nobody budges,
For all matters of the sort
Are decided by the judges
Of the Supreme Court.
(*All repeat*)

CHIEF FLUNKY:

The Secretary of Agriculture!
(*Music: "The Farmer in the Dell"*)

LIPPMAN: (*entering*)

The farmers in the dell,
The farmers in the dell,
They all keep a-asking me:
A boy or a gel?

JUDGES:

On that point nobody budges,
For all matters of the sort

> Are decided by the judges
> Of the Supreme Court.

CHIEF FLUNKY:

> The Secretary of the Navy.
> (*Music: "Sailor's Hornpipe"*)

GILHOOLEY: (*entering*)

> All the sailors in the Navy
> In these great United States,
> Do not eat their bowls of gravy,
> Nor the captains nor the mates.
> They refuse to jib an anchor,
> Strike a boom, or heave a sail,
> Till you've satisfied their hanker:
> Is it female or a male?

JUDGES:

> On that point nobody budges,
> For all matters of the sort
> Are decided by the judges
> Of the Supreme Court.

CHIEF FLUNKY:

> Senator Carver Jones!
> (*Music: "Come Be My Rainbow"*)

JONES: (*entering*)

> Out on the prairie,
> The cowboys all keep asking of me:
> He or a she—
> She or a he?
> Out on the prairie,
> For baby boy or girl they are keen,
> But they want nothing in between.

JUDGES:

> On that point nobody budges,
> For all matters of the sort
> Are decided by the judges
> Of the Supreme Court.

CHIEF FLUNKY:

> Senator Robert E. Lyons!
> (*Music: "Swanee River"*)

LYONS: (*entering*)

> Way down upon the Swanee River,

Folks are filled with joy;
But they want to know what will the stork deliver—
Will it be a girl or a boy?

JUDGES:
On that point nobody budges,
For all matters of the sort
Are decided by the judges
Of the Supreme Court.

ALL:
There's something glorious happening today:
A baby will be born!
A baby will be born!
Oh, trumpeter, trumpeter, blow your golden horn!

(*Enter Wintergreen, followed by Fulton and Jenkins*)

FULTON: Take it easy, Jack! Nothing can happen to her.

WINTERGREEN: I know, but at a time like this—Mary in there alone—

(*A chorus of greeting from all*)

Oh! Hello! God, I'm nervous! Anybody got a drink?

(*Every man brings out a flask*)

Thanks. When I think of Mary in there alone— (*Takes a drink*) Well, I guess it's not going to be so hard for her.

GILHOOLEY: How is Mary?

WINTERGREEN: Finest little woman in the world! When I think of what she's got to—anybody got a drink? (*The flasks come out again. He takes Gilhooley's, although he still has Fulton's in his hand*) Well, I guess I'd better not mix them.

MISS BENSON: Oh, Mr. Wintergreen!

WINTERGREEN: (*Wheeling*) Any news?

MISS BENSON: The baby will be here at any moment.

(*An excited buzz from the crowd*)

WINTERGREEN: Tell 'em I'm ready.

(*Miss Benson goes*)

My God! You hear that? What do I do now? Anybody got a drink?

ON THAT MATTER NO ONE BUDGES

CHIEF JUSTICE:
Gentlemen, duty calls. We have to determine the sex
of the infant.

WINTERGREEN:
> You decide?

CHIEF JUSTICE:
> We do.

JUDGES:
> On that matter, no one budges,
> For all cases of the sort
> Are decided by the judges
> Of the Supreme Court.

ENSEMBLE:
> Are decided by the judges
> Of the Supreme Court.
>
> (*They retire*)

WINTERGREEN: I shouldn't be drinking at a time like this. (*To Jenkins and the Committee*) Here! Take it away! (*Jenkins reaches for the flask. Wintergreen pulls away*) Oh, no, you don't. My wife's the finest little woman in the world! And I can lick anybody that says she ain't!

FLUNKIES: (*Announcing*) The French Ambassador!

WINTERGREEN: Bring him in!

FRENCH AMBASSADOR: Your Excellency! I have another message from France!

WINTERGREEN: Not a nickel!

FRENCH AMBASSADOR: Will you surrender the baby?

WINTERGREEN: Never! Give my baby to France and have it eat snails and get ptomaine poisoning! Never!

FRENCH AMBASSADOR: Then, sir, I am instructed to say that with the birth of the child France severs diplomatic relations!

WINTERGREEN: Hurray!

FRENCH AMBASSADOR: And that is not all, sir. I wish furthermore to report—

> (*Two flunkies enter and blow a fanfare on their trumpets. The Supreme Court re-enters*)

JUDGES:
> Whereas:

CHIEF JUSTICE:
> A child has been born to the President of the United
>   States and his consort.

JUDGES:
> Whereas:

CHIEF JUSTICE:

> The judges of the Supreme Court have been sent to
> determine the sex of the aforesaid infant.

JUDGES:

> Whereas:

CHIEF JUSTICE:

> By a strict party vote it has been decided that—
> (*spoken*)
> It's a boy.

JUDGES: (*Sing*)

> On that matter, no one budges,
> For all cases of the sort
> Are decided by the judges
> Of the Supreme Court.

ENSEMBLE:

> Are decided by the judges
> Of the Supreme Court.
> (*The committee and guests press around Wintergreen to congratulate him*)

WINTERGREEN: A boy! That makes me a father! Thank you! Thank you very much! I certainly am a lucky man! Boy, the cigars! Smoke up, everybody! Here you are, ladies and gentlemen! Have a cigar, Frenchy!

FRENCH AMBASSADOR: My thanks, Monsieur. On behalf of France permit me to offer my felicitations.

WINTERGREEN: Attaboy! Let bygones be bygones! Have another cigar!

FRENCH AMBASSADOR: And permit me also to inform you that France hereby severs diplomatic relations! (*He reaches for the cigar*)

WINTERGREEN: (*Closes the humidor with a bang*) Then the hell with you!

FRENCH AMBASSADOR: You understand what this means, Monsieur?

WINTERGREEN: I do! (*Takes back the first cigar*) It means no smoke!

FRENCH AMBASSADOR: Precisely. And where there is no smoke there is fire. I am instructed to say, Monsieur, that this means that the French government will—
(*The Flunkies re-enter. Another fanfare. The Justices re-enter*)

JUDGES:

>Whereas:

CHIEF JUSTICE:

>A child has been born to the President of the United States and his consort.

WINTERGREEN: (*spoken*) Wait a minute; we've had all that.

CHIEF JUSTICE:

>Yes, but you're having it again.
>This time it's a girl.

JUDGES: (*Sing*)

>On that matter, no one budges,
>For all cases of the sort
>Are decided by the judges
>Of the Supreme Court.

ENSEMBLE:

>Are decided by the judges
>Of the Supreme Court.

(*All crowd around Wintergreen to congratulate him again*)

WINTERGREEN: A girl! That makes me a father *and* a mother. Twins! That's a little more than I counted on!

JENKINS: Cigars, sir?

WINTERGREEN: No. Cigarettes this time! A boy *and* a girl! Well!

FRENCH AMBASSADOR:

>Oh, I can stand no more;
>My temper's getting gingery;
>This certainly will lead to war!
>This insult added to injury!

ENSEMBLE:

>Oh, he can stand no more;
>His temper's getting gingery;
>He says that this will lead to war!
>This insult added to injury!

You realize what you have done, sir? You have taken away from France not one baby, but two!

WINTERGREEN: That's it! Blame me for everything!

FRENCH AMBASSADOR: What you have done to Mlle. Devereaux! That poor little girl! Where is she? What is she doing?

>(*In the distance Diana is heard singing "I was the most beautiful blossom"*)

WINTERGREEN: She's still singing.

(*Diana enters*)

You like that song, don't you?

FRENCH AMBASSADOR: My poor motherless one! My sweet blossom of the Southland!

FLUNKIES: (*Announcing*) The Vice-President of the United States!

THROTTLEBOTTOM: (*Knitting a baby's sweater*) Is the baby born yet? I just got this finished!

WINTERGREEN: Only one? Where's the other one?

THROTTLEBOTTOM: (*Pulls out second sweater*) I thought something like that might happen!

FRENCH AMBASSADOR: Once and for all, Monsieur, what are you going to do? What are you going to do about Mlle. Devereaux and her babies?

WINTERGREEN: Well, she can have her own babies.

DIANA: But I am not married, Monsieur.

WINTERGREEN: What's that got to do with it?

FRENCH AMBASSADOR: Everything. The family has been illegitimate long enough.

WINTERGREEN: Then let her get married!

FRENCH AMBASSADOR: Exactly! But it was agreed, Monsieur, that she was to marry the President of the United States.

WINTERGREEN: But she can't have me! I'm married!

FRENCH AMBASSADOR: Then it is war, sir! When the President of the United States fails to fulfil his duty—

WINTERGREEN: That's it! I've got it!

ALL: Got what?

WINTERGREEN: It's in the Constitution! When the President of the United States is unable to fulfil his duties, his obligations are assumed by—

THROTTLEBOTTOM: The vice-president! I get her!

CHIEF JUSTICE: Article Twelve!

FRENCH AMBASSADOR: Monsieur, you are a genius!

THROTTLEBOTTOM: (*To Wintergreen*) I could throw my arms right around your neck!

WINTERGREEN: Oh, no, you don't! Hers!

(*The Trumpeters re-enter. Another fanfare*)

WINTERGREEN: Oh, my God!

CHIEF JUSTICE: It's all right. The boys are merely practicing.

(*There is a great burst of music, and from the more intimate quarters of the White House there comes into the room a great canopied bed, hung with gold, and silver, and bald-headed eagles. In it is Mary Turner Wintergreen, a twin on each arm. Wintergreen advances to greet her; the crowd bursts into song. And of all the songs in the world, you'd never guess what they pick out. It's "Of Thee I Sing, Baby"*)

THE CURTAIN FALLS

DINNER AT EIGHT

A Play
by
George S. Kaufman
and
Edna Ferber

FROM THE SOCIETY COLUMN
OF THE NEW YORK *TIMES*:

. . . who will sail for Bermuda on the tenth.

————

Mr. and Mrs. Oliver Jordan, of 927 Park Avenue, entertained at dinner last night in honor of Lord and Lady Ferncliffe. Their guests included Miss Carlotta Vance, Mr. and Mrs. Daniel Packard, Dr. and Mrs. J. Wayne Talbot, and Mr. Larry Renault. Following the dinner Mr. and Mrs. Jordan and their guests attended a musical comedy.

————

The list of patronesses for the Riverdale House benefit will include Mrs. G. Orton Stanhope . . .

THE SCENES

Act One

Act Two
A Week Later.

Act Three

ACT ONE

SCENE I

Upstairs sitting room in the Oliver Jordans' home. It is a luxurious and rather feminine room. There are books, flowers, a chaise longue, a charming little desk. Sunlight is streaming in at the window. Double doors, curtained, open into Mrs. Jordan's bedroom. Another door leads into the hall.

It is ten o'clock of a bright November morning.

Millicent Jordan is breakfasting in a negligée. She is a pretty, rather vapid woman of thirty-nine. She is dividing her attention between her orange juice and the letter in her hand. A folded copy of the Times *is at her elbow. If she ever glances at it, it is to ignore the front page as she turns directly to the society column on the inside. Dora, a maid, young and attractive, comes from the bedroom, a dress thrown over her arm. She crosses and goes into the hall. A moment later Gustave, the butler, enters from the hall. Gustave is about thirty-five, of light complexion, and good-looking in a vaguely foreign way. He brings a silver pot of coffee.*

MILLICENT: (*Feeling the side of the coffee pot*) I hope it's hot this time.

GUSTAVE: Very hot, madam.

(*He turns to leave. Her voice halts him.*)

MILLICENT: (*Pouring coffee*) I shan't be home to lunch. Mr. Jordan and I are out to dinner. I don't know about Miss Paula. I'll have to ask her.

GUSTAVE: Very good, madam.

MILLICENT: Has Mr. Jordan gone?

GUSTAVE: No, madam. He's still downstairs. He's just finished breakfast.

MILLICENT: Tell Ricci I want to see him before he takes Mr. Jordan to the office.

(*Gustave nods. Goes.*)

(*Millicent returns to her mail.*)

(*Oliver Jordan enters from the hall. A man in his early*

forties, quiet, well-bred, sensitive. You are rather surprised to learn that he is in business. His topcoat is over his arm, his hat in hand. He has just popped in to say good-morning and good-bye.)

OLIVER: Hello, darling. You're early!

MILLICENT: Oh, hello.

OLIVER: We could have had breakfast together if I'd known. (*He stoops for a perfunctory kiss. She, her eye still on the letter in her hand, presents a cool wifely cheek.*) Unless you think people might talk. (*Catches sight of a plate of thimble-size popovers on the table. Begins to nibble one.*) Mm! They didn't give me any of these.

MILLICENT: (*Absently. Busy with her mail*) I shouldn't have them, either. (*Dashes a printed card into the waste basket.*) Join Cooper Union!

OLIVER: How'd you sleep? Better?

MILLICENT: Never closed an eye. Then the minute I dropped off the fire engines woke me up.

OLIVER: Where do they go every night? I've never seen a fire in New York. I think they go around looking for them.

MILLICENT: (*Who has opened another letter*) Well! This is too shocking! Peggy Mainwaring is starting a night club in her lovely old house in Sutton Place.

OLIVER: Really? Is she as hard-pressed as that?

MILLICENT: (*Still reading*) "Opening attraction—Schnozzle Levine."

OLIVER: Old Lady Mainwaring must be whirling in her grave.

MILLICENT: (*Tosses letter into waste basket.*) Well, at least it'll keep Peggy out of Harlem.

OLIVER: (*About to go*) What's on for tonight? We're home, I hope.

MILLICENT: Oh, now, darling, you know perfectly well tonight's the Hilliards' costume party.

OLIVER: Oh, look here, Millicent. D'you mean I have to go as something?

MILLICENT: Oh, you'll love it. I got you Richard the Conqueror, and I'm a Florodora Girl. (*Returns to her letters.*)

OLIVER: Makes an ideal couple.

MILLICENT: I wanted Tarzan for you, but it's so draughty at the Hilliards'.

OLIVER: Look here—it's a late affair. We can have dinner at home, h'm?

MILLICENT: Oh, dear, no! We're dining with the Cartwrights and going on from there.

OLIVER: And I have to go through dinner in that armor!

MILLICENT: (*A soothing smile*) Well, we're home tomorrow night.

OLIVER: Thank God!

MILLICENT: The Martins are coming in for bridge.

(*His look says, "And you call that an evening at home!"*)

(*Gustave enters, carrying a radiogram on a small tray.*)

OLIVER: (*Picks up his topcoat, starts to put it on*) Oh, well—

GUSTAVE: This just came, Mrs. Jordan. (*Gustave goes.*)

MILLICENT: Oh, good! Wait a minute, Oliver. (*Opens and reads radio to herself, mumbling a word or two as she deciphers its meaning.*) Delighted . . . Friday . . . Listen to this, Oliver. I've got the Ferncliffes!

OLIVER: (*Momentarily arrested*) What?

MILLICENT: Lord and Lady Ferncliffe. They get in this morning—on the *Aquitania*. I sent them a radio last night, and they're coming to dinner Friday. Wasn't that bright of me!

OLIVER: Yes—if you want the Ferncliffes.

MILLICENT: Want them! Why, you know everybody'll pounce on them. Besides, we've got to have them. They entertained us in London.

OLIVER: Yes, and very dull it was, too.

MILLICENT: Oh, I don't know. I like those formal English dinners.

OLIVER: Not that one. All family portraits and Australian mutton and fox-hunting and Lloyd George. And the guests! A lot of people who had been buried for years, and who got up just for that dinner.

MILLICENT: Don't be American, Oliver. It's a great coup for me to get them. Friday. That gives me just a week.

OLIVER: Friday! . . . I was taking Paula to the opera. That Russian singer.

MILLICENT: I'm giving up Bori this morning! The Plaza musicale. All this phoning. (*A gesture with the message in her hand.*)

OLIVER: Bori—in the morning! To sit on a little gold chair and listen to Bori in the morning. Where's the glamour?

MILLICENT: Oh, Oliver, do be sensible and keep your mind on this a minute. After all, it's just as much your dinner as mine. And the Ferncliffes are terribly important. I should think you'd like to talk to him. Hasn't he got something to do with shipping?

OLIVER: (*A little genuflexion*) Mr. Oliver Jordan accepts.

MILLICENT: I thought just a small dinner. What do you think? Ten's a nice number.

OLIVER: (*Overcome*) Oo! Fascinating number.

MILLICENT: Of course it's terribly short notice. I thought I'd ask the Talbots—the Doctor and Lucy. The Ferncliffes and you and I are six. And your precious Carlotta Vance. Would you like me to ask her?

OLIVER: Oh, fine! I haven't seen her.

MILLICENT: I think it's sweet of me. (*Thoughtfully*) Of course, she's never met the Ferncliffes. She goes with a much faster crowd over there.

OLIVER: Carlotta! She knows everybody in Europe.

MILLICENT: Not people like the Ferncliffes. She's too flamboyant. Now let me see. I'll need just one more couple, and an extra man. (*Rummaging through her address book*) I'll be all morning telephoning. . . . Talbot—Talbot. . . . Butterfield eight—six-three-two-five. (*Scribbles it on a slip of paper.*)

OLIVER: (*Who has been turning something over in his mind*) Look here, dear. If you're looking for another couple—

MILLICENT: (*Her eye still on the slip*) Butterfi— What?

OLIVER: If you need another couple I wish you'd ask Dan Packard and his wife.

MILLICENT: You're joking!

OLIVER: I know it sounds funny, but there's a reason.

MILLICENT: I'll not do any such thing!

OLIVER: Now, wait a minute, Millicent—

MILLICENT: Ask that woman to my house!

OLIVER: Oh, they're not as bad as all that.

MILLICENT: But with the Ferncliffes!

OLIVER: They'll like him. Over there they like that two-fisted Western stuff.

MILLICENT: And what about her! I suppose they'll like her, too!

OLIVER: They'll think she's very refreshing. Look here, Millicent, I wouldn't ask this if it weren't important to me. You know that. Packard's become a big man in the last year or so. I don't want to go into details, but it's—damned important.

MILLICENT: (*Realizing his earnestness*) Oh, Oliver.
   (*Paula Jordan enters from the hall. Nineteen, modern, chic. She is dressed for the street.*)

PAULA: (*Pulling on her gloves*) Off to the marts of trade. Hello, mother! Dad, what're you lolling in boudoirs for? What's become of the shipping business?

OLIVER: What indeed! Mm! Don't you look smart!

PAULA: Next year's style. I won't be home for dinner, mother. Ooh, I'm late!

MILLICENT: What about this afternoon, Paula? Where are we meeting?

PAULA: Hm?

MILLICENT: Where am I meeting you this afternoon!
   (*Dora enters with fresh linen over her arm. Crosses and goes into the bedroom.*)

OLIVER: I've got to go to the office. Look here, Millicent, you'll do that for me, won't you?

MILLICENT: Well, if it's as important as you say—

PAULA: What is?

OLIVER: Believe me—it is.

MILLICENT: Oh, well—

OLIVER: That's my brave girl! Thanks . . . Drop you, Paula?

PAULA: (*With a shake of the head*) Walking.
   (*Oliver goes.*)

MILLICENT: (*Calls after him*) I want to see Ricci before you go.

OLIVER: (*From down the hall*) Right!

MILLICENT: (*As Paula manœuvres to the door*) Now, Paula, I'm lunching at the Embassy. I can meet you about—

PAULA: Mother, I can't meet you this afternoon. I simply can't.

MILLICENT: Paula, you've put it off time after time. The monogramming takes months. When do you expect to get things!

PAULA: It can't be today. We're giving a tea at the office for Chanel.

MILLICENT: If that silly magazine is more important to you . . . After all, *I'm* not the one that's being married.

PAULA: But there's loads of time.

MILLICENT: There's not loads of time. You're being married in three months, and not a stitch of trousseau.

PAULA: Oh, I'm not the girl to gloat over a linen closet. All tied up with little pink bows. (*A vicious gesture.*) I'll get everything when the time comes.

MILLICENT: Well, for an engaged girl you're certainly casual. Do you act like that with Ernest?

PAULA: Ernest says I'm a flawless fiancée.

MILLICENT: Oh, by the way, what was all this last night?

PAULA: What?

MILLICENT: Ernest called up this morning in a perfect dither. When you weren't up he asked to talk to me.

PAULA: Oh, yes.

MILLICENT: Did I know how you were feeling, and were you any better? I told him I didn't know there was anything the matter with you, and he said he brought you home at ten last night with a terrible headache.

PAULA: Yes, I did have. But I'm all right now.

MILLICENT: I distinctly heard you come in at four this morning.

PAULA: (*A trifle dashed*) Oh! Yes! Well—I went out again. (*Great frankness.*) I took three aspirins, and my headache vanished, and I felt wide awake and simply superb, and there it was, only eleven o'clock, and some of the crowd called up and said there was a marvelous party going on—so I went out again.

MILLICENT: Well, I hope you've got charm enough to explain that to Ernest. Where was the party?

PAULA: Oh—around. We went over to Twenty-one . . . Look, darling, I've just got to run. I'll be home before dinner. I'm going out with Ernest. Will you be here?

MILLICENT: I suppose so.

(*Dora appears in bedroom doorway.*)

PAULA: 'Bye! (*Goes quickly.*)

DORA: Mrs. Jordan, do you want the pink to go?

MILLICENT: What?

DORA: I didn't pack the pink because I don't think it needs cleaning.

(*Gustave enters.*)

MILLICENT: Oh, I thought it did. I'll look at it. (*Disappearing through bedroom door, her voice coming out from the next room*) I've worn it five times and I'm sure it must be filthy.

(*Dora picks up a torn envelope or two, fallen to the floor. Places them in waste basket.*)

(*Gustave, about to take away the tray, is regarding Dora with a fond eye. As Dora straightens and turns to go to the bedroom Gustave detains her with an affectionate and intimate gesture.*)

DORA: (*Pleased, but fearing discovery. Points toward Mrs. Jordan in bedroom. Whispers.*) I've got to go. (*She leans close to him.*)

MILLICENT: (*In her room*) Dora!

(*Dora scoots.*)

(*Gustave picks up the laden tray. Goes.*)

(*The voices of Millicent and Dora are heard from the bedroom.*)

Oh, no, Dora. I think it looks dreadful. Pack it in with the others. Really, pink is almost as extravagant as white. It's so hard to keep clean.

DORA: It looks lovely on you.

MILLICENT: I wish I looked well in black. It isn't very good on me. I think I'll wear the beige today. Get it out, will you, Dora? I imagine it needs pressing.

DORA: It probably does.

MILLICENT: Goodness, yes! Take it right down.

(*As the voices are heard in the bedroom, the figure of Ricci, the chauffeur, appears in the hall doorway. He stands a moment, hears the voices of Millicent and Dora, and takes a step or two into the room, his eyes on the bedroom doorway. Ricci is a tall, saturnine Italian, slim, graceful, and a little sinister. He is wearing his chauffeur's uniform, cap in hand.*)

Have you got everything there for Ricci? I wonder what in the world's keeping him.

(Dora comes into the sitting room, the beige dress over her arm. She is walking quickly; sees Ricci, who stands regarding her steadily. She stops.)

(Their eyes hold a second. Dora makes herself very small and aloof as she disdainfully passes Ricci. Ricci, slouching insolently toward her, puts out a hand to touch her as she passes him. She evades him.)

DORA: He's here now, Mrs. Jordan.

MILLICENT: Send him right in, will you?

(Ricci straightens as he goes toward the bedroom doorway.)

(Dora goes into the hall.)

RICCI: Yes, madam.

MILLICENT: *(Still unseen in the bedroom)* In the first place, I want you to come back here for me at one o'clock—better make it quarter to one. I'll need you all afternoon. And now listen: after you've taken Mr. Jordan to the office— *(She appears in the bedroom at this point.)* —take this box to Charvet—*you* know—you've been there before—East Fifty-fifth Street. And then you're coming back here for me in time for lunch. Is that clear?

RICCI: *(Takes the box)* Yes, madam.

MILLICENT: And oh, yes! Stop at Cartier's and see if my stationery is ready. *(He half turns; waits for further orders.)* That's all . . . Oh, my goodness! I nearly forgot. *(Goes quickly to her desk. Writes a few words on a card as she continues talking.)* As soon as you drop Mr. Jordan go up to Thorley's and get two dozen Talisman roses—long-stemmed. And remember—Talisman.

RICCI: Talisman.

MILLICENT: That's right. *(Addressing the envelope)* And don't have them sent. Take them over yourself to *(Writing)* Lady Ferncliffe . . . where's that radio . . . *(Searches her desk. Finds the radio.)* Waldorf Astoria. *(Writes.)* They'll know. They get in this morning. Is that clear?

RICCI: Perfectly.

MILLICENT: *(A little abstracted)* I think that's all.

(Ricci goes.)

(Millicent stands a moment, gathering her forces. Sighs deeply. Drops into the chair before her desk. Shuffles a few papers; finds the one she is seeking. With an eye half on this

*paper she dials the telephone number, misses the third figure
of the number, hangs up and starts all over again.*)
Is this Dr. Talbot's home? . . . Is Mrs. Talbot there? This is
Mrs. Oliver Jordan. I want to speak to Mrs. Talbot. . . .
(*She is turning the pages of her own private address book,
hunting down certain telephone numbers as she waits.*) Lucy!
. . . This is Millicent. . . . How are you? . . . Oh, I'm fine.
. . . Listen, Lucy dear, I'm giving a little dinner for Lord
and Lady Ferncliffe. You know they're here from England. I
want you and the Doctor to come. A week from tonight—
Friday. . . . That'll be lovely. I'm only asking a few people
whom I know they'd like. I'm inviting you informally like
this because the time's so short, and anyway it's just a small
dinner. . . . Yes, that's right. Friday, the twenty-third, at
eight o'clock.

(*Hattie Loomis, Mrs. Jordan's sister, appears in the doorway.
A few years older than Millicent, and attractive-looking
in spite of a harassed and rather bitter expression. Her
clothes are modish enough, but not too new. She is not shabby;
neither can she be called smart. As usual, she is carrying a
smallish lumpy brown paper parcel.*)

We'll probably see a play afterward. I think they'd like that.
Though there's nothing to see. But I'm so glad you can
come. I know you'll like the Ferncliffes. They're just as
simple . . . That'll be fine. . . . Good-bye!

HATTIE: What's that? Covers for thirty again?

MILLICENT: No, no. Only ten. The Ferncliffes are over here
and I've just got to entertain them. They gave a dinner for
us in London.

HATTIE: That's fair enough. . . . Listen, Millie, can I have a
look at that blue flat crêpe of Paula's—remember?—that
you promised me for Joan? Everything's got capes this year
and I had this piece of blue velvet— (*Beginning to open her
paper parcel*) —that I thought might do. But if it's the
wrong shade I'll have to pick up something else. So I'd like
to take a look at the crêpe, because if it isn't, Stern's have a
sale on velvets and I could hurry right down there.

MILLICENT: Do you have to have it right now? I'm simply—

HATTIE: Don't you bother. I'll tell Dora. I saw her as I—
(*To hall doorway, quickly. Calls.*) Dora! (*Back into the room a*

step or two.) Because if it doesn't match I want to get right down. Everything gets picked over.

(*Dora appears in the doorway.*)

MILLICENT: Dora, will you go to Miss Paula's room and get that blue crêpe dress of hers? *You* know?

DORA: You mean the evening one?

MILLICENT: Yes. I want to show it to my sister.

(*Dora goes.*)

HATTIE: I hope it's right. Oh, well— When's your dinner?

MILLICENT: A week from tonight.

HATTIE: Just ran into Oliver downstairs. I thought he looked a little under-done.

MILLICENT: (*Absently. She is at her desk.*) What?

HATTIE: As if he could stand a few violet-rays.

MILLICENT: (*Fishes from a desk pigeonhole an impressive announcement card with two colored tickets attached by clips.*) Oh, Hattie, what are you doing— (*Consulting card*) —next Monday afternoon?

HATTIE: (*Cagily*) I don't know. Why?

MILLICENT: That Russian prince of Alison Cruikshank's is giving a talk against Communism in the Rose Room of the Park Lane.

HATTIE: Sorry. I've got to see a man about a dog.

MILLICENT: (*As she turns back to her desk.*) Well, I just thought you might use the tickets if you weren't doing anything.

HATTIE: (*One of those indrawn society laughs*) Than-kyou!

MILLICENT: I wish now I'd never started this miserable dinner. (*An inspiration*) Tommy Van Veen!

HATTIE: What about him?

MILLICENT: My extra man!

HATTIE: He's nothing extra.

MILLICENT: If I can only get him. He'd fit in so— (*Turns to her sister.*) What do you think? Now, here's the list. (*Reaches for her slip of paper.*) I've got the Ferncliffes, of course— that's what makes it so difficult—you see, she's so deaf you have to yell your head off, and all he knows is Parliament and grouse.

HATTIE: Gives you a nice start.

MILLICENT: That isn't the worst. Oliver's got some business thing up his sleeve and insists on my asking those Packards.

You know who they are. All the money in the world, and bellows at the top of his lungs.

HATTIE: (*Brightly*) Put him next to Lady Ferncliffe.

MILLICENT: And as for *Mrs.* Packard! They say she was a check-room girl, or something. Commonest little piece. She's his second wife—years younger. Of course it was his money.

HATTIE: It gets better and better. Tell me more about her.

MILLICENT: I met her at the races once. She was beautifully dressed. But the bracelets and the perfume and the make-up —they gave her away at fifty yards. And when she opened that little rosebud mouth—well, she spoke pure spearmint.

HATTIE: Ferncliffe'll be crazy about her. He'll probably divorce the old girl.

MILLICENT: There's one good thing—I've got the Talbots. They are sweet. And a doctor always fits in. Of course, lately, he's always trying to analyze you. And at dinner, no matter what you talk about, it leads right back to your inhibitions. When it comes to that, he ought to concentrate on his wife. You know Lucy! Talk about inhibitions!

HATTIE: I like Lucy—I think she's got brains.

MILLICENT: Nonsense! If she had any brains she'd have been on to him long ago. That bedside boy! Carrying on with every pretty patient he's got. . . . I think I'll put him next to Carlotta Vance.

HATTIE: Oh, I didn't know she was here. When did she come over?

MILLICENT: A few days ago. I ran into her at the Colony. Of course I think she's poisonous, but I've got to have her here some time. When I think of the way she behaved that summer at Antibes. Trying to steal Oliver under my very nose. You'd think a woman of her age—

HATTIE: Why, she can't be so old.

MILLICENT: Oh, Hattie!

HATTIE: How old was she when she played *"La Vallière"*? Remember how beautiful she was, and how thrilled we were!

MILLICENT: Well, she doesn't thrill me now—but I've got to have her. We were in and out of her house all that summer. Everybody was. Sunning on her rocks and sprawling on her terrace. It's really astonishing, the people she gets around her over there. Michael Arlen and Willy Maugham and Charlie Chaplin—even Shaw came in one day. I've got to have her.

HATTIE: Yes, have her—if you're sure you don't like her. She just fits in.

MILLICENT: Oliver's fond of her. She was one of his college crushes. He says she's a child about business and advises her now and then. If you ask me I think she's a man-eating shark. Look at the fortune she got out of old Stanfield. And that theatre named after her. It's hers, you know.

HATTIE: I wish somebody'd name a theatre after me—The Hattie Loomis.

MILLICENT: You know, 'way down deep I'm really rather glad to have her. I want to show her there are some people she could never hope to meet over there, but that she *can* meet in my house.

HATTIE: I see. Who has the choice of weapons?

MILLICENT: (*Reaches for the telephone directory*) I don't suppose that Packard woman would be up at this hour. Oh, dear, when I think of that voice.

HATTIE: Wouldn't it be wonderful if they couldn't come?

MILLICENT: (*Running a finger down the P's in the directory*) Pablo—Pacific—Packard—

HATTIE: Sometimes I think there are compensations in being a poor relation.

MILLICENT: (*At the number now. Writing it on her pad*) El-do-ra-do. E-l-5—

(*Dora enters, carrying the blue dress.*)

DORA: It was in with her summer things. I had to find it.

HATTIE: (*Snatches up the piece of blue velvet.*) Oh, no! It's a million miles off. (*Takes the dress from Dora.*) I'll have to go down. Thanks, Dora.

(*Dora goes.*)

HATTIE: It's lovely, though, Millie. (*Holding up the blue dress*) Joan'll look sweet in it.

MILLICENT: I never liked it much. (*Consults phone pad.*) Eldo-rado-five—

HATTIE: Joan'll love it. I'll have to run. I'll take the whole thing along. (*Wraps dress, velvet, in a bundle, hastily.*) How I hate matching things.

MILLICENT: Are you going to stay down for lunch? (*About to start dialing. Abandons it.*)

HATTIE: Oh, no, I have to be home.

MILLICENT: Hattie, will you do something for me? If I pick you up at, say, quarter to three, will you go with me to just two places and look at some stuff for Paula? You're so good at that. She won't do anything about it, and the time's so short. (*Starts to dial.*)

HATTIE: I was going to start this little cape for Joan. She wants to wear it tomorrow night.

MILLICENT: (*With a gesture that says, "Wait a second. I'm busy." Finishes dialing her number. Turns now to Hattie.*) You can do it tonight, Hattie. You know you can. You're so quick.

HATTIE: I don't like to sit and sew when Ed's home. He hates it.

MILLICENT: Oh, he won't mind. Tell him to go to a movie. I'll pick you up at quarter to three. (*In telephone.*) . . . Could I speak to Mrs. Packard, please? . . . This is Mrs. Oliver Jordan. Is Mrs. Packard up yet?

HATTIE: Listen, Millie, I—

MILLICENT: (*Waiting, receiver in hand*) Please, darling. Ed won't mind. How *is* Ed? (*Very absent.*)

HATTIE: (*Acidly*) He's got the bubonic plague.

MILLICENT: (*Concentrates on the phone*) That's fine.

(*Hattie, with a grim smile, goes. Millicent has not noticed her departure. Keeps on talking into the phone.*)

Mrs. Packard? How do you do, Mrs. Packard? This is Mrs. Oliver Jordan. How are you? (*Removes the receiver a few inches from her ear, with a wry look, as that voice comes over the telephone.*) . . . I hope I didn't wake you. . . . Well, I thought this might be a strange hour, for you. . . . Mrs. Packard, Mr. Jordan and I are giving a small dinner for Lord and Lady Ferncliffe, two very dear friends of mine from England. We would like so much to have you and Mr. Packard come. (*She sets her teeth.*) . . . Oh, that'll be lovely. . . . Don't you want to know the date? . . . It's a week from tonight. Friday, the twenty-third. I'm inviting you informally like this because the time's so short, and anyway, it's just a small dinner. . . . Friday, the twenty-third.

Dinner at eight. (*The lights start to dim.*) I thought we'd all go to the theatre afterward, and see a play. Though perhaps you and Mr. Packard would prefer a musical comedy. I'll see what there is, and perhaps we can go to one of those . . .

(*The lights are out.*)

SCENE II

The private office of Oliver Jordan, head of the Jordan Line. It is on the fifth floor of an old-fashioned red-brick office building on State Street, facing the Battery. The structure dates back at least fifty years, and now is almost surrounded by modern skyscrapers. With the possible exception of a flat-topped desk, the furnishings of the room are those of the day of old Oliver Jordan, grandfather of the present head of the steamship line.

Prominently hung on the wall is a large colored map showing the routes taken by the various Jordan boats. Printed on this, in large letters, are the words JORDAN LINE. There are mahogany bookcases containing thick volumes on maritime law, shipping, and the like. Atop these cases are models of ships representing the line. There is, too, a portrait of old Oliver Jordan, showing him to be a rather handsome and rockbound old gentleman with side-whiskers and a good deal of watch-chain and collar.

For the rest, there is a wooden filing cabinet; a decrepit and scuffed leather chair whose stuffing is oozing here and there. The chair is placed alongside the desk for callers. Another smaller chair is at the back. A small table or two. An ancient safe whose door is ornamented with a faded painting of a maritime scene, with ships, scrolls, festoons, and border.

As the curtain goes up Miss Copeland enters, a sheaf of documents in her hand.

Miss Copeland is a spare and spinsterish forty-eight. She makes for the filing cabinet, deposits the papers in their proper places. The telephone sounds from the desk. It is not the shrill, insistent ring one usually hears, but a faint single tinkle. The connection has come from the outer office.

Miss Copeland goes to the telephone.

MISS COPELAND: Hello! . . . Who? . . . Yes, put him on. I'll talk to him. . . . Yes, Mr. Kingsberry. . . . No, he isn't. . . . Yes, he's always back by this time. He must have gone some place else after lunch.

(*Fosdick enters. A relic of the old Jordan régime. He is sixty-odd; the shiny alpaca office coat, wing collar, and baggy trousers. Goes to the safe and squats creakingly in front of it, working with the combination knob. He opens the safe door; you get a glimpse of small wooden drawers and musty pigeonholes.*)

Yes, I will. (*Hangs up.*) That's the second time they've called. Did he tell you he was going to be late?

FOSDICK: Didn't tell me anything.

MISS COPELAND: (*As she returns to the filing cabinet*) He nearly always gets back by half-past two. He's got a Mr. Packard coming in at quarter-past three.

FOSDICK: Who?

MISS COPELAND: Mr. Daniel Packard. I was all morning on the telephone trying to get him. He's got an office in the Empire State Building, and a secretary, and she was looking for him herself. I kept calling up and she kept saying try Mr. Untermeyer's office, and try the Amalgamated Copper Company, and try the Jockey Club, and Mr. Al Smith, and try the New York Athletic Club, and they finally paged him there and I got him in the swimming pool.

FOSDICK: Like to know what they have offices for! Commodore— (*A gesture toward the picture of old Oliver Jordan*) —used to get here eight o'clock every morning and stayed till seven. You could set your watch by him. Now it's down at eleven, two hours for lunch, and home at four. Where'd you put those invoices?

MISS COPELAND: What invoices?

FOSDICK: For the *Castillian*. I want them all together twenty-four hours before she sails.

MISS COPELAND: They aren't all in yet. There's plenty of time.

FOSDICK: (*As he rises from the safe*) Don't forget she sails at five.

(*Oliver Jordan enters. In the next moment or two he takes off his topcoat, places it with his hat and stick on a coat tree in the corner. There is plainly something on his mind.*)

OLIVER: (*Rubbing his arm briskly*) Brr! Glad to be indoors. Cold out. It cuts through you like a knife.

MISS COPELAND: I thought it was real pleasant. I sat in Battery Park, lunch time.

OLIVER: (*Striding over to his desk*) It may have been pleasant there; I've been out on the dock.

MISS COPELAND: Oh, it's damp there. . . . Mr. Kingsberry called up twice, Mr. Jordan. He wants you to call him. Shall I get him?

OLIVER: Just a minute.

(*Fosdick starts to leave the room.*)

Don't go, Fosdick.

(*Fosdick halts.*)

The *Castillian* isn't sailing tomorrow.

MISS COPELAND: What!

FOSDICK: Not sailing!

OLIVER: No use sending her out when she hasn't got enough cargo to keep her down in the water.

MISS COPELAND: Why, Mr. Jordan!

FOSDICK: But tomorrow's her regular sailing.

OLIVER: Well, she'll have to go next week, instead. By that time maybe she'll have a cargo.

FOSDICK: But the *Santa Clara* goes next week.

OLIVER: She'll have to wait, too. Those boats aren't going for the ride.

FOSDICK: No Jordan boat has missed a trip in sixty years.

OLIVER: They're going to miss them now, that's sure. Our business doesn't warrant it, Fosdick. We've got to haul in for a while. That's all there is to it.

(*Fosdick goes.*)

MISS COPELAND: (*In a crushed voice*) Shall I get Mr. Kingsberry for you?

OLIVER: All right.

MISS COPELAND: (*Speaks into desk phone.*) Get Mr. Kingsberry for Mr. Jordan.

(*Oliver sits at the desk.*)

OLIVER: When Mr. Packard gets here show him right in.

MISS COPELAND: Yes, sir. (*She goes.*)

(*Oliver drops rather heavily into his desk chair. A little absent-minded rubbing of his chest. A deep sigh. He pulls him-*

*self together a bit now, and, glancing over his desk, lifts a
paper, listlessly opens a drawer.)*

(*The telephone rings.*)

OLIVER: Yes? . . . Oh, hello, Mr. Kingsberry! I'm sorry you've
had trouble getting me. . . . Well, no, I'm afraid I . . .
Can't you tell me over the phone? . . . I see. . . . Oh, they
are? . . . I see. . . . Um . . . Well, no, I'm not prepared to
buy it right now, but you can tell Miss Satterlee and her sister for me that the Jordan stock is just as good today as it
was when their father bought it—allowing, of course, for
these times. I'm sure that if Mr. Satterlee had lived he'd have
advised them to . . . Well, of course. I'll give you any information you want. You know, the stockholders' meeting is a
week from Monday. I wish you'd ask them to hold off
until that time. After all, their father and my father were
friends for half a century. I think they'd regret any hasty action. . . . Thank you very much for your courtesy. . . .
Good-bye.

(*Oliver hangs up the receiver, rises, paces the room back and
forth once or twice, swiftly. He wheels, stands at the window
a moment looking out over the harbor.*)

(*Miss Copeland enters.*)

MISS COPELAND: (*With great impressiveness*) Miss Carlotta
Vance is here to see you.

OLIVER: Carlot—here! Outside! Carlotta! (*Rushes to doorway.*)

(*Carlotta Vance is not one to wait outside. She is already on
the threshold, her hands dramatically outstretched to meet
his. As they meet, Miss Copeland, lost in admiration, backs
out of the door, her eyes on Carlotta until the door is closed.*)

(*Carlotta Vance is a battered beauty of, perhaps, fifty-three.
She cannot be said to be faded, for there still is about her a
magnificent vitality and zest. Her figure is gone, for she likes
good living, and in the past twelve or fifteen years she has
given up the struggle. There clings to her, intangibly, much
of the splendor, the success, the élan of the old days when she
was a famous theatrical beauty and the mistress of millions.*)

(*Her dress is rich, careless, and somewhat fussy, what with
scarfs, veils, chains, furs, muff. She moves and sits with
consciousness of herself. Her speech is racy, biting. She is very
much on to herself.*)

(*There is a little babble of greetings, cooings, exclamations.*)

CARLOTTA: Oliver! Ducky! How are you! How simply marvelous to see you! I never was so glad to see anyone in all my
life! (*She kisses him dramatically, on one cheek, then on the
other, embracing him.*)

OLIVER: Well, for God's sake, Lotta! This is a surprise! What
brings you down here? How've you been? I heard you were
over here. You're looking marvelous!

CARLOTTA: Do I? I do, don't I? And you! You're actually
handsomer than ever. Oh, oh, Oliver! (*Just touches the grey
at his temples.*) Distinguished!

OLIVER: (*Takes her hand.*) Come over here! Sit down! This is
swell! Let me look at you!

    (*Carlotta describes a sweeping circle about the room, for his
inspection, but the little parade ends with her rather shrewd
eye encompassing the outmoded and shabby surroundings in
which she finds herself.*)

CARLOTTA: My God, what a hole! Is this what I own stock in!
Why, I thought it would be all platinum and plush. What do
you make down here? Worm holes!

OLIVER: Well—good enough for my father— Gosh, but I'm
glad to see you again! I read you'd landed. What're you
doing over here?

CARLOTTA: (*Sinks into the depths of the old leather chair.*) Trying
to mend the shattered for-tyune.

OLIVER: You picked a good day for it. And the right part of
town, too. (*A gesture toward the window.*) There are all our
financiers, sitting on those benches. Now, who did you
come way down to the Battery to see? Not *me.*

CARLOTTA: (*Opening her handbag, fishing a paper from among
the débris*) Well, sir, not to deceive you, I came down to
see— (*Gropes a moment; adjusts her lorgnette carefully. Reads
from letter.*) —United States Customs Inspector Isidore J.
Greenbaum—the son of a bitch. (*Looks up.*) Why *shouldn't* I
own six fur coats!

OLIVER: Perfectly reasonable.

CARLOTTA: And then, right in front of the Customs, what did
I sight but Jordan Line? And I says to meself, maybe the old
gentleman is in. And here you are.

OLIVER: I'm very grateful to Mr. Greenbaum.

CARLOTTA: I told him, I said, "I didn't come to this country to *bring* money. I came to take it out." Oliver darling, I'm as flat as a mill-pond. I haven't a sou.

OLIVER: Oh, now, come, Carlotta! How about all those gilt-edged securities? And your theatre! Why, that theatre alone ought to bring you enough to live on.

CARLOTTA: That's my chief reason for coming over. To try to get rid of that rat trap.

OLIVER: What's the matter with it?

CARLOTTA: May I take you for a stroll down Forty-second Street and a little look at the Carlotta Vance Theatre? It's between the Flea Circus and a Hamburg-and-Onion Eatery. It's had six weeks of booking in the past two years. And what were they! Special matinées of a Greek actress named Maria Koreopolous playing Sophocles' *How Are You?* in the original Greek. *That* filled a long-felt want. Then there was a movie week. A big educational film called *The Story of Evolution, or; From Ooze to Hoover* in ten reels. It then swung back to the legitimate with a little gem entitled *Papa Love Mama*. Three days. For the past six months they haven't taken the lock off the door. It's now known as the spiders' rendezvous, but you can't collect rent from *them*!

OLIVER: Well! Then it's not bringing in a cent.

CARLOTTA: So my little problem is to find somebody I can sell it to. Though I don't know what they'd do with it, unless they flood it and use it for a swimming pool. (*A sudden thought.*) I wonder if I couldn't sell it back to the Stanfield estate. There's an idea. You know, when he gave me that theatre I thought it was pretty magnificent of the old boy. I wish now I'd taken a sandwich.

OLIVER: Oh, now, Lotta, you always exaggerated. I'll bet you're rolling in wealth.

CARLOTTA: What've I got? Railroads, oil, cotton. That's what they gave you in my day. I could only take what they had. You know what's happened to *those* things.

OLIVER: Well, you *are* down to cases. "International Beauty Returns To Stage"?

CARLOTTA: Never. I'll have my double chins in privacy. I've seen too many hardened arteries dragged out to make a

first-night holiday. Though I must say I saw Julie Cavendish
last night and she looked wonderful. Forty-five if she's a day.

OLIVER: Look here, Carlotta. Your stuff must bring you in a
little something. It can't cost you an awful lot to live over
there.

CARLOTTA: Oh, no—but you saw what it was like in Antibes—
you and Millicent. Ten and twenty for lunch—cocktails—
most of them stay for dinner. And the house in London.
They drop in there. Noel, and Winston, and now and then
Wales. I've really done pretty well for a little girl from
Quincy, Illinois, but it runs into money. And unless you've
salted down your million! Look at Lily Langtry! Not half
my looks, but she got her Edward. I picked the wrong period. Too young for Edward and too old for Wales. I fell
right between princes.

OLIVER: Why don't you get rid of all that? Live over here for a
while. Get a little apartment, simplify everything.

CARLOTTA: Oliver, I've been in New York four days. It's the
first time I've been back in ten years. I'm lost already. Everything's changed. I'd die here. I belong to the Delmonico
period. A table by the window, facing Fifth Avenue, with the
flower boxes and the pink lampshades and the string orchestra. Oh, I don't know—willow plumes and Inverness capes,
dry champagne and snow on the ground—God, they don't
even have snow any more.

(*Miss Copeland enters. A little timid of interrupting.*)

MISS COPELAND: Pardon me.

OLIVER: Yes, Miss Copeland?

MISS COPELAND: (*A few steps into the room*) Mr. Eaton is on
the phone. He's taking a train, and—

OLIVER: All right. I'll talk to him. . . . Hello, Archie! (*In
phone.*)

(*Miss Copeland is edging off with a lingering glance of admiration at Carlotta Vance. Carlotta looks up from the
depths of her chair with a friendly smile.*)

MISS COPELAND: (*Thus encouraged*) Oh, Miss Vance—I just
want to tell you—I hope you won't mind—I can't help
telling you how exciting it is seeing you right here.

OLIVER: (*At telephone*) Yes?

CARLOTTA: Sweet of you!

MISS COPELAND: I'll never forget—I saw you in *Trelawney*— oh, you were wonderful.

CARLOTTA: Oh, yes. That was the last thing I did.

OLIVER: (*Still at telephone*) I understand.

MISS COPELAND: I remember it as plainly as if it was yesterday. Though I was only a little girl at the time.

(*Carlotta's smile stiffens.*)

CARLOTTA: How extraordinary!

MISS COPELAND: (*Backing off toward the door*) Well, I'm glad I had the chance to tell you. It's wonderful seeing you like this.

(*Miss Copeland goes.*)

OLIVER: (*At telephone*) That'll be Tuesday? . . . All right. (*He hangs up.*) (*To Carlotta*) Sorry. You have to work occasionally, even in business. Well, see here, Lotta, I wish there was something I could do to straighten this tangle out for you. I don't think any of my friends needs a theatre right now. And as far as your stocks are concerned—those things are still good. And, incidentally, so is your Jordan stock. You're not thinking of selling *that*, are you?

CARLOTTA: I don't know. Should I?

OLIVER: Much rather you wouldn't, just at this time. We've been hit, as everybody has. If you sold it now, I'm afraid you wouldn't get what it's worth.

CARLOTTA: I'd expect to lose something on it. But after all, ladies must live.

OLIVER: It's like this, Carlotta. You, perhaps, don't understand. Jordan stock has never been on the market. It's held very closely. Only six or seven people in all. Of course, you've got a very small block. What did you pay for it, anyway? Remember?

CARLOTTA: Sixty-one thousand two hundred and fifty dollars.

OLIVER: (*Amused*) Carlotta, you're wonderful!

CARLOTTA: No. I remember because it's the only stock I ever bought for myself. You said it was a good thing, and it has been, too, for twenty years. Of course, in the last year or two . . . You wouldn't want to buy it back yourself, would you?

OLIVER: I'd like to, but it would be pretty difficult just now.

CARLOTTA: Why, I've always thought of you as having all the money in the world.

OLIVER: I thought so too, for a few years.

CARLOTTA: When I think of Oliver Jordan, 3d!

OLIVER: I dropped that long ago.

CARLOTTA: Oliver Jordan at twenty-one! New York was full of gilded youths, but the gold was encrusted on *you*.

OLIVER: I suppose I was what they called a stage-door johnny—though you will admit I never carried a bouquet.

CARLOTTA: You always sent me roses—those deep velvet roses, hundreds and hundreds of them. And not a pearl necklace in a carload.

OLIVER: And you let me read my plays to you, remember? I was going to be a playwright in those days—and the hell with the shipping business.

CARLOTTA: Dear Oliver, you were sweet! And so serious and respectful. I was very fond of you, Oliver.

OLIVER: I was very much in love with you, Carlotta. You were the most divine creature in the world. I was at your feet, but so was all New York. If you took supper at a restaurant it was made. If you wore a certain hat it became the rage.

CARLOTTA: I was rather gorgeous, wasn't I? Remember, they named everything after me—cigars, and racehorses, and perfumes, and battleships.

OLIVER: How thrilled I was the first time you went out with me. I remember waiting for you, all chills and fever, hoping everyone knew I was meeting Carlotta Vance. Supper at Martin's —"There's Carlotta Vance! There's Carlotta Vance!" —a hansom through the Park, with a moon like a silver platter. You let me kiss you, Carlotta. Remember?

CARLOTTA: Did I? . . . One thing I'll never forget. It was the day you were twenty-one, Oliver. And you asked me to marry you.

OLIVER: What a young fool you must have thought me!

CARLOTTA: I thought it was sweet of you. Remember, I was thirtyish. I even went home and wept a little. They didn't often ask me to marry them.

OLIVER: It broke my heart when you refused me, Carlotta. I took revenge on the theatre. None of *my* plays should it have! So I went back to Papa Jordan and the shipping business.

CARLOTTA: (*She looks around the office*) And here you are.

OLIVER: Yes. Here I am.

MISS COPELAND: (*At door*) Mr. Packard is here now.

OLIVER: Oh! Yes. Send him right in. (*Turning to Carlotta as Miss Copeland goes.*) Do you mind? Dan Packard. Quite a fellow. Big Western stuff. Used to be a miner.

CARLOTTA: I'm just going.

(*Dan Packard's voice is heard booming before he enters.*)

PACKARD: That's no elevator—that's a bird-cage! Hey, Jordan, what kind of a dump— I beg your pardon.

(*He enters, stops abruptly as he sees Carlotta. Miss Copeland, unable to precede him in his rush, has followed fussily behind. She now withdraws, closing the door.*)

(*Dan Packard is one of those big, vital men, bellowing, self-important, too successful. His clothes are noticeable. He seems never to sit down; ramps and gesticulates as he talks, and he talks a great deal. He is always in the midst of a big deal, and curiously enough it really is a big deal. Every now and then, in his talk or in his manner, there crops up a word or gesture reminiscent of his Western mining days.*)

OLIVER: Lotta, this is Dan Packard. Miss Carlotta Vance.

PACKARD: (*As Carlotta acknowledges the introduction with a nod*) Miss Vance, I— Wait a minute! Vance! You don't mean Carlotta Vance! (*He does not stop for her confirmation.*) Why, I know you! Jordan, you old son of a gun!

CARLOTTA: (*To Jordan. Grimly*) Saw me when he was a boy.

PACKARD: Why, your picture was up on the wall of every mining shack in Montana, right 'longside of John L. Sullivan. Bunch of us rode forty miles into Butte just to see you. Sutton's Opera House. What was that piece you were in? You wore pants, I remember. (*A quick glance at her present contour.*) Say!

CARLOTTA: (*Hastily*) That's an exit cue. (*Starts toward door.*)

OLIVER: When'll I see you, Lotta? Soon?

PACKARD: Don't go on my account.

CARLOTTA: I'm at the Barclay.

OLIVER: I'll call you. Look here—you're dining with us next week. Friday, isn't it?

CARLOTTA: Am I?

OLIVER: Of course you are. (*Over his shoulder, to Packard*) So are you, Dan. But I'll see you before that. What did you say? The Barclay?

CARLOTTA: Righto! Good-bye! (*Then, to Packard*) Good-bye,
Lochinvar! (*She goes.*)

PACKARD: What'd she call me?

OLIVER: Sit down, Dan. How've you been?

PACKARD: Only stay a minute. Running down to Washington,
five-thirty. Got to drop up home, pick up a bag. Bunch of us
going down. I'll tell you in confidence what it's about.
Seems the President wants to get right down to the bottom
of things. So he asked a little crowd of us to run over. Jim
Thorne, Whitaker, couple of others. Breakfast at the White
House, gab for a while, jump right back again. Not so bad.
Private car, plenty of stuff, poker game.

OLIVER: That sounds grand. Dan, the reason I asked you to
come in—I want to put something up to you.

PACKARD: Sure! Go right ahead!

OLIVER: It's about the Jordan Line. We find ourselves facing
a—

PACKARD: Holy smoke, I almost forgot! What time is it?
(*Delves for his watch.*) Mind if I use your phone? (*He is al-
ready reaching for it; receiver in hand, he turns inquiringly to
Oliver.*) What kind of a—

OLIVER: Just tell my operator—she'll call you.

PACKARD: (*Into phone*) Get me Ashland four—six one seven
nine, will you, girlie? Say my secretary, Miss Brice. Snap it
up! (*As he talks into the telephone his eye travels appraisingly
over the room.*) Say, who put up this building—Peter Stuy-
vesant? This isn't an office; it's a museum.

OLIVER: Not exactly modernistic. But it was the last word
when the old gentleman built it. (*A gesture to the portrait.*) I
suppose it's sentimental of me, but I don't believe I'd want
to change it. Been like this for seventy-five years.

PACKARD: I hope those tubs of yours don't date with the office— (*The telephone rings. Packard leaps to it.*) Hello! That
you, Miss Brice? . . . Two or three things before I go. I
won't be in. What's that directors' meeting? . . . Monday
morning. . . . Wait a minute . . . (*His quick eye sweeps the
desk, he snatches a piece of paper which is an important letter,
begins to make notes on it. Oliver instinctively flings out a
hand to salvage it. Too late.*) . . . Coast State Waterways. Oh,
yeh. . . . Did you send that South American cable? . . .

Good. . . . Did the Governor call me? Tell him I'll be back tomorrow. . . . And get me ten good seats for that *Vanities* show tomorrow night. And you know—I don't want to sit back of the second row. . . . Now! I want you to send a case of Scotch, with my compliments, to District Attorney Michael G. Slade, Presbyterian Hospital. . . . Cancel my seats for the fight tonight. . . . And get this. This is important. Call up the stables down in Maryland and tell O'Rourke I'm changing the feed on Streak-o'-Lightning. Tell him to try half bran mash from now on. . . . BRAN MASH! MASH! That's all. (*Hangs up. Turns to Oliver.*) Now then, Jordan, what's on your mind?

OLIVER: I'm not intruding?

PACKARD: That's all right. What's troubling you? Kind of up against it?

OLIVER: Not quite that. You probably know about our business. We're strictly freight carriers. New York and Southern Coast—Havana, Port au Prince. I needn't tell you what's happened to trade down there—sugar, coffee. Of course it isn't going to last forever. But what I want to know is, if it does take a little longer than we figure, would you be in a position—you and your associates—to sort of tide us over?

PACKARD: (*Shifts his position as he thinks this over*) H'm.

OLIVER: I realize I might have to turn over some of my holdings. I'd rather not disturb any of the other stockholders. It's a closed corporation. Not many in it. Most of them have had it for years. Inherited.

PACKARD: Well, I'll tell you. Of course I don't know anything about your business, but it looks to me as if it's gone to seed. Only have to look around this office. All those old fogies out there. No wonder you're in a hole. As far as that Southern trade's concerned, I don't see much future in it. Tell you the truth, Jordan, I don't think you've got much to offer.

OLIVER: (*With some indignation*) Just a minute, Packard! You know nothing about my business. The Jordan Line is one of the best known in the shipping world. Our boats have traveled the ocean for a century. We started with clipper ships. And we're not going to stop now. We're not through—not by a damn sight!

PACKARD: Gosh, Jordan, I didn't mean anything. You know—I'm a business man—I may have put it a little—you know how it is these days—everybody after you—I apologize.

OLIVER: (*His hand absently rubbing his chest, as though to still a discomfort there*) That's all right.

PACKARD: Tell you what I'll do. You get together some figures on this thing. Can you do that?

OLIVER: Why—I could.

PACKARD: Balance sheet, assets—total tonnage, and when the boats were built—list of stockholders—not many of them, you said?

OLIVER: No, no. It's held quite closely.

PACKARD: Well, let me have a list of them. Now, when do you want to send this to me?

OLIVER: Oh—it won't take long. You understand, Packard, this is confidential.

PACKARD: (*Getting into his coat*) Sure! Sure! Of course I've got to lay it before my people.

OLIVER: Another thing. We've got a stockholders' meeting on November twenty-sixth. That's a week from Monday.

PACKARD: You give me that dope early next week, and I'll let you have an answer in a few days.

OLIVER: That's very kind of you. (*Again the vague rubbing of the chest.*)

PACKARD: What's the matter there—got a pain? (*Imitating Jordan's gesture.*)

OLIVER: No, no. Little indigestion.

PACKARD: Juice of half a lemon—I get it all the time—half a lemon in hot water. (*A hasty glance at his watch.*) Jumping Jupiter! I've got to travel. You'll send me that stuff? Do what I can for you, anyway. God knows! (*Packard goes.*)

(*Oliver has accompanied him to the door. He now stands a moment, his hand on the knob of the shut door. The other hand passes once more over his chest, absently. Then, slowly, he starts to walk toward his desk.*)

THE LIGHTS DIM.

Scene III

Kitty Packard's bedroom in the Packard's apartment. It is a rather startling room done in the modernistic manner by the newest and most fashionable decorator. The color is white—all the shades of white from cream, through ivory, to oyster. Kitty has just had it done, and finds she doesn't like it very well. It isn't, she thinks, becoming to her. There is a large and luxurious bed; a dressing table bearing bottles, brushes, mirrors, jars; a bedside table, a wardrobe which, when opened, reveals rows of silken things on hangers. There are two doors, one leading into Dan Packard's room, the other into the hall.

It is half-past four in the afternoon. Kitty Packard is in bed. She has been in bed all day.

A pretty woman of twenty-nine, the slightly faded wild-rose Irish type. She was Kitty Sheehan before her marriage. There is, in her face, the petulance of the idle and empty-headed wife. She is sitting up among her pillows and is wearing a charming bed jacket over her nightgown. Her hair is arranged as carefully as though for a more formal occasion. All about her, on the bed, on the table, and even on the floor, are the odds and ends that have accumulated for her amusement during the long day. The tabloid newspapers, four movie magazines, novels in cheap lurid jackets; manicure implements, an opened box of candy, very large; a small tray on which are a chocolate pot, cup, cream pitcher; a puzzle game in a pasteboard box—the trick is to get the ball of mercury and the four colored disks all into their proper places. Costume dolls, in grotesque shapes and positions, sprawl and squirm on dressing table and bed and chair. Kitty admires these childish ornaments. On the floor, near the foot of the bed, where it has fallen open, is a large and imposing volume which has been cast aside by Kitty.

At the rise of the curtain, Kitty is to be seen working over the puzzle held balanced in her hands. Her whole attention is concentrated on it. She fails to make it come right, tosses it aside pettishly, looks about for amusement, takes up a motion-picture magazine, flips its pages idly, throws that aside.

KITTY: (*Calls.*) Tina! TINA!

(*Tina enters from the hall.*)

(*Tina is Mrs. Packard's personal maid. A somewhat hard-faced, capable, and shifty girl of twenty-five or -six. She is wearing a smart maid's uniform.*)

TINA: Yes, Mrs. Packard?

KITTY: What time is it now?

TINA: (*Glances at clock on dressing table.*) Half-past four.

KITTY: What did Dr. Talbot say? What time's he coming?

TINA: He didn't say exactly. He asked were there any symptoms and I said, no, I didn't think so, so he said all right then, some time this afternoon.

KITTY: (*Annoyed*) I've got a cold and my legs ache all over.

TINA: Oh—well—you didn't tell me to *say* that, Mrs. Packard.

KITTY: Well, you should have known it! What'll I do from now until— (*Her eye travels about the bed and bedside, falls on the chocolate tray.*) Oh, take that all away. Wait a minute! (*Reaches swiftly for the spoon, dips it into the whipped cream, licks it with a lingering tongue.*)

(*Tina picks up the tray. Goes to hall door.*)

(*Kitty has picked up the half-empty candy box, rattled its contents, cast it aside.*)

Get me that other candy box—the big one. (*Looks about at her assortment of pastimes. Picks up a large and glittering nail-buffer with which she begins briskly to polish her nails, slows up, casts it aside. A deep sigh. Picks up the discarded puzzle, and again tries to concentrate on this.*)

(*Tina returns with the candy box, an enormous affair of pink satin and gold lace. She comes up to the bedside, stands, box in hand, watching a moment to see if Mrs. Packard is really going to perform the trick this time.*)

TINA: (*After an absorbed second*) If you tip it up this way— (*A gesture with her hand*) —you can get the blue in.

KITTY: (*Throws the puzzle across the room.*) Oh!

(*Tina hastily places the candy box on the bed; goes to retrieve the puzzle.*)

(*Kitty turns over on her side; her glance encounters the candy box; she opens it and begins greedily to inspect its contents. Selects a chocolate, begins to nibble it.*)

(*Tina, in picking up the puzzle, has become momentarily*

interested in it, and even essays a little manipulation of the
colored balls with the hope of getting them into the slots.)

KITTY: (*Nibbling the chocolate, her eye roaming the room*) I don't
like this room. It's all done, and I don't like it. Do you?

TINA: (*Gazing about*) I don't understand it. Is it finished?

KITTY: I think I'll have 'em do it again, not modernistic.

TINA: I liked it the old way, with the pink satin.

KITTY: Yeah, that's what I'll do, I'll change it back again. . . .
Was the dog out?

TINA: I don't know for sure.

KITTY: Well, find out, and have John take him. (*As Tina goes.*)
He's got to have his walk. (*Left to her own devices, Kitty picks
up a largish hand mirror and surveys herself in it, tipping it
at various angles, peering at a tiny blemish on her skin,
smoothing her eyebrows, widening her eyes, and performing
like antics to which women are given when alone with a mirror. Takes a large fluffy powder puff from the bedside table,
pats her face with it.*)

(*Tina returns with a very gay hatbox ornamented with a
brilliant bow.*)

TINA: Your hat's come.

KITTY: Ooh!

TINA: And Mr. Packard's just come in.

KITTY: Bring it here! (*She sits up eagerly. Between them she and
Tina open the box. The hat emerges, a modish winter thing
with an ornament and a little nose-veil.*) Looks cute, doesn't
it?

TINA: Mm.

KITTY: (*Hands Tina the mirror.*) Here! Hold this! (*Adjusts the
hat to her head. Peers at the effect in the mirror held by Tina.*)
No, higher. There! No—let me have it. (*Takes the mirror,
holds it herself, still looking at her reflection in the glass.*)

(*Tina steps back a few paces, the better to see.*)

(*The booming of Dan Packard's voice is heard down the hall
as he approaches.*)

PACKARD: (*He is in topcoat and is wearing his hat.*) You in bed
again? What's the matter?

KITTY: I don't feel good.

(*Tina gathers up the hatbox and goes.*)

PACKARD: (*Notes her hat.*) What's the idea of the hat? Going out? (*Has been making straight for the closed door of his own bedroom. Opens the door. Shouts.*) Hey! John! You know what I want. Just overnight.

JOHN: Yes, Mr. Packard.

PACKARD: (*Glances at watch. To Kitty*) Got held up. Got to get right out. (*Sees candy box.*) What d'you eat all that sweet stuff for? Why don't you get up? Do something!

KITTY: You don't care what I do. Or how I feel.

PACKARD: (*As the scene progresses he takes off his hat and coat which he tosses onto the bed; looks at himself in her dressing-table mirror to see if he needs a shave; unfastens his tie; vanishes into his own room for a second, emerges with a tie of another color.*) Look at me! Never sick a day in my life. And why? I get out, and do things, keep going. . . . Hey, John! I don't want any dinner clothes. . . . (*Again to her*) That's the reason.

KITTY: (*Looking at herself in the mirror*) That's because you're an extravert and I'm an introvert.

PACKARD: A what?

KITTY: Dr. Talbot says you're an extravert and I'm an introvert, and that's why I have to be quiet a good deal and have time to reflect in.

PACKARD: Reflect in! What have you got to reflect about? I've got to think and act at the same time! Do you know why I'm going to Washington tonight? Because the President wants to consult me about the affairs of the nation! That's why!

KITTY: What's the matter with them?

PACKARD: Everything's the matter with them! That's why he's sending for me! And I'll tell you something else, if you want to know. It wouldn't surprise me a bit if he offered me a Cabinet job, and what do you know about that?

KITTY: (*Busy with her own thoughts*) Where'd that buffer get to?

PACKARD: You ought to be married to some of the guys that I see. That'd give you something to reflect about. Why, I went into an office this afternoon—fellow begging me to—and it turns out he can't even keep a little bit of a business going! I juggle fifty things and he can't handle one! And here's the blow-off! I've been trying to get hold of just his kind of layout for the last two years, and the damn fool hands it to me! Only he don't know it. I give him a song and dance—he's sending me a full list of stockholders—I buy up what I need—and it's all over but the shouting! Little Dan Packard owns the best shipping line between here and the tropics, and Mr. Oliver Jordan is out on his ear.

KITTY: (*Bringing that fine mind of hers to bear*) We're going there for dinner next Friday, and I'm going to wear my new pink.

PACKARD: We are what?

KITTY: Mrs. Oliver Jordan called me up, and they're giving a swell dinner, and we're invited.

PACKARD: Oh, that's what he was driving at—well, we're not going.

KITTY: The hell we ain't! Why not?

PACKARD: I can't go and eat his dinner! If he's a sucker that's his funeral! Business is business, but I can't go walking into his house!

KITTY: No! Presidents and Washington, and all those rummies, but you can't go anywheres with *me*! Once in our life we get asked to a classy house, and I've got a new dress that'll knock their eye out, and we're going!

PACKARD: We are *not* going!

KITTY: (*Now on her knees in the bed, the hat still on her head. In high rage.*) We are so! You big crook, you pull a dirty deal and it ruins my social chances! Well, you can't get away with it!

PACKARD: Oh, go lay down! You tell me what I can do! Well, we're not going and that's all there is to it. (*Into his own room.*) Come on now, John—snap into it!

KITTY: (*Kitty, still on her knees, expresses her hatred for the absent Dan with a series of hideous and unadult facial contortions, reminiscent of her past. That finished with, she realizes that she needs a new method of attack. She sinks back among her pillows, taking the hat off as she does so; draws up the covers very thoughtfully, and arrives at her plan of campaign.*) Dan-ny! (*A honeyed voice.*) Danny! Ple-ease! Kitty wants to go. Kitty wants to see all the dreat bid— (*She is now in baby talk of the most revolting kind.*) —lords and ladies in the big booful house. (*No sound from the other room. The baby talk is followed by a dirty look.*) Danny! It's for Lord Ferncliffe and Lady Ferncliffe. Danny!

PACKARD: (*His head through the doorway, his gaze very intent on her*) What did you say?

KITTY: It's for Lord and Lady Ferncliffe, from England.

PACKARD: (*Emerging*) Who says so?

KITTY: *She* did.

PACKARD: Why the hell didn't you say so in the first place?

KITTY: Because you were mean to poor little Kitty.

PACKARD: Ferncliffe? You know who he is, don't you? He's one of the richest men in England.

KITTY: Oh, goody! Then you'll go?

PACKARD: I've been trying to meet him for years.

KITTY: See? And I did it for you.

PACKARD: Ferncliffe, eh? Well, that's different. Do you know what I'll do? (*Thinking it out swiftly as he talks.*) I'll buy up that Jordan stock through dummies. I'll use Baldridge and Whitestone—fellows like that. Keep my name out of it.

KITTY: Out of what?

PACKARD: Oh, for God's—
    (*Tina enters.*)

TINA: Dr. Talbot's come.

PACKARD: (*Grabs his hat and coat; a quick good-bye.*) Good! He'll fix you up all right! Ferncliffe! God, what a break! Bye, Kitten! See you tomorrow. Stick that in the car, John! S'long, Kitten. (*He is gone.*)

KITTY: (*Through Packard's speech*) Good-bye! Good-bye! Yes, that's fine! Good-bye! (*She barely gives Dan time to get out of the room.*) Tina! Quick! Get me the other jacket, with the feathers! (*As Tina goes to the wardrobe Kitty slips off her bed jacket and hurls it across the bed, holding out her arms for the new one.*) Get me my pearls out of the case! Clear the things off the bed! Fix it up a little! (*With a quick movement she slips both a candy box and a tabloid newspaper under the bed; then, mirror in hand, she plies powder puff, lipstick, and comb. Sprays the bed and the air all about her with an atomizer.*) Give me that book! The big one!

TINA: (*With a wild look around*) Where is it?

KITTY: Look around! It fell down!
    (*Tina drops to her hands and knees and begins looking under the bed.*)
Hurry up! It's there some place!

TINA: (*Bringing up a brightly bound detective story*) Is this it?

KITTY: No, no! That Dr. Talbot gave me! It's a big thick one and it says "Aspects of the Adult Mind." (*She manages the two-syllable words with difficulty.*)

TINA: I got it!

KITTY: Give it to me!

(*Tina's lips move silently for a second as she reassures herself about the title.*)

TINA: Yeah, this is it!

KITTY: (*Taking the book*) All right now!

(*She dismisses Tina with a wave of the hand; Tina scurries out.*)

(*A final preening on Kitty's part—a patting of the pillows. She opens the book at random, but decides that she really ought to be further along than that. She slaps over another hundred pages; then, inserting a finger as though to mark her place, she closes the book. She is very much the invalid, interrupted while reading, as the Doctor enters*)

(*Dr. Talbot is happy in the possession of a good figure, a conventionally handsome face, a dark neat mustache, a reassuring bedside manner. Perhaps forty-six.*)

(*Tina has followed him into the room.*)

TALBOT: (*His is a quiet, soothing voice.*) Well! Hello! What's all this?

KITTY: (*Suddenly weak*) Hello, Doctor!

TALBOT: Just ran into your husband downstairs. Tells me he's going to see the President.

KITTY: Yes, he's going to help him fix things.

TALBOT: (*Seats himself on the side of the bed. A finger on her pulse*) Well! What's the trouble with the little lady?

KITTY: Well, Doctor, I don't know. I kind of ached all over, and felt funny, and you've got to be so careful about flu, and I thought maybe if I stayed in bed—

(*Tina, after following Dr. Talbot in, has closed the door into Packard's room, and has gone, closing the hall door after her.*)

(*As she departs, Kitty's voice trails off into nothingness. She is listening intently, as she talks, for the sound of Tina's retreating footsteps. Dr. Talbot's finger is still on her pulse.*)

You don't ever come unless I send for you.

TALBOT: I'm very busy, Kitty. You know how busy I am.

KITTY: But I'm so lonely, Wayne. And you know how I need
    you. I don't do anything all day except long for you.

TALBOT: But you must develop your inner resources. (*A ges-
    ture to the book.*) Didn't you read?

KITTY: I know. You're tired of me.

TALBOT: No, I'm not, dear. But—

KITTY: Oh, Wayne, darling! (*She flings her arms suddenly about
    him. A trifle reluctantly, he responds to her embrace.*)

THE LIGHTS DIM QUICKLY.

SCENE IV

*The Jordan sitting room, late afternoon of the same day. Two or
three shaded lamps are lighted. Dora, the maid, is lighting the
last of them as the scene begins. Takes a last look around to see
that everything is in order. Satisfied that it is, she goes into the
bedroom.*

*Immediately Gustave enters from the hall. Over one arm he
carries, neatly folded, a pair of newly pressed trousers, from
which dangles a pair of suspenders. In the other hand is a lace
tea cloth. As he enters he peers toward the bedroom, having
caught a vanishing glimpse of Dora. He tosses the cloth, folded,
onto the table, another look into the bedroom for a possible
glimpse of Dora. Finds he can't see her, turns, and goes toward
the hall door.*

*The ring of the telephone arrests him. The trousers still over his
arm, he goes to answer it. On the telephone ring, Dora appears at
the bedroom door, peers into the room, sees that Gustave is answering the call, and disappears again into the bedroom.*

GUSTAVE: Hello! Yes, sir. . . . No, sir, Mrs. Jordan has not
    come in yet. Is there any message? . . . Yes, sir. . . . Mr.
    Townsend finds that he will not be able to come to dinner
    on Friday, the twenty-third. . . . Out of town. . . . Yes,
    sir. Very good. I'll tell her. (*Hangs up the receiver.*)
        (*About halfway through this telephone conversation, Dora*

*has reappeared in the bedroom doorway, and, lingering
there, waits for Gustave to finish.*)

DORA: (*From the doorway, smiling, and provocative*) Psst!
(*Gustave turns toward her.*)
Darling! (*Dora comes down toward him.*)

GUSTAVE: My little princess! (*A long embrace and a kiss, during
which the trousers on Gustave's arm suffer a little. Emerging
from the embrace, Gustave feels a fleeting concern for his
freshly pressed burden, and, brushing them lightly with his fingers he places them over a chair-back.*) Where have you been
all afternoon?

DORA: (*A gesture*) I had some sewing to do for *her*. She's
going to a masquerade. You ought to see the hat! And a
pompadour!

GUSTAVE: That's nothing. You should see what he is wearing.
A coal scuttle. (*A little laugh at this sally. Then, tenderly,
Gustave attempts another embrace which she coyly evades.*)

DORA: You ought to be downstairs. She'll be home to tea any
minute.

GUSTAVE: There is yet time. (*Kisses her again. Withdraws a
little, so that she is very near as she now talks to him.*)

DORA: Oh, Gustave, I only feel safe when I am with you like
this. That Ricci!

GUSTAVE: Has he been bothering you again—that snake!

DORA: He tries to grab hold of me. And he says things, in
Italian—like this— (*She hisses these last two words.*) I don't
know what they mean.

GUSTAVE: How could you ever like him, that *ausverflugter
Hund*!

DORA: I didn't really like him. But he had such little soft ways,
and he used to say things that made me feel good, and took
me to the movies, sometimes—besides, that was before you
came here.

GUSTAVE: *Ma petite!* (*He tries to draw her to him. This time she
repulses him definitely.*)

DORA: No, no. I'm not going to kiss you any more.

GUSTAVE: Not going to kiss me! What have I done?

DORA: (*Tidying herself, primly*) Nothing. Only why should I let
you kiss me? We're not engaged or anything.

GUSTAVE: What are you saying? You know I am mad for you! Mad in love with you! I cannot do my work for thinking of you! All day long it is "Dora! Dora!" All night long I cannot sleep! My Dora! (*Another gesture towards her.*)

DORA: No, no! You mustn't.

GUSTAVE: I love you! I adore you! I am mad for you! Why are you so cold to me? At night why do you lock your door, always? You know how much I love you!

DORA: (*In a panic*) No, no, Gustave! No! (*Pulls herself together a little.*) I couldn't be like that! I couldn't!

GUSTAVE: You do not love me!

DORA: I do! I do! But—you come from Europe. You don't understand. I'm not like that. I was brought up strict. If anybody loves me like that they would want me to marry them.

GUSTAVE: Marry! Oh, but, Dora! To marry takes so much money. I have been here in America only a year.

DORA: You don't want to marry me!

GUSTAVE: I love you! I love you!

DORA: You don't love me! You were only fooling with me! You're as bad as Ricci! I hate you! I'll give my notice, and go away! I'll get another place and you'll never see me again! I hate you! I hate you! I hate you!

(*A whistle from down the hall, followed by Paula's voice, calling.*)

(*Gustave snatches trousers from chair, hangs them over his arm.*)

PAULA: (*From the hall*) That you, mother? (*Paula enters.*) Oh, I thought I heard— Mother isn't home yet, h'm?

GUSTAVE: Not yet, Miss Paula. I believe she'll be in soon.

PAULA: Oh! Tell her I'm home. (*Goes off to her room down the hall, whistling a fragment of a popular tune.*)

GUSTAVE: Dora, don't talk like that! Don't say that! I can't stand it. I love you more than anything in the world. I am crazy for you. I will do anything for you. I have never been like this—never!

DORA: You don't love me. If you loved me you would marry me. Good-bye. (*Dora turns to go.*)

GUSTAVE: Wait.

(*She halts.*)

I can't stand it. I will marry you.

DORA: (*In joyful unbelief*) Gustave! When?

GUSTAVE: (*Evasively*) Soon. Soon.

DORA: But when?

GUSTAVE: Well—when we can.

DORA: Thursday! We'll both be off.

> (*Paula's voice, heard in the distance, from her bedroom down the hall.*)

PAULA: Gustave!

GUSTAVE: (*A move toward the door.*) Yes, Miss Paula. (*Pulling himself together.*)

PAULA: (*Still heard in the distance*) I wonder if I could have a cup of hot tea in my room.

GUSTAVE: Very good, Miss Paula. (*In a cautious undertone to Dora*) But remember—no word of this. They wouldn't like it. It must be a secret.

DORA: (*Very low*) All right. I'm satisfied. And we won't tell Ricci. He might do something.

GUSTAVE: (*A whisper*) That's right. Only us.

DORA: Thursday.

> (*With a fond gesture in Dora's direction, Gustave goes.*)
>
> (*With Gustave's departure a little look of triumph comes over Dora's face. She has achieved what she wanted. She stands for a moment in contemplation of her victory, her pleasure visibly mounting. Humming a bit of gay song, she trips into the bedroom, highly pleased with herself.*)
>
> (*The voices of Oliver and Ricci are heard approaching down the hall.*)

RICCI: I would stop here and rest if I were you, sir.

OLIVER: I'd rather go to my bedroom.

RICCI: I'd sit here for just a minute and get your breath. By that time you'll be all right, sir.

> (*Oliver and Ricci enter from the hall. Oliver is being half-supported by Ricci, and seems to be breathing with a little difficulty. Obviously he is not well.*)

Here we are, sir. Now, why don't you sit here just a minute. I'll see if Mrs. Jordan— (*Looks toward the bedroom door.*)

OLIVER: (*Rising, hastily*) No, no, no! Mrs. Jordan mustn't—

> (*The quick movement of rising has been too much for him. Gasping a little, he sinks back into the chair. Ricci returns quickly to his side.*)

(*As Oliver sits, Dora appears in the bedroom doorway, drawn by the men's voices. Comes forward in some alarm.*)

DORA: What's the matter! Mr. Jordan!

OLIVER: I'm all right. I'm all right.

DORA: Anything I can do, sir? What should I get? (*To Ricci*) What's the matter with him?

RICCI: You must not get up, sir. You should lie back. The head down. (*To Dora*) Has Mrs. Jordan come in?

DORA: No, she hasn't. What should we do?

OLIVER: (*Rising again, but cautiously*) Not so much fuss. Please! (*With an effort, pulls himself together.*) I'm quite all right. I'm going to my own room.
     (*Ricci attempts again to assist him.*)
     What happened, Ricci? I don't quite remember.

RICCI: You were stepping out of the car, sir. You—you stumbled.

OLIVER: That's—funny. I didn't—fall? H'm?

RICCI: No, no. I caught you. You did not—no, no, sir.

OLIVER: (*Thoughtfully*) I'm much obliged to you, Ricci. Remember, both of you. Nothing about this to Mrs. Jordan. (*Oliver goes.*)

DORA: Do you think he's all right?
     (*Ricci goes to the door, looks after the retreating figure. Turns.*)

RICCI: Sure. He's all right. (*Comes toward Dora. His whole attention suddenly concentrating ominously on her.*)

DORA: You keep away from me, Tony Ricci! (*Dora backs away from him.*)

RICCI: My little darling Dora, why are you frightened of me? Why do you always run away from me? Tell me, my pretty little Dora. Why? H'm? (*With a swift movement he seizes her waist in a tight grip.*)

DORA: (*Tries to free herself.*) Let me go!
     (*Ricci pulls her closer to him. Holds her in a vise.*)

RICCI: Listen to me, you little she-devil! You think you can run away from Ricci, eh? You were sweet enough to me before he came here. And you think now you can spit on me for that Alsatian pig!

DORA: You crazy fool! Let me go! (*Vainly pulls and tugs away from him.*)

RICCI: (*Again pulls her closer to him.*) I show you who is the fool.

DORA: You let me go! I'll scream!

RICCI: Oh, no, you won't. (*A glance over his shoulder at the hall door.*)

(*Dora begins to pound his chest with her free fist. Ricci twists the wrist he is holding. Dora opens her mouth to scream. Ricci claps a hand over her mouth. In a flash she twists loose and sinks her teeth in his hand. With a curse he frees his other hand and deals her a hard, vicious slap in the face.*)

(*Ricci turns and goes quickly.*)

(*Dora has staggered a little under the blow, crouched a little, her hand to her face, stumbles against the chair in front of the desk, and sits, a bundle of fear and misery, whimpering a little.*)

(*The voices of Millicent and Hattie are heard from the hallway.*)

MILLICENT: (*Off*) Oh, well, come in long enough to have a cup of tea. I'll send you home with Ricci.

HATTIE: I ought to be home now.

(*Dora, hearing their voices, springs to her feet, arranges her attire, smoothes her hair. Darts to the tea table. Spreads the lace cloth.*)

MILLICENT: (*Entering. She is in street attire, as is Hattie, who follows her in. Millicent crosses and goes straight to her bedroom, which she enters, talking as she goes.*) Nonsense. Cup of tea'll be good for you. I'll die if I don't have one in a minute. (*In a higher pitch, from the bedroom*) There's nothing in the world wears me out like shopping. I hate it.

HATTIE: Hello, Dora.

DORA: Good-afternoon, Mrs. Loomis. (*Her hand on the injured cheek.*)

HATTIE: What's the matter—neuralgia?

DORA: (*A nod and a gulp.*) Yes, madam. (*She gets out of the room as quickly as possible.*)

MILLICENT: (*From the bedroom*) Well, this settles it. I am not going to kill myself for Paula. If she doesn't care enough to come along she can be married like a shopgirl for all of me.

(*Gustave enters from the hallway, bringing the tea things. He arranges them on the table; brings the table down into position.*)

HATTIE: Remember that lovely trousseau poor mama got for me? All lace and embroidery?

MILLICENT: (*Still in the next room*) You've probably still got it. I know you.

HATTIE: Those fifteen-foot tablecloths? I sold them to Ringling Brothers for a tent.

MILLICENT: (*Hearing the click of china*) Is that the tea? I'll be right in.

HATTIE: (*Sauntering over to the table and peering into a sandwich*) M'm. What's this, Gustave?

GUSTAVE: I believe that's watercress, madam. With mayonnaise.

MILLICENT: (*Entering. Has taken off her hat and coat.*) I am simply dead. Maybe this'll pick me up. (*Pouring immediately*) Any messages, Gustave?

GUSTAVE: Yes, madam. They telephoned from the costumer's. The dress for Miss Florodora will be here promptly at six-thirty. . . . And Mrs. Fyffe's butler telephoned from Tuxedo about the week-end. Mrs. Fyffe wishes you to know that the ice is very good and suggests that you and Mr. Jordan come up and bring your skates.

HATTIE: You can go right out from the masquerade.

GUSTAVE: And Mr. Townsend regrets very much that he cannot come to dinner on Friday, the twenty-third. He will be out of town.

MILLICENT: Oh, damn!

GUSTAVE: (*Very quietly*) Yes, madam.

(*Gustave goes.*)

MILLICENT: Well, I've got to begin all over again. I'll bet if I called one man this morning, I called ten. Would you believe it! There just isn't an extra man in all New York!

HATTIE: I never could understand why it has to be just even— male and female. They're invited to dinner, not for mating.

MILLICENT: Don't be bohemian, Hattie. I've got to have a balanced table. Now, who is there? I've tried everybody— Morty Beeman and Aleck Fraser, and Bob Randolph and Courtland Hudson—

HATTIE: Good heavens! Is Courty still around? He must be ninety.

MILLICENT: Well, he's a man.

HATTIE: Anybody can get by these days. So long as he's un-married, owns a dinner suit, and can still sit up.

MILLICENT: (*She has her little book listing Extra Men.*) Now, here's the list. There are the good ones. I've tried them all.

HATTIE: I know. It's like one of those boxes of candy. You be-gin with those luscious chocolate creams and at the finish you're down to candied violets and spit-backs. What be-comes of all the men, anyhow? You see men on the street. They're well dressed, they're attractive-looking. Do they set them out in the morning and take them in at night?

MILLICENT: (*Tossing the book onto her desk*) Well, I don't know what I'm going to do. There just isn't anybody, that's all.

HATTIE: Why don't you try a little new blood? They don't have to be those same old set pieces. Don't you know any prize-fighters or politicians or playwrights? Your dinner sounds pretty deadly to me—except for Carlotta. Get a little excitement in it.

MILLICENT: I'd love to have someone exciting—that is, if they'd fit in with the Ferncliffes.

HATTIE: Nothing exciting fits in with the Ferncliffes. Get somebody that'll go with Carlotta. Give *her* a little fun. Get an actor, or something.

MILLICENT: (*Thoughtfully*) An actor. Of course, it would have to be one that's not acting. Let me see . . .

HATTIE: A *movie* star! Aren't there any movie stars around?

MILLICENT: (*Snaps her fingers in triumph*) Larry Renault! He'd be marvelous. I wonder if he's still in town.

HATTIE: He was yesterday.

MILLICENT: How do you know?

HATTIE: Ed. Ed, the movie hound. Read me an interview with him in last night's *Telegram*. He's leaving pictures and going into a play.

MILLICENT: I wonder where he's stopping. Did it say?

HATTIE: (*A great effort of memory*) Yes, it did. Let me see. It's one of those hotels in the Fifties—they all stop at it. Now, just—it'll come to me—

MILLICENT: (*Busy with her own thoughts, while Hattie is recollecting*) You know, he knows Carlotta. We met him three years ago, in Antibes. He was simply a sensation. He'd just made that big picture—*Sins* of something—and he was absolutely mobbed wherever he went. The Casino crowds just gaping, and the girls fighting to get into his car. And on the beach! I must say I never saw such a figure. He wore even less than the girls.

HATTIE: Ed doesn't like him since the talkies. He says he seems different. You can't fool Ed about the movies. He remembers Flora Finch, and Mae Marsh, and Henry B. Walthall—

MILLICENT: Of course, I don't know if he'd even know me now. We met at a dozen dinners. I wonder who'd know where he's stopping.

HATTIE: (*Suddenly*) Versailles! That's it. Hotel Versailles.

MILLICENT: (*Reaches for the telephone book*) Oh, good! Are you sure?

HATTIE: Yes, I remember the whole interview. He was wearing a black moire lounging robe with a white monogram.

MILLICENT: (*Hunting the number*) I don't suppose people like that are ever home.

HATTIE: What's the name of that play he's going to be in?

MILLICENT: (*One finger marking her place, she looks up at Hattie.*) I'll put him next to Carlotta, and then give her Doctor Talbot on the other side—let's see—next to Doctor Talbot—the Packard woman—h'm—Talbot and the Packard woman —no, they'd never get on together.

HATTIE: See if you can get him first and let nature take its course.

MILLICENT: (*Consulting the book again*) Plaza three— (*Scribbles the number on her note pad; starts to dial.*)

HATTIE: (*Jumping up; pulling on her gloves.*) Well, I make you a present of it, darling. At least that's one trouble I haven't got. Three rooms and a kitchenette eliminates the extra-man problem.

(*Paula enters from the hallway.*)

PAULA: Hello, Aunt Hattie. I didn't know you were here.

HATTIE: Hello, Paula. Pour you a cup of tea?

PAULA: I had some in my room. I've been sleeping.

MILLICENT: (*Has finished dialing; the receiver to her ear*) I
  thought you were at the office. That tea for Chanel.
PAULA: (*Nibbling a sandwich*) Oh, she was an awful bust. She
  wore pearls with a sport suit—ropes of 'em.
MILLICENT: (*Into the phone*) Hotel Versailles? . . . (*The word
  catches Paula's attention.*) Is Mr. Larry Renault stopping
  there?
PAULA: (*A little startled*) Who?
MILLICENT: Larry Renault. *You* know. I'm giving a dinner and
  I thought it'd be fun if he came.
HATTIE: See you soon, Millie. I've got to be going.
MILLICENT: (*Carelessly*) Oh, don't be in a hurry.
HATTIE: Yes, got to. Ed's sort of an old-fashioned husband.
  He thinks wives ought to be home before dinner. (*Hattie
  goes.*)
MILLICENT: (*At the telephone*) Hello! . . . I'm waiting for Mr.
  Larry Renault.
  (*Gustave enters with the evening paper.*)
PAULA: How did you happen to think of him?
MILLICENT: (*Turns*) What? . . . Oh, Gustave, has Mr. Jordan
  come in yet? He's late, isn't he?
GUSTAVE: He's been in quite some time, madam. He's in his
  room.
MILLICENT: Really! Does he know I'm home?
GUSTAVE: I'm not sure, madam. I believe he's lying down. I
  understand he has a slight headache.
MILLICENT: Oh—I didn't know. Tell him I'll be right in. (*Into
  the telephone as Gustave departs*) Hello! Can't you get . . .
  Is this Mr. Renault? Mr. Renault, this is Mrs. Oliver Jordan.
  I don't know if you remember me . . . Yes! . . . Antibes!
  . . . Why, you're wonderful! . . . Mr. Renault, I'd like it so
  much if you could come to a little dinner I'm giving a week
  from tonight. Just a tiny dinner. Lord and Lady Ferncliffe
  are coming, and Carlotta Vance—of course you know Carlotta . . . Well, that's so nice. Friday, the twenty-third, at
  eight o'clock. . . . That's right. . . . What? My daughter?
  . . . Well, *what* a memory! . . . (*To Paula*) He remembers
  you, Paula. . . . (*Into phone*) She's right here, and very flat-
  tered. . . . Oh, no, she won't be at the dinner. She isn't

invited. But she's quite grown up now. . . . Wait a minute.
Won't you say hello to her? I know she'd be thrilled to
death. . . . (*To Paula*) Here, Paula . . . go ahead! Don't
be silly. (*Turns the receiver over to Paula. Reluctantly Paula
takes the receiver.*)

PAULA: Hello! . . . Yes, this is Paula Jordan. . . . Indeed I
do. . . . Well, people don't forget *you*, do they? . . . Now,
you're just being whimsical, Mr. Renault.

MILLICENT: (*As she flutters off. In a loud whisper*) Be nice to
him. I want to see how Dad is.

PAULA: (*Telephone*) Oh, no, I'm not.

MILLICENT: (*As she goes into the hallway*) Oliver, I didn't know
you weren't feeling well.

PAULA: (*Very intense. Into the telephone*) You're insane! . . .
You can't come here. . . . No, she's gone. . . . No, I
can't. I tell you I can't tonight. I've got to go out with
Ernest. . . . No, it won't work again. He's furious about
last night. . . . Larry, you've been drinking. Listen, I'll call
you later on another phone. . . . Of course I love you. . . .
Of course. . . . Good-bye. (*Hangs up quickly. Takes a darting look to see if anyone could have been within earshot. Sits a
little huddled figure in the chair.*)

THE CURTAIN FALLS

ACT TWO

Scene I

A week later.

Larry Renault's apartment in the Hotel Versailles. It is a rather smart hotel in the East Fifties, of the type patronized by successful actors and motion-picture people. Its style of furnishing is French in excellent, though conventional, taste. The employees' uniforms are very chic, and a shade too spectacular.

The room which we see is the sitting room. It is bright, tastefully arranged, comfortable. A door leads into a bedroom, unseen. At the back there is a fireplace, furnished with gas logs. On either side of the fireplace are narrow French windows leading to minute twin balconies. There is a second door which leads to the outer corridor.

There are large comfortable chairs, a luxurious davenport couch, with cushions; small convenient tables for cigarettes; a mirror, a small desk. On one small table there is a French telephone. There are photographs, in frames. One, prominently displayed, is a photograph of Paula Jordan, this in a heavy silver frame. On a small table near the couch is an empty whiskey bottle, and a glass. An even larger frame displays a photograph of Renault himself in one of his favorite (and more youthful) poses.

There is no one on the stage at the rise of the curtain. The sound of the buzzer at the outer door is heard. A slight pause. Larry Renault enters from the bedroom.

He is a handsome man in his early forties, with the perfect profile that so gracefully lends itself to a successful motion-picture career. His figure still passes, but about the whole man there are the unmistakable marks of middle age, abetted by pretty steady drinking, increasing failure, and disappointment. It is a vain and weak face, but not unappealing.

He is wearing the black moire dressing gown mentioned by Hattie. The initials L.R., in white, form an impressive monogram on

517

the left side. A white silk shirt with a soft collar, dark trousers and black soft leather lounging slippers complete his costume. He is slightly unshaven, as he means to shave before dressing to go out to dinner. It is now about four o'clock in the afternoon.

As he crosses the room the buzzer sounds for the second time. As he opens the door Eddie, the bellboy, steps into the room. He is carrying a bottle of whiskey rather carelessly wrapped.

LARRY: Where've you been so long?

EDDIE: (*Gives him the bottle.*) Come as quick as I could. (*Turns to go.*)

LARRY: Hey! Wait a minute!

(*The boy stops.*)

Where's my change?

EDDIE: Had to go to a new place. Cost half a dollar more.

LARRY: Who told you to go to a new place?

(*The boy has not stopped. He is out the door before Larry's last word is finished. The door slams behind him.*)

(*Larry stands looking after him for a second, then heads for the couch, unwrapping the bottle as he crosses. The paper flutters from his hand; his eye sweeps the room—he is looking for the corkscrew. Sees it on the desk; goes for it, pausing to pick up the empty bottle as he goes. Shakes the empty bottle to reassure himself as to its emptiness, then drops it into the waste basket by the desk. Takes up the corkscrew; goes to work on the new bottle as he returns to the couch.*)

(*The telephone rings. The bottle still in hand, corkscrew protruding from it, he answers the phone.*)

LARRY: Hello. . . . (*A bit eagerly, as he recognizes the voice*) Oh, hello, Max. . . . Yeah, I'll be here. Why? . . . Well, what's up? . . . Can't you tell me over the phone? . . . How soon'll you be here?

(*The door buzzer sounds.*)

All right—I'll be waiting for you. (*Hangs up. An annoyed glance, then puts the bottle on the table and goes to the door.*)

(*It is Paula Jordan who enters. There is about her the unnatural vivacity of one who has secret and important news.*)

Paula!

PAULA: Mr. Renault! (*Whirls into the room.*) Not Mr. Larry Renault! *NOT* the great motion— (*Snatches off her little béret and throws it at him.*) —picture actor! (*Runs to him. Is in his arms. They kiss.*)

LARRY: Crazy little darling!

PAULA: How've you been and how are you and I want to know how you are! And do you love me?

LARRY: You know I do!

PAULA: Well, I just thought I'd ask.

LARRY: What's happened to you? Why all the animal spirits?

PAULA: Oh, nothing. Just girlish vivacity. *And* hunger.

LARRY: Hunger!

PAULA: Would you give a girl a cup of coffee? Nothing else.

LARRY: Of course. (*Reaches for the telephone.*) What's the matter? Didn't you have any lunch?

PAULA: Well—I had a sort of liquid lunch.

LARRY: Room service, please. (*Turns to her.*) Did you say coffee? You don't drink coffee in the afternoon. Don't you mean tea?

PAULA: I do not mean tea.

LARRY: Well, if you . . . (*Then into telephone*) Room service? This is Mr. Renault, in Nineteen Hundred. Will you send up a pot of coffee, please? (*Turning to Paula*) Anything else?

PAULA: Toast.

LARRY: (*In telephone*) Toast. (*To Paula*) Do you want it buttered?

PAULA: Buttered.

LARRY: (*In phone*) Buttered. That's all. Right away, please. (*Hangs up.*) Now, what's got into you? What're you up to?

PAULA: I had lunch in a speakeasy. I had lunch in a speakeasy with Ernest. I had three double Martini cocktails and Ernest had double lamb chop with spinach a dollar fifty.

LARRY: That sounds like a quarrel.

PAULA: Well—yes. You can get pretty nasty on lamb chops. Larry, I can't face him again, tonight. Listen, darling, let's go somewhere together, you and I. Let's get a car and drive up the river, and have dinner.

LARRY: Look, Foolish, this is the night I'm having dinner at your mother's.

PAULA: Oh, Lord! . . . Oh, what if you are! What do you care about a lot of Ferncliffes and "Hel-lo! So nice to see you!"

LARRY: But I have to go.

PAULA: Yes, we can't do that to poor Millicent. You're the Extra Man. A great big glamorous figure to dazzle the . . . (*A sudden thought.*) Larry.

LARRY: (*A little tender quick kiss.*) What?

PAULA: Promise me something.

LARRY: What is it?

PAULA: Don't drink tonight. At Mother's, I mean.

LARRY: (*Moves away from her.*) Now, Paula, don't get maternal.

PAULA: I know. But I want them to see you at your best.

LARRY: But a man can take a drink or two.

PAULA: That's just it, Larry. If you take one you always take another, and then—

LARRY: Oh, for God's sake, Paula!

PAULA: All right, all right! My darling, my darling! Let's talk about something else. Tell me what you've been doing. Tell me everything you've done since yesterday. Did you see Baumann? Who'd he get for your leading lady? When d'you go in rehearsal? I want to know everything. Only first I want to be kissed, and kissed, and kissed.

LARRY: (*Takes her in his arms.*) My sweet! My marvelous little girl!

PAULA: You love me, don't you, Larry? I know—but *say* it.

LARRY: Yes, yes. You know I worship you. I adore you!

PAULA: Oh, Larry! Darling! Wouldn't it be lovely if we could just stay here all evening. We'd pretend it was our house. We'd order up dinner, and pretend I'd cooked it, and we'd light the gas logs and pretend they were real, and we'd sit together in the firelight, you with a movie magazine, and me with a bit of sewing—doesn't it sound terrible! (*Another kiss, a note of laughter from her.*)

LARRY: It sounds very charming.

PAULA: Just a home boy. (*Opens her handbag to glance at herself in her mirror.*) Oh, what a sight! (*Powder, lipstick, her curls.*) Larry, what about the play? Do tell about it. When do you start rehearsing? Monday?

LARRY: (*Wanders over to the whiskey bottle; draws the cork as he speaks.*) Yes, I think so. Just had a call from Max Kane. He's coming right over. I suppose everything's settled. (*The cork is out. Larry takes up a glass; pours himself quite a drink. Tosses it off.*)

PAULA: (*Trying not to notice the size of Larry's drink.*) That's—fine.

LARRY: I suppose it's a wise thing—Max seems to think so. You know how these agents are—run you, practically. He may be right. A season in the legitimate, before I go back to pictures. Let them *see* me—they like that sort of thing.

PAULA: He's a funny little man, isn't he? I never met anyone like that. (*Has finished with lipstick and powder puff. A look at her hair in pocket mirror.*) May I use your comb? (*Wanders into the adjoining bedroom. Her voice comes up from there, as she disappears.*) But he's amusing. I like that kind of person.

LARRY: Oh, Max is all right. I let him talk. But this play thing is a good notion—I've been thinking about it quite a while.

PAULA: (*Reënters.*) I'm crazy to see you in it. It's such a romantic part. I think you'll be marvelous in it.

LARRY: It's really the only thing I've read that I thought was worth doing. The play's not much, but the part is very interesting. It's practically the only male part in the play.

PAULA: There's the beach-comber.

LARRY: Oh, that doesn't amount to anything—he has one little scene, and I dominate that. (*He is about to pour himself another drink.*)

PAULA: Oh, Larry! Please don't.

LARRY: (*Puts his glass down with a bang.*) God! Are you going to keep on— I can't even— I do wish you'd mind your own business!

PAULA: Don't you talk to me like that!

LARRY: Then why don't you leave me alone!

PAULA: Oh, darling, let's not quarrel. I couldn't stand another. I've been through the most dreadful scene with Ernest. I need you so. That's why I came here.

LARRY: I'm so sorry. Why didn't you tell me? What's the matter?

PAULA: (*Facing him squarely.*) Ernest is being sent to London. He expects me to go with him.

LARRY: London! You mean right away?

PAULA: I don't know. Soon. He was so excited about it, and happy. I just sat there. I couldn't even pretend. Of course he noticed it. He said, didn't I want to go? I made some excuse. He began telling me how wonderful it would be—we could run over to Paris in the spring— I tried to— But it only sounded— Then he got angry. Poor Ernest, he's been so sweet. Finally he said I didn't love him. I wanted to scream, no, I don't! And end the whole thing.

LARRY: You didn't do it!

PAULA: And when I think that I've got to see him again tonight. Tonight! (*Laughs a little hysterically.*) You'll be at Mother's dinner. (*Laughs again, a high little cracked laugh.*) "Tell me about your work. Is Hollywood really . . ." (*Trailing off into something like a whimper.*)

LARRY: Paula, stop that! Pull yourself together! Stop it!

PAULA: Oh, Larry, what are we going to do? I've got to tell him.

LARRY: But you mustn't. (*The door buzzer sounds.*) Come in! . . . It's your coffee.

PAULA: I'd forgotten all about it.

(*The Waiter enters with a portable table balanced on his shoulder. On it is service for one.*)

LARRY: Right over here, waiter. Shall I pour it for you, Paula?

PAULA: Please.

WAITER: Is everything all right, sir?

LARRY: (*Pouring*) Yes, I think so.

(*The Waiter stands, check in hand.*)

Oh. (*Takes the check; signs it. A little futile slapping of the pockets in search of change. None is forthcoming.*) Paula, have you got a quarter? I don't seem to—

PAULA: What? Oh—my bag's there on the table. Help yourself.

(*Larry opens the bag, takes out a quarter, gives it to the Waiter.*)

WAITER: Thank you. (*He goes.*)

(*Paula, who has been detached in mood from all this, now swallows down a cup of coffee, black.*)

LARRY: Hey! You must have needed that.

PAULA: Larry, let me tell Ernest. It's so rotten not to. Poor Ernest, he's a dear. (*A sigh. A hand passed over her forehead.*)

Why, less than a month ago I thought I was in love with him. And you were just one of those million-dollar movie stars. Only a month ago! That was another girl—a different person. What a very young person!

LARRY: Now listen to me, Paula. I want to tell you something.

PAULA: I know, I know. Ernest is just the sort of man I ought to marry. And you're the sort that girls are always warned against. Well, I don't care a hoot what people say. I know your life is different from mine; I know all the things you've done; I know all the times you've been married—

LARRY: But I'm still married.

PAULA: I don't care! I'm sick of hiding my love for you— I'm sick of scheming and pretending. What do I care about my prim little life—Miss Hickson's-on-the-Hudson—"one, two, three—*turn!* One, two—" I tell you I don't care! I want to give it up! I hate it!

LARRY: You're out of your mind!

PAULA: Do you think I could still love Ernest after all this! After what we've been to each other! Oh, Larry!

LARRY: Paula, I've reproached myself a thousand times. If only I'd never touched you.

PAULA: Oh, Larry, don't talk to me as though I were the little country girl, ruined by the city slicker. I knew what I was doing. I'm proud of it.

LARRY: Paula, for the first time in my life I'm thinking of the other person.

(*Paula turns away with a look of impatience.*)

You don't know anything about me. Not a thing. You've read about me in the papers. You've known me a month.

PAULA: But, Larry, how can—

LARRY: I know. It's been a beautiful month. But you don't really know me. You know less about me than—the waiter who just went out of this room.

PAULA: We've been together every day.

LARRY: Yes—as lovers. But we've hardly spoken a sensible word to each other. You know that I don't like pink, and I eat my oysters without cocktail sauce. That's all right for a month. But that isn't me.

PAULA: All right. Tell me you murdered a man in Alaska.

LARRY: That's what I mean. You're not even grown up. You're

a kid of nineteen. You're nineteen and I'm forty-t— I'm almost forty.

PAULA: All the more reason. College boys in coonskin coats— I hate them!

LARRY: It isn't just age—it's everything. You've never known anything but Park Avenue, and butlers, and Pierre's—

PAULA: That's not true. I've got a job. I go to work every day.

LARRY: It's the fashion to have a job in your crowd. You don't know what it means to be up against it. To be fighting 'em every second. To pull yourself up, hand over hand, and have them waiting up there with a knife to cut the rope. Well, I'm not through yet! I'll show them! If they think I'm finished!

PAULA: But, Larry! What's that got to do with it? What's that got to do with our love!

LARRY: Love—love! Do you want to know the truth, Paula? I love you. As much as I can love—any woman. But at my age it isn't real love any more. There's been too many. I've been in love a hundred times. I've had three wives. Would you like to know about them?

PAULA: No!

LARRY: Well, there was Violet. She was a vaudeville hoofer, and still is. I'll bet she hasn't changed her act in twenty years. It was a hell of a marriage—rooming houses and dirty kimonos and fried-egg sandwiches. We used to fight like wildcats. Then I broke into pictures, and I left her. I made three pictures—*Sinners in Eden*—*King of the Desert*—*Desert Love*. Then I married Edith. She was crazy about my profile. Always talking about it. She was society. Good deal like you, Paula. Funny, I never thought of that before. Anyhow, we were happy for about six months. Then Hollywood got her. Parties—drinks—they were pretty rough in those days. Then one night—you know the rest of it—out in her car alone, drunk as the devil—over the cliff.

PAULA: You were really in love with her, weren't you, Larry?

LARRY: As for Diana—well, you know her. She's top of the heap now. Biggest draw of any woman in pictures. Ambitious! I never saw a woman like her. Anything to get on, and knife me to get there. Always saying some day she'd be bigger than I was and now— (*He catches himself as he realizes*

that he has said too much.) Well, there they are, the three of
'em. Pretty picture, isn't it? I won't tell you about the
others. They swarmed on me—every kind and age and de-
scription. And I—oh, what the hell do you want with *me!*

PAULA: I love you, Larry.

LARRY: You're young and fresh. I'm burned out. I've got
nothing left to give. For God's sake, Paula, this is the first decent thing I ever did in my life. Listen to what I'm telling you.

PAULA: I won't listen. I love you. Ernest and London and
Mother and Dad—I love *you*, Larry! Nothing else matters in
the whole world!

LARRY: Paula, don't say that!

PAULA: Larry, it's no use. Nothing you can say will make any
difference. I'm going to tell them! Now! Tonight! Today!
(*Reaches for her hat. Adjusts it excitedly.*)

LARRY: No, you don't! You listen to me.

PAULA: No, I'm sick of all this. I'm going to tell them. I'm
going to tell everybody.

LARRY: You can't do a thing like that. I won't let you! D'you
understand! I won't let you smash up your life.

PAULA: I'll smash it up if I want to! I'm going straight home
and tell Mother and Dad! And tonight I'm going to tell
Ernest!

LARRY: You're not!

PAULA: I am!

LARRY: I tell you—you're not!
(*A noisy, prolonged, and patterned buzz at the door an-
nounces the impending entrance of Max Kane. It has come
insistently in the midst of their argument.*)
(*The noise finally quiets them. They stand a moment.*)
That—that's Max. (*He glances toward the outer door, back to
Paula.*) Paula, I want you to promise me—

PAULA: (*Very low and determined*) No.
(*Max, fearful that Larry is asleep, begins a mild pounding
at the door.*)

LARRY: (*Torn between answering the door and getting a promise
of silence from Paula*) Paula, for God's sake!

PAULA: It's no use, Larry. My mind is made up. (*They stand,
facing each other.*)

(*Larry goes to the door. Paula picks up her bag, her gloves.*)

(*Max Kane, whom Larry now admits, is a small, tight, eel-like man in his thirties; swarthy, neat, and very Broadway. He is unmistakably Jewish, but he does not talk with an accent, unless it is the accent of a Cockney New Yorker. His clothes are extreme in haberdashery and cut. He carries an evening paper which he later drops onto a convenient chair.*)

MAX: Don't you ever get up? (*He sees Paula.*) Oh!

LARRY: (*Ill-at-ease*) You know Mr. Kane. Miss Jordan.

MAX: Oh, sure! How's the little lady?

PAULA: I'm splendid, thank you. And you?

MAX: Top of the bottle!

PAULA: I'll telephone you, Larry—later.

LARRY: Please think of what I said.

MAX: Am I butting in?

PAULA: No, I was just going. Good-bye.

MAX: (*A parting gesture*) Pearls in your oysters!

PAULA: Good-bye, Larry.

LARRY: (*Their eyes meeting*) Good-bye. (*She goes.*)

MAX: (*He has again placed his hat on his head. It now is perched well back, at a precarious angle. He has a habit of talking through the cigarette in his mouth.*) Well, how's the Great Profile! Been out today, or just sticking around here?

LARRY: (*Going over to the desk on which the whiskey stands*) No, I wasn't feeling very well, and I slept kind of late. I'm going out to dinner. (*Is pouring his drink.*)

MAX: Whyn't you go up to McDermott's and get a workout every day? Take some of that blubber off you. (*Lifts cover off of toast dish.*) What's this? Toast? (*Polishes off a slice.*)

LARRY: I'm all right. Once I go into rehearsal I'll get in shape. (*Tosses off a stiff drink.*)

MAX: (*A gesture toward the drink*) Just keep on with that. That'll fix you. (*Another slice of toast, stopping first to add extra butter.*)

LARRY: What's up? Did you see Baumann? I thought maybe he might come up with you.

MAX: Baumann? No, he didn't come up. Uh, look, Larry, I got a little disappointing news for you, kind of.

LARRY: What's the matter?

MAX: You know how Baumann is—this way, that way—you never know when you got him. Well . . .

LARRY: For God's sake, come out with it!

MAX: I'm telling you. I go in there this afternoon, he's sitting there—a face like that— (*A gesture*) I start in talking about the play, and what does he do, he says he's got to go South next month. He's sick.

LARRY: (*Sets down his glass.*) What's that mean?

MAX: Well, there you are. He's got to go South—and you can't do a play if you're South.

LARRY: Why, he's got to do it. Everything was settled.

MAX: Well, it was talked over, but it wasn't really—you see, unless you got it down in black and white—and *then* sometimes it's no good.

LARRY: Well, that's a hell of a— We'll take it away from him. He's not the only producer. The cheap crook!

MAX: Sure, Baumann's no good. That's how he got where he is. But that ain't the point. What does he do, he goes and turns the play over to Jo Stengel.

LARRY: Jo Stengel! I thought he did nothing but highbrow plays—Isben.

MAX: Yeah, he likes to do those kind, but right now he needs a little money and he figures this thing sort of looks like box-office.

LARRY: Yes—of course with my draw.

MAX: (*Absently*) Huh? Yeah.

LARRY: Stengel, h'm? I rather like the idea of going with Stengel. They tell me he's quite a character.

MAX: Look, Larry, I—

LARRY: He understands I'm to be starred, of course?

MAX: Well, that's just it.

LARRY: What?

MAX: Look, Larry—I don't want you to blame me for this—I been plugging for you for months—

LARRY: (*Fixes Max with a glare of suspicion.*) What the hell are you trying to tell me?

MAX: Now, don't go up in the air about it. Because there's sure to be something else.

LARRY: (*Ominously*) Do you mean I'm out! You double-crossing bastard! Do you mean I'm out!

MAX: God, Larry, could I help it!

LARRY: Help it! Why, you dirty little swine—

MAX: Now, hold on! All right. I'm a this and I'm that. But there wasn't any way *I* could stop it. It was all done before I knew anything about it.

LARRY: It's your business to know! That's what you're hired for!

MAX: Now listen, if there's a better agent, you get him. But I'm telling you nobody knew about this. Nobody. They don't know it *yet*.

LARRY: (*Paces a step or two back and forth, trying to get control of himself.*) Who's going to play the part?

MAX: Cecil Bellamy.

LARRY: Ha! That piffling little— Why, he's English, in the first place.

MAX: Well, the part says English explorer.

LARRY: All right! (*Glares.*) I can be English. I can be as English as anybody. (*Pacing in his annoyance; speaking from time to time, throwing lines over his shoulder.*) I've waited for this play for six weeks. I could have had a million things.

MAX: Sure. Sure you could. And you can get 'em yet, Larry. Only—

LARRY: Only what? Go on—say it, you little squirt!

MAX: No—only you been a long time away. And you know the public. Besides, there's a bunch of 'em want to work on the stage again—picture names.

LARRY: Well, good God, you're not going to compare me—

MAX: No—no! But you see, you're not a talkie name—

LARRY: I was in talkies. I made some of the first talking pictures that were made.

MAX: Yeah. But—trouble is, they forget. They forget overnight. You got to get to work again. Get out there and act. Let 'em see you.

LARRY: All right. That's what I got you for. You've got to dig something up. And none of your four shows a day in vaudeville.

MAX: You could have got twenty weeks with that act if you'd behaved yourself.

LARRY: What about those radio people? Didn't you hear from them?

MAX: Well, I'm watching that. The fella's out of town.

LARRY: And the personal appearances—what did you do about that?

MAX: Mm—for personal appearances you got to be right in the limelight. That's my point. They forget about you. The best thing would be a part in a play.

LARRY: All right. But where's the vehicle?

MAX: Well—now—don't jump down my throat again. But I got an idea.

LARRY: What kind of an idea?

MAX: (*Picks up the play manuscript.*) I was thinking about this play again. You know, Larry, I never said anything, but I never did think that was such a hot part for you. (*Fixes Larry now with a finger.*) Do you know the part I would be crazy to play if I was an actor?

LARRY: What?

MAX: That beach-comber.

LARRY: Beach-comber! You're asking me to go on— (*Pounds his chest in outraged vanity*) —and play a part that isn't— Get the hell out of here! Go on! Get out! Get out, you miserable little— Get out, get out, get out!

MAX: (*Soothingly*) Now, Larry, don't make a mistake.

LARRY: (*Between his teeth*) Get out! Get out before I kick you out!

MAX: (*A shrug. Quietly adjusts his hat.*) Have it your own way. (*A gesture with the hand. A last furtive look to see if he means it. He opens the door.*)

LARRY: Wait a minute!

(*Max stands motionless, his hand on the door.*)

Shut the door!

(*Max does so.*)

What makes you think the other part isn't right for me?

MAX: It's no good. They'll get tired of him. But this *other* fellow! Comes on once—hell of a scene—goes off—they keep waiting for him to come back, and he never does! What a part!

LARRY: Of course his one scene is very nice. (*Reaches for the script; turns the pages.*) Where *is* it now?

MAX: It's the high spot of the show. You know what'll happen? At the finish this What's-His-Name'll be trying to take bows, and they'll all be yelling "Renault! Renault!"

LARRY: (*Not unpleased*) You think so, huh?

MAX: A pushover! Now what do you say? (*A quick consulting of his watch.*) I'm seeing Stengel right away—he's an old friend of mine—

LARRY: Well, don't let on you've talked to me yet. Just say maybe you can *get* me to play it.

MAX: Sure! Leave it to me.

LARRY: Of course—I'd be—featured?

MAX: Maybe it'd be smart not to. Sneak up on 'em.

LARRY: Well—but I'd get my regular salary—I mean, what Baumann was going to give me?

MAX: Larry, we gotta be reasonable. That's one part and this is another one.

LARRY: But after all, I'm a star. I got eight thousand a week in pictures. Everybody knows that.

MAX: Mm—that was quite a while ago. And this is the *theatre*.

LARRY: Of course, that's true. What do you think he—would pay?

MAX: Well—you mustn't think of this as salary. Suppose you only get—uh—I'll tell you what— It's quarter to five. I'll run right down to Stengel's office, fix up an appointment, get you in to see him before he leaves there today. I'll call you right back.

LARRY: Hold on a minute. He mustn't think I'm after this part. Make him come to see me.

MAX: Now, Larry, it isn't done that way. You're the actor, and—

LARRY: I'm Larry Renault! I don't go to managers with my hat in my hand. He'd expect to get me for nothing. But if he comes up here, sees this place—

MAX: God, Larry, you don't make things very easy for me— bringing managers to actors! Well, maybe he'll do it as a favor to me. You know, I used to be Jo's office boy. . . . How long you going to be here?

LARRY: Oh—a long time. I'm not dining till eight.

(*Max picks up his overcoat, prepares to leave.*)

MAX: Well! If I can do it, I'm good. Look, Larry— (*One arm in his coat sleeve, he pauses to give these final instructions*) —if he comes up here, you want to watch your step. We can't afford to let this part get away from us.

LARRY: (*A slight pause, while Larry paces, nervously, turning the whole thing over in his mind. Suddenly he wheels.*) Max, I can't do it.

MAX: Can't do what?

LARRY: I can't play that part. Larry Renault can't go on and play a mere character part.

MAX: (*Very low*) You've got to play it. There isn't anything else.

LARRY: No, no. I tell you I can't do it. I won't humiliate myself.

(*The sound of the door buzzer. Larry goes slowly to the door. Max drifts thoughtfully upstage, so that he is not seen from the hall doorway.*)

(*Mr. Hatfield, the assistant manager of the Hotel Versailles, is seen at the door. He comes a step or two into the doorway, a suave figure in cutaway coat and striped trousers. He goes through the form of bowing deferentially from the waist.*)

HATFIELD: (*Professionally cheery*) Good-afternoon, Mr. Renault!

LARRY: Oh! How-do-you-do?

HATFIELD: Beautiful day, isn't it!

LARRY: (*Uneasily*) Yes—ah—

HATFIELD: I've taken the liberty of bringing up your bill again, Mr. Renault.

(*A quick warning gesture from Larry. An apprehensive look over his shoulder toward Max.*)

Our cashier would like to balance his books, so if—

(*Max, as he catches the drift of what is going on, comes cautiously forward a few steps for a look at the proceedings.*)

LARRY: Oh, yes, yes. (*Hurriedly takes the envelope from Hatfield's hand.*) I'll send you down a check. I've someone here now. Thank you very much. (*Quickly closes the door. Stuffs the envelope into the pocket of his dressing gown.*) Damned impertinence!

MAX: (*With a great show of cheerfulness*) Well! I'll bustle on down, get hold of Stengel— (*On his way. Stops to give Larry two or three heartening slaps on the back.*) Come on! Snap out of it! This time next year you'll be riding the high waves!

LARRY: (*With a false air of agreement*) I'm all right.

MAX: Sure! You're swell! Well—good-bye!

LARRY: Oh—Max!

MAX: Huh?

LARRY: (*A transparent attempt at lightness. He even manages a cackle of laughter.*) Here's a funny thing! I wonder if you could let me have five dollars. Taxi fare. I didn't get out to the bank—I'm going to this dinner—and what do you think I've got! (*Plunges his hand in his pocket, brings out a little scattering of coins, at which he glances, very amused.*) Seventeen cents! Ha-ha!

MAX: Say, I got just enough to get to the office. I'll bring it to you when I come back. (*He goes, hurriedly.*)

(*Larry stands alone, jingling the coins in his palm. He tosses them on the table, goes over and pours himself a drink. As he pours it the door buzzer sounds.*)

LARRY: Come in!

(*The Waiter has entered, using his pass key, as Larry calls to him. He leaves the outer hall door open.*)

WAITER: Can I take the table?

LARRY: Yes.

(*The Waiter comes over, picks up the table, hoists it to his shoulder, turns to leave.*)

Oh, waiter!

WAITER: Yes, sir?

LARRY: I just remembered I haven't had a thing to eat all day. I'm not dining till eight. I'll tell you what. Bring me a cup of coffee, good and strong, and—let me see—I think I'll take a caviar sandwich.

WAITER: Yes, sir. (*Hesitates.*)

LARRY: (*Dismisses him with a wave of the hand.*) That's all.

WAITER: I'm sorry, Mr. Renault, but were you going to sign for it?

LARRY: Why?

WAITER: Well, excuse me, but my orders are that if you sign for it, I can't serve any more food here.

LARRY: What's that! Not serve— (*Rushes to the telephone.*) You get that order up here! I'll tell that manager— You get that order—

WAITER: Yessir. (*He goes, closing the door gently behind him.*)

LARRY: (*Just as the Waiter is vanishing. In phone*) Hello! Hello! (*Then very quietly he hangs up. Immediately the phone rings.*) Hello! . . . No, I didn't call. . . . No. . . . Wait a minute. Yes, I did. Send up a bellboy, will you? To go on an errand.

(*An afterthought.*) Listen. I want Eddie—Eddie, the one that always comes up here. (*Hangs up.*)

(*Glances down at his shirt cuffs. Quickly removes his cuff links, regards them a second in the palm of his hand; puts them on the table. Stops and thinks. Slaps himself as though hoping to come upon some hidden valuable. Remembers his gold belt buckle. With a swift desperate gesture strips the buckle from the belt around his waist. Adds that to the links on the table. A look around the room, searching for still another article. The silver frame containing Paula Jordan's picture. He goes quickly to it, removes the photograph, props the picture precariously up against the leather frame containing his own picture, brings the silver frame over to the table, looks about for something in which to wrap it. He sees the newspaper left by Max, rips off a page, wraps the frame up in it.*)

(*He goes to the table on which the bottle stands, pours a big drink, tosses it down his throat as the* LIGHTS DIM.)

SCENE II

Dr. Talbot's office. The room is oval in shape. There is a door at the back, leading into the laboratory and examination rooms. Another door opens on the reception room; a third connects with the Talbots' house proper.

The room is pine-paneled, restful, simply and tastefully furnished as a doctor's consulting room. In a niche over the door at the back there is a bust of Hippocrates. Built-in book shelves extend to the ceiling. The doctor's flat-topped desk is at one side, turned slightly at an angle. On it, in addition to the usual desk furnishings, are two telephones, and a large photograph of the doctor's wife and his fourteen-year-old son. A comfortable chair for patients is at the side of the doctor's desk. There is a clock in a niche above a book shelf.

As the curtain rises Miss Alden, the nurse attendant, enters from the laboratory. She is about twenty-seven, poised, capable without being bustling, intelligent, and attractive in her white uniform. She comes to the doctor's desk, consults the desk pad, turning a page or two, tears off the top page, throws it into the waste basket. A little tidying of the desk. She goes into the reception room.

The stage is empty. The clock strikes five. A clear and pleasing sound. A brief moment of silence. Dr. Talbot enters his consulting room from the house door. He is wearing his topcoat and hat. As he removes hat and coat and tosses them into the chair his whole aspect is that of a man wearied almost to the point of exhaustion.

As he drops into the chair before his desk he pulls himself together with a characteristic shake and a long breath, and a hand run through his hair. He has an hour of consultation work ahead of him. He glances at his desk pad, presses his desk buzzer. It is heard sounding in the reception room.

Miss Alden enters immediately. Between Dr. Talbot and Miss Alden there is a friendly professional understanding. They convey to each other, with a look or a brief sentence, the entire history of a patient's case.

MISS ALDEN: (*There is a slip of paper in her hand. She goes directly to Dr. Talbot's desk, and places the slip of paper before him.*) There are six in the waiting room. And Mr. Trowbridge telephoned. It's his sinus again, but he can't get here till seven. He wants to know if you'll see him.

TALBOT: (*Wearily*) Oh, I suppose so.

MISS ALDEN: Did you see Mrs. Talbot as you came through? She wanted to talk to you.

TALBOT: (*Rather distractedly*) No. No, I didn't.

MISS ALDEN: You look all in. It must have been tougher than you thought it would be.

TALBOT: Fierce! Carcinoma of the pancreas. On the table an hour. It was a beautiful operation.

MISS ALDEN: You must be limp as a rag. Don't you want a cup of coffee?

TALBOT: (*As he rises he takes off his suit coat, and goes toward the laboratory door.*) No, I'll be all right.

MISS ALDEN: (*An afterthought*) Oh, how's the patient? Did he live?

TALBOT: Yes, he's fine. (*He goes into the laboratory.*)

(*As Miss Alden gathers up his hat and coat one of the telephones rings. It is his private wire, and the ring is rather fainter than that of the ordinary phone.*)

MISS ALDEN: (*Coat and hat on her arm. Goes to the telephone.*) Dr. Talbot's office. . . . Who is it, please? . . . Well, who is it? . . . I'm sorry, but I have to have the name. . . . (*A little knowing smile*) . . . Oh, yes, Mrs. Packard. He's in. Just a minute. (*Goes to the door, which is slightly open.*) Doctor!

TALBOT: (*Unseen*) Yes?

MISS ALDEN: (*With no little delight*) Call on your private wire.

TALBOT: Who is it?

MISS ALDEN: (*A little smile*) Mrs. Packard.

TALBOT: (*Quickly*) I'm not here!

MISS ALDEN: (*With devilish elation*) I'm awfully sorry. (*She is going toward reception-room door, very pleased with herself.*) I've already told her you're in. (*Goes.*)

TALBOT: Oh, for God's— (*He enters. He has changed his suit coat to a roomier older coat. He strides into the room, halts a moment, and stands glaring at the waiting telephone. With resignation he goes to his desk, speaks into the phone.*) Hello. . . . Now, Kitty—Kitty! . . . But there's no occa— . . . Kitty, for heaven's sa— . . . Now, Kitty, listen . . . Will you listen a minute! No, I can't come over! You know perfectly well these are my office hours. I've got a whole roomful of— . . . There's nothing the matter with you. . . . Take an aspirin. . . . Well, I've been busy. . . . I'll see you tonight at the Jordans'. . . . Of course you can go. There's nothing the matter with you.

(*Lucy Talbot enters quietly from the house door, right. She does not mean to overhear the telephone conversation, but she finds herself in the midst of it and must stand a moment before she is impelled to make her presence known.*)

(*She is a wren-like, somewhat faded little figure, but possessed of a quiet power, too, as well as poise and gentle breeding. Her dress is dark, almost prim, relieved with white collar and cuffs, very simple and delicate. In her hand she carries an opened letter.*)

(*Talbot, rather frantic at the telephone, does not see her. His hand is pressed to his forehead.*)

Kitty, my time isn't my own. I can't do just as I want to. . . .
Of course I do. I think you're very sweet. . . . Other
women! Of course there's no other woman. . . . Kitty,
you're driving me . . .

(*Lucy, in order to let her husband know that she is in the
room, shuts the door behind her firmly enough to attract his
attention. She advances a few steps into the room as he
rather blunderingly goes on with his conversation, changing
its tone completely, or attempting to.*)

Yes, I think you'd better rest for an hour, and then take a
mild bromide—say an aspirin. . . . Well, I have patients in
the office. You must excuse me. There's no cause for alarm.
(*He hangs up quickly. Then, with a great assumption of ease,
he turns to his wife.*) Hello, Lucy!

LUCY: (*In the same tone*) Hello, Jo!

TALBOT: How are you, dear?

LUCY: I'm fine. And you?

TALBOT: I'm all right.

LUCY: Anything new?

TALBOT: (*Very airily*) No. No.

LUCY: Just the same old thing, h'm?

TALBOT: What?

LUCY: I mean—unreasonable women patients.

TALBOT: Oh—yes—she's not really sick. They get it into their
heads they're not well—you know—women with a lot of
time on their hands. I just prescribed a sedative. She doesn't
need anything.

LUCY: How about an apple a day?

TALBOT: (*Startled*) What's that?

LUCY: Don't bother, dear.

TALBOT: Huh?

LUCY: Don't bother. Because I know all about it.

TALBOT: Why—uh—what are you talking about?

LUCY: Please, Jo! I'm not going to make a scene. You know I
never do, do I? Remember how nicely I behaved about the
others? Mrs. Whiting, and the Dalrymple girl, and that
Ferguson woman, and Dolly, and— (*A swift look around*)
—where do you keep your files?

TALBOT: (*With great dignity*) I tell you, you are quite wrong
about this woman.

LUCY: Now, Jo. I knew when it started, and I knew when you began to tire of her. They came at about the same time, didn't they? And now she's at the insistent stage. It's a great bore, isn't it, darling? (*He turns his eyes away from her, and with that gesture admits the truth of what she has said.*) Don't think that I don't mind, Jo. I pretend not to—but I do. But I can't let it tear me to pieces the way it did that first time. It was just before Wayne was born—remember? I thought the world had come to an end. The noble young physician was just a masher.

TALBOT: Surely, a little more than that.

LUCY: A great deal more, Jo. That's what makes it so pathetic. You are really two people. One is so magnificent, the other so shoddy.

TALBOT: (*His fingers drum nervously for a moment on the table. Then slowly, painfully, he speaks of himself.*) I suppose it's natural enough. Son of a railroad brakeman—what can you expect?

LUCY: Mm. I'm sure he blew the whistle for every hired girl between here and Albany. I wonder how your mother felt about that.

TALBOT: Don't!

LUCY: She's that other side of you—the lovely side, Jo.

TALBOT: Perhaps if she had lived I'd have been different. But turned over to an old maid aunt who wasn't fitted for the job— (*A gesture that breaks the introspective mood.*) I don't know why you've stayed with me all these years. Why did you?

LUCY: A very foolish reason, Jo. Because I'm still in love with you. Isn't that funny? You'd think I'd have more pride.

TALBOT: I don't love anyone but you, Lucy. I never have. Those other women— It's like gambling or drinking or drugs. You just keep on.

LUCY: No, Jo, that isn't it at all. Do you know what I think? I think you're still the little boy living over on Tenth Avenue, a little in awe of the girl from Murray Hill. The little boy who thinks that sex is something to be ashamed of. And that's why—forgive me, Jo—all these women in your life have been a little common—a little bit Tenth Avenue, too. I know you love me, Jo. Try to think of me as a woman, too.

TALBOT: (*His hand tightening on hers*) Lucy, darling, I feel
   closer to you now than I have in years.

LUCY: I'm glad, Jo.

TALBOT: I never want to see that woman again as long as I live.

LUCY: Nonsense! See her as often as you like. You're seeing her
   tonight, aren't you? Isn't she going to the Jordans'?

TALBOT: Good God, yes! I forgot.

LUCY: And I'm forgetting what I'm here for. I've good news
   for you. (*Indicates the letter in her hand.*) Your son and heir
   has decided upon a career. He says that at fourteen a man
   should be— (*Turning the letter over in search of the written
   line.*) —where is it?—"be ready to face the future."

TALBOT: (*Smiles faintly.*) What's it going to be now? Aviation,
   or the mounted police?

LUCY: He's going to follow in your footsteps, Jo.

TALBOT: A doctor?

LUCY: A doctor. (*Returns to the letter, briefly.*) Do you know
   why? He read the Hippocratic oath.

TALBOT: Where did he come across that?

LUCY: The encyclopedia. I fancy he visualized himself as a
   student, standing up in cap and gown— (*Her right hand
   upraised*) —swearing to serve humanity. Do you know the
   part that impressed him, Jo? He quotes it.

TALBOT: What?

LUCY: (*Reads from the letter.*) ". . . In purity and holiness I
   will guard my art, keeping myself free from all wrongdoing.
   Now if I keep this oath, and break it not, may God be my
   helper in my life and art, and may I be honored among all
   men for all time. But if I forswear myself, may the opposite
   befall me."

   (*As she reads, Talbot's head droops a little. He reaches out to
   cover her hand with his own.*)

   (*Miss Alden enters hurriedly from the reception room.
   Though she makes no undue commotion, it is evident that
   she is disturbed.*)

MISS ALDEN: Doctor— Oh, I'm sorry. (*Seeing Mrs. Talbot*) Mr.
   Oliver Jordan is outside, and he seems quite ill. I think
   you'd—

TALBOT: Have him come right in.

   (*Miss Alden goes quickly.*)

(*Talbot's head comes up. He pulls himself together. He is at once the professional man.*)

LUCY: I'll go. (*She goes immediately.*)

(*Talbot has risen. He crosses quickly to the reception-room door, which has stood open. As he stands at the door Miss Alden's voice is heard.*)

MISS ALDEN: You're fine now. Here—let me help you.

(*Oliver Jordan enters, assisted by Miss Alden. Obviously he has had an acute attack, from which he is just emerging. Talbot supports him as he comes through the door. Miss Alden, with her free hand, closes the door behind her.*)

TALBOT: Why, what's this, Oliver? Come over here and sit down. Take it easy. That's right.

OLIVER: (*Being assisted toward the patient's chair. His hand held over the region of the pain*) It's right here.

TALBOT: (*Quickly, to the nurse*) Nitrate of amyl—quick!

(*Miss Alden vanishes into the laboratory.*)

(*As Oliver drops into the chair, Talbot quickly undoes his tie, unbuttons his shirt and undershirt. Miss Alden returns immediately with the amyl, gives it to Talbot, who quickly breaks the covering, holds the drug to Oliver's nose.*)

Sniff that!

(*Almost immediately, under the influence of the strong drug, Oliver revives. Miss Alden leaning over him, her hands resting lightly on his shoulders.*)

There! That's better. (*Talbot takes his stethoscope from his inner coat pocket, applies it over Oliver's heart.*)

OLIVER: (*A feeble gesture of protest.*) I'm all right now.

(*Heedless of Oliver's protest Talbot concentrates on the examination. At its conclusion he straightens, stands completely still for a second, looking down at Oliver. There is a quick exchange of glances between Talbot and Miss Alden.*)

TALBOT: Yes, of course you are.

OLIVER: (*Relieved. Smiles wanly.*) I've got no business doing this. What's the matter with me?

TALBOT: (*As Miss Alden goes into the laboratory. Closes the door.*) How long has this been going on? Have you had it before?

OLIVER: (*Buttoning his shirt*) Why, no, not like this. I started to walk home from the Athletic Club and suddenly I felt—funny. As luck would have it, I wasn't far from here.

I managed to get into a taxi, and—here I am. What is it, anyhow?

TALBOT: Oh, probably a little indigestion. (*A gesture that vaguely points in the direction of the heart.*) What have you been eating? What did you have for lunch?

OLIVER: Why, nothing that would upset me. A little fish—

TALBOT: If I were you I'd watch my diet. Simple food, and not too much of it.

OLIVER: Well, if *that's* all—

TALBOT: I'd like to have you come in again in a day or two. More thorough examination. How's tomorrow?

OLIVER: Tomorrow—that's Saturday. I'd rather make it next week some time.

TALBOT: Now—pretend this is a business appointment. To-morrow—what time? When do you leave your office?

OLIVER: (*Good-natured humoring of the doctor.*) All right, all right! How about two-thirty?

TALBOT: I'm at the hospital until four. Make it at four-fifteen?

OLIVER: Four-fifteen.

(*Talbot makes a note of this on his pad.*)

Well! (*Rises. Finds himself surprisingly steady. Looks about in mild triumph.*) Why, I feel great! I may fool you and not come in at all tomorrow.

TALBOT: You show up here. Broken appointments are charged double.

OLIVER: You boys certainly clean up. What did I get for my money today! A whiff of smelling salts.

TALBOT: Look here—what're you going to do tonight?

OLIVER: Huh? Why, you're coming to dinner, among others.

(*Miss Alden enters from laboratory, carrying a card-index box. Busies herself at desk.*)

TALBOT: Can you sneak out early, and go to bed?

OLIVER: Why—I think we're all going to theatre.

TALBOT: I wouldn't do it, if I were you. Take it easy for a while. Avoid any excitement or emotional strain. Stop worrying. Stop thinking about business.

OLIVER: What does that mean? The old pump out of order?

TALBOT: No, no. But it's bound to feel the effect of any physical disorder. That's all.

OLIVER: (*A pause. Thoughtfully*) I—see.

TALBOT: (*Heartily*) Well, see you later, h'm? Dinner at eight?

OLIVER: Yes, I believe so. Good-bye.

TALBOT: Good-bye, Oliver.

OLIVER: I'm—I'm not fooled. (*Oliver goes.*)

    (*Talbot stands motionless looking after Oliver.*)

MISS ALDEN: How bad is it?

TALBOT: Coronary artery. Thrombosis.

MISS ALDEN: How long will he live?

TALBOT: A few months—weeks—days, even. (*Walks slowly to his desk.*)

MISS ALDEN: You're sure?

TALBOT: Positive. You can tell it like— (*Snaps his fingers.*) —that.

MISS ALDEN: Poor fellow.

TALBOT: (*Sits in his desk chair. Assents, almost unintelligibly.*) Yes.

    (*Miss Alden assumes again her professional manner.*)

MISS ALDEN: Ready?

    (*Talbot nods.*)

    (*Miss Alden goes to the reception-room door, opens it, stands looking into the outer room.*)

All right, Mrs. Beveridge!

    (*She remains at the door, waiting for the new patient to enter. The doctor still sits thoughtfully at his desk. His head comes up, his face assumes the professional look for the next patient.*)

THE LIGHTS DIM

SCENE III

The butler's pantry at the Jordans'. It is a rectangular room, its walls, woodwork, and curtains in a delicate pale yellow, very cool and agreeable. It is a workman-like place, equipped for serving. A single swinging door leads to the kitchen.

At the back there is a large cupboard, its shelves filled with plates, cups, saucers, glassware; flower vases on the topmost shelves; compote dishes. Underneath it are drawers. Just above these is a broad shelf for laying out plates, etc.

In one corner of the room is a sink, to which is attached, at one end, a drain-board which extends around the corner, taking up part of the wall. Against the back wall is a very large built-in electric refrigerator, with a solitary grapefruit on top of it.

There is a second cupboard with a serving shelf, a kitchen table, its narrow end turned toward the audience. Two chairs are alongside this table.

There is a small portable radio on the cupboard shelf at the rear.

The time is about five-thirty.

At the rise the radio is going full tilt—a popular tune played by one of the hotel tea dance orchestras. Dora, the only occupant of the pantry, is bringing down piles of plates from the cupboard in preparation for tonight's dinner. Ten of this, ten of that. As she works she hums happily, a compliment to the radio's music, and occasionally tosses in a few words of the lyric—when she knows them. Presently she pauses, steps back a pace or two, and cranes her neck to an upper shelf.

Finding what she seeks, she pulls out a long drawer and hops up on it, still humming, and breaking her rhythm only in the final reach. She stretches; brings down the final plates.

There is about her a certain elation and bloom, the reason for which now becomes apparent. From her apron pocket she takes a handkerchief, in one corner of which is knotted a ring. She undoes this knot with fingers and teeth, slips her new wedding ring on the third finger of her left hand, and holds the hand, thus orna-mented, up to her own enchanted gaze.

Enter, from the kitchen, Mrs. Wendel, the cook. Mrs. Wendel is Swedish, but with no trace of accent. She is an ample woman in her mid-fifties; is dressed in white, and wears a large apron. Rolled-up sleeves. Her natural amiability is clouded at the mo-ment by a bad tooth, and her face is tied up in a great toothache bandage. Her left arm encircles a yellow mixing bowl, which rests on one broad hip. In the hand that holds the bowl she grasps an envelope containing a letter. With the other hand she busily stirs the mixture as she talks. She drops the letter on the table, goes to the refrigerator. Relinquishing her spoon for a time, she opens the refrigerator, deftly removes the top from a milk bottle, pours a little milk into the mixture within the bowl, replaces the milk bottle, slams the refrigerator door. Dora, in the meantime, having got the necessary number of plates from the cupboard, is now occupied in scanning them to see that they are properly shining. Occasionally she rubs one with a tea cloth, or runs hot water from the tap over a cloudy-looking plate.

MRS. WENDEL: (*At the refrigerator*) I put a letter there for Gustave. It just came.

DORA: What?

MRS. WENDEL: A letter came for Gustave. Turn that lower. (*Indicating radio.*)

> (*Dora modifies the radio music. Drifts over to the table to look inquisitively at the letter.*)

It's from that place he came from over in Europe.

DORA: (*Reads the postmark.*) Lu-cerny. S-u-i-s-s-e. (*Spelling it.*) Where's that, Mrs. Wendel?

MRS. WENDEL: (*Coming down to peer over Dora's shoulder*) It's what they call Switzerland. I got one, too, today, from Sweden.

DORA: It looks like a woman, the writing.

MRS. WENDEL: Mine was from my brother. He wants fifty dollars.

DORA: (*Tucks the letter in her apron pocket. Going to the sink*) Letters from your folks is always money. (*Fills a glass with water, turns, stands sipping it, her gaze on Mrs. Wendel, who is briskly beating her mixture.*) How's your tooth, Mrs. Wendel? Any better?

MRS. WENDEL: I put essence of cloves on it, but it keeps jumping. I wish I could get to the dentist. Only for this dinner I could have.

DORA: Yeah, it had to be just today, or else we could have had a celebration. (*Again her gaze fastens itself upon the new ring.*)

MRS. WENDEL: I have to laugh the way you thought you could fool me. The minute I looked at your face I knew you was married.

DORA: Remember, don't you tell a living soul. I better take my ring off. (*Speaking as she removes her ring, knots it again in the handkerchief, tucks the handkerchief into her pocket.*) If that Ricci sees it, I wouldn't put nothing past him.

MRS. WENDEL: I wouldn't breathe it to him. (*A sudden thought.*) Say, if they're going to the country Sunday, and he drives them, we could have a celebration then. I'd bake you a wedding cake. It don't seem hardly right, getting married yesterday and coming right back to work today.

DORA: It was fun, though. I was all excited and laughing, but Gustave, he was so scared you'd think he was getting hung.

MRS. WENDEL: The men are always like that.

DORA: He was all right, though, after. When we had dinner. You ought to go to that place, some time, where we ate. For a dollar you get choice of crabmeat or soup, and then there's fish, and then choice of pork chops with applesauce, prime ribs of beef au jus, or chicken à la Calcutta. We took that.

MRS. WENDEL: How was it fixed?

DORA: Well, it turned out it was chicken with curry sauce, and I don't like curry sauce, but I was so happy I ate it anyway.

MRS. WENDEL: I got chicken for them tonight. I'm glad because it don't take much fixing. I was two hours on the lobster aspic—they're such a job—and then they'll eat it up in five minutes.

DORA: It's good, though. I hope there's some left over.

MRS. WENDEL: I made the big one so there would be. Wait till you see it. Of course the lobster's in the middle, and I'm going to mix caviar in with the mayonnaise and decorate the whole top with it.

DORA: They got a lord and lady coming, haven't they? I wonder how she'll look.

MRS. WENDEL: They look just like anybody else—only plainer.

DORA: I think they're having mostly old people. Miss Paula won't be there. She's going out with Ernest.

MRS. WENDEL: When they get married, *that*'ll be a lot of cooking.

DORA: If you ask me, I don't think she's going to marry him. He's always calling up and she's always making excuses.

MRS. WENDEL: I don't like him. I peeked in at him once through the door. He hasn't any It.

DORA: I never could see why Mr. Jordan ever married Mrs. Jordan. He's so sweet, and all she thinks of is what she's going to put on and where is she going.

MRS. WENDEL: I've worked for worse. She keeps out of the kitchen, anyway.

DORA: I'm worried about Mr. Jordan. I think he's got something on his mind.

(*Gustave enters, bearing a tray and the remains of a depleted tea. His entrance is preceded by a kick against the swinging door.*)

Oh, hello!

GUSTAVE: (*Puts down the tray with something of a thump.*) Thought she'd never get through. Sip. Sip.

(*He is at Dora's side as soon as he can get there; kisses her tenderly.*)

MRS. WENDEL: (*With a fondly deprecatory gesture*) Oh, you two! (*Goes into the kitchen.*)

DORA: I thought you were never coming back. I was going to go up there and get you.

GUSTAVE: (*A final kiss. Removing his coat and hanging it over the back of a chair.*) I was wishing she'd choke. All I could think of was getting back to my little Dora. (*He takes from a hook a long apron designed for protection in rougher work. Ties it around his waist.*)

DORA: I wish this dinner was over.

GUSTAVE: We'll serve 'em fast. Take the plates away from them. . . . What's the meat course?

DORA: Chicken.

(*Gustave takes from the table a long and vicious-looking carving knife, together with a knife sharpener. He proceeds to wield the two with expert strokes.*)

(*Dora goes back to polishing her plates.*)

I had my ring on again. I wish I could keep it on all the time. (*Puts her hand in the apron pocket. Encounters Gustave's letter.*) Oh, here's a letter came for you. From Switzerland.

GUSTAVE: (*Takes the letter, barely glances at it.*) Oh! Yes. It will be from my sister. (*Puts it in his pocket. He turns away, goes to the cupboard, begins to take down goblets. They are fragile, thin-stemmed wine glasses, to be used for dinner that evening.*)

DORA: Why don't you read it?

GUSTAVE: (*Busy with reaching down the glasses*) It will be the same story. They must buy a new plow—my brother-in-law is sick—there is another baby coming. (*He begins to wipe the glasses, using a tea towel. As they are wiped he brings them, one or two at a time, to the table, going back and forth between cupboard and table.*)

(*Through all of this the radio, tuned very low, is playing, with occasional announcements, also low-pitched, such as "You are listening to Ted Niblo's Musketeers broadcasting from the Pompeiian Room of the Hotel Commonwealth. The next two numbers will be . . ."*)

DORA: I'd like to see what Europe is like. I bet it's inter*est*ing. You been all over, haven't you?

GUSTAVE: A good butler should be a cosmopolitan. I have worked in France, in Germany, in England—even one winter I was in Cairo.

DORA: Oh, how I'd like to go traveling and see all those things with you. Gustave! Couldn't we go! Couldn't we save our money, both of us, and maybe go next summer?

GUSTAVE: No, it takes too much money.

DORA: But we could get jobs over there.

GUSTAVE: You would not like it. Anyway it is finished over there. *Kaput!*

DORA: I would *so* like it! And I could meet your folks. Maybe you're ashamed of me!

GUSTAVE: (*Comes quickly over to her. He has the glass and towel in his hands, she the plate and towel in her hands.*) No, no, my darling! My darling Dora! (*They kiss.*)

DORA: My wonderful husband! My handsome Gustave! When I think how lucky I am! You might have married some other girl. How does it happen some other girl didn't grab you?

GUSTAVE: I was waiting for you, my beautiful Dora.

DORA: Oh, Gustave, I have never been so happy. I would be just perfectly happy, only if it wasn't for that Ricci. I keep thinking about him—what he would do if he finds out.

GUSTAVE: Don't be a silly child! What can he do!

(*Mrs. Wendel enters from the kitchen. In triumph she is carrying the aspic, an imposing structure on a great platter. The aspic is in the form of a hollow ring. Inside the ring are piled the chunks of lobster. In one hand, though both are grasping the platter, Mrs. Wendel carries a very large three-*

pronged fork, the centre prong protruding beyond the other two. The handle is a foot long.)

MRS. WENDEL: God be thanked, this is finished! (*Depositing it on the centre table.*)

GUSTAVE: Look out for those glasses.

MRS. WENDEL: (*Fork in hand, she steps back and surveys her handiwork.*) And it's the best one I ever made, if I do say so. Here it is, almost six, and I've been working on it since three. She couldn't get another cook in New York to do what I've done today, with a toothache killing me. They'd say, "I'm sick and you can cook your own dinner." (*She has been gesticulating with the fork during this speech. She now leans over the dish, using the fork delicately to arrange a bit of lobster here, a bit there, so that they show to greater advantage.*)

DORA: It's just beautiful, Mrs. Wendel.

GUSTAVE: A good thing for the toothache is to hold a little brandy like this. (*Tips his head to one side, to illustrate holding a mouthful of brandy.*)

MRS. WENDEL: I'm afraid to take anything with the dinner to cook.

GUSTAVE: (*Goes to cupboard, brings forth a decanter of brandy.*) Nonsense! A mouthful won't hurt you. Just a *schluck.* (*Reaching for one of three or four of the frail glasses still standing, unwiped, on the cupboard shelf.*)

MRS. WENDEL: Well, all right. I'm half crazy.

(*Gustave pours her a drink.*)

You take one, too—and Dora. We'll drink a toast. The bride and groom!

GUSTAVE: That's fine! Heh, Dora? (*Pouring two more drinks.*)

DORA: All right. I'll turn on the wedding march. (*She goes to radio, turns it up so that the orchestra comes up loudly.*) Oh, that's good! Come on, Gustave! (*Takes his arm. Together they execute a little march, their glasses held high.*)

MRS. WENDEL: (*Very much in the spirit of the thing, her voice high above the music*) To the bride and groom! *Skoal!*

GUSTAVE AND DORA: (*In unison*) *Skoal!*

(*A little excited giggle from Dora.*)

(*The kitchen swinging door flies open from a terrific kick. It is Ricci. He takes one dramatic step into the room and stands, a menacing figure, confronting the three.*

DORA: (*A terrified half-whisper.*) Gustave!

RICCI: You lying little bitch! *Porca di madonna!*

DORA: Gustave! I'm scared!

GUSTAVE: (*A gesture to quiet her.*) I 'tend to him.

MRS. WENDEL: Get out of my kitchen!

RICCI: (*Advances a step or two, crouchingly.*) So! You sneak off and get married, eh?

DORA: No, we ain't! No such thing!

MRS. WENDEL: You're crazy! They ain't married!

RICCI: Oh, no! Then why do you tell Josephine next door, who tell the chauffeur, who tell *me*, that they go to City Hall—

MRS. WENDEL: I did not, you lying Wop! (*Quickly, to Dora*) I didn't breathe it!

DORA: Oh! Oh!

GUSTAVE: Oh, Mrs. Wendel!

RICCI: So! It is true! (*Another step forward.*)

DORA: No! No! (*Cowering behind Gustave.*)

RICCI: It is true! (*He is at the table. His fist comes down on the table with a crash. It encounters the handle of the big knife which Gustave has recently sharpened.*) Ah! (*He grasps it and brings it up slowly into view.*)

DORA: (*Hysterically*) Oh, my God!

MRS. WENDEL: *Og, Hedon!*

GUSTAVE: (*Shoves the two women behind him, protectingly.*) Put down that knife!

    (*Dora is whimpering with terror.*)

RICCI: (*Knife in hand, he pushes back his sleeve as he talks, preparing for battle.*) If Ricci not have her, then no one will have her!

DORA: Oh, God! Oh, God!

GUSTAVE: Put it down, I tell you! (*A wild glance around. Sees the great fork. Seizes it as a desperate weapon.*) Put it down!

DORA: No, no! Gustave!

MRS. WENDEL: *Gud hjälp mig!*

RICCI: Ah-h-h-h! (*To Gustave*) So you think *you* can stop me, eh? First you want me to take care of *you*!

    (*Eyes fixed on his adversary, knife poised, he begins a stealthy advance, around the end of the table. Gustave, fork in hand, is crouched to meet his advance. There is a bit of jockeying* for position. *Gustave retreats a step; shakes off the restraining hands of the women.*)

DORA: Gustave! He'll kill you! He'll kill you! Don't fight him! Don't fight him! Ricci! Oh, my God! Oh, my God! Oh, my God!

MRS. WENDEL: Stop them! Stop them! Get the missus! Somebody stop them! Oh, *min Gud!*

(*For a second there is complete silence, broken only by the music over the radio—a gay and lilting tune.*)

(*Then the moment arrives. Gustave, seeing his opportunity, makes an unexpected lunge, which surprises Ricci, who had meant to make the attack. Stepping quickly backward to avoid Gustave's weapon, he comes into violent contact with the laden table, which overturns with a crash. Down go wine glasses, plates, aspic.*)

(*Gustave follows up his offense. The two men grapple on the floor, knife and fork flashing.*)

(*Screams from the women as the table is overturned.*)

(*A particularly terrifying scream from Dora as the men roll on the floor.*)

(*The music is gayer than ever.*)

BLACKOUT

SCENE IV

Upstairs sitting room at the Jordans'. Six o'clock. The lamps are lighted. Millicent Jordan, in a negligée, is at the telephone.

MILLICENT: Yes, that will be all right. No, I only want those three. . . . I want the ones that played at Mrs. Post's last week. . . . No, no, it isn't for dancing. I explained all that on Monday. It's just music through dinner. And be sure to give me the one with the black mustache that plays the violin. And tell him he's not to come into the dining room and start playing *at* us. He's to stay where he is, with the others. . . . Now, they'll wear their red coats, won't they? They're so romantic. And I don't want anything but Hungarian music. That gypsy stuff, or whatever you call it. . . .

What? . . . Yes, that's it. (*Attempts the word without much assurance.*) Czigane. Yes. And I especially want that one piece—I don't know the name of it—it's *so* well known— No—no—that's not it. . . . No. If I could . . . It goes something like this. . . . (*Goes off into quite a perform- ance, though briefly, doesn't quite make the high note, clears her throat, starts again.*)

> (*Dora enters in the middle of this. She is plainly still agi- tated by the events that have just taken place belowstairs. She is somewhat startled, now, as she catches Mrs. Jordan in the midst of a quite pretentious trill at the telephone.*)

What? . . . Yes, that's it, that's it. And they'll be here no later than quarter to eight. . . . You know the address? . . . That's it. . . . Good-bye.

> (*Hangs up. Dora is standing, plainly waiting to speak to her.*)

Yes, Dora?

DORA: (*In considerable embarrassment*) Madam, Mrs. Wendel wants to know if she can come in. (*A gesture toward the hall.*) She wants to speak to you a minute.

MILLICENT: Why, yes. Tell her to come in.

> (*Wordlessly and a little apprehensively, Dora summons Mrs. Wendel from the hall. Dora retreats a step or two, but can- not bear to withdraw until she has caught at least a bit of the scene to follow.*)
>
> (*Mrs. Wendel advances, a figure of portent. The bandage has been removed, but occasionally, as she talks, her hand goes to the aching face.*)

Yes, Mrs. Wendel?

MRS. WENDEL: It's the aspic.

MILLICENT: The aspic? What about it?

MRS. WENDEL: It didn't turn out right. I think it must have been the gelatine. It didn't set.

MILLICENT: What do you mean? You can't use it?

MRS. WENDEL: No, ma'am. It's no good.

MILLICENT: Do you mean to tell me at this hour!—Why, it's six o'clock! What do you mean, you can't use it?—Let me see it. (*As though to accompany Mrs. Wendel to the kitchen.*)

> (*Dora makes her escape.*)

MRS. WENDEL: It's no use. I threw it away. It was like water.

MILLICENT: This is inexcusable. I particularly wanted this dinner to be . . . You can use the lobster, can't you?

MRS. WENDEL: No, ma'am. It's—uh—I don't know what's the
matter with it. I've never seen lobster like it. I don't think
it's good.

MILLICENT: Not good! You got it at Faulkner's, didn't you?

MRS. WENDEL: Yes, ma'am.

MILLICENT: Well, that's the last time I'll go there. I'll close my
account tomorrow.

MRS. WENDEL: I never liked 'em.

MILLICENT: Well, this is a fine state of things! Where's my dinner? What are we going to do?

MRS. WENDEL: I thought maybe we could send for some crabmeat, all ready, and I'd cook it Newburg.

MILLICENT: But the aspic was so dressy! It looks so smart
when it's served.

MRS. WENDEL: Yes, ma'am. But this one wouldn't have.

MILLICENT: (*A gesture of accepting the inevitable.*) All right.
Send for some crabmeat. I'll tell you what you do. Is Ricci
here?

MRS. WENDEL: (*Hesitatingly*) Yes, ma'am.

MILLICENT: Have him drive over to Schultz's, on Lexington,
and bring it right back.

MRS. WENDEL: Ricci isn't feeling very good.

MILLICENT: What's the matter with him?

MRS. WENDEL: He hurt himself. He slipped and fell, and there
was a thing there, and he—hurt himself. (*A gesture indicating an injury to the face.*)

MILLICENT: Where? When did this happen?

MRS. WENDEL: It was the swinging door. I don't know much
about it. I wasn't there.

(*Dora enters.*)

DORA: Excuse me. Miss Carlotta Vance is calling on Mr. Jordan.

MILLICENT: On the telephone?

DORA: No, ma'am. She's downstairs.

MILLICENT: Downstairs!

MRS. WENDEL: I'll call Schultz up, Mrs. Jordan, and have them
send it right over.

MILLICENT: Yes, do that. Tell them I want it right away. It's an
emergency.

(*Mrs. Wendel goes.*)

Dora, what do you mean—downstairs? Miss Vance is coming to dinner at eight. Are you sure?

DORA: Yes, ma'am. She's calling on Mr. Jordan.

MILLICENT: How did you happen to go to the door? Where's Gustave.

DORA: He isn't feeling very good.

MILLICENT: This is fantastic! What's the matter with him?

DORA: He hurt himself.

MILLICENT: I must be going mad! Why, I never in all my life—

(*Carlotta's voice from the hallway.*)

CARLOTTA: Yoo-hoo! Millicent! Where are you?

MILLICENT: Oh, dear! (*Below her breath. Then raising her voice*) In here, Carlotta! (*A gesture indicating that Dora is to show her the way. But Carlotta does not wait to be ushered.*)

(*Dora goes into the bedroom.*)

CARLOTTA: (*Entering with a rush*) Hello, Millicent darling!

MILLICENT: Carlotta, dear!

CARLOTTA: Oh, what a ducky little room! You don't mind my rushing up, do you? I just popped in to see Oliver.

MILLICENT: Really! How nice! But I don't think he's—

CARLOTTA: Well, I'll wait. Anything to be out of those streets. (*Sinks into a chair.*) Whew!

MILLICENT: (*Appalled to see Carlotta loosen her furs and make preparations for something of a stay.*) Perhaps it's something I could tell Oliver. Sometimes he stops at the club—Dora!

CARLOTTA: No, it's business. I'm afraid I've done something rather naughty. I've come to confess.

MILLICENT: (*As Dora reënters from the bedroom*) Dora, Mr. Jordan hasn't come in, has he?

DORA: No, madam, he hasn't.

CARLOTTA: Oh, could I have a whiskey and soda? Millicent, do you mind? I'm dying!

MILLICENT: Why, of course. Dora, a whiskey and soda for Miss Vance.

(*Dora goes.*)

CARLOTTA: I'm absolutely cracked up. I'm simple depleted. I've been in every office building between the Battery and the Bronx. Do you mind if I take my shoes off?

MILLICENT: No—please do.

(*Carlotta slips her feet halfway out of her pumps, one foot on the floor, the heel out, her knees crossed so that the slipper of the other foot dangles from her toe as she talks.*)

CARLOTTA: Oh! (*A sigh of relief.*) What a city! I left the hotel at eleven this morning, a young and lovely girl, and now look at me! An old woman! I took on ten years just trying to get from the Barclay to Times Square. Then when we reached my building there was a crowd outside worse than Bank Holiday. It took me five minutes to fight my way through it, and it turned out to be a man selling rubberless garters at two for a quarter. I told the taxi driver to wait and he said, "Lady, I ain't got time to wait—I got three children." Then I had a nice, restful luncheon with four lawyers—it was up on the eighty-eighth floor of the Whatsis Building—the Sky Club—a cloud floated right into my soup plate.

MILLICENT: Isn't it awful! But we get used to it.

CARLOTTA: The minute I've seen Oliver I'm going right home and pop myself into bed and not get up until noon. Thank God I don't have to go to some dreadful dinner tonight.

MILLICENT: (*In a tone of ice*) Why—you're coming here.

CARLOTTA: Am I! So I am. How simply enchanting! Why, of course—the Ferncliffes. That means a cozy little game of bridge. Well! I can always stay awake for that.

MILLICENT: But we're going to the theatre.

CARLOTTA: Oh, how delightful! I always enjoy a new play. What are we seeing?

MILLICENT: We're going to see *Say It With Music*.

CARLOTTA: Oh—charming! I thought it was *so* amusing.

MILLICENT: You've seen it?

CARLOTTA: Oh, I don't mind seeing it again. He's very funny— (*A vague gesture*) —with the cigar.

(*Dora enters carrying a large florist's box whose contents are so long that the stems protrude from one end. The cover has been removed; one sees a profusion of roses.*)

DORA: These just came, Mrs. Jordan.

MILLICENT: Ah! (*Takes the box.*) How lovely! (*Tips them toward Carlotta.*) Talisman roses.

CARLOTTA: Exquisite!

MILLICENT: (*Picking up the card envelope*) It's my favorite rose.

(*Reads the card.*) From the Ferncliffes. (*Patronizingly*) Lord and Lady Ferncliffe. How thoughtful of them!

CARLOTTA: Not Bunny! Flowers from Bunny?

MILLICENT: Bunny?

CARLOTTA: Bunny Ferncliffe. All his friends call him Bunny. He *does* look like a rabbit.

MILLICENT: (*A trifle dashed*) Why—I didn't know you knew them.

CARLOTTA: To think of Bunny loosening up for flowers! Why, nobody in London will believe it. Once he dropped a shilling down the grating and he made them dig up Piccadilly to get it.

(*Gustave brings a tray with the whiskey and soda. Down his right cheek and over his left eye are two very noticeable strips of adhesive tape. To offset this his bearing is more magnificent than usual.*)

MILLICENT: Dora, put some water in that tall vase. (*Hands her the flowers.*) And—let me see—I think they'd look well on the console in the drawing room.

DORA: Yes, ma'am. (*Goes to the table toward the rear of the room. Places the box on the table for the moment, picks up the tall vase.*)

GUSTAVE: Shall I mix it for you, madam?

MILLICENT: Why, Gustave! What's happened to your face!

(*Dora, arrested by the question, stands nervously awaiting its outcome.*)

(*At Millicent's tone, Carlotta, too, glances with curiosity at Gustave's face.*)

CARLOTTA: Why, Gustave! It's my Gustave! Gustave, when in the world did— He was my waiter for weeks at the Bauerau-lac in Lucerne. When was it, Gustave? Two winters ago. No—three.

GUSTAVE: (*With an uncomfortable little cough*) Ah—yes, madam.

MILLICENT: How interesting!

CARLOTTA: How is your darling wife and those lovely children? (*Turns to Millicent.*) He's got three of the most— Have you seen them? And his wife!

(*The vase drops from Dora's hands with a thud.*)

MILLICENT: (*Reprovingly*) Dora!

DORA: (*Crushed*) Excuse me—madam. (*She rushes blindly from the room.*)

MILLICENT: Why, what's the matter with her? Gustave, see if anything's the matter.

GUSTAVE: Yes, madam. (*He puts down his tray on a small table near Carlotta; picks up the vase; goes to the other table for the box of flowers.*)

CARLOTTA: Gustave! Bringing those Continental customs over here!

GUSTAVE: Oh, no, madam!

　　(*Oliver enters. He throws a little puzzled backward glance over his shoulder, having passed the fleeing Dora in the hall.*)

OLIVER: (*Sees Carlotta.*) Why, Carlotta! (*To Millicent*) Hello, dear.

　　(*Gustave goes, taking the box of flowers and the vase.*)

MILLICENT: Hello, darling.

CARLOTTA: Well, I've found out about you Big Business Men. Leave your offices at four. What have you been up to for the last two hours?

OLIVER: (*Wanly*) All sorts of mischief.

MILLICENT: (*Goes up to Oliver.*) Darling, you're all mussy. Look at your tie! Been playing squash?

OLIVER: No. No.

MILLICENT: Why don't you try to get a rest before dinner? . . . Oh, Carlotta wants to talk to you.

CARLOTTA: (*Pouring herself a drink, and mixing it*) I shan't be a minute, Oliver dear.

MILLICENT: I'll be tactful and vanish. (*Goes to her bedroom.*)

　　(*Oliver goes to the tray, pours himself a stiff drink, takes it.*)

CARLOTTA: (*Watching this in some surprise*) Mm! Hard day at the office, h'm?

　　(*Oliver wordlessly pats her shoulder, almost as though for companionship.*)

I tried to get you there. Did they tell you?

OLIVER: No. I left early.

CARLOTTA: Then I called up here. They said you'd be in about six. So I took a chance.

OLIVER: What's the matter? Something wrong?

CARLOTTA: Oliver, ducky, you won't be cross with Carlotta, will you? I wanted to ask you first, and I told him, but the man said it had to be today—there was some sort of meeting—and you weren't at your office, so I went ahead. And then I got sort of worried about it—

OLIVER: What are you trying to tell me?

CARLOTTA: Well—Oliver, sweet, poor Carlotta was so stony, and it was such a chance— (*In a rush*) —so I sold my Jordan stock. I hope you don't mind.

OLIVER: (*A moment of blank pause. Then Oliver's mind begins to work, rapidly.*) Who'd you sell it to?

CARLOTTA: (*Fumbling in her handbag*) His name was—he was really quite a sweet fellow—such a charming manner— (*Fishes out the check, scans it*) —Mr. Baldridge—James K. Baldridge.

OLIVER: What'd he look like?

CARLOTTA: Well, do you know, he was really quite handsome. He looked a good deal like Reggie Traymore—you know—around the eyes. You must remember Reggie.

(*Oliver strides quickly to the desk. Opens the phone book, is feverishly finding his number.*)

I hope I didn't do wrong. I did try to reach you. I called the office three times.

(*Oliver starts to dial his number, his gestures quick and terribly decisive.*)

(*Carlotta is silent until he has finished dialing.*)

You said you didn't want to buy it yourself, and there was this nice Mr. Bainbridge with all that beautiful money right in his hand. It's certified.

OLIVER: (*Into the phone*) Is Mr. Kingsberry home? . . . Mr. Oliver Jordan.

CARLOTTA: Oh, dear, you *are* cross with me. I'm just devastated. I never would have done it. I would have gone barefoot and hungry rather than—

OLIVER: (*Sharply, into the phone*) Hello! Is that you, Kingsberry? This is Jordan. Sorry to bother you at home. (*A deep breath. A hand passes over his head. He pulls himself together, reaches for the properly self-controlled opening.*) Did you—uh—have the Satterlee sisters sold their Jordan stock? . . .

You sold it this afternoon. . . . May I ask who bought it? . . . Whitestone? . . . Whitestone. Thank you. Thank you very much! (*Hangs up. Stays a moment, motionless.*)

CARLOTTA: (*A little uncomfortably*) Well, I'll be trotting along. I'm seeing you at dinner. (*Raises her voice.*) Goodbye, Millicent!

OLIVER: What? Oh—I'll take you downstairs, Carlotta.

CARLOTTA: Oh, don't bother.

    (*Millicent appears from the bedroom.*)

    Toodle-oo!

    (*The telephone rings. Oliver makes a half-turn.*)

MILLICENT: I'll go, dear. It's probably for me. . . . See you later, Carlotta.

CARLOTTA: (*Going toward the hall door, with Oliver.*) Now, Oliver, you shouldn't take business so seriously. Smile! Don't be so American. Really, you never used to be . . .

    (*They are gone.*)

MILLICENT: (*At the telephone.*) Yes? . . . This is Mrs. Jordan. . . . Lord Ferncliffe's secretary? Yes? . . . Yes? . . . What's that? . . . But you must be . . . But they can't . . . (*In an absolute frenzy*) But they *can't* go to Florida! They're coming here to dinner. . . . But it's not possible. I'm giving the dinner *for* them . . . They've gone! When? . . . But people don't *do* things like that! . . . But letting me know at this hour—I don't care how sudden it was, you should have let . . .

    (*Paula Jordan enters. She is wearing the costume in which we have seen her at Larry Renault's apartment. She takes off her hat with a little gesture of something like defiance. Stands, tense, waiting for her mother to finish at the telephone.*)

Well, all I can say is, I never heard of such a thing in all my life! Never! (*Bangs the receiver on the hook.*)

PAULA: Mother, I want to talk to you!

MILLICENT: What?

PAULA: It's about Ernest and me! I want to talk to you! I can't—

MILLICENT: Paula, don't bother me now! For pity's sake, don't bother me! I don't want to listen to your silly little—

PAULA: But mother, you don't understand! This is terribly important! Ernest—

MILLICENT: Paula, shut up! Shut up, I tell you! (*Her hand pressed to her head.*) Let me think!

(*Paula is stunned into momentary silence by her mother's tone and words. Millicent stands, seething, her thoughts concentrated on her own problem.*)

(*Into this brief pause Oliver enters quickly from the hall.*)

OLIVER: Millicent, dear, do you mind if I don't go to the theatre? I'm feeling pretty rotten. If I could just go to bed—

MILLICENT: (*As though unable to believe her ears*) What's that you're saying!

OLIVER: I say, I'm feeling pretty rotten— (*His hand on his chest*) —and I'm up against a business thing that—

PAULA: (*Sympathetically*) Oh, Dad, I'm—

MILLICENT: (*In mounting hysteria*) Business thing! At a time like this you talk about a business thing! And feeling rotten. This is a nice time for you to say you're feeling rotten! You come to me with your— (*Turning to Paula*) —and *you*, whimpering about Ernest! Some little lovers' quarrel! I'm expected to listen to Ernest and business and headaches when I'm half out of my mind! Do you know what's happened to *me*! I've had the most hellish day that anybody ever had! No aspic for dinner—and that Vance woman coming in—and Gustave looking like a prize-fighter —and sending for crabmeat—*crabmeat*—and now, on top of everything, do you know what's happened! (*Quivering breath of rage and bafflement as she prepares to launch her final thrust.*) The Ferncliffes aren't coming to dinner! They call up at this hour, those miserable cockneys—they call up and say they've gone to Florida! Florida! And who can I get at this hour! Nobody! I've only got eight people! Eight people isn't a dinner! Who can I get? And you come to me with your idiotic little—*I'm* the one who ought to be in bed! I'm the one who's in trouble! You don't know what trouble is—either one of you!

(*Storms out of the room to her bedroom. Oliver and Paula stand in silence, their eyes following her.*)

CURTAIN

ACT THREE

SCENE I

Kitty Packard's bedroom. The time is 7:30.

Dan and Kitty Packard are dressing for the Jordans' dinner. Kitty is at her dressing table. Dan is in his bedroom adjoining Kitty's. The door is open. The conversation is going on between the two as they dress.

Kitty's dressing table is littered with bottles, jars, atomizers, brushes, toilette articles. Her throat and arms are bare, as she is clad in the slip which belongs under her evening dress. On her feet are mules. She is almost at the point where her dress may be carefully slipped over her head. It is plain that she has spent much time on the details of her toilette. She is marcelled, facialed, manicured, massaged within an inch of her life.

Carefully spread out on the bed is the dress she is to wear at dinner. Vivid satin evening slippers, to be worn with her gown, stand at the foot of the bed, side by side. Her lacy dressing gown hangs over the back of the chair on which she is seated.

At the rise of the curtain, Kitty is giving to her face those last detailed touches—mascara, lipstick, eyebrow pencil. She uses a hand mirror for these operations, but occasionally glances in the larger mirror of the dressing table, in order to get the full effect of her efforts.

From the adjoining room comes Dan's cheerful whistle while dressing. After a moment he appears briefly in the doorway. He, too, is only half dressed for the evening. He has on the trousers of his evening clothes, an undershirt, patent leather shoes. White dress suspenders dangle behind him. His hair is rumpled. He is wiping his hands on a towel, having just finished shaving.

PACKARD: (*As he pops in*) How you coming, Kitten?
    (*Kitty, intent on darkening her eyelashes with mascara, does not answer.*)
  Huh? How you coming?

KITTY: (*Turns, furious, her pencil poised.*) I've told you a million times not to talk to me when I'm doing my lashes!

PACKARD: O.K. Then don't talk to me when I'm shaving! (*He disappears into his bedroom.*)

(*Immediately Tina enters from the hall, at right. She is carrying a small florist's box. From the depths of this she is holding up, for her own admiration, a large cluster of orchids.*)

TINA: I think these are the handsomest ones you ever bought.

KITTY: (*Turning her glare upon Tina*) Will you take those back! I'll tell you when I want 'em!

TINA: Yes'm. (*Goes quickly.*)

KITTY: (*Loudly, after Tina has disappeared*) Put 'em back in the icebox, you nitwit! (*Resumes her carefully detailed work with the eye pencil.*)

(*Dan, in the adjoining room, now bursts into loud song. He is in high spirits. The sound engages Kitty, who suspends her work an instant to glare in the direction of the voice. The song, after its first height, drops a little as Dan reappears in Kitty's bedroom. He is thrusting an arm into the sleeve of his dress shirt.*)

PACKARD: (*As he talks he dons his shirt, fastens the studs, buttons his suspenders.*) Yes, sir, I'd give a thousand bucks to see Jordan's face when he walks into that meeting Monday. There'll be Whitestone and Baldridge each with a big hunk of stock in their fists, and when they begin to count noses— (*A gesture and a whistle indicating that all is over*) —little Oliver can go buy himself a rowboat and start all over again.

KITTY: I guess this is the last time we'll be invited there to dinner. We'd better eat a good one.

PACKARD: How do you mean?

KITTY: He'll be pretty sore, won't he, when he finds out you double-crossed him?

PACKARD: Huh? Jordan'll never know. Didn't I tell you? I stick in Whitestone for president, Baldridge is the treasurer, my name never appears. We can go there to dinner as long as they've got anything to eat.

(*Tina enters from the hall. She is carrying, suspended from its hanger, a magnificent ermine evening wrap. This she suspends from the door by the hook of its hanger.*)

KITTY: You're so smart you're going to land in jail some day. . . . Tina, where the hell are my slippers!

(*Tina scrambles hastily for the slippers, dashes back, kneels at Kitty's feet, removes the mules, puts on the slippers. Kitty is trying on her bracelets, and is holding up her arm to get the effect of the first two or three.*)

PACKARD: Well, they got to go some to get Dan Packard. They've been laying for me ever since the old Montana days. But I got hold of the Copperhead, and I got the Big Emma, and I came to New York and put it over on 'em, and who's got bigger bracelets than you've got!

KITTY: (*To Tina*) Oo! Look out, will you! What you trying to do! Slice my heel off!

PACKARD: And I'm just beginning, Tootsie. Just beginning. Remember what I told you last week?

KITTY: (*Turning back to her dressing table*) I don't remember what you told me a minute ago.

(*Tina goes.*)

PACKARD: Washington. Don't you remember that! How'd you like to be a Cabinet member's wife, mingling with all the other Cabinet members' wives, and senators' wives and ambassadors', and even the President's wife! What'd you think of that! Huh?

KITTY: Nerts!

PACKARD: You don't know what you're talking about. There isn't a woman living wouldn't break her neck to get in with that bunch.

KITTY: (*With definite defiance in her tone*) Yeah! You don't drag me down to that graveyard. I've seen their pictures in the papers—those girlies. A lot of sour-faced frumps with last year's clothes on. Giving medals to Girl Scouts, and pouring tea for a lot of D.A.R.'s, and rolling Easter eggs on the White House lawn. A hell of a lot of fun I'd have! You go live in Washington. I can have a good time right here.

PACKARD: Listen, Stupid, if I get this appointment I'm going to Washington. And if I go to Washington you're going, too. Understand!

KITTY: (*Rising slowly*) Do you mean you're really going to get it?

PACKARD: You're right I am!

KITTY: (*At bay*) I won't go!

PACKARD: Oh, yes, you will!

KITTY: I will not! I won't go 'way from New York! All my friends are in New York!

PACKARD: You'll go if I go!

KITTY: Oh, no, I won't! You can't boss me around! I can yell just as loud as you can.

PACKARD: (*A snarl of rage.*) Oh-h-h! (*Plunges off into his bedroom.*)

(*Kitty stands, victorious, glaring after him. She picks up the buffer from her dressing table, burnishes her nails with vicious energy, glares again after him, seats herself before her mirror, drops the buffer with a little clatter. Sits, doing nothing, thinking a way out of her situation.*)

(*Dan reënters from his bedroom. His shirt has been tucked in, his suspenders fastened. In his right hand he carries his dress collar and white tie. It is with this hand, one finger pointed menacingly, that he gestures toward Kitty.*)

(*Kitty, in queenly contempt following her victory, picks up her hairbrush, ignoring Dan. Begins to smooth her hair.*)

PACKARD: (*Striding back into the room*) You've been acting damn funny lately, my fine lady. And I'm getting good and sick of it.

KITTY: Yeah? And so what?

PACKARD: I'll tell you what. I'm the works around here. I pay the bills. And you take your orders from me.

KITTY: (*Rising, brush hanging idle in her hand*) Who do you think you're talking to? That first wife of yours out in Montana?

PACKARD: You leave her out of this!

KITTY: That poor mealy-faced thing, with her flat chest, that never had the guts to talk up to you!

PACKARD: Shut up, I tell you!

KITTY: Washing out your greasy overalls, cooking and slaving for you in some lousy mining shack! No wonder she died!

PACKARD: God damn you!

KITTY: (*Gesticulating with the hairbrush*) Well, you're not going to get *me* that way! You're not going to step on my face to get where you want to go—you big wind-bag! (*Turns away from him, drops her brush among the bottles and jars on the dressing table.*)

PACKARD: Why, you cheap little piece of scum! I've got a good notion to drop you right back where I picked you up, in the check room of the Hottentot Club, or whatever the dirty joint was.

KITTY: Oh, no, you won't!

PACKARD: And then you can go home and live with your sweet-smelling family, back of the railroad tracks in Passaic. That drunken bum of a father and your jailbird brother that I'm always coming through for. The next time he can go to the pen, and I'll see that he gets there.

KITTY: You'll be there ahead of him—you big crook!

PACKARD: And get this! If that sniveling, money-grubbing mother of yours comes whining around my office once more, I'm going to give orders to have her thrown the hell out of there and right down sixty flights of stairs, so help me God!

(*Tina has entered as Dan is almost at the end of this speech. In her hand is Kitty's evening bag, jeweled and metallic, and containing Kitty's powder compact, lipstick, cigarette case, etc. Finding herself in the midst of a storm, she hesitates briefly.*)

(*Dan, on his last words, and coincident with Tina's entrance, snatches the bag from Tina's hand, dashes it to the floor, gives Tina a shove that sends her spinning out of the room.*)

KITTY: (*White with rage*) You pick that up!

PACKARD: Pick it up yourself!

KITTY: You pick that up!

(*For answer Dan gives the bag a violent kick, sending it into a corner of the room.*)

(*Beside herself.*)

Bracelets, eh? (*She takes off a three-inch jeweled band; drops it onto the floor, and kicks it viciously across the room.*) That shows what you know about women! You think if you give me a bracelet— Why do you give 'em to me! Because you've put over one of your dirty deals and want me to lug these around to show what a big guy you are! You don't do it to make *me* feel good; it's for *you!*

PACKARD: Oh, it is, is it! What about this place and all these clothes and fur coats and automobiles! Go any place you want to, money to throw away! There ain't a wife in the world got it softer than you have! I picked you up out of the gutter, and this is the thanks I get!

KITTY: Thanks for what? Dressing me up like a plush horse and leaving me to sit alone, day after day and night after night! You never take me anywheres! Always playing poker and eating dinner with your men friends—or say you are.

PACKARD: That's a nice crack.

KITTY: You're always either coming in or going out, blowing what a big guy you just been, or going to be. You never think about me, or do any of the nice little things that women like—you never sent me a flower in your life! When I want to wear flowers I got to go out and buy 'em! (*With a gesture toward the door where Tina has lately stood with the orchids.*) What woman wants to buy theirself flowers! You never sit and talk to me, or ask me what I've been doing, or how I am, or anything!

PACKARD: Well, go and find yourself something to do! I ain't stopping you!

KITTY: You bet you ain't! You think I sit home all day looking at bracelets! Hah! Of all the dumb bunnies! What do you think I'm doing while you're pulling your crooked deals! Just waiting for Daddy to come home!

PACKARD: What're you driving at, you little—

KITTY: You think you're the only man I know—you great big noise! Well, you aren't! See! There's somebody that just knowing him has made me realize what a stuffed shirt you are!

PACKARD: Why, you—you—

KITTY: You don't like that, do you, Mr. Cabinet Member! Somebody *else* put over a deal.

PACKARD: Do you mean to tell me you've been putting it over on me with some man!

KITTY: (*She is in for it now. Means to go through with it.*) Yes! And what're you going to do about it, you big gas-bag!

PACKARD: (*Drawing the full breath of the outraged male*) Who is it?

KITTY: (*A purr of pure malice.*) Don't you wish you knew!

PACKARD: (*Seizes her wrist. Kitty screams.*) Tell me who it is!

KITTY: I won't!

PACKARD: Tell me, or I'll break every bone in your body!

KITTY: I won't! You can kill me, and I won't!

PACKARD: I'll find out. I'll— (*Drops her wrist.*) Tina! Tina!

KITTY: She don't know.

> (*There is a moment during which the two stand silent, waiting for the appearance of Tina.*)
>
> (*There comes slowly into the doorway and a step or two into the room a Tina who, in spite of the expression of wondering innocence on her face, has clearly been eavesdropping. She comes forward so that she stands between the two silent figures.*)

PACKARD: Who's been coming to this house?

TINA: Huh?

KITTY: You don't know, do you, Tina?

PACKARD: Shut your face, you slut! (*Turns again to Tina.*) You know, and you're going to tell. What man's been coming to this house?

TINA: (*A frantic shake of the head.*) I ain't seen nobody.

PACKARD: (*Grasps her shoulder. Gives her a little shake.*) Yes, you have! Come on! Who's been here? Who was here last week? Who was here when I went to Washington?

TINA: Nobody. Nobody—only the doctor.

PACKARD: No—no! I don't mean that. What man's been coming here behind my back!

TINA: I ain't seen a soul.

KITTY: Hah! What did I tell you!

PACKARD: (*Looks at her, as though trying to find a way of worming the truth out of her. Decides it is hopeless. Gives her a push toward the door.*) Get the hell out of here!

> (*Kitty stands waiting to see what turn events will take. Packard paces a step this way and that. Wheels suddenly.*)

PACKARD: I'll divorce you. That's what I'll do. I'll divorce you, and you won't get a cent. That's the law for what you've done.

KITTY: You can't prove anything. You've got to prove it first.

PACKARD: I'll prove it. I'll get detectives to prove it. They'll track him down. I'd like to get hold of that guy just once! How I'd like to get my fingers around his neck. And I will, too! I'll get him! I'll kill *him*, and I'll throw you out like an alley cat!

KITTY: Yeah? You'll throw me out. Well, before you throw me out you'd better think twice. Because me, I don't have to get detectives to prove what I've got on you.

PACKARD: You've got nothing on me.

KITTY: No? So you want to go to Washington, do you? And be a big shot, and tell the President where to get off? You want to go in politics. (*Her tone becomes savage.*) Well, I know politics. And I know all about the crooked deals you bragged about. God knows I was bored stiff—but I was listening. Stealing from Delehanty, and the Thompson business, and gypping old man Clarke, and now this Jordan thing. Skinning him out of his eye teeth. When I tell about those it'll raise a pretty stink. Politics! You couldn't get into politics. You couldn't get in anywhere. You couldn't get into the men's room at the Astor!

PACKARD: You snake, you! You poisonous little rattlesnake! I'm through with you. I've got to go to this Ferncliffe dinner, but after tonight we're through. And I wouldn't go there with you, except that meeting Ferncliffe is more important to me than you are. I'm clearing out tonight, get me? Tomorrow I send for my clothes. And you can sit here and get flowers from your soul-mate. We're through. (*Packard stalks off to his own room. Slams the door.*)

   (*Kitty stands looking sullenly after him. Then she drifts over to her dressing table, drops into the chair, regains a measure of composure, picks up her powder puff, dabs at her face with little angry dabs, glances at her right arm, and misses the absent bracelet.*)

KITTY: Tina! Tina!

   (*Tina enters, too promptly.*)

TINA: Yes'm.

KITTY: (*Her tone strangely dulcet*) Tina, would you mind picking up that bracelet. It fell.

TINA: (*Glancing round. Sees it.*) Oh! (*Goes to it. Picks it up. Looks at it admiringly as she brings it to Kitty. She holds it too long, so that Kitty reaches toward it. But Tina, instead of relinquishing it, brings it closer to her own gaze.*) My, it's pretty, ain't it?

KITTY: (*A little uneasily*) Give it to me.

TINA: Look—it just fits me.

KITTY: Give it here, will you!

TINA: You've got so many bracelets, I don't see how you can use 'em all.

KITTY: What are you driving at!

TINA: (*Looking down at it, then up at Kitty with a hard and meaningful eye*) Nothing. Only, I thought with you having so many, maybe you might want to give me one. (*Quickly she picks up the powder puff, begins busily to powder Kitty's back, the bracelet still in her left hand. Kitty's face, as she turns her head slowly toward Tina standing behind her, shows that the sinister meaning of the girl's remark has penetrated.*)

THE LIGHTS DIM

Scene II

Larry Renault's apartment in the Hotel Versailles. It is a quarter to eight.

The room is in considerable disorder—a disorder reflecting the befuddled mind and uncoördinated movements of its occupant. The garments in which we have last seen Larry are now strewn over the room—his trousers on the floor near the bedroom, his shirt over the back of a chair, his shoes in widely separated spots. The black moire dressing gown is draped over the couch. His evening topcoat, folded so as to reveal the glistening black silk lining, is flung over another chair. Two sections of the evening paper are thrown about the room.

The whiskey bottle, now empty, is on the table by the couch, and near it an overturned glass.

The cushions on couch and chairs are awry, and one of them has fallen to the floor. One or two chairs are out of their previous positions.

Larry Renault himself, in full evening dress—tails, white waistcoat, white tie, silk hat on the side of his head—is walking up and

*down the room impatiently. About his walk is a sort of wavering
uncertainty that denotes a degree of intoxication.*

*Pushes up his left sleeve an inch or two to look at his wrist watch;
sees that it is not there; remembers why. Makes for the telephone to
ascertain the time.*

LARRY: (*His speech is slightly slurred.*) Hello! . . . Hello! . . .
What time is it? . . . Time—*time!* What time is it? . . .
Seven forty-five. Thanks. (*Hangs up noisily. Paces the room
with increased impatience. Encounters a pillow on the floor,
kicks it savagely so that it lands in another part of the room.*)
   (*The telephone rings.*)
(*Eagerly he removes the receiver.*) Hello! Yes, this is Mr. Renault. . . . Yes, I got it. Your man brought it up to me. . . .
Listen, my good fellow. I'm not accustomed to being
dunned for hotel bills. I'm a very busy man—my secretary
usually attends to these things—but he's in California, at the
moment. You'll get your money. . . . You'll get it when it
suits my convenience. (*Hangs up. Resumes his striding.*)
   (*The sound of the door buzzer finds him in a far corner of
the room. He wheels in the direction of the door. Shouts.*)
Come in!
   (*Max Kane comes nimbly into the room, with Jo Stengel
following slowly some paces behind him. Jo Stengel is
about sixty; his hair is well grayed; he is kindly-looking;
time has refined his features; his eyes are shrewd, his man-
ner quiet; yet there is about him the indefinable air of the
showman.*)
MAX: Liberty Hall, eh?
LARRY: Where the hell have you been! I told you I was—
   (*Max warns him with a gesture of the right hand as, with
the left, he impressively ushers in Jo Stengel.*)
MAX: I brought up Mr. Stengel, Larry. Meet Larry Renault,
Mr. Stengel.
LARRY: (*A complete change of manner.*) Oh—how are you, Mr.
Stengel.
STENGEL: (*They shake hands.*) Mr. Renault.
LARRY: Well, this is quite an occasion. Meeting of two celebri-
ties. We ought to have the newsreel men here.

(*Max is removing his coat.*)

STENGEL: Yes. (*His eye takes in Larry's costume, including the high hat, which is still on his head.*) Of course, I didn't realize it was a full-dress affair. I just came as I was.

MAX: (*Max appreciates this with a laugh which breaks off rather sharply as his quick eye spots the empty whiskey bottle. He edges unobtrusively toward it, talking, as he goes, with a fine air of carelessness.*) Mr. Renault's got a dinner date with some of his Park Avenue friends. (*Furtively picks up the bottle, shielding it behind his back, gets rid of it behind the convenient couch.*) These big picture boys, they're pretty social. (*Having accomplished his purpose, he turns upon the other two a radiantly glassy smile.*)

STENGEL: Yes. I've heard.

LARRY: They'll wait. Sit down, Mr. Stengel. Don't you want to take your coat off?

MAX: (*Trots hastily over to Stengel.*) Sure he does. Take your coat off, Mr. Stengel.

STENGEL: (*Sitting*) I've only got a minute. I got a classy dinner date too—I got to meet a hamburger, with onions, at Dinty Moore's.

(*Stengel safely seated, Max returns to the couch, and sits down. Larry Renault stays on his feet, pacing as he talks.*)

(*Max laughs his sycophantic laugh.*)

LARRY: I don't care much for those chophouse places. Matter of fact, there isn't a decent restaurant in New York. Take this hotel—class of people they've got, you'd think—but it's terrible. I'm not going to eat here any more.

STENGEL: You don't say!

LARRY: (*Warming to the subject*) You really have to go to Europe for good cooking. The Continent, I mean. English cooking! Foul! But Paris! There's a little place on the Left Bank—nobody knows about it. The way they cook kidneys—their *rognons aux beurre* are absolutely marvelous! And the Restaurant Royale in the Hague! (*Wafts a kiss into the air, very Gallic, in memory of that delectable meal.*) But the most exquisite food I ever ate was—guess where? (*To Stengel.*)

STENGEL: (*Very promptly*) I give up.

LARRY: A little place called Ming Chow's, in Pekin. Better than when I dined with the Emperor—I want to tell you about that, some time.

STENGEL: Some other time, maybe—

LARRY: Of course, most of the time, I carried my own chef. That's really the only way to travel.

STENGEL: (*Rising*) Well, look, Mr. Renault, I haven't got an awful lot of time—

MAX: Yeah, Larry. Suppose we get down to brass tacks.

LARRY: All right, my good fellow. . . . Well, Stengel, you're going to produce this play, h'm? And you want me to act in it?

STENGEL: (*A bit taken aback*) Well, I— (*His alarmed eye goes to Max.*)

MAX: (*Hurriedly*) This is just getting acquainted, Larry. (*With his spurious good nature, to Stengel*) You see, he's crazy to play the part.

LARRY: Just a minute! Let's get this straight. I understood from Mr. Kane, here, that you wanted to know if I would be willing to portray the beach-comber in this thing.

STENGEL: Wait a minute! Not so fast, there.

MAX: (*Comes quickly between the two.*) Now, now! What's the difference which one is—*he* wants to *do* it—and you *want* him to do it—so what's the difference—

LARRY: A lot of difference.

MAX: Now, Larry!

LARRY: In the first place, if I decide to accept this part—and I don't say I will—it'll have to be built up.

MAX: There's the actor for you! No matter how good the part is, right away they want it built up.

STENGEL: Built up! The fella's got one scene, and they find him dead on the beach. This ain't a spiritualism play.

LARRY: No? Well, you're forgetting one thing, Stengel. Don't forget I'm Larry Renault.

MAX: Larry, for God's sake!

LARRY: Shut up! Now listen, Stengel. I'm a Name, and I know it. And so do you. And I'm not going to go on and play second fiddle to any cheap English ham.

MAX: (*In a frantic half-whisper*) Larry!

LARRY: (*Waving Max away*) Eight thousand a week—that's

what I got. And I was going to get ten—only the talkies
came in. So don't think you're doing me a favor, giving me
a part in your ratty little play—because *I'm* doing *you* one.

(*Max, desperate, turns away.*)

STENGEL: I think maybe we're keeping you from your dinner,
Mr. Renault. (*Turns to depart.*)

MAX: Listen, Jo, he doesn't mean—

LARRY: Oh, yes, I do. And just because it's Mr. Jo Stengel
doesn't mean a thing to me. I'm still good. I'm better than
I ever was. See that! (*Runs his hands down his slim flanks.*)
And that! (*Indicates the famous profile.*) Give me the right
part and you'll have the biggest hit that even Mr. Jo Stengel
ever produced.

STENGEL: (*Quietly and conclusively*) Good-night, Mr. Renault.

LARRY: Oh, I see. You're doing a second-rate show. You don't
want real artists. Well, your English ham will give you what
you want. (*Grasps Stengel's arm*) Listen to me, old-timer.
I'm drunk, and I know I'm drunk. But I know what I'm
saying.

(*Stengel breaks from Larry's grasp.*)

MAX: For God's sake, Mr. Stengel!

STENGEL: It's all right, Max. I'll see you tomorrow.

MAX: I'll take you to the elevator.

(*Stengel goes, followed by Max.*)

LARRY: (*Who has continued to talk through the others' speeches*) I
wouldn't be in your rotten show! I didn't come to your office, did I! Not Larry Renault! You came to see me. And
d'you know why! Because I'm an important artist, and
you're a cheap pushcart producer! (*Leans through the door to
shout his final insult.*) Pushcart! (*For a second Renault hangs
precariously in the doorway, glaring after the departing figures down the hall. Sways a little, then lurches back into the
room, coming to a wavering halt at about the middle. He is
muttering a little to himself.*)

(*As Max reënters, Larry is looking toward the door. Max
comes in swiftly, slams the door behind him, fixes Larry with
an eye of utter fury.*)

(*There is a moment's silence as the two men stare at each
other.*)

MAX: You—drunken—fool! Ha! I bring him up here! I go down on my hands and knees to do it. And you!— God, I can't believe it! I can't believe that any man— (*Mutters "God damn fool" under his breath as he crosses the room.*) Well, that's that! (*Snatches up his hat and coat from the couch.*)

LARRY: (*As Max goes toward the door*) Just a minute! I've got something to say to you, too! Telling him I was crazy to play that part! Yessing him all over the lot! You know what I think! It's you got the play away from Baumann and gave it to Stengel! It's you did me out of the part! You double-dealing Kike! I've been suspicious of you all along! You're in with the managers! You've been taking my money and working for them!

MAX: (*Very low—in a cruel level tone*) You don't say! Working for the managers, eh? And taking your money? Me! That you're into for five hundred bucks—in touches. All right. If you think I've been lying to you all this time, you're going to get the truth now.

> (*A deprecatory wave of the hand from Larry; a sneering sound and a half-turn away.*)

Renault, you're through.

LARRY: (*Turns slowly toward him*) Get out!

MAX: I'll get out. And stay out. But get this first. I never worked so hard to put anybody over as I did you. You think I told you all the things I tried! No. Because I couldn't come to you and tell you what they said. I was too sorry for you.

LARRY: (*A little fearfully*) You were sorry for *me*!

MAX: Vaudeville! Why, every time I walked into the booking office they leaned back and roared. Called me Maxie, the grave-snatcher. And the radio—remember I told you I hadn't seen the right fellow! I saw him. Only he saw me first. Last night I sent another wire to the Coast. I knew it was no use, but I sent it anyway. Do you want to see the answer? (*Drawing it out of his pocket.*)

LARRY: (*Backing away, as though from something dreadful*) No.

MAX: (*Reads*) "When we are in the market for extras we will let you know." (*Crushes the telegram into a ball; throws it at Larry's feet.*)

LARRY: Trying to throw a scare into me.

MAX: No. I'm just telling you the truth. Do you know what

Stengel said, out in the hall, there? He said, "Why, he's a wreck of a man." Of course, you never were an actor, but you did have looks. Well, they're gone. And you don't have to take my word for it. Look in the mirror. They don't lie. Take a good look. (*Comes closer to him, while Larry retreats.*) Look at these pouches under your eyes. Take a look at those creases. You got wattles under your chin. (*His taunting hand is up, pointing at this, at that. Larry slaps it down like a frightened child.*) You sag like an old woman. (*A gesture indicates the face of the man before him.*) Get a load of yourself. (*Turns and walks a few jaunty steps toward the door, claps his hat on his head.*) What's the matter! Afraid! You ain't seen nothin' yet! Wait till you start tramping round to offices, looking for a job. No agent'll handle you. Wait till you start sitting in anterooms, hours and hours. Giving your name to office boys who never heard of you. You're through, Renault. You're through in pictures, and plays, and vaudeville, and radio, and everything! You're a corpse, and you don't know it. Go get yourself buried. (*Goes, closing the door decisively behind him.*)

(*Larry stands, as though dazed, swaying a little. He passes a hand over his head, the hat falls off with the gesture, it drops to the floor, Larry does not heed it. He looks about the room, vaguely, his eye falls on the wall mirror, he lunges swiftly toward it, stands before it, peering intently at the reflection of his own face, tries to smooth away, with his fingers, the bags under his chin and beneath his eyes. There they are. He turns away, with something like a shudder. He advances heavily, a step or two, stands. With his handkerchief he wipes the cold sweat from beneath his chin, from his upper lip, from his clammy brow. He espies the crumpled telegram on the floor. Lunges toward that, picks it up, smooths it. A quick look, throws it down, as though sickened.*)

(*A noisy rapping of knuckles on the hall door. As Larry half turns toward the sound, Eddie, the bellboy, enters. He is carrying the silver frame, wrapped in its newspaper, an untidy bundle.*)

(*Eddie's walk is a scuffling swagger that carries with it unmistakable disrespect. He tosses his bundle onto the first chair handy. At the same time he plunges his hand in his pocket,*)

*brings out the cuff links and the belt buckle, which he throws
on the table.)*

EDDIE: They don't want this junk. They wouldn't give me
nothing on it.

LARRY: (*Dazedly*) What? . . . Why—that's a silver frame! The
buckle's solid gold!

EDDIE: All right—*you* take 'em. I lugged 'em to every pawn-
shop on Sixth Avenue. (*Starts to slouch out of the room.*)

LARRY: You little liar! You never took them any place!

EDDIE: (*Turns, his expression ugly.*) Say! Who you calling liar!
What do I get out of all this—you down-and-out ham!

LARRY: You filthy little rat, how dare you talk to me like that!

EDDIE: (*Contemptuously*) O.K.! (*A wave of the hand. He turns
to leave.*)

LARRY: No, no! Wait! I didn't mean that. I didn't mean to call
you that. I'm sorry. Listen! I've got to have some liquor.
I'm sick. You lay it out for me, and I'll pay it back to you.

EDDIE: What kind of a sucker do you think I am!

LARRY: No, no! I've got to have it! I've got to! I'll pay you
back. I'll pay you back tomorrow.

EDDIE: Tomorrow! You won't be here tomorrow.

LARRY: What?

EDDIE: Aw, boloney! (*He goes. Closes the hall door.*)

(*From the sidewalk far below, and muffled by the closed
windows, comes the sound of a hurdy-gurdy rolling out a
sprightly sentimental air.*)

(*This penetrates his dazed mind a little. He stands. Then,
desperate for a drink, he searches the corner for the bottle. He
finds it where Max has tucked it behind the couch, eagerly
holds it up in the hope of finding just a mouthful remaining.
There is nothing. He drops the bottle on the floor.*)

(*The sound of the door buzzer.*)

(*Larry wheels in terror.*)

LARRY: Who's that!

(*The sound of a key in the lock. Fitch, the hotel manager,
and Hatfield, the assistant manager, come into the room.*)

(*Fitch, in his business suit and eyeglasses, is the solid man of
affairs. Hatfield, garbed in the assistant's uniform of cutaway and striped trousers, defers to his superior. Hatfield
carries a sheaf of cards, one for each floor, on which are*

specified the hotel rooms and their occupants. In the other hand is a pencil. The two advance well into the room, as though taking possession, though their manner is, to the end, polite.)

FITCH: How do you do, Mr. Renault? I haven't had the pleasure of meeting you before. Though you've been with us for some time. I'm Mr. Fitch, the manager.

LARRY: (*Vaguely*) Oh, yes.

FITCH: I believe you know my assistant, Mr. Hatfield?

LARRY: (*Wets his lips.*) Yes.

FITCH: (*A little apologetic laugh.*) Mr. Renault, we find ourselves in an awkward predicament. We've just had a communication from some very old clients of our—Mr. and Mrs. Sherman Montgomery—possibly you know them. They've been making this their home for many years—every winter. And have always occupied this particular suite. You know how people are. Nothing'll do but these rooms. They say it's like home to them. Now, we've just been notified that they're coming in tomorrow. Tomorrow—is that right, Mr. Hatfield?

HATFIELD: Yes, sir. Tomorrow afternoon.

FITCH: Well, there you are. Under the circumstances I am afraid we must ask you for these rooms.

LARRY: Oh! Well—what other rooms have you got for me?

FITCH: That's just the trouble. We're terribly full up. The Horse Show, and— Mr. Hatfield, is there any place we can put Mr. Renault?

HATFIELD: (*A great show of consulting his slips.*) I'm—afraid—not, Mr. Fitch. (*A little embarrassed laugh.*) It looks as though everything is taken.

FITCH: (*Throws out his hands in a gesture of helplessness.*) I'm sorry, Mr. Renault—but of course old customers have to be taken care of.

LARRY: That's—that's all right. Funny, I was just about to tell your office I was leaving. Some friends of mine—Palm Beach —private car— When do you want me to—

FITCH: No hurry. Shall we say—tomorrow morning?

LARRY: (*Thickly*) All right.

FITCH: We'd be very glad to have one of our people come in and pack your things tonight. You're probably pretty busy.

LARRY: No. No, I'll—I'll tend to it.

FITCH: Shall we say—noon tomorrow, Mr. Renault?

(*Larry merely nods his assent.*)

Thank you very much. So sorry to have inconvenienced you in this way. (*Clears his throat.*)

(*They give the effect of a little procession as they leave, Fitch first, Hatfield following.*)

(*Throughout this scene the hurdy-gurdy music has continued, faintly.*)

(*Larry stands in the centre of the room, a sagging figure. He stares at the window. You see the thought come into his mind. He strides straight in the window, jerks it open. The full rollicking sound of the hurdy-gurdy comes up. He leans out. A fresh thought. He runs back into the room, scoops the scattered coins that have been thrown on the table into the palm of his hand, wraps them into a scrap of the crumpled telegram which he picks up from the floor, tearing off a corner of it to do so, runs back to the window, leans far out, throws the little ball of coins into the street below.*)

LARRY: Seventeen cents!

(*A slow leaning forward to look into the street below. A shuddering withdrawal. The music stops. He slams the window shut. An indrawn breath that is almost a sob of hysteria. He lurches to the mantel shelf, rests his head on his arm, leans there a moment, turns, leaning his weight against the mantelpiece, facing the room, his desperate gaze on the floor. His gaze encounters the gas logs. An idea is born in his mind. He bends forward, looks fixedly at the gas logs and the little knob which serves to turn on the gas. Swiftly he stoops and tries it. There is heard the hiss of escaping gas. He turns it off, in a kind of triumph.*)

(*A quick look around the room. Runs to the outer door, turns the lock, looks at the crack under the door, whips off his dress coat, stuffs it hurriedly under the crack. He now runs to the bedroom door, closes it, finds his afternoon trousers on the floor, spreads them close to the crack beneath the door. A look at the windows. Uses his evening topcoat to plug up one of these, a few cushions for the other. Strips the heavy seat cushions off the couch and one deep armchair, as he needs them.*)

(*Another survey. He sees Paula's photograph. Leaning over the desk he scribbles a few lines, folds the paper, leans it against her picture. Again gazes around, sees the telephone, dashes to it.*)

(*His voice a croak.*)

Hello! . . . I don't want to be disturbed for a while. . . . I'm—busy. . . . I say, I don't want any calls till I let you know.

(*Summoning his forces again. Surveys all the work he has done. Finds it good. In his survey he comes again to the mirror. His vanity asserts itself. He must make a good exit. Smooths his hair, straightens his crumpled collar. Doesn't like the idea of shirt sleeves. His coat is serving as stuffing for a door. He picks his dressing gown as the thing to wear, dons it, ties it, looks at himself. Backs to the chair, still looking at himself, turning his head this way and that to decide which side of his famous profile is more nearly perfect.*)

(*Sits in the chair. Rehearses his position. It isn't quite right artistically, he decides. He rises and turns out all the lights except one floor lamp which throws a glow over the chair in which he is to sit. There. That is better. A last summoning of courage. You see him pulling together the remnants of his manhood. A deep inhalation and exhalation. A rush to the gas fixture. The sharp hiss as it is turned on. He settles himself in the armchair. The chair is so turned that we see the back of his head, a glimpse only of the famous profile, one arm over the side of the chair, as he has previously rehearsed his position.*)

THE LIGHTS DIM

SCENE III

The Jordan drawing room, eight o'clock. It is a large, gracious, and rich room, well balanced, and furnished with that distinction which comes of the combination of the best of the old and the new. At one side is a fine old marble mantel and fireplace. On the other two semi-cylindrical niches in which stand twin vases holding graceful sprays of flowers. The only opening which we see is at the back, centre; a large arched doorway opening into a foyer. Two steps lead up from the drawing room to the foyer.

Against the back wall of the foyer, facing the drawing room, can be seen, through the archway, the figures of three Hungarian musicians in their red coats.

As the curtain rises the musicians are near the finish of their first number, though no one is in the room to hear them. The Jordans' dinner guests have not yet begun to arrive; the host and hostess are not yet downstairs.

After a moment Millicent Jordan enters. She is in evening dress, and in her haste is fastening and adjusting her pearl necklace, her arms upraised, as she appears. She glances at the musicians as she passes them grouped in the foyer, nods her recognition, and stands on the top step leading down to the drawing room, surveying the scene with the critical eye of the hostess. She comes down into the room, moves an ash tray here, a cigarette box there; adjusts a flower spray at a more pleasing angle, moves a chair an inch or two. She turns back to the foyer just as the musicians are finishing their selection, stands a moment awaiting the concluding bars.

The Leader of the musicians, violin and bow in hand, rises and bows. The other two follow his example.

MILLICENT: That's very nice. But do you mind—not quite so loud? You see, the people will be right in here— (*Indicates the drawing room*) —talking. After we've gone down to dinner you can play louder.
> (*The Leader bows his assent. The other two nod. They sit again as Millicent goes. Before they begin their next number there is the usual preliminary violin bow scraping, adjusting of chairs, mopping of brows, clearing of throats.*)
> (*They begin another number, softly.*)
> (*For a few seconds the music goes on while the room is again empty. Hattie Loomis appears. She gives an interested little glance over her shoulder at the musicians as she passes into the drawing room.*)

HATTIE: (*After a little survey of the room, looks back toward the doorway through which she has just entered.*) Ed! Ed! Where are you?

ED: (*Speaking as he appears in the doorway*) I'm coming.
(*Ed Loomis would be one of those insignificant grayish-looking men if it were not that he is distinguished a trifle by his air of irascibility, due, probably, to faulty digestion and the world in which he finds himself. He is wearing a dinner coat and black tie—the one man, it later turns out, who is not in full evening dress.*)

HATTIE: She's got music.

ED: (*Very cross*) I hear it.

HATTIE: Now, Ed! Are you going to be like that all evening! You ought to be glad to help Millie out. It isn't going to be so terrible.

ED: Not so terrible! Calling up at quarter to seven, just when we're sitting down to dinner—and I got to get into this uniform and come over here and meet a bunch of fatheads I don't want to know, and eat a lot of fancy food I can't digest, and miss that Greta Garbo picture I've been waiting two months for up at Eighty-sixth Street!

HATTIE: You can see that any time.

ED: I can not! I waited all this time because it was two dollars downtown, and it's only *at* the Eighty-sixth one night, and God knows where it'll be tomorrow night.

HATTIE: Don't you want to meet Larry Renault? That's better than going to a movie.

ED: Larry Renault! That has-been!

HATTIE: And Carlotta Vance!

ED: And Jenny Lind—is *she* coming?

HATTIE: Now, Ed, Millie does a lot of things for us. . . . Besides, who can you get at quarter to seven but relatives?

ED: All right. I'm a relative and I'm here.

HATTIE: Wonder why she isn't down. I think I'll run up and see her.

ED: (*Lifting the cover of a cigarette box*) I don't suppose they've got a Lucky.

HATTIE: (*As she goes through the doorway*) Oo-ooh! Where are you, Millie? Upstairs?
(*Ed goes from cigarette box to cigarette box, lifting each lid, inspecting the contents, and slamming the lid down again with increasing irritation. Failing in his search, he turns to the orchestra.*)

ED: One of you boys got a Lucky?

(*One of the men, without breaking his rhythm, tosses him a package of Luckies. Ed removes one cigarette, tosses the pack back, and comes back down into the room, lighting his cigarette as he does so.*)

(*Millicent and Hattie reënter. Millicent's voice is heard just a moment before the two women actually appear.*)

MILLICENT: —and then, on top of everything, the Ferncliffes not coming—I never had such a day in all my life! . . . Hello, Ed. . . . It's all I can do to stand up.

HATTIE: I can imagine.

ED: Where's Oliver?

MILLICENT: He'll be down. He's got a headache, or something.

ED: Me, too.

(*Dan and Kitty Packard appear in the doorway. They give the effect of being in full panoply. Dan's linen seems more expansive, more glistening, his broadcloth richer, than that ordinarily seen. Kitty's dress is the ultimate word in style and a bit beyond that in cut. When later she has occasion to turn her back one modifies one's first impression of the front décolletage, which now seems almost prudish.*)

MILLICENT: (*In that exaggerated tone of the very social hostess*) How nice! It's so lovely to see you!

PACKARD: How-d'you-do, Mrs. Jordan! (*Coming down into the room. Kitty has taken his proffered arm.*) This is indeed a pleasure. You know Mrs. Packard, I believe?

MILLICENT: Of course I do. So pleased to meet you again, Mrs. Packard. So sweet of you to come.

KITTY: (*Who has learned the right answer*) So—uh—so nice of you to have me.

PACKARD: (*To Kitty*) See! We're on time, Sugar! (*To Millicent*) She thought we were going to be late.

KITTY: No, I didn't, sweetheart.

MILLICENT: (*Who has been hovering on the verge of the necessary introductions*) Mrs. Packard, may I present my sister and my brother-in-law—Mr. and Mrs. Loomis. This is Mr. and Mrs. Packard.

KITTY: I'm pleased to meet you.

PACKARD: Hello, there! Glad to know you!

HATTIE: How do you do?

ED: How are you?

PACKARD: Y'know, for a minute there I had you wrong. I figured maybe you were Ferncliffe.

ED: You were close. I'm pinch-hitting for him.

(*Hattie, standing next to him, gives him a vicious nudge.*)

(*Ed turns to glare at her over his shoulder.*)

What's the matter?

MILLICENT: (*A shade too glibly, even for an experienced hostess.
And casting on brother-in-law Ed, meanwhile, a fleeting but
malevolent glance*) Yes, isn't it too bad? Lord Ferncliffe was
taken desperately ill late this afternoon. Neuritis. The doctors said he must have sunshine.

PACKARD: Say, that's too— (*He gets the full import of her remark.*) Wait a minute! Do you mean he's not coming?

MILLICENT: Oh, impossible. They rushed him right down to
Florida on a special train.

KITTY: (*A high shriek of malicious laughter, in a single note, as
she hears Packard thus defeated.*) Ha! (*Immediately smothers
the sound with her palm against her mouth.*)

(*Packard wheels on her in soundless rage. The others, startled, look at her inquiringly. Kitty turns the sound into a
patently false cough.*)

MILLICENT: Would you like a glass of water?

(*Kitty shakes her head in refusal.*)

PACKARD: She don't need anything.

HATTIE: (*Coming to the rescue*) I don't care for Florida, do
you? Have you ever been to Florida?

MILLICENT: I love it—but we're not going down this winter.
(*To the Packards*) Are you?

KITTY: (*In a coo*) No, I don't think we are. (*To Packard*) Are
we going to Florida this winter, sweetheart?

PACKARD: (*Meaningly*) I wouldn't count on it if I were you.

MILLICENT: I shall miss it so. It's so wonderful, not to think
about anything, just to lie all day in the sun.

KITTY: But you got to look out you don't blister. My skin's
awful delicate, I don't dare expose it. (*Turns, as she speaks
this line, so that the extremely low-cut back of her gown is in
full view for the first time.*)

(*Ed casts a comprehensive look at the view.*)

MILLICENT: Who *is* going down this winter, I wonder?

PACKARD: Nobody, I guess. Looks as though the sailfish are going to get the vacation this year.

(*There is a ripple of polite laughter at this little sally. Under cover of the merriment Oliver Jordan enters, stands for a moment on the top step, and then comes down into the room. There is about him an air of detachment—he seems to be no part of the room and its occupants.*)

(*For a moment he is unnoticed by the others, who are gathered together in a little group.*)

MILLICENT: Yes, we've fallen upon queer days, haven't we? Goodness knows where any of us will be this time next year.

PACKARD: Oh, America will come out on top.

ED: Hello, Oliver.

PACKARD: Why, here's Oliver! (*Goes to him with a great show of heartiness and good fellowship.*) Well, how's the boy? Say, I've been wanting to call you up!

OLIVER: How are you? Hello, Hattie. How are you?

HATTIE: I'm fine.

OLIVER: Hello, Ed.

MILLICENT: You've met my husband, haven't you, Mrs. Packard?

OLIVER: Yes, indeed. It's delightful to see you again.

KITTY: Yeah.

PACKARD: (*To Oliver*) You're looking great! How've you been? How's that pain of yours? Better? Did you take that lemon juice?

OLIVER: Yes. Fine—fine!

(*Dr. Talbot and Lucy enter.*)

MILLICENT: Hel-lo! *Darlings!* So glad to see you. Lucy, what a sweet dress!

LUCY: Hello, dear.

TALBOT: Millicent! You're looking very lovely.

MILLICENT: (*Looking about to see where introductions are in order*) Let me see—

LUCY: (*Catching sight of familiar faces*) Hello, Hattie. How are you, Oliver?

(*Hattie and Oliver return Lucy's greetings. At the same time Dr. Talbot and Ed have briefly greeted each other.*)

MILLICENT: (*Performing the necessary introductions*) Lucy— Mrs. Packard. This is Mrs. Talbot, Mrs. Packard. Mr. Packard.

Mrs. Packard, I don't believe you've met Dr. Talbot. Mr. Packard.

(*There is a murmur of "We've met." "Yes, I know Dr. Talbot," from Talbot and Kitty. Packard's voice booms out above theirs.*)

PACKARD: Go on! He's her father confessor. Hello, Doc! (*Goes to him, grasps his hand, claps him on the shoulder.*) How's the old medico! Haven't seen you round my house lately. What's the matter? Patient get well on you?

TALBOT: Yes, she's getting along very well without me—aren't you, Mrs. Packard?

KITTY: I get along better when you're looking after me.

LUCY: (*Not unkindly*) You mustn't become too dependent on Jo. He might fail you.

(*The party now breaks up into three groups: Dan and Dr. Talbot engage in conversation which is dominant in tone. Each group speaks in a natural tone of conversation. An occasional sentence comes clearly out of the babble.*)

PACKARD: Hey, Doc! Saw your name on the members' list out at my golf club. I didn't know you belonged.

TALBOT: Oh, I've been a member there for years. Don't get a chance to play much.

PACKARD: We ought to have a game some time. What d'you go round in?

TALBOT: I'm not very good. Lucky to break a hundred.

PACKARD: Say, that's just about my speed! How about tomorrow afternoon?

TALBOT: Afraid I haven't the time for golf. If I have an hour or two I generally jump on a horse—do a little riding.

PACKARD: Ride? Say, I'll ride with you! You're talking to an old cowboy! Well, what do you think of that!

MILLICENT: Well, Mrs. Packard, and what have you been doing with yourself lately?

KITTY: Oh, I don't know. Nothing much.

MILLICENT: Have you seen any of the new plays?

KITTY: Sure. I go to all the shows.

MILLICENT: We're taking you to see *Say It With Music* tonight. I hope you haven't seen it.

KITTY: I saw it twice.

ED: Where'd you say we're going tonight?

MILLICENT: *Say It With Music.* They say it's so amusing.

HATTIE: Lucy, I never see you any more. Why don't you call me?

LUCY: Why, I love being with you, Hattie. I always think everybody's busier than I am.

OLIVER: Isn't it insane? We never see the people we want to in this New York. The weeks go by, and—

HATTIE: Remember those grand days in that big Murray Hill house of yours?

LUCY: We did have fun when we were kids.

HATTIE: It's positively frightening. You can see life getting the best of you.

OLIVER: Give it the best. What's the difference?

PACKARD: (*Turns to the others, with his genial roar.*) I've found a buddy here! Hey! Mrs. Talbot!

LUCY: Yes, Mr. Packard?

PACKARD: Just discovered your husband and I have got a lot in common.

LUCY: That's so nice. (*Moving toward Packard as she talks*) Why don't you and Mrs. Packard have dinner with us next week? How would Thursday suit you? There's an idea! I want you all to come to dinner at our house next Thursday.

(*There is a murmur of pleasure from the group. "That'll be lovely!" "Oh, so nice!" "We'd be delighted!"*)

ED: (*To Hattie, under cover of this general outburst. With more than his usual irritability*) We're going to see *Say It With Music.*

HATTIE: Well?

ED: We *saw* it!

LUCY: And the Ferncliffes! I'd love to ask the Ferncliffes. Where are they, Millicent?

MILLICENT: My dear, didn't I tell you? Poor dear Bunny— that's what we call Ferncliffe—was taken desperately sick this afternoon, and they had to whirl him down South to save his life.

(*A mildly surprised look from Oliver.*)

LUCY: Why, how ghastly!

TALBOT: What was the trouble?

(*Carlotta Vance appears in the doorway. A resplendent figure. And then, for good measure, a Pekinese dog, which she carries under one arm. She comes straight on into the room, talking as she appears*)

CARLOTTA: Millicent darling, do forgive me. I *am* so sorry. He *wouldn't* stay home. He cried and cried. I just *had* to bring him. He's so spoiled since I brought him to America. Aren't you, Mussolini? He won't be a bit of trouble. He's as good as gold. He'll just sit under my chair as quiet as a mouse. You'll never know he's there. Just throw him a bit of lobster.

MILLICENT: Isn't he sweet? Carlotta, have you met—

CARLOTTA: What do you think of Ferncliffe! Isn't Bunny a swine! Running off to Florida and ruining your whole dinner. (*A sweeping gesture that tosses the other guests into the discard.*) You know, I left here, and went straight to my hotel, and there was his telegram—"Off on a fishing trip—can't you come down—I love your America—never felt so well in my life—Molly and I expect you—telegraph us Palm Beach. Bunny."

(*Lucy and Hattie plunge valiantly forward to cover Millicent's discomfiture. Their voices are high and clear. They speak simultaneously.*)

LUCY: (*In the general direction of Packard*) Have you seen that wonderful German picture at the Europa? Really, they have the most marvelous way of doing things! And their attention to detail—no matter how small the part!

CARLOTTA: Oliver darling, you haven't said a word to me. Aren't you glad to see me?

OLIVER: (*Gracefully*) You know I love you, Carlotta.

CARLOTTA: Then you're not cross with me. (*Turning to Packard*) You'd have thought I'd done something terrible. Just because I sold my Jordan stock. I was stony broke, and a man came along and made me the most wonderful offer, right out of the blue—well, I grabbed it! That wasn't so terrible, was it?

OLIVER: What do *you* think, Packard? Was that so terrible? (*His gaze is fixed on Packard.*)

PACKARD: Well, business is business. Every fellow's got to look out for himself. That's the kind of world it is.

CARLOTTA: It must be wonderful to be a sheltered woman. A man to look after you, so you never have to worry for yourself.

PACKARD: Say, I think that ought to be a cinch for you! (*Laughs at his own witticism.*)

LUCY: The trouble with a shelter is that in a storm it sometimes falls down around your ears.

OLIVER: I suppose we all dream of being something we're not. There was a time when I thought I was Bernard Shaw. (*A little laugh from the group.*)

LUCY: And then you ate a beefsteak? (*Another polite round of laughter.*)

HATTIE: (*Making her leap in the direction of Kitty and Talbot*) Do you know, I'd rather go away in the winter than in the summer? I love New York in the summer. Everybody's out of town and you can just have the city to yourself.

TALBOT: Matter of fact, New York is healthier in the summer. Though it's all one to me—I have to work the whole year round.

ED: I don't envy any doctor, summer or winter.

MILLICENT: I've never been in New York in the summer. I don't think I could stand it. Those buildings must be like ovens.

TALBOT: In time, I think, every building will be artificially cooled, just as it's now artificially heated. After all, why not? There's no reason why we should be more uncomfortable in the summer than we are in the winter, simply because of the elements. We protect ourselves against the cold—why not against the heat?

KITTY: I like it here in the summer. I've had some swell times on penthouse parties.

HATTIE: Oh, all my life I've wanted to be a penthouse girl, like one of Arno's pictures in the *New Yorker*.

ED: Yeah. You'd do well at that. (*A little laugh from the others.*)

MILLICENT: Of course the ideal life is to be in New York just about three months in the year.

TALBOT: Wait a minute! What about us doctors? What have we got to do? Follow you around? (*Again a laugh.*)

MILLICENT: Well, of course then we won't need doctors. (*More light laughter.*)

(*In both groups the conversation has simmered down to polite nothingness. As it nears this stage the figures of Dora and Gustave come through the doorway, stand a moment, and slowly approach the guests.*)

(*Dora is carrying the canapés, Gustave the cocktails. Dora is deathly pale, her eyes are red-rimmed from weeping, her whole face a mask of tragedy. Gustave, too, is pale, his expression stricken and guilty. The adhesive tape bandages are still on forehead and cheek. The pace of both is leaden, funereal.*)

(*Dora goes first to Millicent's group, Gustave goes to Oliver's. In each group there are little murmurs of comment or appreciation as the trays are passed.*)

MILLICENT'S GROUP: Oh, aren't they pretty! . . . What do you suppose this is? . . . Look out! They're hot . . . Mm—caviar! . . . I know I'm going to eat too many of these . . . Nonsense, they can't hurt you. There's nothing to them.

OLIVER'S GROUP: Ah, here we are! Well, I certainly needed this. . . . What's in them? . . . I think Gustave generally uses rum. I don't like gin in my cocktail. . . . Oh, aren't they good! . . . This is the kind you get in Cuba, isn't it?

(*Simultaneously Gustave and Dora, having served their respective groups, move toward the opposite group. As they try to pass each other they come face to face, stop for one second as their eyes meet, Dora's accusing, Gustave's beseeching. For one second the air is charged with emotion, then they cross, and resume their serving.*)

PACKARD: (*His voice breaking the Gustave-Dora tension*) Hey! Don't go far away with those!

(*There is a little desultory conversation.*)

MILLICENT: Let me see—we're all here except Mr. Renault. I hope he hasn't forgotten.

CARLOTTA: Oh, he'll be here. He's just staging an entrance.

KITTY: Oh, I'm crazy to see him. I think he's gorgeous!

(*Paula Jordan appears in the doorway. Being on her way out to dinner with Ernest, she is in evening clothes, with an evening coat. She stands on the top step, her eyes searching the group.*)

PACKARD: Where's that shaker? I want another one of these.

TALBOT: I'm going to break a rule and have another one myself.

MILLICENT: I thought you'd gone, Paula. . . . You all know my daughter, Paula.

(*A little murmur of acknowledgment from the group.*)

OLIVER: Hello, there! Where's your young man?

MILLICENT: Yes, where's Ernest?

PAULA: He's outside in the car. He turned shy on me, and wouldn't come up. I like this party. I may stay here.

LUCY: Hello, Paula dear! How's the future bride? When are you going to be married?

PAULA: Huh? . . . Oh, I . . . Where's Mr. Renault? Wasn't he going to be here?

MILLICENT: Yes, he's coming. He's not here yet.

PAULA: Oh! (*A little fleeting look of anxiety crosses her face.*)

PACKARD: She's hanging around to see the movie star. The rest of us don't stand a chance.

(*A little laugh from the group, in which Paula joins half-heartedly.*)

CARLOTTA: Oh, Larry's always late. He makes a point of it.

MILLICENT: Well, we'll wait a few minutes. He can't be long now. (*Attempts to start the conversational ball rolling.*) Of course, with traffic what it is, it's a wonder anybody gets anywhere.

(*The company has again broken up into groups, busy with chit-chat.*)

(*Gustave and Dora move about with the cocktails and canapés.*)

(*During all this, Paula is restlessly glancing toward the door, never giving her full attention to any one person in the room.*)

(*Bits of conversation come up; one hears a fragment from this and that group. It is all recognizable as something one has heard many times before.*)

PACKARD: Don't know what New York's coming to. Traffic getting worse and worse. Keep on putting up high buildings. What happens!

TALBOT: But if Germany *can't* pay—what then? You can't get blood out of a stone.

KITTY: They say it's getting warmer every winter. It's on account of the Gulf Stream. They say there'll be palm trees growing where the Empire State is.

MILLICENT: Of course, I don't get a minute to read. The only time is when I go to bed at night, and then I'm so sleepy—

ED: The first thing they've got to do is cut salaries. Look at what they pay their stars!

LUCY: But the trouble with children today is that they're blasé at fourteen. They've been everywhere, they've seen everything, they've done everything.

OLIVER: But most people don't go to the opera for the music. They go to be seen.

CARLOTTA: Oh, dear, yes! You become just as attached to them as if they were human beings.

HATTIE: It's just steak and lamb chops over and over again. I wish somebody would invent a new meat.

MILLICENT: (*Speaking to the guests as a whole*) I don't think we'll wait for Mr. Renault. He must have been delayed.

CARLOTTA: Yes, let's have dinner. I'm starving. And so is Mussolini. (*Turns to the Pekinese in her arms.*) Aren't you, Benito?

MILLICENT: (*To Gustave*) All right, Gustave. You may serve dinner.

(*Gustave bows. He and Dora go, leaving their trays.*)
I hope Mr. Renault won't be offended.
(*They all start to move toward the door.*)

PACKARD: Last come, last served. That's the way we used to do out in Montana.

TALBOT: I didn't get a bite of lunch. Reached the hospital at ten o'clock and was there until nearly five. Then I found an office full of patients, and I never did come up for air.

LUCY: Millicent, I hope you haven't got too good a dinner, or mine will suffer by contrast.

KITTY: (*To Carlotta, as they move on*) Isn't he cute! I've had a lot of Pekineses, but I don't have any luck with them. They die on me.

PACKARD: We used to swarm around that cook shack like a bunch of locusts. And the way those beans and biscuits vanished—boy! The guy who was late was out of luck. Believe me, he could eat grass.

MILLICENT: My dear, I'm having just the simplest meal in the world. I couldn't have less.

ED: (*Looking at his wrist watch*) Half-past eight. We won't get to that show till the second act.

HATTIE: I thought you didn't want to see it.

ED: If I've got to go I don't want to get there in the middle.

OLIVER: (*Ushering his guests ahead of him*) I think New Yorkers ought to have their dinner after the theatre instead of before. They do it in Vienna, and Paris, and Berlin. Much more comfortable.

KITTY: I love to eat late. We went to Spain once, Dan and I, and in Madrid they eat dinner at ten o'clock, and the shows don't begin until twelve.

CARLOTTA: Really! What time is sunrise? Noon?

(*Oliver is just behind Kitty and Carlotta, bringing up the rear. The others have ascended the steps and disappeared in the foyer, in the direction of the dining room.*)

(*Paula remains the sole occupant of the room, nervous, distrait, looking toward the foyer in the direction from which the late guest would come.*)

OLIVER: What's the matter, Paula? Something wrong?

PAULA: (*Pulling her wrap up about her shoulders*) No, no. I'm just going, Dad.

OLIVER: (*Comes back to her. Pats her cheek tenderly, just a touch, passes a hand over her hair.*) Good-night, my dear. (*Oliver goes.*)

(*The guests being out of the room, the music slowly comes up in volume.*)

(*Paula, on the steps, turns and peers fixedly out in the direction from which Larry would come. Turns a step or two toward the room. Sees the cocktail tray, goes quickly to it, snatches up a full glass, drains it. Turns, wavers with indecision, then, with a rush, goes.*)

(*Through this we have heard, faintly, the conversation and laughter of the guests on their way to the dining room. Now a burst of laughter comes up at some special sally. For some fifteen or twenty seconds, while the stage is empty, the music plays on, a romantic, throbbing Hungarian waltz.*)

THE CURTAIN FALLS

STAGE DOOR

A Play
by
Edna Ferber
and
George S. Kaufman

THE SCENES

ACT I

ACT II

ACT III

ACT ONE

SCENE I

The Footlights Club. A club for girls of the stage.

It occupies an entire brownstone house in the West Fifties, New York. One of those old houses whose former splendor has departed as the neighborhood has changed.

The room we see is the common living room. It is comfortably furnished with unrelated but good pieces, enlivened by a bit of chintz. The effect is that of charm and livability, what with the piano, a desk, a fireplace with a good old marble mantel. Prominently hung is a copy of a portrait of Sarah Bernhardt, at her most dramatic. There is a glimpse of hallway with a flight of stairs. Near the stairway is a hall table that holds mail, messages, papers; an occasional hat is thrown there.

It is an October evening, just before the dinner hour. The girls are coming home from matinees, from job-hunting, they are up and down the stairs, and presently they will be out again on dinner dates, playing the evening performances, seeing a movie.

Two girls are in the room at the moment, one at the piano, the other at a writing desk.

The girl at the piano, Olga Brandt, is dark, intense, sultry-looking.

Bernice Niemeyer, at the desk, is a young girl definitely not of the ingenue type. This is at once her cross and (in her opinion) her greatest asset as an actress.

For a moment nothing is heard but the music. The girl at the piano is playing, beautifully and with exquisite technique, Chopin's Opus 9, No. 2.

A girl comes in from the street door, stops for a quick look through the mail, tosses a "Hi!" into the room, and goes on up the stairs. Susan Paige.

The piano again.

BERNICE: (*To Olga*) What's that you're playing?

OLGA: (*Her Russian origin evident in her accent*) Chopin.

BERNICE: How did you learn to play like that?

OLGA: Practice. Practice.

BERNICE: How long did it take you?

OLGA: (*Out of patience*) Oh! (*A little discordant crash of the keys*)

BERNICE: Well, I was just asking.

> (*The telephone rings as Mattie, the maid, is descending the stairs, a little pile of towels over her arm.*)
>
> (*Mattie is colored, about thirty, matter-of-fact, accustomed to the vagaries of a houseful of girls, and tolerant of them.*)

MATTIE: Hello! . . . Yes, this the Footlights Club. . . . (*To the girls in the room*) Miss Devine come in yet?

> (*A negative shake of the head from Olga, and a muttered "uh-uh" from Bernice*)

No, she ain't. (*She hangs up.*)

BERNICE: Was it a man?

> (*Meanwhile voices are heard as the street door opens. "Oh, no, let's have dinner here and go to a movie." "Well, all right."*)

BERNICE: (*Pursuing her eternal queries*) Who's that?

OLGA: (*A shade of impatience*) Big and Little Mary.

> (*Big and Little Mary—Mary Harper and Mary McCune —come into view in the doorway. There is a wide gap in stature between the two. One comes about to the other's elbow.*)

BIG MARY: What time is it? Dinner ready yet?

BERNICE: Where've you been? Seeing managers?

LITTLE MARY: (*Drooping*) Yeh. We're dead.

BIG MARY: We've been in every manager's office on Broadway.

BERNICE: Is anybody casting?

BIG MARY: How do *we* know? We only got in to see *one* of them.

BERNICE: Which one? Who'd you see?

LITTLE MARY: Rosenblatt.

BERNICE: What's he doing?

BIG MARY: Take it easy. It's all cast. (*Her tone implies that this is the stereotyped managerial reply.*)

LITTLE MARY: All except a kid part—ten years old.

BERNICE: (*Eagerly*) I could look ten years old! (*She becomes a dimpled darling.*)

LITTLE MARY: No. Big Mary had the same idea, and she's littler than you are.

BIG MARY: You're almost as tall as Little Mary.

(*The Marys go up the stairs.*)

BERNICE: Listen, why is the little one called Big Mary and the big one Little Mary?

OLGA: Nobody knows. Will you for heaven's sake stop asking questions?

BERNICE: Oh, all right. . . . Where've you been?

(*The last remark is addressed to a newcomer who stands in the doorway. She is Madeleine Vauclain, a languid beauty, who runs through a sheaf of letters to discover if there is any mail for her.*)

(*The telephone rings. Bernice picks it up.*)

BERNICE: Footlights Club! . . . (*To Olga*) Terry Randall come in? (*As she shakes her head*) Not yet. (*Hangs up.*)

MADELEINE: I saw her sitting in Berger's office. I guess she gives up hard.

BERNICE: (*Alert at once*) Is Berger doing any casting?

(*Another girl comes in the street door and dashes upstairs at break-neck speed. Bobby Melrose*)

MADELEINE: Listen, if you'd make the rounds once in a while, instead of sitting on your bustle and writing letters—

BERNICE: (*Up the stairs*) I make the rounds, but all you see is the office boys.

MADELEINE: Well, who do you think sees the letters?

BERNICE: Well, if they won't see you and won't read the letters, where do you go from there?

MADELEINE: (*Calling after her*) If you find out I wish you'd tell me.

MATTIE: (*In the dining-room doorway*) Either you girls eating home?

MADELEINE: I'm not.

MATTIE: Anyhow, it's ready. (*Goes*)

OLGA: (*Continues playing*) Yes, yes.

MADELEINE: Look, you don't want to go out tonight, do you? I've got an extra man.

OLGA: (*A shake of the head*) I am rehearsing.

MADELEINE: Tonight?

OLGA: (*With bitterness*) Tonight! I must play the piano for a lot of chorus girls to sing and dance. (*She plays and even sings in a wordless imitation of their infantile tones, a few scornful bars of the music to which the chorus girls are expected to sing and dance. Then she rises, furiously.*) That's what I am doing tonight—and every night! And for that I studied fifteen years with Kolijinsky! (*She storms into the dining room.*)

MADELEINE: (*Mildly astonished at this outburst*) Well, look, all I did was ask you if you wanted to go out tonight.

(*A new figure appears in the doorway. It is Judith Canfield, hard, wise, debunked. She has picked up a letter from the hall table.*)

JUDITH: (*With dreadful sweetness*) Oh, goody, goody, goody! I got a letter from home!

MADELEINE: Hello, Judith!

JUDITH: (*Averting her gaze from the letter as she opens it, she brings herself to look at it with a courageous jerk of the head. A little laugh of false gayety as the letter meets every expectation*) Mmmmm! Pa got laid off. (*Turns a page*) My sister's husband has left her. (*Her eye skims a line or two*) And one of my brothers slugged a railroad detective. . . . I guess that's all. Yes. Lots of love and can you spare fifty dollars.

MADELEINE: Nothing like a letter from home to pick you up. . . . Look, Judy, what are you doing tonight?

JUDITH: (*Who has dropped onto a couch, whisked off her pump, and is pulling out the toe of her stocking*) I don't know. Why?

MADELEINE: I've got an extra man.

JUDITH: (*Brightening*) You mean dinner?

MADELEINE: Yes. Fellow from back home in Seattle. He's in the lumber business. He's here for a convention.

JUDITH: Sounds terrible.

MADELEINE: No, he isn't bad. And he's got this friend with him, so he wanted to know if I could get another girl.

JUDITH: Is the friend also in the lumber business?

MADELEINE: I don't know. What's the difference!

JUDITH: He'll be breezy. "Hello, Beautiful!"

MADELEINE: If we don't like it we can go home early.

JUDITH: Well— (*Weighing it*) —do we dress?

MADELEINE: Sure!

JUDITH: Okay. I kind of feel like stepping out tonight.

MADELEINE: (*Going toward the stairs*) Swell. We'd better start.
It's getting late.

JUDITH: (*Tugging at her stocking*) I'll be ready.

(*Madeleine disappears.*)

(*Judith wriggles her cramped toes, sighs.*)

(*Still another girl, Ann Braddock, has come down the stairs
and goes toward the dining room. She is wearing a hat and
carrying her coat, which she tosses onto the piano as she
passes.*)

ANN: Going in to dinner?

JUDITH: Got a date.

ANN: Well, that's all right for you—you're not working. But I
can't go out to dinner, and run around, and still give my
best to the theater. After all, you never see Kit Cornell
dashing around. (*Righteously, she goes into the dining room.*)

JUDITH: (*Mutters at first*) Kit Cornell! (*Then raises her voice as
the portrait on the wall gives her an idea.*) What about Bernhardt! I suppose *she* was a home girl!

(*From above stairs and descending the stairway the voice of
the House Matron is heard.*)

MRS. ORCUTT: Yes, I'm sure you're going to be most comfortable here. Both of your roommates are lovely girls. Now if
you'll just— (*Sees Judith.*) Oh—

(*Mrs. Orcutt is a woman of about forty-six. In her manner
and dress you detect the flavor of a theatrical past. Her dress
is likely to have too many ruffles, her coiffure too many curls.
She is piloting a fragile and rather wispy girl whose eyes are
too big for her face. We presently learn that her name is
Kaye Hamilton.*)

Uh—this is Judith Canfield, one of our girls— I'm so sorry,
I'm afraid I didn't—

KAYE: Kaye Hamilton.

MRS. ORCUTT: Oh, yes. Miss Hamilton is planning to be with
us if everything—uh—she'll room with Jean and Terry, now
that Louise is leaving.

JUDITH: That'll be swell. Excuse me. (*Shoe in hand, she limps
toward the stairs.*)

MRS. ORCUTT: (*A little gracious nod*) Now, that's our dining
room. (*A gesture toward it*) Dinner is served from six to

seven, because of course the girls have to get to the theater
early if they're working. Now, let me see. You're in the same
room with Terry and Jean, so that's only twelve-fifty a week,
including the meals. I suppose that will be all right.

KAYE: Yes, thank you.

MRS. ORCUTT: Now, about the reference. (*She looks at a piece of
paper she has been holding.*) I'll have that all looked up in the
morning.

KAYE: Morning! Can't I come in tonight?

MRS. ORCUTT: I'm afraid not. You see—

KAYE: But I've got to come in tonight. I've got to.

   (*A girl comes in at the street door, passes through the hallway
   and goes rapidly up the stairs, humming as she goes. Pat
   Devine. Halfway up the stairs we hear her call "Yoo-hoo!"*)

MRS. ORCUTT: (*After the interruption*) Well—uh—it's a little
irregular. However . . . Did you say your bags were near
by?

KAYE: Yes. That is, I can get them.

MRS. ORCUTT: (*Reluctantly*) Well, then, I suppose it's all right.
. . . Now, we have certain little rules. As you know, this is a
club for stage girls. I assume you are on the stage.

KAYE: Yes. Yes. I'm not working now, but I hope . . .

MRS. ORCUTT: I understand. . . . Now about callers—men
callers, I mean—

KAYE: There won't be any men.

MRS. ORCUTT: Oh, it's quite all right. We like you to bring
your friends here. But not after eleven-thirty at night, and—
of course—only in this room.

KAYE: I understand.

MRS. ORCUTT: I try very hard to make the girls feel that this is
a real home. I was one of them myself not many years back,
before I married Mr. Orcutt. Helen Romayne? Possibly you
remember?

KAYE: I'm afraid I—

MRS. ORCUTT: That's quite all right. I think that covers everything. If you wish to go and get your bags— Mattie! (*Peering
toward the dining room*) Will you come here a minute?

MATTIE: Yes, ma'am!

MRS. ORCUTT: (*She gently pilots Kaye toward the doorway.*)
Now, each girl is given a door key, and there's a little charge

of twenty-five cents in case they're lost. Well, good-by, and I'll expect you in a very short time.

(*As Mattie has appeared in the dining-room doorway Bernice comes downstairs; crosses the living room.*)

BERNICE: What have we got for dinner, Mattie?

MATTIE: We got a good dinner.

BERNICE: (*As she disappears*) Smells like *last* night. *Is* it?

(*The sound of the front door closing. Mrs. Orcutt, very businesslike, returns.*)

MRS. ORCUTT: Now Mattie, there's a new girl coming in as soon as Louise Mitchell leaves. You'll only have a few minutes to get that room straightened up.

MATTIE: Yes, ma'am.

MRS. ORCUTT: Let's see, Terry Randall isn't in yet, is she?

MATTIE: No, ma'am.

MRS. ORCUTT: Well, if I don't see her be sure to tell her there's a new girl moving in with her and Jean. Don't forget fresh paper in the bureau drawers, and—

(*Down the stairs like an angry whirlwind comes Linda Shaw. She is clutching a dressing gown about her. Her hair is beautifully done, she is wearing evening slippers; obviously she is dressed for the evening except for her frock.*)

LINDA: Mattie, isn't my dress pressed yet?

MATTIE: Oh! Was you wanting it right away?

LINDA: Right away! When did you *think* I wanted it?

MATTIE: Well, I'll do it right this minute.

LINDA: Oh, don't bother! I'll do it myself! (*Storms out.*)

MATTIE: (*Following after her*) You never give it to me till pretty near half-past five.

(*The telephone rings. Mrs. Orcutt answers.*)

MRS. ORCUTT: Footlights Club! . . . Yes, she is. . . . The Globe Picture Company? . . . Mr. Kingsley himself? . . . Just a minute. (*Impressed*) I'll get her right away. . . . (*Calls toward the stairs*) Jean! Oh, Jean!

(*A voice from above*)

JEAN: Yes!

MRS. ORCUTT: (*In hushed tones*) Mr. Kingsley of the Globe Picture Company wants to talk to you.

JEAN: All right.

MRS. ORCUTT: (*Back to telephone*) She'll be right down.

(*She lays down the receiver with a tenderness that is almost reverence, and takes a few steps away, looking toward the stairway. As Jean appears, Mrs. Orcutt affects an elaborate nonchalance and disappears into dining room.*)

(*Jean Maitland is a beautiful girl in her early twenties. She is, perhaps, a shade too vivacious. A better actress off than on. Her hair is blonde, and that toss of her head that shakes back her curls is not quite convincing. An opportunist; good-natured enough when things go her way; she has definite charm and appeal for men.*)

(*Jean throws her all into her voice as she greets the man at the telephone.*)

JEAN: Hello! Mr. Kingsley! How perfectly— (*Obviously she is met by a secretary's voice. Dashed by this, her tone drops to below normal.*) Yes, this is Miss Maitland. Will you put him on, please? (*Again she gathers all her forces and even tops her first performance.*) Hello! Mr. Kingsley! How wonderful! . . . Well, *I* think it's pretty wonderful. With all the thousands of people at that party I didn't think you'd remember *me*. . . . Yes, I know you said that, but in your business you must meet a million beautiful girls a day. . . . Well, anyhow, half a million. . . . (*Coyly*) Dinner! You don't mean tonight! Oh! . . . Yes, I did have, but it's nothing I can't break. . . . Oh, but I want to. I'd love to. . . . What time? . . . Yes, I'll be ready. I suppose we're dressing? . . . Yes, I'd love to. All right. Good-by.

(*As she hangs up the receiver, figures pop out of the vantage points from which they have been listening. Bernice and Ann come out of the dining room with Mrs. Orcutt; cloppity-clop down the stairs come Big and Little Mary and Bobby Melrose. Bobby is a soft Southern belle, fluffy, feminine. At the moment she is in a rather grotesque state of metal hair curlers, cold cream and bathrobe.*)

BIG MARY: (*A squeal of excitement*) Jean!

BERNICE: I'm dying!

LITTLE MARY: Tell us about it!

BOBBY: What time is he coming?

MRS. ORCUTT: Well, Jeanie, does this mean we're going to lose you to pictures?

BOBBY: Aren't you palpitating?

BERNICE: How soon is he coming? Can I see him?

JEAN: Now listen, you girls, no fair hanging around!

LITTLE MARY: Aw!

JEAN: You've got to promise me—no parading.

BIG MARY: Big-hearted Bertha!

BERNICE: I'll bet you'll let Terry meet him.

JEAN: Well, Terry's different.

ANN: All this fuss about a man! I wouldn't lift my little finger to meet him. (*She stalks into the dining room.*)

LITTLE MARY: She's oversexed!

MRS. ORCUTT: (*Still among her souvenirs*) David Kingsley! You know, he was Al Woods' office boy when I played *The Woman in Room 13*.

BERNICE: (*Not much interested*) Really? (*To Jean*) What are you going to wear?

JEAN: I wonder if Pat'll let me have her rose taffeta.

BERNICE: Sure she would.

JEAN: And I'll wear Kendall's evening coat.

MRS. ORCUTT: (*Insistent*) When he became a producer he wanted me for his first play. But by that time I had married Mr. Orcutt—

(*From abovestairs comes the sound of half-a-dozen voices haphazardly singing: "Here Comes the Bride!" The group in the room at once knows what this means, and their attention is turned toward the stairs.*)

BIG MARY: Oh, here's Louise!

BERNICE: Louise is going!

BOBBY: Oh, my goodness, I promised to help her pack.

LITTLE MARY: Let's get some rice and throw it!

BIG MARY: Oh, for heaven's sake, that's silly.

(*Frank, the houseman, comes down the stairs laden with bags. He is Mattie's husband—thirty-five or so. Close on Frank's heels comes Louise Mitchell in traveling clothes, and wearing a corsage of gardenias. She is accompanied by three girls. One is Susan, a student of an acting school. The others are Pat Devine, a night-club dancer, and Kendall Adams, of the Boston Adamses.*)

(*Mattie, broadly grinning and anticipatory, comes to the dining-room doorway.*)

(*Louise is ushered into the room on a wave of melody.*)

MRS. ORCUTT: Well, my dear, and so the moment has come. But when you see how saddened we are, you will realize that parting is sweet sorrow, after all.

(*Judith comes down the stairs, followed by Madeleine. Both in dishabille*)

JUDITH: Well, Mitchell, you're finally getting the hell out of here, huh?

MRS. ORCUTT: Judith! That seems to me hardly the spirit.

JUDITH: Sorry.

LOUISE: Judy doesn't mean anything.

FRANK: (*In the doorway*) Shall I get you a taxi, Miss Louise?

LOUISE: Oh, yes, thank you, Frank. (*The moment of departure has come. She looks about her for a second.*) Well, I guess there's no use in my trying to— Why, where's Terry? I thought she was down here.

KENDALL: Isn't she here?

SUSAN: No.

JEAN: She hasn't come in yet.

LOUISE: Oh, dear, I can't go without seeing Terry.

BERNICE: What's she up to, anyhow? I haven't seen her for days.

JEAN: I don't know. She's gone before I'm awake in the morning.

LOUISE: Well, anyhow, I guess I'd better get out of here before I bust out crying. You've all been just too darling for words, every single one of you—

(*Linda, having retrieved her dress, flashes through the hall and makes for the stairs.*)

Who's that? Oh, good-by, Linda. I'm going.

(*Linda, no part of this, tosses a "good-by" over her shoulder as she goes up the stairs.*)

And no matter how happy I am, I'll never forget you, and thanks a million times for the perfume, Pat, and you, Susan, for the compact, and all of you that clubbed together and gave me the exquisite nightgown.

BERNICE: (*Accepting the credit*) Oh, that's all right.

LOUISE: So—I hope I'll make a better wife than I did an actress. I guess I wasn't very good at that—

BIG MARY: (*Stoutly*) You were so!

LITTLE MARY: You were swell!

LOUISE: I guess I wasn't *very* swell or I wouldn't be getting mar— (*Catches herself.*) —that is, any girl would be glad to give up the stage to marry a wonderful boy like Bob— anyway, I certainly am. Goodness, when I think that for two whole years he's waited back there in Appleton, I guess I'm pretty lucky.

BIG MARY: (*Obliging, but not meaning it*) Yes.

(*The faces about her, while attentive, do not reflect full belief in Louise's good fortune.*)

LOUISE: Well, if any of you ever come out that way with a show, why, it's only a hundred miles from Milwaukee. Don't forget I'll be Mrs. Robert Hendershot by that time, and Wisconsin's perfectly beautiful in the autumn—the whole Fox River Valley—it's beautiful—

(*It's no use. She cannot convince even herself, much less the rather embarrassed young people about her. The situation is miraculously saved by the slam of the street door and the electric entrance of a new and buoyant figure.*)

(*Terry Randall has the vivid personality, the mobile face of the born actress. She is not at all conventionally beautiful, but the light in her face gives to her rather irregular features the effect of beauty. High cheekbones, wide mouth, broad brow.*)

TERRY: (*Breathless*) LOUISE! Dar-ling! I was so afraid you'd be gone. I ran all the way from Forty-sixth Street. Nothing else in the world could have kept me—look—what do you think! I've got a JOB!

(*This announcement is greeted with a chorus of excited exclamations. "You haven't! . . . Who with? . . . Tell us about it! . . . Terry, how wonderful! . . . Tell us all about it!"*)

I will in a minute. . . . Louise, what a darling crazy hat! I just love it on you.

LOUISE: Oh, Terry, have you really got a job! What in?

JEAN: Who is it? Berger?

TERRY: Yes.

BERNICE: I thought he was all cast.

TERRY: He was, all except this one part. It's not big, but it's good. It's got one marvelous scene—you know— (*With*

*three attitudes and a series of wordless sounds—one denuncia-
tory, one tender, one triumphant—she amusingly conveys the
range of the part.*)

(*From among the group, "It sounds marvelous! . . . Terry,
you'll be wonderful!"*)

FRANK: (*In the doorway*) Taxi's waiting, Miss Louise.

LOUISE: (*A glance at her wrist watch*) Oh, dear, I can't bear to
go. How'll I ever know the rest of it? Why did I ever— I've
got to go— Terry, baby! (*Throws her arms about Terry, kisses
her. There is general embracing and good-bys.*) Jean!

(*She kisses Jean, her other roommate*)

Good-by, good-by!

(*Louise is hurrying from the room, the others streaming
into the hallway to speed her. "Don't forget us! . . . Send
us a piece of wedding cake! . . . We want the deadly details. . . ."* [*From Mrs. Orcutt*] *"I hope you'll be very
happy, dear child. Good-by . . . Good-by . . . Good-by!"*)

(*Mattie, giggling, tosses after Louise a handful of rice that
she has brought from the kitchen. Louise is gone.*)

(*The girls stream back into the room.*)

KENDALL: When do you go into rehearsal, Terry?

OLGA: Yes, when?

TERRY: Right away!

BERNICE: Gosh, Terry, you certainly got a break. Berger
wouldn't even talk to me.

LITTLE MARY: Berger's an awful meany. How'd you get to him,
anyway?

TERRY: I just stood there outside his door for a week.

PAT: And it did the trick?

BIG MARY: *I* tried that.

BOBBY: It never helped *me* any.

JUDITH: Me neither. I laid there for a whole afternoon once
with "Welcome!" on me.

TERRY: I've had a longer run outside his office than I've had
with most shows. This was my second week. I was just going
to send out for a toothbrush and a camp chair when suddenly he opened the door. He was going. I said, "Mr.
Berger!" That's practically all I've said for two weeks—Mr.
Berger. (*She gives an assortment of readings of "Mr. Berger,"
ranging from piteous pleading to imperious command.*)

LITTLE MARY: What did he do?

SUSAN: What happened?

TERRY: He never even stopped. Suddenly I was furious. I grabbed his arm and said, "Listen! You're a producer and I'm an actress. What right have you got to barricade yourself behind closed doors and not see me! And hundreds like me! The greatest actress in the world might be coming up your stairs and you'd never know it."

KENDALL: Terry! What did he say!

TERRY: He said, "Are you the greatest actress in the world?" I said, "Maybe." He said, "You don't look like anything to me. You're not even pretty and you're just a little runt." I said, "Pretty! I suppose Rachel was pretty. And what about Nazimova! She's no higher than this." (*Indicates a level*) "But on a stage she's any height she wants to be."

JUDITH: P.S. She got the job.

TERRY: Yes. (*A deep sigh that conveys her relief at the outcome*) And when I walked out on Broadway again it seemed the most glamorous street in the world. Those beautiful Nedick orange stands, and that lovely traffic at Broadway and Forty-fifth, and those darling bums spitting on the sidewalk—

(*The doorbell rings. Instantaneously the group is galvanized. The girls realize the lateness of the hour.*)

(*Bobby takes a peek out the window.*)

BOBBY: Oh, it's my new young man! Mattie, tell him I won't be a minute!

MADELEINE: Wait a minute, Mattie! Give us a chance to get upstairs.

JUDITH: (*Darting after her, gathering her negligée as she goes*) Yes, Mattie. We don't want to give him the wrong idea of this house.

(*A handful of girls, squealing for time, dash into the dining room.*)

(*Jean starts up the stairs with Terry.*)

JEAN: Terry! What do you think's happened to your little girl friend! I'm having dinner with David Kingsley tonight.

TERRY: Jean, how marvelous! Did he say anything about a picture test?

JEAN: Not yet, but it must mean he's interested. Now look,

when he gets here I want you to come down and meet him, because you never can tell.

(*Mattie, having waited until the coast was clear, now goes to the front door. There is the sound of a man's voice. "Is Miss Melrose in?" Mattie's reply, "Yes, she is. Come right in."*)

(*A Young Man stands in the doorway, a trifle ill at ease in these unfamiliar surroundings. He hasn't the look of a New Yorker. There is about him the rather graceful angularity and winning simplicity of the Westerner.*)

MATTIE: You-all can wait in there.

THE YOUNG MAN: Oh, thanks. Just tell her Sam Hastings is calling for her.

MATTIE: (*As she goes to the dining-room door*) I think she knows about it— She'll be down directly.

(*Sam Hastings mutters a thank-you as Mattie passes into the dining room, closing the doors behind her.*)

(*Left alone, and not yet at ease, Sam Hastings makes a leisurely survey of the room, rather getting in the way of his own big frame as he turns. He decides, unfortunately, on the least substantial chair in the room and sits gingerly on its edge. At once there is a short sharp crack of protesting wood. He is on his feet like a shot. From abovestairs a snatch of popular song. Swift footsteps are heard descending the stairs. He rises expectantly, but it's not his girl. It is Kendall, who is humming a bit of song as she comes. She pauses on the stairs to fix her stocking. She stops abruptly as she sees a stranger. With a glare at the embarrassed Hastings she goes into the dining room. Then a preemptory voice shouts from upstairs; "Judy! You going to stay in the johnny all night?" He clears his throat and looks away, though there's nothing to look away from.*)

(*The doorbell rings.*)

(*Bernice comes out of the dining room. Her eye brightens as she beholds the young man.*)

BERNICE: (*Summoning all her charm*) Pardon me. You're not Mr. David Kingsley!

SAM: No. My name's Hastings.

(*With a syllable of dismissal, Bernice goes on her way, and up the stairs.*)

(*By this time Mattie is opening the front door. A voice inquires, "Miss Paige in?" "Yes, come right in."*)

(*The Boy who appears is even younger than Sam Hastings. Perhaps nineteen. Slight, graceful, dark-haired, rather sensitive looking.*)

MATTIE: (*Calls from the foot of the stairs*) Miss Susan!

(*Susan's voice from upstairs—"All right, Mattie!"*)

(*The two Boys confront each other rather uncertainly. The newcomer in the doorway ventures a mannerly, "How do you do?" "Howdy-do?" There is a little awkward pause.*)

THE NEWCOMER: My name's Devereaux.

SAM: Mine's Hastings.

DEVEREAUX: Yes, I recognized you. I saw you in that Keith Burgess play last month.

SAM: You sure must have looked quick.

DEVEREAUX: I liked that part. You did a lot with it. Too bad the play flopped.

SAM: I don't rightly recall you. Have you done anything lately?

DEVEREAUX: Last month I played Emperor Jones, and I'm cast now for Hamlet.

SAM: Hamlet?

DEVEREAUX: I'm at the New York School of Acting. This is my last year.

SAM: Oh! And then what?

DEVEREAUX: Then I'm going on the stage.

SAM: Did you ever try to get a job on the stage?

DEVEREAUX: Not yet.

SAM: That's more of a career than acting. I've been in New York two years. I'm from Texas. Houston Little Theater. We came up and won a contest, and I stayed. I've had ten weeks' work in two years. Don't ask me how I live. I don't know.

DEVEREAUX: You could go back to Texas, couldn't you?

SAM: Go back! Oh, no! I'm an actor.

(*Susan runs down the stairs, in street clothes.*)

SUSAN: Hello, Jimmy!

DEVEREAUX: Hello, Sue. Do you know Mr. Hastings?

SUSAN: Howdy-do?

DEVEREAUX: Miss Susan Paige. She's up at the school, too. She's going to do Hedda Gabler.

SAM: Well, you have to start somewhere.

SUSAN: (*Laughingly*) Yes.

> (*Devereaux says, "Good-by!" There is a word of farewell
> from Hastings and Susan as the doorbell rings.*)

DEVEREAUX: (*As he and Susan go into the hall*) Where do you
want to eat?

SUSAN: How much money have you got?

DEVEREAUX: Sixty-five cents.

SUSAN: I've got thirty. That's ninety-five.

> (*As they open the door they are accosted by a hearty mascu-
> line voice, subsequently identified as that of Fred Powell.
> "This the Footlights Club?"*)

SUSAN: Yes. Won't you just— Mattie! Somebody at the door.

MATTIE: (*Having appeared in the hallway*) Yes'm, Miss Susan.
. . . You gentlemen calling on somebody?

> (*Fred Powell and Lou Milhauser come into view. They are
> two overhearty Big Business Men out for a holiday. Their
> derby hats and daytime attire will be a shock to the girls, es-
> pecially Judith.*)

POWELL: Yes, we're calling for Miss Madeleine Vauclain.

MILHAUSER: And her friend.

MATTIE: (*At the foot of the stairs*) Miss Madeleine! . . . Couple gentlemen down here say they calling for you and—
somebody.

MADELEINE: Coming down!

MATTIE: She's coming down.

> (*They come into the living room, and finding another man
> there, offer a tentative greeting; a smile and wave of the
> hand. Then they look the room over.*)

MILHAUSER: What'd you say this place was? A Home for Girls?

POWELL: Yeah, all actresses. A whole bunch of 'em live here.

MILHAUSER: Kind of a handy place to know about.

POWELL: Yeah.

MILHAUSER: (*Whisks from his pocket two cellophaned cigars.*)
Smoke?

POWELL: Thanks.

> (*As they light up, having tossed the crumpled cellophane
> jackets to a near-by table, Powell sends a glance of half-
> inquiry at Sam. Hastily, in order to divert any further ad-
> vances, Sam opens his cigarette case and lights a cigarette.*)

MILHAUSER: Certainly is a funny place, New York. Now, you take a layout like this. Wouldn't find it anywhere else in the world.

POWELL: Bet you wouldn't, at that.

MILHAUSER: I—I always thought actresses lived in flats or— uh—hotel rooms.

POWELL: Lot of 'em do.

MILHAUSER: (*Struck by a new thought*) What about men actors—where do they live?

POWELL: I don't know—Lambs' Club, I guess.

MILHAUSER: Oh, yeah.

(*Sam Hastings shifts his position a little, throws them a look.*)

(*Bobby Melrose, finally coming down the stairs, saves the situation. She is at her most Southern.*)

BOBBY MELROSE: (*From the stairs*) Hello there, Texas!

SAM: (*Gathering up his coat and hat*) Oh, hello!

BOBBY: Ah hope Ah didn't keep you waitin'.

SAM: No! No!

BOBBY: One thing about me, Ah'm always prompt.

(*The outer door closes. They are gone.*)

POWELL: That was a cute little trick.

MILHAUSER: Yeah. . . . Look! What about this one you've got on the fire for me? She any good?

POWELL: Sure, sure. You leave it to Madeleine.

MILHAUSER: Oh, well, as long as she's good-natured.

(*There is a rustle of silk on the stairway. "Ah!" exclaims Powell, in anticipation and relief.*)

(*Madeleine and Judith descend the stairs in full evening regalia, gathered from the richest recesses of the club—furs, silks, gloves, jewelry.*)

MADELEINE: (*Furiously, as she catches sight of the men's attire*) Well, is this what you call dressing?

POWELL: Huh?

MADELEINE: Why didn't you come in overalls!

POWELL: Now, now, baby. We got snarled up in a committee meeting, didn't we, Lou?

MILHAUSER: Sure. Sure.

POWELL: This is Ben Dexter, girls. Miss Madeleine Vauclain and—uh—

MADELEINE: (*Sulkily*) This is Miss Canfield.

MILHAUSER: (*Coming right up to Judith's expectations*) Hello, Beautiful! (*Very jovial*) How about it? Shall we step out and go places?

JUDITH: (*Sourly*) Yes, let's.

MILHAUSER: Now don't be like that. We're going to have a good time.

POWELL: Sure we are! The works! (*He is piloting Madeleine out to the hallway.*) Come on, boys and girls! Where do you want to eat?

MILHAUSER: I got an idea. How about a little Italian place?

JUDITH: Little Italian *nuts!* I want a decent dinner.

> (*A slam of the door. They are gone.*)
> (*Kendall comes out of the dining room and busies herself at the mirror. Olga follows, adjusting her hat and cape as she enters.*)

OLGA: Kendall, are you going to your show? I am rehearsing at the Winter Garden, if you want to walk down.

KENDALL: No, it's too early for me. We don't go up till eight-fifty.

OLGA: (*With almost too much Slavic bitterness*) The Winter Garden! The star pupil of Kolijinsky, at the Winter Garden! (*She goes.*)

LITTLE MARY: (*Who, with the inevitable Big Mary at her side, has come into the room just in time to hear this*) Bellyaching, and she's got a job. Look at me. (*She flops into a seat.*) Edwin Booth and I retired from the stage at practically the same time.

KENDALL: I think I'll take a rest before the night show. Matinee days are frightfully tiring. (*She goes up to her room.*)

BIG MARY: Frightfully tiring! Why doesn't she go back to Boston, where she belongs! That'd rest her up.

LITTLE MARY: There ought to be an equity law against society girls going on the stage. "Miss Kendall Adams, daughter of Mr. and Mrs. Roger Winthrop Adams."

BIG MARY: Of Boston and the Lucky Strike ads.

> (*Pat and Ann come out of the dining room. There is the tinkle of china and silver. The doors are shut by Mattie. Dinner is over.*)

ANN: What's it like out? It looked rainy when I came in. (*Goes to the hallway for her coat.*)

BIG MARY: (*At the window*) No, it's all right. . . . Oh, girls, look! There's the Cadillac again for Linda Shaw.

LITTLE MARY: Is *he* in it?

BIG MARY: No, just the chauffeur, same as always.

PAT: Who's the guy, anyhow? Anybody know?

LITTLE MARY: He doesn't ever come. Just sends the car.

PAT: Well, nice work if you can get it.

ANN: (*Righteously*) I think it's disgraceful. A nice girl wouldn't want a man to send for her that way. And if you ask me, it gives the club a bad name.

(*A warning gesture and a "Pss-s-st!" from Little Mary as Linda descends the stairs*)

(*Linda is beautifully dressed for the evening. She is wearing the dress whose pressing had annoyed her; her evening cape is handsomely furred. Enormous orchids*)

BIG MARY: Oo, Linda! How gorgeous!

LINDA: (*Pausing reluctantly*) Oh, hello.

LITTLE MARY: Come on in. Let's see you.

BIG MARY: What a marvelous coat, Linda!

PAT: Yes, and a very nifty bit of jack rabbit, if I may say so. (*Her finger outlines a collar in the air.*)

LINDA: Oh, that! Mother sent it to me. It used to be on a coat of hers.

LITTLE MARY: It's lovely.

PAT: (*Mildly*) Oh—Mother has a nice taste in orchids, too.

LINDA: (*Baring her fangs*) Yes. Don't you wish *you* had a mother like mine? (*She sweeps out.*)

(*The two Marys dart to the window.*)

PAT: What would you two do without that window? Why don't you pull up a rocking chair!

ANN: Linda Shaw's comings and goings don't interest me. Girls make such fools of themselves about men! (*She goes.*)

BIG MARY: Say! What do you know about Jean? Having dinner with David Kingsley!

LITTLE MARY: Some girls have all the luck. Where'd she meet him, anyhow?

BIG MARY: Oh, some cocktail party.

PAT: I wish *I* could meet him. He can spot picture material just like that. (*She snaps her fingers.*) He's got an eye like a camera.

LITTLE MARY: Yeh, he picked three picture stars last year. No-body ever heard of 'em before he sent 'em out there.

PAT: Well, I'll never meet him. (*She indulges in an elaborate yawn and stretch.*) Oh, what to do till eleven o'clock. Except sleep.

LITTLE MARY: Anyhow, you've got something to *do* at eleven. . . . Look at us!

BIG MARY: Yeh, you're working.

PAT: I hate it. Hoofing in a night club for a lot of tired business men. The trouble is they're *not* tired and there's no business.

(*The doorbell rings.*)

BIG MARY: (*At the window*) I think it's David Kingsley! It looks like him.

PAT: Kingsley? Are you sure?

LITTLE MARY: (*Peering*) Yes, that's him. Look, we'd better get out of the way, hadn't we?

BIG MARY: Yes, I guess so.

(*Pat, mindful of her pajamas, also gathers herself together.*)

(*Bernice descends the stairs with rather elaborate unconcern.*)

BERNICE: (*Too polite*) Oh, pardon me, I just want to speak to— Frank—about—something— (*She dashes into the dining room.*)

(*Pat stands looking after Bernice for a second. Then as Mattie crosses the hallway to answer the door Pat makes her own decision and darts up the stairs.*)

(*A man's voice at the door*)

KINGSLEY: (*In the hall*) Miss Maitland, please.

MATTIE: Yessuh. Come right in.

KINGSLEY: Tell her Mr. Kingsley.

(*David Kingsley enters. Perhaps thirty-six or -seven. A man of decided charm and distinction. He is wearing evening clothes. You see his white muffler above the dark topcoat.*)

MATTIE: If you'll just rest yourself—I'll go right up. (*Mattie goes up the stairs with a stateliness that indicates her appreciation of the caller's importance.*)

(*Kingsley glances about the room a bit. He opens his cigarette case, lights a cigarette.*)

(*Bernice comes out of the dining room. Her face is turned toward someone in the room she has just left and it is this person she is addressing, apparently all unaware that any-*)

one (certainly not Kingsley) is in the living room. With one quick twist she has altered—or thinks she has altered—the arrangement of her hair so as to make of herself a more arresting type.)

BERNICE: Yes, Mattie, an actress's life is such an interesting one, if you could only see the different types that I do in the course of a day, Mattie. For example, an English actress came into an office today. (*Goes suddenly very English.*) "My dear, Harry, how definitely ripping to see you. Definitely ripping!" And then Mattie, a little girl from Brooklyn came in. "Listen, I did write for an appurntment! You got a noive!" (*She turns, and to her obvious embarrassment there is Mr. Kingsley. She is a picture of pretty confusion.*) Oh, I am so sorry! I didn't dream anyone was here.

KINGSLEY: (*Politely amused*) That's quite all right.

BERNICE: (*Following up her advantage*) I'm—Bernice Niemeyer. (*Kingsley bows slightly, murmurs her name*)

Well—I just thought— (*She is dangling at the end of her rope.*) (*Here she is mercifully interrupted by Pat's descent of the stairs. The jacket of Pat's pajama suit is missing. Her slim figure is well revealed in the trousers and scant short-sleeved top. Her low-heeled scuffs have been replaced by pert high-heeled mules.*)

PAT: I wonder— (*Makes a slow turn toward Bernice—a turn which by a strange chance serves at the same time to reveal the best points of her figure to the waiting Kingsley.*) You—you didn't see my book anywhere around here, did you?

BERNICE: (*Sourly*) What book? (*She goes up the stairs*)

(*Pat flutters in her quest to a table, goes to the book-shelf, selects a volume, ruffles its pages to make sure that the book meets her mood, then gives a little sigh of delight, clasps the book to her breast and trips up the stairs.*)

(*Kingsley barely has time to seat himself again before another aspirant for his approval appears.*)

(*It is Mrs. Orcutt, who has shed her workaday dress for something very grand in the way of a silk dinner gown.*)

MRS. ORCUTT: (*Outstretched hands*) David Kingsley! Little David Kingsley!

KINGSLEY: (*A little bewildered, rises to meet the emergency*) Why—how do you do!

MRS. ORCUTT: (*Coquettishly*) Surely you remember me.

KINGSLEY: (*Lying bravely*) Of course I do.

MRS. ORCUTT: Who am I?

> (*Kingsley has an instant of panic.*)

Now think. Helen who?—Ro—

KINGSLEY: (*Catches desperately at this straw*) Ro—

MRS. ORCUTT: —mayne! Helen Romayne!

KINGSLEY: (*Repeating it just the barest flash behind her*) Helen Romayne. Why, of course! Well, what a charming surprise. Imagine your remembering me! A scrubby little kid in the office.

MRS. ORCUTT: But that little office boy became one of the most brilliant producers in the theater. Those beautiful plays! I loved them all.

KINGSLEY: So did I. But something happened to the theater about that time. It was sort of shot from under us.

MRS. ORCUTT: But you've gone right on. You've risen to even greater triumphs in the pictures.

KINGSLEY: (*Quietly ironic*) Yes, even greater triumphs.

> (*A step on the stair. Mrs. Orcutt turns.*)

MRS. ORCUTT: Well—it was lovely seeing you. I hope you'll be coming again.

KINGSLEY: I hope so too.

> (*Mrs. Orcutt makes her escape as Jean appears on the stairs, resplendent in her borrowed finery. Pat's rose taffeta, and Kendall's evening wrap*)

JEAN: So glad to see you, Mr. Kingsley.

KINGSLEY: I'm glad you happened to be free.

JEAN: I guess girls generally manage to be free when you invite them.

KINGSLEY: You don't think my being in the motion-picture business may have something to do with it?

JEAN: Why, Mr. Kingsley, how can you say such a thing!

KINGSLEY: You think it's all sheer charm, huh?

JEAN: Of course. . . . Look, would you mind awfully if I— (*Calls up the stairs*) Terry! Come *on*!

TERRY: (*From above*) I'm coming.

JEAN: That's Terry Randall, my roommate. Did you see *Cyclone*? Or *The Eldest Son*?

KINGSLEY: Oh, yes. In *Cyclone*—she was—

JEAN: It was just a tiny part. She came into the drugstore.

KINGSLEY: Oh, yes. Just a bit, but she was good. . . . Yes, she was excellent!

(*Terry comes down the stairs.*)

(*She is still wearing the plain dark little dress in which we have previously seen her. If it were not for the glowing face she would seem rather drab in comparison to the dazzling Jean.*)

TERRY: (*With great directness*) Well, if you will come calling at a girls' club, Mr. Kingsley, what can you expect?

KINGSLEY: I didn't expect anything as charming as this.

TERRY: Mm! You *are* in the moving-picture business, aren't you?

KINGSLEY: I am, Miss Randall. But my soul belongs to God.

JEAN: Don't you think she'd be good for pictures, Mr. Kingsley? Look.

(*Turning Terry's profile to show to the best advantage.*)

TERRY: I think I'd be terrible.

JEAN: Don't talk like that. Of course she's rehearsing now in the new Berger play. That is, she starts tomorrow.

KINGSLEY: Good! I hear it's an interesting play.

TERRY: Do you know the first play I ever saw, Mr. Kingsley?

KINGSLEY: No, what?

TERRY: It was your production of *Amaryllis.*

KINGSLEY: *Amaryllis!* You couldn't have seen that! That was my first production. Ten years ago.

TERRY: I did, though. I was eleven years old, and I saw it at English's Opera House, in Indianapolis. My mother took me. She cried all the way through it, and so did I. We had a lovely time.

KINGSLEY: But *Amaryllis* wasn't a sad play.

TERRY: Oh, we didn't cry because we were sad. Mother cried because it brought back the days when she was an actress, and I cried because I was so happy. You see, we lived seventy-five miles from Indianapolis, and it was the first time I'd ever been in a theater.

JEAN: Now, really, I don't think it's tactful to talk about the theater to a picture man.

TERRY: I'm afraid I'm kind of dumb about pictures. Mother used to say the theater had two offspring—the legitimate stage, and the bastard.

JEAN: (*Taking Kingsley by the hand and pulling him from the room*) Come on! And forget I ever introduced her to you.
   (*He goes, calling, "Good-by, Miss Randall!"*)

TERRY: (*Calling after him*) Oh, I hope I didn't—

KINGSLEY: (*As the door closes on them*) It's all right. I forgive you.
   (*Left alone, Terry suddenly realizes she has had no dinner. As she goes toward the dining room she calls.*)

TERRY: Mattie! (*She opens the dining-room doors.*) Oh dear, is dinner over!

MATTIE: Yes. I'm just clearing away.

TERRY: Oh, Mattie darling, could you let me have just anything! Champagne and a little caviar?

MATTIE: (*In the dining room*) Well, I'll fix you a plate of something.

TERRY: You're an angel.
   (*Kendall Adams comes down the stairs, dressed for the street. At sight of Terry she pauses a moment to chat.*)

KENDALL: Isn't it splendid, Terry, about your getting a job!

TERRY: It seems pretty dazzling to me, after six months. I only hope it's as big a hit as yours.

KENDALL: It's queer about being in a hit. You go through everything to get into one, and after a few months you're bored with it. It's like marriage.
   (*The doorbell rings.*)
   (*Calls*)
   It's all right, Mattie, I'll answer it. . . . Going out, Terry?

TERRY: Not tonight.

KENDALL: (*At the street door*) See you later.
   (*A voice at the door. "Hello there! Who are you!" Kendall's voice, a film of ice over it. "I beg your pardon!" The man's voice explains, "I'm looking for Jean Maitland." Kendall calls, "Mattie!" and goes on her way. The call is unheard by Mattie.*)
   (*Keith Burgess appears in the archway. He is the kind of young man who never wears a hat. Turtle-necked sweater, probably black; unpressed tweed suit; unshaven.*)

KEITH: Where's Jean Maitland?

TERRY: In a taxi with a big moving-picture man.

KEITH: She can't be. She had a date with me.

TERRY: Sorry. It isn't my fault.

KEITH: Who are you?

TERRY: Who wants to know?

KEITH: Are you an actress?

TERRY: Are you dizzy in the morning? Do you have spots before the eyes?

KEITH: My name is Keith Burgess.

TERRY: Is it?

KEITH: Don't you know who I am?

TERRY: Yes. You're a playwright, and you wrote a play called *Blood and Roses* that was produced at the Fourteenth Street Theater, and it ran a week and it wasn't very good.

KEITH: It was the best goddam play that was ever produced in New York! And the one I'm writing now is even better.

TERRY: Mm! *Two* weeks.

KEITH: (*Vastly superior*) I don't think in terms of material success. Who cares whether a play makes money! All that matters is its message!

TERRY: (*Mildly*) But if nobody comes to see it, who gets the message?

KEITH: I write about the worker! The masses! The individual doesn't count in modern society.

TERRY: But aren't the masses made up of individuals?

KEITH: Don't quibble!

TERRY: I'm so sorry.

KEITH: I ask nothing as an individual. My work, my little room—that's all.

TERRY: No furniture?

KEITH: A table, a bed, a chair. My books. My music. And—
   (*The doorbell has rung, and Frank has crossed the hall to answer it. The voice of Kaye Hamilton is now heard at the door. Keith, accordingly, is forced to suspend for a moment.*)

KAYE: I'm Miss Hamilton. Kaye Hamilton.

FRANK: Oh yes. I think Mrs. Orcutt's expecting you.
   (*Mrs. Orcutt appears in the hallway just in time to greet the new arrival.*)

MRS. ORCUTT: Glad to see you again, Miss Hamilton. Everything's in readiness for you. Frank, take Miss Hamilton's things right up. Oh! (*As she sees Terry in the living room*) Terry, this is Kaye Hamilton, who's going to share the room with you and Jean. Terry Randall.

KAYE: I'll try not to be in the way.

TERRY: Oh, don't start that way! Grab your share of the closet hooks.

KAYE: Thank you.

MRS. ORCUTT: Now, if you'll just come with me I'll show you where everything is.

TERRY: (*As they start up*) Let me know if I can be of any help.

MRS. ORCUTT: (*Talking as they ascend*) If you have a trunk check Frank will take care of all that for you.

KAYE: No, no, I haven't got a trunk. (*They are gone.*)

(*Keith, throughout the above scene, has been observing Terry with an old-fashioned eye of appreciation.*)

KEITH: Hey! Turn around! (*She does so, rather wonderingly.*) You shouldn't wear your hair like that. It hides your face.

TERRY: Oh, do you notice faces? I thought you were above all that.

KEITH: I notice everything. Your head's too big for the rest of you, you've got pretty legs, but you oughtn't to wear red.

TERRY: (*Surveying him*) I suppose you're known as Beau Burgess! What the Well-Dressed Man Will Wear!

KEITH: Oh, you like snappy dressers, eh? Monograms and cuff links.

TERRY: No, I don't meet very many monograms.

KEITH: (*His gaze roaming around the room*) What do you live in this place for? Do you like it?

TERRY: I love it. We live and breathe theater, and that's what I'm crazy about.

KEITH: (*Eagerly*) Are you? So am I. What do you want to *do* in the theater? What kind of parts do you want to play?

TERRY: I want to play everything I'm suited for. Old hags of eighty, and Topsy, and Lady Macbeth. And what do I get? Ingenues—and very little of that.

KEITH: Don't take 'em. Wait till you get what you want.

TERRY: Well, it's a nice idea. But did you ever hear of this thing called eating?

KEITH: You mustn't think of that. Why, I've lived on bread

and cocoa for days at a time. If you believe in something you've got to be willing to starve for it.

TERRY: I'm willing. But you don't know what it is to be an actress. If you feel something you can write it. But I can't act unless they let me. I can't just walk up and down my room, being an actress.

KEITH: It's just as tough for a writer. Suppose they won't produce his plays? I write about ironworkers and they want grand dukes. I could write potboilers, but I don't. The theater shouldn't be just a place to earn a living in. It should be thunder and lightning, and power and truth.

TERRY: And magic and romance!

KEITH: No, no! Romance is for babies! I write about *today*! I want to tear the heart out of the rotten carcass they call life, and hold it up bleeding for all the world to see!

TERRY: How about putting some heart *into* life, instead of tearing it out?

KEITH: There's no place for sentiment in the world today. We've gone past it.

TERRY: I suppose that's why you never hear of *Romeo and Juliet*.

KEITH: (*Turning away*) That's a woman's argument.

TERRY: Well, I'm a woman.

KEITH: (*Once more surveying her*) Why haven't I run into you before? Where've you been all the time?

TERRY: Right here, in and out of every manager's office on Broadway.

KEITH: Me too. But I'm going to keep right on until they listen to me. And you've got to keep right on too!

TERRY: I will! I'm going to!

(*Mattie appears in the dining-room doorway.*)

MATTIE: You-all want your dinner now, Miss Terry? It's ready.

TERRY: Why, I'd forgotten all about it, Mattie.

KEITH: (*Taking control*) Never mind, Mattie! . . . How about dinner with me? We'll go to Smitty's and have a couple of hamburgers.

TERRY: (*Not at all unwilling*) With onions?

KEITH: Sure—onions! . . . Say, what the hell's your name, anyway?

(They start for the door. The two Marys are coming down the stairs again, deep in an argument, as usual.)

CURTAIN

Scene II

One of the bedrooms. A pleasant enough but rather cramped room, with three beds, three dressers, three small chairs. There is a bathroom door down left, a window center. A door up left leads to hall.

Each dresser reflects something of the personality and daily life of its owner. Stuck in the sides of the mirrors are snapshots, photographs, newspaper clippings, telegrams, theater programs.

It is night, and through the window we get a glimpse of the city's lights.

At the beginning the room is unoccupied.

Kaye Hamilton comes out of the bathroom, closes the door. She is wearing a bathrobe over her nightgown. Goes to her dresser, which is conspicuously bare of ornaments, souvenirs, or photographs. She opens the dresser top drawer, takes out her handbag, removes her money from a small purse and counts it, a process which doesn't take long. Two dollars and sixty cents.

There is a knock at the door.

KAYE: Yes?

JUDITH: (*As she opens the door*) Can I come in? Where's Terry?

KAYE: She isn't back yet.

> (*Judith is wearing sleeping pajamas and she is in the process of doing her face up for the night. A chin strap is tied about her face and ends in a top-knot. A net safeguards her curls.*)

JUDITH: Look, do you think she'd mind if I borrowed some of her frowners? I forgot to get some.

KAYE: I think there's some in her top drawer.

JUDITH: (*As she pulls open the drawer*) Thanks. . . . You don't go out much evenings, do you?

KAYE: No.

JUDITH: Any sign of a job yet?

KAYE: No, not yet.

JUDITH: Something'll turn up. It always does. (*She waits a moment for Kaye's answer, but there is none.*) You know, you're a funny kid. You've been here a month, and I don't know any more about you than when you came in. The rest of us are always spilling our whole insides, but you never let out a peep. Nobody comes to see you, no phone calls, never go out nights, you haven't even got a picture on your dresser. Haven't you got any folks? Or a beau or something?

(*No sound from Kaye. Judith turns to glance at her.*)

Sorry. My mistake.

(*The voices of Big and Little Mary are heard in the hall. Big Mary: "Mm, somebody's cooking something." Little Mary: "Smells like a rarebit."*)

(*The two Marys, in hats and coats, stick their heads in at the door.*)

LITTLE MARY: Who's cooking? You?

JUDITH: No—Madeleine. Where've you been? Show?

BIG MARY: (*Dourly*) Yeh. We saw the Breadline Players in *Tunnel of Death*.

LITTLE MARY: Come on, let's get some rarebit before it's all gone. (*They disappear down the hallway.*)

JUDITH: Terry's late, isn't she? It's half-past eleven. And she isn't in the last act.

KAYE: She'll be here in a minute. Have you seen the play?

JUDITH: I haven't had time yet. I'm going tomorrow night.

KAYE: I didn't like it very much, but Terry's awfully good. Just a little part, but you always knew she was on.

(*Pat appears in the doorway. She is wearing a tailored suit and hat.*)

PAT: (*Peering around*) Anybody in here? . . . Well, off to the mines.

JUDITH: Hello, Pat. Going to work?

PAT: (*Wearily*) Yeh, the night shift. (*She does a rather listless floor-show dance step; disappears.*)

KAYE: I wonder what it'd be like, working in a night club. I wish I'd learned to dance.

JUDITH: (*Intent on her own reflection in the mirror*) Well, with your looks you'll get along all right. (*She wanders over to Kaye's dresser.*) Where's your hand mirror? Why, where's the whole set?

KAYE: I haven't got it any more.

JUDITH: (*A little too casually*) It was—gold, wasn't it?

KAYE: Uh-huh.

JUDITH: I see. . . . Got any folks you have to support?

KAYE: (*Quietly*) No, I haven't any folks.

JUDITH: Well, if you want some, I'm the girlie that can fix you up. Five brothers and four sisters, and you couldn't scare up a dollar eighty among the lot. I've got a little sister named Doris. Fifteen, and as innocent as Mata Hari. She's coming to New York next year to duplicate my success.

KAYE: (*Somewhat wistfully*) I think it would be rather nice, having a little sister with you.

JUDITH: Yeh, only she won't be with me much. Two weeks, and they'll have her in the Home for Delinquent Girls.

(*Terry enters, a drooping figure. A glance at the two occupants of the room. Her back to the door, she slowly closes it behind her and slumps against it.*)

TERRY: Young lady, willing, talented, not very beautiful, finds herself at liberty. Will double in brass, will polish brass, will *eat* brass before very long. Hi, girls!

KAYE: Terry, what's the matter?

TERRY: We closed. Four performances and we closed.

KAYE: Terry, you didn't.

JUDITH: Tonight! But it's only Thursday!

TERRY: Well, it seems you can close on Thursday just as well as Saturday—in fact, it's even better; it gives you two more days to be sunk in.

JUDITH: But it didn't get bad notices. What happened?

TERRY: We just got to the theater tonight, and there it was on the call board. "To the Members of the *Blue Grotto* Company: You are hereby advised that the engagement of the *Blue Grotto* will terminate after tonight's performance. Signed, Milton H. Schwepper, for Berger Productions, Incorporated."

KAYE: Terry, how ghastly!

JUDITH: Just like that, huh?

TERRY: Just like that. We stood there for a minute and read it. Then we sort of got together in the dressing rooms and talked about it in whispers, the way you do at a funeral. And then we all put on our make-up and gave the best damned performance we'd ever given.

JUDITH: Any other job in the world, if you get canned you can have a good cry in the washroom and go home. But show business! You take it on the chin and then paint up your face and out on the stage as gay as anything. "My dear Lady Barbara, what an enchanting place you have here! And what a quaint idea, giving us pigs' knuckles for tea!"

TERRY: Yes, it was awfully jolly. I wouldn't have minded if Berger or somebody had come backstage and said, "Look, we're sorry to do this to you, and better luck next time." But nobody came around—not Berger, or the author, or the director or anybody. They can all run away at a time like that, but the actors have to stay and face it.

JUDITH: You'll get something else, Terry. You got swell notices in this one.

TERRY: Nobody remembers notices except the actors who get them.

KAYE: The movie scouts remember. What about your screen test?

JUDITH: Yes, how about that? Have you heard from it?

TERRY: Oh, I'm not counting on that. They might take Jean. She's got that camera face. But they'll never burn up the coast wires over me.

JUDITH: Jean can't act. You're ten times the actress that she is.

TERRY: Oh, how do you know who's an actress and who isn't! You're an actress if you're acting. Without a job and those lines to say, an actress is just an ordinary person, trying not to look as scared as she feels. What is there about it, anyhow! Why do we all keep trying?

(*The door opens and Bernice enters—rather solemnly. Her mood fits none too well with the definitely pink pajamas that form the basis of her costume, so you gather that it must have to do with a great filmy bit of black something that she has draped around her head and shoulders, and which trails behind her at enormous length. Obviously, she thinks that*

Modjeska herself could not have achieved a finer characteri-
zation.)

BERNICE: How do I look?

KAYE: Marvelous.

JUDITH: What *are* you?

BERNICE: (*In the voice of a woman anywhere between forty and
eighty*) I'm trying out tomorrow. The Theatre Guild is reviving *Madame X.* (*She goes—the perfect embodiment of
Madame X, or anyhow Little Eva.*)

(*Meanwhile Madeleine has come down the hall and now
stands lounging in the doorway, a plate of food in one hand,
a fork in the other.*)

MADELEINE: Anybody want some chop suey? Terry? Kaye?

TERRY: No, thank you.

KAYE: No, thanks.

JUDITH: (*Tempted by this*) Chop suey? I thought it was rarebit.

MADELEINE: We didn't have any beer, so I'm calling it chop
suey. (*She goes.*)

JUDITH: Certainly sounds terrible. (*Turns, with a hand on the
door*) Look, I guess you want this closed, huh?

TERRY: Yes, please.

(*The door closes. Kaye and Terry are alone. With a sigh
Terry again faces reality. Listlessly she begins to undress.
Kaye is almost ready for bed. As she turns back the bedclothes
she pauses to regard Terry.*)

KAYE: I know how sunk you feel, Terry. It's that horrible let-
down after the shock has worn off.

TERRY: The idiotic part of it is I didn't feel so terrible after that
first minute. I thought, well, Keith's coming around after
the show, and we'll go to Smitty's and sit there and talk and
it won't seem so bad. But he never showed up.

KAYE: Terry, I shouldn't try to advise you where men are concerned. I haven't been very smart myself—but this isn't the
first time he's let you down. Don't get in too deep with a
boy like Keith Burgess. It'll only make you unhappy.

TERRY: I don't expect him to be like other people. I wouldn't
want him to be. One of the things that makes him so much
fun is that he's different. If he forgets an appointment it's
because he's working and doesn't notice. Only—I wish he
had come tonight. (*She is pulling her dress over her head as*

she talks and her words are partly muffled until she emerges.)
I needed him so. (*Suddenly her defenses are down.*) Kaye,
I'm frightened. For the first time, I'm frightened. It's
three years now. The first year it didn't matter so much.
I was so young. Nobody was ever as young as I was. I
thought, they just don't know. But I'll get a good part
and show them. I didn't mind anything in those days. Not
having any money, or quite enough food; and a pair of
silk stockings always a major investment. I didn't mind
because I felt so sure that that wonderful part was going to
come along. But it hasn't. And suppose it doesn't next
year? Suppose it—never comes?

KAYE: You can always go home. You've got a home to go to,
anyhow.

TERRY: And marry some home-town boy—like Louise?

KAYE: I didn't mean that, exactly.

TERRY: I can't just go home and plump myself down on Dad.
You know what a country doctor makes! When I was little I
never knew how poor we were, because Mother made
everything seem so glamorous—so much fun. (*All this time
Terry has continued her preparations for bed. At one point in
her disrobing she has gone to the clothes closet, hung up her
dress, and slipped her nightgown over her head. Unseen there,
for a moment, she has gone on talking.*) Even if I was sick it
was a lot of fun, because then I was allowed to look at her
scrapbook. I even used to pretend to be sick, just to look at
it—and that took acting, with a doctor for a father. I adored
that scrapbook. All those rep-company actors in wooden attitudes—I remember a wonderful picture of Mother as Es-
meralda. It was the last part she ever played, and she never
finished the performance.

KAYE: What happened?

TERRY: She fainted, right in the middle of the last act. They
rang down and somebody said, "Is there a doctor in the
house?" And there was. And he married her.

KAYE: Terry, how romantic!

TERRY: Only first she was sick for weeks and weeks. Of course
the company had to leave her behind. They thought she'd
catch up with them any week, but she never did.

KAYE: Didn't she ever miss it? I mean afterward.

TERRY: I know now that she missed it every minute of her life. I think if Dad hadn't been such a gentle darling, and not so dependent on her, she might have gone off and taken me with her. I'd have been one of those children brought up in dressing rooms, sleeping in trunk trays, getting my vocabulary from stagehands.

KAYE: That would have been thrilling.

TERRY: But she didn't. She lived out the rest of her life right in that little town, but she was stage-struck to the end. There never was any doubt in her mind—I was going to be an actress. It was almost a spiritual thing, like being dedicated to the church.

KAYE: I never thought of the theater that way. I just used it as a convenience, because I was desperate. And now I'm using it again, because I'm desperate.

TERRY: Oh, now I've made you blue. I didn't mean to be gloomy. We're fine! We're elegant! They have to pay me two weeks' salary for this flop. Eighty dollars. We're fixed for weeks. One of us'll get a job.

KAYE: I can't take any money from you. You paid my twelve-fifty last week.

TERRY: Oh, don't be stuffy! I happened to be the one who was working.

KAYE: I'll never get a job. I'm—I'm not a very good actress.

TERRY: Oh, stop that!

KAYE: And there's nothing else I can do and nobody I can go back to. Except somebody I'll never go back to.

TERRY: (*Facing her*) It's your husband, isn't it?

KAYE: (*Looks at Terry a moment, silently.*) I ran away from him twice before, but I had to go back. I was hungry, and finally I didn't even have a room. Both times, he just waited. He's waiting now.

TERRY: Kaye, tell me what it is! Why are you afraid of him?

KAYE: (*She turns her eyes away from Terry as she speaks.*) To most people he's a normal, attractive man. But I know better. Nights of terror. "Now, darling, it wouldn't do any good to kill me. They wouldn't let you play polo tomorrow. Now, we'll open the window and you'll throw the revolver at that lamppost. It'll be such fun to hear the glass smash." And then there were the times when he made love to me. I can't even tell you about that. (*She recalls the scene with a shudder.*)

TERRY: Kaye, darling! But if he's as horrible as that, can't you do something legally?

KAYE: (*A desperate shake of her head*) They have millions. I'm nobody. I've gone to his family. They treated me as though *I* were the mad one. They're united like a stone wall.

TERRY: But Kaye, isn't there anybody—what about your own folks? Haven't you got any?

KAYE: I have a father. Chicago. I ran away at sixteen and went on the stage. Then I met Dick—and I fell for him. He was good-looking, and gay, and always doing sort of crazy things—smashing automobiles and shooting at bar-room mirrors. . . . I thought it was funny, then.

TERRY: (*Reaches out wordlessly to extend a comforting hand.*) And I've been moaning about my little troubles.

KAYE: You know, I'd sworn to myself I never was going to bother you with this. Now, what made me do it?

TERRY: I'm glad you did. It'll do you good.

KAYE: Yes, I suppose it will.

TERRY: (*Taking off her robe*) Well, we might as well get those sheep over the fence. Maybe we'll wake up tomorrow morning and there'll be nineteen managers downstairs, all saying, "You, and only you, can play this part."

KAYE: (*As she settles herself for sleep*) I suppose Jean'll be out till all hours.

TERRY: There's a girl who hasn't got any troubles. Life rolls right along with her. . . . (*At the window*) Well, ready to go bye-bye?

KAYE: I suppose I might as well. But I feel so wide awake.

(*As Terry opens the window a blast of noise comes up from the street. A cacophony made up of protesting brakes, automobile horns, taxi drivers' shouts, a laugh or two.*)

(*Kaye turns out the top light. From her dresser she takes a black eyeshield and adjusts it over her eyes after she is in bed. Terry does the same, then shouts a "Good night!" loudly enough to be heard above the street din. Kaye's good night is equally loud. Simultaneously they turn out their bed lights. For a second—but only a second—the room is in darkness. Then the reason for the eyeshades becomes apparent. A huge*) *electric advertising sign on an adjacent roof flashes on, off, on, off, alternately flooding the room with light and plunging it into darkness.*)

TERRY: (*Shouting*) Funny if we both *did* get jobs tomorrow!

KAYE: Huh?

TERRY: (*Louder*) I say, it would be funny if we both got jobs tomorrow!

KAYE: Certainly would!

(*A moment of silence in the room.*)

(*The door bursts open. Jean comes in, bringing with her a quiver of excitement. She is in dinner clothes.*)

JEAN: (*She turns on the light*) Terry! Wake up!

TERRY: What's the matter?

JEAN: (*Slams the window down.*) We're in the movies!

TERRY: What?

JEAN: Both of us! We're in the movies! They just heard from the Coast!

TERRY: Jean! How do you know? What happened?

JEAN: Mr. Kingsley just got the telegram. They liked the tests, and we're to go to the office tomorrow to sign our contracts. We leave for the Coast next week! Terry! Can you believe it!

KAYE: Oh, girls, how exciting!

TERRY: (*Bewildered*) Yes. Yes. You mean—right away?

JEAN: (*Hardly able to contain herself*) Of course we'll only get little parts in the beginning. But there's that beautiful check every week, whether you work or not. And the swimming and the sunshine and those little ermine jackets up to here. No more running around to offices and having them spit in your eye. And a salary raise every six months if they like us. So at the end of three years it begins to get pretty good, and after five years it's wonderful, and at the end of seven years it's more money than you ever heard of.

TERRY: Seven years! What do you mean—seven years!

JEAN: Yes, it's a seven-year contract—that is, if they take up the options.

TERRY: But what about the stage? Suppose I wanted to act?

JEAN: Well, what do you think this is! Juggling? Motion-picture acting is just as much of an art as stage acting, only

it's cut up more. You only have to learn about a line at a
time, and they just keep on taking it until you get it right.

TERRY: (*Staring at Jean. A stricken pause. Then she shakes her
head slowly. Her decision is made.*) Oh, no.

JEAN: What?

TERRY: I couldn't.

JEAN: Couldn't what?

TERRY: This isn't acting; that's piecework. You're not a human
being, you're a thing in a vacuum. Noise shut out, human
response shut out. But in the theater, when you hear that
lovely sound out there, then you know you're right. It's as
though they'd turned on an electric current that hit you
here. And that's how you learn to act.

JEAN: You can learn to act in pictures. You have to do it till it's
right.

TERRY: Yes, and then they put it in a tin can—like Campbell's
soup. And if you die the next day it doesn't matter a bit. You
don't even have to be alive to act in pictures.

JEAN: I suppose you call *this* being alive! Sleeping three in a
room in *this* rotten dump! It builds you up, eh?

TERRY: I'm not going to stay here all my life! This is only the
beginning!

JEAN: Don't kid yourself! You've been here three years, and
then it's three years more, and then another three, and
where are you? You can't play ingenues forever. Pretty soon
you're a character woman, and then you're running a
boardinghouse, like old Orcutt. *That'll* be nice, won't it?

TERRY: I don't know! You make me sound like a fool, but I
know I'm not. All I know is I want to stay on the stage. I
just don't want to be in pictures. An actress in the theater—
that's what I've wanted to be my whole life. It isn't just a career, it's a feeling. The theater is something that's gone on
for hundreds and hundreds of years. It's—I don't know—
it's part of civilization.

JEAN: (*Screaming at her*) All right, you stay here with your civilization, eating those stews and tapiocas they shove at us,
toeing the mark in this female seminary, buying your clothes
at Klein's! That's what you like, eh?

TERRY: *Yes*, I like it!

JEAN: And I suppose you like this insane racket going on all night! (*She throws open the window.*)

TERRY: (*Yelling above the noise*) Yes, I *do!*

JEAN: And that Cadillac car sign going on and off like a damned lighthouse! (*She turns off the light. Again we see the flash of the electric sign, off, on, off, on.*) I suppose you've got to have *that* to be an actress!

TERRY: Yes! Yes! Yes! Yes! Yes!

JEAN: (*Not stopping for her*) Well, not for me! I'm going out where there's sunshine and money and fun and—

TERRY: (*Shouting above her*) And little ermine swimming pools up to here!

(*The street noise, the flashing light, and their angry shouts are still going on as the curtain descends.*)

CURTAIN

ACT TWO

Scene I

The main room of the Footlights Club. It is mid-morning; the sunlight is streaming in.

Frank, the houseman, is rather listlessly pushing a carpet sweeper, his attention directed toward an open newspaper lying on a chair. He edges nearer and nearer; his movements with the carpet sweeper become slower and slower, until finally they are barely perceptible.

Ann Braddock comes briskly down the stairs with a condescending "Good morning, Frank!" and goes into the dining room, Frank's response having been an absent-minded mumble.

Mattie bustles in from the hall, and her face reflects her irritation as she sees her husband's idling at this busy hour of the day. Lips compressed, she marches straight to him, snatches the carpet sweeper from him and goes off with it. Frank follows meekly after.

Somewhere in the hall, unseen, a clock strikes eleven.

Bobby Melrose, gaily singing, skips down the stairs and stops for a look through the mail. She finds a letter that gets her full attention, so that she is absorbed in it as she walks more slowly toward the dining room.

BOBBY: Oh, girls! Here's a letter from Madeleine.

JUDITH: (*Entering from the dining room*) Where is she this week?

BOBBY: Let's see. This week, Portland and Spokane. Next week, Seattle.

JUDITH: Seattle. That's her home town.
    (*Kendall Adams dashes down the stairs, struggling into one coat sleeve as she comes. She stops for a quick glance at the mail, shrugging into her coat meanwhile.*)
  Heh, where're you going?

KENDALL: Rehearsal!

JUDITH: What's the rush?

631

KENDALL: Late!

JUDITH: (*Calling after her as she dashes for the door*) You're too conscientious. (*The slam of the door*) Never gets you anywhere in this business.

TERRY: (*Coming down the stairs*) Well, what *does* get you anywhere, if I may make so bold?

JUDITH: Clean living, high thinking, and an occasional dinner with the manager.

TERRY: (*Taking a look through the mail*) What time is it? Shouldn't you be at rehearsal?

JUDITH: No, there's plenty of time. The nuns aren't called until eleven-thirty today.

TERRY: (*Turning over the envelope in her hand*) Mrs. Robert Hendershot—why, that's Louise! Appleton, Wisconsin. It's a letter from Louise.

> (*The telephone rings. Terry rips open the envelope and takes a quick look at its pages, which are voluminous.*)

JUDITH: (*En route to the telephone*) Maybe it's a Little Stranger. She's been married a year. . . . Hello! . . . She's right here. . . . (*Hands the telephone to Terry.*)

TERRY: Keith? (*Thrusts the letter into Judith's hand.*) Here. It's addressed to all of us.

> (*As Judith buries herself in the letter Terry's attention goes to the telephone.*)

Keith! Isn't this the middle of the night for you! . . . What about? . . . No, I've got to stay free all afternoon on account of Dad. . . . I don't know what time he gets here. He's driving with a friend. . . . Yes, all the way from Elvira. Well, you don't have to like it. He will. . . . No, I can't, because he's only here a day and a half, and this afternoon he wants to see Radio City and the Medical Center and the Battery.

JUDITH: (*Looking up from her letter*) Has he got a bicycle?

TERRY: And don't forget that you've invited us to dinner. . . . No, not at Smitty's. . . . Well, Dad and Smitty's just don't go together. And look, darling, don't wear a black shirt and don't be one of the Masses tonight. . . .

> (*Susan runs down the stairs and goes to the dining room with a "Good morning!" to the girls.*)

What? . . . Well, you can tell me about it at dinner. . . .
No, I've got a radio rehearsal.

JUDITH: (*Still with the letter*) Say, this is a classic.

TERRY: Well, if it's as vital as all that you can come up here. . . .
That's my brave boy! (*She hangs up.*)

JUDITH: (*Her first opportunity to read from the letter*) Get this:
"I have gained a little weight, but Bob says I look better not
so scrawny. He says maybe I like my own cooking too much,
but then he is always joking." (*To Olga, who has come out of
the dining room*) It's a letter from Louise.

OLGA: What does she say?

BOBBY: (*Appearing in the dining-room doorway*) Who said a
letter from Louise?

TERRY: Yes, it just came.

JUDITH: (*Reading, as Ann and Susan come into the dining-
room doorway to hear the news*) "Dear Girlies: I guess you
all wonder why I have not written for so long. I honestly
don't know where the year has gone to. First there was the
house to furnish. We've got the darlingest six-room bungalow on Winnebago Street. And then of course everybody
was giving parties for me, and after that I had to return the
obligations by giving parties for them. We are all even now.
I gave the last one just yesterday—eighteen girls of the
young married set, three tables of bridge and one of mah
jong, and two people just talked. The luncheon was lovely, if
I do say so. Everything pink."

OLGA: You're making it up.

JUDITH: So help me . . . "I am a member of the Ladies' Committee at the Country Club, which gives wonderful Satur-
day-night dances during the summer." (*She turns to the girls
for a moment.*) Japanese lanterns. . . . "But do not think
that I have lost track of the theater. We take the Milwaukee
Sentinel daily, and last week we drove to Milwaukee and saw
Walter Hampden in *Cyrano.*"

TERRY: (*Reaching for the letter*) Let me see! "So now I've told
you all my news and you've got to write me just everything
about the club. What about you, Terry, have you got a swell
part for this season? I thought I'd die when I saw Jean's
picture in *Photoplay*, all dressed up like a real movie star in a

little ermine jacket and everything. Jean a movie star! I've been bragging to all my friends. Well, if you girls think about me as much as I do about you, my ears would be about burned off. We have supper here around six o'clock, just as you all do at the club, and when it's over I always think, well, the girls are all beating it down to the show shop and making up to go on and just knocking the audience cold. Only I don't say it out loud any more because Bob says, oh, for God's sake, you and your club! Love to old Orcutt and for goodness' sakes, write, write, WRITE!"

JUDITH: (*Very low*) Wow.

TERRY: Well, I'll never complain again. This makes my eighteen a week on the radio look pretty wonderful.

OLGA: (*As she goes up the stairs*) Everything pink.

BOBBY: We've just been livin' in a bed of roses.

ANN: I could have told her when she left it wouldn't work.

(*Bobby, Ann and Susan go back to the dining room. Terry and Judith remain in the living room.*)

JUDITH: (*Getting into her coat*) Well, I might as well get down to the factory.

TERRY: Look, Judith. Think you'll be rehearsing all afternoon?

JUDITH: How do I know! This thing I'm in is a combination of Ringling Brothers and the Passion Play. You never know whether they're going to rehearse us nuns or the elephants.

TERRY: It's just that I'd love you to meet my father, if you have time.

JUDITH: Oh, I want to. He sounds like a cutie.

TERRY: I wonder what's on Keith's mind, getting up so early.

JUDITH: Nothing, is my guess.

TERRY: Judith! Maybe he sold the play!

JUDITH: Maybe. (*Takes the plunge*) Look, Terry. Where're you heading in with that guy, anyhow?

TERRY: Why, what do you mean?

JUDITH: *You* know. He's been coming around here for a year, taking all your time, talking about himself, never considering you for a minute. Sold his play! Well, if he has he can thank *you* for it. It's as much your play as his.

TERRY: That isn't true.

JUDITH: Don't tell *me*. It was nothing but a stump speech the way he wrote it. You made him put flesh and blood into it.

TERRY: (*Quietly*) You're talking about someone you don't understand.

JUDITH: O.K. Forget I ever brought it up. . . . Well—good-by.

TERRY: (*Rather reserved*) Good-by. (*Takes a couple of type-written pages out of her handbag.*)

JUDITH: Oh, now you're sore at me. I never can learn to keep my trap shut. But I only said it because I think more of you than anybody else in this whole menagerie. . . . Forgiven?

TERRY: Of course, Judy darling.

JUDITH: (*Indicating the papers in Terry's hand*) What's that? Your radio?

TERRY: Mmm.

JUDITH: It makes me boil to think of an actress like you reading radio recipes for a living. (*Peers at the script.*) "Two eggs and fold in the beaten whites." The beaten whites! That's us!

TERRY: Anyhow, it's a living for a few weeks. Aunt Miranda's Cooking Class.

JUDITH: Well, you're a hell of an Aunt Miranda, that's all I can say. . . . (*Goes.*)

(*Ann and Bobby come out of the dining room. Ann is carrying a newspaper.*)

ANN: (*Seeing Terry*) Did you read about Jean out in Hollywood? They've given her a new contract with a big raise and she's going to play the lead in *Two for Tonight*.

TERRY: Really! (*Looking over Ann's shoulder*) How marvelous! (*Takes paper from Ann and goes into dining room.*)

BOBBY: It's all a matter of cheek bones. You've got to have a face like this. (*She pushes her round little face into hollow curves.*)

ANN: (*Getting her coat*) What are you doing this morning? Job-hunting?

BOBBY: Uh-huh. Ah thought Ah'd go round to Equity and see what's up on the bulletin board. Maybe there's something new casting.

ANN: (*Applying her lipstick*) I'm going to try a couple of agents' offices. (*Becomes unintelligible as she paints the cupid's bow.*) Sometimes they know about new things.

BOBBY: What kind of lipstick's that?

ANN: It's a new one. It's called "I'll Never Tell."

BOBBY: Let me see. (*Tries a daub on the back of her hand.*) Mm. It's too orangey for me. Ah like Hibiscus—good and red— as if you'd been kicked in the mouth by a mule.

(*They gather up their handbags and go.*)

(*Kaye comes down the stairs like a little wraith. Near the foot of the stairs she glances over the railing and it is evident that she is relieved to find the living room empty.*)

(*As she is about to go to the street door Mrs. Orcutt swoops down on her with a promptness which indicates that she has been waiting for her.*)

MRS. ORCUTT: Oh, Kaye! Could I speak to you just a minute, please?

KAYE: I'm—just on my way to rehearsal.

MRS. ORCUTT: (*As she carefully closes the dining-room door*) I won't detain you but a second. I just want to— (*The door is closed.*) You must know how reluctant I always am to speak to you on this subject. I try to be as easy as I can with the girls, but, after all, I have my bills to pay, too.

KAYE: But Mrs. Orcutt, I'm rehearsing. You know that. And I'm sure they like me. And just the minute we open I can start paying off.

MRS. ORCUTT: Yes, I know. But plays are not always successful, and the amount has grown rather large. So, taking everything into consideration, I wonder if you'd mind a little suggestion.

KAYE: No. No.

MRS. ORCUTT: Well, it occurred to me that perhaps it might be wise if you were to find some place a little cheaper. By a lucky chance I think I know the ideal place. Of course the girls are a little older, and it's not strictly a theatrical club— more the commercial professions. However, I think you'll find it almost as conveniently situated. Forty-ninth Street, this side of Tenth Avenue. Perhaps, when you have time, you might drop in and look at it.

(*Kaye only nods a silent assent.*)

Now, now, we mustn't be upset by this. It's just a little talk. (*A rather grim pause which suggests the alternative.*) Now, let's put it out of our minds. Shall we? And let me see a little smile. (*As there is no response from Kaye, Mrs. Orcutt smiles*

for both.) There! . . . Well, we both have our day's work to
do. (*Mrs. Orcutt goes.*)

(*Pat, singing blithely, comes down the stairs. As she passes
Kaye she chucks her gaily under the chin, says, "H'ya, baby?"
by way of morning greeting, and executes a brief and intricate little dance step, all this without pausing on her way to
the dining room.*)

(*Kaye stands, a little wooden figure. She turns to go as Terry
comes in from the dining room.*)

TERRY: What are you doing—going without your breakfast?

KAYE: I don't want any breakfast. I'm not hungry.

TERRY: (*On her way to the stairs*) Well, you're just an old fool,
rehearsing on an empty stomach.

(*As Kaye goes the two Marys come into sight on the stairs,
talking as they descend. They pass Terry as she goes up.*)

BIG MARY: (*In the throes of trying to memorize a part. Little
Mary, who is cueing her, follows with the part in her hand.*)
"Three weeks now since he first came here. What do we
know about him—uh—anyhow?" Is there an "anyhow"?

LITTLE MARY: Yeh.

BIG MARY: "What do we know about him anyhow? Only that
he spent twelve years in Australia and that he claims to be
your second cousin—second cousin—second cousin—"

LITTLE MARY: "I tell you—"

(*The doorbell rings.*)

BIG MARY: "I tell you there is something mysterious going on
in this house." Well, that's all, give me the cue.

LITTLE MARY: (*Scans the part.*) Uh—huh—

BIG MARY: Oh, for heaven's sakes! "We must call the police."

LITTLE MARY: Oh, yeh. "We must call the police."

BIG MARY: Now let's go back and do it right. "I tell you there
is something mysterious going on in this house."

LITTLE MARY: (*As they go into the dining room*) "We must call
the police."

(*The outer door is opened and we hear a voice subsequently
identified as that of Mrs. Shaw, Linda's mother.*)

MRS. SHAW: Good morning.

MATTIE: How-do.

MRS. SHAW: This is the Footlights Club, isn't it?

MATTIE: Yes, ma'am. Won't you come in?

MRS. SHAW: Oh, thank you.

(*Mrs. Shaw comes into sight. She is a rather cozy little woman of about fifty-five, plainly dressed, sweet-faced and inclined to be voluble.*)

(*She speaks rather confidingly now to Mattie.*)

I'm Mrs. Shaw, Linda's mother. She doesn't know I'm coming. I'm surprising her.

MATTIE: Oh—you Miss Linda's mother! For land's sakes!

MRS. SHAW: She doesn't know I'm here. We live in Buffalo. I just got off the train and came right up. Linda hasn't gone out, I hope?

MATTIE: (*As she goes toward the stairs*) No, I haven't seen her around yet.

MRS. SHAW: Well, you just tell her there's somebody here to see her, very important. Only don't tell her it's her mother.

MATTIE: Yes'm. (*She disappears.*)

(*Mrs. Shaw seats herself and looks about her with bright-eyed interest.*)

(*Susan comes out of the dining room, and seeing a middle-aged woman in the room nods politely.*)

MRS. SHAW: Good morning.

SUSAN: Good morning.

MRS. SHAW: Are you a little actress?

SUSAN: Yes, sort of.

MRS. SHAW: I'm Linda's mother. I've come to surprise her.

SUSAN: Oh, what fun!

MRS. SHAW: Which one of the girls are you? Perhaps Linda's written me about you.

SUSAN: I'm Susan Paige.

MRS. SHAW: Are you acting a part on Broadway?

SUSAN: I'm in *Petticoat Lane*, but I'm only an understudy.

MRS. SHAW: Understudy?

SUSAN: That means I play the part in case the leading woman gets sick.

MRS. SHAW: Oh! That's nice. And does she get sick often?

SUSAN: Never!

(*Susan goes up the stairs as Mattie descends.*)

(*Mattie appears slightly flustered.*)

MATTIE: I'm awful sorry, I must have made a mistake. I guess Miss Linda must have gone out already.

MRS. SHAW: Oh, dear! Does anybody know where she went?

MATTIE: (*Edging toward the hall*) Well, I'll see—maybe Mrs. Orcutt knows.

> (*We have not heard the front door open or close, so silently has Linda Shaw entered the house. She is swiftly tiptoeing up the stairs as Mattie turns and sees her.*)

There she is! Miss Linda! Miss Linda!

> (*Linda has not heeded the first call, but the second one stops her.*)

Your ma's here.

MRS. SHAW: Oh, dear, I was going to surprise you.

LINDA: (*Frozen on the stairs*) Why—Mother!

MRS. SHAW: I guess I have. Well, aren't you going to come down? (*Holds her arms open wide to embrace her daughter.*)

> (*Linda makes a slow and heavy-footed descent, eyeing first her mother, then Mattie. She is wrapped in a camel's-hair ulster, a little too large for her; on her head is a small beret such as might be worn by a man or woman.*)

LINDA: Mother, how—how wonderful. When did—you—

MRS. SHAW: Why, Linda, child, aren't you glad to see me?

LINDA: Of course I am, Mother. (*Kisses her mother quickly.*)

MRS. SHAW: (*As she surveys her daughter's strange attire*) Of all the funny getups!

LINDA: Yes, isn't it silly—I— (*She turns to the gaping Mattie.*) —Mattie, I'm sure you have your work to do. Why don't you run along?

MATTIE: (*Reluctant to leave*) Yes—Miss Linda. (*She goes.*)

MRS. SHAW: Where did you get that coat? I never saw that coat before.

LINDA: It belongs to—to one of the girls. . . . I had to go down to the drugstore.

MRS. SHAW: Why—you've got on evening slippers!

LINDA: I just put on the first thing I could find.

MRS. SHAW: Linda Shaw, if you've run out in your pajamas—

LINDA: (*Backing away from her mother*) No, I haven't. I— (*She realizes she has made a blunder.*) —Yes, I have. Yes.

MRS. SHAW: Linda, what are you wearing under that coat?

> (*Linda stands, holding the coat about her.*)

Take off that coat! Take off that—

> (*She jerks it open so that it slides down the girl's arms and*

drops to the floor, revealing Linda in a black satin evening dress of extreme cut—the narrowest of shoulder straps, bare shoulders, a deep decolletage, the bodice almost backless.)

Linda!

LINDA: I spent the night with a girl friend.

MRS. SHAW: Oh—Linda!

LINDA: Oh, Mother, don't make a scene!

MRS. SHAW: (*With repressed emotion*) Linda, go up and pack your things. You're coming home with me.

LINDA: Oh, no, I'm not.

MRS. SHAW: Linda Shaw!

LINDA: We can't talk here, Mother. And there's no use talking, anyhow. I'm never coming home. I'm twenty-two years old, and my life is my own.

MRS. SHAW: Who—who is this man? Are you going to marry him?

LINDA: He *is* married.

MRS. SHAW: I'm going to send for your father. He'll know what to do.

LINDA: Mother, if you make a fuss about this I'll have to leave the club. That girl knows already. And if I leave here I'll go and live with him, and the whole world will know it. Now take your choice.

(*Mrs. Orcutt enters, apprehension in her face, steeled for an eventuality. Her quick eye goes from the girl to the mother.*)

MRS. ORCUTT: I'm Mrs. Orcutt, Mrs. Shaw. My maid just told me you were here.

MRS. SHAW: Oh, how do you do, Mrs. Orcutt?

MRS. ORCUTT: I understand you arrived unexpectedly.

MRS. SHAW: Yes, I came down to do a bit of shopping and surprise my little girl, here, and we practically came in together. She spent the night with my niece and her husband—Eighty-sixth Street—they had a rather late party and Linda just decided to—I don't see how these young people stand it. . . . (*A little laugh*) Doesn't she look silly—this time of day—Linda darling, do run up and change. Why don't you meet me for luncheon at the hotel? Can you do that?

LINDA: Of course, Mother dear.

MRS. SHAW: I'm at the Roosevelt, darling. Shall we say one o'clock?

LINDA: (*In quiet triumph*) Yes, Mother darling. (*She goes up-stairs.*)

MRS. SHAW: Oh, well, I must run along. I'm only going to be here a day or two and . . . Well, good-by.

MRS. ORCUTT: (*Accompanying her to the door*) Good-by. It's been *so* nice. I'm always happy to meet the parents of our girls. And I hope that whenever you are in the city you won't fail to drop in on us. Well, good-by.

(*As Mrs. Orcutt passes back along the hallway Olga descends the stairs. She is wearing a hat, her coat is over her arm. In one hand she has a few sheets of music, in the other a music portfolio. She tosses her coat over to the piano and props a sheet of music on the rack.*)

(*She sits at the piano, plays a few bars.*)

(*Bernice, in hat and coat, comes down the stairs. She looks in on Olga and listens to the music.*)

BERNICE: Are you going to play that at your concert?

OLGA: (*Playing*) Yes.

BERNICE: When's it going to be?

OLGA: In the spring.

BERNICE: Whereabouts, Town Hall?

OLGA: Yes, yes.

BERNICE: Are you going to play under your own name?

OLGA: Certainly.

BERNICE: Well, you've got an interesting name—Olga Brandt. It sounds like a musician. But Bernice Niemeyer! I think that's what's holding me back in the theater. Do you know what? I thought maybe I'd take one of those one-word names, the way some actresses do. I thought, instead of Bernice Niemeyer, I'd just call myself—Zara. (*Bernice goes.*)

(*Olga continues with her music. The doorbell rings. Mattie answers.*)

(*As the door opens we hear the voice of Dr. Randall, Terry's father. His first words are lost under cover of Olga's music.*)

MATTIE: Just go right in and sit down. I'll tell Miss Terry you're here. (*She goes up the stairs.*)

(*Dr. Randall is a gentle-looking, gray-haired man touching sixty. There is about him a vague quality—a wistful charm—that is not of the modern professional world.*)

(*Olga, as he enters, is about to launch herself on the finale of the selection she has been playing. It entails terrific chords, dissonances, and actual physical effort. The length of the keyboard seems scarcely adequate. Dr. Randall stands arrested by this. Three times the music pauses as if finished, each time Dr. Randall steps forward to speak and Olga starts again. He gives a little nod of approval as Olga finishes, rises, and gathers up her music and her coat. Olga acknowledges this with a little inclination of her head, and goes.*)

(*The front door slams on her going. Immediately the dining-room doors open and the two Marys come out, still deep in rehearsal.*)

BIG MARY: "I tell you there is something mysterious going on in this house."

LITTLE MARY: "We must call the police."

BIG MARY: (*With no particular expression*) "Last night I heard moans and shrieks, and this morning a dead man was found on the doorstep, his head completely severed."

LITTLE MARY: "What about the blood in the library?" (*They disappear up the stairs.*)

(*Pat emerges from the dining room, intent on mastering a fast and intricate dance routine for which she provides her own music. She catches herself at the sight of a stranger, and scampers up the stairs.*)

(*Dr. Randall has barely had time to react to these somewhat bewildering encounters when a gay high voice from the stairs calls, "Dad!" and Terry comes running down. She hurls herself into her father's arms.*)

TERRY: Dad! Darling! I couldn't be more surprised.

DR. RANDALL: Glad to see me?

TERRY: Glad! I should say so! It's been almost a year.

DR. RANDALL: Too long, my dear. Too long to be separated. . . . Let me look at you.

TERRY: Bursting with health, Doc.

DR. RANDALL: Mmm. (*Pulls down first one eyelid, then the other.*)

Look kind of peaked to me. Eat enough greens?

TERRY: Greens! I'm a regular Miss Popeye. Now let me look at you. Say Ah, say Oh, say you love me. (*He laughs as he kisses her.*) Now come on and tell me everything. How's Aunt Lucy? And is she taking good care of you?

DR. RANDALL: Say, you know Lucy! You'd think I was ten years old.

TERRY: I know. Wear your rubbers, have you got a clean handkerchief. Didn't she fuss about your driving all this way?

DR. RANDALL: Carried on like mad.

TERRY: How did you get here so early? You said afternoon. What happened?

DR. RANDALL: Well, when Stacy invited me to come East with him, I didn't know what kind of driver he was. Turned out he's one of those fellows slows down to eighty going through a town. I dozed off a couple of minutes, once, and missed all of Pennsylvania.

TERRY: He shouldn't have done it, but it *does* give me more time with you.

DR. RANDALL: Now maybe you've got things to do. You weren't expecting me till three or four.

TERRY: I've got nothing but a silly radio rehearsal. You know —I'm the big butter-and-egg girl. I'll be all through by quarter-past one. Let's have lunch way up on top of something. Shall we?

DR. RANDALL: That's fine. Gives me time to drop in at the Polyclinic a few minutes. Three forty-five West Fiftieth Street. Where's that?

TERRY: It's not five minutes from here. And I'll pick you up at your hotel. Where are you?

DR. RANDALL: New Yorker. Stacy's idea. Full of go-getters.

TERRY: After lunch we'll whirl all over town. We'll see everything. Tonight we're going to the theater, and Keith's taking us to dinner.

DR. RANDALL: Oh, yes. Your young man. I want to meet the boy.

TERRY: Now, Dad, remember, he's not like the boys back in Elvira.

DR. RANDALL: Say, *they're* not like that any more, either.

TERRY: Yes, but Keith's not like anybody you ever met. He's brilliant, and he's written the most marvelous play, and he hates the government and won't wear evening clothes.

DR. RANDALL: Sounds as if he didn't have a nickel.

TERRY: Oh, but he will have! This play will put him over. It's thrilling and beautiful! And oh, Dad, I'm going to play the lead.

DR. RANDALL: Why, Tress, that's wonderful. Your mother would have been very proud.

TERRY: Of course he hasn't sold the play yet. But he will. He's bound to.

DR. RANDALL: Say, I'm going to come back and see you in that if it takes my last nickel.

TERRY: (*Who has been eyeing him a little anxiously*) Dad.

DR. RANDALL: Yes, Tress?

TERRY: You look as though you'd been working too hard. Have you?

DR. RANDALL: I wish I could say I had. But my waiting room looks pretty bleak these days.

TERRY: Isn't anybody sick at all? How about old Mrs. Wainwright?

DR. RANDALL: Yes, folks get sick, all right.

TERRY: Well, then!

DR. RANDALL: Well, it seems just being a medical man isn't enough these days. If you had a cold, we used to just cure the cold. But nowadays, the question is, why did you get the cold? Turns out, it's because, subconsciously, you didn't want to live. And why don't you want to live? Because when you were three years old the cat died, and they buried it in the back yard without telling you, and you were in love with the cat, so, naturally, forty years later you catch cold.

TERRY: But who tells them all this?

DR. RANDALL: Why—uh—young fellow came to town a few months ago; opened up offices.

TERRY: Oh!

DR. RANDALL: Sun lamps, X-ray machines, office fixed up like a power plant. He's the one's looking after Mrs. Wainwright. She's bedridden with sciatica, arthritis and a heart condition, but, fortunately, it's all psychic.

TERRY: Dad, do you mean he's taken your whole practice away from you!

DR. RANDALL: Mm—not as bad as that. The mill folks still come to me.

TERRY: But they haven't any money!

DR. RANDALL: They still have babies.

TERRY: Never you mind. I'm going to buy you the biggest, shiniest, sun-lamp machine ever invented; and fluoroscopes and microscopes and stethoscopes and telescopes. You'll be able to sit in your office and turn a button and look right *through* Mrs. Wainwright, six blocks away.

DR. RANDALL: How about that new doctor? Will it go through him?

TERRY: It'll *dissolve* him.

(*The front door slams. Keith strides to the foot of the stairs. The black sweater has given way to a black shirt. Otherwise his costume is about the same. No hat, of course*)

KEITH: (*Shouts up the stairs.*) Terry!

TERRY: Why—Keith!

KEITH: Oh! I—the door was open. I came right in.

TERRY: Here's Father! He got here this morning.

KEITH: (*Advancing*) Well! This is indeed a pleasure, sir.

DR. RANDALL: Thank you, young man. I'm glad to know you.

KEITH: Terry has told me so much about you. I've been looking forward to this meeting for a long time, sir.

DR. RANDALL: Oh, that's very good of you.

KEITH: (*Takes out a crumpled pack of Camels.*) May I offer you a cigarette, sir?

DR. RANDALL: Thanks. (*Takes a cigarette.*)

TERRY: (*Who has been observing all this courtliness with a growing bewilderment*) Keith, Dad doesn't understand that kind of fooling.

KEITH: You never told me, Theresa, that you and your father had such a strong resemblance. The same fine brow, the deep-set, thoughtful eyes. Allow me, sir! (*Lights Dr. Randall's cigarette.*)

TERRY: Keith, will you stop it! What is this act, anyhow?

KEITH: (*Blandly*) It's no act. What are you talking about?

DR. RANDALL: (*Pats Keith on the shoulder.*) I guess you'll do. . . . Well, children, I've got to be off. You said quarter-past one, Terry?

TERRY: Yes, Father. I'll come to your hotel.

DR. RANDALL: (*To Keith*) Understand we're seeing you later. That right?

KEITH: (*Absent-mindedly*) What? Oh, yes.

TERRY: (*As she accompanies her father into the hallway, their arms about each other's shoulders*) I can't tell you how grand it is to have you here, Dad. . . . Now, don't cross against the lights, and promise to take taxis. Don't try to find places by yourself.

DR. RANDALL: All right, all right.

TERRY: I'll be at the hotel at one-fifteen.

DR. RANDALL: I'll be waiting.

TERRY: Good-by, darling.

DR. RANDALL: Good-by.

(*Terry returns to the living room and Keith.*)

TERRY: Really, Keith, you can be so maddening. What was all that "Yes, sir," and "How are you, sir?"

KEITH: Can't I be polite?

TERRY: One of the least convincing performances I ever saw.

KEITH: That's right. Hit a fellow when he's down.

TERRY: Keith, what's the matter?

KEITH: I come to you in one of the toughest spots I ever was in in my life, and you jump all over me.

TERRY: I'm so sorry. I didn't know. How could I—what's happened? Is it the play?

KEITH: (*Unhappily*) Yes.

TERRY: They all turned it down?

KEITH: (*Reluctantly*) N-no.

TERRY: Keith! Tell me!

KEITH: (*Unwillingly*) I—I could sign a contract this afternoon.

TERRY: You don't mean it! Who with?

KEITH: Gilman.

TERRY: (*Almost with awe*) Gilman! Why, he's the best there is!

KEITH: That's what makes it so tough.

TERRY: Keith, for heaven's sake, you're not being unreasonable about this! A Gilman production—why, it's— Keith, no matter what he wants you to do, you've got to do it. What's he want you to change? The second act?

KEITH: No. He likes the play all right. He's nuts about it.

TERRY: Well, then, I don't—understand what—

KEITH: (*Squirming*) I just can't let him have it, that's all.

TERRY: (*Something clicks in her mind.*) Keith! It's me. He doesn't want me.

KEITH: Well—you see—Gilman's got Natalie Blake under contract, and she *is* a big star, and it just happens to be the kind of part she's been looking for—

TERRY: (*Crushed*) Did you tell him you thought I would be good in it?

KEITH: Of course. I gave him a hell of an argument. But he just won't do it unless Blake is in it.

TERRY: Well, then, that's—that. I wouldn't do anything to— I bow out, Keith.

KEITH: Gosh, Terry! You mean you really would do that for me!

TERRY: The play is the important thing, Keith. I love every line of it. You didn't think, after the way we've worked on it for a whole year, that I'd stand in the way, did you?

KEITH: God, you're wonderful, Terry! You're a great kid! I'm crazy about you! (*He embraces her.*)

TERRY: (*Evading him*) Please, Keith.

KEITH: There isn't one girl in a million would have taken it like this. And I love you for it. Love you, do you hear!

TERRY: Yes, Keith.

KEITH: Well, look—

> (*He breaks off as Linda comes down the stairs—Linda in a neat little mink cape, and carrying a costly looking dressing case. There is determination written in her face.*)
> (*She gives a swift glance down the hall. Then decides to use Terry as her messenger.*)

LINDA: Terry. Terry, will you do something for me?

TERRY: (*Absorbed in her own thoughts*) What? . . . Oh, hello, Linda.

LINDA: I don't want to see Orcutt. Will you give her a message for me?

TERRY: Yes, of course.

LINDA: Tell her I'm leaving. I'll send for my things this afternoon. And give her this. (*She thrusts some bills into Terry's hand.*) It's for the whole week.

TERRY: Linda, what's the matter? You're moving? Where?

LINDA: You bet I'm moving. Fast. And nobody'll *ever* know where. (*She goes.*)

KEITH: What was all that about?

TERRY: (*Collecting herself*) What? . . . I don't know. She's a strange girl.

KEITH: Well, look, I've got to run. Gilman's waiting in the office for me. He's lining up a hell of a cast. I'm going to meet Natalie Blake this evening. I'm having dinner with her and Gilman.

TERRY: Tonight! Keith, you're having dinner with Father and me.

KEITH: Oh, for God's sake, Terry! I get a chance like this with a top manager and a big star, and you expect me to say (*Lapses into an imitation of a nitwit.*) I can't meet you tonight, I got to have dinner with my girl and her papa. That's what you want me to say, I suppose?

TERRY: No—no.

KEITH: (*About to leave*) I'll do the best I can. You know that. This whole thing is for you as much as for me. You know that, don't you?

TERRY: Yes.

KEITH: Well, then! Now look, darling—
> (*Terry's gaze, chancing to go toward the stairway, sees a quiet little figure stealing up the steps. She halts Keith with a gesture.*)

TERRY: Why, Kaye, what are you doing back?
> (*Kaye turns on the stair; looks at Terry for a moment without speaking. Then she starts slowly into the room.*)

KAYE: Terry, they let me out.

TERRY: Oh, Kaye!

KAYE: There was another girl rehearsing when I got there. I'm fired.

TERRY: But they can't do that! How long had you been rehearsing?

KAYE: They still could. This was the seventh day.

TERRY: Darling, don't let it upset you. It happens to all of us. (*A realization of her own recent disappointment comes over her.*) To me. It's a part of this crazy business.

KAYE: Terry, I haven't a cent.

TERRY: Who cares! I've still got my radio job. We'll get along.

KAYE: (*Dully*) Don't try to fool me. I know about the radio job. You've only got two more weeks. I can't take any more money from you. I owe you more than a hundred dollars.

TERRY: What of it! Now look. Have lunch with Dad and me. Come on down to my radio rehearsal.

KAYE: No, I couldn't, Terry. I just—couldn't. Don't you bother about me. I'm all right.

TERRY: (*Glances at her wrist watch*) Oh, dear, I hate to leave you like this. Don't be low, darling.

KAYE: (*As she goes up the stairs*) I'm all right. Thanks, Terry.

TERRY: Oh, I wish I didn't have to— (*She turns to Keith.*) It meant everything to her.

KEITH: She'll get something else—the season's just begun. . . . Look, darling, you and your dad have a nice dinner some place and leave my ticket at the box office and I'll be along just as soon as I can. Will you do that, sweet?

TERRY: (*Dully*) Yes.

KEITH: Okay! That's my girl! (*He gives her a hasty kiss.*) You're the swellest kid that ever lived! (*Dashes off; the slam of the door*)

(*Terry stands for a moment, trying to pull herself together. Keith and his news; Kaye's terrible situation; even the strange behavior of Linda—all these are in her mind. Then Mattie comes into the room, intent on tidying up. With ash receptacle and dust cloth, she makes the rounds.*)

TERRY: (*Mechanically, as she looks down and finds Linda's money in her hand*) Mattie, where's Mrs. Orcutt?

MATTIE: Back in her room.

(*Terry goes.*)

(*Mattie, continuing her work, hums a snatch of lively song.*)

(*Then suddenly a piercing scream is heard from upstairs. Susan hurtles down the steps, her face distorted with terror. Terry rushes back into the room.*)

TERRY: What is it? What is it?

SUSAN: Up in the hall! She drank something! She's—

TERRY: No! No!

(*She rushes up the stairs, followed quickly by Mattie. Mrs. Orcutt and Frank rush breathlessly into the room.*)

MRS. ORCUTT: What's the matter? What happened?

(*Susan, unable to speak, gestures toward the upper hallway. Mrs. Orcutt and Frank run up.*)

(*Susan, sobbing, staggers further into the room and drops onto the piano bench, a little huddled figure. Meanwhile we*) *hear frantic voices upstairs: "Kaye, can you hear me?" "Oh, Lord, look at her!" "Kaye, darling, why did you do it?" "Want me to carry her in her room?" "What'd she swallow? What was it?" "Here's the bottle. Don't say nothing on it." "I'll get a doctor!")*

(Mrs. Orcutt comes quickly down the stairs; goes to the phone, dials. Before she can even finish, however, Terry comes slowly into view on the stairs. Mrs. Orcutt looks at her; it is almost unnecessary for Terry to speak.)

TERRY: It's—no use.

(Mrs. Orcutt hangs up the receiver mechanically. Terry comes slowly down the remaining steps, her eyes fixed straight ahead of her.)

MRS. ORCUTT: *(In a low voice)* It'll be in all the papers. I never should have let her stay here. I felt it from the start. There was something about her. She was—different from the rest of you.

TERRY: Don't say that! It might have been any one of us. She was just a girl without a job, like— *(She is afraid to finish the sentence.)* It might have been—any one of us.

(Frank and Mattie, huddling together, come into view on the stairs, as—

THE CURTAIN FALLS

Scene II

Again the living room of the Footlights Club. It is seven o'clock in the evening, about two months later.

Again Sam Hastings is waiting for a tardy Bobby. Obviously it has been a long wait and his patience is frayed. He peers up the stairs, paces the room, crosses to the piano and impatiently fingers a few notes.

Bobby floats down the stairs, as Southern as ever.

BOBBY: Hello there, honey bun!
SAM: Hello, sugar!
BOBBY: *(As she kisses him)* Ah didn't keep you waitin', did Ah?

SAM: No. No.

BOBBY: (*Fussing with his necktie*) Just look at your tie! Ah declare, Ah don't see how Ah can keep on lovin' you, the way you get yourself up.

SAM: (*On their way out*) Go on! Everybody knows you're crazy about me.

BOBBY: Ah sure enough am. Ah just can't sleep or eat.

SAM: Honest, honey?

BOBBY: Mhm. Where we going to have dinner?
> (*They go.*)
> (*Two Marys enter from dining room, crossing to stairs deep in an argument.*)

LITTLE MARY: Well, what do you want to do all evening? I'm sick of movies and you don't want to sit around *here*.

BIG MARY: I'll tell you what. Let's go and see Keith Burgess' play.

LITTLE MARY: Keith Burgess' play! We couldn't get into that. The paper says seats eight weeks in advance and fifty standees last night.

BIG MARY: Then two more won't matter. That's all we want to do—stand up.

LITTLE MARY: Yes, but I don't think we ought to ask.

BIG MARY: Good Lord, you don't want to *pay*, do you?

LITTLE MARY: Pay? For theater? You must be out of your mind.
> (*They go up the stairs.*)
> (*Doorbell. Mattie enters from the dining room. Looks back.*)

MATTIE: Did you put a new 'lectric bulb up in Miss Kendall's room?

FRANK: (*From dining room*) I will.

MATTIE: Give Miss Terry that telephone message? From Mr. Kingsley.

FRANK: Land sakes, I forgot.

MATTIE: Well, you better tell her—he's important. And you can close up the dining room—everybody's been in that's going to eat.
> (*Frank closes the dining-room doors. Mattie proceeds to the outer door, and presently we hear her astonished voice.*)

Well, I declare!
> (*The reason for her exclamation becomes apparent as Keith Burgess comes into the room. He is a figure of splendor in*

*full evening regalia—white tie, top hat, white muffler,
beautifully tailored topcoat.)*
*(Mattie goes toward the stairs with her astonished gaze so
fixed on this dazzling apparition as to make her ascent a
somewhat stumbling one.)*
*(Keith, waiting, takes out a platinum-and-gold cigarette
case, symbol of his seduction; taps a cigarette smartly, lights
it.)*
*(Judith, the last to finish her dinner, comes out of the dining
room eating a large banana. As Keith bursts upon her vision she stops dead, and all progress with the banana is temporarily suspended.)*

KEITH: (*Removing his hat*) Hello, Judith.

> *(Judith advances slowly to him, grasps the hand that holds
> the hat, moves it up so that the hat is held at about shoulder
> height, backs up, lifts her skirts a little, and is about to kick
> when Keith, outraged, breaks his position and walks away
> from her.)*

JUDITH: Well, if you don't want to play. (*Takes the final bite of
her banana.*)

KEITH: Pixie, eh?

> *(Judith tosses the banana skin on the floor between them;
> beckons him enticingly.)*

JUDITH: Come to mama!

MATTIE: (*Descending the stairs*) Miss Terry'll be right down.

JUDITH: (*Shakes her head dolefully as she picks up the banana
skin.*) You were more fun in the other costume.

KEITH: You'd better watch your figure, eating those bananas.
Starches and show business don't go together.

JUDITH: They do in my show. I got nothing to compete with
but elephants.

KEITH: Are there idiots who really *go* to those childish things—
pay money?

JUDITH: Say, you can't have *all* the idiots. You're doing pretty
good; give us some of the overflow.

KEITH: I suppose you know we broke the house record last
week.

JUDITH: Oh, sure. I stayed up all Saturday night to get the returns.

KEITH: (*Under his breath*) Wisecracker.
  (*Terry's voice is heard as she comes running down the stairs.*)
TERRY: So-o sorry, Mr. Burgess! At the last minute I had a run
  in my stocking and I had to— (*She stops short as she sees
  Keith's magnificent effect. She herself is wearing her everyday
  clothes.*)
JUDITH: (*Sensing trouble*) Well, I'll—I'll leave you two young
  people together. (*She gives the effect of tiptoeing out of the
  room.*)
TERRY: (*Dazzled*) Keith! How— (*She curtsies to the floor.*) Did
  you remember to bring the glass slipper?
KEITH: What's the idea, Terry? I told you on the phone we
  were dressing.
TERRY: I thought you were joking. You said, "We'll dress, of
  course," and I said, "Of course!" But I didn't dream you
  were serious.
KEITH: We're going to an opening night! And our seats are
  third row center!
TERRY: Downstairs?
KEITH: Down— Where do you think?
TERRY: Darling, we've been to openings before, and we always
  sat in the gallery.
KEITH: Gallery! We're through with the gallery! I've got a
  table at the Vingt-et-un for dinner, and after the theater
  we're invited to a party at Gilman's penthouse. You can't go
  like that!
TERRY: Give me just ten minutes— I'll go up and change. (*She
  suddenly recollects.*) Oh, dear!
KEITH: What's the matter?
TERRY: I loaned my evening dress to Susan.
KEITH: Oh, for God's— (*Turns away in disgust.*)
TERRY: It's all right. I'll borrow Judy's pink— Oh, no! Olga's
  wearing it.
KEITH: This is the god-damnedest dump I was ever in! Sordid
  kind of life! Wearing each other's clothes! I suppose you use
  each other's toothbrushes, too!
TERRY: (*Quietly*) Would you rather I didn't go, Keith?
KEITH: I didn't say that I—
TERRY: (*Still quietly*) Yes—but would you rather?

KEITH: Now you're playing it for tragedy. What's the matter with you, anyhow!

TERRY: There's nothing the matter with me, Keith. I just can't see us as third-row first-nighters. We always went to see the *play*, Keith. That whole crowd—it makes the audience more important than the show.

KEITH: Listen, I don't like those people any better than you do. They don't mean anything to *me*.

TERRY: Then why do you bother with them?

KEITH: They can't hurt me. I watch them as you'd watch a hill of ants. Insects, that's what they are.

TERRY: Keith, you wrote your last play about people you understood and liked. You lived with them, and you knew them, and they gave you something. You'll starve to death in third-row center.

KEITH: I'm going back to them. I'm no fool. They're keeping my room for me just as it was.

TERRY: Keeping it? How do you mean?

KEITH: Oh, I don't want to talk about it now. Come on, let's get out of here.

TERRY: But I've got to know. Do you mean you've moved without even telling me?

KEITH: (*Decides to face the music.*) Well, I was going to break it to you later. I knew you'd jump on me. But as long as you've gone this far— I'm going to Hollywood.

TERRY: Hollywood!

KEITH: Yes, to write for pictures.

TERRY: No, no, Keith!

KEITH: Now don't start all over again! If you don't watch yourself you'll turn into one of those nagging— (*He stops as Kendall comes down the stairs. She throws a glance into the room, in passing, and notices Keith's unusual attire.*)

KENDALL: (*Impressed and very friendly*) Hel-lo!

KEITH: (*With no cordiality*) H'are you?

KENDALL: (*Senses she has walked into a hornets' nest.*) Good-by. (*Beats a hasty retreat via the front door.*)

KEITH: Let's get out of here.

TERRY: Keith, you can't go to Hollywood! I won't let you! You said you'd never go, no matter how broke you were, and now that your play's a big hit you're going.

KEITH: Well, they didn't want me before it was a hit!

TERRY: Keith, listen—

KEITH: I know what you're going to say. All that junk about its shriveling up my soul. Listen! I'm going to use Hollywood. It's not going to use me. I'm going to stay one year at two thousand a week. That's one hundred thousand dollars. I'll write their garbage in the daytime, but at night I'll write my own plays.

TERRY: But will you? That's what I'm afraid of. *Will* you?

KEITH: You bet I will! And in between I'll keep fit with sunshine, and swimming, and tennis, and—

TERRY: Little ermine jackets, up to here.

KEITH: Huh?

TERRY: It doesn't matter.

KEITH: Believe me, they'll never catch *me* at their Trocaderos or their Brown Derbies.

TERRY: (*Quietly*) When are you going, Keith?

KEITH: I don't know. Next week.

TERRY: Well—good-by.

KEITH: What?

TERRY: Good-by, Keith, and good luck. It's been swell. (*She turns; runs swiftly up the stairs.*)

(*Keith goes to the foot of the stairs and calls.*)

KEITH: Terry! What's the— Terry! . . . Terry! (*Only silence from above. He claps his hat on his head and goes. The door slams loudly after him.*)

(*Immediately on the slam of the door Bernice tiptoes down the stairs with a catlike swiftness and soundlessness. Obviously she has been eavesdropping. A quick, comprehensive look around the room, then she scurries to the window, peers out guardedly, so as not to be seen from the street. Turns back from the window just as the two Marys make swift, silent descents of the stairs. The three at once plunge into an elaborate whispered and pantomimic routine revealing their knowledge of the scene which has just taken place between Terry and Keith, and their unbounded interest in its consequences. "Is he gone?" "Yes." "How's Terry?" "Don't know." "Do you think she can hear us!" "Yes." "Wasn't it terrible!" "I thought I'd die." "Poor Terry!" "I never did like him." "Me neither." "We'd better go back up or she'll be suspicious." "Yes, be very quiet.")*

(With elaborate caution they start to tiptoe up the stairs again. On the stairway one of them turns to the girl behind her. "Shall we ask her if we can do anything?" "No.")

(They vanish up the stairs.)

(The doorbell rings. From the back of the house we hear Mattie's complaint to Frank: "Land sakes, I been runnin' my laigs off. Cain't you pick yourself up go answer that doorbell once!")

(Frank appears, getting into his housecoat and casting a resentful glance back at the unseen Mattie.)

(As the door is opened by Frank the voice of David Kingsley is heard: "Does Miss Terry Randall happen to be in?" "Yessuh, I think so. Will you come right in?" Frank comes into sight. "What's the name, suh?")

KINGSLEY: Mr. Kingsley.

FRANK: Oh, yeh. You the gentleman telephoned. I clean forgot to tell Miss Terry.

KINGSLEY: Well, as long as she's here . . .

FRANK: Yessuh. *(Pulls himself together and goes up the stairs.)*

(Kingsley comes into the room. He stands a moment, then takes out his cigarette case and lights a cigarette.)

(Frank comes down again.)

FRANK: I told her you was here.

KINGSLEY: Oh, thank you.

FRANK: And I told her about the phone call, too. *(Frank goes about his business as Terry comes down the stairs.)*

TERRY: Why, Mr. Kingsley, how dramatic! You're just in the nick of time.

KINGSLEY: I'm glad of that. What's happened?

TERRY: Oh—sort of an emotional crisis. I dashed upstairs to have a good cry, buried my head in the pillow just the way you're supposed to, and guess what?

KINGSLEY: What?

TERRY: The tears wouldn't come. In fact, I felt sort of relieved and light, as though I'd just got over a fever.

KINGSLEY: How disappointing. Like not being able to sneeze.

TERRY: Perhaps I'll be able to manage it later. Tonight.

KINGSLEY: If a shoulder would be of any—help?

TERRY: You're very kind. I'm afraid I have to fight this out alone. . . . Do take your coat off.

KINGSLEY: Thanks. This is rather a strange hour for me to drop in. I did telephone—

TERRY: Oh, Frank doesn't believe in phone messages.

KINGSLEY: They do in Hollywood. They just called me up. Can you take a plane for California tomorrow?

TERRY: Me!

(*He murmurs an assent.*)

KINGSLEY: They didn't say what the part was—sort of character-comedy, I believe. Of course they put the picture in production first and then started looking for a cast—the Alice-in-Wonderland method. At any rate, they want a new face in this particular part; they ran off all the screen tests they had on file, and finally came to that one of yours. So there you are. And—oh, yes—they want to know in twenty minutes. Or course it's only four-thirty on the Coast. (*As he glances at his watch.*)

TERRY: You're joking.

KINGSLEY: No, all important things are decided in twenty minutes out there. The more trivial ones take years. Shall I phone them you'll be there?

TERRY: Why—I don't know.

KINGSLEY: You don't mean to say you're hesitating!

TERRY: But it's fantastic! How can I—

KINGSLEY: Dear child, do you mind if I tell you something?

(*Terry looks up at him.*)

I've been watching you for several seasons. You've been in the theater for two—three—what is it?

TERRY: Three.

KINGSLEY: Three years. You've appeared in, perhaps, half-a-dozen plays. I wouldn't call any of them exactly hits—would you?

(*Terry merely shakes her head.*)

And one or two of them closed before the week was over.

TERRY: You've been doing a lot of detective work, haven't you?

KINGSLEY: No, I didn't need to. I know all about you.

TERRY: You do! That's a little frightening.

KINGSLEY: It's part of my business—watching the good ones. And you are good. You've got fire and variety and a magnetic quality that's felt the minute you walk on a stage.

TERRY: (*As he hesitates*) Oh, don't stop!

KINGSLEY: But off stage you're nothing at all.

(*Terry wishes she had left well enough alone.*)

When you walk into an office the average manager doesn't see anything there. You might be the little girl who's come to deliver the costumes. They wouldn't see that spark. If Elizabeth Bergner walked in on them unknown—or Helen Hayes—what would they see! Little anaemic wisps that look as if they could do with a sandwich and a glass of milk. But put them on a stage, and it's as if you had lighted a thousand incandescent bulbs behind their eyes. That's talent—that's acting—that's you!

TERRY: Now I—*am* going to cry.

KINGSLEY: But what if they don't see what's hidden in you? Suppose they never discover you. You might go tramping around for twenty years, and never get your chance. That's the stage.

TERRY: Twenty years!

KINGSLEY: But let's say you go to Hollywood. They'll know what to do with you out there. Light you so as to fill those hollows, only take your— (*He is turning her head this way and that to get the best angle.*) —right profile. That's the good one. Shade the nose a trifle. (*Opens her mouth and peers in as though she were a racehorse.*) Perhaps a celluloid cap over those two teeth. They'd make you very pretty.

(*Terry steals a quick look in the mirror. Her morale is somewhat shaken.*)

Then you play in this picture. Fifty million people see you. Fan mail. Next time you get a better part. No tramping up and down Broadway, no worries about money. A seven-year contract, your salary every week whether you work or not. And if you make a really big hit, like Jean, they'll tear up your contract and give you a bigger one.

TERRY: (*A sudden idea*) Wouldn't they let me do just one or two pictures, instead of this seven-year thing?

KINGSLEY: I'm afraid not. If you make a big hit they don't

want another studio to reap the benefit. That's not unreasonable, is it?

TERRY: No, I suppose not. Oh, dear! Everything you say is absolutely sound and true, but you see, Mr. Kingsley, the trouble with me is—I'm stage-struck. The theater beats me and starves me and forsakes me, but I love it. I suppose I'm just that kind of girl—you know—rather live in a garret with her true love than dwell in a palace with old Moneybags.

KINGSLEY: But it looks as though your true love had kicked you out of the garret.

TERRY: Oh, dear, if there was only somebody. Mr. Kingsley, won't *you* help me? Won't you tell me what to do?

KINGSLEY: Me?

TERRY: Please!

KINGSLEY: But I work for the picture company.

TERRY: But if you didn't.

KINGSLEY: (*Quietly*) I'd think you ought to tell them to go to hell.

TERRY: What!

KINGSLEY: (*Indignantly*) Go out there and let them do all those things to you! (*Again he has a finger under her chin, raising her head as he scans her face.*) That lovely little face! And for what? So that a few years from now they can throw you out on the ash heap! The theater may be slow and heartbreaking, but if you build solidly you've got something at the end of seven years, and seventeen years, and twenty-seven! Look at Katharine Cornell, and Lynn Fontanne, and Alfred Lunt. They tramped Broadway in their day. They've worked like horses, and trouped the country, and stuck to it. And now they've got something that nothing in the world can take away from them. And what's John Barrymore got? A yacht!

TERRY: You're wonderful!

KINGSLEY: Are you going to Hollywood?

TERRY: NO!

KINGSLEY: Will you go to dinner?

TERRY: YES!

KINGSLEY: That's really all I came to ask you.

CURTAIN

ACT THREE

Scene I

A Sunday morning at the Footlights Club. The following October.

The girls are scattered about the room in various informal attitudes and various stages of attire. Pajamas, lounging robes, hair nets, cold cream, wave combs. Four or five Sunday papers, opened and distributed among the girls, are in drifts everywhere; girls are lying on the floor reading bits of this and that; lounging in chairs; coffee cups, bits of toast, a banana or an orange show that Sunday-morning breakfast is a late and movable feast. One of the girls is in riding clothes (Kendall) and bound for a day in the country. All the girls are present except Terry.

During the year two new girls have joined the club, and now are sprawled at ease with the others.

Olga, at the piano, is obliging with the latest popular tune. Now and then a girl rather absent-mindedly sings a fragment of the song, leaving a word half-finished as her attention is momentarily held by something she is reading. A foot is waggled in time to the music. Pat, sprawled full-length on top of the grand piano, is giving a rather brilliant performance of dancing with her legs in the air.

Little Mary, on hands and knees, is making a tour of the recumbent figures in search of a certain theatrical news item. In one hand she holds a half-eaten banana.

LITTLE MARY: Where's the list of next week's openings? (*She finds that Big Mary has the page she wants. She settles down to read over her shoulder.*)

BOBBY: Anybody got a muffin they don't want?

TONY GILLETTE: (*One of the new girls*) Here!

BOBBY: Toss! (*The muffin is hurled through the air.*)

MADELEINE: (*Turning a page of the rotogravure section*) Autumn Millinery Modes. Oh, look at the hats they're going to wear!

SUSAN: Let me see. (*Traverses the distance to Madeleine by two neat revolutions of her entire body, and brings up just behind the outspread papers. Reads:*) "Hats will be worn off the head this winter."

PAT: (*A leg suspended in mid-air as her attention is caught by this remark.*) Where?

SUSAN: That's what it says. "Hats'll be worn off the head this winter."

BERNICE: (*At the desk*) Where're they going to *put* 'em?

LITTLE MARY: (*Busy with the* American) Did you know that in Ancient Egypt five thousand years ago the women used to dye their hair just like we do?

JUDITH: (*Furious*) Who's we?

BIG MARY: (*To Little Mary, who is reading over her shoulder*) Take that banana out of my face, will you!

ELLEN FENWICK: (*The other new girl*) (*Perusing the department store ads*) "Two-piece Schiaparelli suits—$5.98. You cannot tell the model from the copy."

JUDITH: The hell you can't.

SUSAN: (*Emerging from the newspaper*) Oh, they're postponing that Lord Byron play because they can't find a leading man.

LITTLE MARY: What are they looking for?

SUSAN: He's got to be young and handsome.

OLGA: There are no handsome men on the stage now any more.

JUDITH: There's a shortage *off* stage, too.

PAT: Looks don't count any more. It's good old sex appeal.

KENDALL: Would you rather go out with a handsome man without sex appeal, or a homely man *with* it?

BERNICE: I'd rather go out with the handsome one.

JUDITH: Sure, and stay *in* with the other one.

ANN: (*As Judith's sally is greeted with a general laugh*) I think you girls are simply disgusting! Men, men, men! It's degrading just to listen to you.

JUDITH: Isn't it though?

BIG MARY: Say, Terry! . . . Where's Terry?

JUDITH: She's still asleep. It's the only chance she gets—Sundays.

BIG MARY: I see that old beau of hers is coming back.

TONY: Who's that?

BIG MARY: Keith Burgess. He used to hang around here all the time.

TONY: Really? What's he like?

JUDITH: He's one of those fellows started out on a soapbox and ended up in a swimming pool.

LITTLE MARY: Terry was crazy about him, all right.

BIG MARY: Yeah.

PAT: And if you ask me, I think she still is.

LITTLE MARY: Really! What makes you think so?

PAT: Somebody just mentioned his name the other day and you ought to've seen her face!

JUDITH: That's not true. She's forgotten he ever lived—that Left-Wing Romeo.

KENDALL: Well, I should think she might, with David Kingsley in the offing. Now, I call *him* attractive!

PAT: Oh, he isn't her type. Anyway, he's just interested in her career.

KENDALL: If it's just her career they eat an awful lot of dinners together.

LITTLE MARY: If it's her art he's got in mind why doesn't he get her a job? Not much of a career standing behind a sales counter.

BOBBY: Ah think it's perfectly awful the way Terry has to get up at half-past seven every morning. That miserable job of hers.

MADELEINE: It's no worse than what I've got ahead of me.

SUSAN: Well, anyway, you'll be acting.

MADELEINE: Acting! A Number Three Company of *A Horse on You*, playing up and down the West Coast. God! I come to New York to get away from Seattle, and they keep shipping me back there.

BOBBY: You'll be earning some money! Look at Sam and me! We can't make enough to get married. Ah declare Ah'm so bored with livin' in sin.

ANN: Well, really!

LITTLE MARY: Oh, shut up!

JUDITH: Speaking of Seattle, Miss Vauclain, would you be good enough to take that load of lumber off my neck! After all, you put it there.

MADELEINE: It isn't my fault if he fell for you.

PAT: Oh, is Lumber in town again?

JUDITH: (*Drawing a letter from her pajama pocket*) No; but I've had a warning.

ANN: (*Impatiently, rising*) Oh, I'm not going to waste my whole Sunday! What time is Jean coming?

MADELEINE: Stick around. What have you got to lose?

ANN: My time's just as valuable as Jean's is.

MADELEINE: Sure. You're in big demand. Sit down.

ANN: Well, if Jean wants to see me I'm upstairs. I don't find this conversation very uplifting. (*Goes upstairs.*)

OLGA: She should be teaching school, that girl.

TONY: Is Jean Maitland as pretty off the screen as she is on? I've never seen her.

ELLEN: Neither have I.

KENDALL: She's much better looking off. They've made her up like all the rest of them on the screen.

OLGA: I hope she will soon be here. I must be at the Winter Garden at one o'clock.

LITTLE MARY: On Sunday!

OLGA: (*Bitterly*) On Sunday. (*Goes into a few bars of the newest Winter Garden melody. Something very corny.*)

LITTLE MARY: (*Anticipating her*) We know! Kolijinsky!

(*A voice which we later find is that of Louise Mitchell Hendershot calls out from the dining room.*)

LOUISE: What's that you're playing, Olga?

OLGA: (*Not very clearly heard above the music*) "Hillbilly Sam."

LOUISE: (*Off*) What?

OLGA: Come in here if you want to talk.

PAT: Yes, stop stuffing yourself and come in here. . . . Hey, Louise!

LOUISE: (*As she comes out of the dining room*) I was having some pancakes.

PAT: Listen, you've got to cut out those farm-hand breakfasts, now that you're back in New York.

LOUISE: (*Settles herself in the group.*) Imagine getting the *Times* the day it's printed instead of three days later!

JUDITH: You mean you're not lonesome for good old Appleton?

LOUISE: I haven't been so happy in years. (*She turns her attention to the paper.*)

JUDITH: Everything pink.

BIG MARY: Oh, say, Irene Fitzroy has been engaged for the society girl part in *River House*.

> (*A series of highly interested responses to this announcement. "No!" "Really!" "That's wonderful!" "She'll be good in it!" "Isn't that exciting!"*)

BERNICE: I could have played that Fitzroy part. I don't know why I couldn't be a society girl. (*Assumes a supercilious expression to prove her fitness for the part.*)

> (*A chorus of: "Sure!" . . . "We know" . . . "You're always the type."*)

A real actress can play anything. I may play the French adventuress in *Love and War*.

> (*A little chorus of astonishment: "Really!" "No kidding!"*)

KENDALL: Do you mean they offered it to you!

BERNICE: Well, not exactly, but I'm writing 'em a letter.

> (*Another chorus: "Oh, we see" . . . "Letters!" . . . "You and your letters!"*)
>
> (*Mattie comes out of the dining room with a large tray. She is intent on gathering up the coffee cups.*)

MATTIE: You-all knows Mrs. Orcutt don't allow you girls to go laying around downstairs in your pajamas.

JUDITH: (*Dreamily, as she reads*) Don't give it another thought, Mattie. We'll take 'em right off.

MATTIE: Besides, lookit this here room! (*Takes a banana skin off a small bust of Shakespeare, where it has been draped as a hat.*) Banana skins and newspapers and toast! I should think with Miss Jean coming you'd be getting all slicked up. Big moving-picture star. (*She stoops for a hidden coffee cup.*) And fu'thermore, you ain't supposed to eat breakfast in here. What's the dining room's foh! (*She goes back to the dining room with her laden tray.*)

MADELEINE: (*To Bernice*) You still writing that letter about yourself?

BERNICE: Look. How many *l*'s are there in allure?

MADELEINE: Why don't you give up, anyhow?

BIG MARY: Yeh, why don't you take up ballet dancing, or something?

BERNICE: (*Springs suddenly to her feet, her hands clutching the back of the chair behind her.*) Don't you say that to me! I'm never going to give up! I'm as good as— (*She realizes that she is making a spectacle of herself.*) Leave me alone.

KENDALL: Oh, they were just kidding. Can't you take a joke?
  (*Terry runs down the stairs, stopping halfway to toss a word of greeting to the girls below.*)

TERRY: (*A gesture that embraces them all*) Ah! My public!

JUDITH: Well, Terry, the Beautiful Shopgirl!

PAT: Thought you were never going to get up.

TERRY: I wouldn't, if it weren't for Jean's coming. . . . Hey, Mattie!
  (*A "Yes'm," from Mattie in the dining room*)
  Draw one in the dark! . . . Oh, isn't Sunday heavenly! (*Stretches luxuriously.*) I woke up at half-past seven; said, "Nope, I don't have to," and went right back to sleep. Not all day long do I have to say, "This blouse is a copy of a little import that we are selling for $3.95. I am sure you would look simply terrible in it."

JUDITH: I'm going to come down there someday and have you wait on me.

TERRY: If you do I'll have you pinched as a shoplifter.

BOBBY: Honest, Terry, Ah don't see how you tolerate that job of yours. Moochin' down there nine o'clock in the mawnin'. Slaving till six, and after.

TERRY: Oh, it isn't so terrible if you keep thinking that next week that part will turn up. I keep on making the rounds.

ELLEN: But when do you have time for it?

TERRY: Lunch hour.

SUSAN: Then when do you eat lunch?

TERRY: Sundays.

PAT: Just goes to show how cuckoo the stage is. You can act rings around all of us. Well— (*Stretching a bit as she makes for the stairs*) —I guess I'll go up and put the face together. I look like an old popover.

SUSAN: Me too. Don't say anything good while we're gone.

JUDITH: What are you going to do today, Terry, after Jean goes?

TERRY: I don't know. Who's doing what? Kendall, you're going social for the day, h'm?

KENDALL: Yes, I'm going out to Piping Rock.

TERRY: Piping Rock—isn't that where your ancestors landed?

KENDALL: Thereabouts.

JUDITH: Mine landed in Little Rock.

BIG MARY: Oh, say, Terry! The paper says Keith Burgess gets back from the Coast today. Did you know that?

(*A little hush. The eyes of the girls are turned toward Terry.*)

TERRY: Yes, I know. Why do they call California the Coast instead of New York?

LITTLE MARY: I wonder if that sunshine has mellowed him up any.

BOBBY: (*Holding up a paper*) Girls, here's Jean stepping out of an airplane!

BERNICE: (*Jumping up*) Oh, let's see it.

BOBBY: (*As three or four girls cluster around her. Reads:*) "Blonde Hollywood Screen Star Alights At Newark Airport."

LITTLE MARY: That's a darling costume!

BIG MARY: I don't like her hat.

BERNICE: (*Reading*) "Lovely Jean Maitland, Popular Screen Actress, Arrives For Rehearsals Of Broadway Stage Play."

JUDITH: That belle certainly is shot with luck.

BOBBY: That's what she is!

JUDITH: First she goes out and knocks 'em cold in pictures, and now she gets starred on Broadway.

BIG MARY: And she isn't even a good actress.

(*Mattie brings Terry's coffee from the dining room.*)

MATTIE: Here's your coffee, Miss Terry.

TERRY: Thanks, Mattie.

ELLEN: What's she going to do? Quit pictures and stay on the stage?

BIG MARY: No, no. The picture company puts on the play. It's like a personal appearance.

BERNICE: (*Who has drifted over to the window*) Girls! She's here!

BIG MARY: (*Darting to the window*) Let's see!

BOBBY: Look at that car, would you!

LOUISE: Isn't it gorgeous!

LITTLE MARY: There she is! She's getting out!

BERNICE: Oohoo! (*Raps on the window.*) Jean! (*With a concerted rush they make for the front door.*)

(*Little Mary: "She's got on red foxes!"*
Bobby: "She looks marvelous, doesn't she!"

Big Mary: "I wonder if she's changed!"
Bernice: "Isn't it exciting!"
Tony: "Don't forget to introduce me!"
Ellen: "Yes. Me, too!"
Louise: [*Calling up the stairs*] "Girls! Yoohoo! She's here!")
(*Meanwhile, on the part of the remaining girls, there is a wild scramble to tidy up the room. Newspapers, cigarette butts, etc.*)

TERRY: Here—pick up the papers! Give them to me! (*With a great bundle of newspapers she dashes into the dining room and out again.*)

MADELEINE: We should have got all dressed up.

JUDITH: Not me. She's seen me worse than this.

OLGA: She will be dressed up enough.

KENDALL: We're acting like a lot of schoolgirls. We'll be asking for her autograph next.

(*The squealing in the hallway now mounts to a burst of ecstatic greeting. "Jean! Jean!" . . . "DAR-ling!" . . . "WON-derful!" . . . "Look grand!" . . . "Jean! Welcome home!"*)

JEAN: (*Still in the hallway*) Oh, I'm so excited! How darling of you all to be here!

(*Susan and Pat run downstairs.*)

(*From among the group: "Are you glad to be back? . . . You haven't changed a bit."*)

(*Jean comes into view. Her costume is simple and horribly expensive. Her red fox furs are fabulous, her orchids are pure white.*)

JEAN: (*Embracing girls*) Hello, girls! Madeleine! Olga, how's the music? Kendall! Hello, Judy! This is worth the whole trip—

TERRY: Jean darling!

JEAN: Terry! (*They embrace.*)

MRS. ORCUTT: (*Looming up in the dining-room doorway, Frank and Mattie just behind her*) Well, well! My little Jean!

JEAN: Hello, Mrs. Orcutt! Mattie! Frank! (*In turn she throws her arms around all three of them. As she embraces Frank a laugh goes up from the group.*) Well, let me get my breath and have a look at all of you.

BERNICE: It's the same old bunch.

TERRY: No, there are two new ones. Ellen Fenwick and Tony Gillette. Miss Jean Maitland.

TONY: Hello.

PAT: (*The trumpet sound*) Ta-da-a-ah!

JEAN: Hello, girls. I hope you don't think I'm crazy—all excited like this.

ELLEN: Oh, no!

TONY: We think you're darling.

(*Bernice, before the mirror, is having a private try-on of Jean's red fox and orchids. Enchanting effect.*)

JEAN: (*In greeting to Ann, who has come rather sedately down the stairs*) Ann! I was just going to ask for you.

ANN: My, you look Hollywood!

JEAN: (*Recalls the two men who have accompanied her, and who are standing in the hallway. One has a huge camera and tripod.*) Oh, boys, I'm so sorry. Girls, this is Mr. Larry Westcott, our New York publicity man—and a wonder. And this is Billy—uh— I'm afraid I never heard your last name.

BILLY: Just Billy.

LARRY: Just want to snap a few pictures. Do you mind?

MRS. ORCUTT: (*A hand straightening her coiffure*) Not at all.

LARRY: Human-interest stuff.

BERNICE: You mean with us!

JEAN: Of course!

BOBBY: Oh, I've got to go and fix up.

(*A chorus of: "So do I!" . . . "I look a fright." . . . "Me too!" . . . "We'll just be a minute."*)

(*Up the stairs go Bernice, Big and Little Mary, Bobby, and Louise.*)

(*Mattie is doing a little sprucing up, preparatory to being photographed, and Frank buttons his house coat.*)

TERRY: Jean darling, aren't you thrilled at doing a play? When do your rehearsals start?

JEAN: On Wednesday.

BILLY: (*Speaking to Mrs. Orcutt and the two servants. He has his electric apparatus in his hand.*) I've got a pretty strong light here. All right if I plug in?

FRANK: Yes, sah. I'll show you.

(*Billy and Frank disappear into the hallway toward the rear of the house.*)

LARRY: Pardon me, Miss Maitland. You were going to ask about our taking some shots upstairs. (*Glancing from Jean to Mrs. Orcutt*)

JEAN: Oh, yes. Do you mind, Mrs. Orcutt? They want to take some stills of me up in my old room.

MRS. ORCUTT: Of course not.

LARRY: You know—Humble Beginnings in The Footlights Club. They love it.

MRS. ORCUTT: I'd be delighted.

TERRY: Wait a minute! I've got my Sunday wash hanging up there. You can't photograph that!

LARRY: Great! Just what we want!

TERRY: All right. But I never thought my underwear would make *Screenland*.

OLGA: So you are a big actress now, eh, Jean! You are going to be starred in a play.

JEAN: Isn't it silly! I didn't really want them to star me in it. I'm scared stiff.

LARRY: She'll be great in it. Look, Miss Maitland, we haven't got a lot of time. Mr. Kingsley is picking you up here at twelve forty-five and then you're meeting Mr. Gretzl.

TERRY: Who?

JEAN: Mr. Gretzl.

JUDITH: What's a Gretzl?

JEAN: He's the Big Boss—Adolph Gretzl.

LARRY: President of the company.

MRS. ORCUTT: Of course! Adolph Gretzl.

OLGA: (*Dashing to the piano. Improvises and sings.*)
> Of course Adolph Gretzl,
> He looks like a pretzl—

JUDITH: (*Picking it up*) So why should we fretzl—

PAT: (*With an accompanying dance step*) And fume. Boom-boom. (*She times this last with a couple of bumps.*)
(*The two Marys come dashing down the stairs.*)

LITTLE MARY: We're ready!

LARRY: Okay! Everybody here now?

BIG MARY: Oh, no. There's more yet. (*At foot of stairs*) Girls! Hurry!

(*Louise's voice from upstairs: "Coming!"*)

JEAN: Terry darling, when am I going to see you? I've got loads to tell you and I want to hear all about you. Rehearsals start Wednesday. How about lunch tomorrow?

LARRY: Oh, not tomorrow, Miss Maitland. You're lunching with the press.

JEAN: Oh, dear. Let's see—David Kingsley is taking me to that opening in the evening . . . How about tea?

LARRY: Not tea! You've got the magazine people. And you've got photographs all day Tuesday.

JEAN: (*Turns to Terry*) But I want to see her. How about Wednesday? I'll get away from rehearsal and we'll have lunch. One o'clock?

TERRY: You won't believe it, but my lunch hour's eleven-thirty to twelve-thirty.

JEAN: Eleven-thirty! What do you mean?

(*Down come Bobby and Louise, refurbished.*)

BOBBY: Ah hope we didn't keep you waitin'.

LARRY: (*Impatiently glancing at his watch*) All right, Miss Maitland.

JEAN: Oh, fine. Now before we start, everybody, I've got a teentsy-weentsy surprise for you.

BIG MARY: Surprise?

JEAN: Billy, will you bring it in?

BOBBY: Bring what in?

LOUISE: What?

JEAN: It's for all of you, dear Mrs. Orcutt, and the whole dear Footlights Club.

(*Bobby enters from the hallway, carrying what is evidently a large picture, framed and covered with a rich red drapery which conceals the subject.*)

BOBBY: Oh, look!

KENDALL: How exciting!

PAT: What is it?

TONY: Looks like a picture.

LITTLE MARY: What of, I wonder?

JUDITH: Papa Gretzl.

JEAN: All right, girls?

BOBBY: We're ready!

(*Jean steps forward, and with a sweeping gesture, throws*

aside the velvet drape. It is a portrait of Jean. All eyelashes, golden hair and scarlet lips.)

(*A series of delighted and semidelighted exclamations: "It's Jean!"* . . . *"Lovely!"* . . . *"How beautiful!"* . . . *"Darling!"*)

MRS. ORCUTT: (*Her dismayed glance sweeping the walls*) It's lovely, Jean, lovely! Now, if we can only find a fitting place to hang it.

LARRY: Well, let's see. (*With a look that alights on the Bernhardt portrait and rests there*)

(*Judith makes a gallant gesture of Hail And Farewell toward the Divine Sarah.*)

JUDITH: So long, Sarah!

LARRY: Now, if you'll all just gather round the picture . . . Okay, Billy?

BILLY: (*Bringing in his camera*) Ready in a second.

LARRY: Now then, Miss Maitland! You stand right there behind the portrait. And—er— (*He gestures toward Mrs. Orcutt.*)

MRS. ORCUTT: (*Helpfully*) Me?

LARRY: That's right! Right here beside Miss Maitland. And all you girls fill in this space in front. That's it—right in here, all of you. We want a nice little informal group. A nice little— (*He drops back, surveying the group with the eye of an artist. It becomes immediately apparent that it will be a nice group, all right, but that isn't what Larry wants. His concern is Jean Maitland.*) No, no! You'll all have to crouch down. (*He rushes around, pressing them all down on their knees.*) Everybody down! You too, sister! (*This last is addressed to Mrs. Orcutt, who gets down with no little difficulty.*) That's fine! And everybody looking at Miss Maitland!

JEAN: (*Very sweet*) Frank and Mattie have to be in it. Come on, Frank and Mattie!

(*They have been looking a little crestfallen and now take their places at the extreme edge, much elated.*)

LARRY: Sure, sure! It wouldn't be a picture without 'em. We want the whole Twilight Club. Now, then, have we got everybody?

(*Looks over his shoulder just as Billy turns on his special light.*)

LITTLE MARY: No, no, where's Bernice?

BIG MARY: Bernice isn't here!

BERNICE: (*Her voice from the top of the stairs*) I'm ready. Here I am! (*Bernice has seized on this opportunity to register as undiscovered Hollywood star material. She has made herself up to look like a rather smudged copy of Joan Crawford. Her entrance is undulating and regal.*)

PAT: Heh! That's my new dress!

BERNICE: Well, I had to be right, didn't I?

LARRY: Come on, girlie. Right here.

(*Immediately Bernice stares out toward the camera.*)

No, no! Look at Miss Maitland. Everybody look at Miss Maitland. . . . Ready, Billy?

BILLY: Okay.

LARRY: Hold still, now! And everybody look at Miss Maitland! . . . Right!

(*Just as the bulb is pressed Bernice makes a lightning full-face turn toward the camera, all smiles, and back again before they can catch her at it.*)

Now then! For the pictures upstairs . . . Miss Maitland?

JEAN: Want to come along, girls?

(*The girls certainly do want to come along, and they do so. Chattering away, the whole procession streams up the stairs—Mrs. Orcutt, Cameramen, and all. Frank brings up the rear with the electrical apparatus. "You-all using this upstairs too, ain't you?" An answer from Larry: "Yes, bring it right up!"*)

(*Terry and Judith, unable to face a second such scene, remain behind, with only the smiling portrait of Jean as company.*)

(*Their eyes meet understandingly. There goes Jean.*)

TERRY: (*Blandly*) You're not going to be in the—other pictures?

JUDITH: No, if I'm going to work as an extra I want my five dollars a day.

TERRY: I do hope I left my room looking sordid enough.

JUDITH: Say, what about that play they've got her doing? Do you suppose it's really something?

TERRY: Oh, it is. David Kingsley told me about it. He says it's a really fine and moving play.

JUDITH: (*A glance at the portrait*) Then why does he let her do it?

TERRY: He couldn't help it. They got it into their heads out on the Coast. It's Gretzl's idea. What do they care about the theater? They think the stage is something to advertise pictures with.

JUDITH: Listen, Jean can't act. If the play's as good as all that, she'll kill it. It doesn't make sense!

TERRY: Now, Judy, haven't you learned not to—
(*Of all people, Keith Burgess suddenly appears in the archway. Though he has been gone a year, he barges right in as though he had left only yesterday. His clothes represent an ingenious blending of the Hollywood style with his own Leftist tendencies. He still wears the sweater, but it is an imported one; the trousers are beautifully tailored, the shirt probably cost eighteen dollars; no necktie, and, of course, no hat.*)

KEITH: (*His voice heard in the hallway*) Where's Terry Randall? Oh, there you are!

TERRY: Why, hello, Keith!

JUDITH: Well, if it isn't the fatted calf!

KEITH: (*Surveying the room*) God, a year hasn't made any difference in *this* dump! (*He casts an appraising eye over Terry.*) What's the matter with you? You're thin and you've got no color.

TERRY: Well, I haven't been having those hamburgers at Smitty's since you left.

KEITH: That reminds me, I haven't had any breakfast. (*He selects a pear from a bowl of fruit on the table.*) Hope this is ripe . . . Heh! What's her name out there? (*Shouting toward the dining room*) Bring me a cup of coffee!

JUDITH: (*Obsequiousness in her tone*) The deviled kidneys are very nice today.

KEITH: (*Finding the pear too juicy for him*) God! Give me your handkerchief, Terry.

TERRY: You've got one.

KEITH: That's silk. (*Grabs hers.*)

TERRY: Well, Keith, tell us about yourself. Are you back from Hollywood for good?

KEITH: What do you mean? I'm going back there in three

days. I've been working on a plan to put the whole studio
on a commonwealth basis, with the electricians right on a
footing with the executives, and they won't have it.

TERRY: Who won't have it? The executives?

KEITH: The electricians!

TERRY: Well, I must say you look wonderful. All healthy and
sunburned, and I never saw such beautiful trousers.

KEITH: (*Taking a last bite of the pear*) You're looking terrible.
(*The core of the pear in hand, he glances about for some place
to deposit it.*)
   (*Lightning-fast, the perfect servant, Judith is by his side, offering a little ash tray. He drops the pear core on it without
   a word.*)

JUDITH: Thank you.

KEITH: (*Suddenly he notices Jean's portrait.*) What's *this*
chromo?

TERRY: It's Cinderella. She's upstairs.

KEITH: Those autograph hounds out there waiting for her?

JUDITH: No, they want another glimpse of *you*.

KEITH: Did it ever occur to you that I didn't come here to see
you?

JUDITH: You mean there's—no hope for me at all? (*Crushed,
she goes into the dining room.*)

TERRY: Well, Keith! Give me an account of yourself. You've
been gone a year—I hardly know what's happened to you.

KEITH: Why—I wrote you, didn't I?

TERRY: Oh, yes. A postcard from Palm Springs, showing the
cactus by moonlight, and a telegram of congratulations for
my opening in February, which arrived two days after we
closed.

KEITH: I got mixed up.

TERRY: But tell me—what do you mean you're only going to
be here three days? Your year's up, isn't it?

KEITH: Yeh, but they wouldn't let me go. I had to sign for another year.

TERRY: But, Keith, your plays! Aren't you writing another
play?

KEITH: Yes. Sure. I haven't written it yet, but I will this year.

TERRY: I see. I went to see the picture you wrote—what was
the name of it? *Loads of Love.*

KEITH: Oh, did you see that? How'd you like it?

TERRY: Very amusing. Of course, the Masses got a little crowded out.

KEITH: Masses! It played to eighty million people. That's masses, isn't it?

TERRY: Yes. Yes, I guess I didn't get the idea.

KEITH: Now, listen, sweet. You know why I'm here, don't you?

TERRY: No, I don't, Keith.

KEITH: Well, look! You can't go stumbling around like this forever. You're not working, are you?

TERRY: Yes.

KEITH: You are? What in?

TERRY: The blouse department of R. H. Macy & Co.

KEITH: What! You're kidding!

TERRY: I have to live, Keith.

KEITH: Good God! Listen, darling. You spend years on Broadway and finish up in Macy's. And look at Jean! Two years in Hollywood and she's a star.

TERRY: They speed up everything in Hollywood. In two years you're a star, in four you're forgotten, and in six you're back in Sweden.

(*The doorbell*)

KEITH: That's the kind of reasoning that's put you where you are! From now on I'm going to take charge of you. You're going to be— (*Breaks off as Mattie crosses the hall.*) There's always somebody coming into this place. It's like Grand Central Station.

KINGSLEY: (*Heard at the door*) Good morning, Mattie.

MATTIE: Morning, Mr. Kingsley.

KINGSLEY: (*Appearing in the archway*) Hello, Terry. (*As he sees Keith*) Well, hello there!

KEITH: Hello.

TERRY: David! How nice to see you!

KINGSLEY: (*A glance at the portrait*) I see I missed the ceremony.

TERRY: They're still shooting up on Stage Six.

KINGSLEY: No, thanks. I'm the official escort, but there are limits. . . . How are you, Burgess? I heard you were coming back.

KEITH: (*None too graciously*) How are you?

KINGSLEY: So you've served your year, h'm? Well, you're an exception. You've had the courage to quit when you said you would. Another year, and you'd have gone the way they all do. Never written a fine play again.

(*A moment of embarrassed silence*)

TERRY: (*Rather nervously*) Keith is going back to Hollywood for one more year.

KINGSLEY: Oh. I didn't mean to—

KEITH: It always amuses me to hear a fellow like you, who makes his living out of pictures, turn on Hollywood, and attack it. If you feel that way about pictures why do you work in them!

TERRY: (*Hurriedly*) Well, we can't always do what we want to, Keith. After all, you're working in Hollywood, and I'm selling blouses, and David Kingsley is—

KINGSLEY: No, Terry. He's right. I shouldn't talk that way, and I don't very often. But I'm a little worked up this morning. I reread Jean's play last night. (*A gesture toward Jean's portrait*) And I realized more than ever what a beautiful play it is. That's what's got me a little low. When picture people come into the theater—when they take a really fine play and put a girl like Jean in it—when they use a play like this for camera fodder, that's more than I can stand. The theater means too much to me.

KEITH: All right! It's a fine play. And you notice it's Hollywood that's doing it.

TERRY: Oh, Keith, let's not get into an argument.

KEITH: It just shows how little you know about Hollywood. You're five years behind the times. They're *crazy* about fine things. Dickens and Shakespeare—they've got a whole staff digging them up.

TERRY: All right! Let's talk about something else.

KEITH: If you go to a dinner in Hollywood what's the conversation! Books, and politics and art! They never even mention pictures.

KINGSLEY: I suppose they put that on the dinner invitation. Instead of R.S.V.P. it says: Don't mention pictures.

TERRY: Oh, what's got into you two! You're a picture man and you're yelling about the stage, and you're a playwright and you're howling about Hollywood!

KINGSLEY: At least I'm honest about it. I work in pictures, but I don't pretend to like it.

KEITH: Who's pretending? I like it and I'm going back there. And what's more, I'm taking Terry with me.

KINGSLEY: What?

TERRY: Keith, don't be absurd!

KEITH: It's time somebody took her in hand, and I'm going to do it. I'm going to marry her.

KINGSLEY: Terry, you can't do that!

TERRY: (*Hopefully*) Why not, David?

KEITH: Look here, you—

KINGSLEY: I've told you why a hundred times. You belong in the theater.

TERRY: Is that the reason! You certainly *have* told me a hundred times. A thousand! I've sat across a table from you and heard it with the soup and the meat and the coffee. Actress, actress, actress!

KINGSLEY: Of course I've told you. Because you *are* an actress.

TERRY: And I've just realized why. Because you quit the theater yourself, and you've been salving your own conscience by preaching theater to me. That made you feel less guilty, didn't it?

KINGSLEY: Terry, that's not true.

TERRY: Oh, yes, it is. *So* true. Funny I never thought of that before.

KEITH: Look, I've got to get out of here. . . . If I may have just a moment. (*He steps between Terry and Kingsley.*) When are we going to get married?

TERRY: (*In a deadly tone*) When are we going to get married? We are going to get married, Mr. Burgess, when Hollywood to Dunsinane doth come. That's Shakespeare—you know, the fellow they're digging up out there.

KEITH: (*Stunned*) Huh?

TERRY: It's too late, Keith. When you walked out on me a year ago, you walked out on yourself, too. That other Keith was cocksure and conceited, but he stood for something. What was it—"thunder and lightning and power and truth?" Wasn't that what you said? And "if you believe in something you've got to be willing to starve for it." Well, I believed in it, Keith. (*She turns her gaze to Kingsley, then her look includes both of them.*) So—I guess that leaves me just a young lady with a career. Or, shall we say—just a young lady? (*She goes slowly up the stairs.*)

CURTAIN

Scene II

It is midnight, and the main room of the Footlights Club is in semidarkness. There is a pool of light in the hall and on the stairway from the overhead chandelier.

A little later, when the lights go on, we see that Bernhardt has given way to Jean Maitland.

After a moment of stillness there is the sound of the front door opening, and the two Marys are heard coming home.

LITTLE MARY: Well, I didn't like either the play *or* the cast. And I thought Laura Wilcox was terrible.

BIG MARY: She's always terrible. You know how she got the part, don't you?

LITTLE MARY: Sure. Everybody on Broadway knows. The trouble with us is we've been hanging on to our virtue.

BIG MARY: Maybe *you* have.

(*They disappear up the stairs.*)

(*Somewhere in the hallway a clock strikes twelve. Then the door is heard to open again.*)

(*We hear the voice of Judith at the door.*)

JUDITH: Well, good night. And thank you ever so much.

A MAN'S VOICE: Thank *you*.

(*Judith comes into sight. Not a very spirited figure. Meanwhile we hear the man still talking.*)

I certainly had one swell evening, all right.

(*With that he comes into sight. And who is it but good old Lou Milhauser, the lumber man. He is elaborately decked out in evening clothes, in contrast to the simple little street number that Judith has on.*)

JUDITH: (*With a weak smile*) Yes, so did I. What time is it— about two o'clock?

MILHAUSER: No, it's only twelve.

JUDITH: Oh, really? I guess my watch is fast.

MILHAUSER: Look, I'm going to be here all week. What are you doing tomorrow night?

JUDITH: Tomorrow? That's Tuesday— oh, that's my gymnasium night.

MILHAUSER: Well, how about Wednesday?

JUDITH: Wednesday? Oh, I've got friends coming in from Europe. On the—ah—Mauretania.

MILHAUSER: The Mauretania? I thought they took that off.

JUDITH: Did I say Mauretania? Minnetonka.

MILHAUSER: Well, I've got to see you before I go. Of course I'll be back next month.

JUDITH: Next month? Oh, I spend November in the Catskills. My hay fever.

MILHAUSER: Well, I'll call you anyway tomorrow. On a chance.
(*He goes. Judith waits for the closing of the door.*)

JUDITH: Swell chance.
(*She goes grimly up the stairs, just as Frank comes into the room—a final round of inspection before going to bed.*)

FRANK: Evening, Miss Judith. You in early, ain't you?

JUDITH: (*As she disappears*) It may seem early to you.
(*Frank goes on about his business—locks a window, puts out the desk lamp. Then comes a ring of the doorbell.*)

FRANK: (*At the door*) Who's there?

KINGSLEY'S VOICE: Hello, Frank.

FRANK: (*A change of tone as he opens the door*) Why, Mr. Kingsley!

KINGSLEY: (*In the hall*) I hope we didn't wake you up, Frank. May we come in?

FRANK: Yessah, yessah. Pardon my shirt sleeves. I thought one of the young ladies forgot her key.
(*Kingsley and another man have come into view. The stranger is a short thickset man who carries himself with great authority in order to make up for his lack of stature.*

Instinct tells you that this is none other than Adolph Gretzl himself.)

KINGSLEY: We wouldn't have bothered you at this hour, but it's terribly important. We want to see Miss Randall.

FRANK: Miss Terry! Why, she goes to sleep early. She got to get up half-past seven.

KINGSLEY: (*Gently turning Frank around and starting him toward the stairs*) It's all right. Wake her up and ask her to come down.

FRANK: Yessah. You ge'men want to wait in here? (*He turns on the light in the living room, then goes up the stairs.*)

GRETZL: (*Looking about with disfavor*) I don't like the whole idea. A fine actress don't live in a place like this.

KINGSLEY: But she is a fine actress, Mr. Gretzl.

GRETZL: It don't feel right to me. Something tells me it's no good.

KINGSLEY: Mr. Gretzl, you've had this play in rehearsal for two weeks now. And she can't make the grade. You've got to face it—Jean is a motion-picture actress. And that's all.

GRETZL: She is a beautiful girl. When she comes on the stage they will gasp.

KINGSLEY: You saw that rehearsal tonight. And that's the best she'll ever do.

GRETZL: But she's Jean Maitland! People will come to see Jean Maitland.

KINGSLEY: No, they won't. Theatergoers won't come to see movie stars just because they're movie stars. They've got to act.

FRANK: (*Coming down the stairs*) Ah woke Miss Terry up. She's comin' right down. (*He goes down the hall.*)

KINGSLEY: Thank you, Frank. . . . (*Points a stern finger toward the head of the stair.*) Believe me, this girl's an actress.

GRETZL: All right, all right—an actress. Let's see her.

KINGSLEY: She's got presence and authority and distinction! And a beautiful, mobile face. She's exactly right for this play.

GRETZL: If she is such a great beauty and such a wonderful actress, where's she been keeping herself?

KINGSLEY: She's been learning her business.

GRETZL: All right, we'll let her read the part. What else am I here for in the middle of the night? She's got to start

tomorrow morning—tonight, even. It's a great big part.
Everything depends on it.

KINGSLEY: She can do it. She's young and eager and fresh.
Wait till you see her.

GRETZL: That's what I'm—

    (*He stops as Terry Randall comes down the stairs. She is
wearing a loose flowing robe over her long white nightgown.
Her hair falls over her shoulders; her feet are in low scuffs. She
is anything but the dazzling figure described by Kingsley.*)
    (*She comes into the room wordlessly, looking at the two men.*)
    (*Kingsley advances to her.*)

KINGSLEY: It's sweet of you to come down, Terry. I wasn't
sure you would.

TERRY: (*Looking up at him*) You knew I would, David.

KINGSLEY: (*Taking her hand and leading her toward Gretzl*)
Terry, this is Mr. Gretzl. This is Terry Randall.

TERRY: How do you do, Mr. Gretzl?

    (*Gretzl mumbles a greeting. "How do you do?"*)

KINGSLEY: Terry, I suppose I needn't tell you why we're here
at this hour. Could you start rehearsing tomorrow morning
in this play of Mr. Gretzl's, and open in a week?

GRETZL: Wait a minute, Kingsley. Not so fast, there! Let me
look at her. (*He slowly describes a half-circle around her, his
eyes intent on her face. As the inspection finishes she turns her
head and meets his gaze. But Gretzl's inquiring look is now directed at Kingsley.*) This is the party you just now described
to me!

KINGSLEY: (*Pulling a typed "part" out of his pocket*) Terry, I
know what you can do, but Mr. Gretzl doesn't. Will you
read a couple of speeches of this—let him hear you?

TERRY: (*A little terrified at the thought*) Now?

GRETZL: Of course *now*. That's what I came for.

KINGSLEY: Would you, Terry?

TERRY: I'll try.

KINGSLEY: (*Giving her the part*) How about this bit here?

TERRY: May I look at it a second, just to—

KINGSLEY: Of course. (*He turns to Gretzl*) You know, it's
rather difficult to jump right into a character.

GRETZL: What's difficult! We do it every day in pictures. . . .
Come on, young lady. Well— (*He turns a chair around,*

seats himself ostentatiously, and beckons Terry to stand directly in front of him and perform.)

TERRY: (*A deep sigh, and takes the plunge. Reads:*) "Look, boys, I haven't got any right to stand up here and tell you what to do. Only maybe I have got a right, see, because, look—" No, that isn't right. "Because, look—" Do you mind if I start all over?

GRETZL: (*Annoyed*) All right. Start over.

TERRY: (*To Kingsley*) What's she want them to do?

KINGSLEY: Strike.

TERRY: Oh. Uh— (*She is off again, less certain of herself than ever.*) —"Look, boys—" (*A bad start again, but she quickly recovers herself.*) —"Look, boys, I haven't got any right to stand up here and tell you what to do. Only maybe I have got a right, see, because, look, I'm engaged to be married. We were going to be married tomorrow. You all know who it is. He's right here in this hall."

(*Gretzl rises abruptly and begins to pace the floor, his hands behind his back. Terry goes on stumblingly:*)

—"In this hall. So if you fellas vote to go on strike, why, I guess it's no wedding bells for me. Don't kid yourself I don't know what I'm talking about. Because I've been through it before. I've been through it with my old man, and my brothers, so I ought to know."

(*Gretzl has picked up a matchbox from the table, and now strikes a match with a sharp rasping sound and lights a long cigar.*)

"It means hungry, and maybe cold, and scared every minute somebody'll come home with a busted head. But which would you'd ruther do? Die quick fighting, or starve to death slow? That's why I'm telling you—strike! Strike! Strike!

(*Gretzl has again seated himself in front of her, and as he throws back his head, the better to survey her, a cloud of cigar smoke is blown upward toward her face.*)

—That's why I'm telling you—strike! Strike! S—" (*She has been choking back a cough, but it now becomes too much for her. She stops and throws the part to the floor. Tears and anger struggle for mastery.*) I can't do it! I can't! I won't go on!

KINGSLEY: (*Angered*) You're a fool if you do.

GRETZL: (*Rising and buttoning his coat with a gesture of finality*) You must excuse me. I am a plain-speaking man. I don't want to hurt anybody's feelings, but in my opinion this young lady is not anything at all. Not anything.

TERRY: But, Mr. Gretzl, nobody could give a reading under these conditions. It isn't fair. It isn't possible for an actress— you don't understand.

GRETZL: All right. I don't understand. But I understand my business and I know what I see. So I will say good night, and thank you. Come on, Kingsley.

KINGSLEY: I'm sorry, Terry. No one could look a great actress in bathrobe and slippers. And Mr. Gretzl only knows what he sees.

GRETZL: Are you working for me or against me, Kingsley?

KINGSLEY: I'm working *for* you. What are you going to do about your play tomorrow?

GRETZL: I'm going to throw it into the ash can. All I wanted it for was Jean Maitland. So she could make a picture of it. All right. She'll do something else. I can get plenty of material.

KINGSLEY: It's incredible that anyone should be so stupid.

GRETZL: (*Rising to his full height*) Mr. Kingsley, you are *out*! You will hear from our lawyers in the morning.

TERRY: Oh, David!

KINGSLEY: It's all right, Terry. Gretzl, if you've lost your interest in the play, how about selling it to me?

GRETZL: I see. You're going back into the theater, eh?

KINGSLEY: I might. Will you sell it to me?

GRETZL: How much?

KINGSLEY: Just what it cost you.

GRETZL: All right. See Becker in the morning. He'll fix it up. Good night.

KINGSLEY: Good night.

GRETZL: (*As he goes*) And *I* am the stupid one? Huh!

TERRY: David! David, oh, my dear, you mustn't do this just for me.

KINGSLEY: No, I'm not one of those boys who puts on a play just so that his girl can act in it. . . . By the way, you *are* my girl, aren't you?

TERRY: (*Brightly*) Oh, yes sir.

KINGSLEY: I just thought I'd ask. (*He takes her in his arms and kisses her.*) You know, I had a couple of nasty weeks, Terry, after you drove me out into the cold.

TERRY: Weeks? It seemed like years.

(*Again he embraces her—just as Mrs. Orcutt enters, in bathrobe and slippers.*)

MRS. ORCUTT: I'm sorry, Mr. Kingsley, but this is against the rules.

TERRY: Mrs. Orcutt, it's the play!

KINGSLEY: My apologies, Mrs. Orcutt. This may look a little strange. But I came up on business.

MRS. ORCUTT: Frank said there was another gentleman.

TERRY: (*Gaily*) But he's gone! And, oh, Mrs. Orcutt! I'm going to do the play! (*At the end of this announcement, as she says "play," her hand goes to her mouth, like a little girl's; she is surprised to find herself crying.*)

MRS. ORCUTT: Terry, my child!

KINGSLEY: Darling, you're tired. You must get your sleep. (*There is a farewell kiss, with the full approval of Mrs. Orcutt.*) Good night.

TERRY: Good night.

KINGSLEY: Eleven in the morning, at the Lyceum.

TERRY: (*In a low voice*) I'll be there.

(*Kingsley is gone.*)

MRS. ORCUTT: Terry, dear, I'm so happy for you. Aren't you thrilled?

TERRY: (*Her eyes glowing*) It was like Victoria. When they came to tell her she was Queen.

MRS. ORCUTT: Dear child! But now you must run along to bed and get your sleep.

TERRY: No, no. I must learn my part. And I must be alone. I want a room by myself tonight. Please, Mrs. Orcutt.

MRS. ORCUTT: I'll see what I can do. (*She goes, first switching off the main light.*)

(*Terry stands alone in the semi-darkened room. A light from a street lamp shines through the window and strikes her face. For a moment she stands perfectly still. Then the realization of her new position comes over her. She seems to take on height and dignity.*)

TERRY: Now that I am Queen, I wish in future to have a bed, and a room, of my own. (*She stands transfixed as the curtain falls.*)

CURTAIN

YOU CAN'T TAKE
IT WITH YOU

A Play

by

Moss Hart

and

George S. Kaufman

The Scene Is the Home of Martin Vanderhof,
New York

Act One

A Wednesday Evening.

During this act the curtain is lowered to
denote the passing of several hours.

Act Two

A Week Later.

Act Three

The Next Day.

ACT ONE

Scene i

The home of Martin Vanderhof—just around the corner from Columbia University, but don't go looking for it. The room we see is what is customarily described as a living room, but in this house the term is something of an understatement. The every-man-for-himself room would be more like it. For here meals are eaten, plays are written, snakes collected, ballet steps practiced, xylophones played, printing presses operated—if there were room enough there would probably be ice skating. In short, the brood presided over by Martin Vanderhof goes on about the business of living in the fullest sense of the word. This is a house where you do as you like, and no questions asked.

At the moment, Grandpa Vanderhof's daughter, Mrs. Penelope Sycamore, is doing what she likes more than anything else in the world. She is writing a play—her eleventh. Comfortably ensconced in what is affectionately known as Mother's Corner, she is pounding away on a typewriter perched precariously on a rickety card table. Also on the table is one of those plaster-paris skulls ordinarily used as an ash tray, but which serves Penelope as a candy jar. And, because Penny likes companionship, there are two kittens on the table, busily lapping at a saucer of milk.

Penelope Vanderhof Sycamore is a round little woman in her early fifties, comfortable looking, gentle, homey. One would not suspect that under that placid exterior there surges the Divine Urge—but it does, it does.

After a moment her fingers lag on the keys; a thoughtful expression comes over her face. Abstractedly she takes a piece of candy out of the skull, pops it into her mouth. As always, it furnishes the needed inspiration—with a furious burst of speed she finishes a page and whips it out of the machine. Quite mechanically, she picks up one of the kittens, adds the sheet of paper to the pile underneath, replaces the kitten.

As she goes back to work, Essie Carmichael, Mrs. Sycamore's eldest daughter, comes in from the kitchen. A girl of about twenty-nine, very slight, a curious air of the pixie about her. She is wearing ballet slippers—in fact, she wears them throughout the play.

ESSIE: (*Fanning herself.*) My, that kitchen's hot.

PENNY: (*Finishing a bit of typing.*) What, Essie?

ESSIE: I say the kitchen's awful hot. That new candy I'm making—it just won't ever get cool.

PENNY: Do you have to make candy today, Essie? It's such a hot day.

ESSIE: Well, I got all those new orders. Ed went out and got a bunch of new orders.

PENNY: My, if it keeps on I suppose you'll be opening up a store.

ESSIE: That's what Ed was saying last night, but I said No, I want to be a dancer. (*Bracing herself against the table, she manipulates her legs, ballet fashion.*)

PENNY: The only trouble with dancing is, it takes so long. You've been studying such a long time.

ESSIE: (*Slowly drawing a leg up behind her as she talks.*) Only—eight—years. After all, mother, you've been writing plays for eight years. We started about the same time, didn't we.

PENNY: Yes, but you shouldn't count my first two years, because I was learning to type.

(*From the kitchen comes a colored maid named Rheba—a very black girl somewhere in her thirties. She carries a white tablecloth, and presently starts to spread it over the table.*)

RHEBA: (*As she enters.*) I think the candy's hardening up now, Miss Essie.

ESSIE: Oh, thanks, Rheba. I'll bring some in, mother—I want you to try it. (*She goes into the kitchen.*)

(*Penny returns to her work as Rheba busies herself with the table.*)

RHEBA: Finish the second act, Mrs. Sycamore?

PENNY: Oh, no, Rheba. I've just got Cynthia entering the monastery.

RHEBA: Monastery? How'd she get there? She was at the El Morocco, wasn't she?

PENNY: Well, she gets tired of the El Morocco, and there's this monastery, so she goes there.

RHEBA: Do they let her in?

PENNY: Yes, I made it Visitors' Day, so of course anybody can come.

RHEBA: Oh.

PENNY: So she arrives on Visitors' Day, and—just stays.

RHEBA: All night?

PENNY: Oh, yes. She stays six years.

RHEBA: (*As she goes into the kitchen.*) Six years? My, I bet she busts that monastery wide open.

PENNY: (*Half to herself, as she types.*) "Six Years Later." . . .

(*Paul Sycamore comes up from the cellar. Mid-fifties, but with a kind of youthful air. His quiet charm and mild manner are distinctly engaging.*)

PAUL: (*Turning back as he comes through the door.*) Mr. De Pinna!

(*A voice from below. "Yah?"*)

Mr. De Pinna, will you bring up one of those new sky rockets, please? I want to show them to Mrs. Sycamore. (*An answering monosyllable from the cellar as he turns toward Penny.*) Look, Penny—what do you think of these little fire crackers? Ten strings for a nickel. Listen. (*He puts one down on the center table and lights it. It goes off with a good bang.*) Nice, huh?

PENNY: Paul, dear, were you ever in a monastery?

PAUL: (*Quite calmly.*) No, I wasn't. . . . Wait till you see the new rockets. Gold stars, then blue stars, then some bombs, and then a balloon. Mr. De Pinna thought of the balloon.

PENNY: Sounds lovely. Did you do all that today?

PAUL: Sure. We made up—oh, here we are.

(*Mr. De Pinna comes up from the cellar. A bald-headed little man with a serious manner, and carrying two good-sized skyrockets.*)

Look, Penny. Cost us eighteen cents to make and we sell 'em for fifty. How many do you figure we can make before the Fourth, Mr. De Pinna?

DE PINNA: Well, we've got two weeks yet—what day you going to take the stuff up to Mount Vernon?

PAUL: Oh, I don't know—about a week. You know, we're going to need a larger booth this year—got a lot of stuff made up.

DE PINNA: (*Examining the rocket in his hand.*) Look, Mr. Sycamore, the only thing that bothers me is, I'm afraid the powder chamber is just a little bit close to the balloon.

PAUL: Well, we've got the stars and the bombs in between.

DE PINNA: But that don't give the balloon time enough. A balloon needs plenty of time.

PAUL: Want to go down in the cellar and try it?

DE PINNA: All right.

PAUL: (*As he disappears through the cellar door.*) That's the only way you'll really tell.

PENNY: (*Halting De Pinna in the cellar doorway.*) Mr. De Pinna, if a girl you loved entered a monastery, what would you do?

DE PINNA: (*He wasn't expecting that one.*) Oh, I don't know, Mrs. Sycamore—it's been so long. (*He goes.*)

(*Rheba returns from the kitchen, bringing a pile of plates.*)

RHEBA: Miss Alice going to be home to dinner tonight, Mrs. Sycamore?

PENNY: (*Deep in her thinking.*) What? I don't know, Rheba. Maybe.

RHEBA: Well, I'll set a place for her, but she's only been home one night this week. (*She puts down a plate or two.*) Miss Essie's making some mighty good candy today. She's doing something new with cocoanuts. (*More plates.*) Let's see— six, and Mr. De Pinna, and if Mr. Kolenkhov comes that makes eight, don't it?

(*At which point a muffled sound, reminiscent of the Battle of the Marne, comes up from the cellar. It is the sky rocket, of course. The great preliminary hiss, followed by a series of explosions. Penny and Rheba, however, don't even notice it. Rheba goes right on.*)

Yes, I'd better set for eight.

PENNY: I think I'll put this play away for a while, Rheba, and go back to the war play.

RHEBA: Oh, I always liked that one—the war play.

(*Essie returns from the kitchen, carrying a plate of freshly made candy.*)

ESSIE: They'll be better when they're harder, mother, but try one—I want to know what you think.

PENNY: Oh, they look awfully good. (*She takes one.*) What do you call them?

ESSIE: I think I'll call 'em Love Dreams.

PENNY: Oh, that's nice. . . . I'm going back to my war play, Essie. What do you think?

ESSIE: Oh, are you, mother?

PENNY: Yes, I sort of got myself into a monastery and I can't get out.

ESSIE: Oh, well, it'll come to you, mother. Remember how you got out of that brothel. . . . Hello, boys.

(*This little greeting is idly tossed toward the snake solarium, a glass structure looking something like a goldfish aquarium, but containing, believe it or not, snakes.*)

The snakes look hungry. Did Rheba feed them?

PENNY: (*As Rheba re-enters.*) I don't know. Rheba, did you feed the snakes yet?

RHEBA: No, Donald's coming and he always brings flies with him.

PENNY: Well, try to feed them before Grandpa gets home. You know how fussy he is about them.

RHEBA: Yes'm.

PENNY: (*Handing her the kittens.*) And take Groucho and Harpo into the kitchen with you. . . . I think I'll have another Love Dream.

(*Mr. Sycamore emerges from the cellar again.*)

PAUL: Mr. De Pinna was right about the balloon. It was too close to the powder.

ESSIE: (*Practicing a dance step.*) Want a Love Dream, father? They're on the table.

PAUL: No, thanks. I gotta wash.

PENNY: I'm going back to the war play, Paul.

PAUL: Oh, that's nice. We're putting some red stars after the blue stars, then come the bombs and *then* the balloon. That ought to do it. (*He goes up the stairs.*)

ESSIE: (*Another dance step.*) Mr. Kolenkhov says I'm his most promising pupil.

PENNY: (*Absorbed in her own troubles.*) You know, with forty monks and one girl, something ought to happen.

(*Ed Carmichael comes down the stairs. A nondescript young man in his mid-thirties. In shirtsleeves at the moment.*)

ED: Listen!

(*He hums a snatch of melody as he heads for the far corner of the room—the xylophone corner. Arriving there, he picks up the sticks and continues the melody on the xylophone. Immediately Essie is up on her toes, performing intricate ballet steps to Ed's accompaniment.*)

ESSIE: (*Dancing.*) I like that, Ed. Yours?

ED: (*Shakes his head.*) Beethoven.

ESSIE: (*Never coming down off her toes.*) Lovely. Got a lot of *you* in it. . . . I made those new candies this afternoon, Ed.

ED: (*Playing away.*) Yah?

ESSIE: You can take 'em around tonight.

ED: All right. . . . Now, here's the finish. This is me.
   (*He works up to an elaborate crescendo, but Essie keeps pace with him right to the finish.*)

ESSIE: That's fine. Remember it when Kolenkhov comes, will you?

PENNY: (*Who has been busy with her papers.*) Ed, dear, why don't you and Essie have a baby? I was thinking about it just the other day.

ED: I don't know—we could have one if you wanted us to. What about it, Essie? Do you want to have a baby?

ESSIE: Oh, I don't care. I'm willing if Grandpa is.

ED: Let's ask him.
   (*Essie goes into the kitchen as Penny goes back to her manuscripts.*)

PENNY: (*Running through the pile.*) Labor play . . . religious play . . . sex play. I know it's here some place.
   (*Ed, meanwhile, has transferred his attention from the xylophone to a printing press that stands handily by, and now gives it a preliminary workout.*)
   (*Mr. De Pinna comes out of the cellar, bound for the kitchen to wash up.*)

DE PINNA: I was right about the balloon. It was too close to the powder.

ED: Anything you want printed, Mr. De Pinna? How about some more calling cards?

DE PINNA: (*As he passes into the kitchen.*) No, thanks. I've still got the *first* thousand.

ED: (*Calling after him.*) Well, call on somebody, will you? (*He then gives his attention to Rheba, who is busy with the table again.*) What have we got for dinner, Rheba? I'm ready to print the menu.

RHEBA: Cornflakes, watermelon, some of those candies Miss Essie made, and some kind of meat—I forget.

ED: I think I'll set it up in boldface Cheltenham tonight. (*He starts to pick out the letters.*) If I'm going to take those new candies around I'd better print up some descriptive matter after dinner.

PENNY: Do you think anybody reads those things, Ed—that you put in the candy boxes? . . . Oh, here it is. (*She pulls a manuscript out of a pile.*) "Poison Gas." (*The door bell sounds.*) I guess that's Donald.

(*As Rheba breaks into a broad grin.*)

Look at Rheba smile.

ED: The boy friend, eh, Rheba?

PENNY: (*As Rheba disappears into the hallway.*) Donald and Rheba are awfully cute together. Sort of like Porgy and Bess. (*Rheba having opened the door, the gentleman named Donald now looms up in the doorway—darkly. He is a colored man of no uncertain hue.*)

DONALD: Good evening, everybody!

ED: Hi, Donald! How've you been?

DONALD: I'm pretty good, Mr. Ed. How you been, Mrs. Sycamore?

PENNY: Very well, thank you. (*She looks at him, appraisingly.*) Donald, were you ever in a monastery?

DONALD: No-o. I don't go no place much. I'm on relief.

PENNY: Oh, yes, of course.

DONALD: (*Pulling a bottle out of each side pocket.*) Here's the flies, Rheba. Caught a big mess of them today.

RHEBA: (*Taking the jars.*) You sure did.

DONALD: I see you've been working, Mrs. Sycamore.

PENNY: Yes, indeed, Donald.

DONALD: How's Grandpa?

PENNY: Just fine. He's over at Columbia this afternoon. The Commencement exercises.

DONALD: My, the years certainly do roll 'round.

ED: (*With his typesetting.*) M−E−A−T. . . . What's he go there for all the time, Penny?

PENNY: I don't know. It's so handy—just around the corner.
(*Paul comes downstairs.*)

PAUL: Oh, Donald! Mr. De Pinna and I are going to take the fireworks up to Mount Vernon next week. Do you think you could give us a hand?

DONALD: Yes, sir, only I can't take no money for it this year, because if the Government finds out I'm working they'll get sore.

PAUL: Oh! . . . Ed, I got a wonderful idea in the bathroom just now. I was reading Trotzky. (*He produces a book from under his arm.*) It's yours, isn't it?

ED: Yah, I left it there.

PENNY: *Who* is it?

PAUL: *You* know, Trotzky. The Russian Revolution.

PENNY: Oh.

PAUL: Anyhow, it struck me it was a great fireworks idea. Remember "The Last Days of Pompeii"?

PENNY: Oh, yes. Palisades Park. (*With a gesture of her arms she loosely describes a couple of arcs, indicative of the eruption of Mt. Vesuvius.*) That's where we met.

PAUL: Well, I'm going to do the Revolution! A full hour display.

DONALD: Say!

PENNY: Paul, that's wonderful!

ED: The red fire is the flag, huh?

PAUL: Sure! And the Czar, and the Cossacks!

DONALD: And the freeing of the slaves?

PAUL: No, no, Donald—
(*The sound of the front door slamming. A second's pause, and then Grandpa enters the living room. Grandpa is about 75, a wiry little man whom the years have treated kindly. His face is youthful, despite the lines that sear it; his eyes are very much alive. He is a man who made his peace with the world long, long ago, and his whole attitude and manner are quietly persuasive of this*)

GRANDPA: (*Surveying the group*) Well, sir, you should have been there. That's all I can say—you should have been there.

PENNY: Was it a nice Commencement, Grandpa?

GRANDPA: Wonderful. They get better every year. (*He peers*

into the snake solarium.) You don't know how lucky you are you're snakes.

ED: Big class this year, Grandpa? How many were there?

GRANDPA: Oh, must have been two acres. *Everybody* graduated. And much funnier speeches than they had last year.

DONALD: You want to listen to a good speech you go up and hear Father Divine.

GRANDPA: I'll wait—they'll have him at Columbia.

PENNY: Donald, will you tell Rheba Grandpa's home now and we won't wait for Miss Alice.

DONALD: Yes'm. . . . (*As he goes through the kitchen door.*) Rheba, Grandpa's home—we can have dinner.

PAUL: Got a new skyrocket today, Grandpa. Wait till you see it. . . . Wonder why they don't have fireworks at Commencements.

GRANDPA: Don't make enough noise. You take a good Commencement orator and he'll drown out a whole carload of fireworks. And say just as much, too.

PENNY: Don't the graduates ever say anything?

GRANDPA: No, they just sit there in cap and nightgown, get their diplomas, and then along about forty years from now they suddenly say, "Where am I?"

(*Essie comes in from the kitchen, bringing a plate of tomatoes for the evening meal.*)

ESSIE: Hello, Grandpa. Have a nice day?

GRANDPA: (*Watching Essie as she puts the tomatoes on the table.*) Hello-have-a-nice-day. (*Suddenly he roars at the top of his voice.*) Don't I even get kissed?

ESSIE: (*Kissing him*) Excuse me, Grandpa.

GRANDPA: I'll take a tomato, too. (*Essie passes the plate; Grandpa takes one and sits with it in his hand, solemnly weighing it.*) You know, I could have used a couple of these this afternoon. . . . Play something, Ed.

(*Ed at once obliges on the xylophone—something on the dreamy side. Immediately Essie is up on her toes again, drifting through the mazes of a toe dance.*)

ESSIE: (*After a moment.*) There was a letter came for you, Grandpa. Did you get it?

GRANDPA: Letter for me? I don't know anybody.

ESSIE: It was for you, though. Had your name on it.

GRANDPA: That's funny. Where is it?

ESSIE: I don't know. Where's Grandpa's letter, mother?

PENNY: (*Who has been deep in her work.*) What, dear?

ESSIE: (*Dancing dreamily away.*) Where's that letter that came for Grandpa last week?

PENNY: I don't know.

    (*Then, brightly.*)

I remember seeing the kittens on it.

GRANDPA: Who was it from? Did you notice?

ESSIE: Yes, it was on the outside.

GRANDPA: Well, who was it?

ESSIE: (*First finishing the graceful flutterings of the Dying Swan.*) United States Government.

GRANDPA: Really? Wonder what *they* wanted.

ESSIE: There was one before that, too, from the same people. There was a couple of them.

GRANDPA: Well, if any more come I wish you'd give them to me.

ESSIE: Yes, Grandpa.

    (*A fresh flurry of dancing; the xylophone grows a little louder.*)

GRANDPA: I think I'll go out to Westchester tomorrow and do a little snake-hunting.

PAUL: (*Who has settled down with his book some time before this.*) "God is the State; the State is God."

GRANDPA: What's that?

PAUL: "God is the State; the State is God."

GRANDPA: Who says that?

PAUL: Trotzky.

GRANDPA: Well, that's all right—I thought *you* said it.

ED: It's nice for printing, you know. Good and short. (*He reaches into the type case.*) G–O–D — space — I–S — space — T–H–E

    (*The sound of the outer door closing, and Alice Sycamore enters the room. A lovely, fresh young girl of about twenty-two. She is plainly Grandpa's grand-daughter, but there is something that sets her apart from the rest of the family. For one thing, she is in daily contact with the world; in addition, she seems to have escaped the tinge of mild insanity that per-*)

vades the rest of them. But she is a Sycamore for all that, and her devotion and love for them are plainly apparent. At the moment she is in a small nervous flutter, but she is doing her best to conceal it.)

ALICE: (*As she makes the rounds, kissing her grandfather, her father, her mother.*) And so the beautiful princess came into the palace, and kissed her mother, and her father, and her grandfather—hi, Grandpa—and what do you think? They turned into the Sycamore family. Surprised?

ESSIE: (*Examining Alice's dress.*) Oh, Alice, I like it. It's new, isn't it?

PENNY: Looks nice and summery.

ESSIE: Where'd you get it?

ALICE: Oh, I took a walk during lunch hour.

GRANDPA: You've been taking a lot of walks lately. That's the second new dress this week.

ALICE: Oh, I just like to brighten up the office once in a while. I'm known as the Kay Francis of Kirby & Co. . . . Well, what's new around here? In the way of plays, snakes, ballet dancing or fireworks. Dad, I'll bet you've been down in that cellar all day.

PAUL: Huh?

PENNY: I'm going back to the war play, Alice.

ESSIE: Ed, play Alice that Beethoven thing you wrote. Listen, Alice.

(*Like a shot Ed is at the xylophone again, Essie up on her toes.*)

(*Grandpa, meanwhile, has unearthed his stamp album from under a pile of oddments in the corner, and is now busy with his magnifying glass.*)

GRANDPA: Do you know that you can mail a letter all the way from Nicaragua for two pesetos?

PENNY: (*Meanwhile dramatically reading one of her own deathless lines.*) "Kenneth, my virginity is a priceless thing to me."

ALICE: (*Finding it hard to break through all this.*) Listen, people. . . . Listen. (*A break in the music; she gets a scattered sort of attention.*) I'm not home to dinner. A young gentleman is calling for me.

ESSIE: Really? Who is it?

PENNY: Well, isn't that nice?

ALICE: (*With quiet humor.*) I did everything possible to keep him from coming here, but he's calling for me.

PENNY: Why don't you both stay to dinner?

ALICE: No, I want him to take you in easy doses. I've tried to prepare him a little, but don't make it any worse than you can help. Don't read him any plays, mother, and don't let a snake bite him, Grandpa, because I like him. And I wouldn't dance for him, Essie, because we're going to the Monte Carlo ballet tonight.

GRANDPA: Can't do *anything*. Who *is* he—President of the United States?

ALICE: No, he's vice-president of Kirby & Co. Mr. Anthony Kirby, Jr.

ESSIE: The Boss' son?

PENNY: Well!

ALICE: The Boss' son. Just like the movies.

ESSIE: That explains the new dresses.

ED: And not being home to dinner for three weeks.

ALICE: Why, you're wonderful!

PENNY: (*All aglow.*) Are you going to marry him?

ALICE: Oh, of course. Tonight! Meanwhile I have to go up and put on my wedding dress.

ESSIE: Is he good-looking?

ALICE: (*Vainly consulting her watch.*) Yes, in a word. Oh, dear! What time is it?

PENNY: I don't know. Anybody know what time it is?

PAUL: Mr. De Pinna might know.

ED: It was about five o'clock a couple of hours ago.

ALICE: Oh, I ought to know better than to ask you people. . . . Will you let me know the minute he comes, please?

PENNY: Of course, Alice.

ALICE: Yes, I know, but I mean the *minute* he comes.

PENNY: Why, of course.

(*Alice looks apprehensively from one to the other; then disappears up the stairs.*)

Well, what do you think of that?

GRANDPA: She seems to like him, if you ask me.

ESSIE: I should say so. She's got it bad.

PENNY: Wouldn't it be wonderful if she married him? We could have the wedding right in this room.

PAUL: Now, wait a minute, Penny. This is the first time he's ever called for the girl.

PENNY: You only called for me once.

PAUL: Young people are different nowadays.

ESSIE: Oh, I don't know. Look at Ed and me. He came to dinner *once* and just stayed.

PENNY: Anyhow, I think it's wonderful. I'll bet he's crazy about her. It must be he that's been taking her out every night.

(*The door bell rings.*)

There he is! Never mind, Rheba, I'll answer it. (*She is fluttering to the door.*) Now remember what Alice said, and be *very* nice to him.

GRANDPA: (*Rising.*) All right—let's take a look at him.

PENNY: (*At the front door; milk and honey in her voice.*) Well! Welcome to our little home! I'm Alice's mother. Do come right in! Here we are! (*She reappears in the archway, piloting the stranger.*) This is Grandpa, and that's Alice's father, and Alice's sister, and her husband, Ed Carmichael.

(*The family all give courteous little nods and smiles as they are introduced.*)

Well! Now give me your hat and make yourself right at home.

THE MAN: I'm afraid you must be making a mistake.

PENNY: How's that?

THE MAN: My card.

PENNY: (*Reading.*) "Wilbur C. Henderson. Internal Revenue Department."

HENDERSON: That's right.

GRANDPA: What can we do for you?

HENDERSON: Does a Mr. Martin Vanderhof live here?

GRANDPA: Yes, sir. That's me.

HENDERSON: (*All milk and honey.*) Well, Mr. Vanderhof, the Government wants to talk to you about a little matter of income tax.

PENNY: Income tax?

HENDERSON: Do you mind if I sit down?

GRANDPA: No, no. Just go right ahead.

HENDERSON: (*Settling himself.*) Thank you.
  (*From above stairs the voice of Alice floats down.*)
ALICE: Mother! Is that Mr. Kirby?
PENNY: (*Going to the stairs.*) No. No, it isn't, darling. It's—an
  internal something or other. (*To Mr. Henderson.*) Pardon me.
HENDERSON: (*Pulling a sheaf of papers from his pocket.*) We've
  written you several letters about this, Mr. Vanderhof, but
  have not had any reply.
GRANDPA: Oh, that's what those letters were.
ESSIE: I told you they were from the Government.
  (*Mr. De Pinna comes up from the cellar, bearing a couple of
  giant firecrackers. He pauses as he sees a stranger.*)
DE PINNA: Oh, pardon me.
PAUL: Yes, Mr. De Pinna?
DE PINNA: These things are not going off, Mr. Sycamore.
  Look. (*He prepares to apply a match to one of them, as a star-
  tled income tax man nearly has a conniption fit. But Paul is
  too quick for him.*)
PAUL: Ah—not here, Mr. De Pinna. Grandpa's busy.
DE PINNA: Oh.
  (*Mr. De Pinna and Paul hurry into the hall with their fire-
  crackers.*)
HENDERSON: (*Now that order has been restored.*) According to
  our records, Mr. Vanderhof, you have never paid an income
  tax.
GRANDPA: That's right.
HENDERSON: Why not?
GRANDPA: I don't believe in it.
HENDERSON: Well—you own property, don't you?
GRANDPA: Yes, sir.
HENDERSON: And you receive a yearly income from it?
GRANDPA: I do.
HENDERSON: Of— (*He consults his records.*) —between three
  and four thousand dollars.
GRANDPA: About that.
HENDERSON: You've been receiving it for years.
GRANDPA: I have. 1901, if you want the exact date.
HENDERSON: Well, the Government is only concerned from
  1914 on. That's when the income tax started.
GRANDPA: Well?

HENDERSON: Well—it seems, Mr. Vanderhof, that you owe the Government twenty-two years' back income tax.

ED: Wait a minute! You can't go back that far—that's outlawed.

HENDERSON: (*Calmly regarding him.*) What's *your* name?

ED: What difference does that make?

HENDERSON: Ever file an income tax return?

ED: No, sir.

HENDERSON: What was your income last year?

ED: Ah—twenty-eight dollars and fifty cents, wasn't it, Essie?
(*Essie gives quick assent; the income tax man dismisses the whole matter with an impatient wave of the hand and returns to bigger game.*)

HENDERSON: Now, Mr. Vanderhof, you know there's quite a penalty for not filing an income tax return.

PENNY: Penalty?

GRANDPA: Look, Mr. Henderson, let me ask you something.

HENDERSON: Well?

GRANDPA: Suppose I pay you this money—mind you, I don't say I'm going to do it—but just for the sake of argument—what's the Government going to do with it?

HENDERSON: How do you mean?

GRANDPA: Well, what do I get for my money? If I go into Macy's and buy something, there it *is*—I see it. What's the Government give me?

HENDERSON: Why, the Government gives you everything. It protects you.

GRANDPA: What from?

HENDERSON: Well—invasion. Foreigners that might come over here and take everything you've got.

GRANDPA: Oh, I don't think they're going to do that.

HENDERSON: If you didn't pay an income tax, they would. How do you think the Government keeps up the Army and Navy? All those battleships . . .

GRANDPA: Last time we used battleships was in the Spanish-American War, and what did we get out of it? Cuba—and we gave that back. I wouldn't mind paying if it were something sensible.

HENDERSON: (*Beginning to get annoyed.*) Well, what about Congress, and the Supreme Court, and the President? We've got to pay *them*, don't we?

GRANDPA: (*Ever so calmly.*) Not with my money—no, sir.

HENDERSON: (*Furious.*) Now wait a minute! I'm not here to argue with you. All I know is that you haven't paid an income tax and you've got to pay it!

GRANDPA: They've got to show me.

HENDERSON: (*Yelling.*) We *don't* have to show you! I just told you! All those buildings down in Washington, and Interstate Commerce, and the Constitution!

GRANDPA: The Constitution was paid for long ago. And Interstate Commerce—what *is* Interstate Commerce, anyhow?

HENDERSON: (*With murderous calm.*) There are forty-eight states—see? And if there weren't Interstate Commerce, nothing could go from one state to another. See?

GRANDPA: Why not? They got fences?

HENDERSON: No, they haven't got fences! They've got *laws*! . . . My God, I never came across anything like this before!

GRANDPA: Well, I might pay about seventy-five dollars, but that's all it's worth.

HENDERSON: You'll pay every cent of it, like everybody else!

ED: (*Who has lost interest.*) Listen, Essie—listen to this a minute.

(*The xylophone again; Essie goes into her dance.*)

HENDERSON: (*Going right ahead, battling against the music.*) And let me tell you something else! You'll go to jail if you don't pay, do you hear that? There's a law, and if you think you're bigger than the law, you've got another think coming! You'll hear from the United States Government, that's all I can say! (*He is backing out of the room.*)

GRANDPA: (*Quietly.*) Look out for those snakes.

HENDERSON: (*Jumping.*) Jesus!

(*Out in the hall, and not more than a foot or two behind Mr. Henderson, the firecracker boys are now ready to test that little bomber. It goes off with a terrific detonation, and Mr. Henderson jumps a full foot. He wastes no time at all in getting out of there.*)

PAUL: (*Coming back into the room.*) How did that sound to you folks?

GRANDPA: (*Quite judicially.*) I like it.

PENNY: My goodness, he was mad, wasn't he?

GRANDPA: Oh, it wasn't his fault. It's just that the whole thing is so silly.

PENNY: (*Suddenly finding herself with a perfectly good Panama in her hand.*) He forgot his hat.

GRANDPA: What size is it?

PENNY: (*Peering into its insides.*) Seven and an eighth.

GRANDPA: Just right for me.

DE PINNA: Who was that fellow, anyhow? (*Again the door bell.*)

PENNY: This *must* be Mr. Kirby.

PAUL: Better make sure this time.

PENNY: Yes, I will. (*She disappears.*)

ESSIE: I hope he's good-looking.

PENNY: (*Heard at the door.*) How do you do?

A MAN'S VOICE: Good evening.

PENNY: (*Taking no chances.*) Is this Mr. Anthony Kirby, Jr.?

TONY: Yes.

PENNY: (*Giving her all.*) Well, Mr. Kirby, come right in! We've been expecting you. Come right in! (*They come into sight; Penny expansively addresses the family.*) This is *really* Mr. Kirby! Now, I'm Alice's mother, and that's *Mr.* Sycamore, and Alice's grandfather, and her sister Essie, and Essie's husband.

(*There are a few mumbled greetings.*)

There! Now you know *all* of us, Mr. Kirby. Give me your hat and make yourself right at home.

(*Tony Kirby comes a few steps into the room. He is a personable young man, not long out of Yale, and, as we will presently learn, even more recently out of Cambridge. Although he fits all the physical requirements of a Boss' son, his face has something of the idealist in it. All in all, a very nice young man.*)

TONY: How do you do?

(*Again the voice of the vigilant Alice floats down from upstairs. "Is that Mr. Kirby, mother?"*)

PENNY: (*Shouting up the stairs.*) Yes, Alice. He's *lovely!*

ALICE: (*Aware of storms signals.*) I'll be right down.

PENNY: Do sit down, Mr. Kirby.

TONY: Thank you. (*A glance at the dinner table.*) I hope I'm not keeping you from dinner?

GRANDPA: No, no. Have a tomato?

TONY: No, thank you.

PENNY: (*Producing the candy-filled skull.*) How about a piece of candy?

TONY: (*Eyeing the container.*) Ah—no, thanks.

PENNY: Oh, I forgot to introduce Mr. De Pinna. This is Mr. De Pinna, Mr. Kirby.

    (*An exchange of "How do you do's?"*)

DE PINNA: Wasn't I reading about your father in the newspaper the other day? Didn't he get indicted or something?

TONY: (*Smiling.*) Hardly that. He just testified before the Securities Commission.

DE PINNA: Oh.

PENNY: (*Sharply.*) Yes, of course. I'm sure there was nothing crooked about it, Mr. De Pinna. As a matter of fact— (*She is now addressing Tony.*) —Alice has often told us what a lovely man your father is.

TONY: Well, I know father couldn't get along without Alice. She knows more about the business than any of us.

ESSIE: You're awful young, Mr. Kirby, aren't you, to be vice-president of a big place like that.

TONY: Well, you know what that means, vice-president. All I have is a desk with my name on it.

PENNY: Is that all? Don't you get any salary?

TONY: (*With a laugh.*) Well, a little. More than I'm worth, I'm afraid.

PENNY: Now you're just being modest.

GRANDPA: Sounds kind of dull to me—Wall Street. Do you like it?

TONY: Well, the hours are short. And I haven't been there very long.

GRANDPA: Just out of college, huh?

TONY: Well, I knocked around for a while first. Just sort of had fun.

GRANDPA: What did you do? Travel?

TONY: For a while. Then I went to Cambridge for a year.

GRANDPA: (*Nodding.*) England.

TONY: That's right.

GRANDPA: Say, what's an English commencement like? Did you see any?

TONY: Oh, very impressive.

GRANDPA: They are, huh?

TONY: Anyhow, now the fun's over, and—I'm facing the world.

PENNY: You've certainly got a good start, Mr. Kirby. Vice-president, and a rich father.

TONY: Well, that's hardly my fault.

PENNY: (*Brightly.*) So now I suppose you're all ready to settle down and—get married.

PAUL: Come now, Penny, I'm sure Mr. Kirby knows his own mind.

PENNY: I wasn't making up his mind for him—was I, Mr. Kirby?

TONY: That's quite all right, Mrs. Sycamore.

PENNY: (*To the others.*) You see?

ESSIE: You mustn't rush him, mother.

PENNY: Well, all I meant was he's bound to get married, and suppose the wrong girl gets him?

(*The descending Alice mercifully comes to Tony's rescue at this moment. Her voice is heard from the stairs.*)

ALICE: Well, here I am, a vision in white. (*She comes into the room—and very lovely indeed.*) Apparently you've had time to get acquainted.

PENNY: Oh, yes, indeed. We were just having a delightful talk about love and marriage.

ALICE: Oh, dear. (*She turns to Tony.*) I'm sorry. I came down as fast as I could.

RHEBA: (*Bringing a platter of sliced watermelon.*) God damn those flies in the kitchen. . . . Oh, Miss Alice, you look beautiful. Where you going?

ALICE: (*Making the best of it.*) I'm going out, Rheba.

RHEBA: (*Noticing Tony.*) Stepping, huh? (*The door bell sounds.*)

ESSIE: That must be Kolenkhov.

ALICE: (*Uneasily.*) I think we'd better go, Tony.

TONY: All right.

(*Before they can escape, however, Donald emerges from the kitchen, bearing a tray.*)

DONALD: Grandpa, you take cream on your cornflakes? I forget.

GRANDPA: Half and half, Donald.

(*The voice of Boris Kolenkhov booms from the outer door.*)

KOLENKHOV: Ah, my little Rhebishka!

RHEBA: (*With a scream of laughter.*) Yassuh, Mr. Kolenkhov!

KOLENKHOV: I am so hungry I could even eat my little Rhebishka!

> (*He appears in the archway, his great arm completely encircling the delighted Rheba. Mr. Kolenkhov is one of Rheba's pets, and if you like Russians he might be one of yours. He is enormous, hairy, loud, and very, very Russian. His appearance in the archway still further traps Alice and Tony.*)

Grandpa, what do you think? I have had a letter from Russia! The Second Five Year Plan is a failure! (*He lets out a laugh that shakes the rafters.*)

ESSIE: I practiced today, Mr. Kolenkhov!

KOLENKHOV: (*With a deep Russian bow.*) My Pavlowa! (*Another bow.*) Madame Sycamore! . . . My little Alice! (*He kisses her hand.*) Never have I seen you look so magnificent.

ALICE: Thank you, Mr. Kolenkhov. Tony, this is Mr. Kolenkhov, Essie's dancing teacher. Mr. Kirby.

TONY: How do you do?

> (*A click of the heels and a bow from Kolenkhov.*)

ALICE: (*Determined, this time.*) And now we really *must* go. Excuse us, Mr. Kolenkhov—we're going to the Monte Carlo ballet.

KOLENKHOV: (*At the top of his tremendous voice.*) The Monte Carlo ballet! It *stink*s!

ALICE: (*Panicky now.*) Yes. . . . Well—goodbye, everybody. Goodbye.

TONY: Goodbye. I'm so glad to have met you all.

> (*A chorus of answering "Good-byes" from the family. The young people are gone.*)

KOLENKHOV: (*Still furious.*) The Monte Carlo ballet!

PENNY: Isn't Mr. Kirby lovely? . . . Come on, everybody! Dinner's ready!

ED: (*Pulling up a chair.*) I thought he was a nice fellow, didn't you?

ESSIE: Mm. And so good-looking.

PENNY: And he had such nice manners. Did you notice, Paul? Did you notice his manners?

PAUL: I certainly did. You were getting pretty personal with him.

PENNY: Oh, now, Paul . . . Anyhow, he's a very nice young man.

DE PINNA: (*As he seats himself.*) He looks kind of like a cousin of mine.

KOLENKHOV: Bakst! Diaghlieff! *Then* you had the *ballet!*

PENNY: I think if they get married here I'll put the altar right where the snakes are. You wouldn't mind, Grandpa, would you?

ESSIE: Oh, they'll want to get married in a church. His family and everything.

GRANDPA: (*Tapping on a plate of silence.*) Quiet, everybody! Quiet!

(*They are immediately silent—Grace is about to be pronounced. Grandpa pauses a moment for heads to bow, then raises his eyes heavenward. He clears his throat and proceeds to say Grace.*)

Well, Sir, we've been getting along pretty good for quite a while now, and we're certainly much obliged. Remember, all we ask is just to go along and be happy in our own sort of way. Of course we want to keep our health, but as far as anything else is concerned, we'll leave it to You. Thank You.

(*The heads come up as Rheba comes through the door with a steaming platter.*)

So the Second Five Year Plan is a failure, eh, Kolenkhov?

KOLENKHOV: (*Booming.*) Catastrophic! (*He reaches across the table and spears a piece of bread. The family, too, is busily plunging in.*)

THE CURTAIN IS DOWN

SCENE 2

Late the same night. The house is in darkness save for a light in the hall

Somewhere in the back regions an accordion is being played. Then quiet. Then the stillness of the night is suddenly broken

*again by a good loud BANG! from the cellar. Somewhere in the
nether regions, one of the Sycamores is still at work.*

*Once more all is quiet, then the sound of a key in the outer
door. The voices of Alice and Tony drift through.*

ALICE: I could see them dance every night of the week. I think
   they're marvelous.
TONY: They are, aren't they? But of course just walking inside
   any theater gives *me* a thrill.
ALICE: (*As they come into sight in the hallway.*) It's been *so*
   lovely, Tony. I hate to have it over.
TONY: Oh, is it over? Do I have to go right away?
ALICE: Not if you don't want to.
TONY: I don't.
ALICE: Would you like a cold drink?
TONY: Wonderful.
ALICE: (*Pausing to switch on the light.*) I'll see what's in the ice-
   box. Want to come along?
TONY: I'd follow you to the ends of the earth.
ALICE: Oh, just the kitchen is enough.
   (*They go out. A pause, a ripple of gay laughter from the
   kitchen, then they return. Alice is carrying a couple of
   glasses, Tony brings two bottles of ginger ale and an opener.*)
   Lucky you're not hungry, Mr. K. An ice-box full of corn-
   flakes. That gives you a rough idea of the Sycamores.
TONY: (*Working away with the opener.*) Of course, why they
   make these bottle openers for Singer midgets I never *was*
   able to—ah! (*As the bottle opens.*) All over my coat.
ALICE: I'll take mine in a glass, if you don't mind.
TONY: (*Pouring.*) There you are. A foaming beaker.
ALICE: Anyhow, it's cold.
TONY: (*Pouring his own.*) Now if you'll please be seated, I'd
   like to offer a toast.
ALICE: (*Settling herself.*) We are seated.
TONY: Miss Sycamore— (*He raises his glass on high.*) —to you.
ALICE: Thank you, Mr. Kirby. (*Lifting her own glass.*) To you.
   (*They both drink.*)
TONY: (*Happily.*) I wouldn't trade one minute of this evening
   for—all the rice in China.
ALICE: Really?

TONY: Cross my heart.

ALICE: (*A little sigh of contentment. Then shyly.*) Is there much rice in China?

TONY: Terrific. Didn't you read "The Good Earth"? (*She laughs. They are silent for a moment.*) I suppose I ought to go.

ALICE: Is it very late?

TONY: (*Looks at his watch.*) Very.

(*Alice gives a little nod. Time doesn't matter.*)

I don't want to go.

ALICE: I don't want you to.

TONY: All right, I won't. (*Silence again.*) When do you get your vacation?

ALICE: Last two weeks in August.

TONY: I might take mine then, too.

ALICE: Really?

TONY: What are you going to do?

ALICE: I don't know. I hadn't thought much about it.

TONY: Going away, do you think?

ALICE: I might not. I like the city in the summer time.

TONY: I do too.

ALICE: But you always go up to Maine, don't you?

TONY: Why—yes, but I'm sure I *would* like the city in the summer time. That is, I'd like it if— Oh, you know what I mean, Alice. I'd love it if *you* were here.

ALICE: Well—it'd be nice if you were here, Tony.

TONY: You know what you're saying, don't you?

ALICE: What?

TONY: That you'd rather spend the summer with me than anybody else.

ALICE: It looks that way, doesn't it?

TONY: Well, if it's true about the summer, how would you feel about—the winter?

ALICE: (*Seeming to weigh the matter.*) Yes. I'd—like that too.

TONY: (*Tremulous.*) Then comes spring—and autumn. If you could—see your way clear about those, Miss Sycamore. . . .

ALICE: (*Again a little pause.*) Yes.

TONY: I guess that's the whole year. We haven't forgotten anything, have we?

ALICE: No.

TONY: Well, then—

(*Another pause; their eyes meet. And at this moment, Penny is heard from the stairway.*)

PENNY: Is that you, Alice? What time is it? (*She comes into the room, wrapped in a bathrobe.*) Oh! (*In sudden embarrassment.*) Excuse me, Mr. Kirby. I had no idea—that is, I— (*She senses the situation.*) —I didn't mean to interrupt anything.

TONY: Not at all, Mrs. Sycamore.

ALICE: (*Quietly.*) No, mother.

PENNY: I just came down for a manuscript— (*Fumbling at her table.*) —then you can go right ahead. Ah, here it is. "Sex Takes a Holiday." Well—good-night, Mr. Kirby.

TONY: Good-night, Mrs. Sycamore.

PENNY: Oh, I think you can call me Penny, don't you, Alice? At least I hope so. (*With a little laugh she vanishes up the stairs.*)

(*Before Penny's rippling laugh quite dies, BANG! from the cellar. Tony jumps.*)

ALICE: (*Quietly.*) It's all right, Tony. That's father.

TONY: This time of night?

ALICE: (*Ominously.*) *Any* time of night. Any time of *day.* (*She stands silent. In the pause, Tony gazes at her fondly.*)

TONY: You're more beautiful, more lovely, more adorable than anyone else in the whole world.

ALICE: (*As he starts to embrace her.*) Don't, Tony. I can't.

TONY: What?

ALICE: I can't, Tony.

TONY: My dear, just because your mother—all mothers are like that, Alice, and Penny's a darling. You see, I'm even calling her Penny.

ALICE: I don't mean that. (*She faces him squarely.*) Look, Tony. This is something I should have said a long time ago, but I didn't have the courage. I let myself be swept away because —because I loved you so.

TONY: Darling!

ALICE: No, wait, Tony. I want to make it clear to you. You're of a different world—a whole different kind of people. Oh, I don't mean money or socially—that's too silly. But your family and mine—it just wouldn't work, Tony. It just wouldn't work.

(*Again an interruption. This time it is Ed and Essie, re-turning from the neighborhood movie. We hear their voices at the door, deep in an argument. Ed: "All right, have it your way. She* can't *dance. That's why they pay her all that money—because she can't dance." And then Essie: "Well, I don't call that dancing, what she does.*")

(*They come into sight.*)

ESSIE: Oh, hello.

    (*There is an exchange of greetings, a note of constraint in Alice's voice. But Essie goes right ahead.*)

Look! What do *you* think? Ed and I just saw Fred Astaire and Ginger Rogers. Do you think she can dance, Mr. Kirby?

TONY: (*Mildly taken aback by this.*) Why, yes—I always thought so.

ESSIE: What does she do, anyhow? Now, look—you're Fred Astaire and I'm Ginger Rogers. (*She drapes herself against Tony, a la Ginger Rogers.*)

ALICE: Essie, please.

ESSIE: I just want to use him for a minute. . . . Look, Mr. Kirby— (*Her arms go round his neck, her cheek against his.*)

ALICE: (*Feeling that it's time to take action.*) Essie, you're just as good as Ginger Rogers. We all agree.

ESSIE: (*Triumphantly.*) You see, Ed?

ED: Yeh. . . . Come on, Essie—we're butting in here.

ESSIE: Oh, they've been together all evening. . . . Good night, Mr. Kirby.

    (*An exchange of good-nights—it looks as though the Car-michaels are really going upstairs before the whole thing gets too embarrassing. Then Ed turns casually to Essie in the doorway.*)

ED: Essie, did you ask Grandpa about us having a baby?

ESSIE: (*As they ascend the stairs.*) Yes—he said go right ahead.

ALICE: (*When they are gone.*) You see? That's what it would be like, always.

TONY: But I didn't mind that. Besides, darling, we're not going to live with our families. It's just you and I.

ALICE: No, it isn't—it's never quite that. I love them, Tony—I love them deeply. Some people could cut away, but I couldn't. I know they do rather strange things—I never know what to expect next—but they're gay, and they're fun, and—I don't know—there's a kind of nobility about them. That may sound silly, but I mean—the way they just don't care about things that other people give their whole lives to. They're—really wonderful, Tony.

TONY: Alice, you talk as though only you could understand them. That's not true. Why, I fell in love with them tonight.

ALICE: But your family, Tony. I'd want *you*, and everything about you, everything about *me*, to be—one. I couldn't start out with a part of me that you didn't share, and part of you that I didn't share. Unless we were all one—you, and *your* mother and father—I'd be miserable. And they never can be, Tony—I know it. They couldn't be.

TONY: Alice, every family has got curious little traits. What of it? My father raises orchids at ten thousand dollars a bulb. Is that sensible? My mother believes in spiritualism. That's just as bad as your mother writing plays, isn't it?

ALICE: It goes deeper, Tony. Your mother believes in spiritualism because it's fashionable. And your father raises orchids because he can afford to. My mother writes plays because eight years ago a typewriter was delivered here by mistake.

TONY: Darling what *of* it?

ALICE: And look at Grandpa. Thirty-five years ago he just quit business one day. He started up to his office in the elevator and came right down again. He just stopped. He could have been a rich man, but he said it took too much time. So for thirty-five years he's just collected snakes and gone to circuses and commencements. It never occurs to any of them—

(*As if to prove her point, they are suddenly interrupted at this moment by the entrance of Donald from the kitchen. It is a Donald who has plainly not expected to encounter midnight visitors, for he is simply dressed in a long white nightgown and a somewhat shorter bathrobe—a costume that permits a generous expanse of white nightshirt down around the legs, and, below that, a couple of very black shins. His appearance, incidentally, explains where all that music had been coming from, for an accordion is slung over his shoulder.*)

DONALD: (*Surprised, but not taken aback.*) Oh, excuse me. I didn't know you folks were in here.

ALICE: (*Resigned.*) It's all right, Donald.

DONALD: Rheba kind of fancied some candy, and— (*His gaze is roaming the room.*) oh, there it is. (*He picks up Penny's skull, if you know what we mean.*) You-all don't want it, do you?

ALICE: No, Donald. Go right ahead.

DONALD: Thanks. (*He feels that the occasion calls for certain amenities.*) Have a nice evening?

ALICE: Yes, Donald.

DONALD: Nice dinner?

ALICE: (*Restraining herself.*) Yes, Donald.

DONALD: The ballet nice?

ALICE: (*Entirely too quietly.*) Yes, Donald.

DONALD: (*Summing it all up.*) That's nice.
    (*He goes—and Alice bursts forth.*)

ALICE: Now! Now do you see what I mean? Could you explain Donald to your father? Could you explain Grandpa? You couldn't, Tony, you couldn't! I should have known! I did know! I love you, Tony, but I love them too! And it's no use, Tony! It's no use! (*She is weeping now in spite of herself.*)

TONY: (*Quietly.*) There's only one thing you've said that matters—that makes any sense at all. You love me.

ALICE: But, Tony, I know so well . . .

TONY: My darling, don't you think other people have had the same problem? Everybody's got a family.

ALICE: (*Through her tears.*) But not like mine.

TONY: That doesn't stop people who love each other. . . . Darling! Darling, won't you trust me, and go on loving me, and forget everything else?

ALICE: How can I?

TONY: Because nothing can keep us apart. You know that. You must know it. Just as I know it. (*He takes her in his arms.*) They want you to be happy, don't they? They *must*.

ALICE: Of course they do. But they can't change, Tony. I wouldn't want them to change.

TONY: They won't have to change. They're charming, lovable people, just as they are. You're worrying about something that may never come up.

ALICE: Oh, Tony, am I?

TONY: All that matters right now is that we love each other. That's right, isn't it?

ALICE: (*Whispering.*) Yes.

TONY: Well, then!

ALICE: (*In his arms.*) Tony, Tony!

TONY: Now! I'd like to see a little gayety around here. Young gentleman calling, and getting engaged and everything.

ALICE: (*Smiling up into his face.*) What do I say?

TONY: Well, first you thank the young man for getting engaged to you.

ALICE: Thank you, Mr. Kirby, for getting engaged to me.

TONY: And then you tell him what it was about him that first took your girlish heart.

ALICE: The back of your head.

TONY: Huh?

ALICE: Uh-huh. It wasn't your charm, and it wasn't your money—it was the back of your head. I just happened to like it.

TONY: What happened when I turned around?

ALICE: Oh, I got used to it after a while.

TONY: I see . . . Oh, Alice, think of it. We're pretty lucky, aren't we?

ALICE: I know that *I* am. The luckiest girl in the world.

TONY: I'm not exactly unlucky myself.

ALICE: It's wonderful, isn't it?

TONY: Yes . . . Lord, but I'm happy.

ALICE: Are you, Tony?

TONY: Terribly . . . And now—good-night, my dear. Until to-morrow.

ALICE: Good-night.

TONY: Isn't it wonderful we work in the same office? Otherwise I'd be hanging around *here* all day.

ALICE: Won't it be funny in the office tomorrow—seeing each other and just going on as though nothing had happened?

TONY: Thank God I'm vice-president. I can dictate to you all day. "Dear Miss Sycamore: I love you, I love you, I love you."

ALICE: Oh, darling! You're such a fool.

TONY: (*An arm about her as he starts toward the hallway.*) Why don't you meet me in the drugstore in the morning—before you go up to the office? I'll have millions of things to say to you by then.

ALICE: All right.

TONY: And then lunch, and then dinner tomorrow night.

ALICE: Oh, Tony! What will people say?

TONY: It's got to come out some time. In fact, if you know a good housetop, I'd like to do a little shouting.

(*She laughs—a happy little ripple. They are out of sight in the hallway by this time; their voices become inaudible.*)

(*Paul, at this point, decides to call it a day down in the cellar. He comes through the door, followed by Mr. De Pinna. He is carrying a small metal container, filled with powder.*)

PAUL: Yes, sir, Mr. De Pinna, we did a good day's work.

DE PINNA: That's what. Five hundred Black Panthers, three hundred Willow Trees, and eight dozen Junior Kiddie Bombers.

(*Alice comes back from the hallway, still under the spell of her love.*)

PAUL: Why, hello, Alice. You just come in?

ALICE: (*Softly.*) No. No, I've been home quite a while.

PAUL: Have a nice evening? Say, I'd like you to take a look at this new red fire we've got.

ALICE: (*Almost singing it.*) I had a beautiful evening, father.

PAUL: Will you turn out the lights, Mr. De Pinna? I want Alice to get the full effect.

ALICE: (*Who hasn't heard a word.*) What, father?

PAUL: Take a look at this new red fire. It's beautiful.

(*Mr. De Pinna switches the lights out; Paul touches a match to the powder. The red fire blazes, shedding a soft glow over the room.*)

There! What do you think of it? Isn't it beautiful?

ALICE: (*Radiant; her face aglow, her voice soft.*) Yes, father. Everything is beautiful. It's the most beautiful red fire in the world! (*She rushes to him and throws her arms about him, almost unable to bear her own happiness.*)

CURTAIN

ACT TWO

A week later, and the family has just risen from the dinner table. Two or three of them have drifted out of the room, but Grandpa and Paul still sit over their coffee cups.

There is, however, a newcomer in the room. Her name is Gay Wellington, and, as we will presently guess, she is an actress, a nymphomaniac, and a terrible souse. At the moment she sits with a gin bottle in one hand and a glass in the other, and is having a darned good time. Hovering over her, script in hand, is a slightly worried Penny. Ed is watching the proceedings from somewhere in the vicinage of the printing press, and Donald, leisurely clearing the table, has paused to see if Miss Wellington can really swallow that one more drink of gin that she is about to tackle. She does, and another besides.

Penny finally decides to make a try.

PENNY: I'm ready to read the play now, Miss Wellington, if you are.

GAY WELLINGTON: Just a minute, dearie—just a minute. (*The gin again.*)

PENNY: The only thing is—I hope you won't mind my mentioning this, but—you don't drink when you're acting, do you, Miss Wellington? I'm just asking, of course.

GAY: I'm glad you brought it up. Once a play opens, I never touch a drop. Minute I enter a stage door, this bottle gets put away till intermission.

GRANDPA: (*Who plainly has his doubts.*) Have you been on the stage a long time, Miss Wellington?

GAY: All my life. I've played everything. Ever see "Peg o' My Heart"?

GRANDPA: Yes, indeed.

GAY: (*With that fine logic for which the inebriated brain is celebrated.*) I saw it too. Great show. (*She staggers backwards a bit, but recovers herself just in time.*) My! Hot night, ain't it?

DONALD: (*Ever helpful.*) Want me to open a window, Miss Wellington?

718

GAY: No, the hell with the weather. (*She takes a second look at the dusky Donald.*) Say, he's cute.

> (*Rheba, who has entered just in time to overhear this, gives Gay a look that tells her in no uncertain terms to keep out of Harlem on dark nights. Then she stalks back into the kitchen, Donald close on her heels.*)

DONALD: (*Trying to explain it all.*) She's just acting, Rheba. She don't mean anything.

PENNY: Well, any time you're ready, we can go up to my room and start. I thought I'd read the play up in my room.

GAY: All right, dearie, just a minute. (*She starts to pour one more drink, then suddenly her gaze becomes transfixed. She shakes her head as though to dislodge the image, then looks again, receives verification, and starts to pour the gin back into the bottle.*) When I see snakes it's time to lay down. (*She makes for a couch in the corner, and passes right out— cold.*)

PENNY: Oh, but those are real, Miss Wellington. They're Grandpa's. . . . Oh, dear! I hope she's not going to— (*Shaking her.*) Miss Wellington! Miss Wellington!

ED: She's out like a light.

PAUL: Better let her sleep it off.

DONALD: (*Carrying the news into the kitchen.*) Rheba, Miss Wellington just passed out.

> (*From the nether recesses we hear Rheba's reaction—an emphatic "Good!"*)

PENNY: Do you think she'll be all right?

GRANDPA: Yes, but I wouldn't cast her in the religious play.

PENNY: Well, I suppose I'll just have to wait. I wonder if I shouldn't cover her up.

GRANDPA: Next time you meet an actress on the top of a bus, Penny, I think I'd *send* her the play, instead of bringing her home to read it.

ESSIE: (*As Ed starts in with the printing press.*) Ed, I wish you'd stop printing and take those Love Dreams around. They're out in the kitchen.

ED: I will. I just want to finish up these circulars.

ESSIE: Well, do that later, can't you? You've got to get back in time to play for me when Kolenkhov comes.

GRANDPA: Kolenkhov coming tonight?

ESSIE: Yes, tomorrow night's his night, but I had to change it on account of Alice.

GRANDPA: Oh! . . . Big doings around here tomorrow night, huh?

PENNY: Isn't it exciting? You know, I'm so nervous—you'd think it was me he was engaged to, instead of Alice.

ESSIE: What do you think they'll *be* like—his mother and father? . . . Ed, what are you doing *now*?

ED: Penny, did you see the new mask I made last night? (*He reveals a new side of his character by suddenly holding a home-made mask before his face.*) Guess who it is.

PENNY: Don't tell me now, Ed. Wait a minute . . . Cleopatra.

ED: (*Furious.*) It's Mrs. Roosevelt. (*He goes into the kitchen.*)
  (*Paul, meanwhile, has gone to a table in the corner of the room, from which he now brings a steel-like boat model, two or three feet high, puts it down on the floor, and proceeds to sit down beside it. From a large cardboard box, which he has also brought with him, he proceeds to take out additional pieces of steel and fit them into the model.*)

PAUL: You know, the nice thing about these Erector Sets, you can make so many different things with them. Last week it was the Empire State Building.

GRANDPA: What is it this week?

PAUL: The Queen Mary.

PENNY: (*Looking it over.*) Hasn't got the right hat on.
  (*Ed comes in from the kitchen, bringing a pile of about a dozen candy boxes, neatly wrapped, and tied together for purposes of delivery.*)

ED: (*As Mr. De Pinna comes in from the hall.*) Look. Mr. De Pinna, would you open the door and see if there's a man standing in front of the house?

ESSIE: Why, what for?

ED: Well, the last two days, when I've been out delivering, I think a man's been following me.

ESSIE: Ed, you're crazy.

ED: No, I'm not. He follows me, and he stands and watches the house.

DE PINNA: Really? (*Striding out.*) I'll take a look and see.

GRANDPA: I don't see what anybody would follow *you* for, Ed.

PENNY: Well, there's a lot of kidnapping going on, Grandpa.

GRANDPA: Yes, but not of Ed.

ED: (*As Mr. De Pinna returns from the hall.*) Well? Did you see him?

DE PINNA: There's nobody out there at all.

ED: You're sure?

DE PINNA: Positive. I just saw him walk away.

ED: You see? I told you.

ESSIE: Oh, it might have been anybody, walking along the street. Ed, will you hurry and get back?

ED: (*Picking up his boxes.*) Oh, all right.

DE PINNA: Want to go down now, Mr. Sycamore, and finish packing up the fireworks?

PAUL: (*Putting the Queen Mary back on the table.*) Yeh, we've got to take the stuff up to Mt. Vernon in the morning.

(*They go into the cellar. Simultaneously the voice of Alice, happily singing, is heard as she descends the stairs.*)

ALICE: Mother, may I borrow some paper? I'm making out a list for Rheba tomorrow night.

PENNY: Yes, dear. Here's some.

ALICE: (*As she sights Miss Wellington.*) Why, what happened to your actress friend? Is she giving a performance?

PENNY: No, she's not acting, Alice. She's really drunk.

ALICE: Essie, you're going to give Rheba the kitchen all day tomorrow, aren't you? Because she'll need it.

ESSIE: Of course, Alice. I'm going to start some Love Dreams now, so I'll be 'way ahead. (*She goes into the kitchen.*)

ALICE: Thanks, dear . . . Look, mother, I'm coming home at three o'clock tomorrow. Will you have everything down in the cellar by that time? The typewriter, and the snakes, and the xylophone, and the printing press . . .

GRANDPA: And Miss Wellington.

ALICE: And Miss Wellington. That'll give me time to arrange the table, and fix the flowers.

GRANDPA: The Kirbys are certainly going to get the wrong impression of this house.

ALICE: You'll *do* all that, won't you, mother?

PENNY: Of course, dear.

ALICE: And I think we'd better have cocktails ready by seven-fifteen, in case they happen to come a little early. . . . I wonder if I ought to let Rheba cook the dinner. What do you think, Grandpa?

GRANDPA: Now, Alice, I wouldn't worry. From what I've seen of the boy I'm sure the Kirbys are very nice people, and if everything isn't so elaborate tomorrow night, it's all right too.

ALICE: Darling, I'm not trying to impress them, or pretend we're anything that we aren't. I just want everything to—to go off well.

GRANDPA: No reason why it shouldn't, Alice.

PENNY: We're all going to do everything we can to make it a nice party.

ALICE: Oh, my darlings, I love you. You're the most wonderful family in the world, and I'm the happiest girl in the world. I didn't know anyone could *be* so happy. He's so wonderful, Grandpa. Why, just seeing him—you don't know what it does to me.

GRANDPA: Just seeing him. Just seeing him for lunch, and dinner, and until four o'clock in the morning, and at nine o'clock *next* morning you're at the office again and there he is. You just see him, huh?

ALICE: I don't care! I'm in love! (*She swings open the kitchen door.*) Rheba! Rheba! (*She goes into the kitchen.*)

GRANDPA: Nice, isn't it? Nice to see her so happy.

PENNY: I remember when I was engaged to Paul—how happy I was. And you know, I still feel that way.

GRANDPA: I know . . . Nice the way Ed and Essie get along too, isn't it?

PENNY: And Donald and Rheba, even though they're *not* married. . . . Do you suppose Mr. De Pinna will ever marry anyone, Grandpa?

GRANDPA: (*A gesture toward the couch.*) Well, there's Miss Wellington.

PENNY: Oh, dear, I *wish* she'd wake up. If we're going to read the play tonight—

(*Mr. De Pinna comes up from the cellar, bringing along a rather large-sized unframed painting.*)

DE PINNA: Mrs. Sycamore, look what I found! (*He turns the canvas around, revealing a portrait of a somewhat lumpy discus thrower, in Roman costume—or was it Greek?*) Remember?

PENNY: Why, of course. It's my painting of you as The Discus Thrower. Look, Grandpa.

GRANDPA: I remember it. Say, you've gotten a little bald, haven't you, Mr. De Pinna?

DE PINNA: (*Running a hand over his completely hairless head.*) Is it very noticeable?

PENNY: Well, it was a long time ago—just before I stopped painting. Let me see—that's eight years.

DE PINNA: Too bad you never finished it, Mrs. Sycamore.

PENNY: I always meant to finish it, Mr. De Pinna, but I just started to write a play one day and that was that. I never painted again.

GRANDPA: Just as well, too. *I* was going to have to strip next.

DE PINNA: (*Meditatively.*) Who would have thought, that day I came to deliver the ice, that I was going to stay here for eight years?

GRANDPA: The milkman was here for five, just ahead of you.

DE PINNA: Why did he leave, anyhow? I forget.

GRANDPA: He didn't leave. He died.

PENNY: He was such a nice man. Remember the funeral, Grandpa? We never knew his name and it was kind of hard to get a certificate.

GRANDPA: What was the name we finally made up for him?

PENNY: Martin Vanderhof. We gave him *your* name.

GRANDPA: Oh, yes, I remember.

PENNY: It was a lovely thought, because otherwise he never would have got all those flowers.

GRANDPA: Certainly was. And it didn't hurt *me* any. Not bothered with mail any more, and I haven't had a telephone call from that day to this. (*He catches an unwary fly and drops it casually into the snake solarium.*)

PENNY: Yes, it was really a wonderful idea.

DE PINNA: (*With the picture.*) I wish you'd finish this sometime, Mrs. Sycamore. I'd kind of like to have it.

PENNY: You know what, Mr. De Pinna? I think I'll do some work on it. Right tonight.

DE PINNA: Say! Will you?

    (*The door bell rings.*)

PENNY: (*Peering at the prostate Gay.*) I don't think she's going to wake up anyhow. . . . Look, Mr. De Pinna! You go down in the cellar and bring up the easel and get into your costume. Is it still down there?

DE PINNA: (*Excited.*) I think so! (*He darts into the cellar.*)

PENNY: Now, where did I put my palette and brushes? (*She dashes up the stairs as the voice of Kolenkhov is heard at the door, booming, of course.*)

KOLENKHOV: Rhebishka! My little Rhebishka!

RHEBA: (*Delighted, as usual.*) Yassuh, Mr. Kolenkhov!

PENNY: (*As she goes up the stairs*) Hello, Mr. Kolenkhov. Essie's in the kitchen.

KOLENKHOV: Madame Sycamore, I greet you! (*His great arm again encircling Rheba, he drags her protestingly into the room.*) Tell me, Grandpa—what should I do about Rhebishka! I keep telling her she would make a great toe dancer, but she laughs only!

RHEBA: (*Breaking away.*) No, suh! I couldn't get up on my toes, Mr. Kolenkhov! I got corns! (*She goes into the kitchen.*)

KOLENKHOV: (*Calling after her.*) Rhebishka, you could wear diamonds! (*Suddenly he sights the portrait of Mr. De Pinna.*) What is that?

GRANDPA: (*Who has taken up his stamp album again.*) It's a picture of Mr. De Pinna. Penny painted it.

KOLENKHOV: (*Summing it up.*) It stinks.

GRANDPA: I know. (*He indicates the figure on the couch.*) How do you like that?

KOLENKHOV: (*Peering over.*) What is *that*?

GRANDPA: She's an actress. Friend of Penny's.

KOLENKHOV: She is drunk—no?

GRANDPA: She is drunk—yes. . . . How are *you*, Kolenkhov?

KOLENKHOV: Magnificent! Life is chasing around inside of me, like a squirrel.

GRANDPA: 'Tis, huh? . . . What's new in Russia? Any more letters from your friend in Moscow?

KOLENKHOV: I have just heard from him. I saved for you the stamp. (*He hands it over.*)

GRANDPA: (*Receiving it with delight.*) Thanks, Kolenkhov.

KOLENKHOV: They have sent him to Siberia.

GRANDPA: That so? How's he like it?

KOLENKHOV: He has escaped. He has escaped and gone back to Moscow. He will get them yet, if they do not get him.

The Soviet Government! I could take the whole Soviet government and—grrah!

(*He crushes Stalin and all in one great paw, just as Essie
comes in from the kitchen.*)

ESSIE: I'm sorry I'm late, Mr. Kolenkhov. I'll get into my
dancing clothes right away.

KOLENKHOV: Tonight you will really work, Pavlowa.

(*As Essie goes up the stairs.*)

Tonight we will take something new.

GRANDPA: Essie making any progress, Kolenkhov?

KOLENKHOV: (*First making elaborately sure that Essie is gone.*)
Confidentially, she stinks.

GRANDPA: Well, as long as she's having fun. . . .

(*Donald ambles in from the kitchen, chuckling.*)

DONALD: You sure do tickle Rheba, Mr. Kolenkhov. She's
laughing her head off out there.

KOLENKHOV: She is a great woman. . . . Donald, what do
you think of the Soviet Government?

DONALD: The what, Mr. Kolenkhov?

KOLENKHOV: I withdraw the question. What do you think of
this Government?

DONALD: Oh, I like it fine. I'm on relief, you know.

KOLENKHOV: Oh, yes. And you like it?

DONALD: Yassuh, it's fine. Only thing is you got to go round
to the place every week and collect it, and sometimes
you got to stand in line pretty near half an hour. Government ought to be run better than that—don't you think,
Grandpa?

GRANDPA: (*As he fishes an envelope out of his pocket.*) Government ought to stop sending me letters. Want me to be at
the United States Marshal's office Tuesday morning at ten
o'clock.

KOLENKHOV: (*Peering at the letter.*) Ah! Income tax! They
have got you, Grandpa.

GRANDPA: Mm. I'm supposed to give 'em a lot of money so as
to keep Donald on relief.

DONALD: You don't say, Grandpa? You going to pay it now?

GRANDPA: That's what they want.

DONALD: You mean I can come right *here* and get it instead of
standing in that line?

GRANDPA: No, Donald. You will have to waste a full half hour of your time every week.

DONALD: Well, I don't like it. It breaks up my week. (*He goes into the kitchen.*)

KOLENKHOV: He should have been in Russia when the Revolution came. Then he would have stood in line—a bread line. (*He turns to Grandpa.*) Ah, Grandpa, what they have done to Russia. Think of it! The Grand Duchess Olga Katrina, a cousin of the Czar, she is a waitress in Childs' restaurant! I ordered baked beans from her only yesterday. It broke my heart. A crazy world, Grandpa.

GRANDPA: Oh, the world's not so crazy, Kolenkhov. It's the people *in* it. Life's pretty simple if you just relax.

KOLENKHOV: How can you relax in times like these?

GRANDPA: Well, if they'd relaxed there wouldn't *be* times like these. That's just my point. Life is simple and kind of beautiful if you let it come to you. But the trouble is, people forget that. I know I did. I was right in the thick of it—fighting, and scratching, and clawing. Regular jungle. One day it just kind of struck me. I wasn't having any fun.

KOLENKHOV: So you did what?

GRANDPA: Just relaxed. Thirty-five years ago, that was. And I've been a happy man ever since. (*From somewhere or other Grandpa has brought one of those colored targets that one buys at Schwartz's. He now hangs it up on the cellar door, picks up a handful of feathered darts, and carefully throws one at the target.*)

(*At the same time Alice passes through the room, en route from kitchen to the upstairs region.*)

ALICE: Good evening, Mr. Kolenkhov.

KOLENKHOV: (*Bowing low over her hand.*) Ah, Miss Alice! I have not seen you to present my congratulations. May you be very happy and have many children. That is my prayer for you.

ALICE: Thank you, Mr. Kolenkhov. That's quite a thought. (*Singing gayly, she goes up the stairs.*)

KOLENKHOV: (*Looking after her.*) Ah, love! That is all that is left in the world, Grandpa.

GRANDPA: Yes, but there's plenty of that.

KOLENKHOV: And soon Stalin will take that away, too. I tell you, Grandpa—

    (*He stops as Penny comes down the stairs—a living example of what the well-dressed artist should wear. She has on an artist's smock over her dress, a flowing black tie, and a large black velvet tam-o'-shanter, worn at a rakish angle. She carries a palette and an assortment of paints and brushes.*)

PENNY: Seems so nice to get into my art things again. They still look all right, don't they, Grandpa?

GRANDPA: Yes, indeed.

KOLENKHOV: You are a breath of Paris, Madame Sycamore.

PENNY: Oh, thank you, Mr. Kolenkhov.

DONALD: (*Coming in from the kitchen.*) I didn't know you was working for the WPA.

PENNY: Oh, no, Donald. You see, I used to paint all the time, and then one day—

    (*The outer door slams and Ed comes in.*)

ED: (*In considerable excitement.*) It happened again! There was a fellow following me every place I went!

PENNY: Nonsense, Ed. It's your imagination.

ED: No, it isn't. It happens every time I go out to deliver candy.

GRANDPA: Maybe he wants a piece of candy.

ED: It's all right for you to laugh, Grandpa, but he keeps following me.

KOLENKHOV: (*Somberly.*) You do not know what following is. In Russia *everybody* is followed. I was followed right out of Russia.

PENNY: Of course. You see, Ed—the whole thing is just imagination.

    (*Mr. De Pinna comes up from the cellar, ready for posing. He wears the traditional Roman costume, and he certainly cuts a figure. He is carrying Penny's easel, a discus, and a small platform for posing purposes.*)

Ah, here we are! . . . Right here, Mr. De Pinna.

DONALD: (*Suddenly getting it.*) Oh, is that picture supposed to be Mr. De Pinna?

PENNY: (*Sharply.*) Of course it is, Donald. What's it look like—me?

DONALD: (*Studying the portrait.*) Yes, it does—a little bit.

PENNY: Nonsense! What would I be doing with a discus?

KOLENKHOV: Ed, for tonight's lesson we use the first movement of Scheherazade.

ED: Okay.

DE PINNA: (*About to mount the platform.*) I hope I haven't forgotten how to pose. (*He takes up the discus and strikes the classic pose of the Discus Thrower. Somehow, it is not quite convincing.*)

DONALD: What's he going to do with that thing? Throw it?

PENNY: No, no, Donald. He's just posing. . . . Mr. De Pinna, has something happened to your figure during these eight years?

DE PINNA: (*Pulling in his stomach.*) No, I don't think it's any different.

(*With a sudden snort, Gay Wellington comes to.*)

PENNY: (*Immediately alert.*) Yes, Miss Wellington?

(*For answer, Gay peers first at Penny, then at Mr. De Pinna. Then, with a strange snort, she just passes right out again.*)

PENNY: Oh, dear.

(*Essie comes tripping down the stairs—very much the ballet dancer. She is in full costume—ballet skirt, tight white satin bodice, and garland of roses in her hair.*)

ESSIE: Sorry, Mr. Kolenkhov, I couldn't find my slippers.

KOLENKHOV: (*Having previously removed his coat, he now takes off his shirt, displaying an enormous hairy chest beneath his undershirt.*) We have a hot night for it, my Pavlowa, but art is only achieved through perspiration.

PENNY: Why, that's wonderful, Mr. Kolenkhov. Did you hear that, Grandpa—art is only achieved through perspiration.

GRANDPA: Yes, but it helps if you've got a little talent with it. (*He returns to his dart throwing.*) Only made two bull's-eyes last night. Got to do better than that. (*He hurls a dart at the board, then his eye travels to Miss Wellington, whose posterior offers an even easier target.*) Mind if I use Miss Wellington, Penny?

PENNY: What, Grandpa?

GRANDPA: (*Shakes his head.*) Never mind. . . . Too easy. (*Grandpa throws another dart at the target.*)

KOLENKHOV: You are ready? We begin!

(*With a gesture he orders the music started; under Kolenkhov's critical eye Essie begins the mazes of the dance.*)
Foutte temp el levee.

(*Essie obliges with her own idea of foutte temp el levee.*)
Pirouette! . . . Come, come! You can do that! It's eight years now. Pirouette! . . . At last! . . . Entre chat! . . . Entre chat!

(*Essie leaps into the air, her feet twirling.*)
No, Grandpa, you cannot relax with Stalin in Russia. The Czar relaxed, and what happened to *him*?

GRANDPA: He was too late.

ESSIE: (*Still leaping away.*) Mr. Kolenkhov! Mr. Kolenkhov!

KOLENKHOV: If he had not relaxed the Grand Duchess Olga Katrina would not be selling baked beans today.

ESSIE: (*Imploringly.*) Mr. Kolenkhov!

KOLENKHOV: I am sorry.

(*The door bell rings.*)
We go back to the pirouette.

PENNY: Could you pull in your stomach, Mr. De Pinna? . . . that's right.

KOLENKHOV: A little freer. A little freer with the hands. The whole body must work. Ed, help us with the music. The music must be free, too.

(*By way of guiding Ed, Kolenkhov hums the music at the pace that it should go. He is even pirouetting a bit himself.*)
(*From the front door comes the murmur of voices, not quite audible over the music. Then the stunned figure of Rheba comes into the archway, her eyes popping.*)

RHEBA: Mrs. Sycamore. . . . Mrs. Sycamore. (*With a gesture that has a grim foreboding in it, she motions toward the still invisible reason for her panic.*)

(*There is a second's pause, and then the reason is revealed in all its horror. The Kirbys, in full evening dress, stand in the archway. All three of them. Mr. and Mrs. Kirby, and Tony.*)
(*Penny utters a stifled gasp; the others are too stunned even to do that. Their surprise at seeing the Kirbys, however, is no greater than that of the Kirbys at the sight that is spread before them.*)
(*Grandpa, alone of them all, rises to the situation. With a*

*kind of old world grace, he puts away his darts and makes
the guests welcome.*)

GRANDPA: How do you do?

KIRBY: (*Uncertainly.*) How do you do?

(*Not that it helps any, but Mr. De Pinna is squirming into
his bathrobe, Kolenkhov is thrusting his shirt into his
trousers, and Ed is hastily getting into his coat.*

TONY: Are we too early?

GRANDPA: No, no. It's perfectly all right—we're glad to see you.

PENNY: (*Getting rid of the smock and tam.*) Why—yes. Only—
we thought it was to be tomorrow night.

MRS. KIRBY: Tomorrow night!

KIRBY: What!

GRANDPA: Now, it's perfectly all right. Please sit right down
and make yourselves at home.

(*His eyes still on the Kirbys, he gives Donald a good push
toward the kitchen, by way of a hint. Donald goes, promptly,
with a quick little stunned whistle that sums up HIS
feelings.*)

KIRBY: Tony, how could you possibly—

TONY: I—I don't know. I thought—

MRS. KIRBY: Really, Tony! This is most embarrassing.

GRANDPA: Not at all. Why, we weren't doing a thing.

PENNY: Just spending the evening at home.

GRANDPA: That's all. . . . Now don't let it bother you. This is
Alice's mother, Mrs. Sycamore . . . Alice's sister, Mrs.
Carmichael. . . . *Mr.* Carmichael. . . . Mr. Kolenkhov. . . .

(*At this point Mr. De Pinna takes an anticipatory step forward, and Grandpa is practically compelled to perform the
introduction.*)

And—Mr. De Pinna. Mr. De Pinna, would you tell Mr.
Sycamore to come right up? Tell him that Mr. and Mrs.
Kirby are here.

PENNY: (*Her voice a heavy whisper.*) And be sure to put his
pants on.

DE PINNA: (*Whispering right back.*) All right. . . . Excuse me.
(*He vanishes—discus and all.*)

GRANDPA: Won't you sit down?

PENNY: (*First frantically trying to cover the prostrate Gay
Wellington.*) I'll tell Alice that you're—

(*She is at the foot of the stairs.*)

—Alice! Alice, dear!

(*The voice of Alice from above, "What is it?"*)

Alice, will you come down, dear? We've got a surprise for you. (*She comes back into the room, summoning all her charm.*) Well!

GRANDPA: Mrs. Kirby, may I take your wrap?

MRS. KIRBY: Well—thank you. If you're perfectly sure that we're not— (*Suddenly she sees the snakes and lets out a scream.*)

GRANDPA: Oh, don't be alarmed, Mrs. Kirby. They're perfectly harmless.

MRS. KIRBY: (*Edging away from the solarium.*) Thank you. (*She sinks into a chair, weakly.*)

GRANDPA: Ed, take 'em into the kitchen.

(*Ed at once obeys.*)

PENNY: Of course we're so used to them around the house—

MRS. KIRBY: I'm sorry to trouble you, but snakes happen to be the one thing—

KIRBY: I feel very uncomfortable about this. Tony, how could you have done such a thing?

TONY: I'm sorry, Dad. I thought it was tonight.

KIRBY: It was very careless of you. *Very!*

GRANDPA: Now, now, Mr. Kirby—we're delighted.

PENNY: Oh, now, anybody can get mixed up, Mr. Kirby.

GRANDPA: Penny, how about some dinner for these folks? They've come for dinner, you know.

MRS. KIRBY: Oh, please don't bother. We're really not hungry at all.

PENNY: But it's not a bit of bother. Ed!— (*Her voice drops to a loud whisper.*) Ed, tell Donald to run down to the A. and P. and get half a dozen bottles of beer, and—ah—some canned salmon— (*Her voice comes up again.*) —do you like canned salmon, Mr. Kirby?

KIRBY: Please don't trouble, Mrs. Sycamore. I have a little indigestion, anyway.

PENNY: Oh, I'm sorry . . . How about you, Mrs. Kirby? Do you like canned salmon?

MRS. KIRBY: (*You just know that she hates it.*) Oh, I'm very fond of it.

PENNY: You can have frankfurters if you'd rather.

MRS. KIRBY: (*Regally.*) Either one will do.

PENNY: (*To Ed again.*) Well, make it frankfurters, and some canned corn, and Campbell's Soup.

ED: (*Going out the kitchen door.*) Okay!

PENNY: (*Calling after him.*) And tell him to hurry! (*Penny again addresses the Kirbys.*) The A. and P. is just at the corner, and frankfurters don't take *any* time to boil.

GRANDPA: (*As Paul comes through the cellar door.*) And this is Alice's father, *Mr.* Sycamore. Mr. and Mrs. Kirby.

THE KIRBYS: How do you do?

PAUL: I hope you'll forgive my appearance.

PENNY: This is Mr. Sycamore's busiest time of the year. Just before the Fourth of July—

(*And then Alice comes down. She is a step into the room before she realizes what has happened; then she fairly freezes in her tracks.*)

ALICE: Oh!

TONY: Darling, will you ever forgive me? I'm the most dull-witted person in the world. I thought it was tonight.

ALICE: (*Staggered.*) Why, Tony, I thought you—(*To the Kirbys.*) —I'm so sorry—I can't imagine—why, I wasn't—have you all met each other?

KIRBY: Yes, indeed.

MRS. KIRBY: How do you do, Alice?

ALICE: (*Not even yet in control of herself.*) How do you do, Mrs. Kirby? I'm afraid I'm not very—presentable.

TONY: Darling, you look lovely.

KIRBY: Of course she does. Don't let this upset you, my dear—we've all just met each other a night sooner, that's all.

MRS. KIRBY: Of course.

ALICE: But I was planning such a nice party tomorrow night. . . .

KIRBY: (*Being the good fellow.*) Well, we'll come again tomorrow night.

TONY: There you are, Alice. Am I forgiven?

ALICE: I guess so. It's just that I—we'd better see about getting you some dinner.

PENNY: Oh, that's all done, Alice. That's all been attended to.

(*Donald, hat in hand, comes through the kitchen door; hurries across the room and out the front way. The Kirbys graciously pretend not to see.*)

ALICE: But mother—what are you—what did you send out for? Because Mr. Kirby suffers from indigestion—he can only eat certain things.

KIRBY: Now, it's quite all right.

TONY: Of course it is, darling.

PENNY: I asked him what he wanted, Alice.

ALICE: (*Doubtfully.*) Yes, but—

KIRBY: Now, now, it's not as serious as all that. Just because I have a little indigestion.

KOLENKHOV: (*Helping things along.*) Perhaps it is not indigestion at all, Mr. Kirby. Perhaps you have stomach ulcers.

ALICE: Don't be absurd, Mr. Kolenkhov!

GRANDPA: You mustn't mind Mr. Kolenkhov, Mr. Kirby. He's a Russian, and Russians are inclined to look on the dark side.

KOLENKHOV: All right, I am a Russian. But a friend of mine, a Russian, *died* from stomach ulcers.

KIRBY: Really, I—

ALICE: (*Desperately.*) Please, Mr. Kolenkhov! Mr. Kirby has indigestion and that's all.

KOLENKHOV: (*With a Russian shrug of the shoulders.*) All right. Let him wait.

GRANDPA: (*Leaping into the breach.*) Tell me, Mr. Kirby, how do you find business conditions? Are we pretty well out of the depression?

KIRBY: What? . . . Yes, yes, I think so. Of course, it all depends.

GRANDPA: But you figure that things are going to keep on improving?

KIRBY: Broadly speaking, yes. As a matter of fact, industry is now operating at sixty-four per cent. of full capacity, as against eighty-two per cent. in 1925. Of course in 1929, a peak year—

(*Peak year or no peak year, Gay Wellington chooses this moment to come to life. With a series of assorted snorts, she throws the cover back and pulls herself to a sitting position, blinking uncertainly at the assemblage. Then she rises, and weaves unsteadily across the room. The imposing figure of Mr. Kirby intrigues her.)*

GAY: (*Playfully rumpling Mr. Kirby's hair as she passes him.*) Hello, Cutie. (*And with that she lunges on her way—up the stairs.*)

(*The Kirbys, of course, are considerably astounded by this exhibition; the Sycamores have watched it with varying degrees of frozen horror. Alice, in particular, is speechless; it is Grandpa who comes to her rescue.*)

GRANDPA: That may seem a little strange to you, but she's not quite accountable for her actions. A friend of Mrs. Sycamore's. She came to dinner and was overcome by the heat.

PENNY: Yes, some people feel it, you know, more than others. Perhaps I'd better see if she's all right. Excuse me, please. (*She goes hastily up the stairs.*)

ALICE: It *is* awfully hot. (*A fractional pause.*) You usually escape all this hot weather, don't you, Mrs. Kirby? Up in Maine?

MRS. KIRBY: (*On the frigid side.*) As a rule. I had to come down this week, however, for the Flower Show.

TONY: Mother wouldn't miss that for the world. That blue ribbon is the high spot of her year.

ESSIE: I won a ribbon at a Flower Show once. For raising onions. Remember?

ALICE: (*Quickly.*) That was a Garden Show, Essie.

ESSIE: Oh, yes.

(*Penny comes bustling down the stairs again.*)

PENNY: I'm so sorry, but I think she'll be all right now. . . . Has Donald come back yet?

ALICE: No, he hasn't.

PENNY: Well, he'll be right back, and it won't take any time at all. I'm afraid you must be starved.

KIRBY: Oh, no. Quite all right. (*Pacing the room, he suddenly comes upon Paul's Erector Set.*) Hello! What's this? I didn't know there were little children in the house.

PAUL: Oh, no. That's mine.

KIRBY: Really? Well, I suppose every man has his hobby. Or do you use this as a model of some kind?

PAUL: No, I just play with it.

KIRBY: I see.

TONY: Maybe you'd be better off if *you* had a hobby like that, Dad. Instead of raising orchids.

KIRBY: (*Indulgently.*) Yes, I wouldn't be surprised.

ALICE: (*Leaping on this as a safe topic.*) Oh, *do* tell us about your orchids, Mr. Kirby. (*She addresses the others.*) You know, they take six years before they blossom. Think of that!

KIRBY: (*Warming to his subject.*) Oh, some of them take longer than that. I've got one coming along now that I've waited ten years for.

PENNY: (*Making a joke.*) Believe it or not, I was waiting for an orchid.

KIRBY: Ah—yes. Of course during that time they require the most scrupulous care. I remember a bulb that I was very fond of—

(*Donald suddenly bulges through the archway, his arms full. The tops of beer bottles and two or three large cucumbers peep over the edge of the huge paper bags.*)

PENNY: Ah, here we are! Did you get everything, Donald?

DONALD: Yes'm. Only the frankfurters didn't look very good, so I got pickled pigs' feet.

(*Mr. Kirby blanches at the very idea.*)

ALICE: (*Taking command.*) Never mind, Donald—just bring everything into the kitchen. (*She turns at the kitchen door.*) Mr. Kirby, please tell them *all* about the orchids—I know they'd love to hear it. And—excuse me. (*She goes.*)

GRANDPA: Kind of an expensive hobby, isn't it, Mr. Kirby—raising orchids?

KIRBY: Yes, it is, but I feel that if a hobby gives one sufficient pleasure, it's never expensive.

GRANDPA: That's very true.

KIRBY: You see, I need something to relieve the daily nerve strain. After a week in Wall Street I'd go crazy if I didn't have something like that. Lot of men I know have yachts—just for that very reason.

GRANDPA: (*Mildly.*) Why don't they give up Wall Street?

KIRBY: How's that?

GRANDPA: I was just joking.

MRS. KIRBY: I think it's necessary for everyone to have a hobby. Of course it's more to me than a hobby, but my great solace is—spiritualism.

PENNY: Now, Mrs. Kirby, don't tell me you fell for that. Why, everybody knows it's a fake.

MRS. KIRBY: (*Freezing.*) To me, Mrs. Sycamore, spiritualism is —I would rather not discuss it, Mrs. Sycamore.

PAUL: Remember, Penny, you've got one or two hobbies of your own.

PENNY: Yes, but not silly ones.

GRANDPA: (*With a little cough.*) I don't think it matters what the hobby is—the important thing is to have one.

KOLENKHOV: To be ideal, a hobby should improve the body as well as the mind. The Romans were a great people! Why! What was their hobby? Wrestling. In wrestling you have to think quick with the mind and act quick with the body.

KIRBY: Yes, but I'm afraid wrestling is not very practical for most of us. (*He gives a deprecating little laugh.*) I wouldn't make a very good showing as a wrestler.

KOLENKHOV: You could be a *great* wrestler. You are built for it. Look!

(*With a startling quick movement Kolenkhov grabs Mr. Kirby's arms, knocks his legs from under him with a quick movement of a foot, and presto! Mr. Kirby is flat on his whatsis. Not only that, but instantaneously Kolenkhov is on top of him.*)

(*Just at this moment Alice re-enters the room—naturally, she stands petrified. Several people, of course, rush immediately to the rescue, Tony and Paul arriving at the scene of battle first. Amidst the general confusion they help Mr. Kirby to his feet.*)

ALICE: Mr. Kirby! Are you—hurt?

TONY: Are you all right, father?

KIRBY: (*Pulling himself together.*) I—I—uh— (*He blinks, uncertainly.*) —where are my glasses?

ALICE: Here they are, Mr. Kirby. . . . Oh, Mr. Kirby, they're broken.

KOLENKHOV: (*Full of apology.*) Oh, I am sorry. But when you wrestle again, Mr. Kirby, you will of course not wear glasses.

KIRBY: (*Coldly furious.*) I do not intend to wrestle again, Mr. Kolenkhov. (*He draws himself up, stiffly, and in return gets a sharp pain in the back. He gives a little gasp.*)

TONY: Better sit down, father.

ALICE: Mr. Kolenkhov, how could you do such a thing? Why didn't somebody stop him?

MRS. KIRBY: I think, if you don't mind, perhaps we had better be going.

TONY: Mother!

ALICE: (*Close to tears.*) Oh, Mrs. Kirby—please! Please don't go! Mr. Kirby—please! I—I've ordered some scrambled eggs for you, and—plain salad— Oh, please don't go!

KOLENKHOV: I am sorry if I did something wrong. And I apologize.

ALICE: I can't tell you how sorry I am, Mr. Kirby. If I'd been here—

KIRBY: (*From a great height.*) That's quite all right.

TONY: Of course it is. It's all right, Alice. We're not going.

(*The Kirbys reluctantly sit down again.*)

(*A moment's silence—no one knows quite what to say.*)

PENNY: (*Brightly.*) Well! That was exciting for a minute, wasn't it?

GRANDPA: (*Quickly.*) You were talking about your orchids, Mr. Kirby. Do you raise many different varieties?

KIRBY: (*Still unbending.*) I'm afraid I've quite forgotten about my orchids.

(*More silence, and everyone very uncomfortable.*)

ALICE: I'm—awfully sorry, Mr. Kirby.

KOLENKHOV: (*Exploding.*) What did I do that was so terrible? I threw him on the floor! Did it kill him?

ALICE: Please, Mr. Kolenkhov.

(*An annoyed gesture from Kolenkhov; another general pause.*)

PENNY: I'm sure dinner won't be any time at all now.

(*A pained smile from Mrs. Kirby.*)

ESSIE: Would you like some candy while you're waiting? I've got some freshly made.

KIRBY: My doctor does not permit me to eat candy. Thank you.

ESSIE: But these are nothing, Mr. Kirby. Just cocoanut and marshmallow fudge.

ALICE: Don't, Essie.

(*Rheba appears in the kitchen doorway, beckoning violently to Alice.*)

RHEBA: (*In a loud whisper.*) Miss Alice! Miss Alice!
> (*Alice quickly flies to Rheba's side.*)
The eggs fell down the sink.

ALICE: (*Desperately.*) Make some more! Quick!

RHEBA: I ain't got any.

ALICE: Send Donald out for some!

RHEBA: (*Disappearing.*) All right.

ALICE: (*Calling after her.*) Tell him to run! (*She turns back to the Kirbys.*) I'm so sorry. There'll be a little delay, but every-thing will be ready in just a minute.
> (*At this moment Donald fairly shoots out of the kitchen door and across the living room, beating the Olympic record for all time.*)
> (*Penny tries to ease the situation with a gay little laugh. It doesn't quite come off, however.*)

TONY: I've certainly put you people to a lot of trouble, with my stupidity.

GRANDPA: Not at all, Tony.

PENNY: Look! Why don't we all play a game of some sort while we're waiting?

TONY: Oh, that'd be fine.

ALICE: Mother, I don't think Mr. and Mrs. Kirby—

KOLENKHOV: *I* have an idea. I know a wonderful trick with a glass of water. (*He reaches for a full glass that stands on the table.*)

ALICE: (*Quickly.*) No, Mr. Kolenkhov.

GRANDPA: (*Shaking his head.*) No-o.

PENNY: But I'm sure Mr. and Mrs. Kirby would love this game. It's perfectly harmless.

ALICE: Please, mother. . . .

KIRBY: I'm not very good at games, Mrs. Sycamore.

PENNY: Oh, but *any* fool could play this game, Mr. Kirby. (*She is bustling around, getting paper and pencil.*) All you do is write your name on a piece of paper—

ALICE: But mother, Mr. Kirby doesn't want—

PENNY: Oh, he'll love it! (*Going right on.*) Here you are, Mr. Kirby. Write your name on this piece of paper. And Mrs. Kirby, you do the same on this one.

ALICE: Mother, what *is* this game?

PENNY: I used to play it at school. It's called Forget-Me-Not.

Now, I'm going to call out five words—just anything at all—and as I say each word, you're to put down the first thing that comes into your mind. Is that clear? For instance, if I say "grass," you might put down "green"—just whatever you think of, see? Or if I call out "chair," you might put down "table." It shows the reactions people have to different things. You see how simple it is, Mr. Kirby?

TONY: Come on, father! Be a sport!

KIRBY: (*Stiffly.*) Very well. I shall be happy to play it.

PENNY: You see, Alice? He *does* want to play.

ALICE: (*Uneasily.*) Well—

PENNY: Now, then! Are we ready?

KOLENKHOV: Ready!

PENNY: Now, remember—you must play fair. Put down the first thing that comes into your mind.

KIRBY: (*Pencil poised.*) I understand.

PENNY: Everybody ready? . . . The first word is "potatoes." (*She repeats it.*) "Potatoes." . . . Ready for the next one? . . . "Bathroom."

(*Alice shifts rather uneasily, but seeing that no one else seems to mind, she relaxes again.*)

Got that?

KOLENKHOV: Go ahead.

PENNY: All ready? . . . "Lust."

ALICE: Mother, this is not exactly what you—

PENNY: Nonsense, Alice—that word's all right.

ALICE: Mother, it's *not* all right.

MRS. KIRBY: (*Unexpectedly.*) Oh, I don't know. It seems to me that's a perfectly fair word.

PENNY: (*To Alice.*) You see? Now, you mustn't interrupt the game.

KIRBY: May I have that last word again, please?

PENNY: "Lust," Mr. Kirby.

KIRBY: (*Writing.*) I've got it.

GRANDPA: This is quite a game.

PENNY: Sssh, Grandpa. . . . All ready? . . . "Honeymoon." (*Essie snickers a little, which is all it takes to start Penny off. Then she suddenly remembers herself.*) Now, Essie! . . . All right. The last word is "sex."

ALICE: (*Under her breath.*) Mother!

PENNY: Everybody got "sex"? . . . All right—now give me all the papers.

GRANDPA: What happens now?

PENNY: Oh, this is the best part. Now I read out your reactions.

KIRBY: I see. It's really quite an interesting game.

PENNY: I knew you'd like it. I'll read your paper first, Mr. Kirby. (*To the others.*) I'm going to read Mr. Kirby's paper first. Listen, everybody! This is Mr. Kirby. . . . "Potatoes—steak." That's very good. See how they go together? Steak and potatoes?

KIRBY: (*Modestly, but obviously pleased with himself.*) I just happened to think of it.

PENNY: It's *very* good. . . . "Bathroom—toothpaste." Uh-huh. "Lust—unlawful." Isn't that nice? "Honeymoon—trip." Yes. And "sex—male." Yes, of course . . . That's really a wonderful paper, Mr. Kirby.

KIRBY: (*Taking a curtain call.*) Thank you . . . It's more than just a game, you know. It's sort of an experiment in psychology, isn't it?

PENNY: Yes, it is—it shows just how your *mind* works. Now we'll see how *Mrs.* Kirby's mind works. . . . Ready? . . . This is *Mrs.* Kirby. . . . "Potatoes—starch." I know just what you mean, Mrs. Kirby. . . . "Bathroom—Mr. Kirby."

KIRBY: What's that?

PENNY: "Bathroom—Mr. Kirby."

KIRBY: (*Turning to his wife.*) I don't quite follow that, my dear.

MRS. KIRBY: I don't know—I just thought of you in connection with it. After all, you *are* in there a good deal, Anthony. Bathing, and shaving—well, you *do* take a long time.

KIRBY: Indeed? I hadn't realized that I was being selfish in the matter. . . . Go on, Mrs. Sycamore.

ALICE: (*Worried.*) I think it's a very silly game and we ought to stop it.

KIRBY: No, no. Please go on, Mrs. Sycamore.

PENNY: Where was I . . . Oh, yes. . . . "Lust—human."

KIRBY: Human? (*Thin-lipped.*) Really!

MRS. KIRBY: I just meant, Anthony, that lust is after all a—human emotion.

KIRBY: I don't agree with you, Miriam. Lust is not a human emotion. It is depraved.

MRS. KIRBY: Very well, Anthony. I'm wrong.

ALICE: Really, it's the most pointless game. Suppose we play Twenty Questions?

KIRBY: No, I find this game rather interesting. Will you go on, Mrs. Sycamore? What was the next word?

PENNY: (*Reluctantly.*) Honeymoon.

KIRBY: Oh, yes. And what was Mrs. Kirby's answer.

PENNY: Ah—"Honeymoon—dull."

KIRBY: (*Murderously calm.*) Did you say—dull?

MRS. KIRBY: What I meant, Anthony, was that Hot Springs was not very gay that season. All those old people sitting on the porch all afternoon, and—nothing to do at night.

KIRBY: That was not your reaction at the time, as I recall it.

TONY: Father, this is only a *game.*

KIRBY: A very illuminating game. Go on, Mrs. Sycamore!

PENNY: (*Brightly, having taken a look ahead.*) This one's all right, Mr. Kirby. "Sex—Wall Street."

KIRBY: Wall Street? What do you mean by that, Miriam?

MRS. KIRBY: (*Nervously.*) I don't know what I meant, Anthony. Nothing.

KIRBY: But you must have meant something, Miriam, or you wouldn't have put it down.

MRS. KIRBY: It was just the first thing that came into my head, that's all.

KIRBY: But what does it mean? Sex—Wall Street.

MRS. KIRBY: (*Annoyed.*) Oh, I don't know what it means, Anthony. It's just that you're always talking about Wall Street, even when— (*She catches herself.*) I don't know what I meant . . . Would you mind terribly, Alice, if we didn't stay for dinner? I'm afraid this game has given me a headache.

ALICE: (*Quietly.*) I understand, Mrs. Kirby.

KIRBY: (*Clearing his throat.*) Yes, possibly we'd better postpone the dinner, if you don't mind.

PENNY: But you're coming tomorrow night, aren't you?

MRS. KIRBY: (*Quickly.*) I'm afraid we have an engagement tomorrow night.

KIRBY: Perhaps we'd better postpone the whole affair a little while. This hot weather, and—ah—

TONY: (*Smoldering.*) I think we're being very ungracious, father. Of *course* we'll stay to dinner—tonight.

MRS. KIRBY: (*Unyielding.*) I have a very bad headache, Tony.

KIRBY: Come, come, Tony, I'm sure everyone understands.

TONY: (*Flaring.*) Well, *I* don't. I think we ought to stay to dinner.

ALICE: (*Very low.*) No, Tony.

TONY: What?

ALICE: We were fools, Tony, ever to think it would work. It won't. Mr. Kirby, I won't be at the office tomorrow. I—won't be there at all any more.

TONY: Alice, what are you talking about?

KIRBY: (*To Alice.*) I'm sorry, my dear—very sorry . . . Are you ready, Miriam?

MRS. KIRBY: (*With enormous dignity.*) Yes, Anthony.

KIRBY: It's been very nice to have met you all. . . . Are you coming, Anthony?

TONY: No, father. I'm not.

KIRBY: I see. . . . Your mother and I will be waiting for you at home. . . . Good-night. (*With Mrs. Kirby on his arm, he sweeps toward the outer door.*)

(*Before the Kirbys can take more than a step toward the door, however, a new figure looms up in the archway. It is a quiet and competent-looking individual with a steely eye, and two more just like him loom up behind him.*)

THE MAN: (*Very quietly.*) Stay right where you are, everybody. (*There is a little scream from Mrs. Kirby, an exclamation from Penny.*) Don't move.

PENNY: Oh, good heavens!

KIRBY: How dare you? Why, what does this mean?

GRANDPA: What *is* all this?

KIRBY: I demand an explanation!

THE MAN: Keep your mouth shut, you! (*He advances slowly into the room, looking the group over. Then he turns to one of his men.*) Which one is it?

ANOTHER MAN: (*Goes over and puts a hand on Ed's shoulder.*) This is him.

ESSIE: Ed!

ED: (*Terrified.*) Why, what do you mean?

ALICE: Grandpa, what is it?

KIRBY: This is an outrage!

THE MAN: Shut up! (*He turns to Ed.*) What's your name?

ED: Edward. . . Carmichael. I haven't done anything.

THE MAN: You haven't, huh?

GRANDPA: (*Not at all scared.*) This seems rather high-handed to me. What's it all about?

THE MAN: Department of Justice.

PENNY: Oh, my goodness! J-men!

ESSIE: Ed, what have you done?

ED: I haven't done anything.

GRANDPA: What's the boy done, Officer?

ALICE: What is it? What's it all about?

THE MAN: (*Taking his time, and surveying the room.*) That door lead to the cellar?

PENNY: Yes, it does.

PAUL: Yes.

THE MAN: (*Ordering a man to investigate.*) Mac . . .
　　(*Mac goes into the cellar.*)
　　. . . Jim!

JIM: Yes, sir.

THE MAN: Take a look upstairs and see what you find.

JIM: Okay. (*Jim goes upstairs.*)

ED: (*Panicky.*) I haven't done anything!

THE MAN: Come here, you! (*He takes some slips of paper out of his pocket.*) Ever see these before?

ED: (*Gulping.*) They're my—circulars.

THE MAN: You print this stuff, huh?

ED: Yes, sir.

THE MAN: And you put 'em into boxes of candy to get 'em into people's homes.

ESSIE: The Love Dreams!

ED: But I didn't mean anything!

THE MAN: You didn't, huh? (*He read the circulars.*) "Dynamite the Capitol!" "Dynamite the White House!" "Dynamite the Supreme Court!" "God is the State; the State is God!"

ED: But I didn't mean that. I just like to print. Don't I, Grandpa?

(*Donald returns with the eggs at this point, and stands quietly watching the proceedings.*)

GRANDPA: Now, Officer, the government's in no danger from Ed. Printing is just his hobby, that's all. He prints anything.

THE MAN: He does, eh?

PENNY: I never heard of such nonsense.

KIRBY: I refuse to stay here and—

(*Mr. De Pinna, at this point, is shoved through the cellar door by Mac, protesting as he comes.*)

DE PINNA: Hey, let me get my pipe, will you? Let me get my pipe!

MAC: Shut up, you! . . . We were right, Chief. They've got enough gunpowder down there to blow up the whole city.

PAUL: But we only use that—

THE MAN: Keep still! . . . Everybody in this house is under arrest.

KIRBY: What's that?

MRS. KIRBY: Oh, good heavens!

GRANDPA: Now look here, Officer—this is all nonsense.

DE PINNA: You'd better let me get my pipe. I left it—

THE MAN: Shut up, all of you!

KOLENKHOV: It seems to me, Officer—

THE MAN: Shut up!

(*From the stairs comes the sound of drunken singing— "There was a young lady," etc. Gay Wellington, wrapped in Penny's negligee, is being carried down the stairway by a somewhat bewildered G-Man.*)

THE G-MAN: Keep still, you! Stop that! Stop it!

THE LEADER: (*After Gay has been persuaded to quiet down.*) Who's that?

GRANDPA: (*Pretty tired of the whole business.*) That—is my mother.

(*And then, suddenly, we hear from the cellar. Mr. De Pinna seems to have been right about his pipe, to judge from the sounds below. It is a whole year's supply of fireworks—bombs, big crackers, little crackers, sky rockets, pin wheels, every-thing. The house is fairly rocked by the explosion.*)

(*In the room, of course, pandemonium reigns. Mrs. Kirby screams; the G-Man drops Gay right where he stands and dashes for the cellar, closely followed by Mr. De Pinna and*

Paul; Penny dashes for her manuscripts and Ed rushes to save his xylophone. Kolenkhov waves his arms wildly and dashes in all directions at once; every one is rushing this way and that.)

(All except one. The exception, of course, is Grandpa, who takes all things as they come. Grandpa just says "Well, well, well!"—and sits down. If a lot of people weren't in the way, in fact, you feel he'd like to throw a few darts.)

CURTAIN

ACT THREE

The following day.

Rheba is in the midst of setting the table for dinner, pausing occasionally in her labors to listen to the Edwin C. Hill of the moment—Donald. With intense interest and concentration, he is reading aloud from a newspaper.

DONALD: ". . . for appearance in the West Side Court this morning. After spending the night in jail, the defendants, thirteen in all, were brought before Judge Callahan and given suspended sentences for manufacturing fireworks without a permit."

RHEBA: Yah. Kept me in the same cell with a strip teaser from a burlesque show.

DONALD: I was in the cell with Mr. Kirby. My, he was mad!

RHEBA: Mrs. Kirby and the strip teaser—they were fighting all night.

DONALD: Whole lot about *Mr.* Kirby here. (*Reading again.*) "Anthony W. Kirby, head of Kirby & Co., 62 Wall Street, who was among those apprehended, declared he was in no way interested in the manufacture of fireworks, but refused to state why he was on the premises at the time of the raid. Mr. Kirby is a member of the Union Club, the Racquet Club, the Harvard Club, and the National Geographic Society." My, he certainly is a joiner!

RHEBA: All those rich men are Elks or something.

DONALD: (*Looking up from his paper.*) I suppose, after all this, Mr. Tony ain't ever going to marry Miss Alice, huh?

RHEBA: No, suh, and it's too bad, too. Miss Alice sure loves that boy.

DONALD: Ever notice how white folks always getting themselves in trouble?

RHEBA: Yassuh, I'm glad I'm colored. (*She sighs, heavily.*) I don't know what I'm going to do with all that food out in the kitchen. Ain't going to be no party tonight, that's sure.

DONALD: Ain't we going to eat it anyhow?

RHEBA: Well, I'm cooking it, but I don't think anybody going to have an appetite.

DONALD: *I'm* hungry.

RHEBA: Well, *they* ain't. They're all so broke up about Miss Alice.

DONALD: What's she want to go 'way for? Where's she going?

RHEBA: I don't know—mountains some place. And she's *going*, all right, no matter what they say. I know Miss Alice when she gets that look in her eye.

DONALD: Too bad, ain't it?

RHEBA: Sure is.

(*Mr. De Pinna comes up from the cellar, bearing the earmarks of the previous day's catastrophe. There is a small bandage around his head and over one eye, and another around his right hand. He also limps slightly.*)

DE PINNA: Not even a balloon left. (*He exhibits a handful of exploded firecrackers.*) Look.

RHEBA: How's your hand, Mr. De Pinna? Better?

DE PINNA: Yes, it's better. (*A step toward the kitchen.*) Is there some more olive oil out there?

RHEBA: (*Nods.*) It's in the salad bowl.

DE PINNA: Thanks.

(*He goes out the kitchen door as Penny comes down the stairs. It is a new and rather subdued Penny.*)

PENNY: (*With a sigh.*) Well, she's going. Nothing anybody said could change her.

RHEBA: She ain't going to stay away long, is she, Mrs. Sycamore?

PENNY: I don't know, Rheba. She won't say.

RHEBA: My, going to be lonesome around here without her. (*She goes into the kitchen.*)

DONALD: How *you* feel, Mrs. Sycamore?

PENNY: Oh, I'm all right, Donald. Just kind of upset. (*She is at her desk.*) Perhaps if I do some work maybe I'll feel better.

DONALD: Well, I won't bother you then, Mrs. Sycamore. (*He goes into the kitchen.*)

(*Penny puts a sheet of paper into the typewriter; stares at it blankly for a moment; types in desultory fashion, gives it up. She leans back and sits staring straight ahead.*)

(*Paul comes slowly down the stairs; stands surveying the room a moment; sighs. He goes over to the Erector Set; absentmindedly pulls out the flag. Then, with another sigh, he drops into a chair.*)

PAUL: She's going, Penny.

PENNY: Yes. (*She is quiet for a moment; then she starts to weep, softly.*)

PAUL: (*Going to her.*) Now, now, Penny.

PENNY: I can't help it, Paul. Somehow I feel it's our fault.

PAUL: It's mine more than yours, Penny. All these years I've just been—going along, enjoying myself, when maybe I should have been thinking more about Alice.

PENNY: Don't say that, Paul. You've been a wonderful father. And husband, too.

PAUL: No, I haven't. Maybe if I'd gone ahead and been an architect—I don't know—something Alice could have been proud of. I felt that all last night, looking at Mr. Kirby.

PENNY: But we've been so happy, Paul.

PAUL: I know, but maybe that's not enough. I used to think it was, but—I'm kind of all mixed up now.

PENNY: (*After a pause.*) What time is she going?

PAUL: Pretty soon. Train leaves at half past seven.

PENNY: Oh, if only she'd see Tony. I'm sure he could persuade her.

PAUL: But she won't, Penny. He's been trying all day.

PENNY: Where is he now?

PAUL: I don't know—I suppose walking around the block again. Anyhow, she won't talk to him.

PENNY: Maybe Tony can catch her as she's leaving.

PAUL: It won't help, Penny.

PENNY: No, I don't suppose so. . . . . I feel so sorry for Tony, too.

(*Grandpa comes down the stairs—unsmiling, but not too depressed by the situation.*)

(*Anxiously.*) Well?

GRANDPA: Now, Penny, let the girl alone.

PENNY: But, Grandpa—

GRANDPA: Suppose she *goes* to the Adirondacks? She'll be back. You can take just so much Adirondacks, and then you come home.

PENNY: Oh, but it's all so terrible, Grandpa.

GRANDPA: In a way, but it has its bright side, too.

PAUL: How do you mean?

GRANDPA: Well, Mr. Kirby getting into the patrol wagon, for one thing, and the expression on his face when he and Donald had to take a bath together. I'll never forget that if I live to be a hundred, and I warn you people I intend to. If I can have things like that going on.

PENNY: Oh, it was even worse with Mrs. Kirby. When the matron stripped her. There was a burlesque dancer there and she kept singing a strip song while Mrs. Kirby undressed.

GRANDPA: I'll bet you Bar Harbor is going to seem pretty dull to the Kirbys for the rest of the summer.

(*With a determined step, Alice comes swiftly down the stairs. Over her arm she carries a couple of dresses. Looking neither to right nor left, she heads for the kitchen.*)

GRANDPA: Need any help, Alice?

ALICE: (*In a strained voice.*) No, thanks, Grandpa. Ed is helping with the bags. I'm just going to press these.

PENNY: Alice, dear—

GRANDPA: Now, Penny.

(*Ed has appeared in the hallway with a couple of hatboxes, Essie behind him.*)

ED: I'll bring the big bag down as soon as you're ready, Alice.

ESSIE: Do you want to take some candy along for the train, Alice?

ALICE: No, thanks, Essie.

PENNY: Really, Alice, you could be just as alone here as you could in the mountains. You could stay right in your room all the time.

ALICE: (*Quietly.*) No, mother, I want to be by myself—away from everybody. I love you all—you know that. But I just have to go away for a while. I'll be all right. . . . Father, did you 'phone for a cab?

PAUL: No, I didn't know you wanted one.

PENNY: Oh, I told Mr. De Pinna to tell you, Paul. Didn't he tell you?

ED: Oh, he told *me*, but I forgot.

ALICE: (*The final straw.*) Oh, I wish I lived in a family that didn't always forget *every*thing. That—that behaved the

way *other* people's families do. I'm sick of cornflakes, and—
Donald, and— (*Unconsciously, in her impatience, she has
picked up one of Grandpa's darts; is surprised to find it suddenly in her hand.*) —everything! (*She dashes the dart to the
floor.*) Why can't we be like other people? Roast beef, and
two green vegetables, and—doilies on the table, and—a
place you could bring your friends to—without— (*Unable
to control herself further, she bursts out of the room, into the
kitchen.*)

ESSIE: I'll—see if I can do anything. (*She goes into the kitchen.*)
      (*The others look at each other for a moment, helplessly.
      Penny, with a sigh, drops into her chair again. Paul also sits.
      Grandpa mechanically picks up the dart from the floor;
      smooths out the feathers. Ed, with a futile gesture, runs his
      fingers idly over the xylophone keys. He stops quickly as every
      head turns to look at him.*)
      (*The sound of the door opening, and Tony appears in the
      archway. A worried and disheveled Tony.*)

PENNY: (*Quickly.*) Tony, talk to her! She's in the kitchen!

TONY: Thanks. (*He goes immediately into the kitchen.*)
      (*The family, galvanized, listen intently.*)
      (*Almost immediately, Alice emerges from the kitchen again,
      followed by Tony. She crosses the living room and starts
      quickly up the stairs.*)
      Alice, won't you listen to me? Please!

ALICE: (*Not stopping.*) Tony, it's no use.

TONY: (*Following her.*) Alice, you're not being fair. At least let
      me talk to you. (*They are both gone—up the stairs.*)

PENNY: Perhaps if I went upstairs with them. . . .

GRANDPA: Now, Penny. Let them alone.
      (*Essie comes out of the kitchen.*)

ESSIE: Where'd they go?
      (*Ed, with a gesture, indicates the upstairs region.*)
      She walked right out the minute he came in.
      (*Mr. De Pinna also emerges from the kitchen.*)

MR. DE PINNA: Knocked the olive oil right out of my hand.
      I'm going to smell kind of fishy.

GRANDPA: How're you feeling, Mr. De Pinna? Hand still
      hurting you?

DE PINNA: No, it's better.

PAUL: Everything burnt up, huh? Downstairs?

DE PINNA: (*Nodding, sadly.*) Everything. And my Roman costume, too.

GRANDPA: (*To Penny.*) I told you there was a bright side to everything. All except my twenty-two years back income tax. (*He pulls an envelope out of his pocket.*) I get another letter every day.

DE PINNA: Say, what are you going to do about that, Grandpa?

GRANDPA: Well, I had a kind of idea yesterday. It may not work, but I'm trying it, anyhow.

DE PINNA: (*Eagerly.*) What is it?

(*Suddenly Kolenkhov appears in the doorway.*)

KOLENKHOV: (*Even he is subdued.*) Good evening, everybody!

PENNY: Why, Mr. Kolenkhov!

GRANDPA: Hello, Kolenkhov.

KOLENKHOV: Forgive me. The door was open.

GRANDPA: Come on in.

KOLENKHOV: You will excuse my coming today. I realize you are—upset.

PENNY: That's all right, Mr. Kolenkhov.

ESSIE: I don't think I can take a lesson, Mr. Kolenkhov. I don't feel up to it.

KOLENKHOV: (*Uncertainly.*) Well, I—ah—

PENNY: Oh, but do stay to dinner, Mr. Kolenkhov. We've got all that food out there, and somebody's got to eat it.

KOLENKHOV: I will be happy to, Madame Sycamore.

PENNY: Fine.

KOLENKHOV: Thank you. . . . Now, I wonder if I know you well enough to ask of you a great favor.

PENNY: Why, of course, Mr. Kolenkhov. What is it?

KOLENKHOV: You have heard me talk about my friend the Grand Duchess Olga Katrina.

PENNY: Yes?

KOLENKHOV: She is a great woman, the Grand Duchess. Her cousin was the Czar of Russia, and today she is a waitress in Childs' Restaurant. Columbus Circle.

PENNY: Yes, I know. If there's anything at all that we can do, Mr. Kolenkhov . . .

KOLENKHOV: I tell you. The Grand Duchess Olga Katrina has not had a good meal since before the Revolution.

GRANDPA: She must be hungry.

KOLENKHOV: And today the Grand Duchess not only has her day off—Thursday—but it is also the anniversary of Peter the Great. A remarkable man!

PENNY: Mr. Kolenkhov, if you mean you'd like the Grand Duchess to come to dinner, why, we'd be honored.

ESSIE: Oh, yes!

KOLENKHOV: (*With a bow.*) In the name of the Grand Duchess, I thank you.

PENNY: I can hardly wait to meet her. When will she be here?

KOLENKHOV: She is outside in the street, waiting. I bring her in. (*And he goes out.*)

GRANDPA: You know, if this keeps on I want to live to be a hundred and *fifty*.

PENNY: (*Feverishly.*) Ed, straighten your tie. Essie, look at your dress. How do *I* look? All right?

> (*Kolenkhov appears in the hallway and stands at rigid attention.*)

KOLENKHOV: (*His voice booming.*) The Grand Duchess Olga Katrina!

> (*And the Grand Duchess Olga Katrina, wheat cakes and maple syrup out of her life for a few hours, sweeps into the room. She wears a dinner gown that has seen better days, and the whole is surmounted by an extremely tacky-looking evening wrap, trimmed with bits of ancient and moth-eaten fur. But once a Grand Duchess, always a Grand Duchess. She rises above everything—Childs', evening wrap, and all.*)

Your Highness, permit me to present Madame Sycamore—

> (*Penny, having seen a movie or two in her time, knows just what to do. She curtsies right to the floor, and catches hold of a chair just in time.*)

Madame Carmichael—

> (*Essie does a curtsey that begins where all others leave off. Starting on her toes, she merges the Dying Swan with an extremely elaborate genuflection.*)

Grandpa—

GRANDPA: (*With a little bow.*) Madame.

KOLENKHOV: Mr. Sycamore, Mr. Carmichael, and Mr. De Pinna.

(*Paul and Ed content themselves with courteous little bows, but not so the social-minded Mr. De Pinna. He bows to the floor—and stays there for a moment.*)

GRANDPA: All right now, Mr. De Pinna.

(*Mr. De Pinna gets to his feet again.*)

PENNY: Will you be seated, Your Highness?

THE GRAND DUCHESS: Thank you. You are most kind.

PENNY: We are honored to receive you, Your Highness.

THE GRAND DUCHESS: I am most happy to be here. What time is dinner?

PENNY: (*A little startled.*) Oh, it'll be quite soon, Your Highness—very soon.

THE GRAND DUCHESS: I do not mean to be rude, but I must be back at the restaurant by eight o'clock. I am substituting for another waitress.

KOLENKHOV: I will make sure you are on time, Your Highness.

DE PINNA: You know, Highness, I think you waited on me in Childs' once. The Seventy-Second Street place?

THE GRAND DUCHESS: No, no. That was my sister.

KOLENKHOV: The Grand Duchess Natasha.

THE GRAND DUCHESS: *I* work in Columbus Circle.

GRANDPA: Quite a lot of your family living over here now, aren't there?

THE GRAND DUCHESS: Oh, yes—many. My uncle, the Grand Duke Sergei—he is an elevator man at Macy's. A very nice man. Then there is my cousin, Prince Alexis. He will not speak to the rest of us because he works at Hattie Carnegie's. He has cards printed—Prince Alexis of Hattie Carnegie. Bah!

KOLENKHOV: When he was selling Eskimo Pies at Luna Park he was willing to talk to you.

THE GRAND DUCHESS: Ah, Kolenkhov, our time is coming. My sister Natasha is studying to be a manicure, Uncle Sergei they have promised to make floor-walker, and next month I get transferred to the Fifth Avenue Childs'. From there it is only a step to Schraffts', and *then* we will see what Prince Alexis says!

GRANDPA: (*Nodding.*) I think you've got him.

THE GRAND DUCHESS: You are telling *me*? (*She laughs a triumphant Russian laugh, in which Kolenkhov joins.*)

PENNY: Your Highness—did you know the Czar? Personally, I mean.

THE GRAND DUCHESS: Of course—he was my cousin. It was terrible, what happened, but perhaps it was for the best. Where could he get a job now?

KOLENKHOV: That is true.

THE GRAND DUCHESS: (*Philosophically.*) Yes. And poor relations are poor relations. It is the same in every family. My cousin, the King of Sweden—he was very nice to us for about ten years, but then he said, I just cannot go on. I am not doing so well, either. . . . I do not blame him.

PENNY: No, of course not. . . . Would you excuse me for just a moment? (*She goes to the foot of the stairs and stands peering up anxiously, hoping for news of Alice.*)

DE PINNA: (*The historian at heart.*) Tell me, Grand Duchess, is it true what they say about Rasputin?

THE GRAND DUCHESS: Everyone wants to know about Rasputin. . . . Yes, my dear sir, it is true. In spades.

DE PINNA: You don't say?

KOLENKHOV: Your Highness, we have to watch the time.

THE GRAND DUCHESS: Yes, I must not be late. The manager does not like me. He is a Communist.

PENNY: We'll hurry things up. Essie, why don't you go out in the kitchen and give Rheba a hand?

THE GRAND DUCHESS: (*Rising.*) I will help, too. I am a very good cook.

PENNY: Oh, but Your Highness! Not on your day off!

THE GRAND DUCHESS: I do not mind. Where is your kitchen?

ESSIE: Right through here, but you're the guest of honor, Your Highness.

THE GRAND DUCHESS: But I love to cook! Come, Kolenkhov! If they have got sour cream and pot cheese I will make you some blintzes!

KOLENKHOV: Ah! Blintzes! . . . Come, Pavlowa! We show you something! (*With Essie, he goes into the kitchen.*)

DE PINNA: Say! The Duchess is all right, isn't she? Hey, Duchess! Can I help? (*And into the kitchen.*)

PENNY: Really, she's a very nice woman, you know. Considering she's a Grand Duchess.

GRANDPA: Wonderful what people go through, isn't it? And still keep kind of gay, too.

PENNY: Mm. She made me forget about everything for a minute. (*She returns to the stairs and stands listening.*)

PAUL: I'd better call that cab, I suppose.

PENNY: No, wait, Paul. I think I hear them. Maybe Tony has— (*She stops as Alice's step is heard on the stair. She enters— dressed for traveling. Tony looms up behind her.*)

ALICE: Ed, will you go up and bring my bag down?

TONY: (*Quickly.*) Don't you do it, Ed!

(*Ed hesitates, uncertain.*)

ALICE: Ed, please!

TONY: (*A moment's pause; then he gives up.*) All right, Ed. Bring it down. (*Ed goes up the stairs as Tony disconsolately stalks across the room. Then he faces the Sycamores.*) Do you know that you've got the stubbornest daughter in all forty-eight states?

(*The door bell rings.*)

ALICE: That must be the cab. (*She goes to the door.*)

GRANDPA: If it is, it's certainly wonderful service.

(*To the considerable surprise of everyone, the voice of Mr. Kirby is heard at the front door.*)

KIRBY: Is Tony here, Alice?

ALICE: Yes. Yes, he is.

(*Mr. Kirby comes in.*)

KIRBY: (*Uncomfortably.*) Ah—good afternoon. Forgive my intruding . . . Tony, I want you to come home with me. Your mother is very upset.

TONY: (*He looks at Alice.*) Very well, father . . . Good-bye, Alice.

ALICE: (*Very low.*) Good-bye, Tony.

KIRBY: (*Trying to ease the situation.*) I need hardly say that this is as painful to Mrs. Kirby and myself as it is to you people. I—I'm sorry, but I'm sure you understand.

GRANDPA: Well, yes—and in a way, no. Now, I'm not the kind of person tries to run other people's lives, but the fact is, Mr. Kirby, I don't think these two young people have got as much sense as—ah—you and I have.

ALICE: (*Tense.*) Grandpa, will you please not do this?

GRANDPA: (*Disarmingly.*) I'm just talking to Mr. Kirby. A cat can look at a king, can't he?

(*Alice, with no further words, takes up the telephone and dials a number. There is finality in her every movement.*)

PENNY: You—you want me to do that for you, Alice?

ALICE: No, thanks, mother.

PAUL: You've got quite a while before the train goes, Alice.

ALICE: (*Into the phone.*) Will you send a cab to 761 Claremont, right away, please? . . . That's right, thank you. (*She hangs up.*)

KIRBY: And now if you'll excuse us . . . are you ready, Tony?

GRANDPA: Mr. Kirby, I suppose after last night you think this family is crazy, don't you?

KIRBY: No, I would not say that, although I am not accustomed to going out to dinner and spending the night in jail.

GRANDPA: Well, you've got to remember, Mr. Kirby, you came on the wrong night. Now tonight, I'll bet you, nothing'll happen at all.

(*There is a great burst of Russian laughter from the kitchen —the mingled voices of Kolenkhov and the Grand Duchess. Grandpa looks off in the direction of the laughter, then decides to play safe.*)

Maybe.

KIRBY: Mr. Vanderhof, it was not merely last night that convinced Mrs. Kirby and myself that this engagement would be unwise.

TONY: Father, I can handle my own affairs. (*He turns to Alice.*) Alice, for the last time, will you marry me?

ALICE: No, Tony. I know exactly what your father means, and he's right.

TONY: No, he's *not*, Alice.

GRANDPA: Alice, you're in love with this boy, and you're not marrying him because we're the kind of people we are.

ALICE: Grandpa—

GRANDPA: I know. You think the two families wouldn't get along. Well, maybe they wouldn't—but who says they're right and we're wrong?

ALICE: I didn't say that, Grandpa. I only feel—

GRANDPA: Well, what *I* feel is that Tony's too nice a boy to wake up twenty years from now with nothing in his life but stocks and bonds.

KIRBY: How's that?

GRANDPA: (*Turning to Mr. Kirby.*) Yes. Mixed up and unhappy, the way you are.

KIRBY: (*Outraged.*) I beg your pardon, Mr. Vanderhof, I am a very happy man.

GRANDPA: Are you?

KIRBY: Certainly I am.

GRANDPA: I don't think so. What do you think you get your indigestion from? Happiness? No, sir. You get it because most of your time is spent in doing things you don't want to do.

KIRBY: I don't do anything I don't want to do.

GRANDPA: Yes, you do. You said last night that at the end of a week in Wall Street you're pretty near crazy. Why do you keep on doing it?

KIRBY: Why do I keep on—why, that's my *business*. A man can't give up his business.

GRANDPA: Why not? You've got all the money you need. You can't take it with you.

KIRBY: That's a very easy thing to say, Mr. Vanderhof. But I have spent my entire life building up my business.

GRANDPA: And what's it got you? Same kind of mail every morning, same kind of deals, same kind of meetings, same dinners at night, same indigestion. Where does the fun come in? Don't you think there ought to be something *more*, Mr. Kirby? You must have wanted more than that when you started out. We haven't got too much time, you know—any of us.

KIRBY: What do you expect me to do? Live the way *you* do? Do nothing?

GRANDPA: Well, I have a lot of fun. Time enough for everything—read, talk, visit the zoo now and then, practice my darts, even have time to notice when spring comes around. Don't see anybody I don't want to, don't have six hours of things I *have* to do every day before I get *one* hour to do what I like in—and I haven't taken bicarbonate of soda in thirty-five years. What's the matter with that?

KIRBY: The matter with that? But suppose we *all* did it? A fine world we'd have, everybody going to zoos. Don't be ridiculous, Mr. Vanderhof. Who would do the work?

GRANDPA: There's always people that like to work—you can't

stop them. Inventions, and they fly the ocean. There're always people to go down to Wall Street, too—because they *like* it. But from what I've seen of you, I don't think you're one of them. I think you're missing something.

KIRBY: I am not aware of missing anything.

GRANDPA: I wasn't either, till I quit. I used to get down to that office nine o'clock sharp, no matter how I felt. Lay awake nights for fear I wouldn't get that contract. Used to worry about the world, too. Got *all* worked up about whether Cleveland or Blaine was going to be elected President— seemed awful important at the time, but who cares now? What I'm trying to say, Mr. Kirby, is that I've had thirty-five years that nobody can take away from me, no matter what they do to the world. See?

KIRBY: Yes, I do see. And it's a very dangerous philosophy, Mr. Vanderhof. It's—it's un-American. And it's exactly why I'm opposed to this marriage. I don't want Tony to come under its influence.

TONY: (*A gleam in his eye.*) What's the matter with it, father?

KIRBY: Matter with it? Why, it's—it's downright Communism, that's what it is.

TONY: You didn't always think so.

KIRBY: I most certainly did. What are you talking about?

TONY: I'll tell you what I'm talking about. You didn't always think so, because there was a time when you wanted to be a trapeze artist.

KIRBY: Why—why, don't be an idiot, Tony.

TONY: Oh, yes, you did. I came across those letters you wrote to grandfather. Do you remember those?

KIRBY: NO! . . . . How dared you read those letters? How dared you?

PENNY: Why, isn't that wonderful? Did you wear tights, Mr. Kirby?

KIRBY: Certainly not! The whole thing is absurd. I was fourteen years old at the time.

TONY: Yes, but at *eighteen* you wanted to be a saxophone player, didn't you?

KIRBY: Tony!

TONY: And at twenty-one you ran away from home because

grandfather wanted you to go into the business. It's all down there in black and white. You didn't *always* think so.

GRANDPA: Well, well, well!

KIRBY: I may have had silly notions in my youth, but thank God my father knocked them out of me. I went into the business and forgot about them.

TONY: Not altogether, father. There's still a saxophone in the back of your clothes closet.

GRANDPA: There is?

KIRBY: (*Quietly.*) That's enough, Tony. We'll discuss this later.

TONY: No, I want to talk about it *now*. I think Mr. Vanderhof is right—dead right. I'm never going back to that office. I've always hated it, and I'm not going on with it. And I'll tell you something else. I didn't make a mistake last night. I knew it was the wrong night. I brought you here on purpose.

ALICE: Tony!

PENNY: Well, for heaven's—

TONY: Because I wanted to wake you up. I wanted you to see a real family—as they really *were*. A family that loved and understood each other. You don't understand *me*. You've never had time. Well, I'm not going to make *your* mistake. I'm clearing out.

KIRBY: Clearing out? What do you mean?

TONY: I mean I'm not going to be pushed into the business just because I'm your son. I'm getting out while there's still time.

KIRBY: (*Stunned.*) Tony, what are you going to do?

TONY: I don't know. Maybe I'll be a bricklayer, but at least I'll be doing something I want to do.

(*Whereupon the door bell rings.*)

PENNY: That must be the cab.

GRANDPA: Ask him to wait a minute, Ed.

ALICE: Grandpa!

GRANDPA: Do you mind, Alice? . . . You know, Mr. Kirby, Tony is going through just what you and I did when we were his age. I think, if you listen hard enough, you can hear yourself saying the same things to *your* father twenty-five years ago. We all did it. And we were right. How many of us would be willing to settle when we're young for what we eventually get? All those plans we make . . . what happens to them? It's only a handful of the lucky ones that can look back and say that they even came close.

(*Grandpa has hit home. Mr. Kirby turns slowly and looks at his son, as though seeing him for the first time. Grandpa continues.*)

So . . . before they clean out that closet, Mr. Kirby, I think I'd get in a few good hours on that saxophone.

(*A slight pause, then The Grand Duchess, an apron over her evening dress, comes in from the kitchen.*)

THE GRAND DUCHESS: I beg your pardon, but before I make the blintzes, how many will there be for dinner?

PENNY: Why, I don't know—ah—

GRANDPA: Your Highness, may I present Mr. Anthony Kirby, and Mr. Kirby, Junior? The Grand Duchess Olga Katrina.

KIRBY: How's that?

THE GRAND DUCHESS: How do you do? Before I make the blintzes, how many will there be to dinner?

GRANDPA: Oh, I'd make quite a stack of them, Your Highness. Can't ever tell.

THE GRAND DUCHESS: Good! The Czar always said to me, Olga, do not be stingy with the blintzes.

(*She returns to the kitchen, leaving a somewhat stunned Mr. Kirby behind her.*)

KIRBY: Ah—who did you say that was, Mr. Vanderhof?

GRANDPA: (*Very offhand.*) The Grand Duchess Olga Katrina, of Russia. She's cooking the dinner.

KIRBY: Oh!

GRANDPA: And speaking of dinner, Mr. Kirby, why don't you and Tony both stay?

PENNY: Oh, please do, Mr. Kirby. We've got all that stuff we were going to have last night. I mean tonight.

GRANDPA: Looks like a pretty good dinner, Mr. Kirby, and'll kind of give us a chance to get acquainted. Why not stay?

KIRBY: Why—I'd like to very much. (*He turns to Tony, with some trepidation.*) What do you say, Tony? Shall we stay to dinner?

TONY: Yes, father. I think that would be fine. If— (*His eyes go to Alice.*) —if Alice will send away that cab.

GRANDPA: How about it, Alice? Going to be a nice crowd. Don't you think you ought to stay for dinner?

ALICE: Mr. Kirby—Tony—oh, Tony! (*And she is in his arms.*)

TONY: Darling!

ALICE: Grandpa, you're wonderful!

GRANDPA: I've been telling you that for years. (*He kisses her.*)
(*Essie enters from the kitchen, laden with dishes.*)

ESSIE: Grandpa, here's a letter for you. It was in the ice-box.

GRANDPA: (*Looks at the envelope.*) The Government again.

TONY: (*Happily.*) Won't you step into the office, Miss Sycamore? I'd like to do a little dictating.

GRANDPA: (*With his letters.*) Well, well, well!

PENNY: What is it, Grandpa?

GRANDPA: The United States Government apologizes. I don't owe 'em a nickel. It seems I died eight years ago.

ESSIE: Why, what do they mean, Grandpa?

GRANDPA: Remember Charlie, the milkman? Buried under my name?

PENNY: Yes.

GRANDPA: Well, I just told them they made a mistake and I was Martin Vanderhof, Jr. So they're very sorry and I may even get a refund.

ALICE: Why, Grandpa, you're an old crook.

GRANDPA: Sure!

KIRBY: (*Interested.*) Pardon me, how did you say you escaped the income tax, Mr. Vanderhof?

KOLENKHOV: (*Bursting through the kitchen door, bringing a chair with him.*) Tonight, my friends, you are going to eat. . . . (*He stops short as he catches sight of Kirby.*)

KIRBY: (*Heartily.*) Hello, there!

KOLENKHOV: (*Stunned.*) How do you do?

KIRBY: Fine! Fine! Never was better.

KOLENKHOV: (*To Grandpa.*) What has happened?

GRANDPA: He's relaxing.
(*Ed strikes the keys of the xylophone.*)
That's right. Play something, Ed.
(*He starts to play. Essie is immediately up on her toes.*)

THE GRAND DUCHESS: (*Entering from the kitchen.*) Everything will be ready in a minute. You can sit down.

PENNY: Come on, everybody. Dinner!

(*They start to pull up chairs.*)

Come on, Mr. Kirby!

KIRBY: (*Still interested in the xylophone.*) Yes, yes, I'm coming.

PENNY: Essie, stop dancing and come to dinner.

KOLENKHOV: You will like Russian food, Mr. Kirby.

PENNY: But you must be careful of your indigestion.

KIRBY: Nonsense! I haven't any indigestion.

TONY: Well, Miss Sycamore, how was your trip to the Adirondacks?

ALICE: Shut your face, Mr. Kirby!

KOLENKHOV: In Russia, when they sit down to dinner . . .

GRANDPA: (*Tapping on his plate.*) Quiet! Everybody! Quiet! (*Immediately the talk ceases. All heads are lowered as Grandpa starts to say Grace.*) Well, Sir, here we are again. We want to say thanks once more for everything You've done for us. Things seem to be going along fine. Alice is going to marry Tony, and it looks as if they're going to be very happy. Of course the fireworks blew up, but that was Mr. De Pinna's fault, not Yours. We've all got our health and as far as anything else is concerned, we'll leave it to You. Thank You.

(*The heads come up again. Rheba and Donald come through the kitchen door with stacks and stacks of blintzes. Even the Czar would have thought there were enough.*)

CURTAIN

THE MAN WHO
CAME TO DINNER

by

Moss Hart

and

George S. Kaufman

TO
ALEXANDER WOOLLCOTT

*For reasons that are
nobody's business*

THE AUTHORS

SYNOPSIS OF SCENES

The scene is the home of Mr. and Mrs. Stanley,
in a small town in Ohio.

ACT ONE
SCENE I—A December morning
SCENE II—About a week later

ACT TWO
Another week has passed
Christmas Eve

ACT THREE
Christmas morning

ACT ONE

Scene I

The curtain rises on the attractive living room in the home of Mr. and Mrs. Ernest W. Stanley, in a small town in Ohio. The Stanleys are obviously people of means. The room is large, comfortable, tastefully furnished. Double doors lead into a library; there is a glimpse of a dining room at the rear, and we see the first half dozen steps of a handsome curved staircase. At the other side, bay windows, the entrance hall, the outer door.

Mrs. Stanley is hovering nervously near the library doors, which are tightly closed. She advances a step or two, retreats, advances again and this time musters up enough courage to listen at the door. Suddenly the doors are opened and she has to leap back.

A Nurse in full uniform emerges—scurries, rather, out of the room.

An angry voice from within speeds her on her way: "Great dribbling cow!"

MRS. STANLEY: (*Eagerly*) How is he? Is he coming out?
> (*But the Nurse has already disappeared into the dining room*)
> (*Simultaneously the door bell rings—at the same time a young lad of twenty-one, Richard Stanley, is descending the stairs*)

RICHARD: I'll go, Mother.
> (*John, a white-coated servant, comes hurrying in from the dining room and starts up the stairs, two at a time*)

MRS. STANLEY: What's the matter? What is it?

JOHN: They want pillows. (*And he is out of sight*)
> (*Meanwhile the Nurse is returning to the sick room. The voice is heard again as she opens the doors. "Don't call yourself a doctor in my presence! You're a quack if I ever saw one!"*)
> (*Richard returns from the hall, carrying two huge packages and a sheaf of cablegrams*)

767

RICHARD: Four more cablegrams and more packages. . . . Dad is going crazy upstairs, with that bell ringing all the time. (*Meanwhile June, the daughter of the house, has come down the stairs. An attractive girl of twenty. At the same time the telephone is ringing*)

MRS. STANLEY: Oh, dear! . . . June, will you go? . . . What did you say, Richard?

RICHARD: (*Examining the packages*) One's from New York and one from San Francisco.

MRS. STANLEY: There was something from Alaska early this morning.

JUNE: (*At the telephone*) Yes? . . . Yes, that's right.

MRS. STANLEY: Who is it? (*Before June can answer, the double doors are opened again and the Nurse appears. The voice calls after her: "Doesn't that bird-brain of yours ever function?"*)

THE NURSE: I—I'll get them right away. . . . He wants some Players Club cigarettes.

MRS. STANLEY: Players Club?

RICHARD: They have 'em at Kitchener's. I'll run down and get 'em. (*He is off*)

JUNE: (*Still at the phone*) Hello. . . . Yes, I'm waiting.

MRS. STANLEY: Tell me, Miss Preen, is he—are they bringing him out soon?

MISS PREEN: (*Wearily*) We're getting him out of bed now. He'll be out very soon . . . Oh, thank you. (*This last is to John, who has descended the stairs with three or four pillows*)

MRS. STANLEY: Oh, I'm so glad. He must be very happy. (*And again we hear the invalid's voice as Miss Preen passes into the room. "Trapped like a rat in this hell-hole! Take your fish-hooks off me!"*)

JUNE: (*At the phone*) Hello. . . . Yes, he's here, but he can't come to the phone right now . . . London? (*She covers the transmitter with her hand*) It's London calling Mr. Whiteside.

MRS. STANLEY: London? My, my!

JUNE: Two o'clock? Yes, I think he could talk then. All right. (*She hangs up*) Well, who do you think that was? Mr. H. G. Wells.

MRS. STANLEY: (*Wild-eyed*) H. G. Wells? On our telephone?
(*The door bell again*)

JUNE: I'll go. This is certainly a busy house.
(*In the meantime Sarah, the cook, has come from the dining room with a pitcher of orange juice*)

MRS. STANLEY: (*As Sarah knocks on the double doors*) Oh, that's fine, Sarah. Is it fresh?

SARAH: Yes, ma'am.
(*The doors are opened; Sarah hands the orange juice to the nurse. The voice roars once more: "You have the touch of a sex-starved cobra!"*)

SARAH: (*Beaming*) His voice is just the same as on the radio.
(*She disappears into the dining room as June returns from the entrance hall, ushering in two friends of her mother's, Mrs. Dexter and Mrs. McCutcheon. One is carrying a flowering plant, partially wrapped; the other is holding, with some care, what turns out to be a jar of calf's-foot jelly*)

THE LADIES: Good morning!

MRS. STANLEY: Girls, what do you think? He's getting up and coming out today!

MRS. McCUTCHEON: You don't mean it!

MRS. DEXTER: Can we stay and see him?

MRS. STANLEY: Why, of course—he'd love it. Girls, do you know what just happened?

JUNE: (*Departing*) I'll be upstairs, Mother, if you want me.

MRS. STANLEY: What? . . . Oh, yes. June, tell your father he'd better come down, will you? Mr. Whiteside is coming out.

MRS. DEXTER: Is he really coming out today? I brought him a plant—Do you think it's all right if I give it to him?

MRS. STANLEY: Why, I think that would be lovely.

MRS. McCUTCHEON: And some calf's-foot jelly.

MRS. STANLEY: Why, how nice! Who do you think was on the phone just now? H. G. Wells, from London. And look at those cablegrams. He's had calls and messages from all over this country and Europe. The New York *Times*, and Radio City Music Hall—I don't know why *they* called—and Felix Frankfurter, and Dr. Dafoe, the Mount Wilson Observatory —I just can't tell you what's been going on.

MRS. DEXTER: There's a big piece about it in this week's *Time*. Did you see it? (*Drawing it out of her bag*)

MRS. STANLEY: No—really?

MRS. MCCUTCHEON: Your name's in it too, Daisy. It tells all about the whole thing. Listen: "Portly Sheridan Whiteside, critic, lecturer, wit, radio orator, intimate friend of the great and near great, last week found his celebrated wit no weapon with which to combat a fractured hip. The Falstaffian Mr. Whiteside, trekking across the country on one of his annual lecture tours, met his Waterloo in the shape of a small piece of ice on the doorstep of Mr. and Mrs. Ernest W. Stanley, of Mesalia, Ohio. Result: Cancelled lectures and disappointment to thousands of adoring clubwomen in Omaha, Denver, and points west. Further result: The idol of the air waves rests until further notice in home of surprised Mr. and Mrs. Stanley. Possibility: Christmas may be postponed this year." What's *that* mean?

MRS. STANLEY: Why, what do you think of that? (*She takes the magazine; reads*) "A small piece of ice on the doorstep of Mr. and Mrs. Ernest"—think of it!

MRS. MCCUTCHEON: Of course if it were *my* house, Daisy, I'd have a bronze plate put on the step, right where he fell.

MRS. STANLEY: Well, of course I felt terrible about it. He just never goes to dinner anywhere, and he finally agreed to come here, and then *this* had to happen. Poor Mr. Whiteside! But it's going to be so wonderful having him with us, even for a little while. Just think of it! We'll sit around in the evening and discuss books and plays, all the great people he's known. And he'll talk in that wonderful way of his. He may even read *Good-bye, Mr. Chips* to us.

(*Mr. Stanley, solid, substantial—the American business man —is descending the stairs*)

STANLEY: Daisy, I can't wait any longer. If—ah, good morning, ladies.

MRS. STANLEY: Ernest, he's coming out any minute, and H. G. Wells telephoned from London, and we're in *Time*. Look!

STANLEY: (*Taking the magazine*) I don't like this kind of publicity at all, Daisy. When do you suppose he's going to leave?

MRS. STANLEY: Well, he's only getting up this morning—after all, he's had quite a shock, and he's been in bed for two full weeks. He'll certainly have to rest a few days, Ernest.

STANLEY: Well, I'm sure it's a great honor, his being in the

house, but it *is* a little upsetting—phone going all the time,
bells ringing, messenger boys running in and out—

(*Out of the sick room comes a business-like-looking young
woman about thirty. Her name is Margaret Cutler—
Maggie to her friends*)

MAGGIE: Pardon me, Mrs. Stanley—have the cigarettes come
yet?

MRS. STANLEY: They're on the way, Miss Cutler. My son went
for them.

MAGGIE: Thank you.

MRS. STANLEY: Ah—this is Miss Cutler, Mr. Whiteside's secretary.
(*An exchange of "How do you do's?"*)

MAGGIE: May I move this chair?

MRS. STANLEY: (*All eagerness*) You mean he's—coming out now?

MAGGIE: (*Quietly*) He is indeed.

MRS. STANLEY: Ernest, call June. June! June! Mr. Whiteside is
coming out!

(*John, visible in the dining room, summons Sarah to attend
the excitement. "Sarah! Sarah!"*)

(*Sarah and John appear in the dining-room entrance, June
on the stairs. Mrs. Stanley and the two other ladies are
keenly expectant; even Mr. Stanley is on the qui vive*)

(*The double doors are opened once more, and Dr. Bradley
appears, bag in hand. He has taken a good deal of punish-
ment, and speaks with a rather false heartiness*)

DR. BRADLEY: Well, here we are, merry and bright. Good
morning, good morning. Bring our little patient out, Miss
Preen.

(*A moment's pause, and then a wheelchair is rolled through
the door. It is full of pillows, blankets, and Sheridan Whiteside. Sheridan Whiteside is indeed portly and Falstaffian.
He is wearing an elaborate velvet smoking jacket and a very
loud tie, and he looks like every caricature ever drawn of
him*)

(*There is a hush as the wheelchair rolls into the room. Wel-
coming smiles break over every face. The chair comes to a
halt; Mr. Whiteside looks slowly around, into each and every
beaming face. His fingers drum for a moment on the arm of
the chair. He looks slowly around once more. And then he
speaks*)

WHITESIDE: (*Quietly, to Maggie*) I may vomit.

MRS. STANLEY: (*With a nervous little laugh*) Good morning, Mr. Whiteside. I'm Mrs. Ernest Stanley—remember? And this is Mr. Stanley.

STANLEY: How do you do, Mr. Whiteside? I hope that you are better.

WHITESIDE: Thank you. I am suing you for a hundred and fifty thousand dollars.

STANLEY: How's that? What?

WHITESIDE: I said I am suing you for a hundred and fifty thousand dollars.

MRS. STANLEY: You mean—because you fell on our steps, Mr. Whiteside?

WHITESIDE: Samuel J. Liebowitz will explain it to you in court. . . . Who are those two harpies standing there like the kiss of death?

(*Mrs. McCutcheon, with a little gasp, drops the calf's-foot jelly. It smashes on the floor*)

MRS. McCUTCHEON: Oh, dear! My calf's-foot jelly.

WHITESIDE: Made from your own foot, I have no doubt. And now, Mrs. Stanley, I have a few small matters to take up with you. Since this corner druggist at my elbow tells me that I shall be confined in this mouldy mortuary for at least another ten days, due entirely to your stupidity and negligence, I shall have to carry on my activities as best I can. I shall require the exclusive use of this room, as well as that drafty sewer which you call the library. I want no one to come in or out while I am in this room.

STANLEY: What do you mean, sir?

MRS. STANLEY: (*Stunned*) But we have to go up the stairs to get to our rooms, Mr. Whiteside.

WHITESIDE: Isn't there a back entrance?

MRS. STANLEY: Why—yes.

WHITESIDE: Then use that. I shall also require a room for my secretary, Miss Cutler. I shall have a great many incoming and outgoing calls, so please use the telephone as little as possible. I sleep until noon and require quiet through the house until that hour. There will be five for lunch today. Where is the cook?

STANLEY: Mr. Whiteside, if I may interrupt for a moment—

WHITESIDE: You may not, sir. . . . Will you take your clammy
hand off my chair? (*This last to the nurse*) . . . And now will
you all leave quietly, or must I ask Miss Cutler to pass
among you with a baseball bat?

(*Mrs. Dexter and Mrs. McCutcheon are beating a hasty retreat, their gifts still in hand*)

MRS. McCUTCHEON: Well—good-bye, Daisy. We'll call you—
Oh, no, we mustn't use the phone. Well—we'll see you.
(*And they are gone*)

STANLEY: (*Boldly*) Now look here, Mr. Whiteside—

WHITESIDE: There is nothing to discuss, sir. Considering the
damage I have suffered at your hands, I am asking very
little. Good day.

STANLEY: (*Controlling himself*) I'll call you from the office
later, Daisy.

WHITESIDE: Not on this phone, please.

(*Stanley gives him a look, but goes*)

WHITESIDE: Here is the menu for lunch. (*He extends a slip of
paper to Mrs. Stanley*)

MRS. STANLEY: But—I've already ordered lunch.

WHITESIDE: It will be sent up to you on a tray. I am using the
dining room for my guests. . . . Where are those cigarettes?

MRS. STANLEY: Why—my son went for them. I don't know
why he—here, Sarah. (*She hands Sarah the luncheon slip*) I'll
—have mine upstairs on a tray.

(*Sarah and John depart*)

WHITESIDE: (*To June, who has been posed on the landing during
all this*) Young lady, will you either go up those stairs or
come down them? I cannot stand indecision.

(*June is about to speak, decides against it, and ascends the
stairs with a good deal of spirit*)

(*Mrs. Stanley is hovering uncertainly on the steps as
Richard returns with the cigarettes*)

RICHARD: Oh, good morning. I'm sorry I was so long—I had
to go to three different stores.

WHITESIDE: How did you travel? By ox-cart?

(*Richard is considerably taken aback. His eyes go to his
mother, who motions to him to come up the stairs. They disappear together, their eyes unsteadily on Whiteside*)

WHITESIDE: Is there a man in the world who suffers as I do

from the gross inadequacies of the human race! (*To the Nurse, who is fussing around the chair again*) Take those canal boats away from me! (*She obeys, hastily*) Go in and read the life of Florence Nightingale and learn how unfitted you are for your chosen profession.

(*Miss Preen glares at him, but goes*)

DR. BRADLEY: (*Heartily*) Well, I think I can safely leave you in Miss Cutler's capable hands. Shall I look in again this afternoon?

WHITESIDE: If you do, I shall spit right in your eye.

DR. BRADLEY: What a sense of humor you writers have! By the way, it isn't really worth mentioning, but—I've been doing a little writing myself. About my medical experiences.

WHITESIDE: (*Quietly*) Am I to be spared nothing?

DR. BRADLEY: Would it be too much to ask you to—glance over it while you're here?

WHITESIDE: (*Eyes half closed, as though the pain were too exquisite to bear*) Trapped.

DR. BRADLEY: (*Delving into his bag*) I just happen to have a copy with me. (*He brings out a tremendous manuscript*) "Forty Years an Ohio Doctor. The Story of a Humble Practitioner."

WHITESIDE: I shall drop everything.

DR. BRADLEY: Much obliged, and I hope you like it. Well, see you on the morrow. Keep that hip quiet and don't forget those little pills. (*He goes*)

WHITESIDE: (*Handing the manuscript to Maggie*) Maggie, will you take *Forty Years Below the Navel* or whatever it's called?

MAGGIE: (*Surveying him*) I must say you have certainly behaved with all of your accustomed grace and charm.

WHITESIDE: Look here, Puss—I am in no mood to discuss my behavior, good or bad.

MAGGIE: These people have done everything in their power to make you comfortable. And they happen, God knows why, to look upon you with a certain wonder and admiration.

WHITESIDE: If they had looked a little more carefully at their doorstep I would not be troubling them now. I did not wish to cross their cheerless threshold. I was hounded and badgered into it. I now find myself, after two weeks of racking pain, accused of behaving without charm. What would you have me do? Kiss them?

MAGGIE: (*Giving up*) Very well, Sherry. After ten years I should have known better than to try to do anything about your manners. But when I finally give up this job I may write a book about it all. *Cavalcade of Insult*, or *Through the Years with Prince Charming*.

WHITESIDE: Listen, Repulsive, you are tied to me with an umbilical cord made of piano wire. And now if we may dismiss the subject of my charm, for which, incidentally, I receive fifteen hundred dollars per appearance, possibly we can go to work . . . Oh, no, we can't. Yes?

(*This last is addressed to a wraith-like lady of uncertain years, who has more or less floated into the room. She is carrying a large spray of holly, and her whole manner suggests something not quite of this world*)

THE LADY: (*Her voice seems to float, too*) My name is Harriet Stanley. I know you are Sheridan Whiteside. I saw this holly, framed green against the pine trees. I remembered what you had written, about *Tess* and *Jude the Obscure*. It was the nicest present I could bring you. (*She places the holly in his lap, and drifts out of the room again*)

WHITESIDE: (*His eyes following her*) For God's sake, what was that?

MAGGIE: That was Mr. Stanley's sister, Harriet. I've talked to her a few times—she's quite strange.

WHITESIDE: Strange? She's right out of *The Hound of the Baskervilles.* . . . You know, I've seen that face before somewhere.

MAGGIE: Nonsense. You couldn't have.

WHITESIDE: (*Dismissing it*) Oh, well! Let's get down to work. (*He hands her the armful of holly*) Here! Press this in the doctor's book. (*He picks up the first of a pile of papers*) If young men keep asking me how to become dramatic critics— (*He tears up the letter and drops the pieces on the floor*)

MAGGIE: (*Who has picked up the little sheaf of messages from the table*) Here are some telegrams.

WHITESIDE: (*A letter in his hand*) What date is this?

MAGGIE: December tenth.

WHITESIDE: Send a wire to Columbia Broadcasting. "You can schedule my Christmas Eve broadcast from the New York studio, as I shall return East instead of proceeding to Hollywood. Stop. For special New Year's Eve broadcast will have as my guests Jascha Heifetz, Katharine Cornell, Schiaparelli, the Lunts, and Dr. Alexis Carrel, with Anthony Eden on short wave from England. Whiteside."

MAGGIE: Are you sure you'll be all right by Christmas, Sherry?

WHITESIDE: Of course I will. Send a cable to Sacha Guitry: "Will be in Paris June ninth. Dinner seven-thirty. White-side." . . . Wire to *Harper's Magazine*: "Do not worry, Stinky. Copy will arrive. Whiteside." . . . Send a cable to the Maharajah of Jehraput, Bombay: "Dear Boo-Boo: Schedule changed. Can you meet me Calcutta July twelfth? Dinner eight-thirty. Whiteside." . . . Arturo Toscanini. Where *is* he?

MAGGIE: I'll find him.

WHITESIDE: "Counting on you January 4th Metropolitan Opera House my annual benefit Home for Paroled Convicts. As you know this is a very worthy cause and close to my heart. Tibbett, Rethberg, Martinelli and Flagstad have promised me personally to appear. Will you have quiet supper with me and Ethel Barrymore afterwards? Whiteside."

(*The telephone rings*)

If that's for Mrs. Stanley tell them she's too drunk to talk.

MAGGIE: Hello . . . Hollywood?

WHITESIDE: If it's Goldwyn, hang up.

MAGGIE: Hello . . . Banjo! (*Her face lights up*)

WHITESIDE: Banjo! Give me that phone!

MAGGIE: Banjo, you old so-and-so! How are you, darling?

WHITESIDE: Come on—give me that!

MAGGIE: Shut up, Sherry! . . . Are you coming East, Banjo? I miss you . . . No, we're not going to Hollywood . . . Oh, he's going to live.

WHITESIDE: Stop driveling and give me the phone.

MAGGIE: In fact, he's screaming at me now. Here he is.

WHITESIDE: (*Taking the phone*) How are you, you fawn's behind? And what are you giving me for Christmas? (*He roars with laughter at Banjo's answer*) What news, Banjo, my boy? How's the picture coming? . . . How are Wacko and Sloppo? . . . No, no, I'm all right. . . . Yes, I'm in very good hands. Dr. Crippen is taking care of me. . . . What

about you? Having any fun? . . . Playing any cribbage? . . .
What? (*Again he laughs loudly*) . . . Well, don't take all his
money—leave a little bit for me . . . You're what? . . .
Having your portrait painted? By whom? Milt Gross? . . .
No, I'm going back to New York from here. I'll be there for
twelve days, and then I go to Dartmouth for the Drama Fes-
tival. You wouldn't understand . . . Well, I can't waste my
time talking to Hollywood riffraff. Kiss Louella Parsons for
me. Good-bye. (*He hangs up and turns to Maggie*) He took
fourteen hundred dollars from Sam Goldwyn at cribbage
last night, and Sam said, "Banjo, I will never play garbage
with you again."

MAGGIE: What's all this about his having his portrait painted?

WHITESIDE: Mm. Salvador Dali. That's all that face of his
needs—a surrealist to paint it. . . . Now what do *you* want,
Miss Bed Pan?

> (*This is addressed to the Nurse, who has returned somewhat
> apprehensively to the room*)

MISS PREEN: It's—it's your pills. One every—forty-five minutes. (*She drops them into his lap and hurries out of the room*)

WHITESIDE: Now where were we?

MAGGIE: (*The messages in her hand*) Here's a cable from that
dear friend of yours, Lorraine Sheldon.

WHITESIDE: Let me see it.

MAGGIE: (*Reading the message in a tone that gives Miss Sheldon
none the better of it*) "Sherry, my poor sweet lamb, have been
in Scotland on a shooting party with Lord and Lady Cunard
and only just heard of your poor hip." (*Maggie gives a faint
raspberry, then reads on*) "Am down here in Surrey with
Lord Bottomley. Sailing Wednesday on the *Normandie* and
cannot wait to see my poor sweet Sherry. Your blossom girl,
Lorraine." . . . In the words of the master, I may vomit.

WHITESIDE: Don't be bitter, Puss, just because Lorraine is
more beautiful than you are.

MAGGIE: Lorraine Sheldon is a very fair example of that small
but vicious circle you move in.

WHITESIDE: Pure sex jealousy if ever I saw it . . . Give me the
rest of those.

MAGGIE: (*Mumbling to herself*) Lorraine Sheldon . . . Lord
Bottomley . . . My Aunt Fanny.

WHITESIDE: (*Who has opened the next message*) Ah! It's from Destiny's Tot.

MAGGIE: (*Peering over his shoulder*) England's little Rover Boy?

WHITESIDE: Um-hm. (*He reads*) "Treacle Face, what is this I hear about a hip fractured in some bordello brawl? Does this mean our Hollywood Christmas party is off? Finished the new play in Pago-Pago and it's superb. Myself and a ukulele leave Honolulu tomorrow, in that order. By the way, the Sultan of Zanzibar wants to meet Ginger Rogers. Let's face it. Oscar Wilde."

MAGGIE: He does travel, doesn't he? You know, it'd be nice if the world went around Beverly Carlton for a change.

WHITESIDE: Hollywood next week—why couldn't he stop over on his way to New York? Send him a cable: "Beverly Carlton, Royal Hawaiian Hotel, Honolulu—"

(*The door bell rings. Mr. Whiteside is properly annoyed*)

If these people intend to have their friends using the front door—

MAGGIE: What do you want them to use—a rope ladder?

WHITESIDE: I will not have a lot of mildewed pus-bags rushing in and out of this house—

(*He stops as the voice of John is heard at the front door. "Oh, good morning, Mr. Jefferson." The answering voice of Mr. Jefferson is not quite audible*)

WHITESIDE: (*Roaring*) There's nobody home! The Stanleys have been arrested for counterfeiting! Go away!

(*But the visitor, meanwhile, has already appeared in the archway. Mr. Jefferson is an interesting-looking young man in his early thirties*)

JEFFERSON: Good morning, Mr. Whiteside. I'm Jefferson, of the Mesalia *Journal*.

WHITESIDE: (*Sotto voce, to Maggie*) Get rid of him.

MAGGIE: (*Brusquely*) I'm sorry—Mr. Whiteside is seeing no one.

JEFFERSON: Really?

MAGGIE: So will you please excuse us? Good day.

JEFFERSON: (*Not giving up*) Mr. Whiteside seems to be sitting up and taking notice.

MAGGIE: I'm afraid he isn't taking notice of the Mesalia *Journal*. Do you mind?

JEFFERSON: You know, if I'm going to be insulted I'd like it to be by Mr. Whiteside himself. I never did like road companies.

WHITESIDE: (*Looking around, interested*) Mm. Touché if I ever heard one. And in Mesalia too, Maggie dear.

MAGGIE: (*Still on the job*) Will you please leave?

JEFFERSON: (*Ignoring her*) How about an interview, Mr. Whiteside?

WHITESIDE: I never give them. Go away.

JEFFERSON: Mr. Whiteside, if I don't get this interview, I lose my job.

WHITESIDE: That would be quite all right with me.

JEFFERSON: Now you don't mean that, Mr. Whiteside. You used to be a newspaper man yourself. You know what editors are like. Well, mine's the toughest one that ever lived.

WHITESIDE: You won't get around me that way. If you don't like him, get off the paper.

JEFFERSON: Yes, but I happen to think it's a good paper. William Allen White could have got out of Emporia, but he didn't.

WHITESIDE: You have the effrontery, in my presence, to compare yourself with William Allen White?

JEFFERSON: Only in the sense that William Allen White stayed in Emporia, and I want to stay here and say what I want to say.

WHITESIDE: Such as what?

JEFFERSON: Well, I can't put it into words, Mr. Whiteside— it'd sound like an awful lot of hooey. But the *Journal* was my father's paper. It's kind of a sentimental point with me, the paper. I'd like to carry on where he left off.

WHITESIDE: Ah—just a minute. Then this terrifying editor, this dread journalistic Apocalypse is—you?

JEFFERSON: Ah—yes, in a word.

(*Whiteside chuckles with appreciation*)

MAGGIE: (*Annoyed*) In the future, Sherry, I wish you would let me know when you don't want to talk to people. I'll usher them right in. (*She goes into the library*)

WHITESIDE: Young man, that kind of journalistic trick went out with Richard Harding Davis . . . Come over here. I suppose you've written that novel?

JEFFERSON: No, I've written that play.

WHITESIDE: Well, I don't want to read it. But you can send me your paper—I'll take a year's subscription. Do you write the editorials, too?

JEFFERSON: Every one of them.

WHITESIDE: I know just what they're like. Ah, me! I'm afraid you're that noble young newspaper man—crusading, idealistic, dull. (*He looks him up and down*) Very good casting, too.

JEFFERSON: You're not bad casting yourself, Mr. Whiteside.

WHITESIDE: We won't discuss it. . . . Do these old eyes see a box of goodies over there? Hand them to me on your way out.

JEFFERSON: (*As he passes over the candy*) The trouble is, Mr. Whiteside, that your being in this town comes under the heading of news. Practically the biggest news since the Armistice.

WHITESIDE: (*Examining the candy*) Mm. Pecan butternut fudge.

(*Miss Preen, on her way to the kitchen from the library, stops short as she sees Mr. Whiteside with a piece of candy in his hand*)

MISS PREEN: Oh, my! You mustn't eat candy, Mr. Whiteside. It's very bad for you.

WHITESIDE: (*Turning*) My great-aunt Jennifer ate a whole box of candy every day of her life. She lived to be a hundred and two, and when she had been dead three days she looked better than you do now. (*He swings blandly back to his visitor*) What were you saying, old fellow?

JEFFERSON: (*As Miss Preen makes a hasty exist*) I can at least report to my readers that chivalry is not yet dead.

WHITESIDE: We won't discuss it. . . . Well, now that you have won me with your pretty ways, what do you want?

JEFFERSON: Well, how about a brief talk on famous murders? You're an authority on murder as a fine art.

WHITESIDE: My dear boy, when I talk about murder I get paid for it. I have made more money out of the Snyder-Gray case than the lawyers did. So don't expect to get it for nothing.

JEFFERSON: Well, then, what do you think of Mesalia, how long are you going to be here, where are you going, things like that?

WHITESIDE: Very well. (a) Mesalia is a town of irresistible charm, (b) I cannot wait to get out of it, and (c) I am going from here to Crockfield, for my semi-annual visit to the Crockfield Home for Paroled Convicts, for which I have raised over half a million dollars in the last five years. From there I go to New York. . . . Have you ever been to Crockfield, Jefferson?

JEFFERSON: No, I haven't. I always meant to.

WHITESIDE: As a newspaper man you ought to go, instead of wasting your time with me. It's only about seventy-five miles from here. Did you ever hear how Crockfield started?

JEFFERSON: No, I didn't.

WHITESIDE: Ah! Sit down, Jefferson. It is one of the most endearing and touching stories of our generation. One misty St. Valentine's Eve—the year was 1901—a little old lady who had given her name to an era, Victoria, lay dying in Windsor Castle. Maude Adams had not yet caused every young heart to swell as she tripped across the stage as Peter Pan; Irving Berlin had not yet written the first note of a ragtime rigadoon that was to set the nation's feet a-tapping, and Elias P. Crockfield was just emerging from the State penitentiary. Destitute, embittered, cruel of heart, he wandered, on this St. Valentine's Eve, into a little church. But there was no godliness in his heart that night, no prayer upon his lips. In the faltering twilight, Elias P. Crockfield made his way toward the poor box. With callous fingers he ripped open this poignant testimony of a simple people's faith. Greedily he clutched at the few pitiful coins within. And then a child's wavering treble broke the twilight stillness. "Please, Mr. Man," said a little girl's voice, "won't you be my Valentine?" Elias P. Crockfield turned. There stood before him a bewitching little creature of five, her yellow curls cascading over her shoulders like a golden Niagara, in her tiny outstretched hand a humble valentine. In that one crystal moment a sealed door opened in the heart of Elias P. Crockfield, and in his mind was born an idea. Twenty-five years later three thousand ruddy-cheeked convicts were gamboling on the broad lawns of Crockfield Home, frolicking in the cool depths of its swimming pool, broadcasting with their own symphony orchestra from their own radio station. Elias P. Crockfield has long since gone to his Maker, but the little girl of the golden curls, now grown to lovely womanhood, is known as the Angel of Crockfield, for she is the wife of the warden, and in the main hall of Crockfield, between a Rembrandt and an El Greco, there hangs, in a simple little frame, a humble valentine.

MAGGIE: (*Who has emerged from the library in time to hear the finish of this*) And in the men's washroom, every Christmas Eve, the ghost of Elias P. Crockfield appears in one of the booths . . . Will you sign these, please?

(*The door bell is heard*)

WHITESIDE: This aging ingénue, Mr. Jefferson, I retain in my employ only because she is the sole support of her two-headed brother.

JEFFERSON: I understand. . . . Well, thank you very much, Mr. Whiteside—you've been very kind. By the way, I'm a cribbage player, if you need one while you're here.

WHITESIDE: Fine. How much can you afford to lose?

JEFFERSON: I usually win.

WHITESIDE: We won't discuss that. Come back at eight-thirty. We'll play three-handed with Elsie Dinsmore . . . Metz!

(*John, who has answered the door bell, has ushered in a strange-looking little man in his fifties. His hair runs all over his head and his clothes are too big for him*)

WHITESIDE: Metz, you incredible beetle-hound! What are you doing here?

METZ: (*With a mild Teutonic accent*) I explain, Sherry. First I kiss my little Maggie.

MAGGIE: (*Embracing him*) Metz darling, what a wonderful surprise!

WHITESIDE: The enchanted Metz! Why aren't you at the university? . . . Jefferson, you are standing in the presence of one of the great men of our time. When you write that inevitable autobiography, be sure to record the day that you met Professor Adolph Metz, the world's greatest authority on insect life. Metz, stop looking at me adoringly and tell me why you're here.

METZ: You are sick, Sherry, so I come to cheer you.

MAGGIE: Metz, you tore yourself away from your little insects and came here? Sherry, you don't deserve it.

WHITESIDE: How are all your little darlings, Metz? Jefferson, would you believe that eight volumes could be written on the mating instinct of the female white ant? He did it.

METZ: Seven on the female, Sherry. One on the male.

WHITESIDE: Lived for two years in a cave with nothing but plant lice. He rates three pages in the *Encyclopedia Britannica*. Don't you, my little hookworm?

METZ: Please, Sherry, you embarrass me. Look—I have brought you a present to while away the hours.

(*He motions to John, who comes forward bearing a great box, wrapped in brown paper. He unwraps it as he speaks*)

METZ: I said to my students: "Boys and girls, I want to give a present to my sick friend, Sheridan Whiteside." So you know what we did? We made for you a community of *Periplaneta Americana*, commonly known as the American cockroach. Behold, Sherry! (*He strips off the paper*) Roach City! Inside here are ten thousand cockroaches.

JOHN: Ten thousand— (*Heading for the kitchen in great excitement*) Sarah! Sarah!

METZ: Here in Roach City they play, they make love, they mate, they die. See—here is the graveyard. They even bury their own dead.

MAGGIE: I'm glad of that, or I'd have to do it.

WHITESIDE: (*Glaring at her*) Ssh!

METZ: You can watch them, Sherry, while they live out their whole lives. It is fascinating. Look! Here is where they store their grain, here is the commissary of the aristocracy, here is the maternity hospital.

WHITESIDE: Magnificent! This is my next piece for the London *Mercury*.

METZ: With these ear-phones, Sherry, you listen to the mating calls. There are microphones down inside. Listen! (*He puts the ear-phones over Whiteside's head*)

WHITESIDE: (*Listening, rapt*) Mm. How long has this been going on?

(*Mrs. Stanley starts timorously to descend the stairs. She tiptoes as far as the landing, then pauses as she sees the group below*)

(*Meanwhile Prof. Metz, his mind ever on his work, has moved in the direction of the dining room*)

METZ: (*Suddenly his face lights up*) Aha! *Periplaneta Americana!* There are cockroaches in this house!

MRS. STANLEY: (*Shocked into speech*) I beg your pardon!

(*The doorbell rings*)

Mr. Whiteside, I don't know who this man is, but I will not stand here and—

WHITESIDE: Then go upstairs. These are probably my luncheon guests. Metz, you're staying for the day, of course? Jefferson, stay for lunch? Maggie, tell 'em there'll be two more. Ah, come right in, Baker. Good morning, gentlemen.

(*The gentlemen addressed are three in number—two white, one black. They are convicts, and they look the part. Prison gray, handcuffed together. Baker, in uniform, is a prison guard. He carries a rifle*)

Jefferson, here are the fruits of that humble valentine. These men, now serving the final months of their prison terms, have chosen to enter the ivy-covered walls of Crockfield. They have come here today to learn from me a little of its tradition . . . Gentlemen, I envy you your great adventure.

JOHN: (*In the dining-room doorway*) Lunch is ready, Mr. Whiteside.

WHITESIDE: Good! Let's go right in. (*To one of the convicts, as they pass*) You're Michaelson, aren't you? Butcher-shop murders?

MICHAELSON: Yes, sir.

WHITESIDE: Thought I recognized you. . . . After you, Baker. . . . The other fellow, Jefferson— (*He lowers his tone*) —is Henderson, the hatchet fiend. Always did it in a bathtub— remember? (*His voice rises as he wheels himself into the dining room*) We're having chicken livers Tetrazzini, and Cherries Jubilee for dessert. I hope every little tummy is a-flutter with gastric juices. Serve the white wine with the fish, John, and close the doors. I don't want a lot of people prying on their betters.

(*The doors close. Only Mrs. Stanley is left outside. She collapses quietly into a chair*)

THE CURTAIN FALLS

Scene II

Late afternoon, a week later. Only a single lamp is lit.

The room, in the week that has passed, has taken on something of the character of its occupant. Books and papers everywhere. Stacks of books on the tables, some of them just half out of their cardboard boxes. Half a dozen or so volumes, which apparently have not appealed to the Master, have been thrown onto the floor. A litter of crumpled papers around the Whiteside wheelchair; an empty candy box has slid off his lap. An old pair of pants have been tossed over one chair, a seedy bathrobe over another. A handsome Chinese vase has been moved out of its accustomed spot and is doing duty as an ash receiver.

Mr. Whiteside is in his wheelchair, asleep. Roach City is on a stand beside him, the ear-phones, over his head. He has apparently dozed off while listening to the mating calls of Periplaneta Americana.

For a moment only his rhythmic breathing is heard. Then Miss Preen enters from the library. She brings some medicine—a glass filled with a murky mixture. She pauses when she sees that he is asleep, then, after a good deal of hesitation, gently touches him on the shoulder. He stirs a little; she musters up her courage and touches him again.

WHITESIDE: (*Slowly opening his eyes*) I was dreaming of Lillian Russell, and I awake to find you.

MISS PREEN: Your—your medicine, Mr. Whiteside.

WHITESIDE: (*Taking the glass*) What time is it?

MISS PREEN: About half-past six.

WHITESIDE: Where is Miss Cutler?

MISS PREEN: She went out.

WHITESIDE: Out?

MISS PREEN: With Mr. Jefferson. (*She goes into the library*)
    (*John, meanwhile, has entered from the dining room*)

JOHN: All right if I turn the lights up, Mr. Whiteside?

WHITESIDE: Yes. Go right ahead, John.

JOHN: And Sarah has something for you, Mr. Whiteside. Made it special.

WHITESIDE: She has? Where is she? My Soufflé Queen!

SARAH: (*Proudly entering with a tray on which reposes her latest delicacy*) Here I am, Mr. Whiteside.

WHITESIDE: She walks in beauty like the night, and in those deft hands there is the art of Michelangelo. Let me taste the new creation. (*With one hand he pours the medicine into the Chinese vase, then swallows at a gulp one of Sarah's not so little cakes. An ecstatic expression comes over his face*) Poetry! Sheer poetry!

SARAH: (*Beaming*) I put a touch of absinthe in the dough. Do you like it?

WHITESIDE: (*Rapturously*) Ambrosia!

SARAH: And I got you your terrapin Maryland for dinner.

WHITESIDE: I have known but three great cooks in my time. The Khedive of Egypt had one, my great-aunt Jennifer another, and the third, Sarah, is you.

SARAH: Oh, Mr. Whiteside!

WHITESIDE: (*Lowering his voice*) How would you like to come to New York and work for me? You and John.

SARAH: Why, Mr. Whiteside!

JOHN: Sarah! . . . It would be wonderful, Mr. Whiteside, but what would we say to Mr. and Mrs. Stanley?

WHITESIDE: Just "good-bye."

SARAH: But—but they'd be awfully mad, wouldn't they? They've been very kind to us.

WHITESIDE: (*Lightly*) Well, if they ever come to New York we can have them for dinner, if I'm not in town. Now run along and think it over. This is our little secret—just between us. And put plenty of sherry in that terrapin . . . Miss Preen!

(*Sarah and John withdraw in considerable excitement*)

WHITESIDE: (*Raises his voice to a roar*) Miss Preen!

MISS PREEN: (*Appearing, breathless*) Yes? Yes?

WHITESIDE: What have you *got* in there, anyway? A sailor?

MISS PREEN: I was—just washing my hands.

WHITESIDE: What time did Miss Cutler go out?

MISS PREEN: A couple of hours ago.

WHITESIDE: Mr. Jefferson called for her?

MISS PREEN: Yes, sir.

WHITESIDE: (*Impatiently*) All right, all right. Go back to your sex life.

(*Miss Preen goes. Whiteside tries to settle down to his book, but his mind is plainly troubled. He shifts a little, looks anxiously toward the outer door*)

(*Harriet Stanley comes softly down the steps. She seems delighted to find Mr. Whiteside alone*)

HARRIET: (*Opening an album that she has brought with her*) Dear Mr. Whiteside, may I show you a few mementoes of the past? I somehow feel that you would love them as I do.

WHITESIDE: I'd be delighted. (*Observing her*) Miss Stanley, haven't we met somewhere before?

HARRIET: Oh, no. I would have remembered. It would have been one of my cherished memories—like these. (*She spreads the portfolio before him*) Look! Here I am with my first sweetheart, under our lovely beechwood tree. I was eight and he was ten. I have never forgotten him. What happy times we had! What— (*She stops short as she hears footsteps on the stairway*) There's someone coming! I'll come back! . . . (*She gathers up her album and vanishes into the dining room*)

(*Whiteside looks after her, puzzled*)

(*It is Mr. Stanley who comes down the stairs. He is carrying a slip of paper in his hand, and he is obviously at the boiling point*)

(*A few steps behind comes Mrs. Stanley, apprehensive and nervous*)

MRS. STANLEY: Now, Ernest, please—

STANLEY: Be quiet, Daisy. . . . Mr. Whiteside, I want to talk to you. I don't care whether you're busy or not. I have stood all that I'm going to stand.

WHITESIDE: Indeed?

STANLEY: This is the last straw. I have just received a bill from the telephone company for seven hundred and eighty-four dollars. (*He reads from the slip in his hand*) Oklahoma City, Calcutta, Hollywood, Paris, Brussels, Rome, New York, New York, New York, New York, New York, New York— (*His voice trails off in an endless succession of New Yorks*) Now I realize, Mr. Whiteside, that you are a distinguished man of letters—

MRS. STANLEY: Yes, of course. We both do.

STANLEY: Please . . . But in the past week we have not been

able to call our souls our own. We have not had a meal in the dining room *once*. I have to tiptoe out of the house in the mornings.

MRS. STANLEY: Now, Ernest—

STANLEY: (*Waving her away*) I come home to find convicts sitting at my dinner table—butcher-shop murderers. A man putting cockroaches in the kitchen.

MRS. STANLEY: They just escaped, Ernest.

STANLEY: That's not the point. I don't like coming home to find twenty-two Chinese students using my bathroom. I tell you I won't stand for it, no matter *who* you are.

WHITESIDE: Have you quite finished?

STANLEY: No, I have not. I go down into the cellar this morning and trip over that octopus that William Beebe sent you. I tell you I won't stand it. Mr. Whiteside, I want you to leave this house as soon as you can and go to a hotel. . . . Stop pawing me, Daisy. . . . That's all I've got to say, Mr. Whiteside.

WHITESIDE: And quite enough, I should say. May I remind you again, Mr. Stanley, that I am not a willing guest in this house? I am informed by my doctor that I must remain quiet for another ten days, at which time I shall get out of here so fast that the wind will knock you over, I hope. If, however, you insist on my leaving before that, thereby causing me to suffer a relapse, I shall sue you for every additional day that I am held inactive, which will amount, I assure you, to a tidy sum.

STANLEY: (*To his wife*) This is outrageous. Do we have to—

WHITESIDE: As for the details of your petty complaints, those twenty-two Chinese students came straight from the White House, where I assure you they used the bathroom too.

MRS. STANLEY: Mr. Whiteside, my husband didn't mean—

STANLEY: Yes, I did. I meant every word of it.

WHITESIDE: There is only one point that you make in which I see some slight justice. I do not expect you to pay for my telephone calls, and I shall see to it that restitution is made. Can you provide me with the exact amount?

STANLEY: I certainly can, and I certainly will.

WHITESIDE: Good. I shall instruct my lawyers to deduct it from the hundred and fifty thousand dollars that I am suing you for.

(*Mr. Stanley starts to speak, but simply chokes with rage. Furious, he storms up the steps again, Mrs. Stanley following*)

WHITESIDE: (*Calling after him*) And I'll thank you not to trip over that octopus, which is very sensitive.

(*Left alone, Mr. Whiteside enjoys his triumph for a moment, then his mind jumps to more important matters. He looks at his watch, considers a second, then wheels himself over to the telephone*)

WHITESIDE: Give me the Mesalia *Journal*, please. (*He peers at Roach City while waiting*) Hello, *Journal*? . . . Is Mr. Jefferson there? . . . When do you expect him? . . . No. No message. (*He hangs up, drums impatiently on the arm of his chair*)

(*Then he turns sharply at the sound of the outer door opening. But it is the younger Stanleys, Richard and June, who enter. They are in winter togs, with ice skates under their arms. In addition, Richard has a camera slung over his shoulder*)

(*Their attitudes change as they see that Whiteside is in the room. They slide toward the stairs, obviously trying to be as unobtrusive as possible*)

WHITESIDE: Come here, you two. . . . Come on, come on. I'm not going to bite you. . . . Now look here. I am by nature a gracious and charming person. If I err at all it is on the side of kindness and amiability. I have been observing you two for this past week, and you seem to me to be extremely likeable young people. I am afraid that when we first met I was definitely unpleasant to you. For that I am sorry, and I wish that in the future you would not treat me like something out of Edgar Allan Poe. How do you like my new tie?

JUNE: Thank you, Mr. Whiteside. This makes things much pleasanter. And I think the tie is very pretty.

RICHARD: Well, now that we're on speaking terms, Mr. Whiteside, I don't mind telling you that I have been admiring all your ties.

WHITESIDE: Do you like this one?

RICHARD: I certainly do.

WHITESIDE: It's yours. (*He takes it off and tosses it to him*) Really, this curious legend that I am a difficult person is pure fabrication. . . . Ice-skating, eh? Ah, me! I used to cut figure eights myself, arm in arm with Betsy Ross, waving the flag behind us.

JUNE: It was wonderful on the ice today. Miss Cutler and Mr. Jefferson were there.

WHITESIDE: Maggie? Skating?

RICHARD: Yes, and she's good, too. I got a marvelous picture of her.

WHITESIDE: Were they still there when you left?

RICHARD: I think so. Say, Mr. Whiteside, mind if I take a picture of you? I'd love to have one.

WHITESIDE: Very well. Do you want my profile? (*He indicates his stomach*)

JUNE: (*Starting up the stairs*) I'm afraid you're done for, Mr. Whiteside. My brother is a camera fiend.

RICHARD: (*Clicking his camera*) Thank you, Mr. Whiteside. I got a great one.

(*He and June go up the stairs as Maggie enters from the hallway. They call a "Hello, Miss Cutler!" as they disappear"*)

MAGGIE: Hello, there. . . . Good evening, Sherry. Really Sherry, you've got this room looking like an old parrot-cage. . . . Did you nap while I was out?

(*Whiteside merely glowers at her*)

What's the matter, dear? Cat run away with your tongue? (*She is on her knees, gathering up debris*)

WHITESIDE: (*Furious*) Don't look up at me with those great cow-eyes, you sex-ridden hag. Where have you been all afternoon? Alley-catting around with Bert Jefferson.

MAGGIE: (*Her face aglow*) Sherry—Bert read his play to me this afternoon. It's superb. It isn't just that play written by a newspaper man. It's superb. I want you to read it *tonight*. (*She puts it in his lap*) It just cries out for Cornell. If you like it, will you send it to her, Sherry? And will you read it tonight?

WHITESIDE: No, I will not read it tonight or any other time. And while we're on the subject of Mr. Jefferson, you might ask him if he wouldn't like to pay your salary, since he takes up all your time.

MAGGIE: Oh, come now, Sherry. It isn't as bad as that.

WHITESIDE: I have not even been able to reach you, not knowing what haylofts you frequent.

MAGGIE: Oh, stop behaving like a spoiled child, Sherry.

WHITESIDE: Don't take that patronizing tone with me, you flea-bitten Cleopatra. I am sick and tired of your sneaking out like some lovesick high-school girl every time my back is turned.

MAGGIE: Well, Sherry— (*She pulls together the library doors and faces Whiteside*) —I'm afraid you've hit the nail on the head. (*With a little flourish, she removes her hat*)

WHITESIDE: Stop acting like Zasu Pitts and explain yourself.

MAGGIE: I'll make it quick, Sherry. I'm in love.

WHITESIDE: Nonsense. This is merely delayed puberty.

MAGGIE: No, Sherry, I'm afraid this is it. You're going to lose a very excellent secretary.

WHITESIDE: You are out of your mind.

MAGGIE: Yes, I think I am, a little. But I'm a girl who's waited a long time for this to happen, and now it has. Mr. Jefferson doesn't know it yet, but I'm going to try my darnedest to marry him.

WHITESIDE: (*As she pauses*) Is that all?

MAGGIE: Yes, except that—well—I suppose this is what might be called my resignation—as soon as you've got someone else.

WHITESIDE: (*There is a slight pause*) Now listen to me, Maggie. We have been together for a long time. You are indispensable to me, but I think I am unselfish enough not to let that stand in the way where your happiness is concerned. Because, whether you know it or not, I have a deep affection for you.

MAGGIE: I know that, Sherry.

WHITESIDE: That being the case, I will not stand by and allow you to make a fool of yourself.

MAGGIE: I'm not, Sherry.

WHITESIDE: You are, my dear. You are behaving like a Booth Tarkington heroine. It's—it's incredible. I cannot believe that a girl who for the past ten years has had the great of the world served up on a platter before her—I cannot believe that it is anything but a kind of temporary insanity when you are swept off your feet in seven days by a second-rate, small-town newspaper man.

MAGGIE: Sherry, I can't explain what's happened. I can only tell you that it's so. It's hard for me to believe too, Sherry. Here I am, a hard-bitten old cynic, behaving like *True Story Magazine,* and liking it. Discovering the moon, and ice-skating—I keep laughing to myself all the time, but there it is. What can I do about it, Sherry? I'm in love.

WHITESIDE: (*With sudden decision*) We're leaving here tomorrow. Hip or no hip, we're leaving here tomorrow. I don't care if I fracture the other one. Get me a train schedule and start packing. *I'*ll pull you out of this, Miss Stardust. *I'*ll get the ants out of those moonlit pants.

MAGGIE: It's no good, Sherry. I'd be back on the next streamlined train.

WHITESIDE: It's completely unbelievable. Can you see yourself, the wife of the editor of the Mesalia *Journal,* having an evening at home for Mr. and Mrs. Stanley, Mr. and Mrs. Poop-Face, and the members of the Book-of-the-Month Club?

MAGGIE: Sherry, I've had ten years of the great figures of our time, and don't think I'm not grateful to you for it. I've loved every minute of it. They've been wonderful years, Sherry. Gay and stimulating—why, I don't think anyone has ever had the fun we've had. But a girl can't laugh all the time, Sherry. There comes a time when she wants—Bert Jefferson. You don't know Bert, Sherry. He's gentle, and he's unassuming, and—well, I love him, that's all.

WHITESIDE: I see. Well, I remain completely unconvinced. You are drugging yourself into this Joan Crawford fantasy, and before you become completely anesthetized I shall do everything in my power to bring you to your senses.

MAGGIE: (*Wheeling on him*) Now listen to me, Whiteside. I know you. Lay off. I know what a devil you can be. I've seen you do it to other people, but don't you dare to do it to me. Don't drug *yourself* into the idea that all you're thinking of is my happiness. You're thinking of yourself a little bit, too, and all those months of breaking in somebody new. I've seen you in a passion before when your life has been disrupted, and you couldn't dine in Calcutta on July twelfth

with Boo-Boo. Well, that's too bad, but there it is. I'm
going to marry Bert if he'll have me, and don't you dare try
any of your tricks. I'm on to every one of them. So lay off.
That's my message to *you*, Big Lord Fauntleroy. (*And she is
up the stairs*)

> (*Left stewing in his own juice, Mr. Whiteside is in a perfect
> fury. He bangs the arm of his chair, then slaps at the manu-
> script in his lap. As he does so, the dawn of an idea comes
> into his mind. He sits perfectly still for a moment, thinking
> it over. Then, with a slow smile, he takes the manuscript out
> of its envelope.*
>
> *He looks at the title page, ruffles through the script, then
> stops and thinks again. His face breaks out into one great
> smile. Then he quickly wheels himself over to the table and
> hunts hurriedly through a pile of old cablegrams and letters,
> until he finds the one he wants. With this in his hand, he
> takes up the telephone receiver*)

WHITESIDE: (*In a lowered voice*) Long distance, please. I want
to put in a trans-Atlantic call. (*He looks at the cablegram
again for confirmation*) Hello. Trans-Atlantic operator? . . .
This is Mesalia one four two. I want to talk to Miss Lorraine
Sheldon—S-h-e-l-d-o-n. She's on the *Normandie*. It sailed
from Southampton day before yesterday. . . . Will it take
long? . . . All right. My name is Whiteside. . . . Thank
you.

> (*He hangs up as the door bell rings. He goes back to the
> manuscript again and looks through it. John then ushers in
> Dr. Bradley*)

DR. BRADLEY: (*Hearty, as usual*) Well, well! Good evening,
Mr. Whiteside!

WHITESIDE: Come back tomorrow—I'm busy.

DR. BRADLEY: (*Turning cute*) Now what would be the best
news that I could possibly bring you?

WHITESIDE: You have hydrophobia.

DR. BRADLEY: (*Laughing it off*) No, no. . . . Mr. Whiteside,
you are a well man. You can get up and walk *now*. You can
leave here tomorrow.

WHITESIDE: What do you mean?

DR. BRADLEY: Well, sir! I looked at those X-rays again this
morning, and do you know what? I have been looking at

the wrong X-rays. I had been looking at old Mrs. Moffat's X-rays. You are perfectly, absolutely well!

WHITESIDE: Lower your voice, will you?

DR. BRADLEY: What's the matter? Aren't you pleased?

WHITESIDE: Delighted. . . . Naturally. . . . Ah—this is a very unexpected bit of news, however. It comes at a very curious moment. (*He is thinking fast; suddenly he gets an idea. He clears his throat and looks around apprehensively*) Dr. Bradley, I—ah—I have some good news for you, too. I have been reading your book—ah—*Forty Years*— what is it?

DR. BRADLEY: (*Eagerly*) *An Ohio Doctor*—yes?

WHITESIDE: I consider it extremely close to being one of the great literary contributions of our time.

DR. BRADLEY: Mr. Whiteside!

WHITESIDE: So strongly do I feel about it, Dr. Bradley, that I have a proposition to make to you. Just here and there the book is a little uneven, a little rough. What I would like to do is to stay here in Mesalia and work with you on it.

DR. BRADLEY: (*All choked up*) Mr. Whiteside, I would be so terribly honored—

WHITESIDE: Yes. But there is just one difficulty. You see, if my lecture bureau and my radio sponsors were to learn that I am well, they would insist on my fulfilling my contracts, and I would be forced to leave Mesalia. Therefore, we must not tell anyone—not anyone at all—that I am well.

DR. BRADLEY: I see. I see.

WHITESIDE: Not even Miss Cutler, you understand.

DR. BRADLEY: No, I won't. Not a soul. Not even my wife.

WHITESIDE: That's fine.

DR. BRADLEY: When do we start work—tonight? I've got just one patient that's dying and then I'll be perfectly free.

(*The phone rings*)

WHITESIDE: (*Waving him away*) Ah—tomorrow morning. This is a private call—would you forgive me? . . . Hello. . . . Yes, I'm on. (*He turns again to the Doctor*) Tomorrow morning.

DR. BRADLEY: Tomorrow morning it is. Good night. You've made me very proud, Mr. Whiteside. (*He goes*)

WHITESIDE: (*Again on the phone*) Yes, yes, this is Mr. White-side on the phone. Put them through. . . . Hello. Is this my Blossom Girl? How are you, my lovely? . . . No, no, I'm all right. . . . Yes, still out here. . . . Lorraine dear, when do you land in New York? . . . Tuesday? That's fine. . . . Now listen closely, my pet. I've great news for you. I've discovered a wonderful play with an enchanting part in it for you. Cornell would give her eye teeth to play it, but I think I can get it for you. . . . Now wait, wait. Let me tell you. The author is a young newspaper man in this town. Of course he wants Cornell, but if you jump on a train and get right out here, I think you could swing it, if you play your cards right. . . . No, he's young, and very attractive, and just your dish, my dear. It just takes a little doing, and you're the girl that can do it. Isn't that exciting, my pet? . . . Yes. . . . Yes, that's right. . . . And look. Don't send me any messages. Just get on a train and arrive. . . . Oh, no, don't thank me, my darling. It's perfectly all right. Have a nice trip and hurry out here. Good-bye, my blossom. (*He hangs up and looks guiltily around. Then he straightens up and gleefully rubs his hands together*)

(*Miss Preen enters, medicine in hand, and frightened, as usual*)

WHITESIDE: (*Jovial as hell*) Hello, Miss Preen. My, you're looking radiant this evening.

MISS PREEN: (*Staggered*) What?

WHITESIDE: Nothing. Nothing at all. Just said you are ravishing.

(*He takes the medicine from her and swallows it at one gulp. Miss Preen, still staggered, retreats into the library, just as Maggie comes down the stairs. She is dressed for the street*)

MAGGIE: (*Pausing on the landing*) Sherry, I'm sorry for what I said before. I'm afraid I was a little unjust.

WHITESIDE: (*All nobility*) That's all right, Maggie dear. We all lose our tempers now and then.

MAGGIE: I promised to have dinner with Bert and go to a movie, but we'll come back and play cribbage with you instead.

WHITESIDE: Fine.

MAGGIE: See you soon, Sherry dear. (*She kisses him lightly on the forehead and goes on her way*)

(*Whiteside looks after her until he hears the doors close. Then*

his face lights up again and he bursts happily into song as he
wheels himself into the library)

WHITESIDE:
> "I'se des a 'ittle wabbit in the sunshine,
> I'se des a 'ittle wabbit in the wain—"

CURTAIN

ACT TWO

A week later, late afternoon.

The room is now dominated by a large Christmas tree, set in the curve of the staircase, and hung with the customary Christmas ornaments.

Sarah and John are passing in and out of the library, bringing forth huge packages which they are placing under the tree. Maggie sits at a little table at one side, going through a pile of correspondence.

JOHN: Well, I guess that's all there are, Miss Cutler. They're all under the tree.

MAGGIE: Thank you, John.

SARAH: My, I never saw anyone get so many Christmas presents. I can hardly wait to see what's in 'em.

JOHN: When'll Mr. Whiteside open them, Miss Cutler?

MAGGIE: Well, John, you see Christmas is Mr. Whiteside's personal property. He invented it and it belongs to him. First thing tomorrow morning, Mr. Whiteside will open each and every present, and there will be the damnedest fuss you ever saw.

SARAH: (*Bending over the packages*) My, look who he's got presents from! Shirley Temple, William Lyon Phelps, Billy Rose, Ethel Waters, Somerset Maugham—I can hardly wait for tonight.

(*The door bell rings. John departs for the door*)

SARAH: My, it certainly is wonderful. And Mr. Whiteside's tree is so beautiful, too. Mr. and Mrs. Stanley had to put theirs in their bedroom, you know. They can hardly undress at night.

(*It is Bert Jefferson who enters*)

BERT: Hello, Maggie. Merry Christmas, Sarah.

SARAH: Merry Christmas, Mr. Jefferson.

(*She and John disappear into the dining room*)

BERT: (*Observing the pile of packages under the tree*) Say, business is good, isn't it? My, what a little quiet blackmail and a weekly radio hour can get you. What did his sponsors give him?

MAGGIE: They gave him a full year's supply of their product, Cream of Mush.

BERT: Well, he'll give it right back to them over the air.

MAGGIE: Wait until you hear tonight's broadcast, old fellow. It's so sticky I haven't been able to get it off my fingers since I copied it.

BERT: I'll bet . . . Look, I'll come clean. Under the influence of God knows what I have just bought you a Christmas present.

MAGGIE: (*Surprised*) Why, Mr. Jefferson, sir.

BERT: Only I'd like you to see it before I throw away my hard-earned money. Can you run downtown with me and take a look at it?

MAGGIE: Bert, this is very sweet of you. I'm quite touched. What is it? I can't wait.

BERT: A two years' subscription to *Screen Romances*. . . . Listen, do you think I'm going to tell you? Come down and see.

MAGGIE: (*She calls into the library*) Sherry! Sherry, I'm going out for a few minutes. With Horace Greeley. I won't be long. (*She goes into the hallway for her coat and hat*)

BERT: (*Raising his voice*) Noel, Noel, Mr. W.! How about some cribbage after your broadcast tonight?

(*The Whiteside wheelchair is rolling into the room*)

WHITESIDE: No, I will not play cribbage with you, Klondike Harry. You have been swindling the be-jesus out of me for two weeks. . . . Where are you off to now, Madame Butterfly?

MAGGIE: I'm being given a Christmas present. Anything you want done downtown?

WHITESIDE: 'Es. B'ing baby a lollipop. . . . What are *you* giving me for Christmas, Jefferson? I have enriched your feeble life beyond your capacity to repay me.

BERT: Yes, that's what I figured, so I'm not giving you anything.

WHITESIDE: I see. Well, I was giving you my old truss, but now I shan't. . . . Maggie, what time are those radio men coming?

MAGGIE: About six-thirty—I'll be here. You've got to cut, Sherry. You're four minutes over. Oh, by the way, there was a wire from Beverly. It's there somewhere. He doesn't know what train he can get out of Chicago, but he'll be here some time this evening.

WHITESIDE: Good! Is he staying overnight?

MAGGIE: No, he has to get right out again. He's sailing Friday on the *Queen Mary*.

BERT: Think I could peek in at the window and get a look at him? Beverly Carlton used to be one of my heroes.

WHITESIDE: Used to be, you ink-stained hack? Beverly Carlton is the greatest single talent in the English theatre today. Take this illiterate numbskull out of my sight, Maggie, and don't bring him back.

BERT: Yes, Mr. Whiteside, sir. I won't come back until Beverly Carlton gets here.

MAGGIE: (*As they go on their way*) Where are we going, Bert? I want to know what you've bought me—I'm like a ten-year-old kid.

BERT: (*Laughing a little*) You know, you look like a ten-year-old kid right now, Maggie, at that.

(*They are out of earshot by this time*)

(*Whiteside looks after them intently, listens until the door closes. He considers for a second, then wheels himself over to the telephone*)

WHITESIDE: (*On the phone*) Will you give me the Mansion House, please? . . . No, I don't know the number. . . . Hello? Mansion House? . . . Tell me, has a Miss Lorraine Sheldon arrived yet? . . . Yes, that's right—Miss Lorraine Sheldon. From New York. . . . She hasn't, eh? Thank you. (*He hangs up, drums with his fingers on the chair arm, looks at his watch. He slaps his knees impatiently, stretches. Then, vexed at his self-imposed imprisonment, he looks cautiously around the room, peers up the stairs. Then, slowly, he gets out of his chair; standing beside it, he indulges in a few mild calisthenics, looking cautiously around all the while*)

(*Then the sound of the library doors being opened sends him scurrying back to his chair. It is Miss Preen who emerges*)

WHITESIDE: (*Annoyed*) What do you want, coming in like that? Why don't you knock before you come into a room?

MISS PREEN: But—I wasn't coming in. I was coming out.

WHITESIDE: Miss Preen, you are obviously *in* this room. That is true, isn't it?

MISS PREEN: Yes, it is, but—

WHITESIDE: Therefore you came in. Hereafter, please knock. (*Before Miss Preen can reply, however, John enters from the dining room*)

JOHN: (*En route to the front door*) There're some expressmen here with a crate, Mr. Whiteside. I told them to come around the front.

WHITESIDE: Thank you, John. . . . Don't stand there, Miss Preen. You look like a frozen custard. Go away.

MISS PREEN: (*Controlling herself as best she can*) Yes, sir. (*She goes*)

(*At the same time two Expressmen, carrying a crate, enter from the front door*)

JOHN: Bring it right in here. Careful there—don't scrape the wall. Why, it's some kind of animals.

EXPRESSMAN: I'll say it's animals. We had to feed 'em at seven o'clock this morning.

WHITESIDE: Bring it over here, John. Who's it from?

JOHN: (*Reading from the top of the crate as they set it down*) Admiral Richard E. Byrd. Say!

WHITESIDE: (*Peering through the slats*) Why, they're penguins. Two—three—four penguins. Hello, my pretties.

EXPRESSMAN: Directions for feeding are right on top. These two slats are open.

JOHN: (*Reading*) "To be fed only whale blubber, eels and cracked lobster."

EXPRESSMAN: They got Coca-Cola this morning. And liked it. (*They go*)

WHITESIDE: (*Peering through the slats again*) Hello, hello, hello. You know, they make the most entrancing companions, John. Admiral Byrd has one that goes on all his lecture tours. I want these put right in the library with me. Take 'em right in.

JOHN: (*Picking up the crate*) Yes, sir.

WHITESIDE: Better tell Sarah to order a couple of dozen lobsters. I don't suppose there's any whale blubber in Mesalia.

(*At which point Dr. Bradley obligingly enters from the hall. Mr. Whiteside is equal to the occasion*)

WHITESIDE: (*With just the merest glance at the Doctor*) Oh, yes, there is.

DR. BRADLEY: The door was open, so I— Good afternoon, Mr. Whiteside. And Merry Christmas.

WHITESIDE: Merry Christmas, Merry Christmas. Do you happen to know if eels are in season, Doctor?

DR. BRADLEY: How's that?

WHITESIDE: Never mind. I was a fool to ask you.

(*John returns from the library, carefully closing the doors*)

JOHN: I opened those two slats a little, Mr. Whiteside—they seemed so crowded in there.

WHITESIDE: Thank you, John.

(*John goes on his way*)

On your way downtown, Doctor, will you send these air mail? Miss Cutler forgot them. (*He hands him a few letters*) Good-bye. Sorry you dropped in just now. I have to do my Yogi exercises. (*He folds his arms, leans back and closes his eyes*)

DR. BRADLEY: But, Mr. Whiteside, it's been a week now. My book, you know—when are we going to start work on the book?

(*Whiteside, his eyes still closed, places his fingers to his lips, for absolute silence*)

I was hoping that today you'd be—

(*He stops short as Miss Preen returns from the dining room*) Good afternoon, Miss Preen.

MISS PREEN: Good afternoon, Dr. Bradley. (*She opens the doors to enter the library, then freezes in her tracks. She closes the doors again and turns to the Doctor, glassy-eyed. She raises a trembling hand to her forehead*) Doctor, perhaps I'm—not well, but—when I opened the doors just now I thought I saw a penguin with a thermometer in its mouth.

WHITESIDE: What's this? Have those penguins got out of their crate?

MISS PREEN: Oh, thank God. I thought perhaps the strain had been too much.

DR. BRADLEY: (*Incredulous*) Penguins?

WHITESIDE: Yes. Doctor, will you go in and capture them, please, and put them back in the crate? There're four of them.

DR. BRADLEY: (*Somewhat staggered*) Very well. Do you suppose that later on, Mr. Whiteside, we might—

WHITESIDE: We'll see, we'll see. First catch the penguins. And, Miss Preen, will you amuse them, please, until I come in?

MISS PREEN: (*Swallowing hard*) Yes, sir.

(*Meanwhile John has descended the stairs*)

JOHN: The Christmas tree just fell on Mr. Stanley. He's got a big bump on his forehead.

WHITESIDE: (*Brightly*) Why, isn't that too bad? . . . Go ahead, Doctor. Go on, Miss Preen.

(*Richard pops in from the hallway*)

RICHARD: Hello, Mr. Whiteside.

WHITESIDE: Hello, Dickie, my boy.

DR. BRADLEY: (*Still lingering*) Mr. Whiteside, will you have some time later?

WHITESIDE: (*Impatient*) I don't know, Doctor. I'm busy now.

DR. BRADLEY: Well, suppose I wait a little while? I'll—I'll wait a little while. (*He goes into the library*)

WHITESIDE: Dr. Bradley is the greatest living argument for mercy killings. . . . Well, Dickie, would you like a candid camera shot of my left nostril this evening?

RICHARD: I'm sort of stocked up on those. Have you got a minute to look at some new ones I've taken?

WHITESIDE: I certainly have. . . . Why, these are splendid, Richard. There's real artistry in them—they're as good as anything by Margaret Bourke-White. I like all the things you've shown me. This is the essence of photographic journalism.

RICHARD: Say, I didn't know they were as good as that. I just like to take pictures, that's all.

WHITESIDE: Richard, I've been meaning to talk to you about this. You're not just a kid fooling with a camera any more. These are good. That is what you ought to do. You ought to get out of here and do some of the things you were telling me about. Just get on a boat and get off wherever it stops. Galveston, Mexico, Singapore—work your way through and just take pictures—everything.

RICHARD: Say, wouldn't I like to, though! It's what I've been dreaming of for years. If I could do that I'd be the happiest guy in the world.

WHITESIDE: Well, why can't you do it? If I were your age, I'd do it like a shot.

RICHARD: Well, you know why, Dad.

WHITESIDE: Richard, do you really want to do this more than anything else in the world?

RICHARD: I certainly do.

WHITESIDE: Then do it.

(*June comes quietly in from the dining room. Obviously there is something on her mind*)

JUNE: Hello, Dick. Good afternoon, Mr. Whiteside.

WHITESIDE: Hello, my lovely. . . . So I'm afraid it's up to *you*, Richard.

RICHARD: I guess it is. Well, thank you, Mr. Whiteside. You've been swell and I'll never forget it.

WHITESIDE: Righto, Richard.

RICHARD: June, are you coming upstairs?

JUNE: Ah—in a few minutes, Richard.

RICHARD: Well—knock on my door, will you? I want to talk to you.

JUNE: Yes, I will.

(*Richard disappears up the stairs*)

WHITESIDE: (*Brightly opening his book*) June, my lamb, you were too young to know about the Elwell murder, weren't you? Completely fascinating. I have about five favorite murders, and the Elwell case is one of them. Would you like to hear about it?

JUNE: Well, Mr. Whiteside, I wanted to talk to you. Would you mind, for a few minutes? It's important.

WHITESIDE: Why, certainly, my dear. I take it this is all about your young Lothario at the factory?

JUNE: Yes. I just can't seem to make Father understand. It's like talking to a blank wall. He won't meet him—he won't even talk about it. What are we going to do, Mr. Whiteside? Sandy and I love each other. I don't know where to turn.

WHITESIDE: My dear, I'd like to meet this young man. I'd like to see him for myself.

JUNE: Would you, Mr. Whiteside? Would you meet him? He's—he's outside now. He's in the kitchen.

WHITESIDE: Good! Bring him in.

JUNE: (*Hesitating*) Mr. Whiteside, he's—he's a very sensitive boy. You will be nice to him, won't you?

WHITESIDE: God damn it, June, when will you learn that I am *always* kind and courteous! Bring this idiot in!

JUNE: (*Calling through the dining room in a low voice*) Sandy. . . . Sandy. . . .

(*She stands aside as a young man enters. Twenty-three or -four, keen-looking, neatly but simply dressed*)

Here he is, Mr. Whiteside. This is Sandy.

SANDY: How do you do, sir?

WHITESIDE: How do you do? Young man, I've been hearing a good deal about you from June this past week. It seems, if I have been correctly informed, that you two babes in the woods have quietly gone out of your minds.

JUNE: There's another name for it. It's called love.

WHITESIDE: Well, you've come to the right place. Dr. Sheridan Whiteside, Broken Hearts Mended, Brakes Relined, Hamburgers. Go right ahead.

SANDY: Well, if June has told you anything at all, Mr. Whiteside, you know the jam we're in. You see, I work for the union, Mr. Whiteside. I'm an organizer. I've been organizing the men in Mr. Stanley's factory, and Mr. Stanley's pretty sore about it.

WHITESIDE: I'll bet.

SANDY: Did June tell you that?

WHITESIDE: Yes, she did.

SANDY: Well, that being the case, Mr. Whiteside, I don't think I have the right to try to influence June. If she marries me it means a definite break with her family, and I don't like to bring that about. But Mr. Stanley's so stubborn about it, so arbitrary. You know, this is not something I've done just to spite him. We fell in love with each other. But Mr. Stanley behaves as though it were all a big plot—John L. Lewis sent me here just to marry his daughter.

JUNE: He's tried to fire Sandy twice, out at the factory, but he couldn't on account of the Wagner Act, thank God!

SANDY: Yes, he thinks I wrote that, too.

JUNE: If he'd only let me talk to him. If he'd let Sandy talk to him.

SANDY: Well, we've gone over all that, June. Anyway, this morning I got word I'm needed in Chicago. I may have to go on to Frisco from there. So you see the jam we're in.

JUNE: Sandy's leaving tonight, Mr. Whiteside. He'll probably be gone a year. We've simply got to decide. *Now.*

WHITESIDE: My dear, this is absurdly simple. It's no problem at all. Now to my jaundiced eye—

(*The telephone rings*)

Oh-h! Hello. . . . Yes. . . . This is Whiteside. . . . Excuse me—it's a trans-Atlantic call. . . . Yes? . . . Yes, I'm on. Who's calling me? (*His tone suddenly becomes one of keen delight*) All right—put her through. (*He turns to the young pair*) It's Gertrude Stein, in Paris. . . . Hello. . . . Hello, Gertie! How's my little nightingale? . . . Yes, I hoped you would. How'd you know I was here? . . . I see. Well, it's wonderful of you to call. . . . Yes. Yes, I'm listening. Ten seconds more? (*A quick aside to the others*) It'll be Christmas in Paris in ten seconds, and every year—yes? . . . Yes, Gertie, I hear them. It's wonderful. As though they were right outside. . . . June! (*He holds the receiver out to June for a second*) Thank you, my dear, and a very Merry Christmas to *you.* Don't forget we're dining on June tenth. . . . Pourquoi ne pas se réunir chez vous après? Tachez d'avoir Picasso, Matisse, Cocteau. Je serai seulement là pour quelques jours et je veux voir tout-le-monde. N'est-ce pas? Ah! Bon! Au revoir—au revoir. (*He hangs up*) You know what that was you listened to? The bells of Notre Dame.

JUNE: Not really.

WHITESIDE: Miss Stein calls me every Christmas, no matter where I am, so that I can hear them. Two years ago I was walking on the bottom of the ocean in a diving suit with William Beebe, but she got me. . . . Now, where were we? Oh, yes. . . . June, I like your young man. I have unerring instinct about people—I've never been wrong. That's why I wanted to meet him. My feeling is that you two will be very happy together. Whatever his beliefs are, he's entitled to them, and you shouldn't let anything stand in your way. As I see it, it's no problem at all. Stripped of its externals, what does it come down to? Your father. The possibility of making him unhappy. It that right?

JUNE: *Very* unhappy.

WHITESIDE: That isn't the point. Suppose your parents *are* unhappy—it's good for them. Develops their characters.

Look at me. I left home at the age of four and haven't been back since. They hear me on the radio and that's enough for them.

SANDY: Then—your advice is to go ahead, Mr. Whiteside?

MR. WHITESIDE: It is. Marry him tonight, June.

JUNE: (*Almost afraid to make the leap*) You—you mean that, Mr. Whiteside?

WHITESIDE: (*Bellowing*) No, I mean you should marry Senator Borah. If I didn't mean it I wouldn't say it. What do you want me to do—say it all over again? My own opinion is—

(*The voice of Mr. Stanley is heard at the head of the stairs. "Come on, Daisy—stop dawdling"*)

(*June quickly pushes her young man out of the room, as Mr. and Mrs. Stanley descend the stairs*)

STANLEY: (*With deep sarcasm*) Forgive us for trespassing, Mr. Whiteside.

WHITESIDE: Not at all, old fellow—not at all. It's Christmas, you know. Merry Christmas, Merry Christmas.

MRS. STANLEY: (*Nervously*) Ah—yes. Merry Christmas. . . . Would you like to come along with us, June? We're taking some presents over to the Dexters.

JUNE: No—no, thank you, Mother. I—I have to write some letters. (*She hurries up the stairs*)

STANLEY: (*Who has been donning his coat*) Come along, Daisy. (*Turning, he reveals a great patch of court plaster on his head*)

WHITESIDE: (*Entirely too sweetly*) Why, Mr. Stanley, what happened to your forehead? Did you have an accident?

STANLEY: (*Just as sweetly*) No, Mr. Whiteside. I'm taking boxing lessons. . . . Come, Daisy. (*They go*)

(*Harriet, who has been hovering at the head of the stairs, hurries down as the Stanleys depart. She is carrying a little Christmas package*)

HARRIET: Dear Mr. Whiteside, I've been trying all day to see you. To give you—*this*.

WHITESIDE: Why, Miss Stanley. A Christmas gift for me?

HARRIET: It's only a trifle, but I wanted you to have it. It's a picture of me as I used to be. It was taken on another Christmas Eve, many years ago. Don't open it till the stroke of midnight, will you?

(*The door bell rings. Harriet looks apprehensively over her shoulder*)

Merry Christmas, dear Mr. Whiteside. Merry Christmas.

WHITESIDE: Merry Christmas to you, Miss Stanley, and thank you.

(*She glides out of the room*)

(*In the hallway, as John opens the door, we hear a woman's voice, liquid and melting. "This IS the Stanley residence, isn't it?" "Yes, it is." "I've come to see Mr. Whiteside. Will you tell him Miss Sheldon is here?"*)

WHITESIDE: Lorraine! My Blossom Girl!

LORRAINE: (*Coming into view*) Sherry, my sweet!

(*And quite a view it is. Lorraine Sheldon is known as the most chic actress on the New York or London stage, and justly so. She glitters as she walks. She is beautiful, and even, God save the word, glamorous. . . . Her rank as one of the Ten Best-Dressed Women of the World is richly deserved. She is, in short, a siren of no mean talents, and knows it*)

LORRAINE: (*Wasting no time*) Oh, darling, look at that poor sweet tortured face! Let me kiss it! You poor darling, your eyes have a kind of gallant compassion. How drawn you are! Sherry, my sweet, I want to cry.

WHITESIDE: All right, all right. You've made a very nice entrance. Now relax, dear.

LORRAINE: But, Sherry, darling, I've been so worried. And now seeing you in that chair . . .

WHITESIDE: This chair fits my fanny as nothing else ever has. I feel better than I have in years, and my only concern is news of the outside world. So take that skunk off and tell me everything. How are you, my dear?

LORRAINE: (*Removing a cascade of silver fox from her shoulders*) Darling, I'm so relieved. You look perfectly wonderful—I never saw you look better. My dear, do I look a wreck? I just dashed through New York. Didn't do a thing about Christmas. Hattie Carnegie and had my hair done, and got right on the train. And the *Normandie* coming back was simply hectic. Fun, you know, but simply exhausting. Jock Whitney, and Cary Grant, and Dorothy di Frasso—it was *too* exhausting. And of course London before that was so magnificent, my dear—well, I simply never got to bed at all. Darling, I've so much to tell you I don't know where to start.

WHITESIDE: Well, start with the dirt first, dear—that's what I want to hear.

LORRAINE: Let me see. . . . Well, Sybil Cartwright got thrown right out of Ciro's—it was the night before I sailed. She was wearing one of those new cellophane dresses, and you could absolutely see Trafalgar Square. And, oh, yes—Sir Harry Montrose—the painter, *you* know—is suing his mother for disorderly conduct. It's just shocked *every*one. Oh, and before I forget—Anthony Eden told me he's going to be on your New Year's broadcast, and he gave me a message for you. He said for God's sake not to introduce him again as the English Grover Whalen.

WHITESIDE: Nonsense. . . . Now come, dear, what about *you?* What about your love life? I don't believe for one moment that you never got to bed at all, if you'll pardon the expression.

LORRAINE: Sherry dear, you're dreadful.

WHITESIDE: What about that splendid bit of English mutton, Lord Bottomley? Haven't you hooked him yet?

LORRAINE: Sherry, please. Cedric is a very dear friend of mine.

WHITESIDE: Now, Blossom Girl, this is Sherry. Don't try to pull the bed clothes over *my* eyes. Don't tell *me* you wouldn't like to be Lady Bottomley, with a hundred thousand pounds a year and twelve castles. By the way, has he had his teeth fixed yet? Every time I order Roquefort cheese I think of those teeth.

LORRAINE: Sherry, really! . . . Cedric may not be brilliant, but he's rather sweet, poor lamb, and he's very fond of me, and he does represent a kind of English way of living that I like. Surrey, and London for the season—shooting box in Scotland—that lovely old castle in Wales. You were there, Sherry—you know what I mean.

WHITESIDE: Mm. I do indeed.

LORRAINE: Well, really, Sherry, why not? If I can marry Cedric I don't know why I shouldn't. Shall I tell you something, Sherry? I think, from something he said just before I sailed, that he's finally coming around to it. It wasn't definite, mind you, but—don't be surprised if I *am* Lady Bottomley before very long.

WHITESIDE: Lady Bottomley! Won't Kansas City be surprised! However, I shall be a flower girl and give the groom an iron toothpick as a wedding present. Come ahead, my blossom —let's hear some more of your skullduggery.

(*The library doors are quietly opened at this point and the Doctor's head appears*)

DR. BRADLEY: (*In a heavy whisper*) Mr. Whiteside.

WHITESIDE: What? No, no—not now. I'm busy.

(*The Doctor disappears*)

LORRAINE: Who's that?

WHITESIDE: He's fixing the plumbing. . . . Now come on, come on—I want more news.

LORRAINE: But, Sherry, what about this play? After all, I've come all the way from New York—even on Christmas Eve— I've been so excited ever since your phone call. Where is it? When can I read it?

WHITESIDE: Well, here's the situation. This young author—his name is Bert Jefferson—brought me the play with the understanding that I send it to Kit Cornell. It's a magnificent part, and God knows I feel disloyal to Kit, but there you are. Now I've done *this* much—the rest is up to you. He's young and attractive—now, just how you'll go about persuading him, I'm sure you know more about that than I do.

LORRAINE: Darling, how can I ever thank you? Does he know I'm coming—Mr. Jefferson, I mean?

WHITESIDE: No, no. You're just out here visiting me. You'll meet him, and that's that. Get him to take you to dinner, and work around to the play. Good God, I don't have to tell you how to do these things. How did you get all those other parts?

LORRAINE: Sherry! . . . Well, I'll go back to the hotel and get into something more attractive. I just dumped my bags and rushed right over here. Darling, you're wonderful. (*Lightly kissing him*)

WHITESIDE: All right—run along and get into your working clothes. Then come right back here and spend Christmas Eve with Sherry and I'll have Mr. Jefferson on tap. By the way, I've got a little surprise for you. Who do you think's

paying me a flying visit tonight? None other than your old
friend and fellow actor, Beverly Carlton.

LORRAINE: (*Not too delighted*) Really? Beverly? I thought he
was being glamorous again on a tramp steamer.

WHITESIDE: Come, come, dear—mustn't be bitter because he
got better notices than you did.

LORRAINE: Don't be silly, Sherry. I never read notices. I simply wouldn't care to act with him again, that's all. He's not
staying here, is he? I *hope* not!

WHITESIDE: Temper, temper, temper. No, he's not. . . .
Where'd you get that diamond clip, dear? That's a new bit
of loot, isn't it?

LORRAINE: Haven't you seen this before? Cedric gave it to me
for his mother's birthday. . . . Look, darling, I've got a taxi
outside. If I'm going to get back here—

  (*At this point the voice of Maggie is heard in the hallway*)

MAGGIE: Sherry, what do you think? I've just been given the
most beautiful . . . (*She stops short and comes to a dead halt
as she sees Lorraine*)

LORRAINE: Oh, hello, Maggie. I knew you must be around
somewhere. How are you, my dear?

WHITESIDE: Santa's been at work, my pet. Blossom Girl just
dropped in out of the blue and surprised us.

MAGGIE: (*Quietly*) Hello, Lorraine.

WHITESIDE: (*As Jefferson appears*) Who's that—Bert? This is
Mr. Bert Jefferson, Lorraine. Young newspaper man. Miss
Lorraine Sheldon.

BERT: How do you do, Miss Sheldon?

LORRAINE: How do you do? I didn't quite catch the name—
Jefferson?

WHITESIDE: (*Sweetly*) That's right, Pet.

LORRAINE: (*Full steam ahead*) Why, Mr. Jefferson, you don't
look like a newspaper man. You don't look like a newspaper
man at all.

BERT: Really? I thought it was written all over me in neon lights.

LORRAINE: Oh, no, not at all. I should have said you were—
oh, I don't know—an aviator or an explorer or something.
They have that same kind of dash about them. I'm simply
enchanted with your town, Mr. Jefferson. It gives one such

a warm, gracious feeling. Tell me—have you lived here all your life?

BERT: Practically.

WHITESIDE: If you wish to hear the story of his life, Lorraine, kindly do so on your own time. Maggie and I have work to do. Get out of here, Jefferson. On your way, Blossom.

LORRAINE: He's the world's rudest man, isn't he? Can I drop you, Mr. Jefferson? I'm going down to the—Mansion House, I think it's called.

BERT: Thank you, but I've got my car. Suppose I drop you?

LORRAINE: Oh, would you? That'd be lovely—we'll send the taxi off. See you in a little while, Sherry. 'Bye, Maggie.

BERT: Good-bye, Miss C. (*He turns to Whiteside*) I'm invited back for dinner, am I not?

WHITESIDE: Yes—yes, you are. At Christmas I always feed the needy. Now please stop oozing out—*get* out.

LORRAINE: Come on, Mr. Jefferson. I want to hear more about this charming little town. And I want to know a good deal about you, too.

(*And they are gone*)

(*There is a slight but pregnant pause after they go. Maggie simply stands looking at Whiteside, waiting for what may come forth*)

WHITESIDE: (*As though nothing had happened*) Now let's see, have you got a copy of that broadcast? How much did you say they wanted out—four minutes?

MAGGIE: That's right—four minutes. . . . She's looking very well, isn't she?

WHITESIDE: (*Busy with his manuscript*) What's that? Who?

MAGGIE: The Countess di Pushover. . . . Quite a surprise, wasn't it—her dropping in?

WHITESIDE: Yes—yes, it was. Now come on, Maggie, come on. Get to work.

MAGGIE: Why, she must have gone through New York like a dose of salts. How long's she going to stay?

WHITESIDE: (*Completely absorbed*) What? Oh, I don't know— a few days . . . (*He reads from his manuscript*) "At this joyous season of the year, when in the hearts of men—" I can't cut that.

MAGGIE: Isn't it curious? There was Lorraine, snug as a bug in somebody's bed on the *Normandie*—

WHITESIDE: (*So busy*) "Ere the Yuletide season pass—"

MAGGIE: (*Quietly taking the manuscript out of his hands*) Now, Sherry dear, we will talk a bit.

WHITESIDE: Now look here, Maggie. Just because a friend of mine happens to come out to spend Christmas with me—
(*The door bell rings*)
I have a hunch that's Beverly. Maggie, see if it is. Go ahead —run! Run!
(*Maggie looks at him—right through him, in fact. Then she goes slowly toward the door*)
(*We hear her voice at the door: "Beverly!" Then, in clipped English tones: "Magpie! A large, moist, incestuous kiss for my Magpie!"*)

WHITESIDE: (*Roaring*) Come in here, you Piccadilly pen-pusher, and gaze upon a soul in agony.
(*Beverly Carlton enters, arm in arm with Maggie. Very confident, very British, very Beverly Carlton*)

BEVERLY: Don't tell me how you are, Sherry dear. I want none of the tiresome details. I have only a little time, so the con-versation will be entirely about *me*, and I shall love it. Shall I tell you how I glittered through the South Seas like a silver scimitar, or would you rather hear how I frolicked through Zambesia, raping the Major General's daughter and fin-ishing a three-act play at the same time? . . . Magpie dear, you are the moonflower of my middle age, and I love you very much. Say something beautiful to me. Sherry dear, without going into mountainous waves of self-pity, how are you?

WHITESIDE: I'm fine, you presumptuous Cockney. . . . Now, how was the trip, wonderful?

BEVERLY: Fabulous. I did a fantastic amount of work. By the way, did I glimpse that little boudoir butterfly, La Sheldon, in a motor-car as I came up the driveway?

MAGGIE: You did indeed. She's paying us a Christmas visit.

BEVERLY: Dear girl! They do say she set fire to her mother, but I don't believe it. . . . Sherry, my evil one, not only have I written the finest comedy since Molière, but also the best revue since my last one and an operetta that frightens me—

it's so good. I shall play it for eight weeks in London and six in New York—that's all. No matinees. Then I am off to the Grecian islands. . . . Magpie, why don't you come along? Why don't you desert this cannon ball of fluff and come with me?

MAGGIE: Beverly dear, be careful. You're catching me at a good moment.

WHITESIDE: (*Changing the subject*) Tell me, did you have a good time in Hollywood? How long were you there?

BEVERLY: Three unbelievable days. I saw everyone from Adrian to Zanuck. They came, poor dears, as to a shrine. I was insufferably charming and ruthlessly firm in refusing seven million dollars for two minutes' work.

WHITESIDE: What about Banjo? Did you see my wonderful Banjo in Hollywood?

BEVERLY: I did. He gave a dinner for me. I arrived, in white tie and tails, to be met at the door by two bewigged flunkies, who quietly proceeded to take my trousers off. I was then ushered, in my lemon silk drawers, into a room full of Norma Shearer, Claudette Colbert, and Aldous Huxley, among others. Dear, sweet, incomparable Banjo.

WHITESIDE: I'll never forget that summer at Antibes, when Banjo put a microphone in Lorraine's mattress, and then played the record the next day at lunch.

BEVERLY: I remember it indeed. Lorraine left Antibes by the next boat.

MAGGIE: (*Half to herself*) I wish Banjo were here now.

BEVERLY: What's the matter, Magpie? Is Lorraine being her own sweet sick-making self?

MAGGIE: You wouldn't take her to the Grecian Islands with you, would you, Beverly? Just for me?

WHITESIDE: Now, now. Lorraine is a charming person who has gallantly given up her own Christmas to spend it with me.

BEVERLY: Oh, I knew I had a bit of dirt for us all to nibble on.
(*He draws a letter out of his pocket*)
(*Again the library doors are opened and the Doctor's head comes through*)

DR. BRADLEY: Mr. Whiteside.

WHITESIDE: No, no, not now. Go away.
(*The Doctor withdraws*)

BEVERLY: Have you kidnapped someone, Sherry?

WHITESIDE: Yes, that was Charley Ross . . . Go ahead. Is this something juicy?

BEVERLY: Juicy as a pomegranate. It is the latest report from London on the winter maneuvers of Miss Lorraine Sheldon against the left flank—in fact, all flanks—of Lord Cedric Bottomley. Listen: "Lorraine has just left us in a cloud of Chanel Number Five. Since September, in her relentless pursuit of His Lordship, she has paused only to change girdles and check her oil. She has chased him, panting, from castle to castle, till he finally took refuge, for several week-ends, in the gentlemen's lavatory of the House of Lords. Practically no one is betting on the Derby this year; we are all making book on Lorraine. She is sailing tomorrow on the *Normandie*, but would return on the *Yankee Clipper* if Bottomley so much as belches in her direction." Have you ever met Lord Bottomley, Magpie dear? (*He goes immediately into an impersonation of His Lordship. Very British, very full of teeth, stuttering*) "Not v-v-very good shooting today, blast it. Only s-s-six partridges, f-f-four grouse, and the D-D-Duke of Sutherland."

WHITESIDE: (*Chuckling*) My God, that's Bottomley to the very bottom.

BEVERLY: (*Still in character*) "R-r-ripping debate in the House today. Old Basil spoke for th-th-three hours. D-d-dropped dead at the end of it. Ripping."

MAGGIE: You're making it up, Beverly. No one sounds like that.

WHITESIDE: It's so good it's uncanny. . . . Damn it, Beverly, why must you race right out of here? I never see enough of you, you ungrateful moppet.

BEVERLY: Sherry darling, I can only tell you that my love for you is so great that I changed trains at Chicago to spend ten minutes with you and wish you a Merry Christmas. Merry Christmas, my lad. My little Magpie. (*A look at his watch*) And now I have just time for one magnificent number, to give you a taste of how brilliant the whole thing is. It's the second number in the revue. (*He strikes a chord on the piano, but before he can go further the telephone rings*)

WHITESIDE: Oh, damn! Get rid of them, Maggie.

MAGGIE: Hello . . . Oh, hello, Bert . . . Oh! Well, just a minute. . . . Beverly, would you talk to a newspaper man for just two minutes? I kind of promised him.

BEVERLY: Won't have time, Magpie, unless he's under the piano.

MAGGIE: Oh! (*Into the phone*) Wait a minute. (*To Beverly again*) Would you see him at the station, just for a minute before the train goes? (*Beverly nods*) Bert, go to the station and wait for him. He'll be there in a few minutes. . . . 'Bye.

WHITESIDE: The stalls are impatient, Beverly. Let's have this second-rate masterpiece.

BEVERLY: (*His fingers rippling over the keys*) It's called: "What Am I to Do?"

>"Oft in the nightfall
>I think I might fall
>   Down from my perilous height;
>Deep in the heart of me,
>Always a part of me,
>   Quivering, shivering light.
>Run, little lady,
>Ere the shady
>   Shafts of time
>Barb you with their winged desire,
>Singe you with their sultry fire.
>   Softly a fluid
>   Druid
>   Meets me,
>Olden
>   and golden
>   the dawn that greets me;
>Cherishing,
>   Perishing,
>Up to the stars
>   I climb.
>What am I to do
>   Toward ending this madness,
>   This sadness,
>That's rending me through?"

> The flowers of yesteryear
>> Are haunting me,
>> Taunting me,
> Darling, for wanting you.
> What am I to say
>> To warnings of sorrow
>> When morning's tomorrow
> Greets the dew?
>> Will I see the cosmic Ritz
>> Shattered and scattered to bits?
> What *not* am I to do?"

(*As he swings into the chorus for a second time the door bell rings, and John is glimpsed as he goes to the door*)

(*It is a trio of Radio Men who appear in the doorway, their arms filled with equipment for Mr. Whiteside's broadcast*)

WHITESIDE: Oh, come in, Westcott. . . . Beverly, it's superb. The best thing you've ever written. It'll be played by every ragtag orchestra from Salem to Singapore.

BEVERLY: Please! Let *me* say that . . . Ah, the air waves, eh? Well, I shan't have to hear you, thank God. I shall be on the train.

MAGGIE: Come on, Whiteside, say good-bye. Mr. Westcott, he's still four minutes over—you'll have to chisel it out.

WHITESIDE: (*As Maggie starts to wheel him into the library*) Stop this nonsense. Beverly, my lamb—

MAGGIE: You can kiss Beverly in London on July twelfth. (*Then to the technicians*) The microphone set-up is right there, gentlemen, and you can connect up outside. John, show them where it is.

WHITESIDE: Maggie, what the hell are you—

BEVERLY: (*Calling after the fast-disappearing Whiteside*) Au revoir, Sherry. Merry Christmas. Magpie, come get a kiss.

MAGGIE: (*Emerging from the library and closing the doors behind her*) Beverly, I want one minute. I must have it. You'll make the train. The station's a minute and a half from here.

BEVERLY: Why, what's the matter, Magpie?

(*At which the library doors are opened and the Doctor emerges, rather apologetically. He is sped on his way by Mr. Whiteside's roaring voice—"Oh, get out of here!"*)

DR. BRADLEY: I'm—I'm just waiting in the kitchen until Mr. Whiteside is— Excuse me. (*He darts out through the dining room*)

BEVERLY: Who *is* that man?

MAGGIE: Never mind . . . Beverly, I'm in great trouble.

BEVERLY: Why, Magpie dear, what's the matter?

MAGGIE: I've fallen in love. For the first time in my life. Beverly, I'm in love. I can't tell you about it—there isn't time. But Sherry is trying to break it up. In his own fiendish way he's doing everything he can to break it up.

BEVERLY: Why, the old devil! What's he doing?

MAGGIE: Lorraine. He's brought Lorraine here to smash it.

BEVERLY: Oh, it's somebody *here*? In this town?

MAGGIE: (*Nodding*) He's a newspaper man—the one you're going to see at the station—and he's written a play, and I know Sherry must be using that as bait. You know Lorraine —she'll eat him up alive. You've got to help me, Beverly.

BEVERLY: Of course I will, Magpie. What do you want me to do?

MAGGIE: I've got to get Lorraine out of here—the farther away the better—and you can do it for me.

BEVERLY: But how? How can I? I'm leaving.

(*The library doors are opened and Westcott, the radio man, emerges*)

WESTCOTT: Have you a carbon copy of the broadcast, Miss Cutler?

MAGGIE: It's on that table.

WESTCOTT: Thank you. One of those penguins ate the original.

(*The voice of Whiteside is now heard calling from his room*)

WHITESIDE: Beverly, are you still there?

MAGGIE: No, he's gone, Sherry. (*She lowers her voice*) Come out here.

(*Maneuvering him into the hall, we see her whisper to him; his head bobs up and down quickly in assent. Then he lets out a shriek of laughter*)

BEVERLY: I'd love it. I'd absolutely love it.

(*Maggie puts a quick finger to his lips, peers toward the Whiteside room. But Mr. Westcott has gone in; the doors are closed*)

It's simply enchanting, and bitches Sherry and Lorraine at the same time. It's pure heaven! I adore it, and I shall do it up brown. (*He embraces her*)

MAGGIE: Darling, the first baby will be named Beverly. You're wonderful.

BEVERLY: Of course I am. Come to Chislewick for your honeymoon and I'll put you up. Good-bye, my lovely. I adore you. (*And he is gone*)

> (*Maggie comes back into the room, highly pleased with herself. She even sings a fragment of Beverly's song. "What am I to do? Tra-la-la-la-la-la"*)
>
> (*John, entering from the dining room, breaks the song*)

JOHN: Shall I straighten up the room for the broadcast, Miss Cutler?

MAGGIE: No, John, it isn't television, thank God. They only *hear* that liquid voice.

JOHN: He's really wonderful, isn't he? The things he finds time to do.

MAGGIE: Yes, he certainly sticks his nose into everything, John. (*She goes into the library*)

> (*John is putting the room in order when suddenly June comes quietly down the stairs. She is dressed for the street and is carrying a suitcase*)

JOHN: Why, Miss June, are you going away?

JUNE: Why—no, John. No. I'm just— Mr. Whiteside is inside, I suppose?

JOHN: Yes, he's getting ready to go on the radio.

JUNE: Oh! Well, look, John—

> (*And then Richard darts down the stairs. A light bag, two cameras slung over his shoulder*)

RICHARD: (*To June, in a heavy whisper*) Where's Mr. Whiteside? In there?

JUNE: Yes, he is.

RICHARD: Oh! Well, maybe we ought to—

> (*The door bell rings. Richard and June exchange looks, then scurry out quickly through the dining room*)
>
> (*John looks after them for a second, puzzled, then goes to the door*)
>
> (*It is Lorraine who comes in, resplendent now in evening*)

dress and wrap, straight from Paris. At the same time Maggie emerges from the library and John goes on his way)

LORRAINE: Hello, dear. Where's Sherry?

MAGGIE: Inside, working—he's broadcasting very soon.

LORRAINE: Oh, of course—Christmas Eve. What a wonderful man Sheridan Whiteside is! You know, my dear, it must be such an utter joy to be secretary to somebody like Sherry.

MAGGIE: Yes, you meet such interesting people. . . . That's quite a gown, Lorraine. Going anywhere?

LORRAINE: This? Oh, I just threw on anything at all. Aren't you dressing for dinner?

MAGGIE: No, just what meets the eye.

(She has occasion to carry a few papers across the room at this point. Lorraine's eye watches her narrowly)

LORRAINE: Who does your hair, Maggie?

MAGGIE: A little French woman named Maggie Cutler comes in every morning.

LORRAINE: You know, every time I see you I keep thinking your hair could be so lovely. I always want to get my hands on it.

MAGGIE: (*Quietly*) I've always wanted to get mine on yours, Lorraine.

LORRAINE: (*Absently*) What, dear?

(One of the radio men drifts into the room, plugs into the control board, drifts out again. Lorraine's eyes follow him idly. Then she turns to Maggie again)

By the way, what time does Beverly get here? I'm not over-anxious to meet him.

MAGGIE: He's been and gone, Lorraine.

LORRAINE: Really? Well, I'm very glad. . . . Of course you're great friends, aren't you—you and Beverly?

MAGGIE: Yes, we are. I think he's a wonderful person.

LORRAINE: Oh, I suppose so. But when I finished acting with him I was a perfect wreck. All during that tender love scene that the critics thought was so magnificent he kept dropping peanut shells down my dress. I wouldn't act with him again if I were starving.

MAGGIE: (*Casually*) Tell me, Lorraine, have you found a new play yet?

LORRAINE: (*At once on guard*) No. No, I haven't. There was a pile of manuscripts waiting in New York for me, but I hurried right out here to Sherry.

MAGGIE: Yes, it was wonderful of you, Lorraine—to drop everything that way and rush to Sherry's wheelchair.

LORRAINE: Well, after all, Maggie dear, what else has one in this world but friends? . . . How long will Sherry be in there, I wonder?

MAGGIE: Not long. . . . Did you know that Mr. Jefferson has written quite a good play? The young man that drove you to the hotel.

LORRAINE: Really? No, I didn't. Isn't that interesting?

MAGGIE: Yes, isn't it?

(*There is a considerable pause. The ladies smile at each other*)

LORRAINE: (*Evading Maggie's eyes*) They've put a polish on my nails I simply loathe. I don't suppose Elizabeth Arden has a branch in this town.

MAGGIE: (*Busy with her papers*) Not if she has any sense.

LORRAINE: Oh, well, I'll just bear it, but it does depress me. (*She rises, wanders aimlessly for a moment, picks up a book from the table*) Have you read this, Maggie? Everybody was reading it on the boat. I hear you simply can't put it down.

MAGGIE: *I* put it down—right there.

(*Lorraine casually strikes a note or two on the piano*)

(*The telephone rings*)

MAGGIE: (*Taking up the receiver a little too casually*) Hello . . . Yes . . . Yes . . . Miss Lorraine Sheldon? Yes, she's here . . . There's a trans-Atlantic call coming through for you, Lorraine.

LORRAINE: Trans-Atlantic—for me? Here? Why, what in the world—

MAGGIE: (*As she hands over the receiver*) It's London.

LORRAINE: London? . . . Hello. (*Then in a louder tone*) Hello . . . Cedric! Cedric, is this you. . . . Why, Cedric, you darling! Why, what a surprise! How'd you know I was here? . . . Darling, don't talk so fast and you won't stutter so . . . That's better . . . Yes, now I can hear you . . . Yes, very clearly. It's as though you were just around the corner. . . . I see . . . What? . . . Darling! Cedric, dearest, would you wait just one moment? (*She turns to Maggie*)

Maggie, would you mind? It's Lord Bottomley—a *very* personal call. Would you mind?

MAGGIE: Oh, not at all. (*She goes into the dining room; almost does a little waltz step as she goes*)

LORRAINE: Yes, my dearest—now tell me . . . Cedric, please don't stutter so. Don't be nervous. (*She listens for a moment again*) Oh, my darling. Oh, my sweet. You don't know how I've prayed for this, every night on the boat . . . Darling, yes! YES, a thousand times Yes! . . . I'll take a plane right out of here and catch the next boat. Oh, my sweet, we're going to be the happiest people in the world. I wish I were there now in your arms, Cedric . . . What? . . . Cedric, don't stutter so . . . Yes, and I love *you*, my darling—oh, so much! . . . Oh, my dear sweet. My darling, my darling. . . . Yes, yes! I will, I will, darling! I'll be thinking of you every moment . . . You've made me the happiest girl in the world . . . Good-bye, good-bye, darling. Good-bye. (*Bursting with her news, she throws open the library doors*) Sherry, Sherry! Do you know what's happened? Cedric just called from London— He's asked me to marry him. Sherry, think of it! At last! I've got to get right out of here and catch the next boat. How far are we from Chicago? I can get a plane from there.

MAGGIE: (*Emerging, mouse-like, from the dining room*) May I come in?

LORRAINE: Maggie dear, can I get a plane out of here right away? Or I'll even take a train to Chicago and fly from there. I've simply got to get the next boat for England. When is it—do you know? Is there a newspaper here?

MAGGIE: The *Queen Mary* sails Friday. Why, what's all the excitement, Lorraine? What's happened?

LORRAINE: Maggie, the most wonderful thing in the world has happened. Lord Bottomley has asked me to marry him . . . Oh, Maggie! (*And in her exuberance she throws her arms around her*)

MAGGIE: Really? Well, what do you know?

LORRAINE: Isn't it wonderful? I'm so excited I can hardly think. Maggie dear, you must help me get out of here.

MAGGIE: I'd be delighted to, Lorraine.

LORRAINE: Oh, thank you, thank you. Will you look things up right away?

MAGGIE: Yes, I've a time-table right here. And don't worry, because if there's no train I'll drive you to Toledo and you can catch the plane from there.

LORRAINE: Maggie darling, you're wonderful. . . . Sherry, what's the matter with you? You haven't said a word. You haven't even congratulated me.

WHITESIDE: (*Who has been sitting through this like a thundercloud*) Let me understand this, Lorraine. Am I to gather from your girlish squeals that you are about to toss your career into the ashcan?

LORRAINE: Oh, not at all. Of course I may not be able to play this season, but there'll be other seasons, Sherry.

WHITESIDE: I see. And everything goes into the ashcan with it— Is that right?

LORRAINE: But, Sherry, you couldn't expect me to—

WHITESIDE: (*Icily*) Don't explain, Lorraine. I understand only too well. And I also understand why Cornell remains the First Actress of our theatre.

MAGGIE: (*Busy with her time-tables*) Oh, this is wonderful! We're in luck, Lorraine. You can get a plane out of Toledo at ten-three. It takes about an hour to get there. Why, it all works out wonderfully, doesn't it, Sherry?

WHITESIDE: (*Through his teeth*) Peachy!

LORRAINE: (*Heading for the phone*) Maggie, what's the number of that hotel I'm at? I've got to get my maid started packing.

MAGGIE: Mesalia three two.

LORRAINE: (*Into the phone*) Mesalia three two, please . . . Let's see—I sail Friday, five-day boat, that means I ought to be in London Wednesday night. . . . Hello. This is Miss Sheldon. . . . That's right. Connect me with my maid.

MAGGIE: (*At the window*) Oh, look, Sherry, it's starting to snow. Isn't that wonderful, Sherry? Oh, I never felt more like Christmas in my life. Don't you, Sherry dear?

WHITESIDE: Shut your nasty little face!

LORRAINE: (*On the phone*) Cosette? . . . Now listen carefully, Cosette. Have you got a pencil? . . . We're leaving here tonight by plane and sailing Friday on the *Queen Mary*. Start packing immediately and I'll call for you in about an hour . . . Yes, that's right . . . Now I want you to send these cables for me . . . Ready? . . . The first one goes to

Lord and Lady Cunard—you'll find all these addresses in
my little book. It's in my dressing case. "Lord and Lady
Cunard. My darlings. Returning Friday *Queen Mary*. Cedric
and I being married immediately on arrival. Wanted you to
be the first to know. Love.—Lorraine." . . . Now send the
same message—what? . . . Oh, thank you, Cosette. Thank
you very much . . . Send the same message to Lady Astor,
Lord Beaverbrook, and the Duchess of Sutherland . . . Got
that? . . . And send a cable to Molyneaux, in Paris. "Please
meet me Claridge's Thursday of next week with sketches of
bridal gown and trousseau.—Lorraine Sheldon." And then
send one to Monsieur Pierre Cartier, Cartier's, Paris: "Can
you bring over to London the triple string of pearls I picked
out in October? Cable me *Queen Mary*.—Lorraine Sheldon." . . . Have you got all that straight, Cosette? . . .
That's fine. Now you'll have to rush, my dear—I'll be at the
hotel in about an hour, so be ready. . . . Good-bye. (*She
hangs up*) Thank goodness for Cosette—I'd die without her.
She's the most wonderful maid in the world. . . . Well! Life
is really just full of surprises, isn't it? Who'd have thought an
hour ago that I'd be on my way to London?

MAGGIE: An *hour* ago? No, I certainly wouldn't have thought
it an hour ago.

WHITESIDE: (*Beside himself with temper*) Will you both stop
this female drooling? I have a violent headache.

MAGGIE: (*All solicitude*) Oh, Sherry! Can I get you something?

LORRAINE: Look here, Sherry, I'm sorry if I've offended you,
but after all my life is my own and I'm not going to—
(*She stops as Bert Jefferson comes in from the outside*)

BERT: Hello, everybody. Say, do you know it's snowing out?
Going to have a real old-fashioned Christmas.

WHITESIDE: Why don't you telephone your scoop to the New
York *Times*?

MAGGIE: Bert, Miss Sheldon has to catch a plane tonight, from
Toledo. Can we drive her over, you and I?

BERT: Why, certainly. Sorry you have to go, Miss Sheldon. No
bad news, I hope?

LORRAINE: Oh, on the contrary—very good news. Wonderful
news.

MAGGIE: Yes, indeed—calls for a drink, I think. You're not

being a very good host, Sherry. How about a bottle of champagne?

BERT: Oh, I can do better than that—let me mix you something. It's a Jefferson Special. Okay, Mr. Whiteside?

WHITESIDE: Yes, yes, yes, yes, yes. Mix anything. Only stop driveling.

BERT: (*On his way to the dining room*) Anybody admired my Christmas present yet, Maggie?

MAGGIE: Oh, dear, I forgot. (*She raises her arm, revealing a bracelet*) Look, everybody! From Mr. Jefferson to me.

LORRAINE: Oh, it's charming. Let me see it. Oh! Why, it's inscribed, too. "To Maggie. Long may she wave. Bert." Maggie, it's a lovely Christmas present. Isn't it sweet, Sherry?

WHITESIDE: (*Glowering*) Ducky!

MAGGIE: I told you it was beautiful, Bert. See?

BERT: Well, shows what you get if you save your coupons.

LORRAINE: (*Looking from Bert to Maggie*) Well, what's going on between you two, anyhow? Maggie, are you hiding something from us?

WHITESIDE: (*A hand to his head*) Great God, will this drivel never stop? My head is bursting.

BERT: A Jefferson Special will cure anything. . . . By the way, I got a two-minute interview with Beverly Carlton at the station. You were right, Mr. Whiteside— He's quite something.

MAGGIE: (*Uneasily*) Go ahead, Bert—mix the drinks.

BERT: I was lucky to get even two minutes. He was in a telephone booth most of the time. Couldn't hear what he was saying, but from the faces he was making it looked like a scene from one of his plays.

MAGGIE: (*Hiding her frenzy*) Bert, mix those drinks, will you?

WHITESIDE: (*Suddenly galvanized*) Just a minute, if you please, Jefferson. Mr. Carlton was in a telephone booth at the station?

BERT: Certainly was—I thought he'd never come out. Kept talking and making the damnedest faces for about five minutes.

MAGGIE: (*Tensely*) Bert, for goodness sake, will you—

WHITESIDE: (*Ever so sweetly*) Bert, my boy, I have an idea I shall love the Jefferson Special. Make me a double one, will you? My headache has gone with the wind.

BERT: Okay. (*He goes*)
   (*Whiteside, his eyes gleaming, immediately whirls his wheelchair across the room to the telephone*)
WHITESIDE: (*A finger to his lips*) Sssh! Philo Vance is now at work.
LORRAINE: What?
WHITESIDE: Sssh! (*He picks up the telephone. His voice is absolutely musical*) Operator! Has there been a call from England over this telephone within the past half hour? . . . Yes, I'll wait.
LORRAINE: Sherry, what *is* all this?
WHITESIDE: What's that? There have been no calls from England for the past three days? Thank you . . . Now, will you repeat that, please? . . . Blossom Girl. (*He beckons to Lorraine, then puts the receiver to her ear*) Hear it, dear? (*Then again to the operator*) Thank you, and a Merry Christmas. (*He hangs up*) Yes, indeed, it seems we're going to have a real old-fashioned Christmas.
LORRAINE: (*Stunned*) Sherry, what is all this? What's going on? What does this mean?
WHITESIDE: My dear, you have just played the greatest love scene of your career with your old friend, Beverly Carlton.
LORRAINE: Why—why, that's not true. I was talking to Cedric. What do you mean?
WHITESIDE: I mean, my blossom, that that was Beverly you poured out your girlish heart to, not Lord Bottomley. Ah, me, who'd have thought five minutes ago that you would not be going to London!
LORRAINE: Sherry, stop it! What is this? I want this explained.
WHITESIDE: Explained? You heard the operator, my dear. All I can tell you is that Beverly was indulging in one of his famous bits of mimicry, that's all. You've heard him do Lord Bottomley before, haven't you?
LORRAINE: (*As it dawns on her*) Yes . . . Yes, of course . . . But—but why would he want to do such a thing? This is one of the most dreadful—oh, my God! Those cables! (*In one bound she is at the telephone*) Give me the hotel—whatever it's called—I want the hotel—I'll pay him off for this if it's the last thing that I— Why, the cad! The absolute unutterable cad! The dirty rotten— Mansion House? Connect

me with my maid . . . What? . . . Who the hell do you *think* it is? Miss Sheldon, of course . . . Oh, God! Those cables! If only Cosette hasn't—Cosette! Cosette! Did you send those cables? . . . Oh, God! Oh, God! . . . Now listen, Cosette, I want you to send another cable to every one of those people, and tell them somebody has been using my name, and to disregard anything and everything they hear from me—except this, of course . . . Don't ask questions— do as you're told . . . Don't argue with me, you French bitch—God damn it, do as you're told . . . And unpack— we're not going! (*She hangs up*)

WHITESIDE: Now steady, my blossom. Take it easy.

LORRAINE: (*In a white rage*) What do you mean take it easy? Do you realize I'll be the laughingstock of England? Why, I won't dare show my face! I always knew Beverly Carlton was low, but not this low. Why? WHY? It isn't even funny. Why would he do it, that's what I'd like to know. Why would he do it! Why would anyone in the world want to play a silly trick like this? I can't understand it. Do you, Sherry? Do you, Maggie? You both saw him this afternoon. Why would he walk out of here, go right to a phone booth, and try to ship me over to England on a fool's errand! There must have been some reason—there must have. It doesn't make sense otherwise. Why would Beverly Carlton, or anybody else for that matter, want me to— (*She stops as a dim light begins to dawn*) Oh! Oh! (*Her eye, which has been on Maggie, goes momentarily to the dining room, where Bert has disappeared. Then her gaze returns to Maggie again*) I—I think I begin to—of course! Of course! That's it. Of course that's it. Yes, and that's a very charming bracelet that Mr. Jefferson gave you—isn't it, Maggie dear? Of course. It makes complete sense now. And to think that I nearly—well! Wild horses couldn't get me out of here *now*, Maggie. And if I were you I'd hang onto that bracelet, dear. It'll be something to remember him by!

(*Out of the library comes Mr. Westcott, his hands full of papers. At the same time the two technicians emerge from the dining room and go to the control board*)

WESTCOTT: (*His eyes on his watch*) All right, Mr. Whiteside.

Almost time. Here's your new copy. Hook her up, boys. Start testing.

WHITESIDE: How much time?

WESTCOTT: (*Bringing him a microphone*) Couple of minutes.

(*One of the radio technicians is talking into a microphone, testing: "One, two, three, four, one, two, three, four. How are we coming in, New York? . . . A, B, C, A, B, C. Mary had a little lamb, Mary had a little lamb"*)

(*Mr. and Mrs. Stanley, having delivered their Christmas presents, enter from the hallway and start up the stairs. Mrs. Stanley looks hungrily at the radio goings-on, but Mr. Stanley delivers a stern "Come, Daisy," and she follows him up the stairs*)

(*The voices of the technicians drone on: "One, two, three, four, one, two, three, four. O.K., New York. Waiting." Mr. Westcott stands with watch in hand*)

(*From the dining room comes Bert Jefferson, a tray of drinks in hand*)

BERT: Here comes the Jefferson Special . . . Oh! Have we time?

LORRAINE: Oh, I'm sure we have. Mr. Jefferson, I'm not leaving after all. My plans are changed.

BERT: Really? Oh, that's good.

LORRAINE: And I hear you've written a simply marvelous play, Mr. Jefferson. I want you to read it to me—tonight. Will you? We'll go back to the Mansion House right after dinner, and you'll read me your play.

BERT: Why—why, I should say so. I'd be delighted. . . . Maggie, did you hear that? Say! I'll bet *you* did this. You arranged the whole thing. Well, it's the finest Christmas present you could have given me.

(*Maggie looks at him for one anguished moment. Then, without a word, she dashes into the hall, grabs her coat and flings herself out of the house*)

(*Bert, bewildered, stands looking after her. Mr. and Mrs. Stanley come pellmell down the stairs. Each clutches a letter, and they are wild-eyed*)

STANLEY: *Mr.* Whiteside! My son has run off on a freighter and my daughter is marrying an anarchist! They say *you* told them to do it!

MRS. STANLEY: My poor June! My poor Richard! This is the most awful—

WESTCOTT: Quiet! Quiet, please! We're going on the air.

STANLEY: How dare you! This is the most outrageous—

WESTCOTT: (*Raising his voice*) Please! *Please!* Quiet! We're going on the air.

(*Stanley chokes and looks with fury. Mrs. Stanley is softly crying*)

(*In this moment of stillness, Dr. Bradley emerges from the dining room*)

DR. BRADLEY: Oh! I see you're still busy.

STANLEY: (*Bursting forth*) Mr. Whiteside, you are the—

WESTCOTT: (*Yelling*) *Quiet!* For God's sake, quiet! QUIET! . . . All right, boys!

(*From the hallway come six Choir Boys, dressed in their robes. They take their places by the microphone as the voice of the technician completes the hook-up*)

TECHNICIAN: O.K., New York.

(*He raises his arm, waiting to give the signal. Westcott is watching him. There is a dead pause of about five seconds. John and Sarah are on tiptoe in the dining room. Then the arm drops*)

WESTCOTT: (*Into the microphone*) Good evening, everybody. Cream of Mush brings you Sheridan Whiteside.

(*The Leader gestures to the Choir Boys, and they raise their lovely voices in "Heilige Nacht." Another gesture from Westcott, and Whiteside begins to speak, with the boys singing as a background*)

WHITESIDE: This is Whiteside speaking. On this eve of eves, when my own heart is overflowing with peace and kindness, I think it is most fitting to tell once again the story of that still and lustrous night, nigh onto two thousand years ago, when first the star of Bethlehem was glimpsed in a wondrous sky . . .

(*The famous Whiteside voice goes out over the air to the listening millions as—*

THE CURTAIN FALLS

ACT THREE

Christmas morning.

The bright December sunlight streams in through the window.

But the Christmas calm is quickly broken. From the library comes the roaring voice of Mr. Whiteside. "Miss Preen! Miss Preen!"

Miss Preen, who is just coming through the dining room, rushes to open the library doors.

MISS PREEN: (*Nervously*) Yes, sir. Yes, sir.
  (*Mr. Whiteside, in a mood, rolls himself into the room*)

WHITESIDE: Where *do* you disappear to all the time, My Lady Nausea?

MISS PREEN: (*Firmly*) Mr. Whiteside, I can only be in one place at a time.

WHITESIDE: That's very fortunate for this community. . . . Go away, Miss Preen. You remind me of last week's laundry.
  (*Miss Preen goes indignantly into the library and slams the doors after her*)
  (*John emerges from the dining room*)

JOHN: Good morning, Mr. Whiteside. Merry Christmas.

WHITESIDE: (*Testily*) Merry Christmas, John. Merry Christmas.

JOHN: And Sarah and I want to thank you for the wonderful present.

WHITESIDE: That's quite all right, John.

JOHN: Are you ready for your breakfast, Mr. Whiteside?

WHITESIDE: No, I don't think I want any breakfast. . . . Has Miss Cutler come down yet?

JOHN: No, sir, not yet.

WHITESIDE: Is she in her room, do you know?

JOHN: Yes, sir, I think she is. Shall I call her?

WHITESIDE: No, no. That's all, John.

JOHN: Yes, sir.
  (*Maggie comes down the stairs. She wears a traveling suit, and carries a bag. Whiteside waits for her to speak*)

MAGGIE: I'm taking the one o'clock train, Sherry. I'm leaving.

WHITESIDE: You're doing nothing of the kind!

829

MAGGIE: Here are your keys—your driving license. The key to the safe-deposit vault is in the apartment in New York. I'll go in here now and clear things up. (*She opens the library doors*)

WHITESIDE: Just a moment, Mrs. Siddons! Where *were* you until three o'clock this morning? I sat up half the night in this station wagon, worrying about you. You heard me calling to you when you came in. Why didn't you answer me?

MAGGIE: Look, Sherry, it's over, and you've won. I don't want to talk about it.

WHITESIDE: Oh, come, come, come, come, come. What are you trying to do—make me feel like a naughty, naughty boy? Honestly, Maggie, sometimes you can be very annoying.

MAGGIE: (*Looking at him in wonder*) You know, you're quite wonderful, Sherry, in a way. *You're* annoyed. I wish there was a laugh left in me. Shall I tell you something, Sherry? I think you are a selfish, petty egomaniac who would see his mother burned at the stake if that was the only way he could light his cigarette. I think you'd sacrifice your best friend without a moment's hesitation if he disturbed the sacred routine of your self-centered, paltry little life. I think you are incapable of any human emotion that goes higher up than your stomach, and I was the fool of the world for ever thinking I could trust you.

WHITESIDE: (*Pretty indignant at this*) Well, as long as I live, I shall never do anyone a good turn again. I won't ask you to apologize, Maggie, but six months from now you will be thanking me instead of berating me.

MAGGIE: In six months, Sherry, I expect to be so far away from you—

(*She is halted by a loud voice from the hallway, as the door bangs. "Hello—hello—hello!" It is Bert Jefferson who enters, full of Christmas cheer*)

BERT: Merry Christmas, everybody! Merry Christmas! I'm a little high, but I can explain everything. Hi, Maggie! Hi, Mr. Whiteside! Shake hands with a successful playwright. Maggie, why'd you run away last night? Where were you?

Miss Sheldon thinks the play is wonderful. I read her the play and she thinks it's wonderful. Isn't that wonderful?

MAGGIE: Yes, that's fine, Bert.

BERT: Isn't that wonderful, Mr. Whiteside?

WHITESIDE: Jefferson, I think you ought to go home, don't you?

BERT: What? No—biggest day of my life. I know I'm a little drunk, but this is a big day. We've been sitting over in Billy's Tavern all night. Never realized it was daylight until it was daylight. . . . Listen, Maggie—Miss Sheldon says the play needs just a little bit of fixing—do it in three weeks. She's going to take me to a little place she's got in Lake Placid— just for three weeks. Going to work on the play together. Isn't it wonderful? Why don't you say something, Maggie?

WHITESIDE: Look, Bert, I suggest you tell us all about this later. Now, why don't you—

(*He stops as Dr. Bradley enters from the hallway*)

DR. BRADLEY: Oh, excuse me! Merry Christmas, everybody. Merry Christmas.

BERT: God bless us all, and Tiny Tim.

DR. BRADLEY: Yes. . . . Mr. Whiteside, I thought perhaps if I came very early—

BERT: You know what, Doc? I'm going to Lake Placid for three weeks—isn't that wonderful? Ever hear of Lorraine Sheldon, the famous actress? Well, we're going to Lake Placid for three weeks.

WHITESIDE: Dr. Bradley, would you do me a favor? I think Mr. Jefferson would like some black coffee and a little breakfast. Would you take care of him, please?

DR. BRADLEY: (*None too pleased*) Yes, yes, of course.

BERT: Dr. Bradley, I'm going to buy breakfast for *you*—biggest breakfast you ever had.

DR. BRADLEY: Yes, yes. Come along, Jefferson.

BERT: You know what, Doctor? Let's climb down a couple of chimneys. I got a friend doesn't believe in Santa Claus—let's climb down his chimney and frighten the hell out of him. (*He goes out with the Doctor*)

WHITESIDE: (*In a burst of magnanimity*) Now listen to me, Maggie. I am willing to forgive your tawdry outburst and talk about this calmly.

MAGGIE: (*Now crying openly*) I love him so terribly. Oh, Sherry, Sherry, why did you do it? Why did you do it? (*She goes stumblingly into the library*)

(*Whiteside, left alone, looks at his watch; heaves a long sigh. Then Harriet comes down the steps, dressed for the street*)

HARRIET: Merry Christmas, Mr. Whiteside.

WHITESIDE: Oh! . . . Merry Christmas, Miss Stanley.

HARRIET: (*Nervously*) I'm afraid I shouldn't be seen talking to you, Mr. Whiteside—my brother is terribly angry. I just couldn't resist asking—did you like my Christmas present?

WHITESIDE: I'm very sorry, Miss Stanley—I haven't opened it. I haven't opened any of my presents yet.

HARRIET: Oh, dear. I was so anxious to—it's right here, Mr. Whiteside. (*She goes to the tree*) Won't you open it now?

WHITESIDE: (*As he undoes the string*) I appreciate your thinking of me, Miss Stanley. This is very thoughtful of you. (*He takes out the gift*) Why, it's lovely. I'm very fond of these old photographs. Thank you very much.

HARRIET: I was twenty-two when that was taken. That was my favorite dress. . . . Do you really like it?

WHITESIDE: I do indeed. When I get back to town I shall send *you* a little gift.

HARRIET: Will you? Oh, thank you, Mr. Whiteside. I shall treasure it. . . . Well, I shall be late for church. Good-bye. Good-bye.

WHITESIDE: Good-bye, Miss Stanley.

(*As she goes out the front door, Whiteside's eyes return to the gift. He puzzles over it for a second, shakes his head. Mumbles to himself—"What is there about that woman?" Shakes his head again in perplexity*)

(*John comes from the dining room, en route to the second floor with Mrs. Stanley's tray*)

JOHN: Sarah's got a little surprise for you, Mr. Whiteside. She's just taking it out of the oven.

WHITESIDE: Thank you, John.

(*John disappears up the stairs*)

(*Then suddenly there is a great ringing of the door bell. It stops for a second, then picks up violently again—rhythmically, this time. It continues until the door is opened*)

WHITESIDE: Miss Preen! Miss Preen!

(*Miss Preen comes hurrying from the library*)

MISS PREEN: Yes, sir. Yes, sir.

WHITESIDE: Answer the door, will you? John is upstairs.

(*Miss Preen, obviously annoyed, hurries to the door*)

(*We hear her voice from the hallway: "Who is it?" An answering male voice: "Polly Adler's?" Then a little shriek from Miss Preen, and in a moment we see the reason why. She is carried into the room in the arms of a pixie-like gentleman, who is kissing her over and over*)

THE GENTLEMAN CARRYING MISS PREEN: I love you madly—madly! Did you hear what I said—madly! Kiss me! Again! Don't be afraid of my passion. Kiss me! I can feel the hot blood pounding through your varicose veins.

MISS PREEN: (*Through all this*) Put me down! Put me down, do you hear! Don't you dare kiss me! Who are you! Put me down or I'll scream. Mr. Whiteside! Mr. Whiteside!

WHITESIDE: Banjo! Banjo, for God's sake!

BANJO: (*Quite calmly*) Hello, Whiteside. Will you sign for this package, please?

WHITESIDE: Banjo, put that woman down. That is my nurse, you mental delinquent.

BANJO: (*Putting Miss Preen on her feet*) Come to my room in half an hour and bring some rye bread. (*And for good measure he slaps Miss Preen right on the fanny*)

MISS PREEN: (*Outraged*) Really, Mr. Whiteside! (*She adjusts her clothes with a quick jerk or two and marches into the library*)

BANJO: Whiteside, I'm here to spend Christmas with you. Give me a kiss! (*He starts to embrace him*)

WHITESIDE: Get away from me, you reform-school fugitive. How did you get here anyway?

BANJO: Darryl Zanuck loaned me his reindeer. . . . Whiteside, we finished shooting the picture yesterday and I'm on my way to Nova Scotia. Flew here in twelve hours—borrowed an airplane from Howard Hughes. Whiteside, I brought you a wonderful Christmas present. (*He produces a little tissue-wrapped package*) This brassière was once worn by Hedy Lamarr.

WHITESIDE: Listen, you idiot, how long can you stay?

BANJO: Just long enough to take a bath. I'm on my way to Nova Scotia. Where's Maggie?

WHITESIDE: Nova Scotia? What are you going to Nova Scotia for?

BANJO: I'm sick of Hollywood and there's a dame in New York I don't want to see. So I figured I'd go to Nova Scotia and get some good salmon. . . . Where the hell's Maggie? I want to see her. . . . What's the matter with you? Where is she?

WHITESIDE: Banjo, I'm glad you're here. I'm very annoyed at Maggie. Very!

BANJO: What's the matter? . . .

(*To his considerable surprise, at this point, he sees Whiteside get up out of his chair and start to pace up and down the room.*)

Say, what *is* this? I thought you couldn't walk.

WHITESIDE: Oh, I've been all right for weeks. That isn't the point. I'm furious at Maggie. She's turned on me like a viper. You know how fond I am of her. Well, after all these years she's repaying my affection by behaving like a fish-wife.

BANJO: What are you talking about?

WHITESIDE: But I never believed for a moment she was really in love with him.

BANJO: In love with *who*? I just got here—remember.

WHITESIDE: Great God, I'm telling you, you Hollywood nit-wit. A young newspaper man here in town.

BANJO: (*Surprised and pleased*) Maggie finally fell—well, what do you know? What kind of a guy is he?

WHITESIDE: Oh, shut up and listen, will you?

BANJO: Well, go on. What happened?

WHITESIDE: Well, Lorraine Sheldon happened to come out here and visit me.

BANJO: Old Hot-pants—here?

WHITESIDE: Now listen! He'd written a play—this young fellow. You can guess the rest. He's going away with Lorraine this afternoon. To "rewrite." So there you are. Maggie's in there now, crying her eyes out.

BANJO: Gee! . . . (*Thinking it over*) Say, wait a minute. What do you mean Lorraine Sheldon *happened* to come out here? I smell a rat, Sherry—a rat with a beard.

(*And it might be well to add, at this point, that Mr. Sheridan Whiteside wears a beard*)

WHITESIDE: Well, all right, all right. But I did it for Maggie—
because I thought it was the right thing for her.

BANJO: Oh, sure. You haven't thought of yourself in years.
. . . Gee, poor kid. Can I go in and talk to her?

WHITESIDE: No—no. Leave her alone.

BANJO: Any way I could help, Sherry? Where's this guy live—
this guy she likes? Can we get hold of him?

WHITESIDE: Now, wait a minute, Banjo. We don't want any
phony warrants, or you pretending to be J. Edgar Hoover.
I've been through all that with you before. (*He paces again*)
I got Lorraine out here and I've got to get her away.

BANJO: It's got to be good, Sherry. Lorraine's no dope. . . .
Now, there must be *some*thing that would get her out of
here like a bat out of hell. . . . Say! I think I've got it! That
fellow she's so crazy about over in England—Lord Fanny or
whatever it is. Bottomley—that's it!

WHITESIDE: (*With a pained expression*) No, Banjo. No.

BANJO: Wait a minute—you don't catch on. We send Lorraine
a cablegram from Lord Bottomley—

WHITESIDE: I catch on, Banjo. Lorraine caught on, too. It's
been tried.

BANJO: Oh! . . . I told you she was no dope. . . . (*Seeing
Whiteside's chair, he sits in it and leans back with a good deal
of pleasure*)
Well, you've got a tough proposition on your hands.

WHITESIDE: The trouble is there's so damned little time. . . .
Get out of my chair! (*Whiteside gets back into it*) Lorraine's
taking him away with her this afternoon. Oh, damn, damn,
damn. There must be some way out. The trouble is I've
done this job too well. Hell and damnation.

BANJO: (*Pacing*) Stuck, huh?

WHITESIDE: In the words of one of our greatest lyric poets,
you said it.

BANJO: Yeh. . . . Gee, I'm hungry. We'll think of something,
Sherry—you watch. We'll get Lorraine out of here if I have
to do it one piece at a time.
      (*Sarah enters from the dining room bearing a tray on which
      reposes the culinary surprise that John has mentioned. She
      holds it behind her back*)

SARAH: Merry Christmas, Mr. Whiteside. . . . Excuse me. (*This last is to Banjo*) I've got something for you. . . .

(*Banjo blandly lifts the latest delicacy and proceeds to eat it as Sarah presents the empty plate to Whiteside*)

SARAH: (*Almost in tears*) But, Mr. Whiteside, it was for you.

WHITESIDE: Never mind, Sarah. He's quite mad.

BANJO: Come, Petrouchka, we will dance in the snow until all St. Petersburg is aflame with jealousy. (*He clutches Sarah and waltzes her toward the kitchen, loudly humming the Merry Widow waltz*)

SARAH: (*As she is borne away*) Mr. Whiteside! Mr. Whiteside!

WHITESIDE: Just give him some breakfast, Sarah. He's harmless.

(*Mr. Whiteside barely has a moment in which to collect his thoughts before the library doors are opened and Miss Preen emerges. It is Miss Preen in street clothes this time, and with a suitcase in her hand*)

(*She plants herself squarely in front of Whiteside, puts down her bag and starts drawing on a pair of gloves*)

WHITESIDE: And just what does this mean?

MISS PREEN: It means, Mr. Whiteside, that I am leaving. My address is on the desk inside; you can send me a check.

WHITESIDE: You realize, Miss Preen, that this is completely unprofessional.

MISS PREEN: I do indeed. I am not only walking out on this case, Mr. Whiteside—I am leaving the nursing profession. I became a nurse because all my life, ever since I was a little girl, I was filled with the idea of serving a suffering humanity. After one month with you, Mr. Whiteside, I am going to work in a munitions factory. From now on anything that I can do to help exterminate the human race will fill me with the greatest of pleasure. If Florence Nightingale had ever nursed *you*, Mr. Whiteside, she would have married Jack the Ripper instead of founding the Red Cross. Good day. (*And she sails out*)

(*Before Whiteside has time to digest this little bouquet, Mrs. Stanley, in a state of great fluttery excitement, rushes down the stairs*)

MRS. STANLEY: Mr. Stanley is here with June. He's brought June back. Thank goodness, thank goodness. (*We hear her*

at the door) June, June, thank God you're back. You're not
married, are you?

JUNE: (*From the hallway*) No, Mother, I'm not. And please
don't be hysterical.

(*Mrs. Stanley comes into view, her arms around a rebellious
June. Behind them looms Mr. Stanley, every inch the stern
father*)

MRS. STANLEY: Oh, June, if it had been anyone but that awful
boy. You know how your father and I felt. . . . Ernest,
thank goodness you stopped it. How did you do it?

STANLEY: Never mind that, Daisy. Just take June upstairs. I
have something to say to Mr. Whiteside.

MRS. STANLEY: What about Richard? Is there any news?

STANLEY: It's all right, Daisy—all under control. Just take June
upstairs.

JUNE: Father, haven't we had enough melodrama? I don't
have to be taken upstairs—I'll go upstairs. . . . Merry
Christmas, Mr. Whiteside. It looks bad for John L. Lewis.
Come on, Mother—lock me in my room.

MRS. STANLEY: Now, June, you'll feel much better after you've
had a hot bath, I know. Have you had anything to eat? (*She
follows her daughter up the stairs*)

(*Stanley turns to Mr. Whiteside*)

STANLEY: I am pleased to inform you, sir, that your plans for
my daughter seem to have gone a trifle awry. She is not, nor
will she ever be, married to that labor agitator that you so
kindly picked out for her. As for my son, he has been apprehended in Toledo, and will be brought back home within
the hour. Not having your gift for invective, I cannot tell
you what I think of your obnoxious interference in my affairs, but I have now arranged that you will interfere no
longer. (*He turns toward the hallway*) Come in, gentlemen.

(*Two burly Men come into view and stand in the archway*)

Mr. Whiteside, these gentlemen are deputy sheriffs. They
have a warrant by which I am enabled to put you out of this
house, and I need hardly add that it will be the greatest moment of my life. Mr. Whiteside— (*He looks at his watch*) —I
am giving you fifteen minutes in which to pack up and get
out. If you are not gone in fifteen minutes, Mr. Whiteside,

these gentlemen will forcibly eject you. (*He turns to the deputies*) Thank you, gentlemen. Will you wait outside, please?
(*The Two Men file out*)
Fifteen minutes, Mr. Whiteside—and that means bag, baggage, wheelchair, penguins, octopus and cockroaches. I am now going upstairs to smash our radio, so that not even accidentally will I ever hear your voice again.

WHITESIDE: Sure you don't want my autograph, old fellow?

STANLEY: Fifteen minutes, Mr. Whiteside. (*And he goes*)
(*Banjo, still eating, returns from the kitchen*)

BANJO: Well, Whiteside, I didn't get an idea. Any news from the front?

WHITESIDE: Yes. The enemy is at my rear, and nibbling.

BANJO: Where'd you say Maggie was? In there?

WHITESIDE: It's no use, Banjo. She's taking the one o'clock train out.

BANJO: No kidding? You didn't tell me that. You mean she's quitting you, after all these years? She's really leaving?

WHITESIDE: She is!

BANJO: That means you've only got till one o'clock to do something?

WHITESIDE: No, dear. I have exactly fifteen minutes— (*He looks at his watch*) —ah—fourteen minutes—in which to pull out of my hat the God-damnedest rabbit you have ever seen.

BANJO: What do you mean fifteen minutes?

WHITESIDE: In exactly fifteen minutes Baby's rosy little body is being tossed into the snow. My host has sworn out a warrant. I am being kicked out.

BANJO: What? I never heard of such a thing. What would he do a thing like that for?

WHITESIDE: Never mind, never mind. The point is, I have only fifteen minutes. Banjo dear, the master is growing a little desperate.

BANJO: (*Paces a moment*) What about laying your cards on the table with Lorraine?

WHITESIDE: Now, Banjo. You know Dream Girl as well as I do. What do *you* think?

BANJO: You're right. . . . Say! If I knew where she was I could get a car and run her over. It wouldn't hurt her much.

WHITESIDE: (*Wearily*) Banjo, for God's sake. Go in and talk to Maggie for a minute—right in there. I want to think.

BANJO: Could we get a doctor to say Lorraine has smallpox?

WHITESIDE: Please, Banjo. I've got to think.

BANJO: (*Opening the library doors*) Pardon me, miss, is this the Y.M.C.A.?

(*The doors close*)

(*Whiteside is alone again. He leans back, concentrating intensely. He shakes his head as, one after another, he discards a couple of ideas*)

(*We hear the outer door open and close, and from the hallway comes Richard. Immediately behind him is a stalwart-looking Man with an air of authority*)

THE MAN: (*To Richard, as he indicates Whiteside*) Is this your father?

RICHARD: No, you idiot. . . . Hello, Mr. Whiteside. I didn't get very far. Any suggestions?

WHITESIDE: I'm very sorry, Richard—very sorry indeed. I wish I were in position—

STANLEY: (*Descending the stairs*) Well, you're *not* in position. . . . Thank you very much, officer. Here's a little something for your trouble.

THE MAN: Thank you, sir. Good day. (*He goes*)

STANLEY: Will you go upstairs please, Richard?

(*Richard hesitates for a second. Looks at his father, then at Whiteside; silently goes up the steps*)

(*Mr. Stanley follows him, but pauses on the landing*)

STANLEY: *Ten* minutes, Mr. Whiteside. (*And he goes*)

(*John enters from the dining room, bringing a glass of orange juice*)

JOHN: Here you are, Mr. Whiteside. Feeling any better?

WHITESIDE: Superb. Any cyanide in this orange juice, John?

(*The door bell rings*)

Open the door, John. It's probably some mustard gas from an old friend.

JOHN: (*En route to the door*) Yes, sir. . . . Say, that crazy fellow made a great hit with Sarah. He wants to give her a screen test.

(*At the outer door we hear Lorraine's voice: "Good morning! Is Mr. Whiteside up yet?" John's answer: "Yes, he is, Miss Sheldon—he's right here"*)

(*Whiteside groans as he hears her voice*)

LORRAINE: (*Entering, in a very smart Christmas morning costume*) Merry Christmas, darling! Merry Christmas! I've come to have Christmas breakfast with you, my dear. May I? (*She kisses him*)

WHITESIDE: (*Nothing matters any more*) Of course, my sprite. John, a tray for Miss Sheldon—better make it one-minute eggs.

LORRAINE: Sherry, it's the most perfect Christmas morning —the snow is absolutely glistening. Too bad you can't get out.

WHITESIDE: Oh, I'll probably see a bit of it. . . . I hear you're off to Lake Placid, my blossom. What time are you going?

LORRAINE: Oh, Sherry, how did you know? Is Bert here?

WHITESIDE: No, he rolled in a little while ago. Worked rather fast, didn't you, dear?

LORRAINE: Darling, I was just swept off my feet by the play— it's fantastically good. Sherry, it's the kind of part that only comes along once in ten years. I'm so grateful to you, darling. Really, Sherry, sometimes I think that you're the only friend I have in the world.

WHITESIDE: (*Dryly*) Thank you, dear. What time did you say you were leaving—you and Jefferson?

LORRAINE: Oh, I don't know—I think it's four o'clock. You know, quite apart from anything else, Sherry, Bert is really a very attractive man. It makes it rather a pleasure, squaring accounts with little Miss Vitriol. In fact, it's all worked out beautifully. . . . Sherry lamb, I want to give you the most beautiful Christmas present you've ever had in your life. Now, what do you want? Anything! I'm so deliriously happy that—

(*A bellowing laugh comes from the library. She stops, lips compressed*)

That sounds like Banjo. Is he here?

WHITESIDE: He is, my dear. Just the family circle gathering at Christmas. (*A look at his watch*) My, how times flies when you're having fun.

(*Banjo emerges from the library*)

BANJO: Why, hello, Sweetie Pants! How are you?

LORRAINE: (*Not over-cordial*) Very well, thank you. And you, Banjo?

BANJO: I'm fine, fine. How's the mattress business, Lorraine?

LORRAINE: *Very* funny. It's too bad, Banjo, that your pictures aren't as funny as you seem to think *you* are.

BANJO: You've got me there, mama. Say, you look in the pink, Lorraine. . . . Anything in the wind, Whiteside?

WHITESIDE: Not a glimmer.

BANJO: What time does the boat sail?

WHITESIDE: Ten minutes.

LORRAINE: What boat is this?

BANJO: The good ship *Up the Creek*. . . . Oh, well! You feel fine, huh, Lorraine?

LORRAINE: What? Yes, of course I do. . . . Where's that breakfast, Sherry?

(*Maggie emerges from the library, a sheaf of papers in her hand. She stops imperceptibly as she sees Lorraine*)

MAGGIE: I've listed everything except the New Year's Eve broadcast. Wasn't there a schedule on that?

WHITESIDE: (*Uneasily*) I think it's on the table there, some place.

MAGGIE: Thank you. (*She turns to the papers on the table*)

LORRAINE: (*Obviously for Maggie's ears*) New Year's Eve? Oh, Bert and I'll hear it in Lake Placid. You were at my cottage up there once, weren't you, Sherry? It's lovely, isn't it? Away from everything. Just snow and clear, cold nights.

(*The door bell rings*)

Oh, that's probably Bert. I told him to meet me here.

(*Maggie, as though she had not heard a word, goes quietly into the library. Lorraine relaxes*)

You know, I'm looking forward to Lake Placid. Bert's the kind of man who will do all winter sports beautifully.

BANJO: (*Gently*) Will he get time?

(*Voices are heard from the hallway. "Whiteside?" "Yes, sir." "American Express." John backs into the room, obviously directing a major operation*)

JOHN: All right—come ahead. Care now—careful—right in here. It's for you, Mr. Whiteside.

LORRAINE: Why, Sherry, what's this?

(*Into view come two Expressmen, groaning and grunting under the weight of nothing more or less than an Egyptian mummy case. It seems that Mr. Whiteside's friends are liable to think of anything*)

EXPRESSMAN: Where do you want this put?

JOHN: Right there.

WHITESIDE: Dear God, if there was one thing I needed right now it was an Egyptian mummy.

BANJO: (*Reading from a tag*) "Merry Christmas from the Khedive of Egypt." What did you send *him*? Grant's Tomb?

(*Mr. Stanley, drawn by the voices of the Expressmen, has descended the stairs in time to witness this newest hue and cry*)

STANLEY: (*Surveying the scene*) *Five* minutes, Mr. Whiteside! (*He indicates the mummy case*) Including *that*. (*And up the stairs again*)

LORRAINE: Why, what was all that about? Who is that man?

WHITESIDE: He announces the time every few minutes. I pay him a small sum.

LORRAINE: But what on earth for, Sherry?

WHITESIDE: (*Violently*) I lost my watch!

(*From the hallway a familiar figure peeps in*)

DR. BRADLEY: Oh, excuse me, Mr. Whiteside. Are you busy?

WHITESIDE: (*Closing his eyes*) Good God!

DR. BRADLEY: (*Coming into the room*) I've written a new chapter on the left kidney. Suppose I— (*He smiles apologetically at Lorraine and Banjo*) Pardon me. (*Goes into the library*)

LORRAINE: Is that the plumber again, Sherry? . . . Oh, dear, I wonder where Bert is. . . . Darling, you're not very Christmasy—you're usually bubbling over on Christmas morning. . . . *Who* sent this to you, Sherry—the Khedive of Egypt? You know, I think it's rather beautiful. I must go to Egypt some day—I really must. I know I'd love it. The first time I went to Pompeii I cried all night. All those people—all those lives. Where are they now? Sherry! Don't you ever think about that? I do. Here was a woman—like myself—a woman who once lived and loved, full of the same passions, fears, jealousies, hates. And what remains of any of it now? Just this, and nothing more. (*She opens the case, then, with a sudden impulse, steps into it and folds her arms, mummy-fashion*) A span of four thousand years—a mere atom in the eternity of time—and here am I, another woman living out her life. I want to cry.

(*She closes her eyes, and as she stands there, immobilized, the eyes of Banjo and Whiteside meet. The same idea has leaped into their minds. Banjo, rising slowly from the couch, starts to approach the mummy case, casually whistling "Dixie." But just before he reaches it Lorraine steps blandly out*)

LORRAINE: Oh, I mustn't talk this way today. It's Christmas, it's Christmas!

(*Banjo puts on a great act of unconcern*)

WHITESIDE: (*Rising to the occasion, and dripping pure charm*) Lorraine dear, have you ever played Saint Joan?

LORRAINE: No, I haven't, Sherry. What makes you ask that?

WHITESIDE: There was something about your expression as you stood in that case—there was an absolute halo about you.

LORRAINE: Why, Sherry, how sweet!

WHITESIDE: It transcended any mortal expression I've ever seen. Step into it again, dear.

LORRAINE: Sherry, you're joshing me—aren't you?

WHITESIDE: My dear, I don't make light of these things. I was deeply moved. There was a strange beauty about you, Lorraine—pure da Vinci. Please do it again.

LORRAINE: Well, I don't know exactly what it was that I did, but I'll— (*She starts to step into the case again, then changes her mind*) Oh, I feel too silly, Sherry.

(*Banjo's eyes are fixed somewhere on the ceiling, but he is somewhat less innocent than he seems*)

WHITESIDE: (*Returning to the battle*) Lorraine dear, in that single moment you approached the epitome of your art, and you should not be ashamed of it. You asked me a little while ago what I wanted for a Christmas present. All that I want, Lorraine, is the memory of you in that mummy case.

LORRAINE: Why, darling, I'm—all choked up. (*Crossing her arms, she takes a moment or two to throw herself in the mood, then steps reverently into the case*) "Dust thou art, and dust to dust—"

(*Bang! Banjo has closed the case and fastened it. Whiteside leaps out of the chair*)

WHITESIDE: Eureka!

BANJO: There's service for you!

WHITESIDE: Will she be all right in there?

BANJO: Sure—she can breathe easy. I'll let her out as soon as
we get on the plane. . . . What are we going to do now?
How do we get this out of here?

WHITESIDE: One thing at a time—that's the next step.

BANJO: Think fast, Captain. Think fast.

(*And Maggie enters from the library, papers in hand.
Whiteside scrambles back into his chair; Banjo is again the
little innocent*)

MAGGIE: This is everything, Sherry—I'm leaving three car-
bons. Is there anything out here? (*She inspects a small basket
fastened to his chair*) What's in this basket?

WHITESIDE: (*Eager to be rid of her*) Nothing at all. Thank you,
thank you.

MAGGIE: Shall I file these letters? Do you want this picture?

WHITESIDE: No—throw everything away. Wait—give me the
picture. I want the picture.

MAGGIE: The only thing I haven't done is to put all your
broadcasts in order. Do you want me to do that?

WHITESIDE: (*A flash of recollection has come to him as he takes
Harriet's photograph in his hand, but he contrives to smother
his excitement*) What? . . . Ah—do that, will you? Do it
right away—it's very important. Right away, Maggie.

MAGGIE: I'll see you before I go, Banjo. (*She goes into the library again, closing the doors*)

WHITESIDE: (*Watching her out, then jumping up in great excitement*) I've got it!

BANJO: What?

WHITESIDE: I knew I'd seen this face before! I knew it! Now I
know how to get this out of here.

BANJO: What face? How?

(*And, at that instant, Mr. Stanley comes down the stairs,
watch in hand*)

STANLEY: (*Vastly enjoying himself*) The time is up, Mr. Whiteside. Fifteen minutes.

WHITESIDE: Ah, yes, Mr. Stanley. Fifteen minutes. But just
one favor before I go. I would like you to summon those
two officers and ask them to help this gentleman down to

the airport with this mummy case. Would you be good enough to do that, Mr. Stanley?

STANLEY: I will do nothing of the kind.

WHITESIDE: (*Ever so sweetly*) Oh, I think you will, Mr. Stanley. Or shall I inform my radio audience, on my next broadcast, that your sister, Harriet Stanley, is none other than the famous Harriet Sedley, who murdered her mother and father with an axe twenty-five years ago in Gloucester, Massachusetts. . . .

(*At which Mr. Stanley quietly collapses into a chair*)

Come, Mr. Stanley, it's a very small favor. Or would you rather have the good folk of Mesalia repeating at your very doorstep that once popular little jingle:

"Harriet Sedley took an axe
      And gave her mother forty whacks,
      And when the job was nicely done,
      She gave her father forty-one."

Remember, Mr. Stanley, I too am giving up something. It would make a hell of a broadcast. . . . Well?

STANLEY: (*Licked at last*) Mr. Whiteside, you are the damnedest person I have ever met.

WHITESIDE: I often think so myself, old fellow . . . Officers, will you come in here, please?

BANJO: Whiteside, you're a great man. (*He places a reverent kiss on the mummy case*)

WHITESIDE: (*As the Deputies enter*) Come right in, officers. Mr. Stanley would like you to help this gentleman down to the airport with this mummy case. He is sending it to a friend in Nova Scotia.

BANJO: Collect.

WHITESIDE: Right, Mr. Stanley?

STANLEY: (*Weakly*) Yes. . . . Yes.

WHITESIDE: Thank you, gentlemen—handle it carefully. . . . Banjo, my love, you're wonderful and I may write a book about you.

BANJO: Don't bother—I can't read. (*To Maggie, as she enters from library*) Good-bye, Maggie—love conquers all. . . . Don't drop that case, boys—it contains an antique. (*And out he goes with the mummy case, to say nothing of Miss Lorraine Sheldon*)

MAGGIE: (*Catching on to what has happened*) Sherry! Sherry, was that—?

WHITESIDE: It was indeed. The field is clear and you have my blessing.

MAGGIE: Sherry! Sherry, you old reprobate!

WHITESIDE: Just send me a necktie some time. My hat and coat, Maggie, and also your railroad ticket. I am leaving for New York.

MAGGIE: You're leaving, Sherry?

WHITESIDE: Don't argue, Rat Girl— Do as you're told.

MAGGIE: Yes, Mr. Whiteside. (*She goes happily into the library, just as Bert returns*)

BERT: Mr. Whiteside, I want to apologize for—

WHITESIDE: Don't give it a thought, Bert. There's been a slight change of plan. Miss Sheldon is off on a world cruise —I am taking your play to Katharine Cornell. Miss Cutler will explain everything.

(*Maggie brings Whiteside's coat, hat, cane*)

Oh, thank you, Maggie, my darling.

(*And just then the Doctor comes out of the library. Still trying*)

DR. BRADLEY: Mr. Whiteside, are you very busy?

WHITESIDE: Ah, yes, Doctor. *Very* busy. But if you ever get to New York, Doctor, try and find me. (*He takes Maggie in his arms*) Good-bye, my lamb. I love you very much.

MAGGIE: Sherry, you're wonderful.

WHITESIDE: Nonsense. . . . Good-bye, Jefferson. You'll never know the trouble you've caused.

BERT: Good-bye, Mr. Whiteside.

WHITESIDE: Good-bye, Mr. Stanley. I would like to hear, in the near future, that your daughter has married her young man and that your son has been permitted to follow his own bent. OR ELSE. . . . Merry Christmas, everybody! (*And out he strolls*)

(*But the worst is yet to come. There is a loud crash on the porch, followed by an anguished yell*)

(*Maggie gives a little shriek and rushes out. Bert and the Doctor rush after her. Down the stairs come Mrs. Stanley, June and Richard. From the dining room John and Sarah come running. "What's happened?" "What is it?"*)

(*And then we see. Into view come Bert and the Doctor, carrying Mr. Whiteside between them. He is screaming his head off*)

WHITESIDE: Miss Preen! Miss Preen! I want Miss Preen back! . . . Mr. Stanley, I am suing you for *three* hundred and fifty thousand dollars!

(*Mr. Stanley throws up his hands in despair. Mrs. Stanley simply faints away*)

CURTAIN

KAUFMAN CHRONOLOGY

BIOGRAPHICAL NOTES

NOTE ON THE TEXTS

NOTES

Kaufman Chronology

1889 Born November 16, at 6230 Station Street, Pittsburgh, Pennsylvania, the second child of Joseph Kaufman and Henrietta Myers Kaufman. (Father, born in Pittsburgh in December 1856 to German-Jewish immigrant parents, works at a number of jobs, eventually landing a position as superintendent of works for a tool steel company in Pittsburgh. Mother, also of German-Jewish descent, was born in 1859; they married in January 1884.)

1890–1902 Raised in Pittsburgh along with an older sister, Helen (born 1884), and a younger sister, Ruth (born 1895); a brother, Richard, died at age two in 1886. Enjoys reading Edgar Allan Poe, the *Bab Ballads* of W. S. Gilbert, *Argosy* magazine, and Mark Twain. In 1900, the family moves to New Castle, Pennsylvania, where father starts his own company, Vulcan Machine and Foundry.

1903–7 Family returns to Pittsburgh after father's business fails. Attends Pittsburgh Central High School. Collaborates with friend Irving Pichel (later a Hollywood actor and director) on play *The Failure*. Joins Dramatics Club at Rodeph Sholom Community House; plays title role in play *The Queen's Messenger*. Attends religious school, and at 14 is confirmed as a Reform Jew. Travels to Idaho in the summer of 1905, where he works on a cattle ranch. Contributes to high school literary magazine.

1907–8 Enrolls at Western University of Pennsylvania to study law; leaves after first semester after a bout of pleurisy.

1909–12 Father takes job as plant manager for Columbia Ribbon Company, moving family to Patterson and then Passaic, New Jersey. Kaufman works as a surveyor, tax office clerk, stenographer, and ribbon salesman. Publishes essays and poems in Passaic *Herald*. Submits items to Franklin P. Adams' ("F.P.A.") column, "Always in Good Humor," in the New York *Evening Mail*; adds an invented middle initial "S." to his name in imitation of Adams. Attends acting classes at Alveine School for Dramatic Art in New York City. Unsuccessfully manages a theater company in

851

Troy, New York. Rewrites play *The Failure*. On Adams' recommendation, gets job writing a humor column, "This and That with Sometimes a Little of the Other," for the *Washington Times*.

1913–14   Fired from the *Washington Times* by editor Frank Munsey, returns to New York City; lives with parents, who have moved to the city. Again through Adams' intercession, gets a job as drama reporter on *New York Tribune*. Contributes freelance articles to *Puck* and Princeton humor magazine *The Tiger*. Collaborates with friend Herbert Seligman on unproduced play *The Lunatic*. Travels with Seligman to London, Amsterdam, and Paris. Upon return, takes an evening playwriting class at Columbia University.

1915   On Adams' recommendation, takes over his column at the *Evening Mail*, retitling it "Be That As It May" and then "The Mail Chute," and writes various comic observations, light verse, and drama reviews. After five months, new owners of the paper dismiss Kaufman; he returns to the *Tribune* as a drama reporter, under the editorship of Heywood Broun. Takes a course in Contemporary Dramatic Literature at Columbia and, with fellow student Wymberley de Renne, writes one-act play *The Infernal Machine*.

1916   Contributes pieces to *Harper's* and *Musical America*. Travels to Rochester, New York, to attend wedding of sister Ruth; meets Beatrice Bakrow, and soon proposes to her. (Bakrow, born in Rochester on January 20, 1895, is the daughter of a prosperous clothing manufacturer and the granddaughter of German-Jewish immigrants; she had left Wellesley College in 1916 after a year and was engaged, when she met Kaufman, to a Cincinnati rabbi.) In New York, Kaufman writes the unproduced comedy *Going Up*.

1917   Marries Beatrice on March 15; Franklin P. Adams is best man. Forgoing a honeymoon for financial reasons, the couple move to an apartment in the Majestic Hotel at Central Park West and West 72nd Street. Kept out of the army for health reasons, he accepts job as drama editor of *The New York Times*, replacing Brock Pemberton. He will remain at this job until 1930, working under Alexander Woollcott until Woollcott's departure for the *Tribune* in 1922.

1918   In his first professional playwriting assignment, is asked by producer George C. Tyler to take over a crime comedy, *Among Those Present*; retitled *Someone in the House*, it arrives on Broadway at the Knickerbocker Theatre on September 9 and runs for 32 performances. (Kaufman suggests an ad campaign for the failing show, which opened during an influenza epidemic: "Avoid Crowds. See *Someone in the House*.") Beatrice becomes pregnant and they move to an apartment on West 80th Street. In November, a son is stillborn. At the end of the year, Beatrice becomes assistant to the press agent of Norma and Constance Talmadge, silent screen actresses.

1919   Works with Robert Nathan on unproduced political farce *Third Man High*. Meets Marc Connelly, a Broadway reporter for the *Morning Telegraph*. In May, is asked by Tyler to adapt a Danish melodrama; the result, *Jacques Duval*, closes in Boston.

1920   Begins attending informal luncheons at the Algonquin Hotel on West 44th Street, a natural meeting place for the various reporters and show business types around Times Square. The ringleader is Woollcott, but other habitués include Robert Benchley, Dorothy Parker, Robert E. Sherwood, Adams, Broun, and Connelly. Throughout the 1920s, the Algonquin Round Table, as it is called, will be filled out with Edna Ferber, Harpo Marx, Irving Berlin, and Herman J. Mankiewicz, among others. In the spring, Tyler suggests that Kaufman create a comedy for rising actress Lynn Fontanne. Asking for—and getting—Connelly as a collaborator, Kaufman creates a character around a housewife mentioned in F.P.A.'s column. After tryouts in Indianapolis and Chicago, *Dulcy* opens at the Frazee Theatre on August 13 and runs for 246 performances. Kaufman also joins an Algonquin offshoot for poker enthusiasts, the Thanatopsis Literary and Inside Straight Club, which meets on Saturday afternoons.

1921   Continues at the *Times* and begins submitting items to the humor magazine *Life*. Begins work with Connelly on their next play, *To the Ladies*, as a vehicle for Helen Hayes.

1922   *To the Ladies* opens at the Liberty Theatre on February 20 and runs for 128 performances. (Still at the drama desk,

Kaufman is asked by Hayes' manager how he can get more coverage for her in the *Times*. "Shoot her," Kaufman replies.) Moves with Beatrice to apartment on West 58th Street. Joins other clubs in Manhattan: the Regency, a bridge club; the Dutch Treat, a luncheon club; and the Friars, for entertainers. As a rebuke to the various performers who had criticized the reviews meted out to them, the Algonquin set puts on its own show, a one-performance revue called *No Siree!* at the 49th Street Theatre on April 20. Advertised as the work of "the Vicious Circle of the Round Table Hotel," the show includes Robert Benchley's "The Treasurer's Report" and Kaufman and Connelly performing their "Big Casino Is Little Casino." Tyler picks up the show for an extended run; now called *The '49ers*, with various changes, including sketches by Ring Lardner, it runs for 15 performances at the Punch and Judy Theatre. Kaufman and Connelly work on two projects: *West of Pittsburgh*, which closes out of town in the spring, and *Merton of the Movies*, an adaptation of Harry Leon Wilson's *Saturday Evening Post* comic stories about silent movies. Produced by Tyler, the latter show opens at the Cort Theatre on November 13, after a Brooklyn tryout, and runs for 398 performances; it has a successful London production in 1924 and will be made into three different movies over the next 20 years.

1923 Contributes sketch "If Men Played Cards as Women Do" to Irving Berlin's *Music Box Revue of 1923*. Teams up with Connelly and songwriters Bert Kalmar and Harry Ruby for the musical comedy *Helen of Troy, New York*, which is produced by George Jessel at the Selwyn Theatre on June 19 for 191 performances. Writes to novelist Edna Ferber and suggests turning her story "Old Man Minick" into a play. *The Deep, Tangled Wildwood*, a new version of *West of Pittsburgh*, opens on November 5 at the Frazee Theatre and quickly closes. Trading on the trend of expressionist dramas, producer Winthrop Ames brings Kaufman and Connelly a German play by Paul Appel called *Hans Sonnenstrossers Hollenfahrt* to adapt.

1924 *Beggar on Horseback*, as their Appel adaptation is now titled, opens on February 12 at the Broadhurst Theatre and runs for 224 performances, followed by a run in London and a 1925 film. Kaufman and Beatrice, along with others, contribute to Woollcott's purchase of Neshobe

Island in Lake Bomoseen, Vermont, as a summer retreat. Kaufman and Connelly (along with Ira Gershwin, who contibutes lyrics) write the musical *Be Yourself*. While on the road with it, Kaufman begins collaboration with Ferber on what will become *Minick*. *Be Yourself* opens at the Sam H. Harris Theatre on September 3, running for 93 performances; *Minick* opens three weeks later at the Booth and runs 141 performances. Kaufman informally initiates collaboration credit rule: whoever comes up with the basic idea for the play gets top billing.

1925   Collaborates with Dorothy Parker on short play *Business Is Business*, which is put on prior to New York screenings of film version of *Beggar on Horseback*. In May, Kaufman is introduced to Harpo Marx by Woollcott, who has championed the Marx Brothers' first appearance in a Broadway revue, *I'll Say She Is* (1924). Kaufman contributes sketches to the Dutch Treat Club amateur theatricals. Kaufman and Beatrice adopt a girl, whom they name Anne. Writes one of his few solo efforts, *The Butter and Egg Man*, about unscrupulous theater producers, and attempts to direct it, but after several rehearsals turns it over to Howard Lindsay; it opens at the Longacre Theatre on September 23, running for 243 performances, followed by a film version in 1928. In the fall, producer Sam H. Harris hires Kaufman and Berlin to craft a musical comedy for the Marx Brothers. While in Atlantic City working on the show, Berlin writes a ballad called "Always," to which Kaufman responds: "Always is a long time. Shouldn't it be called 'I'll be loving you Thursday'?" Berlin withdraws it from the score. With an uncredited assist from journalist Morrie Ryskind, the final product, *The Cocoanuts*, opens at the Lyric Theatre on December 8 and runs for 218 performances on Broadway and two years on the road; a film version is released in 1929.

1926   Becomes Chairman of the Board of the recently founded Dramatists' Guild, where he is active throughout his career. Collaborates with assistant Herman J. Mankiewicz on *The Good Fellow*, a spoof on civic organizations. It opens on October 5 at the Playhouse and runs for seven performances.

1927   Is hired by producer Edgar Selwyn to write anti-war satire with George and Ira Gershwin, *Strike Up the Band*. In spring, enjoys working with the Gershwins in Atlantic City and, although he is famous for his indifference to music, eventually claims that the title number was his favorite from all of his shows. *Strike Up the Band* opens unsuccessfully in Long Branch, New Jersey, then limps into Philadelphia, where Selwyn closes it in mid-September. ("Satire is what closes on Saturday night," he says of this experience.) Immediately begins work with Ferber on *The Royal Family*, based on the careers of the Barrymore acting clan. When offered the leading role, Ethel Barrymore not only declines, but engages a lawyer, who concludes she has no grounds for a suit. Jed Harris produces *The Royal Family* at the Selwyn Theatre on December 28, the night after the musical adaptation of Ferber's novel *Show Boat* premieres at the Ziegfeld Theatre. *The Royal Family* runs for 345 performances; it is filmed in 1930 as *The Royal Family of Broadway*, and debuts in London in 1934 as *Theatre Royal*, directed by Noel Coward and featuring Laurence Olivier as Tony Cavendish.

1928   Is asked by Jed Harris to direct Ben Hecht and Charles MacArthur's *The Front Page*, a farce about Chicago journalists. As Kaufman prepares for his first real directing assignment in May, Beatrice, accompanied by Woollcott, Harpo Marx, and Alice Duer Miller, vacations on the Riviera. *The Front Page*, opening at the Times Square Theatre on August 14, is a tremendous hit at 276 performances, and leads to a second career for Kaufman as a stage director. (He will go on to direct most of his non-musical projects.) Sam H. Harris asks Kaufman to reunite with Ryskind and the Marx Brothers for a second musical farce. Entitled *Animal Crackers*, with songs by Bert Kalmar and Harry Ruby, the show opens on October 23 at the 44th Street Theatre, after a Philadelphia tryout. It runs 191 performances, followed by a tour and a film version in 1930. Kaufman suggests that Ring Lardner collaborate with him on a stage adaptation of Lardner's 1921 short story "Some Like Them Cold."

1929   Begins work with Lardner, continuing at Lardner's country house in Manhasset, Long Island, on what will become *June Moon*. In late spring, juggles another collaboration, this time with Woollcott on *The Channel Road*, an adaptation of a de Maupassant short story. *June Moon* tries out in Atlantic City in July ("I'm down here with an act," remarks Lardner upon encountering a friend on the boardwalk), while Kaufman works with Woollcott in Katonah, New York. After subsequent rewrites and tours in Washington, D.C., and Newark, *June Moon* opens at the Broadhurst Theatre on October 9 for a 273-performance run, followed by a tour and a film. Opening night of this Sam Harris production is attended by young Moss Hart, sitting in the balcony. Eight days later, *The Channel Road* opens at the Plymouth Theatre, lasting only 60 performances. Kaufman endures the stock market crash at the end of the month with little damage; a mild investor, his fortunes are quickly replenished by his ongoing royalties. In late fall, Hart sends his new play manuscript, a spoof on talking pictures, to various producers, including Jed Harris. Harris, who has had a bitter falling-out with Kaufman over one of his reviews in the *Times*, sadistically suggests Hart send the play directly to Kaufman, who curtly declines to read it.

1930   An associate of Sam Harris intercedes with Kaufman on Hart's behalf and he begins collaborating with Hart on *Once in a Lifetime* on a daily basis at his new home on East 63rd Street. Producer Selwyn gets Ryskind to rewrite *Strike Up the Band* for comedians Clark and McCullough. With additional alterations by the Gershwins, the satire opens on January 13 and runs 191 performances. Kaufman, who is credited as librettist, is pleased with Ryskind's success and they decide to write another political musical together. In February, Kaufman directs a serious drama, *Joseph* by Bertram Block, which quickly folds. Late spring is taken up with more rewrites of *Once in a Lifetime*. Kaufman not only directs the production during its Atlantic City and Brooklyn tryouts, but also plays the supporting part of playwright Lawrence Vail. After Brooklyn, Kaufman pronounces himself unable to fix the troubled comedy, and, to Hart's dismay, withdraws. Hart rewrites the play during the summer, while Beatrice and daughter Anne vacation in Europe, and Kaufman agrees to resume work on the production. Resigns from the *Times* drama desk, due to mounting conflicts of interest. *Once in a Lifetime* opens at the Music Box on September 24 and runs 305 performances. Kaufman announces from the stage that "80% of the show is Moss Hart's." Hart's fortune is made, and Kaufman continues in the part of Vail until April of 1931; Hart himself plays the part in the 1931 Los Angeles production. (A film is made by Universal in 1932.)

1931   Works with Ryskind on *Tweedledee*, a political musical about dueling national anthems. Collaborates with lyricist Howard Dietz on sketches for new revue, *The Band Wagon*, to star Fred and Adele Astaire. (The show, produced by Max Gordon with music by Arthur Schwartz, opens on June 3 at the New Amsterdam and runs for 260 performances.) Producer Sam Harris hires the Gershwins to write the score for the political musical, now called *Of Thee I Sing*, and they begin writing songs while on location in Hollywood. After Kaufman and Ryskind send a draft to the Gershwins, Kaufman begins rehearsals for *Eldorado*, in collaboration with Laurence Stallings; it closes out of town in September. George Gershwin has been playing various songs from *Of Thee I Sing* at parties around town, and Kaufman, annoyed, fears audiences will regard it as a revival when it opens; he directs the show successfully in Boston and at the Music Box, where it opens on December 26. The show runs for 441 performances, the longest run for a Gershwin musical.

1932   Begins working with Ferber on *Dinner at Eight*. Hart achieves success with *Face the Music*, which he writes with Irving Berlin, opening on February 17; Kaufman directs the book scenes and it runs 165 performances. In April, *Of Thee I Sing* is published by Knopf, the first musical ever issued in book form, and in May its creators are awarded the Pulitzer Prize (although George Gershwin is left out—the committee makes its award solely on "literary" merit), making it the first musical thus honored. In the early fall, Kaufman directs *Here Today* by George Oppenheimer and starring Ruth Gordon, which has a brief run at the Ethel Barrymore Theatre, and doctors the Schwartz/Dietz musical *Flying Colors* for Max Gordon. *Dinner at Eight*, with its seven opulent sets, proves too cumbersome to preview out of town, and opens in New York at the Music Box on October 22. It has a run of 232 performances and will become a successful M-G-M film in 1933. After voting for Norman Thomas, the Socialist candidate, in the presidential election, Kaufman sails to London to direct the West End version of *Dinner at Eight*.

1933   Rejoins Ryskind in collaboration on a proposed sequel to *Of Thee I Sing*, a spoof on fascism called *Let 'Em Eat Cake*. Along with Robert E. Sherwood, is hired by film producer Samuel Goldwyn to create a vehicle for Eddie Cantor, called *Roman Scandals*. Refusing to relocate to Hollywood and annoyed by Cantor's interference, the team submits an initial draft of the screenplay and then resigns. In May, Kaufman begins affair in New York with film actress Mary Astor. *Let 'Em Eat Cake*, with a score by the Gershwins, opens in Boston, then in New York at the Imperial on October 21 for a disappointing 90 performances. A second collaboration with Woollcott, a murder mystery entitled *The Dark Tower*, fares even less well, with a run of 57 performances after its November 25 opening.

1934   Meets with Katharine Dayton, a Washington journalist, for a possible collaboration on a political satire. Hoping to collaborate with Hart on another project, travels to Palm Springs in March to work on *Merrily We Roll Along*. One of the most elaborate non-musical plays of its day, with a cast of 91, it opens without a tour at the Music Box on September 29 and runs 155 performances. Beatrice has a small success with a play of her own, *Divided by Three*, written with Margaret Leech Pulitzer and opening in October. A non-musical comedy written by Kaufman with Morrie Ryskind, *Bring on the Girls*, with Jack Benny as its star, closes out of town in December.

1935   Travels to Hollywood in the spring at the urging of M-G-M producer Irving Thalberg to work on screenplay of *A Night at the Opera* for the Marx Brothers; stays on at the Beverly Wilshire Hotel and is given an office on the lot. While writing the script with Morrie Ryskind, visits with such East Coast expatriates as Mankiewicz and Oppenheimer. Plays bridge frequently with Chico Marx. Renews affair with Astor, whose husband has initiated divorce proceedings. While Kaufman returns to the East Coast in April and May, the Marxes tour selected scenes from the screenplay on the road. Kaufman returns in May to help direct dialogue scenes on *A Night at the Opera* and is accompanied by Beatrice and daughter Anne for a three-month visit. Beatrice meets with Sam Goldwyn, who offers her a job as his East Coast literary representative. Kaufman stays until October, then goes back east to collaborate with Dayton on *First Lady*, which opens on

November 26 at the Music Box and runs 246 performances. (A film version with Kay Francis is made in 1937.) Film of *A Night at the Opera*, featuring Kitty Carlisle, is released in December.

1936   Spends New Year's Eve collaborating with Ferber on a new project; in January, travels with her and Beatrice to Palm Beach to continue work on what will become *Stage Door*. At Thalberg's request, returns to Hollywood in May for a prolonged stay, revising scripts for M-G-M, including the Marx Brothers' next film, *A Day at the Races*. Thalberg offers him his own production unit, which Kaufman turns down, preferring to collaborate with Hart (who is busy writing screenplays in Los Angeles) on a new play. He also spends his time trying to cast *Stage Door* and resumes his affair with Astor while Beatrice is on a European cruise. In July, Astor is involved with a child custody case over her daughter, and her husband, Franklin Thorpe, introduces her diary as evidence. The diary is reported to contain many specific references to her sexual encounters with Kaufman and these are quickly leaked to the press. Kaufman is subpoenaed and, as the story makes national headlines, hides out in the homes of various friends. Asks Hart to read the diaries to see what they contain, but on the day he is scheduled to appear in court, August 10, Kaufman fails to do so, having returned to the East Coast on the Santa Fe Chief the day before. The trial ends on the 13th, with Astor awarded joint custody, and two weeks later, Beatrice returns to New York and the couple make several statements to the press affirming the solidity of their marriage. On September 14, Thalberg dies in Hollywood, blunting much of Kaufman's enthusiasm for the film industry. Beatrice and Kaufman buy a country home, Barley Sheaf Farm, in Bucks County, Pennsylvania, in late September. Having found his perfect ingénue in screen actress Margaret Sullavan, Kaufman opens *Stage Door* on October 22, after a tour in Philadelphia, at the Music Box, where it runs 169 performances. (A much-altered film version, with a screenplay by Morrie Ryskind and starring Katharine Hepburn and Ginger Rogers, is made in 1937; Kaufman dubs it "Screen Door.") Immediately afterward, Kaufman and Hart go into rehearsal for their new comedy, *You Can't Take It With You*. While the play is in tryouts in

Philadelphia, Kaufman and Hart attend tryout performances of Clare Boothe's *The Women*, produced by colleague Max Gordon, and offer suggestions. Their own
comedy, produced by Sam Harris, opens at the Booth
on December 14. It is an instant success and runs for a
record 837 performances, with a subsequent tour and
London production. Kaufman and Hart are offered
$200,000 for the film rights by Columbia Pictures, which
hires Frank Capra to direct his own version of the material in 1938; it wins the Academy Award for Best Picture.

1937   Beatrice reads galleys of John Steinbeck's novel *Of Mice
and Men*, and suggests Kaufman option the stage rights
and direct an adaptation. Hart purchases country home
near the Kaufmans in New Hope, and returns to Hollywood, where Kaufman follows in April to work on next
project, a possible musical to include Kaufman, Hart, and
the Gershwins onstage. Eventually, the team opts for a
musical satire of Franklin D. Roosevelt, with a score by
Richard Rodgers and Lorenz Hart, to be called *I'd
Rather Be Right*. In May, Kaufman and Hart receive the
Pulitzer Prize for *You Can't Take It With You*. On July 11,
in the middle of pre-production for the Roosevelt musical, George Gershwin dies unexpectedly of a brain tumor.
After turning down an offer to direct the film version of
The Women, Kaufman retires to Barley Sheaf in the sum-
mer to work with Steinbeck on the stage version of *Of
Mice and Men*. After a tumultuous Boston tryout sur-
rounding the antics of legendary song-and-dance man
George M. Cohan, who comes out of retirement to play
Roosevelt, *I'd Rather Be Right* opens at the Alvin on November 2, where it runs for 290 performances. The next
day, Kaufman goes into rehearsal directing *Of Mice and
Men*, which opens on the 23rd at the Music Box for a run
of 207 performances. Kaufman begins affair with Claire
Luce, the sole actress in the show.

1938   In January, Woollcott visits Barley Sheaf and asks Kaufman and Hart to write a stage vehicle for him to act in;
he spends the rest of the weekend at Hart's home nearby
and proceeds to torment the household staff with his
demands. In February, Kaufman follows Hart to Hollywood, where they work on their next play, continuing on
the return trip home through the Panama Canal; their
project becomes *The Fabulous Invalid*, an epic history of

American theater. Back in New York, Kaufman becomes a
guest on the radio show "Information Please" on CBS
and contributes funds for European Jews to immigrate to
the U.S. Max Gordon asks Kaufman and Hart to serve as
associate producers on Harold Rome's topical revue, *Sing
Out the News*, and they contribute some material as well.
The show opens at the Music Box on September 24 (105
performances) and *The Fabulous Invalid* opens at the
Broadhurst on October 8, for a run of 65 performances.
Kaufman and Hart begin writing another epic, a pro-
democracy play called *The American Way*.

1939   *The American Way*, produced by both Max Gordon and
Sam Harris and starring Frederic March, opens on January 21 at the Center Theatre (part of Rockefeller Center)
and, during an intermittent run, chalks up 244 performances. Kaufman and Hart present Woollcott with their
idea for his vehicle: *The Man Who Came to Dinner*, with
a lead character based on Woollcott. He surprises the team
by turning them down, on the grounds that he would be
overdoing his public persona. (He will play the part of
Sheridan Whiteside in the Los Angeles production the
following year.) With former Yale professor Monty Woolley in the lead, *The Man Who Came to Dinner* opens,
after engagements in Hartford and Boston, at the Music
Box on October 16 and runs for 739 performances. Several touring companies are created and a 1942 film also
stars Woolley. Bennett Cerf of Random House offers to
publish a volume of Kaufman's plays; he declines. On November 11, Kaufman is featured on the cover of *Time*.

1940   In January, travels to Los Angeles to rehearse *The Man
Who Came to Dinner* with Woollcott in the lead and takes
over for him for one performance, when Woollcott falls
ill. Back in New York, Kaufman devotes himself to raising
money and writing sketches for war-relief efforts like the
Theatre Wing. He and Hart begin their next project, a
look at country-house living called *George Washington
Slept Here*. Along with Sam Harris and others, they pur-
chase the Lyceum Theatre on West 46th Street. In June,
Kaufman's father dies; his mother dies in November.
George Washington Slept Here opens at the Lyceum on
October 18 to indifferent reviews; it runs for 173 perfor-
mances and is made into a 1942 film, starring Jack Benny.
Kaufman embarks on directing *My Sister Eileen*, adapted

from Ruth McKenny's *New Yorker* pieces, and mentor its two young playwrights, Joseph Fields and Jerome Chodorov. It opens on December 26 at the Biltmore Theatre and runs for 865 performances. Kaufman goes to Boston to lend advice on *Lady in the Dark*, Hart's musical with Kurt Weill and Ira Gershwin.

1941   *Lady in the Dark* opens in New York on January 20; its immense success allows Hart to pursue a writing and directing career independent of Kaufman, though the pair remain close. In late winter, Kaufman continues war relief efforts and works with Ferber in West Virginia and Atlantic City on a new project, *The Land Is Bright*, a dynastic family drama. The Pasadena Playhouse produces a summer season of eight Kaufman comedies. In July, Sam Harris dies, and, upon the release of the amateur rights to *The Man Who Came to Dinner*, the Bucks County Playhouse produces a version featuring locals Kaufman as Whiteside, Hart as Beverly Carlton, and Harpo Marx in a speaking role as Banjo, a character based on him. *Mr. Big*, written by Arthur Sheekman and Margaret Shane and directed by Kaufman, opens at the Music Box on September 30 and closes later in the week. *The Land Is Bright*, featuring Diana Barrymore in a supporting role, opens at the Music Box on October 28, running for 79 performances. In Hollywood the week before Pearl Harbor, Kaufman discusses a Warner Brothers proposal that he work once again with Herman Mankiewicz on a screenplay, and observe Frank Capra on the set. He returns to New York before the year is over.

1942   In the spring, Warner Brothers offers a contract to Kaufman, who is back east writing sketches with Hart for various war relief events. With Mankiewicz writes *Sleeper Jump*, a comic screenplay about a theater troupe, but it is never produced. Prepares to direct a comedy by Arthur Sheekman and Ruth and Augustus Goetz called *Franklin Street* as a stage vehicle for Groucho Marx. After many negotiations and script rewrites, Groucho bows out. Cast with another actor, the play closes in Washington, D.C., in September. Soon after, Kaufman directs a wartime comedy by Joseph Fields, *The Doughgirls*, which opens at the Lyceum on December 30 for a run of 671 performances. Moves with Beatrice into an apartment at 410 Park Avenue.

1943   On January 23, Woollcott dies of a cerebral hemorrhage. Beatrice begins to collect Woollcott's letters for publication; she and Kaufman sell their share in Neshobe Island. In the spring, Kaufman travels to Hollywood to begin work on projects for Warner Brothers; when he returns, Hart leaves New York City for a two-month tour with the Army Air Corps to research his play *Winged Victory*. In July, Kaufman receives Gypsy Rose Lee as his visitor to Barley Sheaf, as they prepare her play *The Naked Genius*, which he directs on October 26 at the Plymouth (36 performances). Anne marries John Booth in August. Beginning late in the fall, Kaufman works on a production of *Over Twenty One*, written by and starring Ruth Gordon.

1944   *Over Twenty One* opens at the Music Box on January 3 and runs for 197 performances. Kaufman meets with novelist John P. Marquand and discusses adapting his *The Late George Apley* for the stage. Beatrice's collection of Woollcott's letters is published in the spring and by June, Kaufman is working with Marquand at Barley Sheaf. In September, he directs Terence Rattigan's play *While the Sun Shines*, opening on the 19th at the Lyceum for 39 performances. Later in the fall, both Kaufman and Hart contribute sketches to Billy Rose's revue *The Seven Lively Arts*, which opens at the Ziegfeld on December 7. After a Washington tryout, Kaufman opens *The Late George Apley* at the Lyceum on November 23. It runs for 357 performances, his first real success in four years. In December, Hart heads to the South Pacific to lead a U.S.O. tour of *The Man Who Came to Dinner*.

1945   Beatrice retires to Atlantic City for several weeks for health reasons. In the spring, Kaufman prepares *Hollywood Pinafore*, writing book and lyrics to music by Sir Arthur Sullivan. A spoof of the film industry (with Kaufman's only lyrics in 20 years), it opens at the Alvin Theatre on May 31 in Kaufman's own production and runs for 52 performances. On October 6, Beatrice dies of a cerebral hemorrhage. Devastated, Kaufman turns to work and continues with the opening of Mary Chase's *The Next Half Hour* on October 29 at the Empire; it lasts a week. He invests in Max Gordon's production of Garson Kanin's *Born Yesterday*, and gives advice during tryouts.

1946   Anne moves in with Kaufman, after filing for divorce in February. Kaufman goes to Hollywood in March, accompanied by actress Natalie Schaefer, with whom he has been having an intermittent affair since 1941. Collaborates with writer/producer Nunnally Johnson in Los Angeles, and continues to work with him in Bucks County on *Park Avenue*, a musical about Manhattan's elite, with music by Arthur Schwartz and lyrics by Ira Gershwin. In the fall, Hart marries actress Kitty Carlisle, who had been in *A Night at the Opera*. Kaufman's production of *Park Avenue* opens on November 4 at the Shubert and closes after 72 performances.

1947   In May, Anne marries Bruce Colen. In June, Kaufman goes to Hollywood to direct his only film, a political spoof with a screenplay by Charles MacArthur called *The Senator Was Indiscreet*, for Universal. Finds film directing an interesting but uninspiring vocation: "It's all right, if you can stay awake." Produced by Nunnally Johnson, and starring William Powell, the movie opens in December and does poorly at the box office.

1948   A granddaughter, Beatrice Colen, is born on January 10. Working again with Ferber, Kaufman begins a collaboration on a play about European émigrés called *Bravo!* During the fall, he is a frequent guest on the CBS radio show *This Is Broadway* (and continues into the 1950s on its television incarnation *This Is Show Business*). On September 23, Kaufman opens his production of Gertrude Tonkonogy's *Town House* at the National (12 performances). In October, British actress Leueen MacGrath opens on Broadway in *Edward, My Son*. She and Kaufman meet socially on several occasions. After a rocky Boston tryout, *Bravo!* opens at the Lyceum on November 9 and closes after 44 performances.

1949   Without a writing project of his own, Kaufman concentrates on directing three other productions and on his burgeoning romance with MacGrath. On May 26, they marry. The summer and fall bring three theatrical failures: a revue, *Pretty Penny*, closes in Bucks County; a comedy by William Walden, *Metropole*, closes after two performances at the Lyceum in December; and a production of Jean Giraudoux's *The Enchanted*, starring MacGrath, closes at the Lyceum in early March of 1950, after 45 performances.

1950
Kaufman sells his interest in the Lyceum and, in May, travels with MacGrath to Europe for an extended stay, suggesting that they collaborate on a play on the trip home. While in Europe, Kaufman is approached by producers Cy Feuer and Ernest Martin to direct Frank Loesser's musical *Guys and Dolls*. In early fall, Kaufman works with the show's librettist, Abe Burrows (a colleague from *This Is Broadway*) at Barley Sheaf. After a triumphant tryout in Philadelphia, the show opens at the 46th Street Theatre on November 24. Kaufman is so confident of the show's success that, for the only time in his career, he watches the opening night performance from a seat in the orchestra. The musical runs for 1,200 performances, the longest for any show directed by Kaufman, and earns the recently created Tony Award for Best Musical, as does Kaufman for Best Direction. (In 1950, Best Direction included nominees for both plays and musicals.)

1951
The Small Hours, Kaufman's collaboration with MacGrath, opens on February 15 at the National and closes 20 performances later. In the spring, Kaufman travels first to Los Angeles to run rehearsals for the West Coast company of *Guys and Dolls*, then to London in June to collaborate with MacGrath on a new play, *Fancy Meeting You Again*, about reincarnation. When the couple return to New York, they move to an apartment at 1035 Park Avenue. In October, Kaufman suffers a minor stroke, but recovers enough to go into production seven weeks later for *Fancy Meeting You Again*, featuring a young Walter Matthau.

1952
The show opens at the Royale on January 14 and closes within the week. In the spring, Kaufman begins minor revisions to *Of Thee I Sing*, the only Broadway revival of his to be produced in his lifetime. The production, which is updated and interpolates a song from *Let 'Em Eat Cake*, opens at the Ziegfeld on May 5 and runs for only 72 performances. In September, Anne divorces Bruce Colen. On December 21, while appearing on *This Is Show Business*, Kaufman makes a remark about wanting "this to be

one program on which no one sings 'Silent Night.'" In
the ensuing national controversy, CBS lets Kaufman go,
then reinstates him a month later.

1953   Undergoes prostate surgery in the winter. After recuper-
ating, travels with MacGrath to London, where he looks
in on London production of *Guys and Dolls*. The couple
purchase a house at 17 Blomfield Road; in the early fall,
Kaufman sails back to New York while MacGrath makes
a film in London. Kaufman completes a play with
Howard Teichmann, *The Solid Gold Cadillac*, a satire on
big business starring Josephine Hull. Kaufman displays
uncharacteristic insecurity during out-of-town tryouts,
even dismissing the advice of Hart, Burrows, and
Thornton Wilder during the Hartford engagement. In
the final event, the play opens at Belasco on November
5 and runs 526 performances, the last of his plays to be a
success. (A film with Judy Holliday is made in 1956.)
Sells Pennsylvania estate Barley Sheaf and auctions off its
furnishings.

1954   Kaufman and Teichmann attempt a project to star Mac-
Grath; it is never finished. In the meantime, he is con-
tacted again by Feuer and Martin to adapt and direct a
musical version of the film *Ninotchka*, with a score by
Cole Porter. Kaufman selects MacGrath as his collaborator on the book and, after turning in their first draft, they
sail back to London in April to renovate their new home.
In the fall, they considerably revise the new musical,
called *Silk Stockings*. During the out-of-town tryout in
December, Kaufman is fired (along with MacGrath) for
the first time in his career by the producers, who want the
musical to have a broader brand of comedy. Abe Burrows
is brought in to revise the book and Feuer takes over the
direction.

1955   *Silk Stockings*, with Kaufman and MacGrath sharing credit
with Burrows on the book, opens at the Imperial on
February 24 and runs 478 performances (a movie, further
revised, is made with Fred Astaire in 1957). In March,
MacGrath travels to London and in May, Kaufman and
Anne sail over on the *Queen Mary* to join her. MacGrath
has a success acting in Giraudoux's *Tiger at the Gates*,
which he brings to New York in the fall.

1956   In April, Hart has the triumph of his career, directing
        Lerner and Loewe's *My Fair Lady*, which Kaufman ad-
        mires tremendously. In May, Kaufman goes to London to
        collaborate on a play, never produced, with Alan Camp-
        bell, Dorothy Parker's husband.

1957   In February, MacGrath leaves Kaufman; he briefly under-
        goes psychotherapy. On August 21, MacGrath divorces
        him from Mexico. Producer David Merrick asks Kaufman
        to direct Peter Ustinov's political allegory *Romanoff and
        Juliet*. Although fatigued, Kaufman manages to deliver a
        show, opening on October 10 at the Plymouth, that runs
        389 performances. Writes about the growing trend for
        dramatic musical theater pieces (*West Side Story*, et al.) in
        article "Musical Comedy or Musical Serious?" for the
        Times and contributes several humorous pieces to *The
        New Yorker*.

1958   In February, collapses at the opening night of John Os-
        borne's *The Entertainer*. Attempts and then drops several
        projects, including a musical by Ruth Goetz and Schwartz
        and Dietz. Has second minor stroke in the fall. MacGrath
        returns to assist Anne in caring for him.

1959   Appears several times as a guest on Jack Paar's television
        talk show on NBC. (Declines when he is not well,
        claiming he is "not feeling up to Paar.") Grows increas-
        ingly reclusive and impatient. Asks MacGrath to remarry
        him; she declines.

1960   In April, Anne marries Irving Schneider, a theatrical col-
        league of Hart's who appeared as an extra in *Merrily We
        Roll Along* in 1934. In September, Hart gives Kaufman a
        copy of his memoir of his early career, *Act One*. "If it is
        possible for a book of this kind to have a hero," Hart
        writes, "then that hero is George S. Kaufman."

1961   Growing more enfeebled through arteriosclerosis, Kauf-
        man rarely leaves apartment. Dies there on June 2 of
        heart failure. At the funeral, on June 4, Hart delivers the
        eulogy. Hart himself dies of a heart attack in December in
        Palm Springs, California.

Biographical Notes

Edna Ferber was born August 15, 1887, in Kalamazoo, Michigan. Her father was an unsuccessful businessman and the family moved frequently. She attended high school in Appleton, Wisconsin, then, unable to afford college, she found work on a local newspaper and later worked for the *Milwaukee Journal*. She began publishing short fiction in 1910; her first novel, *Dawn O'Hara*, appeared in 1911. She moved in 1912 to New York, where she lived for most of her life. She published four collections of stories, many featuring the character Edna McChesney; with George V. Hobart she wrote a play based on character, *Our Mrs. McChesney* (1915), in which Ethel Barrymore played the lead on Broadway. With Newman Levy she wrote the play *$1,200 a Year*. She collaborated with George S. Kaufman on six plays: *Minick* (1924), *The Royal Family* (1927), *Dinner at Eight* (1932), *Stage Door* (1936), and the less successful *The Land Is Bright* (1941) and *Bravo!* (1948). Her later novels included *The Girls* (1921), *So Big* (1924), which won the Pulitzer Prize, *Show Boat* (1926), adapted as a musical the following year, *Cimarron* (1930), *American Beauty* (1931), *Come and Get It* (1935), *Saratoga Trunk* (1941), *Great Son* (1945), *Giant* (1952), and *Ice Palace* (1958). Her autobiography, *A Kind of Magic*, appeared in 1963, followed by a sequel, *A Peculiar Treasure*. She died in New York City on April 16, 1968.

Ira Gershwin was born in Manhattan on December 6, 1896; his younger brother, **George Gershwin**, was born in Brooklyn on September 26, 1898. Ira attended Townsend Harris Hall and City College and became interested in lyrics and humorous verse. George left school at fifteen to work as a pianist and song plugger for J. H. Remick & Co. He became a prolific Tin Pan Alley composer, selling two million records of "Swanee" (lyrics by Irving Caesar) in 1919. After writing songs with various lyricists for the *George White Scandals* in the early 1920s, he teamed up with Ira in 1924 to write their first Broadway musical comedy, *Lady, Be Good!*, starring Fred and Adele Astaire. This led to one of the most successful collaborations in Broadway history, with George and Ira writing the scores to *Oh, Kay!* (1926), *Funny Face* (1927), *Strike Up the Band* (1927, revised

1930), *Girl Crazy* (1930), *Of Thee I Sing* (1931), and its sequel *Let 'Em Eat Cake* (1933), among others. George began to compose for the concert stage in 1924, when Paul Whiteman commissioned a piece for a concert at New York's Aeolian Hall; the result was "Rhapsody in Blue" (1924). This triumphant score was followed by "Piano Concerto in F" (1925) and "An American in Paris" (1928). In 1931, the brothers went to Hollywood to write the film score to *Delicious*, but soon returned to New York to write *Porgy and Bess* (1935), with a libretto and additional lyrics by DuBose Heyward. The opera's muted reception sent them back to the West Coast to write such scores for RKO as *Shall We Dance* (1937) and *A Damsel in Distress* (1937). During work on the film *Goldwyn Follies of 1938* George was diagnosed with an inoperable brain tumor; he died on July 11, 1937. Ira went into a brief period of retirement, but continued to write with composers such as Kurt Weill (*Lady in the Dark*, 1941), Arthur Schwartz (*Park Avenue*, 1946), Jerome Kern (the film *Cover Girl*, 1944), and Harold Arlen (the film *A Star Is Born*, 1954). Ira died in Beverly Hills, California, on August 17, 1983.

Moss Hart was born into a working-class Jewish family in 1904 and raised in the Bronx and Brooklyn. As a teenager, he worked as an office boy for the theatrical road producer Augustus Pitou, who later produced *The Hold-Up Man* (1925, also titled *The Beloved Bandit*), which Hart had written under a pseudonym. He served as social director at hotels in the Catskills during the summers and started directing at small theaters in New York and New Jersey. In 1929, he wrote *Once in a Lifetime*, a play about Hollywood, and brought it to the stage in collaboration with George S. Kaufman. After its success, he worked with Irving Berlin on revues *Face the Music* (1932) and *As Thousands Cheer* (1933), and he provided the book adaptation for *The Great Waltz* (1934). Again collaborating with Kaufman, Hart wrote *Merrily We Roll Along* in 1934. In 1935, he wrote *Jubilee*, a satire of British royalty, with Cole Porter. He resumed his partnership with Kaufman on *You Can't Take It with You* (1936) and *I'd Rather Be Right* (1937, with a score by Richard Rodgers and Lorenz Hart), *The Fabulous Invalid* (1938), *The American Way* (1939), *The Man Who Came to Dinner* (1939), and *George Washington Slept Here* (1940). In 1941 he wrote and directed the musical *Lady in the Dark*, with a score by Kurt Weill and Ira Gershwin. Another solo effort was *Winged Victory* (1943), a tribute to the Air Force; the sale of the film rights for the play, which Hart also directed, for a million dollars set a record for its time. He had successes as a director with the comedies *Junior Miss* (1941), *Dear Ruth* (1944), Irving Berlin's *Miss Liberty* (1948), and *Anniversary Waltz* (1954); as a Hollywood screenwriter with *Gentleman's Agreement* (1947, Academy Award for Best Picture), *Hans Christian Andersen* (1952), the Judy Garland vehicle *A Star Is Born* (1954), and *Prince of Players* (1955), among others; and as a playwright and director with *Christopher Blake* (1946), *Light Up the Sky* (1948), and *The Climate of Eden* (1952). He married the actress and singer Kitty Carlisle in 1946; the couple had two children. In 1956, he directed Lerner and Loewe's *My Fair Lady*, one of the greatest successes in musical theater history, and won the New York Drama Critics' Award for Best Director; the play was also well received in London in 1958. In 1959 he published a memoir, *Act One*, which became a best seller. Hart worked with Lerner and Loewe again on *Camelot* (1960), a musical version of T. H. White's *The Once and Future King*. During its tryout in Toronto, Hart suffered a heart attack. Lerner took over the direction and brought the musical to Broadway, where it received mixed to good reviews. Hart and his wife moved to Palm Springs, California; he had begun on what he called a "comedy of manners" when died of heart failure, on December 20, 1961.

Ring Lardner was born Ringgold Wilmer Lardner on March 6, 1885, in Niles, Michigan. His father was a prosperous businessman, his mother a poet and the daughter of an Episcopal minister. After high school he briefly attended Armour Institute in Chicago, worked as freight agent and bookkeeper, then became a journalist, writing in Indiana for *South Bend Times* (1905), Chicago *Inter-Ocean* (1907), and Chicago *Examiner*, for whom he covered the White Sox and the Cubs. He edited St. Louis *Sporting News* (1910–11). He married Ellis Abbott in 1911. He wrote a column, "In the Wake of the News" (1913–16), for Chicago *Tribune* and published a collection of poems, *Bib Ballads* (1915). He began publishing stories about baseball player Jack Keefe that were collected as *You Know Me Al: A Busher's Letters* (1916). His stories and articles were widely syndicated. He published collections *Gullible's Travels, Etc.* (1917), *Treat 'Em Rough* (1918), *The Real Dope* (1919), *Own Your Own Home* (1919), *Regular Fellows I Have Met* (1919), *How to Write Short Stories (With Samples)* (1924), *What Of It?* (1925), *The Love Nest and Other Stories* (1926), *Round*

Up (1929), *Lose with a Smile* (1933), novel *The Big Town* (1921), and autobiography *The Story of a Wonder Man* (1927). He collaborated on plays with George M. Cohan (*Elmer the Great,* 1928) and George S. Kaufman (*June Moon,* 1929); contributed sketches to the *Ziegfeld Follies, The '49ers* (1922), and *Smiles* (1930). He died of heart disease in East Hampton, New York, on September 25, 1933.

Harry Ruby, born Harold Rubenstein in New York City on January 27, 1895, met **Bert Kalmar**—also born in New York, on February 16, 1884—in 1917 when they were both playing the piano on various vaudeville circuits. They soon decided to become a songwriting team, equally apportioning the music and lyrics, and had several hit songs on Broadway by the 1920–21 season. Their shows included *Helen of Troy, New York* (1923), *Five O'Clock Girl* (1927), and *Animal Crackers* (1928). Successful songs by the team include "Who's Sorry Now," "I Wanna Be Loved By You," "It Was Meant to Be," "A Kiss to Build a Dream On," and "Three Little Words." They moved to Hollywood in the late 1920s and contributed to numerous screenplays as song and screen writers, among them *Horse Feathers* (1933) and *Duck Soup* (1934), both starring the Marx Brothers. After Kalmar's death on September 18, 1947, Ruby continued to write, but without his former success. In 1950, Hollywood released *Three Little Words*, a movie based on the Kalmar-Ruby partnership. Ruby died in Los Angeles on February 23, 1974.

Morrie Ryskind was born in New York City on October 20, 1895, the son of Russian-Jewish immigrants. He attended Columbia University School of Journalism, from which he was expelled just before his graduation in 1917 for articles he published criticizing the university president. Along with George S. Kaufman and Ira Gershwin, he contributed to Franklin P. Adams' humor column in the New York *Evening Mail*, worked as a reporter for the *New York World* until 1921, and published *Unaccustomed As I Am* (1921), a book of light verse. He contributed dramatic sketches and lyrics to revues *The '49ers* (1922), *The Garrick Gaieties* (1925), and *Merry Go Round* (1927) and assisted George S. Kaufman with *The Cocoanuts* (1925), a musical featuring the Marx Brothers. Later he co-wrote *Animal Crackers* (1928) with Kaufman, and adapted the play for the movie. In 1929 he married Mary House, with whom he had two children. With Kaufman and George and Ira Gershwin, he wrote musical

satire *Strike Up the Band*, which was poorly received at its initial tryouts in 1927 but fared better after he rewrote for a 1930 revival. Also
with Kaufman and the Gershwins, he wrote *Of Thee I Sing* (1931),
which had a theatrical run of more than 400 performances and won
the Pulitzer Prize for drama, the first musical ever to receive the
award. A sequel, *Let 'Em Eat Cake* (1933), ran for 90 performances.
He also adapted the libretto for the Irving Berlin musical *Louisiana
Purchase* (1940), which ran for over 400 performances. He wrote
screenplays for *A Night at the Opera* (1935), *My Man Godfrey* (1936),
Stage Door (1937)—the last two earned him Academy Award nomi-
nations—*Room Service* (1938), *Man About Town* (1939), *Penny Sere-
nade* (1941), and *It's in the Bag* (1945). In 1947 he testified before the
House Un-American Activities Committee about communists in the
Screenwriters' Guild, and felt he was ostracized professionally as a result. In 1954, he helped found the conservative *National Review*, to
which he contributed a column and served as director. He wrote a
syndicated column for the *Los Angeles Times* from 1960 to 1971, and
for the *Los Angeles Herald-Examiner* until 1978. He died in Arling-
ton, Virginia, on August 24, 1985.

Note on the Texts

This volume contains nine plays by George S. Kaufman and various collaborators: *The Royal Family* (1927, with Edna Ferber); *Animal Crackers* (1928, with Morrie Ryskind, music and lyrics by Bert Kalmar and Harry Ruby); *June Moon* (1929, with Ring Lardner); *Once in a Lifetime* (1930, with Moss Hart); *Of Thee I Sing* (1931, with Morrie Ryskind, music and lyrics by George and Ira Gershwin); *Dinner at Eight* (1932, with Edna Ferber); *Stage Door* (1936, with Edna Ferber); *You Can't Take It With You* (1936, with Moss Hart); and *The Man Who Came to Dinner* (1939, with Moss Hart). The texts printed here are taken from the first editions of the plays in book form for general readers, with the exception of the text of *Animal Crackers*, which was not published during Kaufman's lifetime and is now taken from a typescript in the Library of Congress.

All nine plays were also published, in editions intended for actors and directors, by Samuel French or Dramatists Play Service; these editions, meant chiefly to aid in staging, omit prefaces and commentary that are part of the texts of the readers' editions, include more technical stage directions, and incorporate revisions adapting the texts for public performance. (Significant revisions to the texts are recorded in the notes to this volume.) No evidence has been found to suggest the involvement of Kaufman or his collaborators in the preparation of other subsequent reprintings of the plays, including British editions of *Dinner at Eight* and *Stage Door*, the collection of six plays of Kaufman and Hart in the Modern Library series in 1942 (as *Six Plays by Kaufman and Hart*), and annual volumes such as *Famous Plays of 1932* and *Famous Plays of 1933*. The texts of the first hardcover book editions have been chosen for inclusion in the present volume because they are the versions of the plays Kaufman and his collaborators published for general readers after their first presentations on Broadway; the text of *Animal Crackers* has been reprinted from the best available typescript.

The Royal Family was written by Edna Ferber and Kaufman, working in close collaboration, between November 1926 and June 1927; Ferber had had the initial idea for the play and proposed that she and Kaufman write it together. After completing the first act, they showed a draft to the producer Jed Harris, who agreed to bring the finished work to the stage. After tryouts in Newark and Atlantic City, and rehearsals at which both writers were present, the play opened at the Selwyn Theatre on Broadway on December 28, 1927.

The text printed here is taken from the 1928 Doubleday, Doran first edition of the play, which bears a prefatory textual note from the authors: "The printed text of 'The Royal Family' is a shade fuller than the acting version. The exigencies of the theatre compelled occasional elisions, but we are hoping that the reader won't be in quite such a hurry."

Kaufman began writing *Animal Crackers* with Morrie Ryskind early in the summer of 1928 at the suggestion of the producer Sam Harris, who wanted a new play for the Marx Brothers; *The Cocoanuts* (1925), an earlier Kaufman play featuring the Marx Brothers, written with Ryskind's uncredited assistance and with songs by Irving Berlin, had proven highly successful. Bert Kalmar and Harry Ruby were asked to provide music and lyrics. After an initial run in Philadelphia, the play opened on Broadway on October 23, 1928; it closed on April 6, 1929, followed by a regional tour and a 1930 film version (the script of which was extensively revised by Ryskind without Kaufman's involvement). The text of the play was not published during Kaufman's lifetime. An acting edition, based on a 1982 revival at Arena Stage in Washington, D.C., and published by Samuel French in 1984, adapts material from the published film script and unpublished versions of the play. Two significantly different typescript versions of the play are known to be extant: one in Sam Harris's papers at Princeton University, and another in Groucho Marx's papers at the Library of Congress. Both appear to be working documents, drawn from different moments in the play's theatrical history rather than a book-publication process. The Princeton typescript is dated November 1928 on its title page—shortly after the play's October 23 opening night. The Library of Congress typescript is a later version, dating on internal evidence after March 4, 1929, when Herbert Hoover was inaugurated (Coolidge is referred to as the "ex-President"). In some scenes the two versions are nearly identical, varying only in punctuation or an occasional line of dialogue; in others, particularly in the second act, they vary substantially. The differences in the later version are most likely the result, to a large extent, of the Marx Brothers' improvisational revisions of Kaufman and Ryskind's original script. Of the two versions, the Library of Congress typescript is notably fuller in its dialogue and its descriptions of the actors' physical comedy, but the Princeton typescript reproduces the lyrics of Kalmar and Ruby's musical numbers, noted in the Library of Congress typescript only by the title of each number at the point where it was meant to be performed and by a list of numbers in its opening pages. The text of *Animal Crackers* presented in this volume has been taken from the Library of Congress typescript, with the missing lyrics supplied by interpolation from the Princeton typescript. Stage directions have been revised, omitting references to specific stage doors and locations as was Kaufman's practice in editions prepared for general readers; typographical errors have also been corrected.

June Moon had its origins in "Some Like Them Cold," a short story by Ring Lardner first published in *The Saturday Evening Post* in 1921. Kaufman approached Lardner in the fall of 1928 with the suggestion that they adapt the story for the stage. Unhappy with another recent adaptation of one of his stories, Lardner at first declined, but he soon changed his mind, and by early 1929 the pair were at work on their play, which Sam Harris had agreed to produce. Lardner contributed the first draft, Kaufman revised it, and with Lardner's third draft they began rehearsals. Lardner also contributed the music and lyrics. Working together, they continued to revise the play during rehearsals and through a number of productions (in Atlantic City, Asbury Park, Washington, D.C., and Newark) prior to its Broadway opening on October 9, 1929. The text printed here is taken from the 1930 Charles Scribner's Sons first printing of *June Moon*.

Kaufman and Moss Hart began to work together on *Once in a Lifetime* in December 1929. Hart had written the first version of the play and sent a copy to Jed Harris, who commented on it at length. A friend independently sent a copy to Sam Harris, whose initial suggestion that the play be made into a musical Hart declined. Sam Harris went on to offer to produce the play if Hart would agree to rewrite it with Kaufman; Jed Harris was persuaded to give up the play, on which Kaufman and Hart then collaborated. Following a mediocre audience reception to tryout performances in May in Atlantic City and Brighton Beach, Brooklyn, and after further revision, Kaufman told Hart that he had run out of inspiration on the project. Hart proposed extensive changes to the second and third acts, convincing Kaufman to stay on. The pair once again rewrote the third act after the play's run in Philadelphia in early September. It opened at the Music Box Theatre in New York on September 24, 1930. The text presented in this volume has been taken from the 1930 Farrar & Rinehart first edition of *Once in a Lifetime*.

Kaufman and Ryskind decided to collaborate on what became *Of Thee I Sing* in January 1930. At first, they envisioned a musical about competing national anthems to be called *Tweedledee*, and they invited George and Ira Gershwin to contribute music and lyrics. Later in the year, they wrote a 14-page scenario, which they sent to Sam Harris and to the Gershwins; they returned to the project in the summer of 1931, finishing a script in August. The Gershwins completed their score early in the fall. After tryout performances in

Boston beginning on December 8, the musical opened at the Music Box Theatre on Broadway on December 26, 1931. Kaufman prepared a reader's edition of the play, which was published by Alfred A. Knopf in April 1932. The reader's edition omits one of the Gershwin's musical numbers, "Love Is Sweeping the Country," that had been performed at both the Boston and New York openings of the play, and it presents versions of Ira Gershwin's lyrics not consistent with their appearance in his piano-vocal score, also published in April 1932, or in contemporary sheet music. The text of the lyrics in the present volume has been taken from *The Complete Lyrics of Ira Gershwin* (Robert Kimball, ed., New York: Alfred A. Knopf, 1993); Ira Gershwin's song titles have been restored. The rest of the text, aside from the lyrics, is reprinted from the first printing of *Of Thee I Sing*. At 371.29 in this volume, the line "*a line or two of lyric emerges*" has been emended to read "*a few lines of lyric emerge*," to accommodate revisions to the lyrics of the song "Wintergreen for President." At 391.23, the song title "Who Is the Lucky Girl To Be? (*reprise*)" has been supplied in the place of *The Complete Lyrics'* "Exit, Atlantic City Scene." A lyric line "Let's all rejoice!"—included in the Knopf edition but omitted from *The Complete Lyrics*—has been added at 400.6 in this volume; a stage direction, "(*Together*)", has been provided to introduce the line. The song "Love Is Sweeping the Country" has been inserted at 400.23, along with a stage direction, "(*Jenkins and Miss Benson enter*)", to introduce it. The song "On That Matter, No One Budges," printed in *The Complete Lyrics of Ira Gerswin* as a single work, has been reprinted in the present volume in four sections (at 463.36–464.13, 464.34–465.19, 466.1–17, 466.25–36) to accommodate additional dialogue in the reader's edition.

The basic premise for *Dinner at Eight* emerged in conversations between Kaufman and Ferber late in 1931, and they exchanged ideas about the play throughout the winter. In the spring of 1932, they spent ten days together in Atlantic City writing the first act, and they completed the remainder over the summer. The play was ready to be cast by mid-August; its sets were particularly elaborate, so they decided, along with the producer (Sam Harris), to stage several preview performances instead of out-of-town tryouts. *Dinner at Eight* officially opened at the Music Box Theatre on October 22, 1932; the text printed in this volume has been taken from the 1932 Doubleday, Doran first edition.

At the invitation of their producer, Sam Harris, Ferber and Kaufman traveled to Palm Beach in late January 1936 to work on a new play, *Stage Door*, from Ferber's outline; they had first sat down to discuss the collaboration on New Year's Eve. Back in New York, they met daily to write together and sent a finished script to Harris by the end of May. At performances in Philadelphia beginning in late September and then in New Haven, they saw a number of weaknesses, and they delayed the production for a week of intensive revisions before the play opened on Broadway, at the Music Box Theatre, on October 22. The first book edition of *Stage Door*, published by Doubleday, Doran in 1936, provides the text printed in this volume.

Kaufman and Hart wrote *You Can't Take It With You* in close collaboration during the summer of 1936, in Beverly Hills, basing it on an idea that Hart had suggested during a stay in Hollywood in 1934. They finished two acts by the end of July, and by the end of August they had sent copies of a finished draft to the actors, already under contract with Sam Harris. In the course of composition they had considered a number of titles for the play, including *Grandpa's Other Snake*, which they discarded on Beatrice Kaufman's advice; Harris preferred *You Can't Take It With You*. The writers revised the play in a number of minor respects during late October rehearsals and tryout performances in Princeton and Philadelphia; it opened at the Booth Theatre in New York on December 14, 1936. The text printed here is taken from the 1937 first book edition of *You Can't Take It With You*, published by Farrar & Rinehart.

Early in January 1938 Hart and Kaufman decided to write a play that would feature their friend Alexander Woollcott, a critic, lecturer, and radio commentator, and in March 1939 they sat down to write it, incorporating elements of Woollcott's public persona. After hearing the first act, Woollcott began to question the propriety of playing himself and decided to withdraw from the production. Hart and Kaufman completed the play while making alternate casting arrangements; originally titled *Prince Charming* and later *Some Interesting People*, they eventually followed the suggestion of Kaufman's aide Myra Streger and called it *The Man Who Came to Dinner*. After its Hartford opening on September 23, they omitted a character and altered several scenes; further revisions were made during a run in Boston. The play opened on Broadway at the Music Box Theatre on October 16. The text printed in this volume is taken from the 1939 first edition of *The Man Who Came to Dinner*, published by Random House.

This volume presents the texts of the original printings and the typescript chosen for inclusion here, but it does not attempt to reproduce nontextual features of their typographic design. The texts are presented without change, except for the correction of typographical errors (and the few alterations in *Animal Crackers* and *Of Thee I Sing* described above). Spelling, punctuation, and capitalization are often expressive features and are not altered, even when inconsistent or irregular. The following is a list of typographical errors in the published texts, cited by page and line number: 19.18, bottles sherry; 28.4, purpose; 35.38, me.; 36.10, things,; 42.24, *its*; 45.3, *oclock*; 45.6, *doors leading*; 45.9, *term*; 49.7, *steps*. [no closing parenthesis]; 50.37, *etc.*).; 51.3–4, Gettysbury; 55.32, *Fannie*; 68.32, means! you; 69.38, passport Aquitania; 83.12–13, production all built—a new theatre; 83.20, Bagdad; 99.23, the the; 106.18, *is!"* [no closing parenthesis]; 107.36, Sceond; 197.22, death; 228.3, didnt; 234.39, Thee'; 235.14, I've; 261.39, think we; 267.14, can't She; 281.14, 49'ers; 281.34, cash?; 287.15 together I; 293.33, you; 299.1, SUSAN:; 301.13, anywhere anywhere; 320.37, you why?; 332.1, *of of*; 337.21, doctor; 365.21, its'; 417.37, It; 426.10, *panarama*; 601.13, *Women*; 644.40, money?; 672.23, *Camermen*; 675.40, back?; 710.16, "I'll; 733.19, ucers; 748.18, happy.; 761.2, crowd Don't; 814.19, No.

COPYRIGHTS AND ACKNOWLEDGMENTS

Notes

In the notes below, the reference numbers denote page and line of this volume (the line count includes headings). No note is made for material included in standard desk-reference books. Quotations from Shakespeare are keyed to *The Riverside Shakespeare*, ed. G. Blakemore Evans (Boston: Houghton Mifflin, 1974). Cast lists and production information are taken from the first book editions of the plays, with the exception of the cast list for *Animal Crackers*, which is taken from the opening night program. For references to other studies and further information than is included in the Kaufman Chronology and Biographical Notes, see: Richard Anobile, *The Marx Brothers Scrapbook* (New York: Darien House, 1973); Brooks Atkinson, *Broadway* (Macmillan, 1970); Malcolm Goldstein, *George S. Kaufman: His Life, His Theater* (New York: Oxford University Press, 1979); Moss Hart, *Act One* (New York: Random House, 1959); Michael Kantor and Laurence Maslon, *Broadway: The American Musical* (New York: Bulfinch Press, 2004); Scott Meredith, *George S. Kaufman and His Friends* (Garden City: Doubleday, 1974); Rhoda-Gale Pollack, *George S. Kaufman* (Boston: Twayne, 1988); Howard Teichmann, *George S. Kaufman: An Intimate Portrait* (New York: Atheneum, 1972).

1.1   THE ROYAL FAMILY]   *The Royal Family* was presented at the Selwyn Theatre in New York on December 28, 1927. It was produced by Jed Harris and staged by David Burton. The cast was as follows: DELLA: Josephine Williams; JO: Royal C. Stout; HALL-BOY: Wally Stuart; McDERMOTT: Murray Alper; HERBERT DEAN: Orlando Daly; KITTY DEAN: Catherine Calhoun-Doucet; GWEN: Sylvia Field; PERRY STEWART: Roger Pryor; FANNIE CAVENDISH: Haidee Wright; OSCAR WOLFE: Jefferson de Angelis; JULIE CAVENDISH: Ann Andrews; ANTHONY CAVENDISH: Otto Kruger; ANOTHER HALLBOY: Lester Neilson; GILBERT MARSHALL: Joseph King; GUNGA: Hubert Courtney; MISS PEAKE: Phyllis Rose.

7.36   Delaney]   Jack Delaney (1900–1948), a popular French-Canadian boxer, was world lightweight champion from 1925 to 1927.

8.5   *the Lamb's Club*]   A private club founded in 1874 for actors and others in the theater business, on West 44th Street.

10.39–40   The Graphic]   *The New York Graphic*, a leading tabloid newspaper.

11.31   Mansfield]   Richard Mansfield (1857–1907), one of the most prominent American stage actors around the turn of the century.

12.7–8   Mannering . . . Allah"]   Mary Mannering (1876–1953) appeared on
Broadway in *The Garden of Allah*, a romantic melodrama by Robert
Hitchens, in 1911.

12.37   *Piping Rocking*]   Cf. the Piping Rock Club, an exclusive country
club in Locust Valley, Long Island.

12.39   *the Minerva*]   A Belgian-made luxury car.

15.35   Follies]   The *Ziegfeld Follies*, an extravagant musical revue performed beginning in 1907.

18.25   the Astor]   One of the major hotels in the theater district, on
Broadway between 43rd and 44th streets.

21.30   Bendel!]   Henri Bendel, a ladies' department store.

22.16   Camille to The Two Orphans]   *Camille* (*La Dame aux Camelias*),
a popular 1852 play by the younger Alexandre Dumas; *The Two Orphans* (*Les
Deux Orphelines*), 1874 play by Adolphe D'Ennery and Eugene Cormon.

26.7   Beerbohm Tree]   Sir Henry Beerbohm Tree (1853–1917), one of the
leading British stage actors around the turn of the century, built and ran Her
Majesty's Theatre.

26.8   "The Gay Lord Quex"]   1899 play by Arthur Wing Pinero (1855–
1934).

26.30   Otto Kahn's]   Kahn (1867–1934) was a financier and socialite
known for his support of the arts.

31.19   Fanny Ward]   Fannie Ward (1871–1952), an American silent film
actress.

36.12   David Wark Griffith]   D. W. Griffith (1875–1948), the preeminent
American silent film director.

41.6   Lackaye]   Wilton Lackaye (1862–1932), who made his Broadway debut in 1887 and performed in *Trilby* (1895) and *Trelawny of the "Wells"* (1927),
among many other plays.

44.3   Bernhardt . . . Duse!]   Sarah Bernhardt (1844–1923), Helena Modjeska (1804–1909), and Eleanora Duse (1858–1924), all celebrated actresses.

47.3–4   "Ah, the immortal . . . hai!"]   Cf. *Romeo and Juliet*, II.iv.25–26.

47.11–14   Prince, call upon . . . I hit.]   Cyrano's "Envoi," from the duel
scene in Act I of Edmond Rostand's play *Cyrano de Bergerac* (1897).

48.28   "Fauntleroy."]   The title character of Frances Hodgson Burnett's
Little Lord Fauntleroy (1886), in which an American boy is revealed to be the
heir to an English title.

48.30   Ascher]   Hungarian violin virtuoso Ascher Oszkár (1897–1965).

48.33   Krishnamurti]   Jiddu Krishnamurti (1895–1986), an exponent of theosophy, was the author of *Who Brings the Truth* (1927), *Life in Freedom* (1928), and many other books.

52.1–2   Isotta Fraschini . . . Hispano Suiza]   Luxury cars.

54.13   Pink lights]   Pink gels were traditionally added to footlights to make actors look younger.

57.9   "Diplomacy."]   1843 play by Victorien Sardou, set in the time of Louis XVI.

58.36   Elsie Dinsmore]   Main character of a multivolume series of books by Martha Finley (1828–1909); the first in the series was *Elsie Dinsmore* (1867).

60.20–21   "She Stoops . . . Paper"]   *She Stoops to Conquer*, a comedy (1773) by Oliver Goldsmith frequently revived in the late 19th century; *A Scrap of Paper*, a play (1860) by Victorien Sardou.

62.34   rabbit's foot]   Used to apply powder.

75.25   a radio]   A radiogram, sent from ship to shore.

79.3   eight o'clock!]   Until the 1960s, the curtain for most Broadway shows went up at 8:30. "Eight o'clock" would have been an actor's half hour call.

90.8   Sir Charles Wyndham]   Wyndham (1837–1919) was a touring actor in the U.S. and an actor-manager in London; he founded Wyndham's Theatre in London in 1899.

94.7–10   Hungarian play . . . Theatre Guild.]   The Theatre Guild, the most prestigious producing organization on Broadway in the 1920s and 1930s, had successfully staged plays by Hungarian dramatist Ferenc Molnár (1878–1952), including *Liliom* in 1921 and *The Guardsman* in 1924.

103.6–7   Reinhardt's . . . Pitoeff's]   Max Reinhardt (1873–1943), Austrian director and producer; Georges Pitoeff (1887–1939), Russian émigré director active in Paris after World War I.

104.12   Hopkins]   Arthur Hopkins (1878–1950), Broadway producer and director, known for staging classical plays starring John Barrymore.

109.1   ANIMAL CRACKERS]   *Animal Crackers* was presented at the 44th Street Theatre in New York on October 23, 1928. It was produced by Sam H. Harris, with music and lyrics by Bert Kalmar and Harry Ruby and staging by Oscar Eagle. The cast was as follows: MARY STEWART: Bernice Ackerman; MRS. RITTENHOUSE: Margaret Dumont; HIVES: Robert Greig; MRS. WHITEHEAD: Margaret Irving; M. DOUCET: Arthur Lipson; EMANUEL RAVELLI: Chico Marx; CAPTAIN SPAULDING: Groucho Marx; THE PROFESSOR: Harpo Marx; JAMISON: Zeppo Marx; WALLY WINSTON: Bert Mathews;

GRACE CARPENTER: Bobbie Perkins; ROSCOE W. CHANDLER: Louis Sorin; JOHN PARKER: Milton Watson; ARABELLA RITTENHOUSE: Alice Wood.

113.9   Spaulding] In the Princeton typescript of *Animal Crackers* in Sam Harris's papers at Princeton: "Spalding."

114.13   Fanny Ward] See note 31.19.

116.2   Marion Davies] A stage and silent film actress (1897–1961).

116.7   There's an idea.] The Princeton typescript contains additional dialogue:

> GRACE: There's an idea, let's bust it wide open.
> MRS. WHITEHEAD: Now, let's see, what can we do?
> GRACE: Set the house on fire?
> MRS. WHITEHEAD: No, she's insured. How about kidnapping Spalding?
> GRACE: No. Poison Mrs. Rittenhouse.
> MRS. WHITEHEAD: She doesn't drink.
> GRACE: It's too bad.

116.32   *Exit Grace and Mrs. W.*] In the Princeton typescript, Grace and Mrs. Whitehead remain on stage for a brief exchange with Winston:

> GRACE: Little Wally Winston, just the person I want to see. What's the idea of telling the world that I'm going to marry Sir Henry Buxbaum?
> WINSTON: Well, aren't you?
> GRACE: Yes, but I didn't want him to know it yet.
> WINSTON: But it was Buxbaum who told me.
> GRACE: Why the dirty so and so.
>   (*Enter Two Girls*)
> FIRST GIRL: Why, if it isn't Wally.
> SECOND GIRL: Hello, eavesdropper.
> WINSTON: Hello, weakness. How are the heels today, any stronger?
> GRACE: Well, sis, I don't think I can stand this kind of competition.
> MRS. WHITEHEAD: Well, don't forget, I want two husbands at the Yale Bowl.

118.19   the Benches] The Princeton typescript reads: "The bench at seventy second street."

120.35   the Movietone] An early technique for the reproduction of talking pictures, pioneered by Twentieth Century Fox.

121.7   a corporation] The Princeton typescript reads: "positively ridiculous."

121.18   the Dolly Sisters] "Jenny" and "Rozika," a vaudeville tandem dance act in the 1910s and 1920s. (The Princeton typescript reads: "the Fairbanks sisters.")

121.34   The ex-President] The Princeton typescript reads: "The cow-boy, Cal, the President."

130.9   ring for the wagon.] The Princeton typescript reads: "give him a brisk rub down."

131.8–9   Run along . . . good luck.] The Princeton typescript varies:
        (*To Grace*) Run along, my dear. See you again sometime.
    GRACE: Very well. I'll go and trample on some little children.

132.38   Last year] In the Princeton typescript, John's line is preceded by an additional sentence: "Mary, I can't ask you to wait forever."

133.33   You're not Abe Kabibble?] Kabibble was the stereotypically Jewish title character in Harry Hershfield's comic strip *Abie the Agent*, which ran from 1914 to 1940. (The Princeton *Animal Crackers* typescript varies: "I never see the funny pictures.")

134.8   Byzon] Paisan.

134.18   Ivan Pidulski, the Fish-Peddler] Here and in subsequent instances, the Princeton typescript reads "Rabbi Cantor" for "Ivan Pidulski".

136.1   *Chandler storms off*] In the Princeton typescript, this stage direction is followed by an additional line, spoken by Ravelli: "Well you're a fine crook. All you got is a tie, a bad check and a bum set of teeth."

136.23–24   Texas Guinan's] Mary Louise Cecila ("Texas") Guinan (1884–1933) was the nominal owner and flamboyant hostess of the El Fay Club and other nightclubs, where she famously greeted customers "Hello, suckers!"

137.18   two Irishmen?] Varies in the Princeton typescript: "traveling salesman?"

138.21   do it at night . . . looking.] The Princeton typescript varies: "if you kept off the grass."

138.34–36   Saturday at three . . . Pardon me,] The Princeton typescript varies: "Saturday at three. We can get in nine holes anyhow. No, we'd better make it Tuesday. I'm going to Europe Monday. I'll tell you what between Saturday and Tuesday sharp. Pardon me,".

138.39–139.1   Well, you see . . . Everybody was complaining] The Princeton typescript varies:
    CHANDLER: Well, in the first place it is a Presidential year.
    SPALDING: Isn't it though. Everybody is complaining.

139.4–5   locusts after . . . marriage problem?] The Princeton typescript varies: "The whole thing is Locust-Pocust. What do you think of Free Silver? What do you think of Free Lunch?"

140.8–9   I'll go mine.] In the Princeton typescript, the remainder of the scene varies as follows:
    CHANDLER: What about Guatemala?
    SPALDING: Well, that's a totally different problem. Guatemala every night

or you can't Mala at all. Of course, that takes a lot of Honduras. How did this ever start anyhow? Let's talk about something else. Take the foreign situation. Take Abyssinia. I'll tell you what. You take Abyssinia, and I'll take plain White Rock. No, make mine the same. Let's see what the boys in the back room'll have.

141.6   How much we make?]   In the Princeton typescript, Ravelli continues: "Not enough to pay over-the-head."

144.26–145.14   Well, what should I . . . *All exit.*]   The Princeton typescript varies:

RAVELLI: See, he's an expert. Ace of Clubs.

(*Ravelli then spreads his hand on the table. Professor plays one of Ravelli's cards*)

Deuce of Clubs.

(*Professor then takes a card from Mrs. Whitehead's hand and plays it*)

King of Clubs.

(*Professor trumps the trick*)

You trump it? No clubs, partner?

(*Professor tears up a club*)

Look again.

(*Professor tears up another club*)

MRS. WHITEHEAD: But what did he trump with?

RAVELLI: What do you care? You can't start an argument in the middle of the game.

MRS. RITTENHOUSE: I insist upon knowing what's trump.

(*Ad lib talk between Mrs. Rittenhouse, Mrs. Whitehead, and Ravelli. During the argument, Spalding enters*)

SPALDING: What's the trouble? What's the argument?

MRS. RITTENHOUSE: Why, it's ridiculous, here we are playing a game of bridge, and we can't find the trump.

SPALDING: Did you look under the table?

RAVELLI: If we tell her what trump is, we can't win the game.

SPALDING: That sounds reasonable. (*To Mrs. Rittenhouse*) You don't want to cheat, do you?

MRS. RITTENHOUSE: Captain Spalding, I've never played, without knowing what's trump. I refuse to stay here any longer. (*Ad lib between Mrs. Whitehead and Mrs. Rittenhouse and both exit*)

SPALDING: Ah, ha, the great trump mystery. Where is my secretary? Jamison, Jamison. Ah, the great Jamison mystery. You don't often get two mysteries in one day. (*Jamison enters*) Oh, there you are. Jamison, we've got to find out what's trump. Lock the doors and be very careful you don't get lost again.

JAMISON: Yes, sir.

SPALDING: Well spoken, my lad. I wish I'd have said that. Are the doors locked?

JAMISON: Yes, sir.

SPALDING: No one can enter or leave the room?

JAMISON: No sir.

SPALDING (*Indicating door*): Is that door locked over there? (*Professor nods yes*) Try it. (*Professor blows at the door, it opens and he exits*) Now then, not a man of you moves, until the coroner comes. (*To Ravelli*) Out with it, man, what's trump? (*Ravelli in unintelligible dialect, explains the whole game to Spalding*) Oh, you won't talk, eh? Well, maybe you'll talk after we give you the third degree. Jamison, give him the third degree.

JAMISON: I'm sorry, sir, but we left that in Africa.

SPALDING: So we did. Sorry old man, some other time. We've got some very nice second degrees, just came in this morning. (*To Jamison*) And where were you while all this was going on?

JAMISON: I was with you, sir.

SPALDING: Come, come, no evasions, where was I?

JAMISON: None of your business.

SPALDING: Well, there's something in that. That's the first clue we've had. Now all we've got to do is find the trump. Whatever became of Jamison?

JAMISON: Right here, sir.

SPALDING: Well, I find you anyhow. And where's that Italian Ravelli. (*To Ravelli*) You thought you got away, didn't you?

RAVELLI: You don't get rid of me so easy.

SPALDING: You stay right here. Jamison, are the doors locked?

JAMISON: Yes sir.

SPALDING: Nobody can get in or out?

JAMISON: No sir.

RAVELLI: Well, goodbye.

SPALDING: Goodbye. Take care of yourself. Give my regards at home. (*Exit Ravelli*) I must remember to send him a basket of fruit. Jamison, you and I have got to think this thing out together. Are the doors still locked?

JAMISON: Yes sir.

SPALDING: Nobody can get in or out?

JAMISON: No sir.

SPALDING: You're going to stick by me, aren't you, Jamison?

JAMISON: Absolutely.

SPALDING: Through thick and thin, aren't you, Jamison?

JAMISON: Absolutely. Well, goodbye.

SPALDING: Goodbye. (*Jamison exits*) Drop me a line some time. Always glad to hear from an old friend. Jamison, Jamison. Now I've lost Jamison. And Spalding. Jamison was one of my best friends. Well, he was my friend. Well I was acquainted with him. Ah, there was a friendship for you, and for me, and for Jamison, yes and for Spalding. You don't often see a friendship like that. Ah, friendship, friendship. What a wonderful thing it is.

(*Business with chair*)
Did you ever sit and ponder as you walk along the Strand
That life's a bitter battle at the best,
And if you only knew it, and would lend a helping hand
Then every man could meet the final test.
The world is but a stage, my friend, and life is but a game.
And how you play it is all that matters in the end,
For whether a man is right or wrong
A woman gets the blame.
And your mother is your dog's best friend.
Then up came mighty Casey
And strode up to the back
And Sheridan was fifteen miles away
For it takes a heap of lovin'
To make a home like that
On the road to where the flyin' fishes play.
(*In song*)
So be a Pagliacci, and laugh clown laugh.
(*Exit Spalding. Enter Grace and Chandler.*)

145.34   Well, sometimes I—]   Chandler's line is followed in the Princeton typescript by an additional line of Grace's: "You do. You dear old-fashioned thing."

151.27–28   Well, you wouldn't . . . out of that.]   The Princeton typescript varies: "I'd rather see your hand before your face."

153.4–20   My friends . . . six-thirty.]   In the Princeton typescript, Spaulding's speech varies: "My friends, I am here tonight to tell you about that great and wonderfully mysterious continent known as Africa. Africa is God's country and he can have it. We left New York drunk and early on the fatal morning of February Second. We landed on the coast of Africa. On February Fourth, having lost an entire day crossing the Fifty-ninth Street Bridge, we at once proceeded four-hundred miles into the interior, where we were met by Grover Whalen. Well, of course, we turned right around, and went out five hundred miles in the opposite direction, and were again met by Grover Whalen. Well anyhow, there we were in the middle of Africa, by this time it was beginning to get dark and the jungle closes at two, with the customary matinees on Wednesday and Saturday. I don't know whether any of you people have ever seen darkness descend on the jungle. It is so dark you can hear a pin drop. For a moment it is pitch black, then mysterious little lights appear in the distance. First a red light, and then a green light, so we knew it was the Lenox Avenue Express, and we got out at one hundred and thirty fifth street, and found ourselves again in Africa. Are there any questions? From the day of our arrival we led an active life. The first morning saw us up at six, breakfasted and back in bed at seven. This was our routine for the first three months. Then we finally got so we made it by six-thirty, where we were again met by Grover Whalen."

154.32   Victor Herbert]   A musician and composer of comic operas, Herbert (1859–1924) also wrote musical scores for the *Ziegfeld Follies* of 1919, 1921, and 1924.

154.33   *"Gypsy Love Song."*]   From the Victor Herbert musical *The Fortune Teller* (1898).

154.40   *"Some of these Days."*]   1910 song by Shelton Brooks.

155.7   *"Collegiate,"*]   1925 college song by Moe Jaffe and Nat Bonx.

155.16–21   (*Indicating the gift . . . left of painting.*)]   The Princeton typescript varies:

> (*Indicating actual chest*)—which has been handed down from Zulu to Zulu for eight hundred generations, now takes its place among the treasures of your beautiful home. Fashioned by primitive hands, aeons and aeons ago, it stands today as a superlative example of the unparalleled art of ancient men.
> RAVELLI (*reading tag on chest*): Grand Rapids.
> (*Spalding immediately tears tag off*)

156.18–19   *dance step.*) . . . CHANDLER]   The Princeton typescript includes the following additional lines:

> CHORUS: The Captain is a very moral man, he's moral.
> JOHN: My star has descended, there goes my career, all my hopes are ended, dear.
> MARY: Looking for the sun, fighting the battle till it is won, then what joy and fun, watching the clouds roll by.
> CHORUS: When it's dark or fair, what does it matter, what do you care, if you both are there, watching the clouds roll by.
> SPALDING: It's about time I took a hand in this little affair. Jamison, are the doors locked?
> JAMISON: Yes, sir.
> SPALDING: Nobody can get in or out?
> JAMISON: No, sir.
> SPALDING: Well, I'll throw a little light on this subject.
>   (*Black out. Exclamations from All*).
> ALL: The lights. What happened to the lights? Where are the light? Lights.
>   (*Lights up. The "Beaugard" is missing.*)

161.1   the Lambs]   See note 8.5.

161.25–26   soused to the gill.]   The Princeton typsecript varies: "a Goddamn fool."

162.16   bisschen]   German: bit, small amount.

163.29   giggle water.]   The Princeton typescript varies: "laughing soup."

166.17   Oh, he . . . riding.]   In the Princeton typescript, Jamison's line reads: "Oh he had a very bad night."

166.33   dinner you served?]   The Princeton typescript reads: "piano-playing?"

169.17–20   Now listen, you boys . . . *Policemen exit.*)]   The Princeton typescript varies:

> SPALDING: Yes—you see Mae West is opening a new show tonight.
>
> MRS. RITTENHOUSE: Well I hope Monsieur Doucet will be satisfied. Mr. Jamison, would you mind conducting the officers to Monsieur Doucet?
>
> JAMISON: With pleasure.
>
> SPALDING (*to Policemen*): Now listen you boys: you can get some good steady work here if you play your cards right. We're planning a lot of robberies and you know the heads of the firm won't last forever. That means that there'll be vacancies for some bright young men—so of course that lets you out. Good luck and good riddance. (*They march out headed by Jamison. Spalding calls after them*) And remember no matter what else you do—no music.

169.31–36   Nothing interferes . . . feel that way.]   The Princeton typescript varies:

> SPALDING: Nothing ever does. When the King of Siam invited me down for the week-end the King died—but I stayed for the week-end just the same. In fact I stayed all summer—I'd have been there yet if the Queen hadn't made a nasty crack. That's me—every time. Pleasure before pleasure—and after too.
>
> MRS. RITTENHOUSE: I'm glad you feel that way.

171.8–15   If I were Eugene . . . Marsden]   Spalding's speech parodies the soliloquizing "thought asides" for which O'Neill's *Strange Interlude* (1928) was noted; Charlie Marsden is a character in O'Neill's play.

171.17   Will you marry me?]   In the Princeton typescript, Spalding's question is followed by two additional lines:

> MRS. WHITEHEAD: What?
>
> SPALDING: What? As if they hadn't heard me. As if they both weren't waiting to leap into my arms. Strangling me with their desires. Hot afternoons of love. Back home in Montana. Well, what do you say, will you marry me?

171.23–25   This would be a better world . . . spinach.]   The Princeton typescript varies: "I still think Dempsey can beat Tunney."

171.35   DeWolf Hopper] A popular singer and comic actor (1858–1935) who played the lead in a number of comic operas on Broadway.

172.1   companionate marriage] *The Companionate Marriage* (1927), by Ben B. Lindsey and Wainwright Evans, advocated greater sexual freedom among consenting couples and liberalization of divorce laws.

172.4   you could sell Fuller brushes.] The Princeton typescript varies: "you could get a room some place."

176.1   (*Spaulding and Mary enter.*)] In the Princeton typescript, Spaulding and Mary's scene is preceded by an exchange between Chandler and Ravelli:

> RAVELLI: Well you're a fine partner. We're broke. So far they steal more from us than we steal from them. We lose on the week. Some times I think we make more money if we'd be honest.
>
> (*Chandler enters flourishing a newspaper*)
>
> CHANDLER: So—at last I find you. What have you done to me. You— you— See what you have done to me. (*Extends the paper*) See what it says there. Read it. (*Business*) You told this man Winston that I came from Czecho Slovakia.
>
> RAVELLI: I no say nothing.
>
> CHANDLER (*to Professor*): Then it was you—you snake in the grass.
>
> RAVELLI: No—he no tell. I know him for nineteen years—he never tell anything.
>
> CHANDLER: But only the three of us knew. Who could it have been?
>
> RAVELLI: I didn't do it. He didn't do it. (*A second's thought. Levels a finger at Chandler*) You did it. You tell our secret. You crook in the grass.
>
> CHANDLER: No—I wouldn't do a thing like that. But you—my land-man—du robber—du—du robber. Du du—(*Song and all exit*)

176.9–10   the Charles Ross disappearance] Charles Ross, a New Jersey boy kidnapped in 1875, was offered for ransom but never found; his case became a cause célèbre.

176.23   *for his watch.*)] Followed in the Princeton typescript by a number of additional lines:

> SPALDING: Now they've got my watch. This is going too far.
>
> JOHN: Can you imagine the painting was locked in a closet in my room.
>
> SPALDING: You know what it is: it's an inside job.
>
> JOHN: You think so?
>
> SPALDING: They had to get inside to take it, didn't they? It's an outside job, too.
>
> MARY: Really?
>
> SPALDING: Sure. They had to get outside to take it away. You know what it is: it's an inside outside job.
>
> JOHN: Not only that, but the door to my room was locked too.

MARY: How did they get in? Who could it have been?

SPALDING: Wait a minute—I think I've got a clue. (*Approaching John— picks off something from his shoulder*) No—it's a hair. A red hair.

MARY: The professor? No—it couldn't be.

SPALDING: Maybe it couldn't be but he's a good fellow to search. He's the only fellow I know with red hair—except Elinor Glyn. (*Calling off stage*) Hey you. (*First Policeman enters*) You know that little red headed fellow, the Professor—

FIRST POLICEMAN: Yes, sir.

SPALDING: Well, get your orchestra together and see if you can find him. And keep an eye on your uniform. (*First Policeman whistles to off-stage crew. As they march on he puts himself at the head of the procession. As they are exiting, it is discovered that at the very end of the line dressed in Policemen's clothes, is the Professor. He is carrying a painting under his arm*) Hey, you. (*The Professor turns enough to let audience recognize his face. Drops painting and runs off. John recovers the painting*)

177.26–27   the trial of Mary Dugan]   *The Trial of Mary Dugan*, a 1927 play by Bayard Veiller about a chorus girl who murders her financier boyfriend.

178.2–3   Say, would you . . . against you?]   In the Princeton typescript, Spalding has a variant line: "You know sometimes I think it would have been better if your mother had remained single."

178.39   Chic Sales]   Charles "Chic" Sales (1884–1936) was known for his vaudeville act about a carpenter who specialized in the construction of out-houses, and published *The Specialist* (1929) based on it.

179.27–29   Well, I'm going out . . . you're wrong]   In the Princeton type-script, Spalding has a variant line: "Do you mind if I go outside and get a hot towel? I've got black spots before my eyes and most of them are you."

181.11   "Habie's Irish Rose."]   *Abie's Irish Rose*, a play by Anne Nichols, ran on Broadway for five years beginning in 1922; a film version appeared in 1928.

182.24–25   the House of David]   A Michigan-based religious sect that owned and operated an exhibition baseball team and operated an amusement park, among other enterprises. (The Princeton typescript varies: "the Battle Creek Sanitarium.")

183.13–14   RAVELLI: No . . . section]   Varies in the Princeton typescript:
RAVELLI: No but I saw a woman in Paris.
SPALDING: Well that's your story.

183.38–39   How would you like . . . pageant?]   In the Princeton type-script, Spalding's line varies: "You wouldn't eat green apples, would you? Not if you had my stomach you wouldn't."

186.12   His Excellency, the Premier.]   In the Princeton typescript, Doucet
and Spaulding respond differently to Hives' announcement:
> DOUCET: My compliments, your Majesty. Herzogovnia has declared war
> upon us.
>
> SPALDING: Who?
>
> DOUCET: Herzogovnia.
>
> SPALDING: If you think I'm going to let my army fight with a Pullman
> car, you're crazy.

186.23   Your]   The Princeton typescript varies: "You're".

187.15   *"Old man river*]   "Ol' Man River," song from Kern and Hammerstein's *Show Boat* (1927).

187.23   I'll give her a divorce.]   In the Princeton typescript, Spaulding
continues: "I wonder if I could not put some guillotine in the queen's coffee—it might improve it. (*There is a knock at the door*) Entre—entre nous.
They laughed when I told them I could speak French."

187.40   Essex]   A racing automobile of the 1920s.

188.16   No, as you were . . . will.]   In the Princeton typescript, Spaulding
says instead: "Well that's duberries."

188.34–40 $350.60 . . . the wine.]   In the Princeton typescript, Spauld-
ing's response varies: "Get a load of this, Du. Cover charge thirty seven dollars and fifty cents. Is that a blanket charge or you charge them separate?
Baloney and eggs—sixty-five cents—without baloney seventy cents. That's a
lot of baloney for seventy cents. War tax forty dollars. What war was that?
Coffee and cake thirty four dollars and seventy cents—toothpicks two dollars
and fifty cents. Income from fiduciaries and trust fund—five thousand two
hundred and eighty dollars. Say you forgot to charge me for the wine."

189.18   *Enter Professor and Ravelli.*]   In the Princeton typescript, the
stage direction continues: "*They are dressed as Musketeers.*"

190.33   Konjola]   A patent medicine.

192.28   Somebody trumped him.]   In the Princeton typescript, there are
additional lines:
> MRS. RITTENHOUSE: I repeat! Where is the King?
>
> SPALDING (*In a disguised voice*): He's out on the Queen's Boulevard.

192.31–32   (*Ravelli . . . toward center.*]   Following this stage direction, the
Princeton typescript notes that a musical number, "Musketeers," is to be performed. The text of the number, not included in the typescript, is reprinted
here from the musical score:
> We're four of the three musketeers
> We've been together for years
> Eenie, meenie, minee, (*honk*)

Four of the three musketeers
We live by the sword, by the sea, by the way,
And we fight night and day.
My country 'tis of thee
Land of light wines and beers
We're cheered from Des Moines to Algiers
Each time our motto appears
It's one for all and two for five
We're four of the three musketeers.

When the Queen needs recreation
And she strolls along the path
Where are we?
Right by her side!
When she's filled with jubilation
Or consumed with ragtime wrath
Where are we?
Right by her side
We've sworn that we'd shield and protect her
We're her guardsmen, true and tried,
When she gets up in the morning
And she slips into her bath
Where are we?
Far from the old folks at home.

We're four of the three musketeers
We've been together for years
It's one for all and two for five
We're four of the three musketeers.

193.35   *Hives bows.*)]   In the Princeton typescript, the stage direction is
followed by an additional line:
    SPALDING: Well everything is clearing up nicely. In ten minutes I'll be in
    a speakeasy.

194.7–12   from the President! . . . *Music* . . .]   The ending of the Princeton typescript varies as follows:
    It is from the President. I am appointed the new Minister to Czecho
    Slovakia. He read about it in the "Traffic."
    WINSTON: All the big men read the Traffic.
    CHANDLER: Young man you are hired again at a big salary—and as for
    you my boy—(*Turns to John*)—your next commission is to paint me.
    SPALDING: And now friends I want to say—
        (*Music*)

195.1   JUNE MOON]   *June Moon* was presented at the Broadhurst Theatre in New York on October 9, 1929. It was produced by Sam H. Harris, and
Milano Tilden was the stage manager. The cast was as follows: FRED

STEVENS: Norman Foster; EDNA BAKER: Linda Watkins; PAUL SEARS: Frank Otto; LUCILLE: Jean Dixon; EILEEN: Lee Patrick; MAXIE SCHWARTZ: Harry Rosenthal; GOLDIE: Florence D. Rice; A WINDOW CLEANER: Frank Conlan; A MAN NAMED BRAINARD: Emil Hoch; BENNY FOX: Philip Loeb; MR. HART: Leo Kennedy; MISS RIXEY: Margaret Lee.

202.26   Benny Davis] Tin Pan Alley lyricist (1895–1979) whose hits included "Baby Face" and "Margie."

202. 39   Friars' Club] Created in 1904 by vaudeville performers and comedians as an alternative to the Lambs' Club.

209.30   Dillingham] Charles Dillingham (1868–1934), Broadway manager and producer.

209.31   "Nanette"] No, No, Nanette, a musical comedy, opened at the Globe Theatre on Broadway in 1925.

210.31   Dave Stamper] Stamper (1883–1963) was house composer for Florenz Ziegfeld's Ziegfeld Follies in the late 1910s and early 1920s.

211.14   Georgie White] George White (1890–1968), a one-time Ziegfeld dancer who began his own revue, George White's Scandals, in 1919.

213.11   Rogers to Peet] Rogers Peet was a men's haberdashery in Manhattan. (The 1931 Samuel French acting edition of June Moon reads "Roebuck to Sears.")

214.6   Harms] T. B. Harms, a major Tin Pan Alley publishing house.

218.4   a popular tune] The acting edition specifies: "What Have You?"

220.38   good mechanical break] Solid sales in phonograph record or player piano roll form.

222.32   Holland Tunnel] Named after engineer Clifton Holland, a tunnel between lower Manhattan and New Jersey completed in 1927.

224.22–23   "All Those Endearing Young Charms"] Traditional Irish folk song, published by Thomas Moore in his Irish Melodies (1808–1834).

231.19   "The Rosary."] 1903 devotional song, written by Georgia B. Welles and Robert Cameron Rogers.

233.14   Buddy De Sylva] George Gard "Buddy" De Sylva (1895–1950), one of Tin Pan Alley's most successful songwriters.

233.20   "Swanee River"] Cf. "Old Folks at Home," 1851 song by Stephen Foster.

233.23   "Show Boat."] 1927 musical by Jerome Kern and Oscar Hammerstein II.

233.26   Ruby Keeler . . . Duck."]   Keeler (1909–1993), a featured dancer in the 1928 *Ziegfeld Follies* and later a film actress, never appeared in Henrik Ibsen's *The Wild Duck* (1884). (In the Samuel French acting edition of *June Moon*, the line reads "Sophie Tucker in *Strange Interlude*.")

234.5–6   Gil Boag, and Earl Carroll]   Gallaird T. "Gil" Boag, a nightclub owner; Earl Carroll (1892–1948), a producer, director, performer, and theater owner.

236.20   Hesperus]   A ship wrecked on the Massachusetts coast in 1839, the subject of Henry Wadsworth Longfellow's poem "The Wreck of the Hesperus" (1842).

243.1   Wayburn's]   Ned Wayburn (1874–1942), director and choreographer of musical revues for Florenz Ziegfeld and others.

244.31   Make him]   The acting edition reads "Let him".

253.19   Harry Ruby]   Ruby (1895–1974), a vaudeville pianist, wrote many hit songs in the 1920s with lyricist Bert Kalmar, including "Three Little Words" and "Who's Sorry Now?"

259.17   the Happiness boys]   A vaudeville singing duo popular in the 1920s, formed by Billy Jones (1889–1940) and Ernest Hare (1883–1939).

272.4–5   "In a bungalow . . . and coo—"]   In the acting edition of the play, Maxie rather than Fred sings "In a Bungalow for Two," and each character has an additional line:

FRED. Say, that's great.

MAXIE. I thought you'd like it.

273.1   ONCE IN A LIFETIME]   *Once in a Lifetime* was presented at the Music Box in New York on September 24, 1930. It was produced by Sam H. Harris. The cast was as follows: GEORGE LEWIS: Hugh O'Connell; MAY DANIELS: Jean Dixon; JERRY HYLAND: Grant Mills; THE PORTER: Oscar Polk; HELEN HOBART: Spring Byington; SUSAN WALKER: Sally Phipps; CIGARETTE GIRL: Clara Waring; COAT CHECK GIRL: Otis Schaefer; PHYLLIS FONTAINE: Janet Currie; MISS FONTAINE'S MAID: Marie Ferguson; MISS FONTAINE'S CHAUFFER: Charles Mack; FLORABEL LEIGH: Eugenie Frontai; MISS LEIGH'S MAID: Dorothy Talbot; MISS LEIGH'S CHAUFFER: Warner Bliss; BELLBOY: Payson Crane; MRS. WALKER: Frances E. Brandt; ERNEST: Marc Loebell; HERMAN GLOGAUER: Charles Halton; MISS LEIGHTON: Leona Maricle; LAWRENCE VAIL: George S. Kaufman; WEISSKOPF: Louis Cruger; METERSTEIN: William McFadden; FIRST PAGE: Stanley Fitzpatrick; SECOND PAGE: Edwin Mills; THREE SCENARIO WRITERS: Kempton Race, George Casselbury, Burton Mallory; RUDOLPH KAMMERLING: Walter Dreher; FIRST ELECTRICIAN: Jack Williams; SECOND ELECTRICIAN: John O. Hewitt; A VOICE PUPIL: Jane Buchanan; MR. FLICK: Harold Grau; MISS CHASEN: Virginia Hawkins; FIRST CAMERAMAN: Irving Morrow; THE BISHOP: Granville Bates; THE SIXTH

BRIDESMAID: Frances Thress; THE LEADING MAN: Edward Loud; SCRIPT GIRL: Georgia MacKinnon; GEORGE'S SECRETARY: Robert Ryder; HOTEL GUESTS, POLICEMEN, BRIDESMAIDS, STUDIO EMPLOYEES, CAMERAMEN, LIGHT MEN: not credited.

277.39   Automat] A self-service restaurant chain founded in 1912; its flagship was located at Broadway and 45th Street.

278.5–9   pre-Roxy . . . ushers] The Roxy Theatre, opened in 1927 at Broadway and 50th Street, had ushers who dressed in elaborate uniforms.

280.5–6   Al Jolson's . . . "The Jazz Singer."] A film that was widely popular for its innovative use of sound. Released on October 10, 1927, by Warner Brothers, it included about 20 minutes of talking and songs; Jolson's first line was "You ain't heard nothing yet."

280.11   the Vitaphone!] A patented process for synchronizing sound with images, developed by Western Electric in 1925.

280.36   De Milles . . . Laskys] Cecil B. De Mille (1881–1959), a pioneering film director; Jesse L. Lasky (1880–1958), a Hollywood producer.

283.36   "California . . . come."] Cf. 1924 song of the same title, from the show *Big Boy* by Buddy de Sylva, Joseph Meyer, and Al Jolson.

287.8   Gloria Swanson] Silent film actress (1897–1983) who made a successful transition to talkies in 1928.

287.26   ritzed] Snubbed.

289.29–30   Gary Cooper . . . Horse] Cooper (1901–1961), a bit player in silent films of the early 1920s, had a major success with *Lilac Time* in 1928; Rex the Wonder Horse appeared in a number of serials in the 1920s, ridden by cowboy star and stunt man Yakima Canutt.

291.35–36   that Armenian . . . plays and things] Michael Arlen (1895–1956), an Armenian-born British novelist and playwright.

294.7   that's more like it.] In the acting edition of *Once in a Lifetime* (Samuel French, 1930), Helen continues: "Because Mr. Glogauer is a big man and he does things in a big way!"

294.30–32   "Sonny Boy," . . . Jolson.] 1928 song, performed by Al Jolson in the film *The Singing Fool*.

294.36   *Greta Garbo*] Swedish film actress (1905–1990) who made her American debut in 1925.

297.17   John Gilbert] Leading American film actor (1899–1936).

299.7   Buddy Rogers] Film actor (1904–1999) made famous by his role in *Wings* (1927).

301.1–3   "It takes . . . Home"]   From Edward A. Guest's 1916 poem "Home."

301.22   "Ring Out, Wild Bells,"]   Section CVI of Tennyson's "In Memoriam" (1850).

302.28   We'll take a chance on that.]   In the acting edition of the play, May's line is "That's when I sing 'Aida.'"

304.37   *"Pale hands I love!"*]   "Kashmiri Song" (1902), with music by Amy Woodforde-Finden and lyrics by Lawrence Hope.

306.9–10   Lou Jackson—sings these mammies]   Al Jolson was widely known for his "mammy" songs, such as "Mammy" in *The Jazz Singer* (1927). Glogauer's "Lou Jackson" is a conflation of the names of Jimmy Durante's vaudeville partners Lou Clayton and Eddie Jackson.

310.15   *Elinor Glyn*]   An English novelist and socialite (1864–1943), Glyn worked in Hollywood from 1920 to 1929 as a screenwriter and film director.

316.31   fine Italian hand.]   Craftiness, subtlety.

317.1–4   "Yes, I'm a tramp . . . handsome—"]   From "Tale of a Tramp," a folk song.

317.16–17   Duse . . . D'Annunzio]   Gabriele D'Annunzio revealed his relationship with Duse in an erotic novel, *Il fuoco* (*The Flame*, 1900).

319.6–9   Thanks . . . see us.]   This exchange varies in the acting edition:
>   MAY: Thanks. Just tell Mr. Walker for me that I'm doing the best I can and that the Red Cross is helping me.
>   MRS. WALKER: They do so much good, don't they? It's really a wonderful organization.

320.24   Ufa]   Universum Film Aktien Gesellschaft, Berlin's major commercial film studio.

320.27–28   Reinhardt . . . Schauspielhaus]   Max Reinhardt (1873–1943), an Austrian-born director known for his spectacular epics including *Faust* and *Everyman*, worked in Germany until Hitler came to power, when he fled to the United States; the Grosses Schauspielhaus ("Theater of the Five Thousand"), a state-of-the-art theater, was built for him in Berlin in 1919.

320.39–40   in Russia with Eisenstein]   Sergei Eisenstein (1898–1948), leading Soviet film director.

322.31   Will Hays]   Hays (1879–1954) headed the Motion Picture Producers and Distributors of America, an industry self-regulatory agency that in 1930 created the Motion Picture Production Code.

325.22   Chief Engineer]   In the acting edition of the play, "'Barber Shop.'"

336.3   "I love you."]   After Susan's line, the acting edition continues:
KAMMERLING: "I hate you."
SUSAN (*In exactly the same tone as before*): "I hate you."
KAMMERLING: She can do it!
GLOGAUER: That's wonderful!

337.11   twenty-four sheets]   Large-format posters.

340.19   Simmons]   A mattress manufacturer.

342.33   exhibitionist.]   In the acting edition, Lily has an additional line:
"I can't stay out late tonight—I've got to be home by dawn."

344.33–35   They were with Cecil DeMille . . . met 'em.]   The acting edi-
tion varies:
They were in "The Seven Commandments."
BISHOP: Oh, yeah—I was a rabbi in that one.

345.12–14   MAY: Well, maybe . . . That's it!]   The acting edition varies:
MAY: Well, maybe she could perform the ceremony—then she could do
all the talking.
GEORGE: But that wouldn't fit the scenario!

345.35–37   lay that cornerstone . . . fifteen.]   In the acting edition, Glogauer "will look at 'Foolish Virgins' at two-fifteen."

349. 31   Biograph . . . Maurice Costello]   Lawrence (1886–1938), the first
American actress to have her name used to advertise a movie, was also known
as "The Biograph Girl," after the studio promoting her; she made several
films in the 1910s with Costello (1877–1950), a stage and silent film actor.

353.8–16   GEORGE: Well . . . right picture—]   The acting edition varies:
GEORGE: Well, I've been trying to think. You know that thing in my office where we keep the new scenarios? Well, if you're in a hurry it
looks just like the wastebasket, and so I reached into it—only it was
the wastebasket.
MAY: Well, you certainly produced it.

355.9–10   under contract . . . gaff.]   The acting edition varies: "to write
scenarios, but he couldn't stand the sitting."

355.37   has plenty of time]   The acting edition varies: "and getting worse
right along."

358.34–35   an Eastern Star]   The order of the Eastern Star is a women's
organization affiliated with the Masons.

359.19   the Pacific Ocean. . . .]   The acting edition includes an additional
line, spoken by Vail: "(*chiming in, talking simultaneously*) And then you can
take the bathroom and put it where Glogauer is and then take Glogauer and
do as your fancy bids you."

369.1   OF THEE I SING]   *Of Thee I Sing* was presented at the Music
Box Theatre on December 26, 1931. It was produced by Sam H. Harris, and
the cast was as follows: LOUIS LIPPMAN: Sam Mann; FRANCIS X. GILHOOLEY:
Harold Moffet; MAID: Vivian Barry; MATTHEW ARNOLD FULTON: Dudley
Clements; SENATOR ROBERT E. LYONS: George E. Mack; SENATOR CARVER
JONES: Edward H. Robins; ALEXANDER THROTTLEBOTTOM: Victor Moore;
JOHN P. WINTERGREEN: William Gaxton; SAM JENKINS: George Murphy;
DIANA DEVERAUX: Grace Brinkley; MARY TURNER: Lois Moran; MISS BEN-
SON: June O'Day; VLADIMIR VIDOVICH: Tom Draak; YUSSEF YUSSEVITCH:
Sulo Hevonpaa; THE CHIEF JUSTICE: Ralph Riggs; SCRUBWOMAN: Leslie
Bingham; THE FRENCH AMBASSADOR: Florenz Ames; SENATE CLERK: Martin
Leroy; GUIDE: Ralph Riggs; PHOTOGRAPHERS, POLICEMEN, SUPREME
COURT JUSTICES, SECRETARIES, SIGHT-SEERS, NEWSPAPERMAN, SENATORS,
FLUNKEYS, GUESTS, ETC.: The Misses Ruth Adams, Olgene Foster, Peggy
Greene, Yvonne Gray, Billie Seward, Grenna Sloan, Adele Smith, Jessica
Worth, Kathleen Ayres, Bobbie Brodsley; Martha Carroll, Mary Carroll,
Anne Ecklund, Virginia Franck, Dorothy Graves; Georgette Lampsi, Terry
Lawlor, Lillian Lorray, Martha Maggard, Mary Mascher, Anita Pam, Barbara
Smith, Baun Sturtz, Peggy Thomas, Patricia Whitney; The Messrs. Robert
Burton, Ray Clark, Charles Conklin, Frank Erickson, Jack Fago, Frank
Gagen, Hazzard Newberry, Jack Ray, Bruce Barclay, Tom Curley, Leon
Dunar, Michael Forbes, David Lawrence, Charles McClelland, Richard
Neely, John McCahill; THE JACK LINTON BAND: Jack Linton, Dave Allman,
Charles Bennett, Walter Hinger, Milton Hollander, Frank Miller, Pete
Shance, Jake Vander Meulen.

The 1932 first book edition of *Of Thee I Sing* included the following fore-
word by critic George Jean Nathan:

In "Of Thee I Sing," I believe that we discover the happiest and most successful native music-stage lampoon that has thus far come the way of the
American theatre. With it, further, I believe that American musical comedy
enters at length upon a new, original and independent lease of life. That its
genealogical tree betrays traces of the plum juices of the late W. S. Gilbert
and certain minor blood strains of the later Charles H. Hoyt is more or less
evident but, once the fact is allowed it may quickly be dismissed, for the ex-
hibit is fully able to stand on its own feet and to offer itself in its own au-
thentic light.

The reading of a music-show script imposes upon the library armchair a
somewhat different attitude from the reading of a dramatic play. That difference is the same difference that attaches to the mood of theatregoing in the
instance of a music-show on the one hand and a dramatic play on the other.
In the case of a music-show, a volitional predisposition to light pleasure and
even gaiety, a humor for intellect-on-the-loose, a leaning to confetti criticism,
are essential. The music-show is not for pundits in their punditical moments
but for pundits, if at all, in such rare moments as they think and argue with
laughter. I accordingly invite the more sober species of reader to engage this

script with his top hat cocked saucily over his mind, with his ear filled with the hint of gay tunes and with his eye made merry by the imagined picture of all the relevant and appropriate clowns in the persons of actors, and of appetizing femininity. Only by so approaching it will he get from it what its authors would wish him to.

A glance backward over the modern American musical stage will disclose it to have followed, with little deviation, routine and rusty tracks. In endless succession that stage has given us the so-called romantic musical comedies with their proud princesses in love with humble naval lieutenants and their humble slaveys cinderellaed by proud princes, the revues with their vaudeville comedians and peafowl ladies, the shows laboriously manufactured out of dull comedies previously displayed on the legitimate stage, and the German and Austrian importations adapted to what has been believed to be the American taste by the insertion into their books of a sufficient number of facetious allusions to Congress, Yonkers and Miss Aimée Semple McPherson. Here and there, there has, occasionally, been a mild effort to break away from the established patterns, but the effort has been so mild that it has come to naught, and what has resulted has been, at bottom, much the same old thing. It remained for the authors of "Of Thee I Sing" two years ago to introduce into this swamp, in a show called "Strike Up the Band," the novel bloom that paved the way for the fuller and more highly perfumed sardonic hothouse that the present show is.

In "Strike Up the Band," a sound brand of broad satire was applied to the American music-show stage of our time. That broad satire, smeared generously upon a slapstick, is now applied again, and very much more thwackingly and amusingly, in "Of Thee I Sing." Pour a couple of cocktails into your sobriety and turn the page.

372.13   *White Rock*]   A brand of sparkling mineral water.

384.18–19   Coolidge . . . words on love]   After he retired from the presidency, Calvin Coolidge wrote a newspaper column, "Thinking Things Over with Calvin Coolidge."

390.13   Clara Bow]   American film actress (1905–1965).

395.22   March the Fourth]   Inauguration Day (changed to January 20 in 1937).

402.22–24   Jack Sharkey . . . Schmeling]   Jack Sharkey and Max Schmeling fought for the world heavyweight title in 1930; Sharkey was disqualified for hitting below the belt. He beat Schmeling in a 1932 rematch.

408.5–13   WINTERGREEN . . . obviously you.]   Wintergreen's verse for "Of Thee I Sing," included in the April 1932 piano-vocal score, was not sung in the original New York production of the play.

410.36   Walter Hampden]   American actor (1879–1955), known for his portrayals of historical characters (Washington, Richlieu) and Cyrano de Bergerac.

411.8   Primo Carnera] Italian boxer (1906–1967), world heavyweight champion (1933–34).

411.9   Man O'War] A celebrated racehorse (1917–1947).

414.17   A.K.s] Alter kockers (Yiddish: old farts, crochety old men).

426.29   Friars' Club] See note 202.39.

426.35–427.2   Queen . . . Carol.] Queen Marie of Romania (1875–1938), who visited the United States in the 1910s and 1920s; her son Carol, who lived openly in Paris with his mistress for a time, ascended to the Romanian throne in 1930.

428.6   Jackie Cooper] Juvenile actor (b. 1922), nominated for an Academy Award for *Skippy* (1931).

435.33   six of the fifty . . . wrong] Cf. "Fifty Million Frenchmen Can't Be Wrong," a 1927 song performed by Sophie Tucker, with music by Fred Fisher and lyrics by Willie Raskin and Billy Rose.

452.26–27   the Frankie . . . wrong] "Frankie and Johnny," a folk ballad; its refrain runs "He was her man, he done her wrong."

454.38   CHIEF JUSTICE] In the 1932 Knopf edition of *Of Thee I Sing*: "SENATOR FROM MASSACHUSETTS".

461.14, 16   Supreme] In the 1932 Knopf edition of *Of Thee I Sing*: "*Su*preme".

469.1   DINNER AT EIGHT] *Dinner At Eight* was presented at the Music Box Theatre in New York on October 22, 1932. It was produced by Sam H. Harris, and Robert B. Sinclair served as stage manager. The cast was as follows: MILLICENT JORDAN: Ann Andrews; DORA: Mary Murray; GUSTAVE: Gregory Gaye; OLIVER JORDAN: Malcolm Duncan; PAULA JORDAN: Marguerite Churchill; RICCI: Cesar Romero; HATTIE LOOMIS: Margaret Dale; MISS COPELAND: Vera Hurst; FOSDICK: Clarence Bellair; CARLOTTA VANCE: Constance Collier; DAN PACKARD: Paul Harvey; KITTY PACKARD: Judith Wood; TINA: Janet Fox; DR. J. WAYNE TALBOT: Austin Fairman; LARRY RENAULT: Conway Tearle; THE BELLBOY: Robert Griffith; THE WAITER: James Seeley; MAX KANE: Sam Levene; MR. HATFIELD: William McFadden; MISS ALDEN: Ethel Intropodi; LUCY TALBOT: Olive Wyndham; MRS. WENDEL: Dorothy Walters; JO STENGEL: Frank Manning; MR. FITCH: George Alison; ED LOOMIS: Hans Robert.

474.15   Cooper Union] A private college, the Cooper Union offered lectures and public programs through its Peoples Institute, from 1898 to 1933.

474.37   Florodora Girl] *Florodora*, a British musical by Owen Hall and Leslie Stuart, opened on Broadway in 1900; it featured a sextet of chorus girls.

475.38   Bori]   Lucrezia Bori (1887–1960), a Spanish soprano.

478.33   Twenty-one]   The "21" Club, opened in 1922 as a speakeasy.

480.18   Charvet]   A men's haberdashery.

483.28   the Colony]   A private women's club, established in 1903.

491.11   the Carlotta Vance Theatre]   Actress Maxine Elliott, on whom Ferber and Kaufman based the character of Carlotta Vance, opened the Maxine Elliott Theatre in 1908, on West 39th Street.

492.1   Julie Cavendish]   A character in Ferber and Kaufman's *The Royal Family*.

492.20   Delmonico]   A classic New York restaurant, opened in 1827.

493.1   *Trelawney*]   *Trelawny of the "Wells,"* a popular British play (1898) by Arthur Wing Pinero.

495.26   John L. Sullivan]   A boxer and vaudeville performer (1858–1918), also known as "The Boston Strong Boy."

496.2   Lochinvar]   Hero of Sir Walter Scott's *Marmion* (1808), who abducts his beloved on the evening of her betrothal to another man.

497.2   *Vanities*]   *Earl Carroll's Vanities*, a Broadway revue (1923–32).

507.28–29   *ausverflugter Hund*]   Accursed dog.

514.11   Flora Finch . . . Walthall]   Flora Finch (1867–1940), Mae Marsh (1895–1968), and Henry B. Walthall (1878–1936), actors who began their careers in the silent era but who were no longer well-known.

546.7   *Ted Niblo's Musketeers*]   Fred Niblo (1874–1948), born Federico Nobile, directed *The Three Musketeers* in 1921.

547.22   *schluck*]   German: sip, swig.

553.28   *Say It With Music*]   Cf. Irving Berlin's 1921 *Music Box Revue*, which opened with the song "Say It With Music."

569.20–21   Dinty Moore's]   A popular theater district restaurant, on Broadway and 46th Street.

571.21   Mr. Stengel!]   In the 1932 Samuel French acting edition of *Dinner at Eight*, "Larry!"

577.17   *his famous profile*]   John Barrymore, who played Larry Renault in the 1933 film version of *Dinner at Eight*, was sometimes referred to as "the Great Profile."

586.29   Arno's pictures]   Peter Arno (1904–1968) contributed cartoons to *The New Yorker* beginning in 1925.

591.1   STAGE DOOR]   *Stage Door* was presented at the Music Box Theatre in New York on October 22, 1936. It was produced by Sam H. Harris, and E. John Kennedy served as the stage manager. The cast was as follows: OLGA BRANDT: Sylvia Lupas; BERNICE NIEMEYER: Janet Fox; SUSAN PAIGE: Lili Zehner; MATTIE: Dorothea Andrews; MARY HARPER (Big Mary): Beatrice Blinn; MARY McCLUNE (Little Mary): Mary Wickes; MADELEINE VAUCLAIN: Grena Sloan; JUDITH CANFIELD: Lee Patrick; ANN BRADDOCK: Louise Chaffee; MRS. ORCUTT: Leona Roberts; KAYE HAMILTON: Frances Fuller; PAT DEVINE: Virginia Rousseau; LINDA SHAW: Jane Buchanan; JEAN MAITLAND: Phyllis Brooks; BOBBY MELROSE: Juliet Forbes; LOUISE MITCHELL: Catherine Laughlin; KENDALL ADAMS: Margot Stevenson; FRANK: William Andrews; TERRY RANDALL: Margaret Sullavan; SAM HASTINGS: Robert Thomsen; JIMMY DEVEREAUX: Alex Courtney; FRED POWELL: Walter Davis; LOU MILHAUSER: Edmund Dorsay; DAVID KINGSLEY: Onslow Stevens; KEITH BURGESS: Richard Kendrick; MRS. SHAW: Helen Ray; DR. RANDALL: Priestly Morrison; ELLEN FENWICK: Judith Russell; TONY GILLETTE: Draja Dryden; LARRY WESTCOTT: Tom Ewell; BILLY: William Atlee; ADOLPH GRETZL: Ralph Locke.

592.3   the Footlights Club]   While writing *Stage Door*, Ferber visited the Rehearsal Club, a subsidized club for young actresses on West 53rd Street, founded in 1913.

597.16   Kit Cornell]   Katharine Cornell (1893–1974), an American stage actress; Alexander Woollcott described her as "First Lady of the American Theater."

601.12–13   Al Woods' . . . *Room 13*]   Woods, a Broadway producer (1870–1951), presented *The Woman in Room 13*, by Samuel Shipman and Max Marcin, in 1919.

605.13   Rachel]   Stage name of Elisa Felix (1821–1858), a French classical actress.

605.14   Nazimova]   Alla Nazimova (1879–1945), Russian-born actress famous for her performances in Chekhov, Ibsen, and O'Neill plays.

607.19   Emperor Jones]   Title character of a one-act play (1920), set in the Caribbean with a mostly black cast, by Eugene O'Neill.

609.38   Ben Dexter]   Revised, in the acting edition of *Stage Door* (Dramatists Play Service, 1941), to read "Lou Milhauser."

610.17   the Winter Garden]   A large theater on Broadway between 50th and 51st streets, built by the Schubert brothers in 1911. In 1937, it featured *The Ziegfeld Follies*.

610.25–26   Edwin Booth]   A leading classical actor (1833–1893), famous for his Shakespearean roles.

617.12–13   Fourteenth Street Theatre]   Built in 1866 and revived in 1926 by actress Eva Le Galliene as a home for her Civic Repertory Company; Clifford Odets, on whom Ferber and Kaufman based the character of Keith Burgess, presented his one-act play *Waiting for Lefty* there on January 6, 1935.

618.34   Topsy]   A young slave girl in Harriet Beecher Stowe's *Uncle Tom's Cabin* (1852); a dramatization of the novel by George L. Aiken played around the country from 1852 to the late 1920s.

624.8–9   reviving *Madame X . . . Little Eva*]   *Madame X*, a 1910 play by Alexandre Bisson, revived at the Earl Carroll Theatre in 1927; Little Eva, a young white girl in *Uncle Tom's Cabin*.

629.38   Klein's]   A modestly priced women's department store on Union Square.

630.14   *curtain descends*.)]   Followed in the acting edition by an additional line of Jean's: "(*As curtain falls.*) I'm going to make something out of my life. I'm not going to stay in this lousy dump."

633.34   Walter Hampden]   See note 410.36.

648.32   the seventh day]   Actors' Equity allows producers to fire an actor without severance pay up to the end of the seventh day of a contract.

655.15–16   Trocaderos . . . Brown Derbies]   Fashionable Hollywood restaurants of the 1930s.

658.10–11   Elizabeth Bergner . . . Helen Hayes]   Bergner (1897–1986), who began her career as a stage actress in Switzerland, Austria, and Germany, went on to work on stage and in film in England and the United States; Hayes (1900–1993) was a stage, film, and later television actress.

659.38   CURTAIN]   In the acting edition of *Stage Door*, Terry is given a curtain line: "Just a minute, I'll get my hat. (*Runs for stairs as curtain falls.*)"

661.17   Schiaparelli]   Elsa Schiaparelli (1890–1973), an Italian fashion designer.

664.35   How many . . . allure?]   The acting edition varies: "How many X's are there in sexy?"

665.38   Piping Rock]   See note 12.37.

677.32–33   Hollywood to Dunsinane . . . Shakespeare]   Cf. *Macbeth*, V.v.43–44.

685.1–2   I wish in future . . . of my own.]   Terry is quoting the Victoria of Laurence Housman's *Victoria Regina: A Dramatic Biography*, published in 1934 and performed on Broadway in 1936: "As I may now do as I like, I wish in future to have a bed, and a room of my own!"

687.1   YOU CAN'T TAKE IT WITH YOU]   *You Can't Take It With You* was presented at the Booth Theatre in New York on December 14, 1936.

It was produced by Sam H. Harris, and William McFadden was the stage manager. The cast was as follows: PENELOPE SYCAMORE: Josephine Hull; ESSIE: Paula Trueman; RHEBA: Ruth Attaway; PAUL SYCAMORE: Frank Wilcox; MR. DE PINNA: Frank Conlan; ED: George Heller; DONALD: Oscar Polk; MARTIN VANDERHOF: Henry Travers; ALICE: Margot Stevenson; HEN-DERSON: Hugh Rennie; TONY KIRBY: Jess Barker; BORIS KOLENKHOV: George Tobias; GAY WELLINGTON: Mitzi Hajos; MR. KIRBY: William J. Kelly; MRS. KIRBY: Virginia Hammond; THREE MEN: George Leach, Ralph Holmes, Franklin Heller; OLGA: Anna Lubowe.

690.36–37   El Morocco]   A nightclub and former speakeasy on East 54th Street.

695.17   Porgy and Bess]   Title characters of the 1935 opera by George and Ira Gershwin and DuBose Heyward.

696.17   "The Last Days of Pompeii"]   Cf. Edward Bulwer-Lytton's 1834 novel, frequently adapted for the stage.

697.7   Father Divine]   African-American charismatic religious leader (c. 1879–1965).

698.12–13   the Dying Swan.]   A ballet standard, first choreographed for Anna Pavlova in 1907 by Mikhail Fokine.

699.18   Kay Francis]   Stage and screen actress (1905–1968) noted for her elegant couture.

709.7   Bakst! Diaghlieff!]   Leon Bakst (1866–1924), a Russian set designer, worked exclusively with Sergei Diaghlieff (1872–1929), who ran the Ballets Russes from 1920 to 1929.

710.26   Singer midgets]   A performing troupe first assembled in 1914 by Leopold von Singer (1877–1951).

711.4   "The Good Earth"]   Pearl S. Buck's 1931 novel about a Chinese peasant family.

712.11–12   "Sex . . . Holiday."]   Cf. Death Takes a Holiday (1929), a popular Broadway play by Walter Ferris.

718.28–29   "Peg o' My Heart"]   Popular 1912 play by J. Hartley Manners.

725.7   Pavlowa]   Anna Pavlova (1885–1931), a Russian ballerina.

727.14   WPA]   The Works Progress Administration, formed in 1935, employed actors, writers, musicians, and artists, among others, in national projects.

728.3   Scheherazade]   Symphonic suite (1888) by Nicolai Rimsky-Korsakov.

729. 3   Foutte temp el levee]   Fouetté, temps levé (a whipping movement, a hopping movement).

746.4   *Edwin C. Hill*]   Edwin Conger Hill (1884–1957), journalist and radio commentator.

746.22   Union Club]   One of New York's most exclusive clubs, founded in 1836.

753.27   Hattie Carnegie's]   Couture house on East 49th Street owned by designer Hattie Carnegie (1886–1956).

753.35   Schraffts']   A chain of ice-cream parlors catering to a genteel clientele, first opened in 1898.

763.1   THE MAN WHO CAME TO DINNER]   *The Man Who Came to Dinner* was presented at the Music Box Theatre in New York on October 16, 1939. It was produced by Sam H. Harris. Cole Porter provided the music and lyrics. Bernard Hart served as stage manager, and Donald Oenslager made the sets. The cast was as follows: MRS. ERNEST W. STANLEY: Virginia Hammond; MISS PREEN: Mary Wickes; RICHARD STANLEY: Gordon Merrick; JUNE STANLEY: Barbara Wooddell; JOHN: George Probert; SARAH: Mrs. Priestley Morrison; MRS. DEXTER: Barbara Adams; MRS. McCUTCHEON: Edmonia Nolley; MR. STANLEY: George Lessey; MAGGIE CUTLER: Edith Atwater; DR. BRADLEY: Dudley Clements; SHERIDAN WHITESIDE: Monty Woolley; HARRIET STANLEY: Ruth Vivian; BERT JEFFERSON: Theodore Newton; PROFESSOR METZ: LeRoi Operti; THE LUNCHEON GUESTS: Phil Sheridan, Charles Washington, William Postance; MR. BAKER: Carl Johnson; EXPRESSMAN: Harold Woolf; LORRAINE SHELDON: Carol Goodner; SANDY: Michael Harvey; BEVERLY CARLTON: John Hoysradt; WESTCOTT: Edward Fisher; RADIO TECHNICIANS: Rodney Stewart, Carl Johnson; SIX YOUNG BOYS: Daniel Leone, Jack Whitman, Daniel Landon, Donald Landon, DeWitt Purdue, Robert Rea; BANJO: David Burns; TWO DEPUTIES: Curtis Karpe, Phil Sheridan; A PLAINCLOTHES MAN: William Postance.

769.37   Dr. Dafoe]   Allan Roy Dafoe (1883–1943), Canadian physician famous for delivering the Dionne quintuplets in 1934.

770.28   *Good-bye, Mr. Chips*]   Best-selling 1934 novel by James Hilton, about a British public school teacher.

772.14   Samuel J. Liebowitz]   Samuel Simon Leibowitz (1893–1978), a prominent criminal defense lawyer, defended the widely publicized case of the Scottsboro Boys (nine black youths accused, in 1937, of raping two white women on a freight train).

773.2   my chair?]   The acting edition of *The Man Who Came to Dinner* (Dramatists Play Service, 1939) continues: "You have the touch of a sex-starved cobra!"

773.36   How did you . . . ox-cart?]   The acting edition of the play reads: "You were gone long enough to have a baby!"

775.31–32   If young men . . . critics—]   The acting edition of the play reads: "I see no reason why I should endorse Maiden Form Brassieres."

776.2–3   Jascha Heifetz . . . Anthony Eden]   Jascha Heifetz (1901–1987), a Russian violinist; Katharine Cornell (1893–1974), a stage actress; Elsa Schiaparelli (1890–1973), Italian fashion designer; Alfred Lunt (1892–1977) and Lynn Fontanne (1887–1983), actors, married in 1922; Alexis Carrel (1873–1944), the 1912 Nobel Laureate in Medicine; Anthony Eden (1897–1977), British politician who served as foreign minister from 1935 to 1939 and later as prime minister.

776.6   Sacha Guitry]   French playwright and film director (1885–1957).

776.18   Tibbett . . . Flagstad]   Opera singers Lawrence Tibbett (1896–1960), an American baritone; Elisabeth Rethberg (1894–1976), a German soprano; Giovanni Martinelli (1885–1969), an Italian baritone; and Kirsten Flagstad (1895–1962), a Norwegian soprano.

776.20   Ethel Barrymore]   A leading American stage actress (1879–1959).

776.40   Dr. Crippen . . . of me]   The acting edition of the play varies: "I've got the best horse doctor in town. . . ."

777.4   Milt Gross]   Comic writer and cartoonist (1895–1953) whose "Nize Baby" and "Hiawatta" parodied myths and legends, in Yiddish dialect.

777.8   Louella Parsons]   American journalist (1893–1972) who wrote a widely syndicated movie gossip column for the Hearst newspapers from 1922 to 1965.

778.4   "Treacle Face]   The acting edition of the play reads: "Dear Baby's Breath,".

778.26   counterfeiting!]   The acting edition reads "white-slavery!"

779.19   William Allen White]   White (1868–1944), owner and editor of the *Emporia Gazette*, won a 1923 Pulitzer Prize for editorial writing; he was also the author of several books.

779.39   Richard Harding Davis]   American journalist and author (1864–1916), noted for his dramatic war reporting.

780.36   Snyder-Gray case]   In 1928, Ruth Snyder and her lover Judd Gray murdered her husband, a crime for which she was later executed.

781.17   Maude Adams]   American actress (1872–1953) best known for her performance in *Peter Pan* (1905).

782.21   Elsie Dinsmore]   See note 58.36.

783.20–30   Here in Roach City . . . *Mercury*.]   The acting edition of the play varies:

METZ. And in one week, Sherry, if all goes well, there will be *fifty* thousand.

MAGGIE. If all goes well—? What can go wrong? They're in there, aren't they?

WHITESIDE. (*Glaring at her.*) Quiet, please.

METZ. You can watch them, Sherry, while they live out their whole lives. Look! Here is their maternity hospital. It is fascinating. They do everything that human beings do.

MAGGIE. Well!

WHITESIDE. Please, Maggie, these are *my* cockroaches.

MAGGIE. Sorry.

WHITESIDE. Go ahead, Metz.

784.28   did it in a bathtub] The acting edition reads: "chopped them up in a salad bowl—".

785.23–24   Lillian Russell] Also known as "The American Beauty," Russell (1861–1922) was one of the leading vaudeville and music hall performers around the turn of the century.

788.14   William Beebe] American naturalist and oceanographer (1877–1962).

789.4   is very sensitive.] The acting edition of the play reads "once belonged to Chauncey Depew." Depew (1834–1928) was a leading figure in the New York State Republican Party.

791.11   Zasu Pitts] American film actress (1898–1963) best known for her dithering comic persona.

792.30   Joan Crawford fantasy] In *Grand Hotel* (1932) and other films, Crawford (1904–1977) played women of modest means who married wealthier men.

793.4   Big Lord Fauntleroy] See note 48.28.

797.22   William Lyon Phelps] Phelps (1865–1943), an English professor at Yale, popularized the arts through his lectures and essays.

798.19   Horace Greeley] American journalist and editor (1811–1872).

800.19–20   Admiral Richard E. Byrd] Polar explorer (1888–1957).

802.24   Margaret Bourke-White] Photographer and photojournalist for *Life* and other publications (1904–71).

803.21   Elwell murder] Joseph Elwell, a bridge expert, card shark, and ladies' man, was found shot to death in 1920. His murder was unsolved.

804.31   John L. Lewis] American labor leader (1880–1969).

804.34   Wagner Act]   The National Labor Relations Act of 1935 guaranteed workers the right to unionize and authorized a board to investigate unfair employment practices.

805.9–29   All right . . . she got me . . .]   The acting edition, incorporating changes made in the play after Paris fell to the Germans in June 1940, describes a call from Walt Disney instead of Gertrude Stein:

> Oh! Put him on! (*Again an aside.*) It's Walt Disney in Hollywood. (*Into phone.*) Hello . . . Hello . . . Walt. How's my little dash of genius? . . . Yes, I hoped you would. How'd you know I was here? . . . I see . . . Yes. Yes, I'm listening. Now? Ten seconds more? (*To Sandy and June.*) Mr. Disney calls me every Christmas—(*Into phone again*).) Yes, Walt . . . I hear it. It sounds just like static . . . June! (*He extends receiver to her; she listens a second.*) Hello . . . Thanks, old man, and a very Merry Christmas to *you* . . . Tell me, is there any news in Hollywood? Who's in Lana Turner's sweater these days? . . . I see . . . Well, goodbye, and don't worry about "Fantasia." It wasn't your fault . . . Beethoven hasn't written a hit in years . . . Good-bye. (*He hangs up and turns to June.*) Do you know what that was you listened to? The voice of Donald Duck.
>
> JUNE. Not really?
>
> WHITESIDE. Mr. Disney calls me every Christmas, no matter where I am, so that I can hear it. Two years ago I was walking on the bottom of the ocean in a diving-suit, with William Beebe, but he got me . . .

805.20–23   Pourquoi . . . au revoir.]   Why don't we get together at your place afterwards? Try to invite Picasso, Matisse, Cocteau. I'm only going to be there for a few days and I want to see everybody. Isn't that right? Oh, fine! Goodbye, goodbye.

806.8–9 Senator Borah]   William E. Borah (1865–1940), an Idaho Republican. (The acting edition of the play replaces Borah with Hamilton Fish, a Republican congressman from upstate New York.)

807.35   Hattie Carnegie]   See note 753.27.

807.37–38   Jock Whitney . . . di Frasso]   John Hay Whitney (1904–1982), a philanthropist and socialite; Cary Grant (1904–1986), a Hollywood actor; Dorothy di Frasso (1888–1954), a Hollywood socialite.

808.7   Ciro's]   A Hollywood nightclub frequented by celebrities, opened in 1939.

808.13–16   and he gave me . . . Nonsense]   The acting edition of the play reads:

> and Beatrice Lille gave me a message for you. She says for you to take off twenty-five pounds right away and send them to her parcel post. She needs them.
>
> WHITESIDE: I'll pack 'em in ice.

808.15   Grover Whalen]   New York City's "official greeter" from 1919 to 1953, Whalen (1886–1962) also organized the 1939 World's Fair.

810.1–2   your old . . . fellow actor]   Lorraine Sheldon and Beverly Carlton were based on actors Gertrude Lawrence and Noel Coward, who often appeared on stage together in London and New York.

814.2   Charley Ross]   See note 176.9–10.

815.13–14   "What Am I to Do?"]   Written for *The Man Who Came to Dinner* by Cole Porter, after the manner of Noel Coward. (Porter signed his manuscript "Noel Porter.")

820.16   Elizabeth Arden]   Beautician and manufacturer of luxury cosmetics (1878–1966).

823.8   the Duchess of Sutherland]   In the acting edition, "my mother in Kansas City."

825.4   Philo Vance]   An effete, debonair detective featured in a number of mystery novels by S. S. Van Dine.

828.26   *"Heilige Nacht."*]   "Holy Night."

828.32   two thousand years ago,]   The acting edition of the play includes the following additional text:
> (*At this point there is a piercing scream from the library. Everybody turns at interruption as Miss Preen rushes on, holding her hand. The choir continues to sing during all this.*)

MISS PREEN: A penguin bit me!

WHITESIDE: (*raising his voice to top the sobbing Miss Preen, continues*)

830.5   Mrs. Siddons]   Sarah Siddons (1755–1831), British actress known for tragic roles.

831.19   Tiny Tim]   Character in Charles Dickens' *A Christmas Carol* (1843).

833.6   *"Polly Adler's?"*]   Adler (1900–1962) ran an upscale Manhattan brothel.

833.31   Darryl Zanuck]   Film producer (1902–1979) who headed Twentieth Century Fox.

833.37   Hedy Lamarr]   Viennese-born actress (1913–2000) whose films included *Extase* (1932)—in which she appeared nude—and *Algiers* (1938).

836.7   Petrouchka]   Title character of a 1911 Ballets Russes ballet by Igor Stravinsky.

836.10   *Merry Widow waltz*]   From the opera *Die Lustige Witwe* (*The Merry Widow*, 1905), by Franz Lehàr.

Library of Congress Cataloging-in-Publication Data

Kaufman, George S. (George Simon), 1889–1961.
   Kaufman & Co. : Broadway comedies / George S. Kaufman
   with Edna Ferber . . . [et al.].
      p. cm. — (The Library of America ; 152)
     Contents: The royal family / George S. Kaufman and Edna
  Ferber — Animal crackers / George S. Kaufman and Morrie
  Ryskind — June moon / George S. Kaufman and Ring Lardner —
  Once in a lifetime / George S. Kaufman and Moss Hart — Of thee
  I sing / George S. Kaufman and Morrie Ryskind — Dinner at
  Eight / George S. Kaufman and Edna Ferber — Stage Door /
  George S. Kaufman and Edna Ferber — You can't take it with you
  / George S. Kaufman and Moss Hart — The man who came to
  dinner / George S. Kaufman and Moss Hart.
ISBN 1–931082–67–7 (alk. paper)
    1. American drama—20th century. 2. American drama (Comedy)
  3. Broadway (New York, N.Y.) I. Ferber, Edna, 1887–1968. II. Title:
  Royal family. III. Title: Animal crackers. IV. Title: June moon.
  V. Title: Once in a lifetime. VI. Title: Of thee I sing. VII. Title:
  Dinner at eight. VIII. Title: Stage door. IX. Title: You can't take it
  with you. X. Title: Man who came to dinner. XI. Title. XII. Series.

PS3521.A727A6   2004
812'.52—dc22

                                             2004044200

THE LIBRARY OF AMERICA SERIES

The Library of America fosters appreciation and pride in America's literary heritage by publishing, and keeping permanently in print, authoritative editions of America's best and most significant writing. An independent nonprofit organization, it was founded in 1979 with seed money from the National Endowment for the Humanities and the Ford Foundation.

This book is set in 10 point Linotron Galliard,
a face designed for photocomposition by Matthew Carter
and based on the sixteenth-century face Granjon. The paper
is acid-free Domtar Literary Opaque and meets the requirements
for permanence of the American National Standards Institute. The
binding material is Brillianta, a woven rayon cloth made by
Van Heek-Scholco Textielfabrieken, Holland. Composition
by Dedicated Business Services. Printing and
binding by Courier Companies, Inc.
Designed by Bruce Campbell.

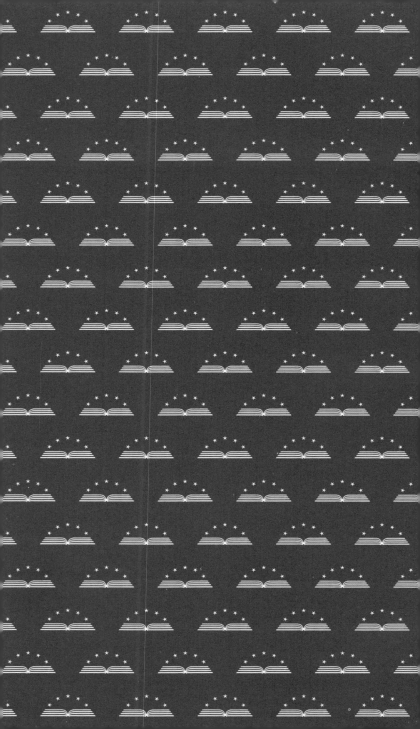